The
Church

BOOKS BY G.C. BERKOUWER

MODERN UNCERTAINTY AND CHRISTIAN FAITH
RECENT DEVELOPMENTS IN ROMAN CATHOLIC THOUGHT
THE TRIUMPH OF GRACE IN THE THEOLOGY OF KARL BARTH
THE SECOND VATICAN COUNCIL AND THE NEW CATHOLICISM

STUDIES IN DOGMATICS SERIES —

THE PROVIDENCE OF GOD
FAITH AND SANCTIFICATION
FAITH AND JUSTIFICATION
FAITH AND PERSEVERANCE
THE PERSON OF CHRIST
GENERAL REVELATION
DIVINE ELECTION
MAN: THE IMAGE OF GOD
THE WORK OF CHRIST
THE SACRAMENTS
SIN
THE RETURN OF CHRIST
HOLY SCRIPTURE
THE CHURCH

Studies in Dogmatics

The
Church

BY

G.C. BERKOUWER
PROFESSOR OF SYSTEMATIC THEOLOGY
FREE UNIVERSITY OF AMSTERDAM

WILLIAM B. EERDMANS PUBLISHING COMPANY
GRAND RAPIDS, MICHIGAN

Translated by James E. Davison
from
the Dutch edition, *De Kerk,* I and II
published by J.H. Kok N.V., Kampen, The Netherlands,
1970 and 1972

Library of Congress Cataloging in Publication Data

Berkouwer, Gerrit Cornelis, 1903-
   The church.

   (His Studies in dogmatics)
   Translation of De kerk.
   Includes bibliographical references and index.
   1. Church—Marks. I. Title.
BV601.B4513   262   75-45202
ISBN 0-8028-3433-7

CONTENTS

ABBREVIATIONS

B.C. — Belgic Confession

C.D. — Canons of Dort

C.D. — K. Barth, *Church Dogmatics*

Denz. — *Enchiridion Symbolorum,* ed. H. Denzinger

Denz.-Schönm. — *Enchiridion Symbolorum,* 34th edition, ed. H. Denzinger and A. Schönmetzer

DV II — *The Documents of Vatican II,* 1966, ed. W. Abbott and J. Gallagher

ET — English Translation

Geref. Dog. — H. Bavinck, *Gereformeerde Dogmatiek*

H.C. — Heidelberg Catechism

Inst. — J. Calvin, *Institutes of the Christian Religion,* ed. J.T. McNeill, trans. F.L. Battles

LXX — Septuagint

TCT — *The Church Teaches: Documents of the Church in English Translation,* 1955, trans. Jesuit Fathers of St. Mary's College, Kansas

TDNT — *Theological Dictionary of the New Testament,* ed. G. Kittel and G. Friedrich, trans. G. Bromiley

Z.N.T.W. — *Zeitschrift für die Neutestamentliche Wissenschaft*

Z.Th.K. — *Zeitschrift für Theologie und Kirche*

6

CHAPTER ONE

CREDO ECCLESIAM

WHOEVER FEELS URGED TO REFLECT ON THE
Church, on her reality for faith (*credo ecclesiam*), finds
himself face to face with a long series of varied questions, all
closely linked to the fact that there are so many churches as
well as so many differing views of the essence of the Church. In
our day, especially, still another question looms behind these
questions: in view of the Church's place in the world today,
is such reflection really relevant? Every traditional ecclesiology
speaks of the great, unique significance of the Church — her
mystery, her divine origin, her relationship to Christ, her continuity, and her future. In light of such exalted language, the
question of the Church's relevance becomes even more challenging and serious.

The more the Church claims to be, the more the question
arises as to how obvious the statements made about the Church
really are. Are such statements really credible? More broadly,
is it meaningful to concentrate so much attention on the Church
when everyone's attention, in the first place, at least, is directed to the world around us? Memories of an earlier time,
of an ecclesiastical milieu, often seem to be present in this
latter question. The Church's interest in the world appeared
to be relatively small, and it seemed that in the Church one
lived in a "world" other than the real world where we live,
where there are heights and depths, troubles and threats.
Is it true that the joys and the hopes, the griefs and the anxieties
of contemporary man — especially of the poor and of all those
who suffer — "are also the joys and the hopes, the griefs and
the anxieties of the followers of Christ"? Is it true that there
is nothing genuinely human that fails to find an echo in their

7

hearts?[1] Or are those people correct who feel that all of this has been said too beautifully? Is the actual situation really like that? Is it not or — in earlier times, at least — was it not much different?

These doubts were often influenced by particular verses of Scripture that seemed to exclude true concern for the world. Is it not true that Christ's kingship is not of this world (John 18:36)? Can anything be clearer than the exhortation to followers of the Lord to "set your minds on things that are above, not on things that are on earth" (Col. 3:2)? And can there be any meaningful relationship between the Church and the everyday concerns of men, when the Church's program appears of necessity to be: "Here we have no lasting city, but we seek the city which is to come" (Heb. 13:14)? Can the faith of earlier ages, the faith of Abraham, throw light on the present, since he looked forward to the city with foundations, whose builder and maker is God (11:10)? In summary, is this not simply an escape from all that our hand now finds to do, because no connection could be made between the expectation of Him Who makes all things new (Rev. 21:5) and the suffering and want in the world today?[2]

These questions are closely related to the nature of the Christian faith and, consequently, to the Church's confession of that faith. They become even more intense when one deals with the history of the Church — with her voice in the past and in the present, her divisions and strife, her failings, her self-assurance, her often irritating pronouncements, and her frequently impotent silences. These questions and others like them arise because of the accessibility of the Church: her earthly reality in the midst of the world, her claims, and her words and deeds. When one reflects on the Church, one may not concentrate on an idealistic picture or on the question of how, "properly speaking," the Church ought to be. In that case, one could dissociate oneself from her history, because history cannot be relevant for the ideal of the Church. But no

---

1. The beginning of Vatican II's "Pastoral Constitution on the Church in the Modern World" (*Gaudium et Spes*, December 7, 1965). Cf. in this connection the reflections on the mystery and the presence of the Church, her solidarity (*conjunctio*) with and love for "the entire human family" (*DV II*, pp. 200f.).

2. One may think of the discussion of this theme in Uppsala, where the attempt was made to show that it is a misunderstanding to characterize this verse as an "escape."

suggestion is made in the *credo ecclesiam* of such an idealistic picture. This belief does not intend to speak about some alien, inaccessible thing, but about the reality of the Church.[3] Not even for a single instant may one avoid this reality because it is customary to speak here of a reality *of faith*. By "believing" in the Church *(credo ecclesiam)*, we do not mean to blur the outlines of the *ecclesia,* but rather to testify to her reality. All questions concerning the Church are connected inseparably to her actual history, her concrete existence in the world, and her visibility and accessibility. And when we speak of the "mystery" of the Church, we do not mean to view the Church abstractly or unhistorically. Rather, from first to last we must deal with the Church as she really is. Even though one emphasizes that the Church may never be explained from her historical, psychological, and social components,[4] one may still not deny that the intention of the *credo ecclesiam* is to point to nothing other than what is customarily called the "empirical" Church. What other "Church" could the *credo* mean, when it is clear that the whole of the *credo* speaks of reality: *credo resurrectionem carnis* and *credo vitam aeternam?*

Even if one were able to construct an "ideal" picture of the Church with the help of various data from the Old and New Testaments, one would not yet have done justice to the *credo ecclesiam*. No matter how significant the Scriptural testimony to the Church (which we will discuss later) may be, to refer simply to a normative concept of the Church will not suffice. Actually, everything that the biblical witness itself tells us about the *ecclesia* intends to refer to reality! This is already clear from the fact that, with regard to the Church, mention is made not only of a norm, but also of a subjection to this normativity. The Church is made up of concrete, living men — a *congregatio fidelium,* a *communio sanctorum* — who assent to this normativity and accept it as "being" the Church *(esse ecclesiae)*. The *credo ecclesiam* does not direct our attention only to what ought to be and what ought to happen, but to what obviously has happened in the lives of those who, according to the words of the Belgic Confession, "bow their necks under the yoke of Jesus Christ" (Art. 28). And likewise, the

---

3. Cf. H. Bavinck, *Geref. Dog.,* IV, 285: the Church is "not a platonic state, which exists only in the imagination and never becomes a reality." Cf. *idem, Magnalia Dei,* p. 500.
4. Cf. G. Voigt, *Die Bedeutung der Soziologie für das Verständnis der Kirche (Fuldaer Hefte,* 18, 1968), p. 103, on "the Church's center of origin."

Confession speaks utterly concretely and historically about the Church, which has been from the beginning of the world and will be to the end thereof (Art. 27). It is precisely this reality of the Church that makes everything we say about her so serious. One cannot excuse oneself for the defects in the "empirical" Church by hiding behind unreachable ideals and unfulfillable norms. The *credo ecclesiam* makes the Church vulnerable, since, in the midst of her past and present existence, she witnesses so emphatically to her reality. This situation becomes even more concrete, because the Church does more than speak only of her own life and reality: she presents herself to the world with an urgent, unique appeal, inviting all to join her.

What "is" this Church? What is the reason for her tendency to penetrate into the lives of others? What riches does she possess, and what reality underlies her? The seriousness of these questions requires that we reflect on that unique reality which the Church has continually claimed to be, since it cannot be denied that the Church has always asserted much about her own reality: her riches, her blessedness, her gifts, her continuity, and her future. It is remarkable that in the *credo* the Church not only confesses her faith in God the Father, the Son, and the Holy Spirit, but also speaks about herself: *credo ecclesiam, credo communionem sanctorum.* Understandably enough, it has often been noted that the formulation does not read *credo in ecclesiam,* but *credo ecclesiam.* This is not merely accidental. According to Calvin, even where the "in" is used in antiquity, it can only be an improper expression.[5] Believing *in* God as the One Who is True, resting in Him with complete confidence, and abandoning oneself to Him form a particular mode of faith and trust that definitely cannot be applied in the same way to the Church.[6] But in spite of this great difference between belief in God and the *credo ecclesiam,* it is highly significant that the Church speaks of herself in this manner, and such language obliges the Church to continuously reflect on this reality of faith. We might say that a searching

---

5. "*Loquutio impropria,*" *Inst.,* IV, 1, 2. The intention was always to say, "I believe the Church," not "I believe in the Church."
6. Cf. H. de Lubac, "Credo Ecclesiam," in J. Daniélou-H. Vorgrimler, *Sentire Ecclesiam,* 1961, pp. 13f. K. Rahner, too, sees this as anything but "merely an idle, somewhat hair-splitting distinction," and suspects that it "has more significance for present-day piety in the Church than it did earlier" ("Dogmatische Randbemerkungen zur 'Kirchenfrömmigkeit,'" *Sentire Ecclesiam,* p. 781).

"introspection"[7] becomes necessary, not in the sense of an introverted self-complacency, but in the sense of a critical, testing self-investigation in the light of the gospel. Is she really what she confesses herself to be? Is she really what her weighty words — drawn from the gospel — claim: the people of God, the disciples of the Lord, the flock of the sole Shepherd, the city set on the hill, the salt of the earth, and the light of the world?

In this connection, we might mention the distinction that is often made between the ideal Church and the empirical Church. The intention is not to designate a pair of churches, but to direct attention to what is lacking in the empirical Church. Very seldom has anyone used totally perfectionistic terminology about the Church. It has almost always been admitted that the Church does not measure up to the ideal in all respects and that her actual appearance is not in harmony with what Christ wanted, i.e., the "absolute and perfect image" of the Church.[8] It is always wise to ask what this admission signifies concretely. Is it only a vague, general admission of the Church's failings, which no one would deny? Or is it a sharp, searching exposure of all the words and deeds of the empirical Church?[9] To the degree that the criticism increases in sharpness and vehemence, revealing many shortcomings within the Church, the question becomes more urgent with respect to the meaning and significance of that liturgical expression, *credo ecclesiam.*

Attributes and marks

That a critical self-examination is necessary is made even clearer when we consider the grand, wonderful things that have constantly been confessed concerning the Church amid all the

7. Pope Paul VI in *Ecclesiam Suam,* 1964 (para. 9): "This is the hour in which the Church should deepen its consciousness of itself, in which it ought to meditate on that mystery which is peculiar to it." Cf. also *Salvete* (Sept. 29, 1963) on the duty of the Church "to come at last to a full understanding of her true nature."
8. Thus Pope Paul VI in *Ecclesiam Suam,* para. 10. Cf. on the *pure* features and on not corresponding perfectly to the ideal.
9. Cf. H. Küng, *The Church,* 1967, pp. 6ff., concerning the establishment of the criterion or norm for determining "what is legitimate in any historical and empirical manifestation of the Church." Here there are many unbiased, frank, and critical concretizations with respect to the historical reality of the Church, for instance, concerning the Church and the Jews (pp. 132ff.) and the Church's power (pp. 34ff., 99f.).

complications of her history. We are thinking especially of those
ancient words in the *credo* that are usually called the attributes
of the Church: unity and catholicity, apostolicity and holiness.
We can hardly interpret the terminological consensus here —
the same words have been used throughout all ages — other
than as a reference to wonderful riches and unprecedented
perspectives. The formulation is so exuberant that one may
wonder whether this is not some idealistic, romantic picture
of the Church, in which scarcely any attention is paid to the
things that contradict this wealth and these perspectives. Even
if one assumes on faith that the Church is not consciously self-
complacent when she uses these words, is there not still a real
danger that the constant repetition of such words can create
an atmosphere in which such self-complacency is scarcely avoidable? And are there not phases in the history of the Church
when this temptation was not resisted? What is the intention and
meaning of these words in the *credo* that make profession of
the reality of the Church? By speaking about herself in this way,
has the Church not become extremely vulnerable? Does her *credo*
not present a measuring rod to which she wishes to be compared,
a criterion that can judge her whole life — her coming and
going, her speaking and being silent? Generally, when the
Church is judged, not all four words are used as criteria; rather,
for many people two of them spring immediately to mind,
namely, unity and holiness. But the Church's vulnerability is
implicit in all four words, since they attest to what is proper
to the Church. How is one to reflect on the Church with these
attributes?

When we reflect on the way the Church confessionally designates herself — what we might in a certain sense call a "pretension"[10] — it is not surprising if, unintentionally, we conceive of
the Church's attributes as analogous to the attributes of other
"things," which can be established by means of observation and
analysis. We distinguish various realities via such attributes. The
way something appears forces itself upon us of its own accord;
thus, one can speak of great and powerful peoples, poor and

10. Cf. A.A. van Ruler, "De Pretentie van de Kerk" (*Wending*, 13, 1958,
pp. 567f.), where various descriptions are given, such as, "The Church
is the reality of *agape* in the world" (p. 574). Further, cf. the Christian
Church's recognition "that she and only she had the true morality"
(p. 578), and her "going out in absolute openness to everyone and
everything" (p. 580). Van Ruler speaks of this pretension as a challenge
(p. 581).

rich lands, and good and bad characters. In comparison to this kind of observation and analysis, the Church's attributes are much more controversial and much less obvious than are the attributes of many other objects. It is apparent that, in this context, everything is less easily accessible and less straightforward than in common usage. Not only have intensive discussions and differences in interpretation developed in the history of the Church with respect to those four words, but also the question can arise as to whether a multitude of less pleasant facts and facets of her existence should not have led us to designate other "attributes" of the Church!

Surveying the history of the Church, we meet with a striking distinction that is very closely tied to the questions mentioned above, namely, the distinction between the attributes and marks of the Church. At first sight, the distinction is quite unclear, since one might expect that the Church can be known and precisely demarcated by means of her "attributes." However, closer inspection shows that there is an explicit motive underlying this distinction, which played a far-reaching role in the controversy between Rome and the Reformation and was related to the question of how one ought to view the Church's attributes. Bavinck considered the Roman Catholic error to be the lack of a distinction between attributes and marks, because they saw the attributes as the marks to point out the one, true Church.[11] Thus, all emphasis was laid on substantial attributes, which became apparent in the reality of the Church.[12] However, the judgment of the Reformation was that one had not yet said everything when one had referred only to the Church's attributes. In speaking of the marks of the Church, the *notae ecclesiae*, the Reformation introduced a criterion by which the Church could be, and had to be, tested as to whether she were truly the Church.

This motif of testing in ecclesiology adds an entirely new and important perspective to the doctrine of the Church's attributes, and it is of decisive significance for the nature of the Church and her attributes. The notion of *notae*, with its unmistakable implications of criticism and testing, is directed against every

11. *Geref. Dog.*, IV, 304.
12. Cf. B. Bartmann, *Dogmatik*, II, 198, concerning catholicity as "not only an inner attribute of the Church, but also an external mark." Cf. *Theologisch Woordenboek*, II, 2711: "Marks *are* attributes which become knowable in their external appearance for our natural, human experience." Marks are "the external radiation of an attribute."

presumption of the presence and verifiability of the attributes —
in other words, against every static ecclesiology, in which everything is decided simply from the basis that a church "exists"
and that she possesses a number of immediately recognizable,
unassailable "attributes." Ultimately, such a static ecclesiology
no longer allows room for discussion about the ecclesiastical
reality; and to the extent that one is willing to embark on such
a discussion, it can have relation only to the Church's periphery,
which is separated from her unassailable "essence." In contrast,
in the Reformation it was precisely the *notae* that took on decisive significance, with the result that it was impossible to use
the "attributes" apologetically as an unthreatened and unassailable, aprioristic reality. The Reformers could not refer
simply to the factual reality of the Church: *una, catholica,
apostolica,* and *sancta.*

The question of the *notae* reached an apex in various tensions in Church history in connection with the question of the
true Church, the *ecclesia vera.* It is striking in this connection
that the four words themselves were never disputed, since the
Reformers did not opt for other "attributes." There is a common attachment everywhere to the description of the Church
in the Nicene Creed: one, holy, catholic, and apostolic.[13] Even
after the Reformation, in spite of all the differences in interpretation which appeared with respect to the four words, this
usage remained the same.[14] But in the midst of this consonant
terminology, the Reformers' notion of the *notae* remained a
disquieting element.[15] Via the *notae,* the Reformers wanted to
indicate from the Word of God "which is the true Church,
since all sects which are in the world assume to themselves the
name of the Church" (B.C., Art. 29). The striking thing here
is that the general question about whether the Church is truly
one and catholic, apostolic and holy, is not asked; rather, a number of marks are mentioned, viz., the pure preaching of the

13. *Et unam sanctam catholicam et apostolicam,* Denz., 86.
14. One may think of various Reformed confessions and the repetition by
    the Roman Catholics in *De unicitate Ecclesiae* of 1864 (Denz., 1686;
    TCT, 181): "The true Church of Jesus Christ is constituted by divine
    authority and is known by four notes." There is clear reference here
    to the authority "in the Roman Chair," as "principle, root, and never-
    failing source," that results from these marks.
15. Cf. E. Kinder, *Der evangelische Glaube und die Kirche,* 1960[2], pp. 50ff.,
    103ff., concerning the fundamental distinction between attributes and
    marks. See also E. Wolf, "Die Einheit der Kirche im Zeugnis der
    Reformation," in *Peregrinatio,* I, 1954, pp. 154ff.

gospel, the pure administration of the sacraments, and the exercise of church discipline *(ibid.).*

Within the Reformation there was much difference of opinion about the number of *notae.* This was especially the case between the Reformed and Lutherans, since the latter wanted to recognize only the preaching of the Word of God and the administration of the sacraments as *notae.*[16] But in spite of such differences, the motive underlying the *notae* is perfectly clear. The decisive point is this: the Church is and must remain subject to the authority of Christ, to the voice of her Lord. And in this subjection she is tested by Him. That is the common Reformation motive underlying the *notae.* According to Bavinck, there are more differences "in name than in fact,"[17] because there is actually only one mark, the Word. It comes to expression in various ways and is directed to conformity with the gospel. The *notae* — concentrated in one *nota* — imply a judgment, a testing of the Church.[18] They "assume a standard that lies far above the Church by which she may be judged by everyone."[19]

There is a refusal here to proceed from an *esse ecclesiae* according to which the very fact that there is a Church makes all testing superfluous,[20] and in which it was sufficient simply to ascertain substantial attributes, visible to all. The *notae* bring up the question of what actually happens in and with the Church. Thus, they bring a new element into ecclesiology. One could speak of a dynamic aspect, not in the sense of a denial or actualization of the Church's being, but as a different view of the Church's reality, which sees her existence as inseparable from such testing. If the Church does not honor the "abiding" mark, the Word *(Inst.,* IV, 2, 4), she must fall

---

16. Augsburg Confession, Art. 7.
17. *Geref. Dog.,* IV, 296.
18. We see this concentration of the *notae* in one *nota* clearly in Luther, who can enumerate many marks and still say: "the sole, uninterrupted, infallible mark of the Church has always been the Word," and "therefore, the papacy errs in supposing that there are other marks of the Church than the Word" (in E. Wolf, *op. cit.,* p. 157). Calvin *(Inst.,* IV, 2, 4) says that the continual mark of the Church is this: "Everyone who is of the truth hears my voice." Christ has provided the Church with a mark that is not in the least doubtful *(minime dubium symbolum).*
19. *Geref. Dog.,* IV, 292.
20. Cf. O. Weber, *Grundlagen der Dogmatik,* II, 596, against an "objective reality that is not open to any further inquiry and is not in need of any actualizing action."

into a type of introspection which will only result in a reference
to the obviousness of the presence of the attributes (or *notae!*).
For a long time this tendency played a decisive role in traditional Roman Catholic ecclesiology, as is clear from the way
the First Vatican Council speaks about the Church.[21] It deals
with God's foundation of the Church and with the manifest
marks that are intended to be recognized by all. Reference is
made to the Church's propagation, sanctity, fruitfulness, and
stability, all of which are a continuing motive for the Church's
credibility.[22]

In our day one still finds traces of this apologetical use of
the Church's attributes in various of Pope Paul VI's speeches, for
instance, when he speaks of "the *celebration* of the attributes of
the Church."[23] It is recognized that the whole life of the Church
has been subjected to Christ and that shortcomings and imperfections are found in her — specifically in her members.[24] But this
recognition does not make any room for functional, critical *notae*
that test the Church. The "attributes" belong to the Church as
substantial attributes. Therefore, a concentration of the *notae*
is possible here too, for everything is, as it were, summarized
in one indisputable sign that belongs to the Church's essence.
This happens, for instance, in the so-called *via primatus*, that
is, the attribute of being under the rule of the papal primacy.[25]

21. "... its marvelous propagation, its exalted sanctity, and its inexhaustible
     fruitfulness in all that is good, ... its catholic unity and its unshaken
     stability" (Denz., 1794; *TCT*, 68).
22. "... a great and perpetual motive of credibility and an irrefutable proof"
     (*ibid.*).
23. *In Signa Sanctae Crucis*, 1964, "Here the unity is celebrated; here the
     Catholic *nota* of the Church is celebrated," in which she testifies "to
     her marvelous power and her unique ability to unite men as brothers."
     In all of this the Church's being is seen simply as a fact, and the
     critical *notae* no longer function. So the conclusion comes as no surprise:
     "And therefore here is the Church, here also the Spirit, the Paraclete."
24. Cf. my *Nabetrachting op het Concilie*, 1968, p. 33. The distinction
     "specifically in her members," a papal addition inserted in the decree
     on ecumenism, has a parallel in the (Eastern Orthodox) view of N.A.
     Nissiotis ("Die qualitative Bedeutung der Katholizität," in *Theol.
     Zeitsch.*, XVII, 1961, p. 279): "Therefore, for Orthodoxy the Church as
     catholic is both: she is the infallible Church that does not do penance,
     because 'she has no spot or wrinkle' (Eph. 5:27); at the same time,
     she embraces those sinners who must do penance in her unceasingly."
     This far-reaching problematic can be discussed in detail only when
     we deal with the holiness of the Church.
25. Bavinck considers this view characteristic: "Actually, the pope is the

Here all attributes are really founded in and guaranteed by the obvious actuality of the Church, and no disquiet arises about the presence of the Church because of the distinction between attributes and marks. The Church can be examined by a *via empirica,* and thus she *is* one and catholic, apostolic and holy. This talk of the Church's visible clarity and know-ableness is not intended as ecclesiastical self-praise[26] — the attributes are also called gifts — but the attributes do contain a type of apriority that excludes any special function for the *notae.* Hence, the beauty of the Church can also be mentioned. Although it is not a *nota specialis* beside the others, it does reflect the four attributes or marks of the Church.[27] It is as if the "common" actuality of the Church, with her shortcomings and imperfections, remains completely hidden from sight. The "reality" of the Church begins to lead its own life, and then this beauty can begin to function apologetically again.

Recent Catholic emphasis on testing

In our time, however, this apologetical aspect of referring to ascertainable attributes has receded more and more into the background, and there is less and less talk of the splendor *(resplendentia)* of the attributes. That is closely connected to a strong anti-triumphalism with respect not only to individual believers, but also to the whole Church. It is a call to humility, seeking to avoid any assumption of the self-evidence of the Church.[28] Another important factor here is the changed insight into the relationship with other churches. One has gradually begun to speak much less exclusively about the Church's attributes, so that everything now is more complicated than it was in the time of Bellarmine, or even at the time of Vatican I,

one, sufficient mark of the true Church" (*Geref. Dog.,* IV, 305). Nevertheless, one often accepted gradations in the *notae,* for instance, when unity was seen as "the primary mark from which the other three derive their origin" (G. Thils, *Les nôtes de l'Eglise dans l'Apologétique cath. depuis la Reforme,* 1937, p. 118).

26. Bavinck (*Geref. Dog.,* IV, 294) does use the word "self-complacency" (*zelfbehagen*) concerning the unity of the Church.
27. J.V. de Groot, *Summa Apol.,* p. 150.
28. As we have seen, Pope Paul VI, too, speaks of a searching renewal and humility (*Salvete,* 1963); but in recent Roman Catholic theology all of this acquires a much stronger — and different — accent.

when the Church's being and attributes could be determined without difficulty. [29]

In all of this there is new and more critical reflection on the concrete Church in the light of the gospel. The cautioning question is asked about whether the Church is not in danger of becoming imprisoned in self-complacency and self-overestimation. Such critical questioning of the legitimacy and reality of the Church could not be interpreted *a priori* as a lack of love for the Church, as an alienation from Christ's authority in His Church, or as offense at the *skandalon* of the gospel. The relatedness to the *skandalon* of the cross was precisely — whether or not in recollection of Luther's *theologia crucis* — the deepest motif of all the warnings directed to the Church in her pilgrimage through the world.[30] At the background there was also a protest against a simplistic identification of Christ and His congregation, whereby criticism of the Church was all too quickly seen as "opposing" Christ. One saw more and more how vulnerable the Church was, as was clear from her history and reality. In our time more than ever before, we see the truth that Bavinck expressed in this way: the Reformation denied that the Church is *autopistos* (self-authenticating).[31] He referred to the higher authority to which she is subjected and in which her being is founded. Here an unproblematic, devout description of her beauty is impossible, since this beauty cannot be understood apart from the decisive normativity above the Church. Thus, ecclesiology cannot ascertain phenomenologically the Church's essential marks, because what happens in the Church under the power of the Word and the Spirit belongs to her

---

29. Cf. Thils, *op. cit.*, p. 292, concerning the 17th century. Cf. p. 345 on the "romantic apologetic." B. van Leeuwen ("De Kenbaarheid der Katholieke Kerk als de ware Kerk volgens de Weg der Kentekenen," *Bijdragen Tijdschr. filos.-theol.*, XXVI, 1965, pp. 188ff.) speaks of the "recognition of a certain presence of the attributes outside the Catholic Church" and of doubt with respect to the so-called "positive mark" (cf. on this Thils, *op. cit.*, pp. 94f.). A positive mark belongs only to the true Church (*Theologisch Woordenboek*, II, 2711).

30. Cf. A. Brandenburg, "Luthers *theologia crucis* und die Auffassung von der pilgernde Kirche," *Volk Gottes. Festgabe für J. Höfer*, 1967, pp. 323f. Many lay special emphasis on the function of the pilgrimage (*peregrinatio*) in *Lumen Gentium*. Cf. P. Bormann, "Das wandernde Gottesvolk" — die "Exodusgemeinde," *idem*, pp. 563ff.: the idea of pilgrimage is directed against all triumphalism and, therefore, is critical to the Church's being the true Church.

31. *Geref. Dog.*, IV, 296.

essence.[32] In the same way as there are *notae* of Christians, indicated in the activities of love, struggle, and faith (B.C., Art. 29), the nature of the Church's *notae* lies in a dynamic which, in Word and sacrament, is decisive for the reality of the true Church. Thus, the real — visible and approachable — reality of the Church comes into view in contrast to the abstractness of the earlier way of speaking about the Church;[33] and so the question is asked not only about whether other churches can possess something of the attributes, but likewise about whether the attributes cannot also be temporarily and partially obscured in the Catholic Church![34]

K. Schilder's dynamic motif

It is in some sense understandable that the emphasis of the Reformation on testing was often seen as attacking the Church's objectivity — her *a priori*, ontic existence. However, the fear that this correlative view of the Church would subjectivize her reality rests on a profound misunderstanding. In a static ecclesiology this reality is lifted out of the only framework in which the Church can be and can remain the Church of the Lord: the framework of faith and prayer, obedience and subjection. Isolated from this framework, the Church with her attributes becomes petrified, and nothing of the Church's actual life of discipleship and imitation remains recognizable. That it is impossible to speak differently about the Church is totally apparent from the framework indicated in the New Testament for the Church's true life. Thus, we should not be surprised that the deep meaning of this motif of testing has been understood more and more clearly. We want to further illustrate concern for this dynamic and testing by referring to K. Schilder's view, in which it occupies a large place. Frequently, insufficient attention is given to this aspect because his ecclesiological ideas stand especially in the context of a passionate struggle against the doctrine of the pluriformity of the Church. Because of this, his view is often seen as a certain form of churchism, where one

32. E. Kinder, *op. cit.*, p. 51, on the question of legitimacy: we pay attention not so much to the "constancy of being" (*Seinsbestand*) as to criteria that refer to the Church's authenticity.
33. Cf. G. Thils, *op. cit.*, p. 94, concerning "a neo-platonic conception of the marks of the Church."
34. Asked already by T. Spacie in articles in *Zeitsch. für kath. Theol.*, in 1912 and 1915 (cf. in van Leeuwen, *op. cit.*, p. 186).

has eye only for one's own Church. In this interpretation, however, one does not pay sufficient attention to a special, clear
motif that decisively determines Schilder's ecclesiology. One can
call it the dynamic motif. He continually reminds us that the
Church is not only an assembly *(coetus)* but also a congregation
(congregatio).[35] By the latter Schilder understood the deed of
Christ Himself in His work of gathering, apart from which one
cannot correctly understand the Church as she proceeds into the
future. Nor can one understand the possibility of a critical
examination of the history of the Church.[36]

From this critical viewpoint, Schilder attacked various "phe-
nomenological" theories of the Church and pointed to the concrete confrontation with Christ's active gathering of the Church,
not as a static datum, but rather as the Church "in the unfinished — present time."[37] He refused to disengage the attributes
of the Church from the dynamic of Christ's rule and testing,
and he called the attributes "static givens, as soon as they are
isolated."[38] The words static and dynamic, especially, attract
attention again and again. They point to a decisive ecclesiological motif when Schilder combats making the Church "static"
and designates the Church as "in a state of becoming."[39] Schilder
does not want to see the Church standing still, but rather in
motion. This is connected to "that wonderful, mobile covenantal
tension between God's work and man's" and to "the mobility
of the Spirit."[40] By refusing to abstract the attributes of the

35. In connection with Article 28 of the Belgic Confession: "since this holy
    congregation is an assembly" (Latin: *hic coetus et congregatio*). Cf.
    K. Schilder, *Verz. Werken. De Kerk,* I, 1960, pp. 155f.
36. Cf. Schilder, *ibid.,* pp. 303ff.; *idem,* II, 1962, pp. 343ff., 124ff.
37. *Ibid.,* II, 246.
38. *Ibid.,* pp. 409ff. Schilder writes: "One of the points that has occupied
    me for a long time now concerning the problem of the Church is that
    of the Church's 'being' and 'becoming.'" He also points out that
    Lord's Day 21 of the Heidelberg Catechism, while not giving a definition
    of the Church, does answer the question "What do you believe con-
    cerning the Church?" with a sentence about Christ's work of gathering
    (p. 381).
39. *Ibid.,* pp. 411ff., in connection with the Church as still being built,
    and on the *fieri* in the *Synopsis Purioris Theologiae* of 1625 (XI, 34:
    the *ecclesia visibilis* is "not properly another Church from the invisible
    one, but it is only considered of another kind; the former in becoming
    [*fieri*], the latter in fact").
40. *Ibid.,* p. 415. Cf. the remarks about "the mobile stream of the Spirit"
    as "unfinished present time." Schilder also cautions against abstracting
    one attribute of the Church from another (cf. water as H_2O) in the
    light of the dynamic power of Christ as the Living One (p. 411).

Church from the Lord's present will and deeds, the self-evidentness of the historical process is rejected — the immobility that no longer can be corrected or put in proper order. We are not concerned here with a complete analysis of Schilder's ecclesiology and its many practical consequences; rather, we want only to point out the central motif in many of his considerations, whereby he warned against a static understanding of the Church, in which attributes and marks are separated from the tension of daily obedience and of "bowing the necks under the yoke of Christ" (B.C., Art. 28). According to Schilder, whoever speaks abstractly about the Church and her attributes has not understood the reality of the Church. In contrast to that, he proposes what I would like to describe as the correlative motif of the relatedness of the Church to faith.[41] This faith rests in the Word and, therefore, does not open the way to the ecclesiastical quietism that Schilder thought he perceived everywhere in the theory of pluriformity.

Concerning the "being" and "becoming" of the Church, Schilder did not direct himself first of all against the traditional Roman Catholic view that marks are attributes (nota est proprietas), but much more generally against legitimizing the "status quo" and against any rash pluriformity with its quietistic consequences.[42] According to him it was impossible — no matter in what phase of the Church — to fall back simply on her actuality, as if this actuality were removed from all testing and active normativity. Understandably, therefore, Schilder rejected the reproach of "churchism" and explained that he had "repeatedly and emphatically" opposed the conclusion that the Reformed Church is the only true Church.[43] Such a conclusion was too static for him, and it fails to appreciate that the Church proceeds in the midst of many dangers that threaten her true being. Because she is the Church of the Lord, room remains for critical, testing questions — also because we confess the unity and catholicity, apostolicity and holiness of the Church. This attention for testing does not overshadow the mystery of the Church, but

41. Cf. ibid., p. 349, on the activity of believers in connection with the unity of the Church. For the dynamic in being the Church, see further pp. 185ff. Here the heavenly Jerusalem, our mother (Gal. 4:26), is contrasted to misuse of the concept of mother, lack of appreciation for the mother's function in bearing children, and, consequently, resting in the "actuality" of the institution.
42. On pluriformity, see chapter 3 below.
43. Verz. Werken, II, 343.

rather takes it into consideration. It is precisely in the questioning, criticism, and testing that the Church is reminded of her deep origin, her true mystery. Every church that closes herself off from this, as if she were self-sufficient, shows that she has not correctly understood this mystery. She confuses the critical questions with being anti-ecclesiastical, with lacking appreciation for the riches of the Church's "substantial" attributes. She also forgets that the Church is not an unassailable "transcendent" event, unreachable by critical questions about her way through the world, but rather an earthly reality, the congregation of the faithful (congregatio fidelium).

Ultimately, this view of the real, earthly Church is also at the background of Schilder's criticism of the distinction made between the Church as creatio (a deed of God) and as creatura (an affair of men).[44] Schilder wanted to replace this distinction with the one between coetus and congregatio. He started from an understanding of creation as a deed of God "without intermediary."[45] Therefore, he considered it incorrect to view the Church as creatio on account of the danger that, starting from the Church as "an institution of God" with "elevated predicates," one would relativize the sin of the Church.[46] There is a place in the Church for testing, but such testing is unthinkable with respect to what God "creates." Whoever makes the Church simply creatio can no longer prevent the entrance of false pride. There is no mention in the Church of strict creatio, but only of its result "to the extent that she is the Church."[47] Thus, one may not conclude that Schilder would have objected to Luther's description of the Church as creatura Verbi, through which he expressed the relation of the Church to her origin — the gospel.[48] But Schilder did want to reject any romanticizing and idealizing of the Church by which one forgets that Paul, while naming the Church God's building, can speak in the same context of God's

44. Thus W.J. Aalders, Om de Kerk, 1931, pp. 206ff., in order to indicate the tension, or "ambiguity," in the Church's being. It seems to me that, in essence, Schilder had in view the same tension as did Aalders, who could also use the description "institution of God" for "creatio" (cf. I Cor. 3:9).

45. Verz. Werken, II, 345.

46. Ibid., pp. 346ff.

47. Ibid., p. 349. Schilder himself makes a connection here with his criticism of the pluriformity of the Church.

48. Cf. K. G. Steck, "Ecclesia–creatura Verbi," in Von der Einheit und Wesen der Kirche, 1960, pp. 40ff.; and U. Asendorff, Eschatologie bei Luther, 1967, pp. 129ff., in connection with Matt. 16:18f.

fellow workers with their own calling, not in competition with God, but received from Him.[49] All the problems and dangers concerning fellow-workmanship cannot detract from the fact that the Church is the congregation of the faithful and, therefore, stands under her Lord, directed to Him and tested by Him concerning her obedience.

In times of tension and conflict, when many critical questions are directed at the Church from the outside, there is a great danger that the Church will become apologetic and defensive and will neglect the significance of the question of marks. However, reflection on the Church may not and cannot consist in placid "contemplation" of her attributes, but only in a profound realization of the responsibility that is implicit in the *credo* — precisely because of the width and depth of the words in the *credo* themselves! Because of this, reflection on the Church cannot do without a correcting function. Here, if anywhere, one must hold the Church to her words. We may take Barth as an example of such critical questioning. He finds a hiatus in the Protestant dogmatic tradition. "Holy egoism" led to "that pronounced lack of joy in mission."[50] The result is that "the community does not give those around something to think about in this regard." In this connection, he calls the Church's being for the world "a true *nota ecclesiae*," i.e., "an eternal sign by which the true community of Jesus Christ may be infallibly shown."[51] This example of critical questioning could be multiplied by many others, also with respect to the unity, apostolicity, and holiness of the Church. Such concern for the marks of the Church is and remains of decisive importance for the Church as the Church of Jesus Christ. If forgotten, the Church begins to look like the church of Laodicea, whose speaking about her riches contrasted with her actual poverty (Rev. 3:17). It is a radical misunderstanding to isolate the *credo ecclesiam* and to view all critical questions as an attack on the riches of the Church. To understand that such critical questioning intends

49. I Cor. 3:9. Cf. also Schilder, *Verz. Werken,* II, 377ff., and the varied aspects of the word "build" *(oikodoméō)* in the New Testament, for instance in Matt. 16:18. It has a "typically ecclesiastical ring" *(TDNT,* V, 139), namely, as a "task."

50. K. Barth, *C.D.,* IV/3, pp. 767ff.

51. *Ibid.,* p. 772. Cf. the remarks on this mark as "fundamental criterion" connected with universality. It appears that this "mark" is not intended as an addition to the well-known marks, but is closely connected with catholicity.

precisely the opposite is one of the most essential elements of
reflection on the Church!

Why four attributes?

When we deal successively with the four well-known attributes, the question could be asked whether this approach allows
the whole reality of the Church to come into view. In fact, some
difference still exists with respect to the number of the Church's
attributes. Sometimes other attributes have been added to the
four, especially indefectibility and infallibility. According to
Bavinck, these two also belong to the attributes of the Church.[52]
Obviously, it is not a matter of a closed number of four
attributes seen as exhaustively and adequately describing the
reality of the Church. However, it is reasonable to ask whether
various newer words do not simply bring to light implications
of these four words. For instance, has the confession of the
Church concerning, respectively, her apostolicity and catholicity
not contained essentially what is intended by infallibility and
indefectibility?[53] Yet one must always be open to all the revealing light that falls on the reality of the Church. Here we cannot
help thinking of the many images and characterizations of the
Church in the Scriptures, especially in the New Testament.
From the nature of the case, it is impossible to add up all such
images to arrive at a total sum. Each points to a different aspect
of the one Church, and all need to be considered seriously. This
multiplicity itself can guard us from onesidedness.[54] Repeatedly,

52. *Geref. Dog.*, IV, 308. Bavinck says that the infallibility of the Church
    is gladly recognized by Protestants too. Naturally, this statement re-
    quires further reflection in connection with the meaning of the word
    "infallibility." Cf. A.A. van Ruler, *Reformatorische Opmerkingen in
    de Ontmoeting met Rome*, 1965, pp. 108ff., on the idea that infallibility
    is essential to the pretension of the Church (i.e., pneumatological, in
    distinction from christological, infallibility).
53. See the sections on apostolicity and catholicity below (especially the
    chapter on continuity).
54. Cf. P.S. Minear, *Images of the Church in the N.T.*, 1960, especially
    chapter 7 ("The Interrelation of the Images"). All the images have
    the same "direction," although none of them dominates: "One should
    not ask how one image is superior to another. We would be on sounder
    grounds if we asked how one image benefited from its associations with
    another" (p. 228). This must be remembered when Minear speaks
    about "minor images," for the intention is not to detract from their
    significance (for instance, "the salt of the earth"! See pp. 29ff., 222).
    Cf. also J.R. Nelson, "Many Images of the One Church," *The Ecu-*

one particular aspect has been isolated from the whole or, at least, has been designated as the most central and primary aspect. The dangers of such centralizing are obvious. Other aspects can recede into the background and interest in them can lessen.[55] It is good to remember this when we reflect on the attributes of the Church, since the whole life of the Church is at stake in the pure understanding of the *credo ecclesiam,* the one reality of the Church.

By dealing first with the unity and catholicity of the Church — so much in the center of interest at present — we do not mean to attach priority to these attributes at the expense of apostolicity and holiness. All aspects are so closely connected that any such priority is unthinkable. It is never possible to isolate the different aspects, and it would be possible to put unity and apostolicity or holiness and catholicity together at the beginning.[56] Only from the way in which one deals with the one Church of Jesus Christ in all her aspects can it be clear whether or not the temptation to give priority to one of the attributes has been overcome. So, starting from the mystery of the Church, we call attention to what is undeniably obvious: unity and catholicity, or, phrased differently, the catholicity of the one Church.

menical Review, IX, 1957, pp. 105ff., and H. Schlier, "The Unity of the Church according to the N.T.," *The Relevance of the N.T.,* 1968, pp. 193ff.

55. As we shall see in chapter 4, the problems of precedence and centrality have played an important role in the description of the Church as the "people of God" and the "body of Christ."

56. We are also thinking of the relation between catholicity and apostolicity, and specifically of the problem of continuity. We will discuss continuity in connection with catholicity (chapter 7) and will return to it when we deal with the problematic of apostolic succession (chapter 10).

I. The Unity
of the Church

CHAPTER TWO

UNITY AND DIVISION

AT THE BEGINNING OF REFLECTION ON UNITY, is it not necessary to ban any thought of the division of the Church? If not, ought we not at least avoid beginning with a chapter that carries such a paradoxical title and intends to deal with both the unity and the division of the Church? These questions are understandable, but they suppose the possibility of reflecting abstractly on this attribute, on the "idea" of the Church, while ignoring — for the present, at least — the disunity. However, such a possibility is not open to us, since, as we have already seen, the *credo* does not have an abstract idea, an ideal, or even a norm exclusively in view, but the reality of the Church. The *credo* is related to that reality: "that I am, and forever shall remain, a living member thereof" (H.C., Q. 54). In the Church where we live and move, and where we reflect on her, we are aware of that "paradox," her real history. Thus, we must inquire about the concrete significance of the *credo unam ecclesiam,* since it does not mean to fantasize about the Church. No matter how far-reaching the normativity of God's Word may be in all reflection on the Church, the problematic of unity and division affects the *credo* from the beginning on. There is no other Church than the earthly Church — in Corinth, in Philippi, in Smyrna, or in any other part of the world. As a result, whoever speaks confessionally about the unity of the Church must give account of what is in full view, namely, the Church in her disunity. Can some sort of "synthesis" possibly call us away from the wailing wall of division? Or are we confronted here with a painful, insoluble paradox that — even if it does not entirely annul the *credo ecclesiam* — at least radically relativizes it?

Indeed, it is not surprising that the question has continually been raised not simply how we might possibly explain the divi-

29

sion but how it is possible. What kind of strange, enigmatic reality is it that we call the "divided" Church? When Berkhof speaks of "God's Church and our many churches," he intends to indicate an enigmatic tension, not a dual "actuality."[1] The latter is impossible, since the *credo ecclesiam* cannot have anything else than God's Church in view: "You are God's field, God's building" (I Cor. 3:9). Berkhof's formulation attempts to stimulate us to reflection, since we cannot speak in any respect of "our many churches" next to God's Church. We touch here on one of the most important themes in ecclesiology. Because of the nature of the Church, as described in the gospel, one could take unity for granted, not in a simplistic or trivial sense, but because the being of the Church, as willed by God, implies unity. This is so clear from the entire New Testament that all disunity, rupture, and schism within Christ's Church, which is His body, appear to be ridiculous and impossible. The New Testament does speak in the plural of "churches" *(ekklēsiai)*, but that does not signify any rupture or disunity, since different groups of believers in different places are meant; they together form the Church of Christ (cf. Gal. 1:2; Acts 15:41; 16:5, etc.). It is a unity that cannot be affected by any "diaspora."[2] The light of grace and of reconciliation falls on this one Church. She has not arisen from her own initiative, but has been called, gathered, and chosen as the people of God, obtained by the blood of the cross (cf. Acts 20:28). Who can think here of multiplicity, of many churches, or of divided churches?

Menoud has pointed out that the expression "one Church" *(mia ekklēsia)* does not appear in the New Testament. This is not because of a lack of interest in unity, but because this unity belongs essentially to the Church's being: the expression "one Church" is really a pleonasm.[3] The unity of the Church is most closely connected with God's express intention to gather a people for His name; its background is the one call of God out

1. H. Berkhof, *Gods Kerk en onze vele Kerken*, p. 15.
2. I Pet. 1:1. Cf. *TDNT*, III, p. 505: "It is not that the *ekklēsia* divides up into *ekklēsiai*. Nor does the sum of the *ekklēsiai* produce the *ekklēsia*." From this "diaspora," one does not first have to be brought to the place where God's Name dwells (Neh. 1:9 LXX; cf. Ps. 147:2).
3. P.H. Menoud, *Mía Ekklēsia, Hommage et Reconnaissance*, 1946, pp. 87ff.: "The Church is one by definition," and "the formula '*mia ekklēsia*' would almost have shocked as a pleonasm." See also K. Barth, *C.D.*, IV/I, 668f.: unity "follows necessarily from all that we have seen concerning it." The unity is "a single unity. Otherwise it is not what the New Testament knows as the *ekklēsia*."

of darkness into His marvelous light, the call of the one people to the gracious election of God, to be His possession (Acts 15:14; I Pet. 2:9). Because of the nature and the purpose of this election,[4] unity is so unquestionable that, apart from a number of low points, the Church has never become completely comfortable with "our many churches." She never ceased to realize that multiplicity almost inevitably leads to the conclusion: "a plurality of churches in this sense means a plurality of Lords, a plurality of spirits, and a plurality of gods."[5] Anyone who would be a realist here, one who starts from the "empirical situation" and gives special emphasis to the undeniable division and to the many "churches," would speak about the Church without making the relationship to the Lord of the Church decisive. Realists often forget that, from the nature of the case, there can be only one Church, and multiplicity is by definition impossible.[6]

Is division "necessary"?

More than ever before, our time is aware of how self-evident this is in the Bible, even though one often has no idea of what to do with it in concrete, everyday reality. Because of the origin and mystery of the Church, her unity had to become more and

4. Cf. R.E. Clements, *God's Chosen People. A Theol. Interpretation of the Book of Deuteronomy,* 1968, p. 50, on the "gifts of God" and the clarity of election (Deut. 7:7f.; 9:4f.; 26:5-9). This clarity is not affected by hesitations about the relation between *"ekklēsia"* and the Old Testament (LXX). Cf. *TDNT,* III, 504f., 517f. *et al.;* and (differently) W. Schrage, *"'Ekklesia' und 'Synagoge,'"* *Z.Th.K.,* 60, 1963, pp. 178ff. Cf. also Bavinck, *Geref. Dog.,* IV, 261.
5. K. Barth, *C.D.,* IV/1, p. 675. Cf. *idem, Die Kirche und die Kirchen,* 1935. One may also think of the title of Section I at Evanston in 1954: "Our Oneness in Christ and Our Disunity as Churches." K.M. Beckmann (*Unitas Ecclesiae. Eine syst. Studie zur Theol. Geschichte des 19. Jahrhunderts,* 1967, p. 173) asks whether this formulation is "bearable theologically": "In connection with oneness in Christ, is it at all possible to hold to a disunity as churches? Or does disunity as churches in important questions of faith indicate precisely a lack of oneness in Christ?"
6. Cf. K. Barth, *Die Kirche und die Kirchen,* p. 7: "The question about the unity of the Church must be identical with the question about Jesus Christ as the concrete Head and Lord of the Church." Cf. *TDNT,* II, 442: "This means that early Christianity knows only one saving event, the cross, and only one Church." This aspect has been under discussion continuously in all the assemblies of the World Council of Churches, for instance at Evanston, New Delhi, and Lund. Cf. G.H. Weissgerber, *Die Frage nach der wahren Kirche. Eine Untersuchung zu den ekklesiologischen Problemen der ökum. Bewegung,* 1963; and H.L. Althaus, *Ökum. Dokumente. Quellenstücke über die Einheit der Kirche,* 1962.

more the ecumenical question in ecclesiology in opposition to
every escape into realism or idealism. Disquiet about division
arose neither from a general, natural desire for unity, in which
the slogan of "one Church" was placed next to that of "one
world," nor from the conviction that there is strength only in
unity. It arose rather from the concentrated light of divine
revelation, which reveals the reality of the Church *in Christ*.
Because of that light the question of the "meaning" of all the
tensions and conflicts, which have lasted not only years but sometimes for centuries, is inescapable. Are we not dealing here with
an entirely different reality from the reality that the New Testament calls the Church of God — not an alien, faraway ideal, but
"at Corinth" (I Cor. 1:2; II Cor. 1:1) and wherever the Word
of the Lord resounded, "in Macedonia and Achaia" and everywhere (I Thess. 1:8)? Must we conclude that we can speak only
of a "fall" from unity into an almost "self-evident" division, so
that, although we can grieve over this fall, we have no chance
of bringing the depths and perspective of the *credo* to expression? How should one think of our reality in the light of the
God of peace, Who brought again from the dead the great
Shepherd of the sheep (Heb. 13:20), and Who therefore deserves
glory for ever and ever (13:21)? Is it still possible in one way or
another to build the disunity of the Church into a biblically
normed understanding of the Church, so that everything becomes at least somewhat "understandable"? Can we perhaps
think of the "permission of God"? Or can we make a connection
between the Church's "actuality" and God's (ultimate) intention, His will? This sometimes happened in dogmatics when
the enigmatic, inexplicable statement was made that sin had
been taken up in the counsel of God, although it was attempted
in vain to maintain the biblical *a priori* that God is not the
cause of sin.[7] In these ways, one could easily land on the idea
of a "necessity" that mitigates the tension of disunity. But this
idea of necessity does not fit at all with the urgent admonition
of the whole of Scripture, with the mystery of the Church's
origin, or with God's intentions.

A statement of Paul's in I Cor. 11:19 occasionally plays a
role in these discussions: "For there *must (dei)* be factions among
you." Do we touch here upon a "necessity" that relativizes responsibility and suggests a certain inevitability? This statement
appears remarkably in the same letter in which, as we will see

7. On the biblical *a priori*, cf. my *Sin*, chapter 2.

later, Paul places disunity so sharply under the criticism of the gospel. Clearly, Paul in no sense places the situation in Corinth under the iron grip of "necessity."[8] The context points in a different direction, since Paul adds: "in order that those who are genuine among you may be recognized." This is generally seen as a crisis in which the Church is threatened and is put before a decision or choice. In that framework heresy can receive an indirect "function,"[9] but one must immediately interpret the words "the necessity and significance of heresy" in this way: "Against its own will and precisely by means of the danger that it caused the early Church, heresy has contributed essentially to the formation of ecclesiastical doctrine and to the preservation of the Church's unity."[10] Certainly, Paul's "in order that" points in this direction. Nothing is in common here with a necessity that causally assimilates the sin of disunity, so that its horror, its total disorder in contrast to God's election, calling, and intention, is eliminated.[11]

In the history of the Church, various attempts have been made to clarify the reality of the one Church and the many churches. There is an overwhelming consensus, first of all, that the division of the Church has its origin in human sin. It has been repeatedly pointed out that one's personal life always embraces continuing sinfulness, nearly unavoidable imperfection, a "not yet," and that this continuing resistance can also be

8. Calvin (*Commentary on the Letters of Paul to the Corinthians*, I, 367) does put *oportere* ("to be necessary"; Vulgate: *Nam oportet et haereses esse*) in the light of God's sure providence, but then he says that God "has it in view to try his people, as gold in the furnace." Calvin warns against "labyrinths as to a fatal necessity," blaming the necessity on Satan's attack on the Church: "From this — not from fate — comes that necessity of which Paul makes mention."

9. H.M. Fiolet (*De Tweede Reformatie*, 1969, pp. 20ff.) speaks of "the salvation-function of schism" (in addition to its meaning as disaster). He does not intend a "necessity" by that, but "the ecumenical salvation-function" in the encounter of the churches. K. Rahner-H. Vorgrimler (*Kleines Theologisches Wörterbuch*, s.v. *Häresie*) speaks of "a positive salvation-historical function for the Church" (with reference to Paul). Cf. the "salvation-historical 'must.' "

10. J. Brosch, *Das Wesen der Häresie*, 1936, p. 38. Cf. *TDNT*, II, 259, on "the patient perseverance of faith in Christ" as "the teaching of Paul to the Corinthians."

11. *Dei* ("it is necessary") in the New Testament may never be interpreted as "the neutral necessity of fate" or "cosmic necessity" (*TDNT*, II, 22). It is not connected to an "*anánkē* deity" and cannot be thought of apart from history. Cf. my *The Providence of God*, chapter 5, and *Divine Election*, chapter 8.

noted in the Church. One can speak here of avowed opposition to every ecclesiological perfectionism, that is, to every over-estimation of the "newness" of life in Christ due to an unreal romanticism that prematurely takes hold of a triumph of grace. But, on the other hand, there is a great danger here of forgetting the destructive character of sin and becoming resigned to it; one can underestimate "the dark riddle" (Barth) in ecclesiastical relations. And one can practically begin to use the Roman Catholic distinction between venial and mortal sins, without even cautioning — as Roman Catholic dogmatics does — that venial sins can create a "disposition" for mortal sin. Moreover, one can forget that Christ's concern for His Church was pre-cisely to bring together in love and reconciliation all the chil-dren of God who are scattered abroad.[12] Thus, whoever wants to speak of division as an "attribute" of the real Church, a property that belongs to her between Pentecost and the parousia, actually obliterates the reality of the one Lord, the one Shepherd of the sheep. The reference to continuing sin and to our limited-ness may never lead to ecclesiastical quietism and may never explain away the status quo, since the Church owes her reality as *Christ's* Church precisely to her being called out of darkness into marvelous light.[13]

Every "realistic" explanation threatens to blur the riddle of the disunity. Sin never lends itself to an explanation. Speaking about it here in the midst of the division itself is possible only in the form of a deep confession of guilt, so deep that one might expect unimaginable things to result from it![14] To speak about sin other than in this context is illegitimate; it is an escape from the clarity of God's intention and from the reality of the sole Shepherd. It is good to remind oneself of one of Christ's state-ments with an ominous ring to it: "Every kingdom divided against itself *(meristheisa kath' heautēs)* is laid waste, and no city or house divided against itself will stand" (Matt. 12:25). This "argument," which counters the Pharisees' claim that

12. John 11:52. Cf. W.A. Visser 't Hooft, *Heel de Kerk voor heel de Wereld. Balans van de Oecumene,* 1968, pp. 101ff.
13. I Pet. 2:9. Cf. K. Barth, *C.D.,* IV/1, 677, who says rightly: "The dis-unity of the Church is not grounded in the nature of the matter — in the existence of the Church, for example, in the temporary and im-perfect conditions of the time between the ascension and the coming again of Jesus Christ."
14. Cf. K. Barth, *Die Kirche und die Kirchen,* p. 10; and Ps. 32:3-5 on con-fession after withering silence. The end result is great joy.

Christ drove out evil spirits only by means of Beelzebub, the prince of demons, contains a warning against the "possible" catastrophe of destruction,[15] since it bears a "general" character: kingdom, city, and house. There is no reason to banish this warning from our minds when we reflect on this dividedness in the Church — the churches!

Unity only in the eschaton?

One particular form of this danger is the habit of placing the division in the light of the eschaton: only then will unity be realized. This is not so much a theoretical ecclesiology as it is a feeling that the division and disunity of the Church are as good as certain "in this dispensation" and that it hardly makes sense to look expectantly for the opposite. Thus, the unity of the Church gradually becomes a subject of the eschatological expectation, particularly because of the failure of various attempts to achieve unity. And a certain distrust of all vast, concrete appeals for unity can arise because of the fear that one may force unity and see it as the result of human initiative. In this framework one pointed repeatedly to the Roman Catholic view of unity *(una ecclesia Romana)*, which prematurely strove for the unity of the coming Kingdom and, in fact, proved its impossibility, since this unity often was more apparent than real. All such "eschatological" considerations can give rise to a form of defeatism, characterized by forbearance, resignation, and immobility, that is not willing to seek for unity with all its power and to pray that the status quo of division might be penetrated. One views this as an illusion because of the facts. We remember Kuyper's view of various endeavors to reach unity that started from the assumption that "as long as the unity of the Church has not been restored, the power of the Christian life cannot awake." Then Kuyper makes this striking statement: "There is no power at all in all such endeavor." One can only look down on such attempts "with the pity of melancholy,"

---

15. *Erēmoútai:* "is laid waste" (RSV). The KJV reads "brought to desolation"; and the Vulgate, *desolabitur.* Cf. *TDNT*, II, 658, on the desert as "the place without inhabitants." Parallel to that is "will not stand" *(ou stathēsetai).* We are reminded here of the *articulus stantis et cadentis ecclesiae* ("the article by which the Church stands and falls")! Cf. also the judgment in James 1:8 of the double-minded *(dipsuchos)* man, unstable in all his ways.

because "one knows beforehand that they have been striven for with absolute unfruitfulness."[16]

With this understanding of "reality" and of the course of history, the eschaton can easily begin to function as consolation and reassurance in the midst of the disunity of the Church. But in the New Testament, the eschaton never gives reassurance with respect to what belongs to human guilt. We do get a consoling outlook in connection with the sufferings of the present time that is not worth comparing with the glory to be revealed later (Rom. 8:18), and we are told that God will wipe away every tear (Rev. 21:4); but the eschatological outlook never weakens concrete calling and evangelical admonition. The eschaton does not leave room for any form of defeatism. Rather, it is a stimulus to live in this world, where the Church is called the light of the world (Matt. 5:14) — not in competition with Christ, Who is the Light of the world (John 8:12), but on account of His unique presence.

Therefore, the expectation of the consummation cannot detract from present unrest and anxiety, and no future splendor can take away the shadows that fall on the life of the Church. The call to unity and concord resounds in the Church's present, and the earnestness of this call entirely excludes every eschatological "alibi." In the confusion and darkness of sin, Paul does not console with what will one day be reality, but he calls to mind what has happened and what has been given. So also, reflection on unity is pointed not to the future but to the past. There is a kind of realism that lacks appreciation for God's intention: His will, His love, and Christ's being the Shepherd of the one flock. Christ's intention is to make the Church holy and to present her to Himself "in splendor (éndoxon), without spot or wrinkle or any such thing, that she might be holy and without blemish" (Eph. 5:27). The intention is not an isolated future,[17] but a concrete aim, full of admonition for the Church as she follows after the Lord. It forms the foundation for concrete deeds of love within the Church (Eph. 5:28ff.). Every escapist futurism is impossible, since the Church is summoned as unblemished children to be "blameless and innocent in the midst

16. A. Kuyper, *De Gemene Gratie*, III, 235. He points out how difficult it is to reunite churches "even where there is no difference in confession." For the connection with his doctrine . of pluriformity, see below, chapter 3.

17. *Ámōmos* ("without blemish") appears beside *hágios* ("holy") also in Eph. 1:4, as the purpose of election. Cf. also Col. 1:22: "holy, blameless, and irreproachable."

of a crooked and perverse generation, among whom you shine as lights of the world" (Phil. 2:15). The urgent perspective implies zeal in the present (cf. II Pet. 3:14), and this zealousness touches on the whole life of the one Church. The call to unity is not an eschatological plus; it rather points to unity in the present: unanimity, being in full accord and of one mind, on the basis of Christ's power (Phil. 2:2). Thus only can the Church live in expectation.[18]

Visible and invisible Church?

In addition to this eschatological motif in ecclesiology, there is another approach, which does not view everything from the point of view of the eschaton, but is related to the present. Here the distinction between the visible and invisible Church plays an important role. Often, this distinction was used to moderate to some degree the tension between unity and division by pointing to a certain unity that is present now in the "invisible Church." This distinction has had far-reaching effects in reflection on the Church. However, we also perceive great variation in its usage. For instance, in the polemic of the Reformation against Rome, the "invisible Church" was used to indicate that an institutional view of the Church cannot give a correct view of the reality of Christ's Church.[19] The intention here was not to flee from visibility to invisibility, to a docetic, unearthly ecclesiology; rather, it was to remind us of the Church's essence as the congregation of the faithful in the fellowship with Christ through the Spirit.[20] The intention was definitely not to suggest that there are two churches. True, Bellarmine, especially, did interpret the Reformation in this way,[21] but the Reformers em-

---

18. In connection with *ámōmos*, *TDNT*, IV, 831, speaks of "the perfect moral and religious piety," which obligates the believers to be blameless "before the judgment."
19. Cf. K. Holl, "Die Entstehung von Luthers Kirchenbegriff," in *Ges. Aufs. zur K.G.*, I, 1923, pp. 296ff.
20. Cf. Melanchthon, *Apology of the Augsburg Confession:* "We are not dreaming about some platonic republic, as has been slanderously alleged, but we teach that this church actually exists, made up of true believers and righteous men scattered throughout the world" (in T.G. Tappert, *The Book of Concord*, 1959, p. 171). The critical aspect of the distinction still functions even when the distinction shifts in connection with the "hypocrites and wicked men" (*hypocriti et mali*) in the Church and in connection with the invisibility of the true Church. Cf. Bavinck, *Geref. Dog.*, II, 290.
21. "They imagine two churches" (Bellarmine, *De conciliis*, III, 2). He saw the distinction in the light of the earlier condemnation of the

phatically rejected this reproach. Their concern in using this terminology — which is imperfect, since the distinction can suggest two churches — was the testing of the Church's heart and life before the face of God, a testing about whether she is truly the Church and about whether she truly belongs to the flock of the Shepherd. To the degree that Roman Catholic circles recognize this necessary motif of testing, there is more understanding that this distinction is intended as a critical distinction,[22] making it possible to avoid a capitulation to the identification of ecclesiastical facts with normativity. Such an identification would make the history of the Church sacrosanct and would have made all reformation impossible.[23] Certainly, this distinction was intended as a reference to God's *cognitio ecclesiae,* a reminder of His examination of the Church (cf. II Tim. 2:19; Acts 15:8; I Thess. 2:4; Rev. 2:23), parallel to His testing of individual believers.

But the concept of the invisible Church is also used differently, not so much to expose the tensions and responsibility of the visible Church as to "solve" those tensions, especially with respect to unity. The tensions and the guilt of division are lessened through reassurance of "invisible" unity and fellowship. Thus, the impression is given — the outlines of two churches loom up here — that sin has penetrated into the visible, but not into the invisible, Church. A dualizing element could easily

Fraticelli by John XXII: "He imagines two churches, one carnal and the other spiritual" (*Gloriosam Ecclesiam,* Denz., 485). Cf. H. Bacht, "Die Sichtbarkeit der Kirche im kontroverstheol. Gespräch der Kirche," *Einsicht und Glaube,* 1962, pp. 447ff. Bellarmine's starting point was a very static *ecclesia visibilis;* hence, he could not perceive the viewpoint of the Reformation.

22. Cf. H. Jedin, *Ekklesiologie um Luther (Fuldaer Hefte,* 1968, p. 28). However, the interpretation of the distinction as an escape has lasted for a long time. See the encyclical *Satis Cognitum* in 1896. Criticism of the Reformation can run parallel to the rejection of modern Catholic streams that undervalue the visible, juridical, institutional aspect of the Church. In 1943 *Mystici Corporis Christi (TCT,* 240) stated that the Church "must also be something definite and perceptible." Further, "The Church is visible because she is a body" (a quote from *Satis Cognitum*); she is not merely "pneumatological," as in "many Christian communities."

23. That the intention of the Reformation was not to escape to an "ideal" Church is proved not only by the rejection of the *civitas Platonica* in the *Apology,* but also by the way one spoke of the *ecclesia abscondita* and the *ecclesia latens.* Cf. G. Gloege, *Heilsgeschehen und Welt. Theol. Traktate,* I, 1965, pp. 219ff.; and H. Fagerberg, *A New Look at the Lutheran Confessions (1529-1537),* 1972, p. 251.

penetrate ecclesiology in this way and could bind itself to the eschatological motif, since the assumption was made that the unity, already present though hidden and invisible, would be disclosed not in this world but in the future.[24]

Division in Scripture

Let us leave these impossible paths and return to the New Testament, where the unity of the Church is self-evident. Or is it? Is not the New Testament full of threats to and frustrations of unity in Christ? Does not the admonition to unity, which occurs so frequently, itself point towards the continuing danger of actual division? Undoubtedly, there is reference in the New Testament to actual unity — for example, when Paul considers it unnecessary to speak about love of the brethren, "for you yourselves have been taught by God to love one another" (I Thess. 4:9). But this does not alter the fact that various urgent admonitions give the impression that the concrete Church knew of no such self-evidence of unity and love.[25] An appeal *(paráklēsis)* is made to the Church for unanimity over against everything that threatens concord (Phil. 2:1f.). The Church must lead a life worthy of her calling, and she must be eager to maintain the unity of the Spirit in the bond of peace (Eph. 4:1, 3). All admonition assumes that the attack on unity is a real danger, and nowhere do we meet with evidence that this danger has been radically precluded.[26] In this connection I Cor. 1 is especially striking because Paul deals with actual dissensions *(schismata)* and quarrels *(érides)* among the Corinthians (vss. 10 and 11), who are called at the beginning of the letter "the Church of God, those sanctified in Christ Jesus, those called to be saints" (vs. 2)! The differences at Corinth become spectacularly clear in various slogans; relatedness to a particular person has come to determine the modality of belonging to the Church: Paul, Apol-

---

24. In the Evanston Declaration, 1954, the aspects of "already" and "not yet" come to expression in the words: "It is certain that the perfect unity of the Church will not be totally achieved until God sums up all things in Christ. But the New Testament affirms that this unity is already being realized within the present historical order."

25. Cf. A.A. van Ruler, *Ik Geloof*, 1968, p. 138, on the Church as "the cathedral of love." That is not a simple diagnosis, but is connected with "enormous tensions."

26. See the tension already in Acts 6:1 between the Hellenists and Hebrews.

los, Cephas, or . . . Christ (vs. 12).[27] Clear facts are involved here
(everything has been reported to Paul — vs. 11), and the apostle
takes all of this seriously. Paul's approach to these slogans is a
striking one. He does not simply make a general admonition to
unity but asks an amazing question: "Is Christ divided?" (vs.
13 — *meméristai ho Christós*). Paul's pastoral leadership is assuredly filled with the admonition to unity, with the call to agreement; and he forbids dissensions because the Corinthians must
be united in the same mind and judgment (vs. 10 — *tó autò
légēte pántes*). But all of this stands in the revealing light of
that question about Christ.[28] Essentially, it is the question of
how all of this is possible or even thinkable, and it expresses
great surprise at this "reality" in the Corinthian Church.[29] How
is it possible that there are dissensions here among those who
have been called and sanctified in Christ Jesus, among those
over whom grace and peace have been pronounced (vss. 2-3)?
How is all of this possible without affecting Christ Himself?

The seriousness of Paul's question has not always been understood. Its core is not simply regret at or rejection of the situation
in Corinth, but rather the direct connection that the question
makes between the Church and Christ. Apparently, Paul cannot
acquiesce to an almost inevitable, human "not yet." So he asks
about Christ and about the "possibility" of this dark reality in
Corinth. In the light of the undivided Lord, all motivations for
quarreling and schism are undermined. This situation is truly
"impossible," not as if it were unreal, but because of the meaning, the origin, and the reality of the Church. If shadows are

---

27. Cf. 3:4ff., where only Paul and Apollos are mentioned. The most re-
    markable group in 1:12 is the Christ-faction. Cf. J. Wendland, *Die
    Briefe an die Korinther*, 1954, p. 15; K. Barth, *Die Auferstehung der
    Toten*, 1934, pp. 3ff.; and especially P.A. van Stempvoort, *Eenheid en
    Schisma*, 1950. It is apparent from the schismatic character of the
    Christ-faction that the context is entirely different than when Paul
    says "You are Christ's" (3:23) and speaks of "boasting in the Lord."
28. H. Schlier (*Die Einheit der Kirche nach dem N.T. Catholica*, 1960,
    p. 164) underlines the seriousness of Paul's question: "He means: if the
    Church — or even the local Church alone — divides, Christ is divided.
    He does not mean that only figuratively, but really." Cf. also H. Volk,
    Die Einheit der Kirche und die Spaltung der Christenheit. Catholica,
    1960, pp. 241ff.
29. Cf. the dissensions in contrast to being united in 1:10. Cf. *TDNT*,
    VI, *s.v. schízein. Schízein* is to "tear" or to "rip up," as clothes are
    rent (Isa. 36:22 LXX; Mark 15:38).

cast here, then they are cast on Christ too. Is Christ divided?[30]

The conflicts in the Church of Corinth prove that the Christians there did not understand what the Church is: God's field and building.[31] To be tempted into use of slogans and into separation within the Church is nothing other than the revelation of a fleshly disposition (3:3 — *sarkikós*), behaving like ordinary men (3:3 — *katà ánthrōpon peripateíte*), or babes (3:1f. — *népios*) — just as to celebrate the Lord's supper in division is really to despise the Church of God (11:22 — *kataphronein*). The disunity is not understandable; it is an *alienum* in the congregation. Calvin was very impressed by Paul's question to the Corinthian Church and by the dreadful fact that factions were tearing apart the unity of faith. He says that nothing is more alien to the Christian faith than that one separates oneself from another and, thus, attacks and abandons the center.[32] Dissension in the congregation is an intolerable evil; it is absurd and senseless. It is not enough to deplore the phenomenon of imperfection. To express it one must use the sharpest terms, ones that border on impossibility.[33] In asking whether Christ is divided, Paul seeks to point out that such a division means alienation from Christ. Thus, Calvin reminds us that "there could not be two or three churches unless Christ be torn asunder — which cannot happen" *(Inst., IV, 1, 2)*.

In the New Testament the outlook on the one Lord of the Church makes it impossible and senseless to replace the singular with a plural for the Church. We hear, for instance, of Paul's zeal for and watchfulness over the Church, which he has betrothed "to Christ to present you as a pure bride to her one husband" (II Cor. 11:2). We hear also of Christ's concern for the Church (Eph. 5:2) and for the Church as bride (cf. John

30. F.W. Grosheide *(Commentary on the First Epistle to the Corinthians)* understands *merizein* as "apportioned," i.e., Christ as belonging only to a part, not to all. This interpretation has different ecclesiological consequences, which are connected with the "modalities." Cf. chapter 4.

31. I Cor. 3:9. Paul opposes the lack of understanding again and again in I Cor. with the recollection of what one could know. See in differing contexts the question "Do you not know?" (3:16; 6:2, 3, 9, 15, 16, 19).

32. "Nothing is more inconsistent on the part of Christians than to be at variance among themselves, for it is the main article of our religion that we be in harmony among ourselves" *(Commentary on the Letters of Paul to the Corinthians, I, 62)*. Cf. D. Nauta, "Calvijns Afkeer van een Schisma," *Ex Auditu Verbi*, 1965, pp. 130ff.

33. Paul so abhors all of this that he cannot sufficiently execrate it *(Inst., IV, 13, 14)*.

3:29; Rev. 21:2). The unity is unquestionably clear: the Church is the household of God (I Tim. 3:15), the temple of God (I Pet. 2:9f.), the one flock of the one Shepherd (John 10:16). All such characterizations make any thought of the plural simply ridiculous. Verbally, at least, this always seems to have been understood: we still hear the word "churches," but no one wants to transpose house, temple of God, bride, or flock into the plural! Already in Israel schism casts a deep shadow on the existence of the entire people. The Old Testament places schism in the context of God's judgment,[34] but that does not lessen its seriousness; rather, it makes it totally clear. And when the promises break through this darkness, they relate, first of all, to a breakthrough of the schism between Israel and Judah: Judah will join Israel, and they will come together to the land of the fathers (Jer. 3:18; cf. Hos. 1:11). In Ezekiel, the promise throws the light of a "gathering from all sides" on the darkness of schism: "And they shall be no longer two nations, and no longer divided into two kingdoms."[35] This outlook reaches back to the origin of the one people whose one calling is to bear His name in the world and thus to be a blessing. In the New Testament, we meet the same theme of gathering, the same light of unity and fellowship. There is no longer Jew nor Greek, slave nor free, because "you are all one in Christ Jesus" (Gal. 3:28); and with regard to Jew and Gentile, the dividing wall of hostility is broken down and the two are made one (Eph. 2:14f.).

Why is there such urgency about unity, about broken walls, about restoration and reconciliation? One cannot answer by giving the singular as such priority over the plural. One cannot view the Church in the abstract any more than one can place monotheism in the abstract above polytheism. Israel's monotheism is inseparably connected to the complete uniqueness and incomparability of Yahweh in distinction to all other gods.[36] He

---

34. I Kings 11:29ff. Cf. 12:24, where Shemaiah brings the word of the Lord that Judah may not fight against Israel (her kinsmen), because "this thing is from Me."
35. Ezek. 37:21ff. It goes without saying that one must beware of various "analogies" with the schism in Israel. In spite of a passionate ecumenical attitude, Gregory Baum (*Kerk en Eenheid*, 1964, p. 70) falls victim to this when he draws a parallel between Judah as the "authentic heir" of God's promise and the Catholic Church: "a genuine analogy." He does add, though, that where the inheritance is present sins are even more dreadful, which likewise applies to the Catholic Church (pp. 71f.).
36. Cf. Ps. 135:5 ("above all gods"); 72:18; Isa. 44:25ff.; 45:20. Cf. Rahner-Vorgrimler, *Kleines Theologisches Wörterbuch*, s.v. *Monotheïsmus*, p.

alone is God, the One Who can redeem. He alone does wonders. That is the proclamation to Israel: "Was it not I, the Lord? And there is no other god besides me, a righteous God and a Savior; there is none besides me."[37] The uniqueness of Israel is founded in this singularity of Yahweh, in His gracious election of her as the people of God. The plural is unthinkable here, while the horribleness of a change of gods and the abandonment of Him Who is the source of living water (Jer. 2:11ff.) becomes clear. The whole witness to the unity and incomparability of Israel's God, which implies the uniqueness of Israel as the people gathered by Him, points to an *Einzigartigkeit*, a uniqueness, that leaves no room for the plural.[38] Hence, the Church rests in her unique foundation: the complete sufficiency of Christ. Every other name is out of the question here; all other ways have been cut off. The decisive "once for all" of Hebrews testifies to this sufficiency and radicalness and makes all repetition senseless, because everything has already happened (9:26)! Here the decisive and definitive singular stands opposite the plural;[39] it is a concentration of the promise to Abraham, in the singular, not in the plural.[40] Thus, "together" becomes the decisive aspect of the Church (cf. Eph. 3:17f.; I Cor. 1:2), while rupture and quarreling are stamped as radical alienation and as the source of unending disquiet in the light of God's intention "from the beginning."[41]

Unity "so that the world may believe"

From Christ's high priestly prayer in John 17, we see how significant the unity of the Church was for the Lord as He stood

246: "not some numinous power or other ('a' God), but that one, single, absolute God." See also J.J. Durand, *Una Sancta Catholica in Sendingsperspektief,* 1961, p. 26; and H. Bavinck, *Geref. Dog.,* II, 141.

37. Isa. 45:21. Cf. also 46:5, 9ff.; 40:25f.; Mic. 7:18ff.; Mark 10:18; I Cor. 8:6; and especially Deut. 6:4 ("Hear, O Israel: The Lord our God is one Lord").

38. Cf. K. Barth, *C.D.,* IV/3, 2, 730ff. See Deut. 33:29 with respect to Israel: "Happy are you, O Israel! Who is like you, a people saved by the Lord." The uniqueness is expressed also in the gathering together again "from the nations" (Ezek. 38:12). Cf. van Stempvoort, *op. cit.,* pp. 10f.; and K.H. Miskotte, *De Praktische Zin van de Eenvoud Gods,* 1945.

39. Cf. I Pet. 3:18; and *TDNT,* II, 435: "Early Christianity has a comprehensive awareness of the astonishing import of the single and unique."

40. Gal. 3:16f. *(Eph' henós* in contrast to *epì pollón).*

41. Acts 15:14 *(próton).* Cf. the fulfillment of Amos 9:11f. in Acts 15:16-18.

at the gateway to His *passio magna*. But is there not "tension" here between Christ's supplication and the Church's actual division? What, then, is the power of Christ's prayer? In James, we are told that the prayer of a righteous man has great power in its effects, because power is given to it (5:16f.); and we are reminded of what happened after Elijah's prayer in the barrenness of a beaten land: in a little while the heavens grew black with clouds and wind, and there was a great rain (I Kings 18:45). Hence, it is not at all strange that one ask about the power of the prayer of Him Who in a unique sense is called "the righteous" (I John 2:1). Bavinck says that this prayer ("that they may all be one") "has not resulted from lack of knowledge about her [the Church's] history, nor from lack of power to rule her." His solution is that the prayer "is heard daily in and through the division and is led towards its complete fulfillment." Moreover, he sees a guarantee in this prayer "that it exists already in Him and in His own good time will be disclosed also in all believers."[42]

It is not easy to understand the meaning of these words, at least not as a solution. Christ's prayer for unity is connected to a specific goal: "so that the world may believe that thou hast sent me."[43] The unity of believers does not emerge here as something isolated, but the world comes into view. John 17 says expressly that Jesus does not pray for the world (vs. 9 — *ou perì toú kósmou erōtô*). Rather, via the "detour" of the Church's unity, the world is mentioned.[44] In this way alone does the "so that" get its full meaning, since via the Church's unity faith and recognition also arise in the world, and that world is related to the salvation of God.[45] In this prayer there is no mention of a mystical or inner unity, but of an obvious "accessibility": the unity is a manifest reality open to all, an unassailable concord founded in the sending of Christ into the world. One could call

42. H. Bavinck, *Geref. Dog.*, IV, 301. Cf. also his *Magnalia Dei*, p. 501, on the growing unity. Unity is present, "but it is effected and applied gradually."
43. John 17:21 *(pisteúę)*. Cf. also 17:23: "that the world may *know (ginóskę)*."
44. On concern for the world, cf. also 17:20: belief in Christ through their word. Bultmann *(Das Evangelium des Johannes,* 1950, p. 394) sees Christ's prayer as "intercession for the world."
45. C. Bouma *(Korte Verklaring. De Evangelie naar Johannes,* II, 142) sees belief here not as "saving belief through true faith," but as a necessity due to "the course of things."

the unity of the Church a letter of Christ, in the words of Paul, "to be known and read by all men."[46]

Clearly, this is not of minor importance, something that is not necessary for the "essence" of the Church. In the light of Christ's prayer, the Church may not be viewed as a hidden, mystical, mysterious present reality full of inner richness, which the world cannot perceive. Rather, the world is essentially important here, and we are reminded of what Philip says to Nathanael in the midst of all his hesitations: "Come and see" (John 1:46)! The decisive thing in Christ's prayer is this discovery, the perception of an unbreakable unity and fellowship. It is a wonder awakened by the crucified and raised Lord Who is the Head of this Church. To flee here to the continuing sinfulness of the Church as an "explanation" of her disunity or into the reassurance that a hidden unity can survive in the division does not take Christ's prayer seriously. In the high priestly prayer, "realism" as an evasion certainly has no place. For Christ also asks that this Church be protected from evil (John 17:15) and that she be consecrated in the truth of God (John 17:19). Because of her function and purpose in relating salvation to the world, one cannot boast here of a solidarity that is sufficient in God's eyes, but one must think of the eyes of the world.

It is striking to what a high degree, in the whole of the New Testament, the Church is related to the discovery of the gospel by the world. On one side stands the god of this age, who blinds the minds of men and hinders them from seeing the light of glory (II Cor. 4:3f.). On the other side stands the Church, which has been taken up in the process of convincing the world. She is the salt of the earth (Matt. 5:13) and the light of the world (5:14). Her light shines before men (5:16) that the Father may be glorified. Her preaching must go out into the world (28:19), and she proclaims the wonderful deeds of God (I Pet. 2:9). But the function of the Church manifests itself also in her being, her unity, which becomes visible and thus summons up reactions of faith and acknowledgment. This "being" always has a goal, just as Christ placed love for one another in a broad connection: "By this all men will know that you are my disciples, if you have love for one another" (John 13:35). In that love a window is thrown open on the Lord, and He is perceived as its

---

46. II Cor. 3:2 (*ginōskoménē kaì anaginōskoménē hupò pántōn anthrópōn*). Cf. *phaneroúmenoi* in 3:3: "You show that you are a letter from Christ."

source. Likewise, Christ prays for unity to be such a window, which gives an outlook on His mission in this world.

Unity has a radical transition in view, a conversion from unbelief to belief. But unity is neither a logical conclusion nor an automatic consequence. Faith and acknowledgment, the discovery, do not stand apart from the preaching of the Word (John 17:20); but, apparently, this preaching can result in repentance only if it is a single witness, a symphony and harmony without dissonance, resounding from clear unity. The only way to miss these connections is to take the way of spiritualism, which does not allow for an intermediary and expects everything from the direct working of the Holy Spirit apart from men. But that is the diametrical opposite of Paul's insight that the way to faith is closed apart from preaching, i.e., human proclamation (Rom. 10:14). It is the same with regard to the reality of unity. Therefore, the severance of unity is a catastrophe for the world. John 17 says as much, but we are so accustomed to disunity that we are in danger of becoming immune to its warning.

The Church's guilt for disbelief

One may not offer profound psychological views of the "causes" of unbelief, unless one also does justice to the connection between unbelief and division. Bavinck writes "that the endless division of the Church gives the world *cause* for joy and derision, a *reason* for its unbelief in the One sent by the Father."[47] This brings up the question of the Church's guilt with regard to unbelief, which is one of the deepest "ecclesiological" problems. On the surface that does not seem to be the case because hardly anyone completely distantiates himself from all guilt with regard to division. In general, one recognizes that the Psalmist's statement "but who can discern his errors?" (Ps. 19:12) has more than simply individual significance; but difficulties usually arise when the attempt is made to concretize participation in guilt. Barth writes that "every division as such is a deep riddle, a skandal."[48] Bavinck says the same — in his dogmatics! —

---

47. *Geref. Dog.*, IV, 300. Cf. also his *Magnalia Dei*, p. 502: "a most deplorable sight." Cf. proposition 18 from H.M. Kuitert's dissertation, *De Mensvormigheid Gods*, 1969[3], which reads: "The intelligibility and credibility of the gospel are both frustrated by the plural number of preaching churches."

48. *C.D.*, IV/1, p. 675. Cf. p. 677 on "the effects of this disunity on the mission fields of Asia and Africa" in connection with the illusion of "a Christian West." The Church is in danger of "a repetition of the

when he summons us to humility: "We cannot be humble enough as Christians about the disruptions and the discord that have existed in the Church of Christ through all ages; it is a sin against God, in conflict with the prayer of Christ, and caused by the darkness of our mind and the lack of love in our heart."[49] Naturally, these categories of disorder and darkness bring to mind many questions when we survey the history of the Church, where the concrete occasions and causes of schism and division automatically come into view. Even if we understand the truth of Scheler's statement that, although guilt usually seems one-sided on the surface, it is usually mutual "in the depths," we must admit that to assign equal guilt to everything leads only to vagueness and never serves true reconciliation. Thus, the struggle for a true confession is undoubtedly meaningful,[50] and if we start from some vague concept of schism that is not determined historically, the question of guilt loses its profound significance.

A general statement that avoids all concretions and nuances in the historical life of the Church eventually becomes false and unfruitful. Nevertheless, one cannot deny that the general statements made by Kuyper, Bavinck, and Barth — "all," "we," and "every" — point to something essential. They can be understood, however, only in light of the origin and background of the unity of the Church and in light of her relatedness to the world. The factors influencing the continuing separation and alienation within the one Church are often inscrutable and unverifiable. Neither the accentuation of the institution nor that of the confession can offer any protection here, since the whole of the Church's life in word and deed must be taken into account. Whoever rejects every inclusive statement about the Church because of the danger of vagueness can do so only out of a self-exaltation and in an unjustified aversion to all actual solidarity in guilt.[51] The result is that interest in the world becomes

---

plurality and contradictions of the world of heathen religions and the conflicts of secular totalitarianism."

49. *Geref. Dog.*, IV, 300. Cf. below, chapter 3, footnote 21.
50. Cf. below on the apostolicity of the Church.
51. Occasionally, we meet with a confession of guilt that transcends the individual to a realization of the concrete "we," for instance, in Adrian VI's confession of guilt in 1523, with respect to the sins "especially of the spiritual and ecclesiastical dignitaries." It is a confession "of the last, non-Italian pope" (B. Schneider, "Bemerkungen zur Kritik an der Kirche," *Gott in Welt*, II, 1964, pp. 254ff.).

languid, and one has little trouble with disunity in the Church. But all criticism of the unbelief and, frequently, the enmity in the world is senseless and illegitimate when the obstruction caused by the disunity of the Church is not seen. This criticism, then, casts shadows on the reality and care of the Shepherd of the sheep, and it threatens all intercession for the world and all proclamation of this Shepherd, Who has been brought again from the dead (Heb. 13:20). The "so that" in John 17 sharply sets out the mystery of this unity. It is not a tactical maneuver, but is part of God's plan of salvation, a way of revealing His ultimate, reconciling intentions in a world characterized by disunity.

Trinitarian unity and the Church

The significance of unity also appears from other aspects of the high priestly prayer.[52] We have in mind the reference to the unity between Father and Son: "that they may all be one; even as thou, Father, art in me, and I in thee, that they also may be in us, so that the world may believe that thou hast sent me" (John 17:21). Unity cannot be indicated more deeply than in this analogy. To see it as "a lofty comparison coming from edifying rhetoric" is to envelop it in a pious mist,[53] whereas a new context of reference is introduced here, namely, the trinitarian mystery (17:11, 21f.). Thus, this prayer embraces the command that arises from this mystery.[54] One does have to search for words here: analogy, parallel, reflection, parable. The unity between Father and Son is the great mystery of Christ's messianic life (cf. 10:30, 38), and it forms the deep foundation for what belongs to the essence of the Church.[55] Who would dare make comparisons here if the Lord Himself had not given the right and the duty to do so? Even though the Church confessed that the trinitarian mystery "far surpasses all human understanding" (B.C., Art. 9), there can apparently be no doubt about the accessibility of this analogy, since the Church in the world

---

52. Cf. John 17:23: "that they may become perfectly one." From John 17, it is apparent also how senseless it is to play off truth against unity or unity against truth, for the concern is with this unity: the Word (17:14); truth (17:19); the name (17:26). Cf. also E. Käsemann, *The Testament of Jesus*, 1968, p. 56.

53. Käsemann, *op. cit.*, pp. 57ff.

54. *Ibid.*

55. Cf. Bultmann, *op. cit.*, p. 392, on "the nature and ground of unity."

is in question.[56] For the connections that are made here are the connections of glory: "The glory *(doxá)* which thou hast given me I have given to them, that they may be one..." (17:22). We are not speaking here of far-off, unreal things, but rather of a reality for which we pray, the background of which is the will of Christ and His emphatic vision: "And I have other sheep, that are not of this fold; I must bring them also, and they will heed my voice. So there shall be one flock, one shepherd" (10:16).

The high priestly prayer forms for John the entrance hall of the Lord's way to the cross. The earnestness with which Christ has prayed to the Father will become clear along that way, and also with respect to the Church's unity. To forget the "so that" of John 17 is to lose the outlook both on the meaning of the *passio magna* and on the world, which God has loved in sending His Son.[57] That world is related to this love not through a "miracle," but through the witness of the Word and through the undisrupted oneness of the Church. If the being and proclamation of the Church are to be characterized by fruitfulness in and on behalf of the world, unity is the only possibility.[58]

In times of distress and threat, the necessity of the unity of the Church has often been strongly emphasized out of fear that she would be so engrossed with internal conflicts that she might lose sight of other, external dangers. In such situations a prophetic admonition could sound forth: the jealousy of Ephraim must depart and Judah may not harass Ephraim any longer, because together they must wage war against the Philistines

56. A "nevertheless" *(nihilominus)* of belief and expectation follows these confessional words. Cf. on the "effects" that we feel in ourselves. The "nevertheless" must also be confessed with respect to the comparison, although the Confession does not speak about it.

57. John 3:16. Cf. the statement by the Samaritan believers about Christ: "this is indeed the Savior of the world" (4:42). He is the bread that gives life to the world (6:33, 51), and He has come for the salvation of the world (3:17; 12:47; 9:5). According to Käsemann *(op. cit.,* p. 59), there is "an unmistakable restriction" in the Gospel of John, parallel to that in the Qumran community. He speaks of John 3:16 (the world) as "this statement that is nowhere repeated." Thus, according to him, the exclamation of the Samaritan believers does not characterize the Johannine Christ "adequately." To my mind that is an incomprehensible view of John.

58. Cf. F.W. Grosheide *(De Evangelie naar Johannes,* II, 416), who says in connection with the analogy: "Here even the appearance of any difference of opinion is lacking. Thus it must be among those whom Jesus received from the Father." Cf. also Käsemann, *op. cit.,* pp. 56f., on unity as the dominant criterion of the true Church.

(Isa. 11:13f.). But the call to unity is not a pragmatic endeavor, and the deepest ground of unity does not lie in particular circumstances. If that were the case, disunity would return again when the danger had passed; the unity would be nothing more than a temporary settlement of the differences.

The foundation of unity is the nature of the Church itself. Nothing else than one flock and one Shepherd (John 10:16) is conceivable. Christ is disclosed as Shepherd in His love for the crowds, who were harassed and helpless, like sheep without a shepherd (Matt. 9:36; Mark 6:34). In the context of that mercy, we also hear of the plentiful harvest, along with a call to pray for laborers (Matt. 9:37f.). The Church may forget neither the harvest nor the Shepherd of the sheep, for the Shepherd is known and recognized in the one flock. The picture of the Shepherd shows us Christ's unique work of gathering, which brings and holds the flock together. He gives His life for the sheep, and it is as the Shepherd that He is struck (Mark 14:27; cf. Zech. 13:7). Christ's role of Shepherd shows us the universality of His work, since what was scattered abroad is gathered into one in Him.[59] That is the great light shining on the Church in promise and admonition: the light of glory and the perspective for the world. To be actively and responsibly related in this perspective cannot lead to an *ecclesiologia gloriae* because everything has been founded in the cross.

Finally, one might ask whether we have not spoken too idealistically and unrealistically. Are these not simply distant and unreal ideals? This question belongs to the many great temptations that continually threaten the Church, and it signifies nothing other than alienation from the norm of the Church, as well as from her reality as it is tested by this norm. One must definitely ask what we are to think of the undeniable "plural" that dominates our speech, particularly in light of the self-evident singular. But no "explanation" may moderate the tension, especially if we understand to some degree how greatly the *mysterium iniquitatis,* the mystery of sin, contradicts the genuine "mystery."[60] With the history of the Church in view, we can question further here only in dismay and terror. That is the deeply moving responsibility of the Church's confession: *credo unam ecclesiam.*

59. John 11:51f. Cf. O. Hofius, "Die Sammlung der Heiden zur Herde Israels" (John 10:16; 11:51f.), *Z.N.T.W.,* 58 (1967), 289ff.
60. Cf. my *Sin,* 1971, chapter 5.

CHAPTER THREE

PLURIFORMITY?

IN DIFFERENT PHASES OF THE HISTORY OF THE
Church, the paradoxicality of unity and division has given
new impulse to reflection. As we have seen, the attempt has
been made to accentuate unity through an escape into the
eschaton or into an *ecclesia invisibilis*. But in such attempts lies
the danger of losing the outlook on the Church as the flock of
the good Shepherd. Realizing this danger, others have taken
different paths and have tried to account for both unity and
division. We want to take a separate look now at a remarkable
and suggestive ecclesiological theory, the doctrine of the pluriformity, or multiformity, of the Church. The purpose of this
theory is neither to shift the unity of the Church into the future
nor to make everything dependent on the already present, but
hidden, unity of the invisible Church; rather, it seeks to examine
the concrete, visible Church, and does so by placing her in the
light of pluriformity.

At first glance this formulation is clear. It points to an undeniable state of affairs, the multiplicity of churches. "Pluriformity" immediately forces us to open our eyes to the many
and the multiform. Moreover, the concept of "pluriformity" implies that, at its deepest level, there is only one Church! Thus,
one does not usually speak of a plurality of churches, but of
the pluriformity of the Church.[1] Multiplicity, however, is not
disregarded, because it is discussed in connection with the many
forms, figures, or revelations of the one Church. Thus the pluriformity of the Church is intended, on one hand, to protect the
outlook on one flock and one Shepherd, and, on the other hand,
to keep us from closing our eyes to the actual multiplicity. At

1. However, see Kuyper (*Principles of Sacred Theology*, pp. 662ff.): "the
multiformity of the churches."

51

the same time the theory rejects all churchism, which, resting in the exclusive truth of one's own church, draws simple, radically critical conclusions regarding the other churches. Further, we sense a certain richness in the doctrine of pluriformity. The word itself has always suggested a rich, blessed multiformity in contrast to all uniformity, which Kuyper called the curse of modern life, since uniformity left no room for genuine variation and meaningful differentiation.[2] Pluriformity, then, makes room for variegation and distinction, both of which are so valuable for all human life: because reality is not captive to uniformity, it is richer, not poorer![3]

Criticism of the "riches" in pluriformity

This "creational" motif frequently is perceptible in the doctrine of pluriformity. Along with that goes the notion that God loves multiformity. Nevertheless, critical questions have been raised concerning this creational motif. Pluriformity is a much too beautiful word for the concrete multiplicity of churches. The common meaning of pluriformity is the disclosure of one "essence" in many "forms," but that eliminates the actual problem in disunity. This criticism was pointedly expressed once in the question whether one can still speak of a broken vase as a "pluriform" vase.[4] Is the pluriformity of creaturely life really a good analogy for the multitude of churches, which present themselves in rupture, schism, and contradiction, in separation and alienation? Naturally, this critical question is not intended as a denial of all difference and variation in the Church. Great riches are discernible in the variation, but all of this has its place within the one Church, where there is no rupture, conflict, and disharmony: though many, one body in Christ (I Cor. 12:12; cf. 12:29). The diversity within the congregation is willed and given by God (12:5ff.), and it secures fellowship without discord "in the body" (12:25), since all variation is related to the same Lord (12:5) and is serviceable for the common good.[5]

2. Cf. Kuyper, *Eenvormigheid, de Vloek van het moderne Leven*, 1869.
3. Cf. the descriptions of nature in Pss. 8 and 104 and the diversity of which Paul speaks: the difference between the glory of the sun and that of the moon and between the stars (I Cor. 15:39ff.). See also Pss. 148 and 150.
4. I recall this image from an examination in dogmatics by Rev. D. Sikkel in Classis Amsterdam.
5. I Cor. 12:7. See below, chapter 4.

In the "separateness" there is no place for "separation." Thus, the opponents of the doctrine of pluriformity do not plead for uniformity, as if such uniformity alone could guarantee the truth. In revelation itself we see variation and multiformity. For instance, we are told that God has spoken to the fathers "in various ways."[6] One can also think of the "plurality" of the gospels, which, although they are so varied, are still related in their diversity to the one message of salvation.[7] One has always been aware of this multiplicity in revelation and has seen it as a reference to the depths and the inexhaustibleness of the truth of God.

Still, it is not justified to use all of this in order to explain the division of the Church. What the doctrine of pluriformity calls the different "forms" of the Church are anything but harmonious; they are not directed to the well-being of all, to the equipment of the saints, to the work of ministry, or to the building up of the body of Christ (Eph. 4:12). Criticism, therefore, always concentrates on the mixing of creaturely pluriformity and the division of the Church, asking whether this analogy does not make a virtue of necessity. It is unjust to explain away all criticism of the doctrine of pluriformity as a churchistic view that leaves room only for one's own church.[8] The core of the criticism strikes especially at the stress on "riches," since there is great danger that the division will not be taken seriously enough. Naturally, this can lead to churchism. Yet the questions themselves need arise only from honest concern as to whether the doctrine of pluriformity really clarifies the contradiction between unity and division in the Church. All the criticism can be concentrated in one question: in talking about the multiplicity of churches, may we speak of the manifold wisdom of

6. Heb. 1:1 *(polutrópōs)*. Cf. O. Michel, *Der Brief an die Hebräer*, 1949, p. 34: "as a sign of the riches of God," which is now followed by, and incorporated in, speech about the last days.
7. Cf. O. Cullmann, "Die Pluralität der Evangelien als theol. Problem im Altertum," *Vorträge und Aufsätze*, 1966, pp. 548ff., on attempts to replace the four gospels by one gospel.
8. V. Hepp ("De Pluriformiteit van de Kerk," *Almanak N.D.D.D.*, 1934, pp. 127ff.) makes the following criticism of opponents of pluriformity: "The view of one's own church as *a* true church is narrowed to this: our own church is *the* true Church, while whatever else claims to be a church is a false church or a sect; thus, it is not a church." In my view, this does not deal with the actual problem raised by critics of pluriformity. Cf. K. Schilder's reaction in *Verz. Werken., De Kerk*, I, 303-358, 384-445.

God, which Paul mentions (Eph. 3:10 — *hē polupoíkilos sophía*),[9] and Peter's thankfulness for God's varied grace (I Pet. 4:10 — *oikonómoi poikílēs cháritos*)? It is impossible to answer this question in the affirmative, because the disunity of the Church stands under God's criticism! Rather, disunity obscures God's manifold wisdom and varied grace, since Paul says that the Church is the instrument to make known this manifold wisdom of God.[10]

Providential aspect to pluriformity?

Undeniably, the doctrine of the pluriformity of the Church does not originate in the biblical portrait of the one Church; rather, it has arisen in close connection with the actual course of development in the history of the Church. The question was asked whether her long history of division and disunity is simply alien and enigmatic, in flagrant conflict with God's intention, a senseless and guilty destruction of the mystery of the Church. Or can one think also of positive aspects in the multiplicity? Since the Church is built not by us but by Christ (Matt. 16:18 — *oikodomḗsō mou tèn ekklēsían*), is God's field and building (I Cor. 3:9), and has the promise that the Holy Spirit will guide her into all truth (John 16:13), does there not have to be a providential aspect to the history of the Church? Can we not at least think of God's meaningful and purposeful "permission" here (without getting too involved in the difference between permission and providence)?

In this connection, Bavinck writes that history, just as much as nature, is a work of God and does not stand outside His providence.[11] Bavinck is deeply shocked by the poignant disunity of the Church; but he says that, even though the destructive

---

9. N.A. Dahl ("Das Geheimnis der Kirche nach Eph. 3, 8-10," *Zur Aufer-bauung des Leibes Christi. Festg. P. Brunner,* 1965, p. 19) speaks of manifoldness or variegation, for instance, of beautifully woven garments, as "very bright, diverse, complicated, rich, and splendid." Cf. also the designation of the riches of Christ as unsearchable (Eph. 3:8) and the mention of the depth of the riches (Rom. 11:33).

10. Eph. 3:10 *(dià tēs ekklēsías).* Kuyper *(Gemene Gratie,* III, 328) connected Eph. 3:10 emphatically with the pluriformity of the Church when he spoke of many differences that enrich, rather than impoverish, the Church: "as in general in the whole of nature and history, the full revelation of the manifold wisdom of God becomes known in this pluriformity."

11. *Geref. Dog.,* IV, 301.

aspect in the multiplicity and the disunity "unquestionably has its origin in sin," God still loves the diversity in unity. Even though it is degenerated by sin, there is still something good in the dividedness "that is brought into the Church and is thus preserved forever." The great ecclesiastical rupture of the 16th century plays an important role here. Bavinck speaks of the dawn of a new period, i.e., that of pluriformity: "Since the Reformation the Church has passed over into the period of pluriformity."[12] When Bavinck says that he admits pluriformity "in the historical sense,"[13] he does not mean that he does not find any perspective in it in connection with God's love for pluriformity and in connection with the eternal value of what is good in the division. Thus, to put Bavinck's view of pluriformity in opposition to that of Kuyper is simply incorrect.[14]

Kuyper's doctrine of pluriformity

Without doubt, Kuyper worked out all of these elements into a doctrine much more than Bavinck did and, in many respects, his conception gives a different impression.[15] That is already true with respect to the significance of the "transition" to the "period" of pluriformity. In Kuyper, pluriformity is placed in a more genial light: he speaks of its "unfolding."[16] All Kuyper's discussions of the progress of history make it clear

12. *Ibid.,* p. 304.
13. In a discussion of his speech, "Het Begrip en de Noodzakelijkheid der Evangelisatie," in *Handelingen Congres,* 1913, p. 39.
14. In my view, C. Veenhof does this too much in his important study on Bavinck, *Volk van God,* 1969, p. 168, although he does give the citations from Bavinck to which we have just pointed with respect to God's intentions and the continuing division. Cf. also Bavinck's *Katholiciteit,* 1968², p. 39, on the harmfulness of splits in the Church. Yet the resulting testimony is not entirely adverse: "the richness, the versatility, the multiformity of the Christian faith are disclosed in it." One may also remember Schilder's criticism in *Verz. Werken,* I, 437ff., which applies not only to Kuyper, but also to Bavinck. Cf. "no more justified" and "equally weak" in the proof from Scripture.
15. We have the impression that the common motifs in Kuyper and Bavinck functioned for Bavinck especially in opposition to all forms of churchism. This appears, for instance, from his discourse on catholicity, which is strongly anti-sectarian.
16. *Principles of Sacred Theology,* pp. 658ff. According to Hepp (*op. cit.,* p. 135), the new element in Kuyper is development, but that appears to me to be incorrect. If there is a new element, it is the great significance that Kuyper attaches to human subjectivity. See further in this chapter. Veenhof (*op. cit.,* pp. 201f.) deals in detail with this.

that there is a positive element in his terminology. According to him one was not yet aware in the 16th century of how far-reaching this transition was, because one felt that one's own confession "bore an absolute and exclusive character." One did not yet appreciate pluriformity; rather, one saw one's own church as the legitimate successor of the apostolic Church, since one was accustomed to the idea that absolute truth must also appear in unity of form and content. In that situation the idea of the pluriformity of the Church could not yet arise.[17] Only when one's own church acquired a continuing character — and unity proved to be illusory — did pluriformity become an accomplished fact, not simply as a regrettable evolution, but as an "actuality" containing this "lesson of history": "the Church of Christ was bound to reveal herself in more than one form."[18]

Many of Kuyper's statements speak of this development as decided, inevitable, and necessary. He was convinced that a further development of history could scarcely change this.[19] He did not simply want to establish a historical fact, as Paul did in the divided situation in Corinth, but he tried to make the development to a certain degree understandable and to stamp it as inevitable. "We are completely convinced that pluriformity is a phase of development that the Church of Christ too had to arrive at visibly."[20] One may not conclude from this that Kuyper

17. According to Kuyper (*Gemene Gratie*, III, 269), the Belgic Confession assumes the "absolute" conception. In his view, all the Reformers originally stood on the standpoint of the absolute unity of the Church (p. 233). Therefore, he speaks of a time when this idea had to be abandoned and of a chasm between the Confession and "the conviction that was formed later under the pressure of life" (p. 235). If this insight had been evident already in the 16th century, the Confession would have had a totally different, less absolute shape (p. 271). That is a rather sharp criticism of the Confession.

18. *Principles of Sacred Theology*, p. 662. Cf. p. 664, on the truth of God and the great salvation in Christ as too rich and too aboundingly precious "to reach their full expression in one human form."

19. Cf. *ibid.*, p. 660, on the delusion of unity among the Lutherans.

20. *Gemene Gratie*, III, 235. The word "too" refers to a general, historical, organic event of differentiation. We see that also with regard to the scientific development "in the circle of palingenesis," which does not have to be uniform and does not always have to "arrive *at harmonious results*" (*Principles of Sacred Theology*, p. 169). Here, too, the idea of the varying subjective assimilation of the truth comes to the fore (p. 170). See also in this connection "the organic multiformity of social life." In this light, the "had to" also means that pluriformity has been willed by God (*Gemene Gratie*, III, 274). Kuyper's *Calvinism*, 1898, p. 135, is very enlightening here.

had no awareness of the guilt of division. Not only does he find something "unsatisfying" in pluriformity, but he also sees a sinful disturbance in it: he admits that without sin unity would not have been abandoned.[21] It is a satanic work that must be discerned, since "he [Satan] has succeeded so frighteningly in striking apart Christ's Church on earth." But all these words about guilt and disturbance do not detract from Kuyper's stress on historical necessity, on inevitability, and on the "unfolding" of pluriformity. For he was especially captivated by the multiformity of the whole of creaturely life, and he often recalled it in his reflections on the Church. To show that variegation he points, for instance, to the different ways of speaking of Isaiah and Amos, Paul and James, and to the variation in Paul's way of speaking to Rome, Ephesus, and Corinth.

Kuyper is especially impressed by the "organic" aspect in all variations, as in the picture of the family: every child thinks and feels differently, but the bond of the one family is not affected. The same is true of different races. He considers it unthinkable and absurd that men of an entirely different race than ours "will find the fitting expression for their faith in our confession and in our catechism." Even though "objective" truth is one, the "subjective" application and confession must differ.[22] A beam of light "shines through a window of red, yellow, and blue glass" and "colors the things that are in the apartment in different ways."[23] Thus, multiformity is given a certain halo, as in the image of a fabric, which shows its beauty in varying shadings. For Kuyper, all of this is closely connected to the fact that revelation has entered into human life; it is not an "objective truth" suspended above human life. Consequently, Kuyper characterizes opposition to pluriformity as a form of dualism that does not allow the gospel to penetrate the fabric of life. Then one does not see the pluriformity that is detectable in

---

21. Cf. *Heraut,* May 20, 1900, on the injury to love and on unholy quarrels. So Kuyper does reject a kind of pluriformity, because it "has quenched the fire of love in a pitiful way by bitter hate. And that is the sin *of all" (Gemene Gratie,* III, 268).

22. *Gemene Gratie,* III, 237f. For Kuyper this did not mean ecclesiastical relativism, as if this standpoint meant that our own Church would cease "to be for our own mind the true Church" (p. 272). One can decide whether or not the mark of the Church "in its principal appearance" is present and then find "a purer revelation of Christ's Church" in one's own Church (p. 273).

23. Kuyper, *Band aan het Woord,* p. 23.

contacts with Christians of different races, countries, and traditions.[24]

All of this is concentrated in Kuyper's conception of the distance between "absolute" truth and what we men assimilate of it in our subjective perception. Our knowledge of the truth is always imperfect and inadequate. This admission, the core of Kuyper's ecclesiological epistemology,[25] makes pluriformity intelligible. To a certain degree, apart from the *modus quo,* which is contaminated by sin, it even makes it meaningful and inevitable. A *modus vivendi* was reached in the Reformation which "seemingly continued to maintain the grandeur of one single Church, but nevertheless actually admitted pluriformity as a new way of existence for ecclesiastical life."[26] The fact of pluriformity not only cannot be denied, but it also has its cause in an organic development, so that all attempts to turn back the clock are illusory. The differences between one man and another had also, "wedge-like," to penetrate "into the phenomenal life of the Church upon earth."[27] For Kuyper this is connected to freedom of conscience and to the recognition of the subjective element, which, as the basic element of the confession, "by logical necessity had to lead to the Church's splitting into more formations, often leading to the destruction of every visible Church establishment as such."[28] Since all subjective appropriation is subject to limitedness, the different forms of the Church are inevitable. Certainly, revelation is one, and truth in Christ is one;[29] but when Christ is formed in believers,[30] the law of development and subjectivity comes into operation along the way of a meaningful pluriformity.

The problem with respect to the doctrine of pluriformity is the combination of rich multiformity with the historical course of rupture and disunity. Kuyper's perception of "satanic" aspects,

---

24. *Gemene Gratie,* III, 237f.
25. His view of the true and the false Church is connected to this. Cf. van Leeuwen, *Het Kerkbegrip in de Theologie van A. Kuyper,* 1946, pp. 201f.
26. *Gemene Gratie,* III, 235.
27. *Calvinism,* pp. 78f.
28. *Gemene Gratie,* III, 244. Cf. the crass statement in *Calvinism,* p. 263: "Furthermore our inborn onesidedness will always necessarily lead to the manifestation of the church of Christ in many forms."
29. *Gemene Gratie,* III, 242.
30. Cf. Gal. 4:19 (*morphōthḗ*). W. Elert gave a morphology of Lutheranism (*Die Morphologie des Luthertums,* I, 1931, cf. pp. 1f.). Likewise, Kuyper gave a "morphology" of all Christian life in its variation, and especially of Calvinism. Cf. Elert on the morphology of the Confessions.

of lack of love, of quarrels and bitterness, and of schism and heresy leads to the question of whether we can speak of an "unfolding" of pluriformity in order to characterize the post-Reformation development. Can one refer here to a "necessity" of differentiation that brings in a new, blessed phase of church history? Kuyper criticized the fathers for not seeing that there had to be divisions and splits, for deluding themselves that they grasped "nothing else than the objective," and, thus, for not doing justice to the subjective element.[31] But is ecclesiology not structured too much from the basis of anthropology here?[32] Can we still observe the biblical understanding of the Church of Christ here? Kuyper himself felt something of the seriousness of this question when he admitted that the original standpoint of the Reformation "rested on everything that appears so movingly in the New Testament about the unity of the Church."[33] But he did not see this as signifying the insufficiency of his ecclesiological epistemology. In contrast to earlier, external unity, the multiformity that was now becoming visible had to be accepted and honored.[34] But this anthropological line of thought has little force when we hear how the New Testament speaks of the Church's unity and when Paul perceives the "spread of subjectivity" in the church of Corinth. Rather than honoring it as pluriformity, he points to Christ! But Kuyper ascertained an inevitable shift in the historical consciousness in both the world and the Church. And references to sin as a factor in the shift (the *modus quo*) could not diminish the significance of this spread for him.

Pluralism

What Kuyper speaks of here as the plurality of human subjectivity has come to the fore strongly in our time in Roman Catholic attention for what is usually called pluralism. Pluralism

31. *Gemene Gratie,* III, 242.
32. In my view, this danger comes to expression most pointedly in Kuyper's view of Calvinism, whose confession "is so deeply religious, so highly spiritual, that, excepting always periods of profound religious commotion, it will never be realized by the large masses, but will impress with a sense of its inevitability only a relatively small circle" (*Calvinism,* p. 263).
33. *Gemene Gratie,* III, 233.
34. That earlier unity was the "fruit of mechanical manipulation" (*ibid.,* p. 242). Cf. *Calvinism,* p. 79: Denominations owe their origin "to a deep-rooted opposition to sacerdotalism."

is not, however, simply a reflection on the general problem of the incompleteness of knowledge, applying to all men in all times. Rather, it is especially concerned with a specific modern complication of the problem of knowledge due to the enormous amount of information that deluges us and impresses upon us the inadequacy of our knowledge — including our knowledge of faith. More than ever before the multiplicity of information makes clear the limitedness of our insight and, thus, the possibility of a plural assimilation of the data. Our broadened horizon of knowledge has influence also on our understanding of truth and on theological thinking.

In spite of the difference in the historical situation — for Kuyper, the "variation" began in the time of the Reformation — there is a striking similarity between Kuyper's chief foundation for pluriformity and present-day attention for pluralism. The common element is the recognition of subjectivity in the understanding of truth. That explains why the rise of a stronger sense of plurality coincides with new openness for the ecumenical problematic. Here, too, limitedness plays a much greater role than earlier, opening the possibility of varying insight without making all fellowship in faith impossible. One became aware that one is not simply isolated from the other, separated by a "no man's land" and lacking any points of contact. Rather, in the plurality it is necessary to grope for that which truly binds and unites. It would be erroneous to interpret this concern for pluriformity and pluralism as relativism or subjectivism. In 1909, the Roman Catholic Bensdorp drew this conclusion about Kuyper; and, in spite of Kuyper's short — too short — defense, he did not change his criticism of ultra-subjectivism.[35] Yet Kuyper was dealing with a real problem, and he definitely touched on present-day problems when he asked whether varying interpreta-

---

35. Th. Bensdorp, *De Pluriformiteit der Waarheid,* 1916[2]. Bensdorp asked how flatly contradictory confessions can both be "forms" of one revealed truth. How can there be harmony in the contradiction? Kuyper replied that he did not mean to say that in the doctrine of the Lord's supper, for instance, both transubstantiation and consubstantiation are true. But there is a certain "harmony" in the sense that "the mystical fellowship with Christ is partaken of in the sacrament; however, the way that that fellowship comes about cannot be expressed by us in an adequate form." The differing formulations are attempts to understand the same mystical reality (*Heraut,* Feb. 17, 1901; included in Bensdorp, *op. cit.,* pp. 69f.). Bensdorp, however, while recognizing all Kuyper's images, would do so only within the boundaries of the one Church.

tion as such already breaks fellowship with respect to the reality
to which the varying understanding is directed.[36] Neither Kuyper
nor Rahner[37] postulates that truth is not one, but they touch
each other with respect to the limited, and therefore varied,
understanding of truth. From the nature of the case, there are
profound problems here, both for Rahner in connection with
the old tradition of the infallible confession of the Church and
for Kuyper in connection with pluriformity in confessions.

In our time, more than ever before, one is confronted with
pluriformity. One cannot escape it, even if one does not accept
Käsemann's view that pluriformity is explainable already from
the contradictory plurality of "theologies" in the New Testament itself![38] Even if we accept the "canonical" gospel, we must
continue to give consideration to the way in which that gospel
is understood in different times.[39] Naturally, though, giving subjectivity a voice does encompass many dangers, and the Christian
Church has always recognized the limitedness of human knowledge, specifically in opposition to rationalism.[40] Holy Scripture
itself has given a definition, as it were, of this limitedness when
Paul states that "our knowledge is imperfect" (I Cor. 13:9, cf.
13:12 — ek mérous). This is connected to the fact that "now"
we see in a mirror dimly (13:12). Thus, a limit is assigned to
the Church; this incomplete knowledge stands vis-à-vis that
which is coming, i.e., that which is perfect and complete.[41] This
incompleteness of knowledge can easily be minimized if Paul's

---

36. Kuyper's example of the Lord's supper (cf. n. 35 above) touches on
    recent questions with regard to the fellowship between Lutherans and
    Reformed in the 16th century (presentia realis, communio cum Christo)
    as well as on the recent Roman Catholic questions about the presentia
    realis and transubstantiation, concentrated in concern for the deepest
    intentions of the Church in the Lord's Supper.
37. In connection with the well-known ten questions of Ottaviani to the
    bishops' conferences, cf. K. Rahner, "Über den Dialog in der plural-
    istischen Gesellschaft," Schriften zur Theol., VI, 1965, pp. 46ff.; and
    idem, "Kirchliches Lehramt und Theologie nach dem Konzil," Schriften
    zur Theol., VIII, 1967, pp. 111ff.
38. E. Käsemann, "Begründet der N.T. Kanon die Einheit der Kirche?",
    Exeg. Versuche und Besinnungen, I, 1960, pp. 214ff.
39. Cf. the section on apostolicity below, especially chapter 11.
40. Bavinck, Geref. Dog., II, 21.
41. I Cor. 13:10, 12: "Then I shall understand fully, even as I have been
    fully understood (epignósomai)." Cf. K. Barth, C.D., IV/2, p. 838: knowl-
    edge "in part" (im Stückwerk) is not worthless, but "also in their rela-
    tivity, so that they cannot be confused with the true reality, but are
    asked only concerning their content as love."

positive statements that "we know" are seen as actually taking away or reducing the incompleteness. However, if this does not happen — and it is very important to take Paul seriously in I Corinthians 13! — one cannot view the questions about "subjectivity" and its "partial" character as insignificant.

Kuyper's anti-dualism in itself is irrefutable; revelation is fully intended to be understood and known, to enter into human conceptions, experiences, feelings, knowledge, and understanding. This "entrance into" does not cast shadows on revelation; nevertheless, the Church must be aware of the incompleteness in all her speaking and confessing.[42] Yet the decisive question arises precisely at this point. Must the so greatly varied subjectivity inevitably lead to the pluriformity of the Church (in the sense of many concrete churches)? Convinced that this question must be answered in the negative, we want to point out that a different conclusion can be derived from the variations in subjectivity and the plural assimilation of new, modern information than the conclusion that Kuyper drew from history: precisely when plurality becomes more visible than ever before, the call to unity and fellowship gains more force! The stress on inadequacy and incompleteness does not legitimize the Church's pluriformity, but rejects it because of the necessity of unity. In New Testament times, when the "spread" of subjectivity had also become a reality, it was subjected to the discipline of unity in Christ. Imperfection is recognized, but it is taken up in the call — in antithesis to the individualizing of our knowledge — to understand the love of Christ "with all the saints" (Eph. 3:18f.).

There is simply no road from the incompleteness that has its place within the framework of love (I Cor. 13; Eph. 3:17) to a pluriformity whose form is division, disunity, and contradiction. The "riches" of Ephesians 3, the riches of His glory (3:16), certainly encompass many dimensions — including length and breadth, height and depth (3:18) — but therein, they are directed to unity in strengthening with might (3:16), in comprehending with all the saints;[43] and thus, Christ dwells in their hearts (3:17). When Paul speaks in this connection of the love of Christ "which surpasses knowledge" (Eph. 3:19), he does not make possible a problematic of absolute truth and inadequate perception, which thus includes pluriformity. Rather, he refers to

---

42. Cf. Bavinck, *Geref. Dog.*, II, 20ff., 74ff., 97ff.
43. Eph. 3:18 (*katalabésthai sùn pásin toîs hagíois*). Cf. *katalábō* ("make it one's own") in Phil. 3:12.

fellowship in understanding these "pluriform" dimensions. That knowledge is surpassed does not devaluate it, but rather directs faith to the inexhaustibleness of love. And Paul bows his knees (3:14) that the one Church will live out of that love (5:2, 25).

Vestigia of the Church

The rejection by Rome of various forms of "pluriformity" throughout her history was undoubtedly connected to the realization that the Church is by definition one. Hence, multiformity and variation are possible only within the one Catholic Church. The sharp rejection of the so-called theories of the Ramists *(theoria ramorum)* contains a striking example of this. In a letter to the English bishops in 1864, Rome spoke against the idea of different "branches" of the one Church, namely, the Roman Catholic, Greek Catholic, and Anglican Churches.[44] Rome said that it was impossible to adorn all these churches "by right" *(jure)* with the name catholic by reason of the letter to the Ephesians: "one Lord, one hope, one baptism" (4:5). According to the will of Christ, we can speak only of one Church, and that one Church is an undeniable fact.[45] It excludes every pluriformity that causes separation, because pluriformity contradicts the constitution of the Church with her origin in the cross.[46] All attention is directed to the one Shepherd and the one flock, and we must speak "exclusively" of this Church, this institution — not in haughtiness, but in respect for the work of God, which has been directed to the one people of God.

This consistent reference to the unique reality of the one Church, which can be ascertained everywhere in earlier ecclesiology, has now lost much of its simplicity and self-evidence. The possibility of faith and piety in individual believers outside the institution of the Church had been recognized already, and now the question of recognition of Christian communions outside the Church took on interest. Thus, Roman Catholic ecclesiology touched on the same problem that had already played an important role in Protestant churches and that at present has be-

44. *De Unicitate Ecclesiae, contra theoriam ramorum,* Denz.-Schönm., 2885-2888. See also *Mortalium Animos* in 1928 against the different member churches in the ecumenical movement.
45. "Nor is any other church catholic except that which has been built upon Peter alone and which rises into one body closely joined and knit together in the unity of faith and love" (Denz.-Schönm., 2888; *TCT,* 181).
46. Cf. H.U. von Balthasar, in *Mysterium Salutis,* III, 2, 1969, pp. 219ff.

come of central significance to ecumenism: the admission of "traces" (*vestigia*) of the Church in other churches.

Clearly, one may not rashly identify the admission of vestiges of the Church in other churches with the doctrine of the pluriformity of the Church. The concept *"vestigia"* includes a critical note, because one admits only "traces" of the true Church of Christ in other churches. The traces are also described as "remnants" (*reliquiae*). Here recognition is limited much more than in the doctrine of pluriformity and, frequently, the recognition of vestiges is not a genuine sign of ecumenical rapprochement. Speaking of "traces" of the Church can even cause irritation in other churches, because the concept of *vestigia* includes a relativizing and disqualifying element that seems to exclude full, integral recognition.[47] Is there not a certain ecclesiastical arrogance in the concept of vestiges, which threatens the relation between different churches?[48] Does it not suggest the well-known distinction between pure and less pure churches — a criticism that assumes one's own purity?

A clear illustration of this problematic is Calvin's frequent reference to the concept of *vestigia*. It is avowedly critical, although there is a definite element of "recognition" in it. Calvin states that he does not want to deprive the "papists" of "those traces of the Church which the Lord willed should among them survive the destruction" (*Inst.*, IV, 2, 11). He draws a parallel between the Church and Israel, which retained its covenant with God in spite of everything because of His goodness and faithfulness. Similarly, in the history of the Church under the tyranny of the Antichrist, the Lord has made the covenant inviolable; He has preserved His baptism, the witness of the covenant that maintains its power in spite of the godlessness of men. He has done the same with other vestiges too, "in order that the Church might not utterly die" (*Inst.*, IV, 2, 11). Since the vestiges are directly connected to God's goodness and faithfulness, one may certainly not minimize them. But neither may one use them too simply in a doctrine of pluriformity, because, in the context, Calvin speaks extremely critically about Rome. He uses the

---

47. From the extensive literature we mention: G. Miegge, "Vestigia Ecclesiae," *Verbum Caro*, II, 1967, pp. 211ff.; W. Dietzfelbinger, *Die Grenzen der Kirche nach röm.-kath. Lehre*, 1962, chapter 7; J. Hamer, *Le Baptême et l'Eglise à propos des "Vestigia Ecclesiae,"* *Irenikon Tome*, XXV, 1952, pp. 142ff., 263ff.; and J. Faber, *Vestigium Ecclesiae. De Doop als "Spoor der Kerk,"* 1969.

48. Hamer, *op. cit.*, p. 148; Miegge, *op. cit.*

image of a building that has been pulled down, the foundations and ruins of which remain. Although God did not will "that his Church either be destroyed to the very foundations by Antichrist or be leveled to the ground" *(Inst., IV, 2, 11)*, Calvin still "categorically" *(simpliciter)* denies the title "church" to Rome, although he does not deny "the existence of churches among them" *(Inst., IV, 2, 12)*. The word "nearly" also fits within this tension between recognition and criticism. Calvin mentions sacrilege and oppression: "Well-nigh killed as if by poisoned drinks." Christ is half buried, the gospel is overthrown, piety is scattered, and the worship of God is nearly wiped out *(Inst., IV, 2, 12)*.

In the concept of traces, recognition and criticism come together. Thus, in Calvin's answer to Sadolet a clear element of recognition is followed by pointed criticism of the papacy.[49] The papacy has made the Church a ruin; and Calvin recalls the Antichrist, who has set himself in the temple of God, and cautions that we are not to be misled "by the name church" *(ecclesiae nomine)*. Nevertheless, there are churches "to the extent that the Lord wonderfully preserves in them a remnant of his people, however woefully dispersed and scattered" *(Inst., IV, 2, 12)*. Some marks of the Church do continue to exist, especially those that neither the devil nor human depravity can destroy. Yet many signs have been wrecked, so that "every one of their congregations and their whole body lack the lawful form of the Church" *(Inst., IV, 2, 12)*. Calvin recalls that, because of Israel's apostasy, God "moves elsewhere and strips the place of holiness" *(Inst., IV, 2, 3)*. The name of the Church, which one prides oneself in, may not lead us to think that the Church exists where God's Word is not found *(Inst., IV, 2, 4)*. The mark of the Church that is unmistakable *(Inst., IV, 2, 4 — minime dubio symbolo)* is listening to the voice of the Shepherd. Nothing else than that can correctly indicate the Church.

Contemporary ecclesiological discussions often appeal to Calvin in one of two ways. One person lays strong emphasis on the elements of recognition, while another points to the extremely critical elements in Calvin's view of the Roman Church. This is a clear indication of the influence of such ecclesiological in-

---

49. "Reply to Sadolet," in Calvin, *Theological Treatises. Library of Christian Classics*, XXII, 241: "We indeed, Sadolet, do not deny that those over which you preside are Churches of Christ; but we maintain that the Roman pontiff [and the bishops] are savage wolves, whose only interest has hitherto been to scatter and trample upon the kingdom of Christ, filling it with devastation and ruin."

sight on the interpretation of Calvin.[50] However, one may not approach Calvin's statements from particular emphases and play recognition and criticism off against each other. For precisely the extremely sharp criticism makes Calvin's recognition the more remarkable! The vestiges do not stand next to the ruins, but have reference to them. There is not simply recognition of individual belief among "the papists," but also reflection on the Church on the basis of God's preservation and faithfulness. Schilder said that one may not expand the *vestigia* which Calvin mentions to a Church;[51] but the *vestigia* are *vestigia ecclesiae*, and Calvin denies that he is dealing here only with a reference to the "elect."[52] The elements of recognition in connection with the continuance of the Church are not a friendly ecumenical concession since that would be in conflict with the sharp criticism; rather, they are connected to the outlook on God's preservation and faithfulness, in which the *vestigia ecclesiae* are founded.[53]

Obviously, by using the concept of traces one does not imply a static, unchangeable judgment about other churches. We can never speak of a standstill in the history of the Church, but only of a dynamic process for better or for worse, of growth in one direction or another, of continuing alienation and deformation, or of reformation to true service of God. The judgment about *vestigia* is most intimately connected to this dynamic nature of history. For instance, Calvin pointed out that the situation in the time of Bernard of Clairvaux was much more

50. While V. Hepp (*op. cit.*, pp. 132ff.) saw Calvin's statements as the prelude to Kuyper's doctrine of pluriformity, K. Schilder ("Enige onjuiste Dilemma's in Pluriformiteitsvertoogen," *Almanak F.Q.I.*, 1940, pp. 14ff.) accentuated the critical elements, especially in "Calvin's resolute refusal to attribute the name 'church' to Rome." Cf. further, in opposition to Schilder, P.J. Richel, *Het Kerkbegrip van Calvijn*, 1942, pp. 120ff.

51. *Almanak F.Q.I.*, 1940, p. 15.

52. Calvin, "Letter to Socinus," *Corpus Reformatorum: Johannes Calvini Opera*, XIII, 487: "When I say that remnants of the Church *remain* in the papacy, I do not restrict that to the elect who are dispersed therein; but I judge that ruins of the broken Church still exist there."

53. One may also recall what the Gallic Confession says about the *vestigia ecclesiae*. In article 27 there is a warning against rash use of the name "church." Then, in article 28, after the proposition that where the Word of God is not received "there can be no Church," we read "Nevertheless, as some trace of the Church is left in the papacy, and the virtue and substance of baptism remain, and as the efficacy of baptism does not depend upon the person who administers it, we confess that those baptized in it do not need a second baptism."

bearable than that in Calvin's own day.[54] Naturally, such changes influence the extent of recognition of vestiges. Thus, it would also be unfair to criticize contemporary considerations of these *vestigia a priori*, because they do not coincide in all respects with Calvin's picture of them; for the *vestigia* are always most closely connected to the Church's actual situation in a particular time. Their mention at present in the relation between churches is due not to a general concept of *vestigia*, but to serious analysis of the path of the churches in the present. There is clear continuity in usage of the concept of *vestigia*, namely, to do justice to what is recognized in other churches in the midst of, and in spite of, all separation. The concept of *vestigia* is frequently used today much less critically than earlier. This appears, among other things, from the fact that the Roman Catholic and the Reformed in the Netherlands have officially recognized each other's baptisms.[55] Today, although the recognition of *vestigia* continues to embrace a critical element, there are scarcely any radical characterizations like the earlier ones of traces or relics in the midst of ruins. A change that runs parallel has taken place: on the Reformed side, the abandonment of simple identification of the Pope with the Antichrist; and on the Roman Catholic side, a striking formulation of elements of the Church in other churches, directly and essentially connected to Christ and the Holy Spirit.

Changed usage today

In this connection, the well-known declaration in Toronto by the World Council of Churches is of far-reaching significance for the history of the ecumenical movement. The word "elements" is used in practically the same sense as the concept of vestiges: "The member churches of the ecumenical council rec-

---

54. "Yet how much more tolerable was its condition then than now!" ("Reply to Sadolet," *Library of Christian Classics*, XXII, 242).

55. Cf. the brochure "Dooperkenning tussen R.-K. Kerk in Nederland en Ned. Herv. Kerk," as well as the declaration of mutual recognition of baptism by the Roman Catholics and the Gereformeerde Kerken (*Acta Gen. Syn.*, Amsterdam, 1967-68, art. 311). Naturally, such recognition can give rise to many ecclesiastical questions. Schilder, for instance, asks whether the recognition of baptism involves the legality of the baptizing church (*Verz. Werken*, I, 274). According to him, recognition does involve "a taking account of the catholicity of Christianity." Schilder's formulations (see also *Verz. Werken*, II, 281ff.) show how clearly his concern is especially to protest against the pluriform, self-evident "legality" of all churches, no matter how they have arisen.

ognize elements of the true Church in other churches. They are of the opinion that this mutual recognition obligates them to meet with one another in earnest dialogue; they *hope* that these elements of the truth will lead to a recognition of the full truth and to the unity that is founded on the full truth."[56] Various traditions are recalled in which the elements or *vestigia* have a place, such as the preaching of the Word, the interpretation of the Holy Scriptures, and the administration of the sacraments.[57] It is striking to note here that these elements are spoken of very positively. Even though "elements" obviously contrasts with "fullness" — and thus relativizes it — the elements still have positive value. "These elements are more than pale shadows of the life of the true Church. They contain a real promise, [and the churches] should not underestimate them, as though they were only elements of the truth." The vestiges are "not dead remnants of the past, but powerful instruments through which God does His work."

The question has been asked whether the Toronto statement does not give greater significance, more positive value, to the vestiges than Calvin did. But one cannot speak about more or less positiveness, since Calvin honors the *vestigia* — among other things, baptism — as the work of God and indicates their continuing power; for Calvin too, the *vestigia* are not "dead remnants of the past." Toronto does speak about the *vestigia* from a broader perspective and with stronger expectation for the Church in connection with the direction of her path. However, that does not require a fundamental difference between usage of the *vestigia* earlier and in the document of Toronto, because *vestigia* have reference to the Church's situation *in a particular time*.[58] Today, then, we recognize the same problem of recogni-

56. "The Church, the Churches and the World Council of Churches" (the Toronto Declaration of the Central Committee of the World Council, 1950). The declaration adds, though, that "membership does not imply that each Church must regard the other member Churches as Churches in the true and full sense of the word." This shows clearly the problematic that is present in the relationship of the many "churches."

57. This formulation reminds one strongly of the marks of the Church in the Augsburg Confession, article 7.

58. J. Hamer (*op. cit.*, p. 146) speaks of optimism. Naturally, there can be different grounds for this optimism, but that does not imply a different view of the *vestigia* as such. According to J. Faber (*op. cit.*, p. 185), the Toronto Declaration placed the image of the *vestigia* in a different framework and used the concept in a different way than Calvin did. But this position does not do sufficient justice to the actual (historically-determined) problematic of the *vestigia*. In my view,

tion and criticism, because, by speaking about traces, we intend to recall what the Church should be according to the Word of God. That explains why the problem of *vestigia*, in spite of the unmistakable critical element, is being discussed everywhere.

This is also the case in the Roman Catholic Church. It is apparent that reference to the one, unique Roman Church (*una et unica ecclesia Romana*) does not say everything. More than ever before, the sense of relationship with Christ and with one another arose. The elements of the Church in other churches, hence, are not seen as "dead remnants" of the past; rather, their positive significance as a means in the hand of the Holy Spirit is stressed. The elements have their origin in Christ, and the Church is also built through them. Even though there is no mention of complete recognition (*plena communio Ecclesiae catholicae*) which would involve the pope and his authority, the elements are still valuable and offer an important ecumenical perspective. This change of front is possible only from an ecclesiological view that no longer approaches the Church exclusively from the institutional aspect. Gradually, the conviction has grown that, even if full due is given to the significance of institution and office, the essence of the Church nevertheless lies in a spiritual relationship with Christ in faith; where that is present, the "ecclesiastical" reality cannot and may not be denied.

So, Rome too faces similar problems of recognition with the same difficulties in ecclesiology. Connections are sought between the unique institution, willed and established by Christ, and the pneumatic-ecclesiastical aspect. One sees positive elements in other churches but, at the same time, says that they not only "arise from Christ and lead to him," but that, "by right," they belong to the only Church of Christ.[59] This "by right" (*jure*)

Schilder's "dynamic" concept of the Church makes a fairer judgment of the problematic possible because of what can, and often does, happen in history through elements of reformation and deformation, which then influence the concrete fixation of the *vestigia*.

59. "All of these, which come from Christ and lead back to Him, belong *by right* to the one Church of Christ" ("Decree on Ecumenism," *DV* II, pp. 345ff.). The *jure* was introduced on Nov. 19, 1964, "on higher authority." It implies the connection with the earlier ecclesiological tradition, which, however, is placed in a wider ecumenical context. *Jure* is not exclusively a Roman Catholic conception; the same idea sometimes appears in Protestant literature. For instance, H. Steen (*De Kerk*, p. 112) writes that "those who are truly believers" in a different church are "in the deepest sense members of *our* church." W. Tom (*Pluriformiteit en Pluraliteit*, 1948, p. 56) called this a fiction.

shows the tension between recognition and criticism and accentuates the impossibility of many shepherds and many flocks. The tension becomes especially visible because this "by right" does not supplant recognition. The formulations are too positive for that, since they are related to the Holy Spirit, to faith, hope, and love, and to all the inner gifts of the Holy Spirit. The conviction has grown that belonging to the institution does not yet offer a guarantee for fellowship and that not belonging to the institution does not *per se* exclude one from salvation.[60] One can ask whether this "complementary" view of fellowship and institution is capable of solving the ecclesiological problem. Can they be separated so simply, since the Church is so deeply anchored, also as an institution, in the will of the Lord?[61] Will not the institutional aspect eventually lead again to a relativizing of the ecclesiological elements? Others ask whether the positive recognition will not eventually lead to a minimization of the significance of the institution and of the necessity of the Catholic Church for salvation. In any case, though, we can say that the problem of unity and division concerns everyone and the solutions are never totally satisfying.

Further, the solution clearly cannot be a reassuring pluriformity which assigns meaning to the division of the Church in the light of riches and variegation. There is in reality much more tension than is expressed in the doctrine of pluriformity. Even if the *jure* in Roman Catholic ecclesiology — and in Protestant parallels — does not offer a solution, it does at least point to the anomaly of the one Church and the many churches. This anomaly can never be theologically solved by making it an explanatory factor, which eventually legitimizes the *status quo*. The moment this occurs, the outlook on the one flock and the one Shepherd is obscured. Neither Rome, with its far-reaching recognition, nor Toronto has solved the problem. One can only

60. G. Baum especially ("The Ecclesial Reality of the Other Churches," *Concilium*, 4, 1965, pp. 62ff.) has pointed to the dominance of the aspect of communion at the Council and sees it as a correction of the encyclical *Mystici Corporis Christi* (1943), which called Catholics alone "genuine" *(reapse)* members of the Church. The Council speaks of being incorporated fully *(plene)*, which assumes modes of incorporation. Cf. p. 82 on the Spirit's not being dependent on the institution and on incomplete realizations of the Church.

61. Cf. W. Dantine, "Die kontroverstheol. Problematik der 'ekklesialen Elemente,'" *Erneuerung der einen Kirche*, pp. 148f.; and J.J. von Allmen, *Gedanken zur dogm. Konstitution über die Kirche "Lumen Gentium,"* 1968.

say that a pathway has become visible which is not without perspective if all sloppy, superficial leveling of the differences is shut out. Both Rome and the ecumenical movement have wanted to avoid this leveling by continuing to question each other. The questions are also of the greatest significance for one's own ecclesiastical life, since they touch upon both the institution and fellowship in confrontation with the gospel. That the *vestigia* today are spoken of more positively than before, as footprints of Christ and the Spirit, does not signify a weakening, but rather a strengthening of one's sense of the Church. But it must not embrace haughtiness and exclusiveness, and it must be more and more concerned with being the light of the world. Repeatedly, "purer" has been simply a pretension in opposition to "less pure," and there has been no realization of the degree to which "purity" in the whole life and confession of the Church means an unprecedented strengthening of responsibility! If this "consequence" of purity is understood in the current ecumenical problematic, it will be possible to avoid turning away from the divided Church in disappointment and defeatism, but rather to probe her division according to Christ's will, to seek her unity in Christ, and to bring it to light in word and deed.

Proselytism

Lastly, we want to turn to a much discussed concrete problem — namely, proselytism. This problem came to the fore strongly after the Toronto declaration. Various motifs of recognition (fellowship in spite of and within division) led to the question of whether there is still room for a plea on behalf of "one's own church," for recruitment from one church into another. In general, strong aversion to "proselytism" can be perceived in the ecumenical movement of our day.[62] It is seen as an attitude that starts from the contradiction between light and darkness and projects it on the "transfer" from one church or confession to another; and it is precisely this attitude that

---

62. Proselytism was discussed already at Evanston (1954), St. Andrews (1960), and New Delhi (1961). On proselytism see J.A. Hebly, *Het Proselitisme. Verkenning van een Oecumenisch Vraagstuk*, 1962, especially chapter 3; J.C. Hoekendijk, "Over het Proselytisme," *Oecumene in het Vizier*, 1960, pp. 101ff.; *Die Religion in Geschichte und Gegenwart, s.v. Proselytismus;* and "Christian Witness, Proselytism and Religious Liberty in the Setting of the World Council of Churches (A Provisional Report)," *The Ecumenical Review*, 1956, pp. 48f.

one wants to deny in ecumenical reflection on the unity of the Church in Christ.

Opposition to proselytism comes partly from perverted "recruitment" due to very human, dubious consideration of competition and rivalry. The word has been used less and less because of the association of making proselytes with Pharisaism,[63] even when the word "true" is added to it, as in "true proselytism."[64] One usually sees proselytism as nothing other than worldly propaganda, in conflict with the essence of the Church and her mission.[65] But the actual problem goes deeper. Others are no longer spoken of as "aliens," who by their transfer "come over" (i.e., the meaning of *prosélutos*); but they are spoken of as other churches that know themselves to be related to Christ, and one does not want to deny this relationship. Consequently, the relationship among churches becomes entirely different than when aliens are taken up into the sphere of life in Israel.[66]

If this recognition of positive traces of the Church in other churches is not to result in relativism, how is one to think concretely of the relation to other churches? The question is particularly acute in the Roman Catholic Church, because of her traditional view of the uniqueness *(unicitas)* of the Catholic Church.[67] But the problem is also visible in the ecumenical

63. Matt. 23:15 *(poiêsai)*. Christ's judgment is "Hypocrites!" Cf. Hebly, *op. cit.*, pp. 8f.

64. H. Kraemer did call missions "true proselytism" in spite of the bad connotation of the word (cf. Hebly, *op. cit.*, p. 15). Cf. differently: "it does not seem possible, in practice, to restore the good connotation, which the word 'proselyte' once carried" *(The Ecumenical Review,* 1956, p. 51).

65. The word "propaganda" (propagation) does not have a bad sense in itself, and it was used earlier in connection with missions. For example, Kuyper *(Calvinism,* p. 263) speaks of "absolute and unconditional propagandism" and recalls Paul before Agrippa. Paul prays that Agrippa become "as I am" (Acts 26:29).

66. Whoever "comes over" is an alien *(gēr)*. The relationship that then arose within the theocratic fellowship of Israel resembled assimilation more than deep, true fellowship. For this reason, too, one can hardly use the word "proselytism" in the relation of the churches. Cf. the articles in *TDNT* on *pároikos* (V, 843) and *prosélutos* (VI, 727). For the relationship with Israel, see Judg. 1:16; I Sam. 15:6; Ex. 22:21; Deut. 26:12f.; 27:19.

67. Cf. K. Rahner ("Some Remarks on the Question of Conversions," *Theological Investigations,* V, 1966, pp. 315-355) on the Roman Catholic "claim" that the individual must join the Catholic Church freely. This does not change because of the fact "that the individual concerned is already a Christian" (thus not an alien). Cf. p. 316 on the right and

movement: along with the rejection of proselytism, the statement is made that no single church need be silent about her own affirmation of faith.[68] The mode of that affirmation is then of decisive significance, also with regard to other churches. Because of the nature of the Church, there must be appreciation for the free, inner choice of others; and there can be no pressure, as is true in the activity of missions. One's testimony must be clearly separated from seeking for one's own honor and also clearly separated from *our* cause, from *our* group, or from a transformation according to *our* model. Otherwise, the essence of being the Church is violated. That danger looms up frequently in history when the impression is given that one's distinctive structure shows originality, particular qualities that distinguish it from and set it above other churches. When that happens the Church and the confession have been secularized in a particular form of distinctive "identity," and the gospel is misunderstood.

The sole identity here can only be an actual lack of originality with respect to the gospel of the Lord of the Church, and only in those categories can whatever is distinctive of one's own Church and confession be understood and described. Only in this way can what is irritating be cleaned out of the testimony and out of one's distinctive affirmation.[69] Every "identity" that does not bear the marks of true subjection to the Lord, of imitation of Christ, must eventually result in an unsalutary proselytism and propaganda. Therefore, it is impossible to act self-

duty to make them members of the Church, which is "the true Church of Jesus Christ to the exclusion of all others." However, there is another side to this, which contains more complications than one would suspect with this "objective" starting point. The central problem lies in the meaning of the necessity for salvation of the Catholic Church. Cf. further G. Holtz, "Wird sich die Konvertiten-praxis Ändern?" *Erneuerung der einen Kirche*, 1966, pp. 251ff., particularly on Przywara and Congar (pp. 253ff.).

68. Cf. the Toronto Declaration on the right and duty of the different churches in connection with their own convictions, although there may be no pressure.

69. It has always been noticed that Paul asked others to imitate himself (I Cor. 4:16; I Thess. 1:6). That this imitation is not independent is clear from the fact that Paul imitates Christ (I Cor. 11:1). Cf. W.P. de Boer, *The Imitation of Paul*, 1962, pp. 92ff. The reference to Paul as a "model" before Agrippa (Acts 26:29) cannot be isolated either. The imitation of Paul can be understood only in connection with Paul's "example" in receiving Christ's mercy and patience *(en emoì prṓtǫ —* I Tim. 1:16), the correlate of Paul's foremost place among sinners *(prōtós — 1:15).*

assuredly with one's distinctiveness, since, first of all, it accentuates one's own responsibility. Since it is the Church that we are discussing, the foundation for that which is one's own can be neither psychological, historical, nor sociological. Rather, only true listening to the voice of the Shepherd can legitimize distinctiveness. One's own identity must be nothing other than the manifestation of love, in abundance of knowledge and discernment, in order to approve what is excellent (Phil. 1:9-10) — nothing other than simple devotion to Christ.[70] That applies to the whole life of the Church, whose "approval of what is excellent" must give an outlook on what is decisive for truly being the Church. Therefore, the Church cannot rest in the status quo or in the "riches" of pluriformity as a name for division.[71]

In spite of all the disappointments and all the frustrations in the unity of the Church, the disquiet is a continuing commission. To seek "what is excellent" for one's own life and for the lives of others belongs essentially to the sanctification of the Church. This sanctification, the center and periphery of distinctiveness, makes it evident that the testimony can be nothing else than the reverse side of following the Lord. Where that is no longer understood, one can seize upon pluriformity for reassurance, or one can become indifferent to the calling by the Church to knowledge and discernment due to the misuse of proselytism. The horror of pharisaic proselytism was that it worsened the situation: the person became a child of hell "twice as much as yourselves" (Matt. 23:15). All blessing is gone from this "recruitment," since the key of knowledge has been taken away (Luke 11:52), in spite of all the activity of traversing sea and land. The real situation is then revealed: not entering and hindering those who were entering. But this shocking picture may not lead us to capitulate to the dispersion and to weaken the meaning of testifying to the truth. That pathway would be inevitable only if the discussion were about the multitude of one's own *a priori*'s

70. Paul points to undivided devotion "for your own benefit" in I Cor. 7:35. One may say that the antithesis between centripetal and centrifugal (Hoekendijk, *op. cit.*, p. 197) has been overcome here, and also with respect to ecumenism.

71. The fact that "dialogue" is spoken of everywhere today does not signify *a priori* a relativizing approach to ecumenism. That is decidedly not the intention of Pope Paul VI's emphasis on dialogue (*Ecclesiam Suam*, 1964). Rather, emphasis on dialogue can be a reflection of the preparedness to make a defense (I Pet. 3:15): the Church may not shrink back from any question, whether it be in regard to her confession, her mission, or her *hope* (in which Peter concentrates the defense).

and opinions, about that "contentiousness" of which Paul says that the churches of God do not have this "practice."[72] Where this practice is recognized as a temptation, the Church is cautioned not only to guard against the appearance of evil, but also to know that her division threatens to render every trip over sea and land meaningless, hindering others from entering — precisely while her commission is to represent and to reflect the Lord in His invitation and in His standing at the open door (John 10:9), where He calls all who labor and are heavy laden (Matt. 11:28).

The misunderstanding that the Church, in pointing out the way of life, really seeks her own honor can be overcome only if her words and deeds are evident. The deepest meaning of distinctiveness is imitation. Here wanting to be first is the antithesis of haughtiness, of all churchism, and of misunderstood identity. All the relationships of life that have been blurred by sin are broken through here. Whoever would be first and would be great must be the servant of all (Mark 10:43-45); he will not be among the first who will be last.[73] With respect to this "example," who would want to make a separation between the personal way of faith and that of the Church?[74]

The extreme concentration and responsibility of the Church's whole life does not require a forced, unattractive uniformity (in place of "pluriformity"). The Lord of the Church Who is the Shepherd of the flock, knows all the sheep — in all variation, in need and threat, and in the dangers of doubt and temptation. In only one thing are they "uniform": He cares for them all,[75] in their individuality, their history, their problems, their time, their cares, their new tasks, their gifts, and their lacks. This care makes room for an unexpected, enriching pluriformity, which is manifold and inexhaustible; and here there is room for all of Kuyper's fascinating images. Yet this pluriformity is possible only within the one fellowship, within which the possibilities of all times, lands, and circumstances are unlimited. Because the many questions today are so different and complicated, there

---

72. I Cor. 11:16: the practice *(sunétheia)*, namely, of being contentious *(philóneikos einai)!*
73. Matt. 19:30; Mark 10:31, in contrast to "the only ones qualified" in their own eyes *(TDNT, VI, 868)*.
74. In addition to the imitation of Paul, cf. the imitation of the churches of God in Judea (I Thess. 2:14).
75. In contrast to the hireling who "cares nothing for the sheep" *(ou mélei autô perì tôn probátōn* — John 10:13).

cannot be uniformity in all solutions. But "pluralism" in various provisional solutions[76] is subject to "necessity" as the decisive aspect of the good Shepherd's messianic life-work. The necessity was related to a new reality, to deep fellowship in Him: "I have other sheep, that are not of this fold; I *must* bring them also, and they will heed my voice. So there shall be one flock, one shepherd" (John 10:16). Whoever abstracts in this pluralism even for an instant from the necessity of Christ's bringing the others must despair of unity and fellowship in the Church, since there is so much variation in the many problems that face the Church. That can make us so anxious that we end up quite removed from Paul's calm statement in a concrete situation: "and if in anything you are otherwise minded, God will reveal that also to you" (Phil. 3:15f. — *ei ti heterōs phroneite*). This calm can only be recovered when we bear in mind that Paul begins by holding true to what has been attained (3:16) — not as absolute solutions, and not as if it had been made his own already, but as having been made Christ Jesus's own, and thus of pressing on toward the goal for the prize of the upward call of God (3:13f.). Here is where the light shines in all pluriformity, and this pluriformity must be preserved and protected in the reality of an unassailable fellowship.

76. Cf. on pluralism in the assimilation of the countless actual pieces of information and the dialogue connected with this, K. Rahner, "A Small Question Regarding the Contemporary Pluralism in the Intellectual Situation of Catholics and the Church," *Theological Investigations*, VI, 1969, pp. 21ff.; and "Reflections on Dialogue Within a Pluralistic Society," *ibid.*, pp. 31ff.; and Ervin Válvyi Nagy, *Das dialogische Wesen der Kirche*, 1967.

CHAPTER FOUR

FELLOWSHIP

OUR CONVICTION THAT THE PLURAL FOR "Church" is an inner contradiction is confirmed by the numerous characterizations of the Church of Christ in the whole of the New Testament: the one people of God, the temple of the Holy Spirit, the building of God, the flock of the good Shepherd. These images indicate in various ways the one reality of the Church.[1] Each image points in the same direction, toward the one mystery of the Church, the origin of which is the love and mercy of God. A new fellowship is constituted here, not in uniform synchronization, but in a truly binding unity, evoked by the coming of Christ, Who brings together again what was scattered, divided, and disunited. To think of a plural here[2] is to ignore that the plural is connected with Christ only in the environs of false christs (Matt. 24:24 — *pseudóchristoi*)!

The background of the call to unity and fellowship is God's saving, reconciling action. The individual does not disappear behind the vague contours of a "totality," but he is liberated from individualization and solitariness in order to have a place in this new fellowship. That the Lord cares for the sheep includes, not excludes, specific attention for one lost sheep (Luke 15:4ff.). Every individual need receives His undivided attention; yet, at the same time, ways are opened by which the individual receives a place in a human fellowship, ending all individualism. A new, clear light breaks through into human relationships, in struggle and frustration, fragmentation and dispersion. From

1. *Lumen Gentium (DV II,* p. 18) refers to the many images that indicate the "inner nature of the Church."
2. Cf. above, chapter 2. One may also think of the image of the temple with its evidentness and uniqueness. R.J. McKelvey (*The New Temple. The Church in the N.T.,* 1969, p. 183) writes that "temples in the plural is a characteristic of paganism and unthinkable."

what was disclosed in Christ "through the tender mercy of our God,"[3] a reality comes into view that can scarcely be described with the words "effect" or "consequence"; for the mercy itself is directed to the restoration of life and fellowship, and, against all resistance, it appropriates that restoration in the new commandment (cf. John 13:34f.; I John 2:8).

The body of Christ

Nowhere are we more impressed with this aspect of new fellowship than when the New Testament describes the Church as the body of Christ. Because this description is so peculiar, these words have frequently been seen as a special, unique characterization of the Church, the deepest description of the mystery of the Church. Contemporary discussions about the Church often deal with whether the characterization "body of Christ" or that of "the people of God" speaks more deeply and revealingly about the Church. Van der Linde, for instance, considers "body of Christ" to be deeper and more universal than "people of God," because what is new in the re-creation because of Christ's death and resurrection does not come out in the latter description.[4] Others lay more emphasis on the vast significance of the characterization "people of God," because the salvation-historical perspective comes to expression in it.[5]

Clearly, a preference for a particular characterization is often influenced by the special stress given to specific aspects of the Church at present. We are thinking of the exceptional significance that was attributed to the Church as the people of God at the time of the Second Vatican Council: the Church is the pilgrim Church, still "underway" in danger, threat, and responsibility, and called to watchfulness in comparison with

3. Luke 1:78 (*tà splánchna eléous*). Cf. *splánchna* in I John 3:16f., where the reaction to need is mercy and the laying down of one's life.
4. H. van der Linde, "Ecclesiologisch Perspectief voor de Oecumene, *Oecumene in het Vizier*, 1960, p. 135. Cf. W. Grossouw, *In Christ*, 1952, p. 124: "the most intimate nature of the Church." The encyclical *Mystici Corporis Christi* of 1943 (*TCT*, 239) writes that there is nothing more noble, more sublime, or more divine as a description of the Church than the expression "the mystical body of Jesus Christ."
5. For instance, E. Kinder (*Der evangelische Glaube und die Kirche*, 1960, 29ff.), who is of the opinion "that the idea of the people of God is basic; the conception of the body must be seen in its framework, and not the reverse."

every triumphalistic ecclesiology.[6] Motives of competition often
come to light when one gives such a preference for one's own
one-sided ideals for the Church, so that the outlook on the
fullness of the Church — typified in many images — is in danger
of being lost. In salvation-historical terms, one can say that
the characterization "body of Christ" is a more precise christological determination of the people of God,[7] but that does not
necessarily imply that this expression should dominate as the
deepest and most essential "definition" of the Church. Other
pictures in the New Testament also bring to expression this
direct relatedness to Christ. Therefore, the content that one
gives to a particular characterization is of decisive importance,
for one-sidedness due to various preferences can obscure the
many-sidedness of the biblical witness about the Church.[8]

By saying this, though, we certainly do not want to minimize the great significance of the designation of the Church
as the body of Christ. Paul himself deals extensively with it
and draws profound "consequences" from it for the life of the

6. One may think of R. Grosche's *Pilgernde Kirche*, 1938, which again
   plays a more important role in our time. Cf. Y. Congar, "The Church:
   the People of God," *Concilium*, 1, 1965, pp. 11ff. Congar speaks of a
   revival of the idea of the people of God in contemporary theology,
   beginning with the perspective and dynamic of salvation history. Congar
   wants to supplement this characterization with that of the body of
   Christ as the relation *after* the incarnation, Easter, and Pentecost (pp.
   35ff.). Cf. also *Lumen Gentium*, which has a separate chapter on "The
   People of God" (*DV II*, pp. 24ff.).
7. H.N. Ridderbos (*Paul*, 1975, p. 395) speaks of the body of Christ as
   describing the peculiar character and the newness of the people of God
   in a very pregnant and special way, because it indicates a more precise christological definition and concentration of the people of God.
   Naturally, no formulation may be isolated. One can see how relative
   the search for a "key conception" is when McKelvey (*op. cit.*, p. 180),
   who is intrigued by the aspect of the "temple," draws attention to
   perhaps the "most significant conceptions for our understanding of the
   N.T. doctrine of the Church," specifically because of her theocentric
   character (the Church's relation to God).
8. Cf. M. Schmaus, "Das gegenseitige Verhältnis von Leib Christi und Volk
   Gottes im Kirchenverständnis," *Volk Gottes. Festgabe für J. Höfer*, 1967,
   p. 25: "not competing conceptions," but "ones that complement each
   other." Schmaus sees the salvation-historical continuity expressed especially in the "people of God." This is something that cannot be said of
   the expression "body of Christ." According to him, "'people of God'
   is the "comprehensive" concept (p. 27). Cf. also N.A. Dahl, *Das Volk
   Gottes. Eine Untersuchung zum Kirchenbewusstsein des Urchristentums*,
   1941, pp. 209ff., 248ff.

Church.[9] It can be assumed that the Church as the body of
Christ stands in the full light of unity, concord, and fellowship;
and all opposition, rivalry, and conflict are out of the question
on account of the relatedness of the one body and all its members to Him, Who is the Head of the body, the Church (Col.
1:18). In reflecting on this description, one usually begins
with the deep relatedness and fellowship that comes to expression in Paul's letter to the congregations in Rome and
Corinth. The starting point here is a clear analogy: the Church
is compared to a human body. "For as in one body we have
many members, and all the members do not have the same
function, so we, though many, are one body in Christ" (Rom.
12:4ff.). Great diversity, unity, and fellowship are indicated in
these words. In no respect is one threatened by another. Rather,
the diversity of gifts is totally directed towards serving the
fellowship. No member is independent or has his destination
in himself. "Separateness" is mentioned in a particular sense,
but not in the sense of separation and isolation, because
"everyone" has a meaningful place in the whole, just as there
is no tension and disruption when the Holy Spirit is poured
out on "each one of them" (Acts 2:3f. — *eph' héna hékaston*).

As in Romans, variety is placed in I Corinthians in the
light of relatedness to the same Spirit, the same Lord, and the
same God (I Cor. 12:4, cf. 8f., 11). The multiformity is real,
but is directed to the common good (12:7). Here, too, we meet
with the analogy of the body: it is one, and all the members,
though many, are one body (12:12). To make that clear, Paul
points to the dependency of every member of the body (hand,
foot, eye, ear, and head). The members need one another and
thus have a place in the whole, so that there can be no discord
or schism (12:25). There is immediate clarity in this analogy

9. From the abundant literature we mention only the following: L.
Deimel, *Leib Christi. Sinn und Grenze einer Deutung des innerkirchlichen
Lebens*, 1940; M.D. Koster, *Ekklesiologie im Werden*, 1940; H.M. Matter,
De Kerk als het Lichaam van Christus; J.A.T. Robinson, *The Body*,
1953; H. Berkhof, "Corpus Christi," *In de Waagschaal*, May 4, 1957;
J. Reuss, "Die Kirche als 'Leib Christi' und die Herkunft dieser Vor-
stellung bei dem Apostel Paulus," *Bibl. Zeitschr.*, 1958, pp. 103ff.; W.D.
Jonker, *Mistieke Liggaam en Kerk in die Nuwe Rooms-Katolieke Theologie*, 1955; F. Malmberg, *Eén Lichaam en één Geest. Nieuwe Gezichts-
punten in de Ecclesiologie*, 1958; J.J. Meuzelaar, *Der Leib des Messias*,
1961; C. Colpe, "Zur Leib Christi-Vorstellung im Epheserbrief," *Judentum, Urchristentum, Kirche. Festschrift Jeremias*, 1964, pp. 172ff.; and
Ridderbos, *Paul*, pp. 362ff.

of the human body, of which Paul makes use to show the unity of the Church.[10] Paul's view of the Church is by nature strongly anti-individualistic. The Church does not consist of independent "monads"; rather, she is a fellowship in which isolation is replaced by "sympathy": if one member suffers, all suffer; and if one member is honored, all rejoice together (12:26). It is hardly possible that there be difference of opinion about this relatedness in the one body of Christ. "Now you are the body of Christ and individually members of it" (12:27). Because the reality of this relatedness is so strong for Paul, he reproaches the Corinthians for the schism that they have caused with their practice of the Lord's supper: they despise the Church of God, since those who have nothing are humiliated (11:22).

Real or figurative

But does Paul not have more in view than a reference to the essential relatedness with each other on the basis of Christ? Does he not go beyond all "figurative language" to an avowed "realism"? Does he not view the Church as "the body of Christ" in the sense of an "ontic" reality? These questions arise especially in connection with Paul's letters to Colossae and Ephesus, where various special, new aspects appear, although no one can deny that the aspect of communion, or fellowship, is not lacking here (cf. Eph. 3:15). It is of great importance to know what one understands by "ontic" and "realism." That is even more important if one feels that Paul's deepest ecclesiological intention comes to expression here and, therefore, attaches a certain priority to the description "body of Christ." One points out especially that Paul is concerned with much more than simply figurative language; he has a specific bodily reality in view. This is an unenlightening dilemma, however, because there cannot be a contradiction between figurative language and reality: figurative language undoubtedly intends to refer to reality. A metaphor is not a vague, unreal expression, but intends, in the service of revelation, to open one's eyes to a deep, fascinating reality. And so, the question is not "real or not real?" but is directed to the nature of the reality that is pointed out.[11]

10. Cf. Matter, *op. cit.*, pp. 17ff.
11. "Metaphor" is often spoken of as *"only* a metaphor," as Col. 2:16f. speaks of things that are "only a shadow" in contrast to the "substance *(sóma)* that belongs to Christ. But this is a salvation-historical

Now it is evident what is intended with the dilemma. Saying that it is "not simply figurative language" points out that the expression "body of Christ" refers to an entirely peculiar reality. Something is pointed out in addition to relatedness: the "body of Christ" in the actual sense, namely, in connection with the crucified and glorified body of Christ, with which the Church is identified in a particular way. We continually meet with this "identification" as the actual mystery of the Church. Paul's transition from the division in Corinth to Christ's being divided (I Cor. 1:12f.) is pointed out, and reference is made to Christ's question to Paul when he is persecuting the Church: "Saul, Saul, why do you persecute me?"[12] It is extremely important to know what is understood by this identification, since it is connected with the characterization of the Church as the "body of Christ." One begins with the Church's undeniable, deep relatedness to Christ, which the New Testament speaks of continually and which one may never minimize.[13] For example, Paul points out the horribleness of the immorality in Corinth by recalling that the bodies are members of Christ, and therefore by becoming one with a prostitute they break the relatedness to Christ (I Cor. 6:15ff.). We see two sorts of "fellowship" here as two realities. Paul is concerned with real relatedness in being "of Christ." He sets fellowship with Christ (10:21), with His blood and His body (10:16), over against fellowship *(koinōnía)* with demons *(daimónia)*, which arises from sacrificing to idols (10:18ff.).[14]

Do all these references to the reality and depth of fellowship and to being the body of Christ not lead naturally to the

comparison (cf. Heb. 10:1 — *skiá*) and may not be transferred to the meaning of metaphor, which precisely testifies that the substance has come! Cf. Ridderbos, *Paul,* p. 376, who speaks of a "figurative, metaphorical significance" in which, however, the unity and communion with Christ is "real and literal." For the dilemma, see the statement of Faith and Order at Lund: "The Pauline image of the Church as the body of Christ is no mere metaphor, but expresses a living reality" (*Report,* p. 13). Naturally!

12. Acts 9:4. Cf. J.A.T. Robinson, *The Body,* p. 58. *Mystici Corporis Christi* also refers to this text.
13. H. Berkhof, "Corpus Christi," *In de Waagschaal,* May 4, 1957.
14. The antithesis starts from the reality of fellowship. That does not conflict with I Cor. 8:5 ("so-called gods" — *legómenoi theoi*) or Gal. 4:8 ("beings that by nature are no gods"). Cf. the warnings against "partaking" of the table of demons (I Cor. 10:21) and against taking part in the unfruitful works of darkness (Eph. 5:11). Cf. further Hos. 4:17 ("joined to idols" — LXX, *métochos eidólōn*) and Deut. 32:17.

word identification? This question has been affirmatively answered not only by those who interpreted Paul's view as a *physisch* and as a *naturhafte* relatedness and identification,[15] but also by Bonhoeffer, who spoke of an identification in the words "Christ exists as the Church."[16] Bonhoeffer found a clear identification: "If we take the thought of the body seriously, then it means that 'this image' identifies Christ and the Church, as Paul himself clearly does."[17] Yet that is not the last word for Bonhoeffer. He adds that "Paul does not wish to make this complete identification because Christ for him is also with God," and he speaks here of "this dogmatic problem." Bonhoeffer's intention is clear. On one hand, he wants to follow the New Testament in not minimizing the connection of the Church to Christ;[18] on the other hand, he does not want to take that relatedness out of the framework of calling, subjection, and admonition. Thus he definitely does not want to understand it as a simple, ascertainable identification from which one can draw equally simple conclusions. With that, however, the word "identification" loses its clarity and can easily raise various impure associations.[19]

15. A. Schweitzer, *The Mysticism of Paul the Apostle*, 1931, p. 127: the body of Christ is "for Paul not a pictorial expression, nor a conception which has arisen out of symbolical and ethical reflections, but an actual entity." Cf. *eine naturhafte Gemeinschaft; naturhaft leiblich* (pp. 128f.).
16. D. Bonhoeffer, *The Communion of Saints*, 1960, p. 101.
17. *Ibid.*, p. 100. Cf. p. 138: "Paul could even say that Christ himself is the Church."
18. I Cor. 12:12: "just as the body is one..., so it is with Christ" (not "so it is with the Church"). This text has been discussed again and again in connection with the identification. Calvin (*Commentary on the Letters of Paul to the Corinthians*, I, 405) points to the significance of the reality: "The name of Christ is used here instead of the Church." The text is "full of choice consolation, inasmuch as he calls the Church Christ," since Christ "is willing to be esteemed and recognized, not in himself merely, but also in his members."
19. Cf. K.M. Beckmann, "'Christus als Gemeinde existierend.' Der Begriff der Kirche in D. Bonhoeffers 'Sanctorum Communio' im Blick auf die Ökumene," *Evang. Theol.*, 1961, pp. 327ff. Beckmann also considers the formulation unsatisfying and points out that Bonhoeffer himself lays strong emphasis on Christ as *Lord of the Church* (p. 337). Cf. also H. Ott, *Wirklichkeit und Glaube*, I, 1966, pp. 195ff., and II, 1969, pp. 254ff.; and Bonhoeffer, *The Communion of Saints*, pp. 97ff. How greatly Bonhoeffer was concerned with this problem is apparent from his *Christology*, 1966, p. 61, where he says that "the separation between head and members" first arose in Ephesus and then says that "it is not originally Pauline." Nevertheless, there is no "contradiction" (Ott, *op. cit.*, I, 195).

It is necessary to take into account that the "being of Christ" (His body) can be purely understood only in all the connections and aspects of the Church's being. This fellowship in "being of Him" is indicated in numerous ways. Not only can Paul speak about the body as a temple of the Holy Spirit (I Cor. 6:19) and describe union with the Lord as being one spirit with Him (6:17), but also, in another connection, partaking in Christ does not clearly signify identification, but fellowship! At the footwashing Christ speaks to Peter about having a part in Him by His washing him.[20] It is a new relatedness like that of becoming partakers in Christ (Heb. 3:14), in the heavenly call (3:1), and in the Holy Spirit (6:4). Moreover, fellowship with Christ can be described as Christ's "dwelling" in our hearts through faith (Eph. 3:17 — katoikḗsai), just as there is mention of a coming and dwelling by the Father and the Son.[21] There is an urgent warning in these many-sided descriptions against allowing the description of the Church as the body of Christ to stand alone. Otherwise, as the history of exegesis and dogmatics makes clear, it becomes static and appears to be an object for a "contemplative" theology, which removes "the Church" far from the earthly Church as we know her and as she stands out in the various images of the New Testament.

"Mystical" union with Christ

The tendency to isolate the designation "body of Christ" has often been connected with a specific characterization of fellowship with Christ being "mystical" by nature: a "mystical union" (unio mystica). Then the body of Christ was more precisely defined as corpus Christi mysticum. It is not easy to say what is meant exactly by this addition to the body of Christ and to unio cum Christo. Various further qualifications distinguish the unio mystica from any "substantial" union or identification. But the intention is to indicate the reality of this union. Thus, the unity of the Church in this union comes to the fore. Mention is made not only of a subjective belief

---

20. John 13:8 (méros met' emoú). Cf. sharing in the first resurrection, Rev. 20:6.
21. John 14:23 (eleusómetha kaì monḗn). Cf. Rev. 3:20: Christ's entrance through the opened door (eiseleúsomai) and the mutuality of eating together that follows. Cf. God's dwelling among His people (Ex. 29:45) and the eschatological dwelling of God with men (Rev. 21:3).

with all its possible, pluriform variations, but also of fellowship, of Christ's presence, which radically excludes any plural.

As is generally known, Reformed theology has frequently dealt with this "mystical union." As far as I can see, there was no special concern about the implications of this doctrine for the unity of the Church. One was especially concerned with the nature of this union. With regard to the "mystical" union, reference is always made to the hidden, unsearchable nature of this union with Christ. Through this fellowship, in which Christ becomes ours, we are engrafted into His body, and we are made one with Him.[22] It is emphasized that fellowship is not simply with the gifts given by Him, but rather with His person, with Himself. This excludes all isolation of His gifts and accentuates the personal character of fellowship with Christ.[23] At the same time, however, the Reformed tradition rejects all identification and mixture, as, for instance, is the case with Calvin in opposition to Osiander.[24]

The word "mystical" itself is open to varied associations and is, in fact, used in many different ways.[25] One calls Paul "mystical," while another calls him "completely unmystical." And, as a result, there is great confusion. This confusion is also apparent in the intense Roman Catholic interest in this "mystical" aspect, especially in connection with the Church as "the mystical body of Christ." This formulation has long played an important role, and it has been connected to the (self-evident) unity of the Church, for instance, when the statement is made: "the mystical body of Christ, which is the Church."[26] The

22. Calvin, *Inst.*, III, 11, 10: "that joining together of Head and members, that indwelling of Christ in our hearts." Cf. "because we put on Christ and are engrafted into his body."

23. Cf. my *The Sacraments*, 1969, p. 227; G.P. Hartvelt, *Verum Corpus*, 1960, pp. 93ff., 113ff.; W. Kolfhaus, *Christus gemeinschaft bei Calvin*, 1939; and H. Bavinck, *Geref. Dog.*, IV, 234, 543ff.

24. *Inst.*, III, 11, 10. Cf. on the one hand: "so that Christ, having been made ours, makes us sharers with him in the gifts with which he has been endowed." On the other hand, it is a "spiritual bond," rather than Osiander's "gross mingling of Christ with believers," by which "God pours himself into us."

25. Cf. W. Elert, *The Structure of Lutheranism*, I, 1962, pp. 154ff.; and W. Koepp, "Wurzel und Ursprung der orthod. Lehre von der unio mystica," *Z.Th.K.*, 1921, pp. 46ff., 139ff.

26. The beginning of the encyclical *Mystici Corporis Christi*, 1943. The formulation "mystical body of Christ" appears already in 1302 in the papal bull *Unam Sanctam*: "one mystical body" *(unam corpus mysticum* — Denz., 468; *TCT*, 153). Cf. especially H. de Lubac, *Corpus Mysticum*.

encyclical of 1943 about the mystical body of Christ has greatly stimulated reflection on the nature of fellowship in the body of Christ. The occasion of the encyclical was an interpretation of "mystical" that strongly tended towards identification, against which protests had arisen already before 1943.[27] The encyclical rejects all mystical identification and states that Paul "spoke only metaphorically about these things." One must not understand it in the sense of a fusion into one physical person. Here the encyclical brings up an important viewpoint: Paul does make a wonderful connection between Christ and His mystical body, but he can also place both opposite each other, as the bridegroom stands opposite *(gegenüber)* the bride.[28] It is not that an antithesis is postulated here; the *Gegenüber* does not threaten fellowship, but rather belongs essentially to it. Basically, the protest is against the connection of mystical reality with a vague, irrational, and occult reality that loses sight of the concrete, visible Catholic Church. Identification is inherent in her too, but it makes room for concrete, juridical, and hierarchical structures, where Christ is also honored as Head of the Church. This concrete identification can then be opposed to false mysticism, which lacks appreciation for the essence of the "perfect society" *(societas perfecta)* because of its view of the inner fellowship of grace.[29] In contrast to this, the encyclical understands "mystical" as the wonderful, supernatural aspect of union, which becomes a reality here in the concrete, visible Church.[30]

L'Eucharistie et l'Eglise au Moyen Age, 1948, pp. 116ff., on the way from the Eucharist to the Church as *"corpus mysticum."*

27. M.D. Koster *(op. cit.,* p. 163) was of the opinion that "mystical" originally meant simply "pictorial, figurative, metaphorical, allegorical," and thus aimed at a spiritual reality. Pius X *(Ad Diem Illum,* 1904) had already spoken of "a 'spiritual' or, as one says, a 'mystical' body."

28. *"Opponit,"* *Mystici Corporis Christi* (Denz.-Schönm., 3816). Cf. F. Malmberg *(op. cit.,* p. 50), who does not consider it impossible that there be a mystical identity that "transcends our natural categories of unity."

29. *Mystici Corporis Christi* (Denz.-Schönm., 3816). Cf. W.D. Jonker, *op. cit.,* pp. 140ff., in detail on the encyclical.

30. *Lumen Gentium (DV II,* p. 20) speaks of union "in a hidden and real way" *(arcano ac reali modo).* And it is said of the calling of Christ's brothers from all peoples by the communication of the Spirit: "Christ made them *mystically (mystice)* into His own body." In *Mystici Corporis Christi* the error of fusion is rejected *(in physicam unam personam coire et coalescere).*

Union and communion

Even though the intention here is particularly to resist mysticism and to resist an antithesis between a juridical Church and a Church of love, the viewpoint of the *Gegenüber* plays an auxiliary role and undoubtedly draws upon what is said in the New Testament about the relatedness of the Church to Christ. Here distance *(distantia)* is in the foreground, not as separation and alienation, but as a distinction that belongs to the essence of "communion," separating it from all identification. For example, Calvin points out that the distinction does not injure the union and that it does not mean we contemplate Christ "outside ourselves from afar."[31] Many formulations in the New Testament bring to expression the reality of the nearness of Christ and fellowship with Him. We hear of being "in" Christ,[32] of Christ's life in Paul (Gal. 2:20), of Christ's dwelling in our hearts (Eph. 3:17) — all of which refer to the reality of fellowship.

In this connection, the way in which the letters to Ephesus and Colossae show Christ as Head of the Church has always played an important role.[33] I Corinthians also speaks about the head, but there it appears next to foot, hand, eye, and ear. Thus, it is a part of the human body and does not dominate the other members.[34] But in Colossians and Ephesians, the head is the dominating *Gegenüber* and excludes all identification. A specific relation between Christ and the Church is clearly indicated, as is apparent when we are told that Christ is the Church's Savior (Eph. 5:23) and that she is subject to Him (5:24 — *hupotássetai tǫ̃ Christǫ̃*). The Church must hold

31. *Inst.,* III, 11, 10: *extra nos procul.* Calvin does not contest what Osiander says: "Christ is one with us, and we, in turn, with him" (III, 11, 5). Calvin uses such strong expressions to describe this bond that Bavinck will not take responsibility for all the formulations, since they create misunderstanding *(Kennis en Leven,* p. 176).
32. Cf. in detail, A. Schweitzer, *op. cit.,* pp. 123ff.; A. Wikenhauser, *Pauline Mysticism,* 1960, pp. 17ff. See also II Cor. 5:17 and Rom. 8:1. "In" also plays an important role in I John (with respect to God). Cf. "abiding in Him" (4:13, 15) in the extremely concrete context of keeping His commandments and God's abiding in us (3:23f.).
33. Col. 1:18; Eph. 1:22f.; 4:15; 5:23. Cf. I.J. du Plessis, *Christus as Hoof van Kerk en Kosmos,* 1962; Ridderbos, *Paul,* pp. 387ff.; J.J. Meuzelaar, *op. cit.,* pp. 117ff.; and F.W. Grosheide, "Die Zijn Lichaam Is," *Gereformeerd Theologisch Tijdschrift,* 1947, pp. 193ff.
34. I Cor. 12:21: "'The head cannot say to the feet, 'I have no need of you.'" See Ridderbos, *Paul,* p. 380.

fast to her Head (Col. 2:19) and thus be freed from all fleshly thinking, which does not understand that Christ is and remains the first, the Head of the body, the Church.[35] Paul deals constantly with that relation *(unio ut relatio)*.[36] Not that we get a uniform, exhaustive "definition," but one aspect calls up another, although they do not limit or contradict each other. Fellowship is delineated in many relations. For example, in the context of Christ's Headship, Paul can also speak of growth: growth towards Christ, Who is the Head (Eph. 4:15) through Whom the Church, the Church on earth, receives all her growth.[37]

Because of the various ways in which this one reality is described, we must not place the aspects in contradistinction to one another or see one aspect as referring to the "actual," "deepest" reality of the Church.[38] There can be no theoretical "contemplation" of being "in itself," an isolated "essence" of the Church as a "mystical" reality. Rather, there can only be a penetrating, indissoluble connection with the concrete life of the Church on earth, directed to a unique "representation" of Christ's work of salvation and of His fullness.[39] It is precisely these connections which keep the Church from all vagueness, abstraction, and mysteriousness, since she is placed in the framework of relatedness and growth, of fellowship and subjection, and of calling and service. The Church as the body of Christ signifies her essential functionality in Christ, not as an antithesis to her "being," but as the mode of this reality

35. On submissiveness cf. also I Cor. 11:3: "the head of every man is Christ, the head of a woman is her husband, and the head of Christ is God." Cf. also 11:8 (woman-man), and Meuzelaar, *op. cit.*, p. 119.

36. Cf. Th. Kreider, *Unsere Vereinigung mit Christus, dogmatisch gesehen,* 1941, p. 171.

37. Eph. 4:15f.; Col. 2:19. In all the characterizations, one can say that Paul was "completely engrossed by the realities that metaphors were intended to express" (W. Goossens, *L'Eglise Corps du Christ d'après Saint Paul,* 1949², p. 45).

38. Being open to the riches of all the descriptions in the New Testament prevents one from giving a single exhaustive definition; one can speak of varying "independent" aspects that cannot be reduced to one or the other (see Ridderbos, *Paul,* pp. 380ff. on *kephalê*). We find a striking mixture of the images in *Mystici Corporis Christi* (Denz.-Schönm., 3805), where the head in I Cor. 12 is transferred into the framework of Colossians and Ephesians. The conclusion is that the head (i.e., the Head) cannot say to the feet, "I have no need of you." Cf. "But this too must be maintained, although it may seem utterly astonishing: Christ needs his members."

39. Ridderbos, *Paul,* pp. 391f.

in the light of and under the beneficial power of her Lord. One cannot reflect on this "being" of the Church without doing justice to all the connections of gift and admonition. Then all the "images" are understandable against the ever-present background of the parenesis *(parainesis)*, in which the Church is placed precisely for the sake of her true being.[40]

If a contemplative interpretation of being gives the "mystical" union with Christ the form of an isolated, religious mysticism, we often see justified protest against it.[41] For the Church, as a supernatural, hidden mystery, is no longer accessible for testing and admonition. She gives the impression — in conflict with Christ's prayer (John 17:15) — of having been taken away out of the world. In direct opposition to this, emphasis was then laid on fellowship with Christ in the midst of concrete life. The "mystical" was replaced by the "concrete" and an unworldly piety was rejected.[42] This protest against isolating piety in a central, cultic, or liturgical sphere was a search for the meaning of communion in the sense of its fruitfulness and functionality, its inner-worldly mystery. There are often reactive influences in this protest, since one was grasped by the biblical data about the "being" of the Church in her earthly contours of indicative and imperative, of gift and task, of a union with Christ. These did not make life in the world irrelevant, but gave "being" meaning and perspective. Thus, the danger of a dilemma arose;[43] and, with both sides making

40. On "functionality" see especially H.M. Matter, *op. cit.*, p. 36 (the image of the body "in the framework of an appeal"). Further, see J.J. Meuzelaar (*op. cit.*, p. 172): not a "mystical elevation of the Church, but a stimulus for the messianic fellowship to love and to common service." Lastly, cf. E. Käsemann, *Exeg. Vers. und Besinn.*, I, 285 (on "ontology" and "the sphere of sovereignty of the Spirit of Christ"); and II, 246f. (the Church is described as "not a prolongation of the earthly Jesus," and the testimony to the body of Christ is described as "solely parenetical").

41. In close connection with this, we want to point out Ridderbos' important exposition of the indicative and the imperative (*Paul*, pp. 253ff.). Cf. p. 254 on the irreversible order and p. 255 on the misunderstanding that the indicative vindicates "a given situation that exists apart from the imperative." These radical statements are decisive also for the Church's "being."

42. Cf. A. Ritschl's opposition to the *unio mystica*, which he sees as pietistic. Cf. also W. Herrmann, *Der Verkehr des Christen mit Gott*, 1886; and H. Bavinck, *Kennis en Leven*, pp. 182f.

43. See especially K. Barth's valuable considerations on the danger "of possible distortions" and of replacing "one distorted picture" by another in a vicious circle of reactions. Barth uses monasticism as an

selective use of Scripture, the problem of the first and second commandment, horizontality and verticality, became practically insoluble. Union with Christ and earthly communion threatened to compete senselessly as each other's antipodes.

In the New Testament, these dilemmas are overcome not by a balance of different emphases, but on account of the meaning and perspective of union with Christ.[44] It is not a far-off, abstract union, but a reality that cannot be isolated, since the union is with Christ, relatedness to Him. Attention for earthly fellowship is not cut off here, but is rooted and grounded in love (Eph. 3:17); it is not isolated, but understood in the outlook on the earthly reality of the Church and on the glory of Christ (3:21). Fellowship arises here among those in whose midst He dwells and is present, fellowship in unity and concord, in knowledge, faith, and love. His nearness excludes "schism" in the body. It is not a secondary result, but is due to the nature of His being Lord and Redeemer. The Church is gathered around Him and is assigned to testify to her common faith (Titus 1:4 — katà koinḕn pístin) and to our common salvation (Jude 3 — perì tḗs koinḗs hēmṓn sōtērías). In this light the fiery, passionate character of the admonition is understandable, because an attack on fellowship signifies a violation of the mystery of Christ through a dark resistance, in which the Spirit is grieved (Eph. 4:30) and the fellowship of the Spirit is obscured (cf. Phil. 2:1; II Cor. 13:14).

The decisive significance of communion and concord has often not been completely understood, and the impression has been given that frustrations of this concord can scarcely be avoided in the human phenomenon of the Church. But this signified a lack of appreciation for the radical transfer that takes place in and through Christ (Eph. 4:20ff.), in which all bitterness, wrath, and anger are banished, and in which there is kindness, tenderheartedness, and forgiveness on the analogy of Christ's forgiveness (4:31f.). This is not a shallow, moralistic admonition, but is directly connected to grieving the Holy

illustration (C.D., IV/2, pp. 11ff.). Cf. p. 794 on Ritschl and the love of God and on a reaction to mysticism and pietism that left one "only too wise and superior." In this connection Barth recalls Jesus' anointment in Mark 14:3 and his indignation at the suggestion that the ointment was wasted.

44. Cf. H. Berkhof's "dream" in connection with extroversion and introversion, where he reflects on the visibility of the body of Christ and the recruiting-power it contains ("Tweeërlei Ekklesiologie," Kerk en Theologie, 1962, p. 157).

Spirit and the sealing for the day of redemption (4:30). On account of the unity of the body, the one life of the Church is called away from and lifted out of schism and quarreling. Nothing else is tolerable or acceptable here, since, in another metaphor, the darkness is passing away and the true light is already shining in Him and in the Church (I John 2:8). Whoever does not understand this radicalness misses the meaning of the Church as the body of Christ. The body of Christ is far from being an object of theoretical, speculative dispute; rather it is the proclamation of great disquiet in and for the Church! No view of inert, obstinate "structures" and no reference to psychological or sociological backgrounds can ever take away from the fact that only in this confrontation can we speak meaningfully and fruitfully about the "being of the Church."[45] When Paul encourages the Church (Phil. 2:1 — *paráklēsis*) to be of the same mind, to have the same love, and to be in full accord and of one mind (2:2), he points to the calling to have a "mind" that can be compared to Christ's. The decisive thing is the directedness of one to another, humility against the background of Christ's emptying and humbling Himself (2:5ff.). Paul longs for his joy to become complete and asks for the reflection of Christ's act, of the "form" that He took on, that of a servant.[46] Only in this mind is the being of the Church possible, and only thus, in Christ, is her reality, her meaning, and her fruitfulness disclosed.

45. This is of immediate significance for the correct understanding of the confession of the Name of the Lord. The meaning of fellowship in the union with Christ must not lead to a reduction, but to a concentration that is related to union and fellowship. This makes the confession more, not less, serious. That this problem — one of the most far-reaching in ecumenism — cannot be dealt with until later does not detract from the evidentness of the meaning of union and fellowship in the light of what is "of Christ" (His body). Cf. already O. Cullmann, "Die ökumenische Aufgabe heute im Lichte von Universalismus und Konzentration als ökumenisches Problem," *Basler Univ. Reden*, 1968; and my *Verontrusting en Verantwoordelijkheid*, 1969, chapter 8.

46. Phil. 2:7. The analogy is described as follows: "Have this mind among yourselves, which you have in Christ Jesus" *(toúto phroneite en humin hò kaì en Christõ 'Iēsoú)*. Cf. K. Barth, *Erklärung des Philipperbriefes*, 1928, p. 53: "But it now becomes clear whence comes that absolute tone in which it is discussed." Cf. "the self-evident task" and the "order" and the members of His body. Cf. also the one-sided, but intriguing, book by H. Dembowski, *Grundfragen der Christologie*, 1969.

Credo communionem sanctorum

Since the fellowship indicated in the New Testament is so obvious, we should not be surprised that it has received a place in the *credo* of the ancient Church: *credo communionem sanctorum*. This article of faith did not belong to the original Apostles' Creed, but was added later. We will not go into the symbolic-historical question of whether the original intention of this article was to speak of the fellowship in holy things *(sancta)*, especially the Lord's Supper, or to speak of the fellowship of the saints *(sancti)* — thus a more sacramental or a more personal interpretation.[47] Neither form of communion can be separated from the other — partaking together of one bread.[48] Moreover, the personal aspect of fellowship with one another strongly dominated in the later interpretation of the *communio sanctorum*. So, the insertion of *communio* was understood as a more exact explication of *ecclesia*.

Naturally, everything depends on how one understands this communion. One can reflect on it institutionally — i.e., the *corpus mysticum*, the Church, is present simply in the institution. In that case, *communio* in the *credo* is not simply a more exact explication of *ecclesia* (her riches and calling), but qualifies her as *societas perfecta*, as has so long been the case in traditional Roman Catholic theology.[49] However, communion can be better understood as implied in the reality of the Church of Christ, thus speaking confessionally of what the New Testament says about *koinōnia* as fellowship in Christ and through the Holy Spirit. In this way we can see that the dilemma of the interpretation of the symbol is not nearly so far-reaching. It is also understandable that in the Heidelberg Catechism, for instance, the two-fold aspect almost automatically becomes obvious in the description of communion, where the Catechism

47. Cf. F. Kattenbusch, *Das apost. Symbol*, II, 1900, pp. 930ff.; P. Althaus, *Communio Sanctorum*, 1929; Bonhoeffer, *op. cit.*; my *The Conflict with Rome*, chapter 8; and E. Wolf, *Peregrinatio*, I, 1954, pp. 285ff.

48. According to Kattenbusch (*op. cit.*, p. 938), this was not a problem in the ancient Church either.

49. Wolf (*op. cit.*, p. 289) calls this the romanticizing of the concept of the Church (as the continuation of Christ) via a sociological concept of structure. Cf. also pp. 325ff., where Wolf mentions Bonhoeffer's *The Communion of Saints*, which does not approach fellowship from free, human initiative *(animal sociale)*, but says that it is "not possible" (Bonhoeffer, *op. cit.*, p. 53). Wolf's opposition is wholly directed against replacing *credo ecclesiam* by *credo in ecclesiam* (as the secondary cause of salvation) via an organic concept of Church and fellowship.

deals with partaking in Christ and His treasures and gifts, and being bound *(conferre debeant)* to "employ [all the gifts] readily and cheerfully for the advantage and salvation of other members" (Q. 55). This hardly looks like a precise "definition" in the usual sense of the word.[50] No static description is given, but wherever this communion is mentioned, the Catechism includes an appeal.

This is a clear reflection of what the New Testament says about the fellowship of believers in Christ. A peculiar "must" or "obligation" is spoken of — not in the sense that a new law is set up, but on the basis of a clearly indicated foundation. In I John, especially, these connections are clearly expressed. Love for one another in this fellowship belongs to the proclamation from the beginning (3:11; cf. II John 5), and it rests in the love of God: "if God so loved us, we also ought to love one another" (4:11 — *opheílomen*), and "we love, because he first loved us" (4:19). A deep, essential relation (actually, this word is still too weak) is indicated in order to make the new reality in Christ clear. It is a totally different "reality" than what Cain experienced vis-à-vis Abel (3:11 — *ou kathòs Káïn*). The admonition is so penetrating that, if one does not listen closely, it sounds as if a new law were being instituted.[51] The "ought," the necessity of love, eliminates every escape — even in a case where one pleaded that love for God was present. Only he who loves is born of God (4:7); and whoever does not love, saying that he loves God while hating his brother, has not known God (4:8). He is a captive of his lies, "for he who does not love his brother whom he has seen, cannot love God whom he has not seen" (4:20).

The new reality cannot be described apart from this "ought," since it constitutes the fellowship in Christ and brings it to expression.[52] It illuminates this reality of the fellowship of

---

50. We perceive the same thing in the description of the Church (Q. 54). Christ's active gathering, protecting, and preserving are connected to the personal relatedness of the confessor to this Church.

51. Cf. H.M. Schenke, "Determination und Ethik im ersten Johannesbrief," *Z.Th.K.*, 1963, pp. 203ff.; and *TDNT*, V, *s.v. opheílō.*

52. Reflection on I John 3:9 ("No one born of God can sin" — *ou dúnatai hamartánein*) is also connected to this "ought." When von Dobschütz characterizes it as "not a physical impossibility, but rather a moral inadmissibility," one cannot contradict Schenke *(op. cit.,* p. 207), who calls this a contracted *(verkürzende)* interpretation. Cf. Schenke further on the positive statements and admonitions in I John: John "did not experience the contradiction that exists here in the same way that we experience it" (p. 215). Schenke's concept of determination is con-

love in the one body, in suffering together and rejoicing together (I Cor. 12:26), in understanding together the love of Christ (Eph. 3:17f.), in the relatedness of participation in the Spirit (Phil. 2:1), in the love for the poor who have been chosen by God (James 2:5), in the relation of the strong to the weak (Rom. 15:1; I Cor. 8:7ff.), in bearing each other's burdens (Gal. 6:2), and in the unsearchable power of intercession, which breaks through all isolation.[53] We meet here with a mutual dependency that embraces mutual service as being at the disposal of one another and as an unceasing interest in the other (Phil. 2:4). In the whole New Testament, all of this stands in the full light of fellowship with the Lord, and there is never any obscuring or dividing of attention. In the midst of very concrete admonitions to have fellowship, Paul can write, "Serve the Lord" (Rom. 12:11). In that service the windows open on love of the brothers, not only those of a similar mind, but also the hungering enemy, the cursing opponent (Rom. 12:10, 13ff.), and the unsought-for neighbor. Thus, all opportunities are taken in order to do good to all men (Gal. 6:10).

Fellowship and material blessings

Christ warns His disciples strongly against ruling over each other: "But it shall not be so among you" (Mark 10:43f.). Christ identifies greatness with being a servant. Whoever wants to be counted as first therefore must be the slave of all. This is a very radical reversal of what would appear to be "normal": the greatest becomes as the youngest and the leader as the servant (Luke 22:26). This change does divert attention from the Lord but means that "I am among you as one who serves."[54] The depth and radicalness of true communion stands in opposition here to all apostate "normality." This radicalness is not moralistic and constricted, but is the kind of relaxation that is taught here, when Christ's deed of love is imitated.[55]

nected to his view of the "particular Johannine, i.e., dualistic, imprint of the notion of predestination."

53. James 5:14f.; II Thess. 3:1. One may recall Bonhoeffer's concrete considerations of intercession. Cf. in detail H. Ott, *Wirklichkeit und Glaube*, I, 192ff.; II, 265ff.

54. Luke 22:27; cf. Mark 10:45. See on this H.J.B. Combrink, *Die Diens van Jezus*, 1968.

55. One may recall Paul's reminder of the words of Jesus: "It is more blessed to give than to receive" (Acts 20:35).

Therefore, communion always becomes concrete in earthly reality; it does not pass by life in the world, any more than Christ's love for, His honoring of, and His obedience to the Father is outside human life.

Communion does not contain any dualism between "spiritual" and "material," as is clear from the aspect of communion that Paul indicates in the collection, with which he deals so fully. The word is known from everyday ecclesiastical life in recommendation for assistance by deacons, but it has special depth and significance for Paul. When Paul speaks of the "contribution" (Rom. 15:26 — koinōnia) of Macedonia and Achaia to the poor among the saints, he brings this "indebtedness" into connection with the Gentiles who have come to share in spiritual blessings.[56] Life — especially life in need — is not irrelevant because it is "less spiritual," but it is included in a "mutuality" of fellowship. And according to Paul, the liberality of the churches in Macedonia reveals the grace of God (II Cor. 8:1). Their service, their work of love, is characterized by superabundance, since they gave beyond their means (8:3). Spiritual blessings (pneumatiká) and service (leitourgía) with material blessings are linked by an "ought" (Rom. 15:27; cf. Gal. 2:10). Paul seldom makes it clearer than this that any competition is out of the question, since he says that the Macedonians gave themselves first to the Lord "and to us" (II Cor. 8:5). This "first" (próton) does not make the rest secondary or irrelevant, but fills it with the earnestness of communion. In this context Paul can also point out that the poverty of the Lord was directed to the riches of others.[57] An "analogy" becomes visible, just as in Philippians 2, where the light of Christ's self-emptying — His never-ending service, concern, and mercy — radiates in the fellowship. In this communion God's love goes out to the cheerful "giver."[58] This is not a new doctrine of "merit," but the disclosure of the meaning, depth, and responsibility of a new fellowship. The cheerfulness corresponds to the abundance of God's grace (9:8) and the praise

56. It was not only their desire (ēudókēsan), but also their duty (opheilétai), Rom. 15:27.
57. II Cor. 8:9. For various questions concerning "the collection," see O. Cullmann, A Message to Catholics and Protestants, 1959, pp. 34ff.; D. Georgi, Die Geschichte der Kollekte des Paulus für Jerusalem, 1965, pp. 58ff.; D.W. Oostendorp, Another Jesus, 1967, pp. 75ff.; and Combrink, op. cit., pp. 65ff.
58. II Cor. 9:7: without reluctance (lúpē) or compulsion (anánkē). Cf. "cheerful" (hilarós).

of God; for this service praises God for the obedience in acknowledging the gospel of Christ (9:13)!

Consequently, it is no wonder that we are more aware that this human serviceability and true fellowship is not secondary. It is not a "worldly" ideal, nor a moralism, nor a secularization, but rather a plain understanding of the gospel — in other words, an understanding of the Church as the one body of Christ. Against this background, the sharp protest against breaking apart, hearing the Word (I John 3:18; James 1:22), and doing God's will (Matt. 7:21; cf. 12:50; I John 2:27) is understandable. Whether the word ·"analogy" or the word "example" is used here is not the most important thing. What is important is that one understand how seriously fellowship is taken because of Christ! Because He laid down His life, we have come to know love (I John 3:16), and everything is founded in that. Whoever makes a mistake here — not an intellectual, but a religious error — does not understand that a break between love to God and love to our neighbor is impossible. It is impossible on the basis of the one heart, which cannot be closed to our brother's need if it is open to the love of God: "How does God's love abide in him?"[59]

The question of how the fellowship of believers is disclosed in the world as union with Christ has been dealt with variously. To what extent does it represent Him to us as a pointer to His love and lordship? The Church cannot be "hidden" reality without visible significance. In times of ecclesiastical triumphalism, the radiating glory of the Church in the world has been sought by pointing out Isaiah's prophecy that Yahweh would raise an ensign for the nations.[60] That ensign (signum levatum in nationes) was seen in the Church's continuity, dissemination, and fruitfulness.[61] However, it gradually became clear that "signum" did not lend itself to any triumphalism —

---

59. I John 3:17. Closing the heart (tà splánchna) is an indivisible, catastrophic event.

60. Isa. 11:12, cited by the First Vatican Council (Denz., 1794). Cf. Pope Paul VI's first radio message, Qui Fausto Die (June 22, 1963), which refers to Isa. 5:26.

61. The idea of the Church as the "sacrament of the world" (sacramentum mundi) plays a striking role in contemporary Roman Catholic theology, as well as in Lumen Gentium (sign and instrument, DV II, p. 26). See already O. Semmelroth, Die Kirche als Ursakrament, 1953. Further, see P. Smulders, "De Kerk als Sacrament van het Heil," and J.L. Witte, "De Kerk 'Sacrament der Eenheid' voor geheel de Wereld," in De Kerk van Vatikanum II, I, 1969, pp. 372ff. and 507ff.

neither because of divine initiative nor because of the "empirical" reality of the Church! The true being of Christ's body is revealed only in the imitation, in fellowship, of all His ways.

Once again it is apparent that the unity of the Church is not simply a numerical description. The Church is understandable only as unity in fellowship. A general protest against individualism will not suffice here. Clearly, there is no place for individualism or isolationism — something that is radically revealed in the horribleness of Cain's question, "Am I my brother's keeper?" (Gen. 4:9). The small horizon of individual life is penetrated by wondrous attention and receptiveness, by true discipleship. It is not merely a dull "imitation." True discipleship is following Christ on His way, with His interest, His compassion, His affection, and His servanthood. It would be extremely sad if the reaction to the secularization of love were to be a lack of appreciation for this depth of the heart opened in Christ — in correlation with God's continuing love (I John 3:17). In that case, everything would be lost, specifically, the outlook on the Lord of this fellowship in His unending interest in man, as God finds him in his isolation and guilt, his lost and threatened existence in the midst of conceit, his rebellion and selfishness, his pride and ignorance. The Church may not advocate less interest in this man! Rather, she must be a *signum levatum in nationes* a reflection of the "loving kindness" (Titus 3:4 — *hē philanthrōpía*) that has appeared in Christ. This reflection is not a lesson to be learned theoretically, and it can easily be made into a new slogan, by which one forgets that the reflection begins with one's own life, with that small horizon in the call to discipleship.[62] It then reaches out to all the horizons that are opened for us in historical development. This interest, concentrated in the one fellowship for which the divine call in Christ went forth (Col. 3:15), has its essential structure in the

---

62. Seeing only this limited horizon without a perspective on the relationship with "the Church of all ages," one also demonstrates a radical impoverishment of life (see further, chapter 7). By breaking through one's own limited horizon with regard to the knowledge and understanding of salvation, one does not signify a *sacrificium intellectus*. Instead, one belongs to the "communion of the saints." H. Ott (*op. cit.*, II, 1969, pp. 226ff.) describes this when he speaks of *perichorosis* and of "anticipatory participation" with regard to past and present. The danger of traditionalism cannot nullify this aspect of fellowship any more than the cloud of witnesses (Heb. 12:1) can become irrelevant for the individual struggle of faith.

summons not simply to act, in word and deed, but to act *in the name of Christ* (3:17)!

The Church has usually been aware that the reality of communion in word and deed alone can truly be a reflection of what Christ had in view in discipleship, in "abiding in Him" and thus bearing fruit. Warnings are continuously given against the fatal discrepancy between "orthodoxy" and "orthopraxy" — i.e., right doctrine and right practice. Likewise, Paul speaks to the Jews about breaking apart what is unbreakably united. Boasting in God, approving the law, being instructed, and wanting to be a guide to the blind, a corrector, and a teacher (Rom. 2:17-20) do not remove the concrete question about one's own life, about teaching oneself (2:21). Such a discrepancy blurs the meaning of fellowship, which is founded in the *unio cum Christo*. This concentrated attention for reality and visibility does not arise out of giving priority to life above doctrine. It arises out of the outlook on this doctrine, that *didachê* to which the Church devoted herself on the day of fulfillment, together with prayers, the breaking of bread, and fellowship (Acts 2:42). Here the "liturgy" is not lacking — they are together in the temple — nor is the praise of God (2:42). The *skandalon* of the proclamation has not perished in a self-evident humanity, as if that were the reason that the believers at Pentecost had the favor *(cháris)* of all the people (2:47). In the midst of this new obviousness, in the midst of this shining light before which the darkness is yielding, and in the midst of glad and generous hearts (2:46), God's action is manifested day by day in the enlargement of the Church: *signum levatum in nationes.*

One may ask whether it is still possible today to make clear what is signified by saying that the Church *is* the body of Christ. The question is not simply a hermeneutical problem of understanding words about the Church; it goes deeper, because all the words about Christ's Church speak of something that does not lie in our hands, but rather in His: *His* Church, *His* body, *His* flock. Is it not possible, therefore, that every word about the Church be understood as a simplistic identification, due to an irritating self-complacency on the part of the Church?

In some circles the image of "the apple of the eye" has played a greater role than the designation "body of Christ" for the Church. The image did not arise from a particular sort of piety, since it is in Scripture itself. It points to what belongs to God, since His people, Israel, are kept by Him as the apple of His eye (Deut. 32:10). And sacrilege against God is possible in that "he who touches you [Israel] touches the apple of His [God's] eye."[63] But where this "belonging to Him"[64] — the apple of the eye, the body — is separated from true fellowship in faith and love and then used for self-justification, all the depth and richness of the "images" for the Church is lost. Then only a sterile claim remains, which must become the object of razor-sharp, prophetic criticism. Nothing creates more responsibility than thinking and speaking about the Church as the body of Christ, as the mystery of belonging to Him — My Church (Matt. 16:18). That is the source of danger in all the discussions about the *corpus Christi mysticum:* in a contemplative analysis, one can lose sight of the reality of being the Church, which can be understood only in connection with calling and commission, with concrete unity and fellowship both with the Lord and with one another.[65]

Impatience for unity and fellowship

In a day when it is asked whether the Church has not outlived her time, when she is in danger of becoming a marginal phenomenon of the modern world, one can feel powerless and can question the meaning and reality of the Church. In such times defeatism can set in. Yet one can also long for a new understanding and a new experience of being in Christ, of unity and fellowship. Hoekendijk has pointed out that, in recent times, the question is again being asked "about the meaning of Pauline haste."[66] Impatience also arises, and it becomes a messianic category next to the apostolate. For Hoekendijk, this is connected with a return to "an almost primitive

63. Zech. 2:8. Cf. also I Sam. 8:27: the rejection of Samuel is a rejection of Yahweh.
64. One may recall the background of Christ's question to Paul, "Why do you persecute me?" (Acts 9:4f.). By his answer, "Who are you, Lord?" Paul reveals that he is thinking of an isolated encounter. He does not yet understand the meaning of "persecution."
65. It is good to remember that these aspects remain relevant and critical in all attempts to give a "definition" of the Church. The discussions of the *corpus mysticum* at the First Vatican Council are especially instructive. Cf. F. van der Horst, *Das Schema über die Kirche auf dem I. Vatik. Konzil,* 1963, pp. 75ff. Every "definition" contains a danger of confusion which can affect all aspects of the definition (office, institution, *societas perfecta,* etc.).
66. J.C. Hoekendijk, *Getemperd Ongeduld* (Inaugural Oration, 1953), pp. 6f.

naiveté" with which the biblical witness is examined anew. What is remarkable in Hoekendijk's analysis is not so much his aversion to "shuddering at impatience," as it is his more precise description of impatience as "tempered" impatience. "Deeds and things are recognized in their provisionality. They call for the consummation. Impatience does not signify here, therefore, chafing rebellion against the status quo, but believing anticipation of the more and the greater, which has been held out in prospect, and of which the signs testify that it is already under way."[67] The nuances in impatience are not easily analyzed, but one can ask how tempered impatience is possible considering the biblical witness about the unity and fellowship of the Church. Belonging to Him and belonging to the Spirit — His temple (and the repeated question of surprise in I Corinthians that arises from this: "Do you not know?") — point to a form of impatience that cannot rest in provisionality.[68] Rather, it places the shadows surrounding fellowship and imitation in the full light of fellowship with Christ, Who is the Light of the world. One cannot temper this impatience by pointing to the imperfections throughout the history of the Church. It is true that ecclesiological perfectionism must be rejected, but the necessary rejection of a "triumphal Church," even if the rejection were to appeal to the words "more than conquerors" in Romans 8,[69] does not solve the problem of unity and fellowship. Even the reference to the reserve of God's final action cannot diminish Paul's impatience at the violation of fellowship, since unity and fellowship are founded in what has decisively happened.[70]

In the tension between the biblical "almost primitive na-

---

67. *Ibid.*, p. 7. Cf. on the tempering of impatience: "It does not have free play," because it does not abolish the provisionality of the signs, although deeds do result in the apostolate (p. 8). Compare also "being impatient in principle" (p. 7).

68. Cf. chapter 2 above.

69. Rom. 8:37 (*hupernikômen*). There can be misunderstanding here because of the explication: "through him who loved us" (*dià toú agapêsantos hēmás*).

70. Here we touch on questions that K. Barth has discussed in detail in connection with "The Promise of the Spirit" (*C.D.*, IV/3, 1, pp. 274ff.): after Easter — and after Pentecost! — things are not yet "unambiguous" (*unzweideutig*). Cf. in detail my *The Return of Christ*, 1972, pp. 133ff., especially on the "interpretation" of the not yet in the light of Christ's mercy. In spite of the depth of the outlook indicated here, the question of disruption still remains unanswered;· for unity and fellowship have their foundation in the merciful Lord.

iveté" and the many resistances against the fellowship of the
Spirit, Hoekendijk wants to stimulate the Church to put herself totally in service of the confrontation of the world with
the Kingdom. According to him, she will then "refrain from
saying much about herself. She lacks time, interest, and patience for that. It is sufficient for her that the Church comes
into the field of view in passing."[71] There is a necessary warning in this rejection of all introverted ecclesiastical self-complacency. We must bear in mind that the Church has every
reason not to say a great deal "about herself,"[72] and every reason
to consider that she "belongs to the Lord" — with all the inexhaustible consequences entailed by that. Only in the light
of admonition and calling can the impatience be, not tempered,
but made holy. It cannot be "chafing rebellion" — teaching
others (cf. Rom. 2:21). It can only be a cry out of the depths
(de profundis). Impatience does not explain or excuse anything;
it only demonstrates that we are thrown back upon unity and
fellowship in Christ. The Church is not founded on our ex-
ertions or initiative, and she does not lie secure in our hands.
This is a lesson not only of the biblical witness but also of
history. The Church is founded, rather, on the mercy of God.

The fact of belonging to Christ — in indicative and imperative, in gift and calling — entrusts a great deal to the
Church, specifically the right, even in brokenness, to testify to
true, new fellowship. It makes her understand that she can
be a true witness to her Lord only when, in the light of her
undeniable reality, opposition loses its foundation (I Pet. 2:15).
The reality of new life in Christ can result in replacing opposition (blasphemy) by praise of God "on the day of visitation."[73] Although the credibility of the Church's proclamation

71. Hoekendijk, *op. cit.*, p. 9 (viz., when the messianic action with the
    world is praised in christology).
72. Her commission is to "declare the wonderful deeds of him who called
    you out of darkness into his marvelous light" (I Pet. 2:9). Even though
    many of Pope Paul's addresses speak of the Church on account of
    her mystery, one cannot escape the impression that it is "too much":
    it does not make the *credo* in *ecclesiam* impossible *in principle.*
73. I Pet. 2:12. Cf. R. Schnackenburg, *Die Petrusbriefe*, 1961, pp. 71ff. Cf.
    also Matt. 5:16. Blasphemy can also concern the Name of God: "blas-
    phemed among the Gentiles because of you *(di' humás).*" This is one
    of the most moving aspects of the testing of the Church. Cf. the recog-
    nition of the danger — in the explication of a petition — in Q. 122 of
    the Heidelberg Catechism (blaspheming of the Name on our account
    as compared with its being "honored and praised." *Credo ecclesiam!*)

has its deep foundation in the truth of that proclamation itself, the Church is related to God's will of salvation in this credibility by removing the *skandalon* of the occasion to disbelief.[74] Whoever remembers the origin of the Church (cf. I Cor. 1:31) will be able to take this route without self-praise. True boasting in the Lord is possible only along that way. That the *credere ecclesiam* rather than the *credere in ecclesiam* found a place in the *credo* shows the realization that the being of the Church excludes boasting. But relating the *credere ecclesiam* to Christ does not weaken its responsibility. Only a "monophysitic" ecclesiology, which is based on a view of the Church as a "divine-human" reality, could produce such a conclusion. This form of ecclesiology has often influenced thinking about the Church when the meaning, the justice, and the possibility of critical questions were no longer correctly understood. Because the confession reads, *credo ecclesiam, communionem sanctorum,* we can see the impossibility of following such paths — including the subtle escape of "humility," a path which does not take seriously what Christ takes seriously: "you are the light of the world" (Matt. 5:14).

74. Cf. Calvin on I Pet. 2:12 (*Commentaries on the Catholic Epistles*, 1948, pp. 78f.): "lest we become a scandal to them," and "to give no occasion to those who seek occasion." Calvin does not want to relate the "day of visitation" to Christ's return, but to leading the wandering in this way, through life "as a preparation."

II. The Catholicity
of the Church

CHAPTER FIVE

THE MEANING OF CATHOLICITY

BECAUSE OF THE ACTUAL DEVELOPMENT OF
Church history, whoever reflects on the catholicity of the
Church is confronted with a complex of far-reaching questions,
all of which are connected to the meaning of the familiar *credo
ecclesiam catholicam*. For many people the word "catholic" is
not known in any other way than in the name Roman Catholic
Church; but the existence of a Greek Catholic Church, which
reminds us of the early schism between the two Churches, automatically leads to the question of the meaning of the word.
The word "catholicity" is immediately related to a pretension
to catholicity, a situation in which a particular church considers this attribute to be realized in her own ecclesiastical life,
whereas other churches do not possess it — at least not in the
full sense of the word. When we consider that the original word
katholikós means "universal," we realize how important the
meaning of universality is and how it takes on concrete form.
Even though a kind of intuitive supposition of what is included
in catholicity has arisen in the course of ecclesiastical development, a clear insight as to its meaning and significance is not
necessarily present. The word seems too general — i.e., it does
not seem to be concrete enough to be of service to us.

Nevertheless, the particular background of the word is not
without significance. The word "catholic," which does not
appear in the New Testament anywhere in relation to the
Church,[1] signified in extra-biblical literature that which is universal in contrast to that which is special or localized. For instance, a "catholic" depiction of history was distinguished from
what was only partial, related to a limited time. The concept

1. The word *kathólou* does appear in Acts 4:18, where the disciples are
   charged not to speak or teach in the name of Jesus "at all."

"catholic," then, always includes a certain wideness and space, which thus play an important role in reflection on the catholicity of the Church.[2] When Rome, for instance, speaks of the *catholic* Church, the aspect of wideness is always emphasized in contrast to limitation and isolation in time and space. The word "catholic" does appear in connection with Rome (Roman Catholic), but that is not meant as a contradiction; the reference to Rome is used in connection with the wideness and the universality of this church spread over the whole world. Catholicity was intended, as was also the case in the Greek Catholic Church, to be a reference to the decisive importance of the gospel for all times and all peoples and, in that context, a reference to the decisive importance of the Church in which this gospel had been preserved and proclaimed. But outside the Roman Catholic and Greek Catholic Churches, the word "catholic" was not abandoned. Here, too, the perspective of universality plays an important role.[3] Catholicity is connected with the commission to Christ's disciples: "Go therefore and make disciples of all nations,"[4] or, in the words of Mark 16:15: "Go into all the world *(eis tòn kósmon hápanta)* and preach the gospel to the whole creation *(pásę tę̨ ktísei)*." In using the word "catholic," one was often aware of a breaking through of all boundaries in connection with the eschatological expression of salvation which is universal: "thy blood didst ransom men for God from every tribe and tongue and people and nation" (Rev. 5:9). It is also the outlook on the great multitude that no one can num-

---

2. Cf. W. Beinert, *Um das dritte Kirchenattribut*, I, 1964, pp. ·23ff.; J.N. Bakhuizen van den Brink, "Credo Sanctam Ecclesiam Catholicam," *Ecclesia*, II, 1966, pp. 264ff.; and Y. Congar, *Sainte Eglise. Études et Approches Ecclésiologiques*, 1963, p. 154.
3. We meet this meaning of the word "catholic" in practically all ecclesiastical and confessional persuasions. Diverse characterizations can be used, such as "the universal, all-embracing, all natural-relations-transcending character of the church" (H. Hoeksema, *Reformed Dogmatics*, 1966, p. 608). From the formulation of catholicity alone, one cannot tell which church is speaking. Cf. Bavinck, *Katholiciteit*, p. 6; E. Fascher, "Ökumenisch und Katholisch. Zur Gesch. zweier, heute vielgebrauchte Begriffe," *Theol. Lit. Zeitung*, 1960, pp. 7ff.; and E. Kinder, "Der Gebrauch des Begriffs 'ökumenisch' im älteren Luthertum," *Kerugma und Dogma*, I, 1955, 180ff. (especially on catholic and ecumenical, which were often used as "interchangeable concepts").
4. Matt. 28:19. Cf. O. Weber, *Grundlagen der Dogmatik*, II, 619, on catholicity as "clearly intended."

ber "from every nation, from all tribes and peoples and tongues."[5]

Because of the associations inherent in catholicity — e.g., boundaries and walls that have been broken, open windows, wideness, and universality — no church has wanted to abandon the name "catholic." To do so would be to accept implicitly a limitation that conflicts with the Church's essence. This joint appreciation for catholicity automatically leads, however, to the necessity of a more concrete interpretation. And it quickly becomes clear that it would not suffice to ascertain the purely geographical extension of the Church in contradistinction to all local or national limitedness.[6] There is a deeper motif behind this extension — just as with the Old Testament prophets and with the Apocalypse — namely, a universal significance that touches all. The gospel had to go out to all nations on account of this significance (Matt. 28:19) and witnesses had to go out to the ends of the earth (Acts 1:8). The penetration of Christ's messengers in all directions (Paul even wanted to go to Spain[7]) gives an indication of the unique importance of the message, in conformity with the song of praise to the name of the Lord that must be sung "from the rising of the sun to its setting" (Ps. 113:2ff.). Space is incorporated in the framework of God's deeds of salvation in and for the world. The call to repentance resounds "everywhere" *(pantachoú)* in light of the coming day, when God will judge "the world" *(tèn oikouménēn)* in righteousness.[8]

Quantitative and qualitative

An important distinction has been made between quantitative and qualitative catholicity with respect to the concrete world.[9] This is not a subtle distinction that blurs catholicity,

---

5. Rev. 7:9. Cf. A.J. Visser, *De Openbaring van Johannes*, 1965, p. 64: "Every Jewish particularism is foreign to this form of apocalypticism." Cf. the perspective of salvation in Isa. 60 and Zech. 8:13.
6. Cf. J.N.D. Kelly, *Early Christian Doctrines*, 1960, pp. 189ff.
7. Rom. 15:24. Cf. G. Eichholz, "Der ökumenische und missionarische Horizont der Kirche," *Tradition und Interpretation*, 1965, p. 90f., on the horizon of the world for Paul, who is not a "world conqueror," but a witness "who has a message that he owes to the world." Cf. H.N. Ridderbos, *De Brief aan de Romeinen. Commentaar op het Nieuwe Testament*, 1959, on Rome as the new "home front."
8. Acts 17:30f. Cf. calling on the name of Jesus "in every place *(en pantì tópō)*," in I Cor. 1:2.
9. Cf. already F. Kattenbusch, *Das Apostolische Symbol*, II, 925ff.

but an approach that is grounded in catholicity itself. The distinction fixes our eyes upon both the spatial extension and the depth of the salvation that is preached to all.[10] One is often fascinated by the geographical, universal dimension in the history of the Church. It is also fascinating that the gospel enters into all times, peoples, and cultures. There was always an acute danger that one would cling to the empirical externality and perceptibility of the Church and would see the breadth more than the depth, the quantitative more than qualitative catholicity.[11] In traditional Roman Catholic theology, specifically, quantitative catholicity frequently took on an avowed apologetic function, as reference was made to the universality and extension of the Roman Catholic Church through all centuries and among all peoples.

However, reactions to such a quantitative catholicity were bound to occur, since extension *per se* does not assure legitimacy and riches. In our time, the word "ecumenical" is used especially in connection with the perspectives and the calling of the Church. On the surface, this word appears to suggest a quantitative catholicity, since it has such a clear "geographical" significance. The word is used in this way already in the New Testament, when it is said that the gospel of the Kingdom "will be preached *throughout the whole world* as a testimony to all nations."[12] "Ecumenical" does indeed suggest the wideness and the horizons of the world rather than any limitation, but it would be incorrect to understand "ecumenical" and "ecumenical movement" only from this aspect of extension. Just as in the gospel, the perspective of the end of the earth is inseparably connected to the decisive significance of the proclamation of the gospel in the whole world. Just as in the word "catholicity," depth leads to breadth. There has always been a very close connection in the ecumenical movement between world and mission, and this outlook on the universality of the preaching of the gospel continues to play a dominating role.[13]

10. Cf. N.A. Nissiotis, "Die qualitative Bedeutung der Katholizität," *Theol. Zeitsch.*, XVII, 1961, pp. 259ff., on "the infinite dimension of depth of genuine catholicity," viz., "deep under the surface of the quantitative meaning." See especially H. Berkhof, *De Katholiciteit der Kerk*, 1962.

11. Cf. Kattenbusch (*op. cit.*, p. 925) on the development by which the deeper, religious meaning "remained, but sank into the empirical."

12. Matt. 24:14 (*en hólē tē̦ oikouménē̦*). Cf. the word also in Luke 2:1 and Acts 17:31. See further *TDNT*, V, 157, on Heb. 2:5.

13. From the great amount of literature, we mention only W.A. Visser 't Hooft, "Geschiedenis en Betekenis van het Woord 'Oecumenisch,' "

Naturally, all reflection on the world carries the danger that the perspective of ecumenicity and catholicity will be formalized,[14] but the actual situation of divided churches forces us to reflect on the foundation of true relatedness in Christ. In contrast to the striving for unity that does not take diversity seriously, the ecumenical movement strives to reflect on the nature and content of catholicity. Moreover, it is, as it were, forced to such reflection by the membership of churches that do not intend to weaken their confession that catholicity is really present in their own churches. So we see that attention has become concentrated on the qualitative aspect of catholicity. One is increasingly aware that quantitative extension does not necessarily guarantee the truth of what is presented to the world.[15] There is also an extension that only casts shadows on the world. This can be called an overawing catholicity in the form of temptation: in the Apocalypse, when "the earth" and all who dwell on it (Rev. 13:12, 14; 11:10) begin to worship, the whole earth will follow the beast with wonder on account of its power "over every tribe and people and tongue and nation" (13:3, 7; cf. 20:8ff.). Universality, extension, and catholicity, though not yet filled, are in themselves only a formal schematic, and whoever formalizes or quantifies catholicity misses the depth of the actual mystery.[16] Only the relatedness of quantitative extension to qualitative catholicity can protect the Church from externally striving for power and unity.

Apologetics on this point is gradually becoming a thing of the past, undoubtedly because quantitative, directly perceiv-

Heel de Kerk voor Heel de Wereld, 1968, pp. 249ff.; S. Neill, De Groei der Oecumenische Beweging, 1962; L. Volken, L'Action Oecuménique, 1966; and G. Thils, L'Eglise et les Eglises. Perspectives nouvelles en Oecuménisme, 1966.

14. Cf. Visser 't Hooft, op. cit., p. 268.
15. Cf. K. Rahner-H. Vorgrimler, Kleines Theologisches Wörterbuch, pp. 194f., on "the actual, external universality in the heyday of apologetics."
16. J. Kamphuis ("Oecumene en Tolerantie," Onderweg Aangesproken, 1968, pp. 16ff., 22) sees the present-day ecumenical movement totally as a false endeavor for unity, resulting in far-reaching tolerance. Thereby the red carpet is rolled out for the Antichrist. Naturally, the decisive question is whether the official documents of the World Council of Churches contain any basis for this deep distrust. The obvious change in the posture of the Gereformeerde Kerken of the Netherlands to the World Council has nothing to do with capitulation to relativism and syncretism. Rather, the change is due to an analysis of the motives of the ecumenical movement and its avowed view of unity and catholicity.

able catholicity seems to be decreasing rather than increasing and because boundaries have become visible everywhere to catholicity.[17] This has inevitably led to deeper reflection on the meaning of catholicity according to its qualitative grade, starting from the origin and mystery of the Church, her "being" in the world, apart from her varying extension. Warnings began to sound against an excessively easy, apologetic appeal to quantitative universality, which has played such a dominant role specifically in the ecclesiology of the Counter Reformation.[18] Using "obvious" catholicity as a proof for all became increasingly difficult.[19] The necessity of reflecting more deeply on the dimension of depth in catholicity was felt. This did not mean a lack of appreciation for the dimension of breadth. The outlook on the many — i.e., on the nations — belongs essentially to genuine catholicity, when the many become a sign of the superior power of the Spirit.[20] That is not a cult of numbers,[21] nor is it a suggestion of "legion."[22] Rather, it is a perception of the depth that also seeks breadth — the end of the earth — in an irreversible order of succession.[23] So the question of the meaning of catholicity remains a critical question, which breaks

17. According to Bavinck (Geref. Dog., IV, 307), the Church Fathers themselves began to exaggerate the expansion of Christianity among the nations. He speaks of a billion non-Christians and "scarcely five hundred million Christians." Cf. on the decline in numbers, H. Küng, Damit die Welt Glaube!; and Berkhof, op. cit., pp. 17ff.

18. The two aspects were never totally separated. For instance, Augustine's struggle against the Donatists was more than an appeal to the extension of the Church in contrast to the limited Donatist Church. See Kattenbusch, op. cit., II, 922ff. However, a certain isolation of the aspect of extension continued to play a role for a long time in Roman Catholic theology — for instance, in the "marvelous propagation" of the Church as a "motive of credibility" at the First Vatican Council (Denz., 1794; TCT, 68). Cf. Bavinck, Katholiciteit; idem, Geref. Dog., IV, 265, 305; and Berkhof, op. cit., pp. 17ff., on the movement of the idea of catholicity from the confession to apologetics.

19. Beinert, op. cit., I, 147: "The proof of the catholicity of the Roman Catholic Church is no longer furnished by statistics."

20. Acts 2:14 (3000); 2:47 (daily expansion by God's action — prosetithei); Rev. 7:9.

21. Cf. the warning against "too many" in Gideon's combat (Judg. 7:2f.) and in David's numbering of the people (II Sam. 24:1-4; I Chron. 21:1-13; 27:23f.).

22. Mark 5:9: "My name is Legion; for we are many (polloi esmen)." Cf. Luke 8:30 (daimónia pollà).

23. For example, it is said that the gospel bears fruit in the whole world (Col. 1:6) and is preached to every creature under heaven (1:23). Cf. the progress of the gospel in Acts 16:9ff.

through all self-evident, ascertainable catholicity.[24] In what is the depth, wholeness, fullness, and completeness of catholicity founded? From what depth and fullness do perspectives emerge on all horizons in and for the Church?[25] She cannot be an esoteric group of the like-minded or initiates, accessible only for supporters and members who are disposed to her. She cannot be the aristocracy of a people, a nation, or a race, nor can she be bound to a particular time or culture. Rather, her universality is founded in God's love for the world; and then space, extension, and quantitative catholicity automatically become meaningful.[26]

These universal notes of the gospel are so clear that they have met with some response in all eras of the Church. This does not necessarily mean, though, that all conflict about catholicity has thus been ended. The common "intuition" of catholicity does not exclude the question about where it is understood and rightly practiced and where it is more than simply an uncredible pretension. To the degree that the close connection of catholicity and apologetics is broken, the question about the meaning of the "absolute universalism" of catholicity increases.[27] We hear a protest — for the sake of catholicity — against confining salvation to "the narrow circle of a small church or convent," because that derogates "from the love of the Father, and grace of the Son, and the fellowship of the Spirit."[28] But the question remains concerning how one formulates the concrete meaning of catholicity, since everyone agrees that that meaning gives an outlook on the whole, on fullness, and on catholicity, which has been described by Bavinck in contrast to sectarianism and isolation as "of captivating beauty."[29]

24. The dangers are discerned clearly by the Scots Confession of 1560, which — in connection with the tokens for distinguishing the true Church from the false — rejects the prerogative of antiquity as well as that of "the numbers of men approving an error." Even if the number of those who truly believe is only a few, "there, beyond any doubt, is the true Church of Christ." Cf. K. Barth, *C.D.*, IV/1, p. 704.
25. Berkhof, *op. cit.*, pp. 14ff. Cf. "The Catechism of the Church of Geneva" (*The Library of Christian Classics*, XXII, 103): "one Church spread throughout the whole earth."
26. Cf. Bavinck, *Kaholiciteit*, 1968, p. 6.
27. *Ibid.*
28. *Ibid.*, p. 10.
29. *Ibid.* Cf. C. Veenhof, *Volk van God. Enkele Aspecten van Bavincks Kerkbeschouwing*, 1969, pp. 28ff.

Fullness in Christ

We need not be surprised that contemporary discussions of catholicity continually reach back to what the biblical witnesses said about fullness.[30] For fullness also contrasts with what is partial, limited, and narrow. In the New Testament, we meet first of all with a kind of fullness that can be related only with difficulty to the Church. For instance, fullness *(plērēs)* is spoken of with respect to Jesus Christ: full of grace and truth (John 1:14), and full of the Holy Spirit (Luke 4:1). He received the Spirit "not by measure" (John 3:34 — *ou ... ek métrou*). Paul, too, emphatically speaks about fullness with respect to Christ when he writes that all the fullness of God was pleased to dwell in Him (Col. 1:19) and that "in Him the whole fullness of deity dwells bodily" (2:9). Yet it is not as if the divine mystery were isolated, because the Church is also related to the fullness of Christ and the fullness of God. The purpose of the knowledge of Christ is to be filled with all the fullness of God (Eph. 3:18f.); and in the unity of faith and knowledge, everything is directed to mature manhood, to the measure of the stature of the fullness of Christ (4:13). The sentences relating fullness to the Church are difficult to understand, but one cannot deny that we are offered an outlook on fullness and richness.[31] Only if one honors, not minimizes, the Church's "riches" and fullness, does one get a correct view of Paul's understanding of the Church. And whoever hesitates to do that should consider a statement that appears to be a simple fact: "you have come to fullness of life in Him, Who is the head of all rule and authority" (Col. 2:10 — *estè en autǫ peplērōménoi*).

All of this is undoubtedly a profound, doxological interpretation of what the Church came to partake in, of her undeniable "being."[32] Yet the question has been asked over and

30. J.L. Witte, "Die Katholizität der Kirche," *Gregorianum*, XVII, 1961, p. 200.
31. The word *"plērophoria"* is used of Paul's preaching: "in power and in the Holy Spirit and with *full conviction"* (RSV; Dutch: "fullness"). Paul comes with the *"fullness* of the blessing of Christ" (Rom. 15:29 — *en plērōmati eulogías Christoú;* Vulgate: *in abundantia benedictionis*).
32. According to E. Lohmeyer (*Der Brief an die Kolosser*, 1930, p. 106), this statement ("You have") is an exception in Paul's letters, since it appears elsewhere as a prayer. Cf. Rom. 15:13 ("May the God of hope fill you...") and II Thess. 1:11 (Paul's prayer for fulfillment). However, Colossians, too, contains the prayer for fulfillment (1:9); thus, one cannot isolate 2:10, as if Paul had a different "accomplished fact" in view here. Lohmeyer's exegesis (the totality of salvation in Christ

over again whether it is possible to speak meaningfully about the Church in this way. Is this view of the Church too idealistic? Does it not let her speak unproblematically about her fullness and catholicity? Are we confronted here by a mysterious "mystical" reality? Closer inspection shows us, however, that the words "fullness" and "fulfillment" do not describe a tensionless "being," as if the Church had already achieved the final purpose of all her ways; rather, they appear in living and relevant connection with her concrete life on earth. As we saw earlier, the Church as the body of Christ appears in the context of riches and continuous parenesis. The same is true here with regard to fullness, which appears in the context of the Church on her way. The outlook on fullness overflows with promise and proclamation, prayer and admonition, and only in that framework can fullness be rightly understood.

In the fullness that the Church received, she is directed towards fullness. That is the fantastic dynamic characterizing Paul's view of the Church, and through it he wants to make the Church rest in Christ's all-sufficient work.[33] All that is said about fullness in Christ, aimed polemically against any confusion, is inseparably connected to the fact that in Christ all the treasures of wisdom and knowledge are hidden (Col. 2:3) and that the Christians' lives are hid with Christ in God (3:3). This is not ontological speculation, but comfort and encouragement for the Church in opposition to all powers, which, for that matter, have been disarmed and dethroned through Him.[34] All of the perspectives for the present and future are located in the relationship to Him. Therefore, the fullness that the Church received in no sense removes her from the calling to preserve this relatedness to Him, not to be disqualified (Col. 2:18), and to be on her guard against all that could draw her away from this fullness. Her life is led according to God's will "until we all attain to the unity of the faith and of the knowledge of the Son of God" (Eph. 4:13). She has learned Christ (4:20), and from that knowledge a summons resounds through all the corridors of concrete, daily life (4:25-32). Not even for a moment is the Church left to her own, independent existence, as if her acquisition of fullness meant that she could find and go her

vis-à-vis various amplifications on the part of the teachers of false doctrine) is essentially the same as that of Ridderbos (*Aan de Kolossenzen*, 1960, p. 178). Cf. also Eph. 3:17ff.

33. Cf. Ridderbos, *Aan de Kolossenzen*, p. 105.

34. Col. 2:15. Cf. H. Berkhof, *Christus en de Machten*, pp. 36ff.

own ways. Rather, in the light of fullness, the commandment of God becomes clear, urgent — sealed as the Church is "for the day of redemption" (4:30) and taken up in growth and maturity, which are not automatic, but are structured by holding fast to Him (Col. 2:19), in Whom salvation in the absolute sense is found.[35] Therefore, the Church, after receiving this fullness, must set her mind on and seek many things (Col. 3:1f.); and from the fullness, the whole life becomes visible in a radical, utterly concrete admonition (Col. 3:5f.; cf. Eph. 4:17ff.).

When one makes a connection between catholicity and fullness, one may not neglect any of this. Otherwise, a deformation of genuine catholicity inevitably takes place, since it can never be abstracted from Christ Himself.[36] This correlative language of the Scriptures frequently has not received its sufficient due.

Catholicity was dealt with as an acquired fullness, which was then more precisely localized and thus made demonstrable. True, it was not denied that the Church remains under the precept and admonition of her Lord, but these were concretely understood as an "addition" to the actuality of fullness and catholicity. This static view of the Church's catholicity has always held great fascination, because one could clearly and unambiguously speak about the grand fact of the Church. This actual "catholicity," which universally valid conclusions could be drawn from and which could be referred to in witnessing and recruitment, can be made concrete in many ways. In the midst of the division of the churches, particularly, Roman Catholic ecclesiology could relate catholicity and the institutional aspect of the Church, so that the presence of fullness and catholicity could be clear to everyone. Catholicity was, as it were, ascertainable and verifiable, and it was lacking in the other churches.[37]

In spite of the radical change in the Roman Catholic judgment of other churches, this aspect of fullness has continued to play a role, since the other churches — in spite of their relatedness to Christ and the Holy Spirit — still do not partake in

---

35. Ridderbos, *Aan de Kolossenzen*, pp. 194f.
36. Cf. many worthwhile remarks and formulations in Berkhof, *Katholiciteit*, pp. 61ff., especially against H. Schlier's ontological conception (in *Der Brief an die Epheser*, p. 202, n. 1). The rejection of this insight into fullness has nothing to do with an antithesis between being and function, but rather with a different view of being itself, which is inconceivable in abstraction from Christ.
37. "He has poured out His full abundance in Christ and in His mystical body, which is the Church" (*Divinum Illud Munus*, 1897).

this concrete, institutional condensation and centralization of fullness.[38] This is definitely not intended as a replacement of the pneumatic aspect by the institutional, hierarchical aspect.[39] But the conviction is present that the fullness has received the density willed by Christ in the institutional form of the Catholic Church and that the Spirit wanted to give fullness here. The context of fullness and the outlook on catholicity is so essential that, without this concrete form of fullness — i.e., without the pope — the Church would no longer be what she now is and her unity would fall to pieces.[40] At this point, the deficiency in the other churches becomes visible, and the Church may not abandon the honor and jurisdiction of the primate, because it is a direct inheritance of Christ. In it, fullness has been constituted and the Church has been called and fitted to be the guardian of catholicity.

Heresy and catholicity

In Roman Catholic thought today, the realization is growing more and more that the institutional aspect has significance only when it is totally and directly related to Christ and the Holy Spirit. Then the institutional aspect can no longer be used as an independent criterion to determine whether or not fullness and catholicity are present.[41] Consequently, catholicity is given much more content than was given in the past, although its original signification (wholeness) remains of im-

38. Cf. *Lumen Gentium* (*DV II*, pp. 33f.): "though they do not profess the faith in its entirety or do not preserve unity of communion with the successor of Peter." Cf. also the *Decree on Ecumenism* (*DV II*, p. 346): "For it is through Christ's Catholic Church alone, which is the all-embracing means of salvation, that the *fullness* of the means of salvation can be obtained." That is true even though the "fullness of eternal glory" is present only in the heavenly Jerusalem.

39. Cf. *Mystici Corporis Christi, TCT,* 256, 258. It is often admitted by Roman Catholics today that the emphasis on the institutional aspects in the post-Tridentine period resulted in lack of interest for the relevance of the pneumatic aspect. Cf. Bavinck, *Geref. Dog.,* IV, 385ff.; R. Sohm, *Wesen und Ursprung des Katholizismus,* 1912², pp. 16f., 67; and E. Brunner, *The Misunderstanding of the Church,* 1952, pp. 84ff.

40. *Ecclesiam Suam,* para. 110: "Without the Pope the Catholic Church would no longer be Catholic." Cf. below, chapter 10, footnote 82, on the *ubi Petrus, ibi ecclesia.*

41. Cf. A.A. van Ruler, "De Betekenis van het Institutaire (in de Kerk)," *Kerk en Theologie,* 1967, pp. 309ff., especially on institution and spirit (pp. 315f.). Cf. also K. Blei, "Kan de Gemeente zonder het Ambt?" *Kerk en Theologie,* 1967, pp. 1ff.; and Berkhof, *Katholiciteit,* pp. 86ff.

portance. Reflection on catholicity can then assume this form: one perceives a lack in other churches of the fullness of truth, causing a certain disharmony that makes it difficult to experience and preserve catholicity integrally. Other churches do not possess the whole truth; the connecting, harmonious, organic center is lacking because of various one-sided elements. We touch here on a specific aspect of the problem of catholicity that is connected to an old problem in the Church — viz., heresy, the opposite of true catholicity. In true catholicity all one-sidedness is harmoniously surmounted.

In the New Testament, *hairesis* (heresy) at first signified a choice, membership in a special group. The word was not yet filled with a particular content and thus did not have the bad connotation that it later received.[42] The New Testament speaks of the "party" *(hairesis)* of the Pharisees (Acts 15:5) or of the Sadducees (5:17). In this sense, too, the Jews called the adherents of the Christian faith a "party" (28:22; cf. 24:5). But as a specific content is given to choice, the word "heresy" gradually came to mean a genuine deviation from the truth. This usage appears already in the New Testament when heresy was seen to be in conflict with the truth: it is a fruit of the flesh (Gal. 5:20), destructive (II Pet. 2:1), false doctrine and apostasy from the truth for the sake of various fabrications (Titus 3:8ff.). With the advent of this usage, Church and heresy became mutually exclusive.

Heresy must not be simply identified with schism, which is a serious thing in itself; rather, it is, as it were, an intensification of schism. In traditional Roman Catholic ecclesiology, both schism and heresy were viewed as an attack on catholicity. This is immediately clear with respect to schism, because separation from the whole, from the catholic Church, occurs. With heresy, though, other factors are involved due to the element of choice. Frequently, heresy is not in a radically antithetical position in opposition to the truth, but rather intends to make a stand for the truth along the way of subjective emphases and selection. Then it is not a denial of or an attack on the truth, but a process of living and thinking that pulls the truth out of shape. Truth is no longer confessed in its wholeness and organic connections, because particular aspects are neglected

42. For instance, II Thess. 2:13 speaks of God's "choosing" *(haireō):* "God chose you from the beginning to be saved...." Cf. also Phil. 1:22, where Paul is faced with a choice: "Yet which I shall choose I cannot tell."

in favor of others. The process is not always immediately visible but, in the end, it destroys the outlook on catholicity.[43]

One cannot say that this view of heresy appears in the New Testament, since the element of one-sidedness is not present — at least not explicitly present.[44] In the New Testament, we do find heresy concerned with the truth, and it often pretends to possess deeper insight into the truth of the Christian faith. Yet this "choice" is not really a selection of partial aspects, but a radical transformation of the truth. Paul is concerned not so much with what we understand by "one-sidedness" as he is with destruction, although destruction can, of course, result from choice, preference, and selection. Paul passes strict judgment on that destruction, on heresy as apostasy from the apostolic truth,[45] as another gospel that radically obscures the truth of salvation (II Cor. 11:4; Gal. 1:6). And Paul confronts this with an anathema (1:8), even though one wants to give a fuller and richer gospel than Paul's, as was the case with the Judaists in Galatia with their view of the Mosaic law. The decisive point is not one-sidedness, but the attack on what is essential, for "if justification were through the law, then Christ died to no purpose" (2:21), and if one expects justification from the law, one is severed from Christ (5:4 — *katērgēthēte apò Christoú*). Paul is not concerned with partial aspects, but with the transformation of the truth (the appeal to the law of God), which he opposes by means of the preaching of the cross. Hence, there is a great deal of emphasis on the pseudo-character of

43. For the view of heresy which we have just discussed, see J. Brosch, *Das Wesen der Häresie*, 1936, pp. 82ff., 85, 98, 111. Cf. also K. Rahner-H. Vorgrimler, *Kleines Theologisches Wörterbuch*, *s.v. Häresie*, on the the "choice" of a "partial truth," pulled out of its organic relatedness to the whole. A. Harnack (*History of Dogma*, II, 90f.) already includes this element in his characterization of heresy in the ancient Church: "The designation *hairesis* implies an adherence to something self-chosen in opposition to the acknowledgment of something objectively handed down, and assumes that this is the particular thing in which the apostasy consists."

44. Brosch himself (*op. cit.*) admits that there is not much to go on in Scripture for this approach to heresy, because it designates concrete false doctrine more than the essence of heresy.

45. At the present there is intense discussion about whether one can really speak of a kind of heresy that can be judged on the basis of apostolic authority and the New Testament. Can heresy be separated so simply from the wholeness of truth in the New Testament as the normative authority? We will deal with this more fully in chapter 8 below, pp. 225-231.

heresy which compels one to watchfulness, and on repudiation, wandering away from faith (I Tim. 6:10), making shipwreck of faith (1:9), and upsetting the faith of others (II Tim. 2:18). There can be a "profession" in heresy, but it is connected to denial and disobedience (Titus 1:16). Thus, Paul's radical judgment is not diminished because heresy deals with the "truth." That this is the case (in Galatia and Colossae) only accentuates the calling of the Church to watchfulness, and the antithesis is in no sense weakened.[46]

Consequently, one can say that the contemporary view of heresy — in its relationship to catholicity — is on a different level than Paul's usage. Even though heresy does appeal to elements in tradition — the appeal to the law of God — Paul's concern is with the resulting lack of appreciation for full salvation in Christ; it is a bewitchment that loses the outlook on the crucified Christ (cf. Gal. 3:1). This does not mean, however, that to approach heresy from emphases, selection, and one-sidedness[47] is to contradict Paul's rejection of the concrete heresy of his days, which was scarcely distinguishable from apostasy. The analysis of heresy today touches on historical-ecclesiastical developments, different insights into the truth of God, and confessional contrasts. No church has the courage simply to transpose the radicality of Paul's rejection of heresy onto the present division among churches and confessions or to apply Paul's words about shipwreck, apostasy, and rupture to "the others." This does not signify relativism or confessional indifference — any more than it did among the Reformers.[48] Rather, it signifies

---

46. That is apparent from, among other things, the prohibition against disputing about words in II Tim. 2:14, because it is senseless. Cf. L. Goppelt, "Kirche und Häresie nach Paulus," *Gedenkschrift W. Elert*, 1955, p. 21.

47. According to E. Schillebeeckx (*Theologisch Woordenboek*, II, 2784), a one-sided emphasis can also arise in the defense against heresy, and he finds that to be the case in the Counter Reformation. Heresy is a "one-sided affirmation of a definite truth of faith, which is unhooked from the totality of dogma."

48. There is an example of this in one of the propositions from M.J.J. de Kroon's dissertation, *De Eer van God en het Heil van de Mens*, 1968. De Kroon speaks of Calvin's hermeneutical principle in attempting to understand Luther's conception of the presence of Christ on the basis of Luther's intention: "because he could not express his intention otherwise." Cf. Calvin, "Petit Traicté de la Sainte Cene" (1541), *Opera Selecta*, I, 527. This approach is even more striking because Calvin begins his exposition by pointing out that this holy sacrament "has been confused for a long time by several large errors."

the willingness to continuous reflection and testing with regard to the integral understanding of the message of salvation. In that reflection one must, for the sake of catholicity, be conscious of one-sidedness, choice, preference, and selection; but, at the same time, one must guard oneself against the danger of prematurely passing sentence on every one-sided view as signifying that Christ has died "to no purpose."

In our day the problem of heresy and catholicity once again plays a significant role. It is not that the possibility of genuine, destructive heresy is disregarded, but that the far-reaching question is asked of where and when this heresy is present.[49] That question can only be answered by serious analysis with an eye to the whole. One need not be delighted with the word "organic"[50] to admit that the "inorganic" has often played a role in the domain of our "imperfect" knowledge. Hence, on account of the dynamic, alluring character of all selection and preference, it is meaningful to give attention to it. But that is never possible with a criterion that is used legalistically — by which the religious-pneumatic confession of the Church is weakened — but only with the decisive norm of Paul, which is related to the reality of cross and resurrection.[51] Then the question of the outlook on the whole in contrast to arbitrariness automatically takes on great significance. It stands against the background of a great commission: the joint understanding

49. We are thinking of, among other things, Bavinck's distinction between doubt and heresy. He sees heresy as obstinate error in the fundamental articles (*Katholiciteit*, 1968[2], p. 27). The error is "in the substance of the truth," and Bavinck warns against all lack of caution in judging. Cf. my *Verontrusting en Verantwoordelijkheid*, 1969, pp. 32ff.; and H. Küng, *The Church*, pp. 241ff.

50. Apparently, Bavinck also did not know a better word for the problem of minimum and maximum, which he pointed to in Rome (organic in contrast to addition and quantity). Cf. *Geref. Dog.*, I, 583.

51. At what point a deviation is observed is always irrelevant in a legalistic, quantitative concept of heresy (which is connected to a quantitative view of faith). Cf. Bavinck, *ibid*. A formalistic application of ecclesiastical law renders any nuances in connection with Paul's "all or nothing" superfluous. Cf. C. Dietzfelbinger, *Was ist Irrlehre?*, 1967, especially with regard to Galatians, where heresy adopts the form of the destructive plus. The rejection of the quantitative, simple approach to heresy does not signify a lack of appreciation for doctrine, but a recognition of the depth and richness of doctrine! On Luther's new understanding of heresy as compared with the Middle Ages, cf. U. Mäuser, *Der junge Luther und die Häresie*, 1968; and H.W. Gensichen, *Damnamus. Die Verwerfung von Irrlehre bei Luther und in Luthertum des 16. Jahrh.*, 1955, pp. 38ff.

of the whole, which may also be called the center or the one thing that is necessary. Then we find ourselves in the midst of the ecumenical problematic, where catholicity has become a decisive, critical question. Since the relationship between churches is not simply a question of confession or denial of the truth, the problem arises as to degrees of catholicity in the understanding of God's truth. "Fullness" is not always contrasted to "emptiness," but also to incompleteness and partiality. Bavinck's statement that heresy is a "fluctuating" concept is misunderstood if it is seen as confessional relativism, since he does justice to the variation in the historical process and refuses to make flat, black and white judgments about others.[52]

Gift and task

This refusal gives the discussion about the outlook on the whole, about the catholicity of the truth and the Church, new meaning and responsibility. The possibility arises of mutual recognition of the dangers of "one-sidedness" and of a new readiness to be called back by the gospel from all arbitrary preferences, which can often be determined by psychology or sociology instead of theology. Then it is possible, in spite of the difference in insight, to learn from other churches and to become attentive to what, in varied circumstances and in necessary, legitimate polemics, no longer meant very much.[53] It becomes clear that the whole life of the Church — both doctrine

---

52. Cf. especially C. Veenhof, *Volk van God. Enkele Aspecten van Bavincks Kerkbeschouwing*, 1969, pp. 147ff.; and J. Veenhof, *Revelation en Inspiratie*, 1968, 109ff., 575ff., *et al.*

53. There are many examples in the history of the Church where interest in particular aspects of the truth of salvation (and Scripture) acquired a one-sided function in reaction to other churches. One may think of the reactions in the relationship between pietism and orthodoxy or of the "accents" in opposition to the Roman Catholic doctrine of the meritoriousness of good works. These reactions can obscure the genuine outlook on sanctification by not recognizing sufficiently such biblical motifs as "laying up for themselves a good foundation for the future" (*apothēsaurizontes*, I Tim. 6:19; cf. also Phil. 4:17). K. Rahner (*Theological Dictionary*, p. 203) speaks of the *heilsgeschichtlich* function of heresy, in that a heresy can contain actualizations of the essence of Christianity that, although they are present in the Catholic Church, have never reached the same level of actualization there. Thus, they can provide a "stimulus to the development of the Church's doctrine and practice." Rahner refers here also to I Cor. 11:19 for the positive meaning of heresy. Cf. chapter 2 above.

and practice — is related to the critical testing of catholicity, for every violation of the mystery of the truth of salvation — in word and deed, in confessional, political, or social heresy — can obscure the outlook on the qualitative richness of the whole.[54] It becomes impossible to live with the comfortable notion "of the Church taking up a static position, when she is confronted by heresies, and simply persevering in the defense of truths which she has already adequately understood."[55] Once again, catholicity received its place in the dynamic, total life of the Church on the way to fullness, and to that extent one can speak of a shifting in the experience of catholicity.

So, it is not surprising, in view of the biblical light on catholicity, that not only the indicative, but also the imperative of catholicity has drawn more and more attention.[56] A Roman Catholic, for instance, has acknowledged that the fullness of catholicity "is realized here on earth only imperfectly."[57] Subtle distinctions such as that between "fullness" and "completeness" point to a view of catholicity that is full of nuances and draw attention to stronger and weaker "manifestations." Witte makes a connection here with the "renewal" (renovatio) that always remains necessary in the Church. Catholicity, then, stands in the light of gift (Gabe) and task (Aufgabe). The gift is not relativized, but its significance is understood: the call to catholicity in the concrete life of the Church. This catholicity is "understood not only statically but dynamically, not only as a safeguarding datum but as a binding task."[58] Catholicity can no longer be ascertained in isolation, for a "condition" begins to play a role: "provided that we can be certain that a Church has not lost contact with its original nature, has not contradicted that nature."[59] This explains the fear that the Church with her catholicity will once again fall into apologetics. Catholicity cannot be

54. See the many aspects in W.A. Visser 't Hooft, Heel de Kerk voor Heel de Wereld, 1968, not beside, but on account of the one catholicity.
55. K. Rahner, op. cit., p. 155. Cf. "What is Heresy?", Theological Investigations, V, 468ff.
56. Cf. J. Ratzinger, Introduction to Christianity, 1969, pp. 261ff., on the imperatives that are set loose by the claim of catholicity. The imperatives summon one to confess catholicity "not only in the credo."
57. J.L. Witte, "De Kerk 'Sacrament der Eenheid' voor geheel de Wereld," in De Kerk van Vatikanum II, I, 1969, p. 235.
58. H. Küng, Structures of the Church, 1964, p. 48. Notice the tension in the formulation; it does not read, as one would expect, "also dynamically." Cf. his The Church, pp. 296ff.
59. Küng, The Church, p. 304 (italics added).

a proud challenge to other churches, but only a special obligation
— in humility — to one's own church.[60] The statements of the
Church about fullness and catholicity may never let her forget
the gap between pretension and reality. True catholicity "is a
grace given to the Church and constantly renewed by its Lord."[61]
And therefore, it asks for continuing prayer.

This approach to catholicity undeniably shows strong kin-
ship to the Reformed confession of catholicity. What is presently
called the dynamic in the concept of catholicity got a strong
accent in the Reformation, for the Reformers refused to speak
simplistically about the Church's "attributes" on the analogy
of various "things" that have attributes. Actually starting from
a self-evident, unassailable "catholicity" apart from testing and
responsibility, the Reformation itself would have been neither
possible nor conceivable![62] The Reformers knew the dynamic
of gift and task, of a catholicity that could be confessed only
in fear and trembling. It would be wholly unjust to see this
new approach to catholicity, which is closely connected to the
dominating aspects of the New Testament, as a form of "actu-
alism" that bypasses the "reality" of the Church and her catholicity, viewing it only as a contingent event apart from any
continuity. Such a criticism can only arise from the uneasy
feeling that catholicity is not so easily determinable and usable
as one had thought earlier, when the essence of the Church was
defined, as it were, ontologically and *a priori*. But this usability
is in flagrant contradiction with the essence of catholicity, since
catholicity can only be confessed on the way of faith and prayer,
word and deed, a way toward the fullness of Christ.

No ecclesiastical determination or givenness as such offers a
guarantee of true catholicity. Just as the appeal to the institution can conceal catholicity behind closed windows, so also the
appeal (as a reaction) to the "spirit" *(pneúma)* can obscure the
outlook on that catholicity. A docetic protest against the forms
of the earthly Church, which calls for an anti-institutional
"spiritual Church" *(ecclesia spiritualis)* in the era of the Holy

---

60. *Ibid.*, p. 311.
61. *Ibid.*, p. 313.
62. Cf. *Inst.*, IV, 9, 6, where Calvin refers to the "council" convened by
    Ahab (I Kings 22:6, 22), which cast Micaiah into prison as a "heretic."
    Calvin also mentions the "council" that convened against Christ in
    John 11:47 (*Inst.*, IV, 9, 7). None of this is "a cheap anti-ecclesiastical
    protest" (see my "Calvin and Rome," *John Calvin Contemporary
    Prophet,* 1959, p. 191).

Spirit, can bypass the depth of catholicity without understanding that the Spirit — *Veni, Creator Spiritus!* — makes the Church responsible in the midst of earthly reality![63] For the sake of the mystery of (concrete) catholicity, the Church was sent into the world with a commission. Only thus do the perspectives of universality and world-wideness, of doors and windows opened by the Holy Spirit to villages, cities, and new continents emerge (cf. Acts 14:27; 16:9; Col. 4:3). If the Church loses sight of these perspectives, the meaning of her "internal" life becomes illusionary, and she lacks the power to bear fruit. She will also lack that power if she does enter the world, but no longer correctly understands her own catholicity and the outlook on the fullness of Christ. The result will be that her mission no longer exhibits the structure of the message of salvation, but that of an uncredible propaganda.

The catholicity of the Church can be misunderstood in many ways. The formal frame of catholicity can suggest a concrete, earthly "realization" as the Church's exercise of power and influence over the whole world and over all the fields of life, a striving for world domination in the name of Christ. But then, even though appearance suggests the contrary, the Church becomes powerless, as do the branches that do not remain in Christ, the Vine (John 15:4ff.). The Church can act as a Christian empire, clothed in the appearance of catholicity. The aspects of world-wideness and universality remain, but they have lost their true catholic meaning, since they assume the form of power and force, of imperialism and totalitarianism. That is a temptation which has often been very real in the history of the Church. But it is a total misunderstanding of Christ's universal role. This appearance has often blinded the eyes, even to the extent of "compelling them to enter," and has done unexpressible damage to the Church whose gospel is the cross.[64] The gospel could hardly be understood anymore as

63. Cf. especially the captivating book by E. Benz, *Ecclesia Spiritualis. Kirchenidee und Geschichtstheologie der Franzisk. Reformation*, 1964, specifically on Joachim v. Floris (pp. 32ff.), Petrus Joh. Olivi (pp. 256ff.), and, generally, catholicity and sectarianism in one of the most dramatic collisions in the history of the Church.

64. Cf. H. Küng, *The Church*, pp. 250ff., on the inquisition with its intolerant fanaticism and madness. Cf. also pp. 474ff. on the Petrine ministry. Further, see A. Adam, *Lehrbuch der Dogmengeschichte*, II, 1968, pp. 60ff., on the change of the Church's essence into the worldly might of the pope, and the total picture of the Church's structure in the bull *Unam Sanctam* (1302).

the message of salvation, as redemption and liberation, and as
the testimony of salvation and righteousness, of the opening
of the prisons and of the gospel for the poor (cf. Matt. 11:2-6;
Luke 4:18f.). Going beyond all boundaries is an ambivalent
thing. Everything depends on who gave the commission to do
so and how those boundaries were crossed — how one goes forth
and bears fruit.

From her history the Church has clearly had difficulty with
the deep meaning and the consequences of catholicity.[65] Even
if catholicity is not denied, it is often practiced and realized
only with difficulty. Already in the New Testament, we meet
with all sorts of resistance. Over and over again, it is necessary
to re-open the doors and to indicate the perspectives, just as
Christ Himself does when He announces that the hour is coming when limitation and localization will be broken through:
"neither on this mountain nor in Jerusalem will you worship
the Father." Rather, worship will be in spirit and truth (John
4:20-24). The gospel centers the world in the form of limitation
(Israel), but it is a misunderstanding to think that this is its
final purpose. In contrast to particularistic narrowness, an outlook on greater and wider perspectives is offered. This perspective was not immediately understood by everyone, a situation that
is clearly seen from the difficulties about the entrance of the
heathen, when Peter refused, in his vision, to eat what is common and unclean (Acts 10:14). But the light of the revealed
mystery falls upon Peter's discriminating attitude, and Peter
says later that God has shown him that he should not call any
man common or unclean (10:28 — *theòs édeixen*). No prior
distinction is made that as such determines the relationship to
salvation (Rom. 10:12 — *diastolè*). Salvation is not automatically
connected to certain situations or predispositions, since any one
"in every nation" who calls upon Him is acceptable to Him in
Jesus Christ (Acts 10:35), Who is Lord of all (Rom. 10:12).
Peter's distinctions fall away, since God does not discriminate,
and Peter's "discovery" is that there is no partiality with God.[66]

---

65. "Already in antiquity it was immensely difficult for her to be at once
the Church of the barbarians and of the Romans; in modern times
she was unable to prevent the strife among the Christian nations; and
today she has still not been able to unite rich and poor in such a way
that the abundance of the one is turned to the satisfaction of the other.
The sign of the table fellowship remains to a large extent unrealized"
(Ratzinger, *op. cit.*, p. 262).

66. Acts 10:34 (*prosōpolêmptēs*). The KJV reads: "no respecter of persons."
Cf. also Acts 15:9, 11.

These words are not intended to be an antithesis to God's gracious, electing action, but they thwart every distinction that sets up walls between men, whereby a particular group *a priori* receives more consideration for God's grace and friendship than another group.[67] So "showing no partiality" can function in many connections. For instance, it can signify a warning to believers when it is stressed that the poor in shabby clothing may not be treated as inferior to the rich (James 2:1). On account of God's "impartial" action,[68] it is illegitimate also for the believers to "believe in Christ and at the same time show partiality."[69] Therefore, placing boundaries and establishing walls along the way of the Kingdom and of the preaching of the gospel are a "hindrance" to God's intention.[70] It is opposition to universality and catholicity, which, on account of its depth and richness, seeks breadth in order, without any discrimination, to bless Jew or Greek, slave or free, male or female "because you are all one" in Christ Jesus (Gal. 3:28; cf. Rom. 1:14; Col. 3:11). In light of this, to point to the significance of various real distinctions is senseless, for whatever differences there may be, in those differences there is no "distinction" in Christ.

Catholicity and the Church's mission

In connection with the many human distinctions that affect catholicity, it is necessary to recall that the confession of catholicity is preceded by that of the Holy Spirit: *credo in Spiritum Sanctum.* Uppsala took a meaningful approach when it dealt

67. One may think of the election of Israel, which is not based on Israel's qualities (Deut. 7:7). Cf. Israel's origin and birth, Ezek. 16:3. Cf. also J. Verkuyl, *Break Down the Walls: A Christian Cry for Racial Justice*, 1973, pp. 40f. God's lack of partiality is not opposed to election, but forms its reverse side.

68. That "God shows no partiality" (Rom. 2:11) does not conflict for Paul with Israel's "precedence" ("to the Jew first" — 1:16; cf. 3:1f.; 9:4f.; 11:17f.). That is due not only to the "and also to the Greek" (1:16), but also to the goal and directedness of these salvation-historical prerogatives. Cf. Ridderbos, *Paul*, pp. 37ff., 58; and Rom. 3:29: "Or is God the God of Jews only? Is he not the God of Gentiles also?" On the problem of the prerogative see also the (temporary) limitation of the proclamation: Matt. 10:5f.; 15:24; Mark 7:27 (*próton*). See J. Jeremias, *Jesu Verheissung für die Völker*, 1956, pp. 24ff.

69. *TDNT*, VI, 779f. Cf. Eph. 6:9; Gal. 2:6; I Pet. 1:7; Col. 3:25.

70. "Can any one forbid water for baptizing these people who have received the Holy Spirit just as we have?" (Acts 10:47 — *kōlúsai*). Cf. Matt. 19:14: "Let the children come to me, and do not hinder them (*mè kōlúete*)."

with "the Holy Spirit and the catholicity of the Church."[71]
Here, too, strong emphasis is laid on gift and task. Catholicity
is possible only by the Spirit and the perspectives opened by
Him. This is applicable both with regard to the pure understanding of God's salvation and to the Church's going out into
the world. They are immediately related to each other, since
the meaningful entrance into the world is determined by what
is preached in this world. More than ever before, the mission
work of the Church is confronted with the pressing question of
the background and meaning of the catholicity of the gospel.
In her proclamation, the Church came into contact with all
times and cultures, with life that is already brimful, and she
came to that life with the commission to be a true blessing in it.
Does the Church come into this world, characterized more and
more by oneness, with a liberating message? Or can she at most
give expression in another — Western — way to what is already
present in the world? Do not the ideals, activity, and religion
of this world show the pretension of a unique catholicity to
be exaggerated or even illusionary?[72] And when the Church
spoke of God's new, surprising concern for salvation for the
world, was that really more than words?

Here the question of the meaning of catholicity reaches its
culminating point. Catholicity as "universality" could easily perish in a "syncretistic" assimilation that leaves nothing of the
original meaning of (qualitative!) catholicity.[73] Precisely the
"comprehensiveness" of syncretism appears to take over the
formal structures of catholicity, but apart from any connection
to the fullness of Christ. All new reflection on syncretism, thus,
is closely connected to the problem of catholicity.[74] So we meet
with various attempts to give new form to catholicity and universality and, once again, it is the letter of Paul to the Colos-

71. Cf. *Uppsala 1968* on what the Church is and ought to be.
72. Cf. the Second Vatican Council's *Ad Gentes Divinitus (DV II*, pp. 595f.)
on the "truth and grace that are to be found among the nations as
a sort of secret presence of God *(quasi secreta Dei presentia)*."
73. Syncretism is usually spoken of in connection with the relationship
between the Christian faith and world religions. It is used in a different
sense — although still as an amalgamation — in the so-called "syncretistic"
struggle (Calovius' *Historia Syncretistica*, 1682), when the question
was whether there could be a "consensus" of the Protestant confessions on the basis of the unity of the first five centuries *(consensus
quinquesaecularis*, Calixtus).
74. Cf. W.A. Visser 't Hooft, *Heel de Kerk voor Heel de Wereld*, pp. 775ff.;
J.J.F. Durand, *Una Sancta Catholica in Sendingsperspektief*, 1961, pp.
123ff.; and G. Thils, *Syncrétisme ou Catholicité?*, 1967.

sians that plays a striking role here. Strong emphasis is laid
on the universal aspects of this letter. There is the outlook
on the "cosmic" Christ, on the frequency of the phrase "all
things" *(tà pánta)*, in which all limits are exceeded,[75] and on
Christ as the proclaimed Light of the world, full of new perspectives in this opportune time *(kairós)*, to which the Church
must witness.[76]

There can be no doubt about the universal aspects of the
Letter to the Colossians, although the letter may not be isolated from other letters in this respect.[77] Moreover, it is clear
that the Church is related to this universality in a very special
way. Someone has remarked that, after the "discovery" of Paul's
letters to the Romans and to the Galatians during the Reformation, it is especially in our time that the chance and the
calling to understand the exceptional significance of Colossians exists! What is the nature of the perspectives that emerge
here? What are the motives and what is the background of
this universality, which leads to the proclamation of the gospel
"to every creature under heaven" (Col. 1:23)? These questions
are so important and decisive because this background discloses
the meaning of this universality.

In a vehement defense against all transformation of and
every addition to the gospel, Paul finds the message concentrated in salvation, in the all-sufficient Christ, in His power
above all powers, and in the exclusion of every other possibility of finding salvation (cf. Col. 1:13). This is not an as-
tonished, cosmic contemplation of the world in universal perspectives, but a dwelling on the mystery of what has happened
in the cross for reconciliation and redemption (2:14ff.). Nothing
can be understood here from the aspect of power, which has

75. See especially Col. 1:15-20. In all the commentaries the aspect of totality
    is stressed, for instance: "the total validity of Jesus Christ's authority"
    (W. Bieder, *Der Kolosserbrief*, 1943, p. 162). Cf. also H. Ridderbos, *Aan
    de Kolossenzen*, 1960, p. 135: "all-embracing and of paramount im-
    portance."
76. See J. Sitler's report, "Zur Einheit berufen," *Neu Delhi 1961*, 1962, pp.
    512ff. at New Delhi, particularly on the dimensions of salvation in Christ
    and on the meeting place of Christ and the chaos, where the Church is
    called to testify in opposition to all that detracts from His universality.
77. Cf. the "superior power" in Rom. 8:38f. and standing firm against
    "the world rulers of this present darkness" in Eph. 6:12 *(kosmokrátores)*
    together with Col. 1:16. Ridderbos, *Aan de Kolossenzen*, p. 132, refers
    also to Heb. 1:1ff.; I Cor. 8:6; and II Cor. 4:4.

frequently played a role in the history of the Church when a "theology of glory" *(theologia gloriae)* supplanted the "theology of the cross" *(theologia crucis)*.[78] Adherents of this theology did not understand that the glory arises from the cross, and thus they stamped the meaning of universality forever (cf. 1:11, 27; 3:4). Therein, for Paul, lies the unique universality, the way from the depth to the breadth, and every mistake about the breadth as in itself a formal category, as "world-wideness," is unthinkable for him. With respect to the depth of the mystery of the cross that has now been revealed, no synthesis is possible for Paul — neither by addition or completion, nor by self-abasement,[79] which finds a reason in the "not yet" to abandon its security; neither dependence on the worship of angels, nor an escape into a "mystery" as a compensation in the face of powerlessness in the midst of the encircling powers (2:18). This vehement defense is derived from the heights of the proclamation, which excludes all of this because of Christ.

Therefore, the Church is continuously warned against "abstract" world-wideness and is called back to the understanding of her all-sufficient salvation. Apart from that understanding, universality becomes a formal frame or scheme, which will constantly be refilled with components of power, influence, and pretension. In view of this temptation, we can better understand that the unity and catholicity of the Church are inseparably connected. Division inevitably gives the impression of a degradation of relevance in a multitude of opinions. That there is verbal agreement in the Church as to the *credo ecclesiam catholicam* is not a sufficient reply. The relatedness of unity and catholicity is connected not to the worldly adage, "in unity there is strength," but to the Church's seeking for universality, for breadth, for the end of the earth. In times when the oneness of the world is disclosed, there is a danger that isolated, quantitative catholicity may once again come to

---

78. H. Dembowski's book, *Grundfragen der Christologie, Erörtert am Problem der Herrschaft Jesu Christi*, 1969, is determined by this truth, although it cannot be denied that various motives due to reaction are present too. The problematic of *gloria* and *crux* comes to expression without this reaction in K. Barth, for instance, *C.D.*, IV/2, pp. 29f.

79. Col. 2:18 *(thélōn en tapeinophrosúnę̄*, distinguished from the lowliness — *tapeinophrosúnēn*, 3:12! — that is required of Christ's Church). Cf. Bieder, *op. cit.*, p. 162; and Lohmeyer, *op. cit.*, p. 125, who speaks of "cultic practices of 'humility'" along a wearisome road, opposed completely to the knowledge of the mystery that has been made manifest (1:26) and to the transferal to the Kingdom (1:13).

dominate the thought of the Church about her place in the world. But the result is that what she hopes to win in breadth, she loses in depth. And so, the authentic catholicity of the Church urges her to new reflection on the content of her confession and proclamation.

There are not two separate, independent domains — viz., the hermeneutical adventure with all its complications on one hand, and the world-wide preaching of the gospel on the other. And, conceivably, an explosion in one domain would not immediately be felt in the other.[80] "Schizophrenic" thinking here can lead only to uncredible dualism and to internal duplicity, since the gospel, as it was understood by the Church, opened eyes for the perspectives of the end of the earth. There can be no talk here of an esoteric mystery which secludes itself from the world and permits itself to have a "plus" that the Church feels no need to justify. Rather, the confession of her own identity — that of catholicity — contains the conviction that this gospel is intended to enter every age. Therefore, the proclamation must have a fearless character, not as self-overestimation of the "servant" of this gospel, but as trust in the importance of the doors that are opened and the freedom that is given here. This fearlessness can be too easily practiced when a confrontation with the actual thinking and feelings of a particular age is avoided, and the questions that are asked of the Church by the world are scarcely heard at all. Then the height of the letter to the Colossians is forsaken, since Paul, starting from the radicalness, universality, and comprehensiveness, calls for wisdom toward outsiders (4:5) and for the correct answer to all questions, not in underestimation of the questions, nor in simplistic "answers," but in a falling back on the mystery of Christ and the ways that are indicated in it (4:6 — *heni hekásto apokrinesthai*).

Therefore, in every word that the Church says in the world, she is tested concerning her true catholicity and her existence as the light of the world. It will have to be clear from the life of the Church why she continues to seek breadth. Even when struck by various failures, by many embarrassments to the Church, and by answers that were either premature or not forthcoming, one may not expect too little of the Church and

---

80. That is visible constantly in the repercussions of biblical hermeneutics on the understanding of the missionary commission. One may recall E. Troeltsch's "Die Mission in der modernen Welt," *Ges. Schriften*, II, 789ff., as an example.

her calling. Rather, one must maximize that expectation and calling, since in the light of the Church — no matter how strange it may sound — the light of Christ becomes visible in earthly reality. This perspective, which regardless of every disappointment may never be abandoned, resembles the perspective that is pointed out in Corinthians in the searchlight of sharp criticism: when all prophesy, the secrets of the unbeliever's heart are disclosed and he will worship and declare "that God is really among you."[81]

81. I Cor. 14:25 (óntōs). Cf. Zech. 8:23. Once again we encounter the "being" of the Church in the light of the manifold "is with you" in the promise. The statement seems to be very obvious; but it has, nevertheless, become the object of intense study, since it appears about a hundred times already in the Old Testament. What kind of "being" (das Mitsein Jahwes — Yahweh's being-with) is intended in I Cor. 14:25? Is it simply observation of an indisputable reality, or is it a reality along a way of ever new responsibility, since the correlate of the Mitsein Jahwes is "walking with your God" (Mic. 6:8)? To ask the question is to answer it. See especially H.D. Preuss, "Ich will met Dir Sein!" Zeitschrift für Alttestamentliche Wissenschaft, 80, 1968, pp. 139ff., 172ff. This correlation does not do injury to the óntōs, but raises it above every misunderstanding.

CHAPTER SIX

THE BOUNDARIES OF THE CHURCH

A FTER REFLECTING ON THE MEANING OF CATHO-
licity, we have good reason to turn our attention to the
boundaries of the Church, since limitation raises the question
whether we are not attaching too much significance to catholicity by relating it to the whole, to universality, and to the
widest perspectives. Even apart from the problematic of catholicity and unity, we meet many people who do not belong to
the Church and do not want to. Their number exceeds the
number of those who have a place in the Church. Since the
reference to catholicity means that no one is excluded in the
proclamation of the Church in the world, what kind of "reality"
are we dealing with here? These questions about catholicity
and limitedness involve some of the deepest questions of ecclesiology. For it is a limitation of that fellowship which is
interested in the world, which seeks to relate all to the proclaimed salvation. In that light, the limitedness of the Church
seems to overshadow catholicity in a radical way. So it is not
surprising that in the history of theology and the Church there
has often been intense reflection on the boundaries of the
Church.

However, we also see that the boundaries which were designated sometimes acquired a certain self-evidence, because one
grew accustomed to the fact that there had always been belief
next to unbelief, believers next to unbelievers, and felt that
the situation would always remain so. But in this way, there
could scarcely be astonishment any more; and in this condition, one could hardly have much appreciation for Jesus, Who
marveled because of the unbelief of the men of Nazareth,
because of the resistances that arose right around Him (Mark
6:6). For Him, this unbelief is obviously anything but self-

131

evident, and recollection of the general rule that a prophet is not without honor except in his own country does not exclude amazement. Obviously, it is not an "explanation" that clarifies everything. Rather, the Lord confronts the limits of His thinking, His empathy. He does not understand this resistance. He does not understand what moves hearts here. Unbelief is seen as an alien way, a way other than the one that He intended and designated for them and where He waited for them to go with Him.[1] To live on the basis of self-evidence of unbelief next to belief is nothing else than to level the gospel and to attack the care and directedness of the proclamation of salvation. Once in a while we meet with a certain romanticization of the Church as a minority in reaction to the triumphalism of quantitative catholicity. Some say that the Church, because of her minority position, is called to take the lead along the way of God's dealings with the world.[2] Yet it is extremely important to reflect on and be concerned with that limitedness — but not apart from astonishment, as was the case with "someone" in the gospel who, in connection with "actual" resistances, asked why only a "few" would be saved (Luke 13:22f.; cf. Matt. 7:13f.). Even though we recall how Jesus reacted to this question — "strive to enter!" — it is impossible to acquiesce to the boundaries as if they were inevitable. We are speaking of those boundaries which we constantly run across in the vicinity of Jesus and with which He Himself was so often concretely confronted.[3] We find that many of the first circle of disciples no longer walked with him (John 6:66), and the smaller circle of his "brothers" also did not believe in him (7:5). Various boundaries and resistances become visible; and those boundaries often harden, becoming so fixed that apostolic, missionary zeal can come no further than individuals.[4]

Thus, we are automatically confronted with the relationship between this limitation *and* the *catholic* directedness of the gospel and the *catholicity* of the Church. The Church herself, in accordance with the Scriptures, has always spoken of the salva-

---

1. Cf. Jesus' astonishment at the faith of the centurion from Capernaum (Matt. 8:10), which is connected to Israel's unbelief.
2. Cf. *Ketters of Voortrekkers?* ed. H.A. Oberman, 1970, p. 38; and H. Küng, *De Christenheid als Minderheid*, 1966.
3. Cf. the Lord's question about faith on earth at the coming of the Son of man (Luke 18:8).
4. Rom. 11:14 *(kaì sốsõ tinàs ex autốn)*. Cf. also, however, I Cor. 9:19: "that I might win the more" *(hína toùs pleíonas kerdḗsõ)*.

tion of God for the world (John 3:16) and the reconciliation of the world (II Cor. 5:19). God, Who is the Savior of all men (I Tim. 4:10), has come with the wide perspective of peace and reconciliation for "all things, whether on earth or in heaven" (Col. 1:20). Christ is an expiation for our sins, "and not for ours only but also for the sins of the whole world" (I John 2:2). The words "not only but also" exceed particular limitations.[5] Do we not meet here with a perspective that connects the whole world to Christ, to the love of God for the whole world that has appeared in Him? What is the significance of Bavinck's statement that the work of Christ is of eternal value *intensively,* "but spreads also *extensively* to the whole world"? In this context, he says that the Church Fathers before Augustine usually spoke very "universalistically" about God's saving will.[6] In analyzing this aspect, he concludes that universalists win in quantity, but lose in quality; yet, Augustine does not want to deny the universal aspect, i.e., that "all men have much to

5. A. Kuyper combatted the universalistic appeal to this text by pointing out, among other things, that "expiation" does not, as in Rom. 3:25, indicate the means of expiation (by which the expiation is effected, *hilastêrion),* but the deed, the essence of expiation *(hilasmós;* cf. also I John 4:10), as Christ is the Way and the Truth ("inclusive of all expiation"). In other words, the passage is concerned not simply with our personal sins, but "also and even much more" with our imputed guilt in Adam in a fellowship of guilt with the whole world *(Uit het Woord,* II, I. *Dat de Genade Particulier is,* 1884, pp. 29ff.). The force of this argument is weakened already by the reference to I John 4:10: God's deed is love and expiation. Cf. *TDNT,* III, 317f. on the "setting aside of sin" as "the reality by which he [John] lives."

6. Bavinck, *Geref. Dog.,* III, 450. Bavinck speaks also of "universalistic" texts *(ibid.,* IV, 709) and of the calling to salvation, which is "for all without distinction the proof of God's unending love" *(ibid.,* IV, 6). Further study of universalism is very desirable in view of the unsatisfying attempts to minimize these texts (according to Kuyper, I John 2:2 is the "principal bulwark" of universalists, *op. cit.,* p. 31). H.N. Ridderbos *(Paul,* p. 337) speaks of the universalization of salvation and the universal character of the Church, of Christ's universal mercy (p. 338) and the universality of salvation revealed in Christ. When he speaks in this connection of a new limitation and, in a certain sense, of a new particularism (p. 340), that is a different "limitation" than is usually understood by "particularism." Cf. "No one is excluded, but neither does anyone belong to the people of God as a matter of course by virtue of birth, or by virtue of his humanity." However, this is not at all in conflict with the universality. If one wants to speak of "limitation" here, it is in any case of a totally different sort than every spatial limitation; thus, it is better not to speak of a new particularism here.

thank to Christ."[7] How then should we reflect on the "boundaries"? How do they determine our thinking and action, our feelings, and our expectations?

Inside and outside

It is perfectly understandable that some have often been concerned with boundaries. In the New Testament, we meet with very marked boundaries and distinctions. And when the Church's calling toward those who stand "outside" is accentuated, it is assumed that such an unmistakable standing outside is the case.[8] We read that believers and unbelievers have nothing in common (II Cor. 6:15) and that there is no agreement between the temple of God and idols (6:16 — *sunkatáthesis*). All of this ends in a "we" that is connected to being children of God. In many ways we meet with a concrete "outside" (cf. I John 2:19), with a living problematic of "inside" and "outside." It is of great importance to ask whether it is clear that this distinction is entirely different from discrimination. That question is even more urgent because of the way "I" and "we" often function in human life. From the history of this "we" in the Church, there are obviously many dangers; but, no matter how many dangers there may be, there is a different possibility in the vicinity of the Lord. There, while inside and outside do play a role in the proclamation of the gospel, there are no static, fixed distinctions or boundaries. Rather, it is essential to the gospel that it attempt to cross the boundaries. It does not come to rest with those who are inside, while losing sight of those who are outside.

That the gospel does not stop at a fixed state of affairs is clear, for our attention is called to two transitions, two ways of crossing boundaries. In Matt. 8:11-13, Christ speaks revealingly of two transitions: one from inside to outside (the sons of the Kingdom), and the other from outside to inside (many from east and west will sit at table with Abraham, Isaac, and

---

7. Bavinck, *Geref. Dog.*, III, 468. The Church has always been concerned with universality in connection with Christ's death, which is "of infinite worth and value, abundantly sufficient to expiate the sins of the whole world" (C.D., II, 3). Unbelief does not arise because of "any defect or insufficiency in the sacrifice offered by Christ" (II, 6). Cf. H.C., 37: Christ bore God's wrath "against the sin of the whole human race."

8. Cf. W.C. van Unnik, "Die Rücksicht auf die Reaktion der nicht-Christen als Motiv in der altchr. Paränese," *Judentum-Urchristentum-Kirche. Festschr. J. Jeremias*, pp. 221ff.

Jacob in the Kingdom of heaven)! Whoever reflects on the boundaries must also fix his eyes on this critical aspect. Then he can also discover that the proclamation of the gospel does not halt in the face of boundaries, but is unceasingly concerned with them. Nowhere is there mention of a neutral analysis, a fixed state of affairs, or a closed situation. That would be nothing less than an annulment of the gospel, as with Jonah, who abandons Nineveh and its sins, setting it beyond the favor of Yahweh. Jonah never trusted God to respect boundaries, since he knew of God's grace, mercy, slowness to anger, and repentance (Jonah 4:2); and he has no "interest" in the way God's action with Nineveh will end, but would rather die (4:3). In the same way, the Pharisees felt no compulsion to weep for the multitudes; they wrote them off with an anathema. They did not have the same emotion that filled Christ about sheep without a shepherd and moved Him to weep for a city (Luke 19:41; cf. Phil. 3:18).

It is extremely dangerous to write off all emotion too quickly as "sentimental," since that emotion makes it possible to keep reflection on the boundaries from lacking commitment. Nothing legitimate can be said about inside and outside apart from the light of the reversal that is intended, apart from the open situation.[9] The reality of being outside can never be isolated; it stands in the light of commission and perspective. Therefore, the proclamation is precisely the opposite of discrimination. It forbids acquiescence to a state of affairs that is supposedly unchangeable. Where this commandment is disregarded, one misunderstands not only the outside but also the inside. The inside is no longer understood in the light of the original experience of the Church — viz., that her life can be explained only from her own transition from outside to inside, the transition of mercy! Apart from this fundamental recollection of one's own transition, every "ascertainment" of who is outside becomes boundless self-exaltation (Col. 1:13; I Pet. 2:9; Lev. 19:34; Deut. 24:17ff.; Ezek. 16:1ff.). So, if Gentile Christians

9. It is a profound misunderstanding to think that one cannot take the open situation absolutely seriously any more because of election. Rather, it is meaningful to do so precisely because of the nature of election. See Ridderbos, *Paul*, p. 350: the Church belongs not to a definite number, but to Christ! For the "open situation" see further *idem, Aan de Romeinen,* particularly p. 230, on the continuing openness on account of the teleological character of God's unlimited power. Only in this way is it possible to understand that the proclamation is not contrary to "divine election," but is based in it. Cf. my *Divine Election,* 1958, chapter 7.

exalt themselves without remembering their transition, then that other transition from inside to outside comes into view: that they will be cut off from the richness of the olive tree (Rom. 11:17ff.). Then those who are inside could come to be "outsiders"! From the nature of the gospel, the "inside" can never become a self-sufficient, introverted prerogative that is "turned in upon itself" *(incurvatus in se)*. For then all the perspectives of the Old and New Testaments would be obscured, and the prophetic vision of the procession of all nations toward the inside, to the house of the Lord (Isa. 2:2-5), would not be understood, and neither would the vision of those who come from afar, thrilling the hearts of all who look upon it (Isa. 60:4-9), because of which the gates shall be open continually and "day and night they shall not be shut" (60:11). To misunderstand inside and outside is to lack appreciation for the glory of the "catholic" perspective of the ten men "from the nations of every tongue," who "take hold of the robe of a Jew, saying, 'Let us go with you, for we have heard that God is with you' " (Zech. 8:23).

The boundaries here cannot be compared to those between two lands, which are simply there and can be outlined on a map. It is impossible to stop at the boundaries of the Church, as if they were an accomplished fact, and then to turn to internal problems, to the Church's riches and joy, her calling, and her eschatological perspective. Israel believed that Jesus did not respect the boundaries, since he was a friend of tax collectors and sinners (Matt. 11:19; cf. Mark 2:15ff.). To them, this blurred the boundaries, since it was not clear beforehand in which environs Jesus would be found,[10] and His attitude had a disastrous influence on the attitude of His disciples. Jesus' attitude became clear in the concreteness of the commandments to love one's neighbor[11] and to love one's enemies (Matt. 5:43ff.; cf. Rom. 12:14, 20). These commands point to a peculiar picture of the boundaries.[12] To stop at these boundaries and to with-

---

10. Cf. Simon the Pharisee's judgment about Jesus, since He (apparently) does not know who (a sinner, Luke 7:39) has touched Him. Cf. also Luke 15:2.

11. The "neighbor" is not qualified as the man who belongs to one's own circle, but is unqualified; he is the man who is in need (Luke 10:25-37).

12. Cf. *TDNT*, VI, 316, on the "universalizing of the concept of *neighbor*" in contrast to *ecumenical* association with men. G. Hasenhüttl (*Charisma. Ordnungsprinzip der Kirche*, 1969, pp. 31ff.) speaks of *Entgrenzung* ("removal of boundaries"), a word that expresses the peculiarity of the problem of "boundaries."

draw from the others would be possible only if one radically misunderstood that the first can become last and the last first (Luke 13:30). Hence, the relation of the Church to the many who are outside the Church, *extra ecclesiam*, is of far-reaching significance for the whole of her thinking and acting. A daily reality is at stake here in all our relationships in the one world, where distance and isolation are not possible. When boundaries do become visible in the New Testament, they are not concerned with the world "in general,"[13] but with the critical disclosure of the situation inside the Church: the command is given not to associate with the idolater and reviler, "if he bears the name of brother."[14] So, the boundaries between the "Church" and the "world" cannot be determined *a priori*. The whole gospel of transition is at stake here and, in Corinth, Paul puts judgment under discipline: "For what have I to do with judging outsiders? Is it not those inside the Church whom you are to judge? God judges those outside."[15]

Boundaries and judgment

The boundaries bring us into contact with living men whose lives are characterized either by quiet rejection or by an unambiguous "No," and there are very different motives and backgrounds involved here. It would a misunderstanding of reality and of "freedom of religion" to blur these boundaries and to have no interest in them. But has not the Church, in fact, often made a judgment — and even a condemnation — about others? For being inside or outside is connected with salvation. So, do not experience and the *credo* of the Church involuntarily signify an "excommunication," or discrimination, of those who do not believe and are thus outside the Church? In light of the history of the Church, it is difficult to deny that this impression has often been awakened. Even though one hears that there is a place and a dwelling for all peoples under the dome of the Church, "which overarches the whole earth like God's firmament," and that "the mother-heart of the Church" is spacious enough to embrace every development,[16]

13. Cf. I Cor. 5:10: "since then you would need to go out of the world." Paul does not want to suggest that at all *(ou pántōs)*.
14. Cf. I Cor. 5:11. The concern here is "the order in the Church" (H. Conzelmann, *Der erste Brief an die Korinther*, 1969, p. 121). Belief occurs *in* the world; cf. John 17:20.
15. I Cor. 5:12f. On God's knowledge, cf. Jer. 11:20; I Thess. 2:4.
16. Thus Pius XI in *Mit Brennender Sorge*, 1937.

one nevertheless understood that a condition was also accentuated — i.e., that one had to place oneself under her protection in order to participate in her riches.

All thinking and speaking about real boundaries, although legitimate, contains the danger of a rash and haughty judgment on others. Can the Church not begin to look like the Pharisees who "trusted in themselves that they were righteous and despised others" (Luke 18:9 — *toùs loipoùs*)? In many situations, this question has been answered in the affirmative by those outside the Church. Even if we understand that such a judgment has nothing to do with the Church that Christ had in mind, the question remains whether the essence of the Church does not inevitably lead to such judgment of others. The question is all the more urgent because judgment seems to be passed on their lot, their status before God, and their present and future. Was an anathema not pronounced implicitly in the Church? Is it possible to differentiate structurally between this judgment by the Church and the anathema on "this crowd, who do not know the law" (John 7:49 — *epáratoi eisin*)? Can such a judgment about men, whether explicit or implicit, be anything other than Pharisaism, haughtiness, and discrimination?

These boundaries of the Church automatically bring us to the statement of the Lord: "Judge not, that you be not judged. For with the judgment you pronounce you will be judged, and the measure you give will be the measure you get" (Matt. 7:1f.). In what framework can we mention a judgment that does not have those fateful consequences, since judgment cannot be isolated from one's own life "before the face of God"?[17] Is judgment not a divine privilege in opposition to all human presumption to judge others and to pass definitive judgment on them?[18] Where we are speaking of men rather than things and events, does Paul's admonition not apply: "Therefore do not pronounce judgment before the time, before the Lord comes, who will bring to light the things now hidden in darkness and will disclose the purposes of the heart"?[19] Büchsel says that because

17. Cf. also the connection in Rom. 2:1-4. Cf. H.N. Ridderbos, *Aan de Romeinen*, pp. 51f., on the man who judges "especially the sinners named in 1:18-32" and on the "attitude of onlookers."
18. Cf. James 4:11 (judging a brother, along with speaking evil against him); Rom. 14:4, 10; Jer. 11:20.
19. I Cor. 4:5. Cf. the withdrawal of vengeance from man in Rom. 12:19. Cf. H.N. Ridderbos, *Aan de Romeinen*, p. 285, on "wanting to sit in God's judgment seat, not standing in awe of the divine privilege."

this admonition not to judge is so emphatic, "the Church cannot practice discipline with merciless severity. It means that Church discipline must take predominant, if not exclusive, use of means which promote edification and pastoral care."[20] Nevertheless, the questions remain whether the *credo* of the Church does not imply judgment and knowledge, and how it can be separated from the kind of judgment that falls under the verdict of the gospel. Is it possible to see the Church's boundaries in the light of the prophetic commission to Jeremiah: "I have made you an assayer and tester among my people, that you may know and assay their ways" (Jer. 6:27)? Does that assaying not extend also to the many who are "outside"? Is there not still a judgment — even if it is not concretized or applied individually — that is closely connected to the Church's boundaries?[21]

Extra ecclesiam nulla salus

These questions have acquired extraordinary relevance today in the well-known, traditional dictum connecting membership in the Church directly to salvation: "outside the Church [there is] no salvation" *(extra ecclesiam nulla salus [est])*." Summarizing the problem of the Church's boundaries in this way has caused much annoyance and resistance, because one feels that it contains the height of ecclesiastical haughtiness.[22] The radicalness of these words is not simply that they testify in the world to the salvation of God, but that this testimony is made concrete by belonging to the Church. Has the Church here gone the way of a radical institutionalization of the mystery of redemption in order to have a clear-cut criterion with which to judge men? And does that usage not give the impression that it was the Church that, as a sort of border police, had salvation at her disposal, making everyone dependent on her?

Enormous dangers undeniably threaten here. Not unjustly, these dangers call to mind John's story about meeting someone who was casting out demons. John forbade the man on this

---

20. *TDNT*, III, 439.
21. The problem has been discussed frequently in connection with the anathema in the Decrees of Trent. Does it concern the *person* or the *error?* On the *damnamus* cf. H.W. Gensichen, *Damnamus. Die Verwerfung von Irrlehre bei Luther und in Luthertum des 16. Jahrh.*, 1955, pp. 145ff.
22. Cf. the judgment of J.J. Rousseau *(Social Contract,* IV, 8): "anyone who dares to say 'Outside the Church there can be no salvation,' should be banished from the State...."

basis: "he was not following us" (Mark 9:38). John directed interest not so much to what happened — the driving out of
demons — as to the person who effected this triumphant event.
We need not think that the strong consciousness of one's own
group was in this situation totally isolated from Christ,[23] but
isolation did occur, as is clear from Christ's reaction. He broke
the criterion to pieces: "Do not forbid him; for no one who does
a mighty work in my name will be able soon after to speak evil
of me. For he that is not against us is for us" (9:39ff.). True,
Christ did not distinguish between following Him and following
His disciples: "Do not forbid him; for he that is not against
you is for you."[24] Nevertheless, He did point out that an impure
standard of judgment — conclusions from "not following us" —
was being used. It is not so simple to make a clear judgment
about situations in which Christ's name is used and to employ
legitimately the categories of inside and outside. Misunderstanding is obviously possible, and the consequence is a blurred
insight into the powers of the Kingdom. Since "following Jesus"
embraces the promise of not walking in darkness (John 8:12),
judging negatively here is the most serious thing that one can
imagine. Who can avoid recalling the disciples' fierce judgment
on the Samaritans who did not want to receive Jesus? Jesus rejected that judgment with a rebuke (Luke 9:51-56). Fire from
heaven does not appear, since Jesus has more "difficulty" with
it than do the disciples![25] The Church receives an urgent warning here against thoughtlessness and rashness. Hence, the recommendation has been made that the *extra ecclesiam* might better
be replaced by a testimony that directly corresponds to Scripture:
extra Christum nulla salus.

Nevertheless, it would be unjust to designate *a priori* the
background of the phrase *extra ecclesiam nulla salus* as ecclesiastical haughtiness. Rather, these words contain an insight into
the relatedness of Christ and the Church. One is impressed that

23. Cf. the differences between Mark and Luke. Mark reads: "because he
    was not following us *(ēkoloúthei hēmin),*" while Luke (9:49) reads:
    "because he does not follow with us *(akolouthei meth' hēmōn)."* The
    new Dutch translation, 1969, translates the Lukan version as follows:
    "because he does not follow you with us."
24. Luke 9:50. Mark 9:40 reads "us" instead of "you." We come across "me"
    in Luke 11:23 and Matt. 12:30 (with me and against me as gathering
    and scattering).
25. Cf. Jonah with regard to the hundred and twenty thousand children
    of Nineveh, where Jonah could do what Yahweh could not find it in
    His heart to do (4:11).

the Church in the New Testament was not simply an historical phenomenon, but was described from her essential relationship to God and Christ: the people of God, the flock of the Shepherd, and His body. Although no identification was intended, one wanted to say that salvation is not found along a strictly individual or solitary way of personal piety, but along the way of the Church of the Lord. A voice sounded, calling the one flock to one discipleship in fellowship and relatedness. Thus, the proclamation of the gospel automatically took the form of an invitation to participate in the life and fellowship of the Church. And so, the preaching of Pentecost ended with baptism (Acts 2:38, 41) and with the addition of about 3000 souls (2:41 — *prosetéthēsan*). This addition was described as an act of God, an addition to "those who were being saved" (2:47). Becoming a believer is made visible by partaking in the fellowship of the Church. That Church is disclosed in prayer and perseverance, in the breaking of bread, and in fellowship (2:44ff.). The proclamation was a summons to go together along a new way, and it contains something of the Old Testament summons to Israel: "Let us go to the house of the Lord!" (Ps. 122:1).

In the whole of the New Testament, the relationship to Christ has everything to do with the Church. When Paul persecutes the Church, Christ calls that a persecution of Himself (Acts 9:4f.). "Gathering" with Him is also mentioned, and directly opposite to it is "scattering" (Luke 11:23). Christ brings together the children of God who are scattered abroad (John 11:52 — *sunagágē eis hén*), and the outlook on salvation is always connected to fellowship, to discipleship, to the one Church. These connections undoubtedly form the background of the words that found acceptance already in the ancient Church: "outside the Church there is no salvation." The original intention was certainly not to put *extra ecclesiam* in place of *extra Christum*. The intention was not to push Christ into the background for the sake of an institutionalistic pretension, but to attract attention to the way Christ gathers His Church. Although that does not yet prove the legitimacy and clarity of the dictum, one cannot judge it rightly unless one also honors this motif.[26]

This dictum is inseparably connected to the name of Cyprian, and his considerations clearly show that he is concerned with

26. Cf. on the dictum my *The Second Vatican Council and the New Catholicism*, 1965, pp. 188ff. At present I am giving a summary with various amplifications.

the relationship of the Church to Christ. The Church, according to him, is the house of God, the bride of Christ. She is full of great light, of the stream of life, which gives blessings as it discharges itself into the world.[27] She is the mother in ever new fruitfulness. Christ and His Church are so closely joined to each other that one cannot partake of Christ and His salvation if one is not joined to the Church, His Church. Whoever breaks with her cuts himself off from the promises to the Church as an alien, an enemy, and a worldling. The decision is made at the boundaries of the Church: "you cannot have God for your Father unless you have the Church for your Mother."[28] To clarify this, Cyprian uses the image of the ark: "If there was any escape for one who was outside the ark of Noah, there will be as much for one who is found to be outside the Church." There was only one ark, so the consequence is clear. According to the analogy of the ark, the Church is the place of salvation. Who could have a part in that salvation outside the Church, even if he were to die as a martyr?[29] One cannot enter the Kingdom of heaven if one abandons the Church. Thus, the *extra ecclesiam nulla salus* stands at the center of Cyprian's passionate admonitions that speak about the richness and uniqueness of the Church.

It would be incorrect to see this as only a form of haughty clericalism, particularism, or unspiritual triumphalism. Cyprian was concerned with the Church of Christ through the Holy Spirit, with the riches of grace and fellowship that are received in her;[30] he thinks of true discipleship, of the sheep of the one

27. Cyprian, *De unitate Ecclesiae*, 5.
28. *Ibid.*, 6: "*Habere non potest Deum patrem qui ecclesiam non habet matrem.*" Cf. "If a man does not keep this unity, he is not keeping the law of God; he has broken faith with the Father and the Son, he is cut off from life and salvation." One finds a variation at the conclusion of Leo XIII's encyclical *Satis Cognitum:* "they can never be reckoned among God's children if they do not accept Jesus Christ as their brother and, at the same time, the Church as their mother." Leo appeals to what Augustine says against the Donatists: "Therefore, most beloved, persevere; and let all hold fast unanimously to God, Who is your Father, and to the Church, which is your Mother."
29. Cyprian, *op. cit.*, 14.
30. Cf. J.N. Bakhuizen van den Brink (*Cyprianus van Carthago*, 1958, pp. 22ff.), who lays strong emphasis on this (not an antithesis with the "Church of the Spirit"). See the same sort of words of praise for the Church with Clement of Alexandria in, among other places, F. Hofmann, "Die Kirche bei Clemens von Alexandrien," *Vitae et Veritati. Festschr. für K. Adam*, 1956, pp. 11ff. For the dangers in this view of the Church,

flock. Hence, Cyprian did not lack awareness of the essential, pneumatic aspect of the Church,[31] but was concerned with the concretization in the visible Church: salvation is to be found in the concrete, institutional Church on earth. Thus, the dictum *extra ecclesiam nulla salus* is connected to a certain identification. Cyprian could no longer speak abstractly about God and faith, since God's plan of salvation has taken on form in the concrete Church.[32] There is no ambiguity to the boundary between inside and outside. One can know where one is headed with respect to one's salvation! Later, while honoring Cyprian's motives, some have asked whether it was legitimate to draw such far-reaching conclusions from the connection between Shepherd and flock. In spite of all the praise for the Lord, was the Church not allowed a certain independence? And was the freedom of divine grace not limited? Although it was certainly not Cyprian's intention to say that the Church "has become an individual self next to God,"[33] an exclusivism could arise from this identification that draws boundaries not drawn by Christ Himself.[34]

Cyprian's views became established in the Church's thought, confession, and practice. Although the Western Church did not follow him in his rejection of the validity of heretic baptism,[35] there was hardly any hesitation about concretely localizing the *extra*. The clear criterion of inside and outside func-

---

cf. G. Klein, "Die hermeneutische Struktur des Kirchenbegriffs bei Cyprian," *Z. f. Kirch. Gesch.*, 1957, pp. 48ff.; J. Faber, *Vestigium Ecclesiae*, 1969, especially pp. 30ff.

31. Cf. Bakhuizen van den Brink, *Handb. der Kerkgeschiedenis*, I, 1965, p. 121.

32. Calvin took up this motif clearly when he wrote that God is pleased to have His sons gathered into the bosom of the Church; one may not put asunder what God has joined together. Therefore, for those to whom He is Father the Church is a Mother (*Inst.*, IV, 1, 1). Cf. H. Bavinck, *Magnalia Dei*, p. 493: "in the good sense."

33. A. Adam, *Lehrbuch der Dogmengeschichte*, I, 172.

34. For example, the conclusion that the historical boundaries have an eschatological character and are "demonstrable" in the institution and bishops (cf. Klein, *op. cit.*, p. 67). Cf. also A. Harnack, *History of Dogma*, II, 113ff., on the Church as the condition for salvation and a means of grace.

35. B. Neunheuser, *Handb. der Dogmengeschichte*, IV, 1956, pp. 49ff. There is an element in the attitude of the Western Church to heretic baptism that later became of great significance in the acknowledgment of what is possible *extra ecclesiam*. The problem was acute in the Middle Ages with respect to ordination. Cf. M.D. Knowles, *Geschiedenis van de Kerk*, III, 1968, pp. 168ff.

tioned everywhere in the Middle Ages. Jews, Gentiles, schismatics, and heretics were outside.[36] The decree for the Jacobites, which has often been seen as the most rigorous description, placed belonging or not belonging to the Church under the threat of final, eschatological seriousness.[37] Although "excommunication" from the Roman Catholic Church is not definitive, since conversion is possible,[38] the present does stand in the light of this clear exclusivity. There is no subtlety, no account of the background or motives for remaining *extra ecclesiam,* nor any reflection on the possible guilt of the Church itself. Therefore, very different groups of people can be collected under the same common denominator, and they appear as shadowy forms outside the Church and outside salvation. This explains why no other earlier pronouncement has been so critically spoken of as this one.[39] Although the pneumatic elements of Cyprian's ecclesiology did continue to play a role, the dictum nevertheless led to a simple, hard conclusion because of the identity of the flock and the ark with the *ecclesia unica Romana.*[40]

The new interpretation of the extra ecclesiam

Although there are traces of a less exclusive view of the *extra,* and although a timid attempt is made here and there to take account of the disposition and motives for remaining outside the Church,[41] these are only incidental traces in the general view through the centuries. The Lord's word of rebuke when the disciples want to bid fire to come down from heaven

36. The formulation traces back to Fulgentius of Ruspe, who had already named these four groups.

37. Denz., 714. See the text in my *Second Vatican Council,* p. 189.

38. Denz., 714 *(TCT,* 165): "unless before the end of life they are joined to the Church."

39. Cf. Y. Congar ("Hors de l'Eglise, pas de Salut," *Sainte Eglise,* 1963, pp. 417ff.), who calls Fulgentius' enumeration, "the most explicit, indeed, the most brutal."

40. Denz., 469 *(TCT,* 154): "it is absolutely necessary for the salvation of every human creature to be subject to the Roman Pontiff *(subesse Romano Pontifice)."* With regard to the Greeks it is said: "If, therefore, the Greeks or others say that they are not committed to Peter and to his successors, they necessarily say that they are not of the sheep of Christ, as the Lord says in John that there is one fold and one shepherd" (see John 10:16) (Denz., 468; *TCT,* 153). Cf. Congar, *op. cit.,* p. 421; Denz., 570b; 1000; 1473.

41. According to Congar *(op. cit.,* pp. 422, 443), the credit goes especially to Abelard — with his "analysis of the bad conscience" — and, after him, to Thomas Aquinas.

(Luke 9:54f.) has not restrained the Church from speaking of that fire in a generalized condemnation of many, many men. Only in a much later time can one speak of a real, far-reaching change, a reversal whereby living men again become visible and their background and motives are no longer seen simply as irrelevant. There can be no doubt that this change is far-reaching, as is clear from the emphatic rejection of the most rigorous attitude. Cyprian's dictum, which was taken over by the Church, can be spoken of as a "dubious" dictum, a hard saying.[42] We are told that the formulation can no longer be understood as "condemning some person, as concrete as he is, to hell," but only as a confirmation of "the exclusive value" of the Church as the divinely empowered institution of salvation for all men.[43] Some even point out that it is no longer justified to understand the *extra* in the earlier exclusive sense because of the famous letter from the Holy Office in 1949, which rejected the standpoint that the *extra ecclesiam catholicam nulla salus* should finally be taken literally and earnestly again. The consequence is that anyone who holds this viewpoint faces excommunication.[44] This is even more remarkable because Cyprian's words were not taken back and still play a role with regard to the boundaries of the Church. They fall into the sphere of interpretation.

The great shift is chiefly that, while the *extra* was a clear-cut indicator of those who did or did not partake of salvation, this is now no longer the case. This shift is an extremely fascinating aspect of the history of the Church. It has been credited to the widening horizon of later times and, with respect to Rome, to the impression made by the great multitude since the Reformation who no longer belong to the sheepfold of Rome. According to Bavinck, exclusivism could no longer be maintained because of the facts, and "concessions" were gradu-

---

42. B.A. Willems, *Verlossing in Kerk en Wereld*, 1967, p. 105. Cf. p. 109 on Fulgentius' "disastrous catalogue." Cf. further his "Who Belongs to the Church"?, *Concilium*, 1, 1965, pp. 131ff.

43. Congar, *op. cit.*, p. 444.

44. *Ibid.*, p. 420: "Saint Cyprian's formula is no longer held — it is not even permitted to be held — in exactly the sense that he who conceived it intended." The letter of the Holy Office was originally published in the *American Ecclesiastical Review*, Oct., 1952, pp. 307-11, but has now been incorporated in the new Denzinger-Schönmetzer (3866-3873) and appears in English translation in *TCT*, 266-280. Leonard Feeney was excommunicated as a rigorist — "obstinate against the warnings of ecclesiastical authority" — on February 4, 1953.

ally being made.[45] In any case, it is incorrect to derive the change from the widening horizon that has occurred in our time. In the Roman Catholic Church, at least, we can perceive a decisive change of climate already in the 19th century in the pronouncements of Pope Pius IX. He brings a surprising new viewpoint to the fore. Despite the shadows that fell over Abelard's motifs, they are taken up, specifically where attention is asked for the background and motives in the lives of those who are *extra ecclesiam*. Although Pius was convinced that the Church is the ark of salvation, and although it is a "well-known Catholic dogma" *(notissimum catholicum dogma)* that no one can be saved outside the Catholic Church,[46] a view with more nuances is adopted in connection with the question of whether one is outside the Church because of obstinacy or because of "invincible ignorance."[47] Thus, the "psychology" of the outsider is important.

Although Pius IX does not doubt the exceptional significance of the Church and although he wants to limit excessively strong expectations,[48] the simplicity of the judgment nevertheless fades away. From then on, one had to take invincible ignorance, obedience to God's commandments by keeping "natural law," and a pure and honest life into account. Thus, a wider perspective for the attainment of salvation exists here than in the identification of catholicity and the Roman Catholic Church.[49] These new possibilities have since been affirmed and sanctioned by the rejection of rigorism in 1949. The dictum is maintained

---

45. H. Bavinck, *Geref. Dog.,* IV, 295.
46. Denz., 1677; *TCT,* 178.
47. Denz., 1647. Already in the 18th century, nuances appear in Roman Catholic catechisms with regard to whether one is or is not guilty. Cf. M. Ramsauer, "Die Kirche in den Katechismen," *Zeitschrift für Kath. Theol.,* 1951, pp. 335ff. F. Hofmann *(Der Kirchenbegriff des h. Augustin,* 1933, pp. 233ff.) points out how little this aspect is present in Augustine, because he did not have any realization of the "persistent credulity of a heretic"; he felt he had to assume obstinacy when one remained outside in spite of the evidentness of the Church and the truth.
48. Cf. Denz., 1646 *(TCT,* 173) on the destructive error that has already spread (1854!) of those "who think there is good hope for the eternal salvation of all those who in no wise live in the true Church of Christ." This was later repeated at Vatican I against relativism (Denz., 1717).
49. Cf. L. Smith, "Extra Ecclesiam nulla Salus," *Werkgem. Kath. Theol.,* 1951, p. 6.

as an infallible pronouncement,[50] but one must understand the dogma in the sense that the Church gives to it and not according to a private judgment.[51]

It is not necessary for us to go into the subtle problems that come up here.[52] Our interest is in the new and wider concern for what occurs outside the Church. The continuing stress on the necessity of the Church for salvation does not detract from the wider outlook, but makes it even more striking.[53] The Second Vatican Council declared that the Spirit of Christ does not refrain from using other churches as means of salvation.[54] One cannot maintain that "actually" everything has remained the same.[55] For what was of decisive significance earlier is now surrounded by questions. Institutional membership in the Church is no longer identical to participation in salvation. Possibilities

50. Denz.-Schönm., 3866 (TCT, 267): "infallible dictum" (infallibile effatum). It is "among the truths that the Church has always taught and will always teach."

51. The problem was precisely that Feeney felt he had to stand up for the clear boundaries of the Church in opposition to every "lenient" interpretation, which caused uncertainty at the boundaries. Feeney is opposed as a "defender of the faith" (defensor fidei) because he does not hesitate to assail the Church's authority (Denz.-Schönm., 3873).

52. We recall the well-known problematic of the votum, or desire, which played a role in the letter of 1949—not only in the sense of an explicit, but also in the sense of an implicit desire.

53. Cf. my Nabetrachting op het Concilie, pp. 19f., on the necessitas medii ("the necessity of means"). Cf. the discussion in 1870 on the question of whether one can speak of a medium ordinarium, an ordinary means, in view of the suggestion that there are still other means (in F. van der Horst, Das Schema über die Kirche auf dem 1. Vatik. Konzil, 1967, p. 218).

54. "Non renuit tamquam salutis mediis" (Decree on Ecumenism, DV II, p. 346). Cf. DV II, p. 345, on incorporation into Christ through baptism. E. Fischer (Kirche und Kirchen nach Vatik. II, 1967, p. 74) sees a revocation here of Mystici Corporis Christi, which does postulate this "renuit": the Spirit "refuses (renuit) to dwell with sanctifying grace in members that are wholly severed from the body" (Denz., 2288; TCT, 258).

55. Mystici Corporis Christi's statement in 1943 about the impossibility of being certain of salvation outside the Church is taken from the invitation to Protestants for Vatican I (cf. Denz.-Schönm., 3821 and 2999). When Rahner ("Membership of the Church," Theological Investigations, II, 1963, 51) understands the "apparent harshness of these statements" in the sense that one's theme was the Church's essence — with the result that one did not reflect on the positive possibilities of salvation outside the Church — we may ask whether one had not actually reflected here constantly with a negative conclusion!

arise for "relations" not dreamed of earlier.[56] This applies not only to ecumenism, but also to the many others who once were grouped under the same anathema.[57] In order not to relativize the Church and her function, the words remain standing, but they are elucidated in a way that takes away their exclusivism.

Anyone who feels that this is a specifically Roman Catholic problem and therefore quickly rejects the interpretation as erroneous should remember that the *extra* has also played a role in Protestant churches. We meet the literal words of the dictum in the Belgic Confession, where the Church is described as the holy congregation of those who are saved. To this is added: "and outside of it there is no salvation" (Art. 28). There has been much difference of opinion about the meaning of these words. Is ecclesiastical exclusivism present here? How does this "outside" function in the Reformed view of the Church? The statement in the Belgic Confession is not isolated. The Second Helvetic Confession of 1562 denies that one can live "before God" *(coram Deo)* if one does not have fellowship with the Church, but separates oneself from her.[58] And just as with Cyprian, it maintains that "outside the ark" there is no salvation. The Geneva Catechism speaks of damnation and ruin outside the Church in contrast to the forgiveness of sins, in which one participates "inside" the Church.[59] Even though it can be said at the same time that there is no salvation outside Christ,[60] the Church continuously plays an important role; hence, a question about the significance of the *extra* arises. In general, the Reformed churches have been of the opinion that this statement was not intended in an exclusivistic sense. But can the many who are "outside the Church," outside every church, be expected to hear the words in any other way than they sound: *extra ecclesiam nulla salus?*

Extra ecclesiam or extra Christum?

Thus, the question arose whether these words were indeed

56. *Lumen Gentium (DV II,* p. 33): "joined to her" *(cum ea conjunguntur").* Cf. G. Barauna, *De Kerk van Vaticanum II,* 1966, p. 647.
57. Cf. B.A. Willems, *Verlossing in Kerk en Wereld,* 1967, p. 108.
58. Second Helvetic Confession, chapter 17: "we deny that those can live before God who do not stand in fellowship with the true Church of God, but separate themselves from it."
59. "Catechism of the Church of Geneva," in *Library of Christian Classics,* XXII, p. 104 (in connection with the question: "Why do you subjoin the forgiveness of sins to the Church?").
60. The Scots Confession, chapter 16.

intended so radically and so exclusively. Were they final words, or were they penultimate words that were still subject to "interpretation"? Would it not be desirable to replace the *extra ecclesiam nulla salus* by *extra Christum nulla salus*, in order to be directly linked to the preaching of the New Testament about the only name (Acts 4:12) and the only way (John 14:6)? The question was asked in 1917 by C.M. Buizer in the Reformed Churches of Holland, later by H. Kraemer, and emphatically in our time by Hans Küng.[61] Küng wants to analyze the formula in dogmatics "in its narrowness and ambiguity," in order to show that salvation is *in Christ*. Proclamation should no longer use the old formulation, because it is "an ambiguous formula that is detrimental to the Church's service." The ambiguity has "misled many Catholics and non-Catholics alike" and is usually interpreted as intolerance.[62] Moreover, it is a negative axiom; it must be abandoned in order to say clearly where salvation is to be sought and found. This confessional clarity is indeed of the highest importance, for the Church is responsible also for the impression that her words make. Too much "further interpretation" must be avoided. Clarity was present earlier because of the institutional usage.[63] But later, further elucidation became necessary;[64] and so, the call today is to speak unambiguously in order to avoid any misunderstanding.

That there is a problem in the *extra,* especially in light of the past, is clear. This is clear, for example, from the formulation in the Westminster Confession, which, while speaking of the "visible Church," says: "out of which there is no *ordinary* possibility of Salvation."[65] We do not come across this nuance in the other confessions any more than in the Roman Catholic formulations. In general, one was satisfied with a non-exclusive

61. C.M. Buizer, *Een Aanslag op de Gewetensvrijheid in de Geref. Kerken,* 1918; H. Kraemer, *Het Vergeten Ambt in de Kerk,* 1962³, p. 128; H. Küng, "Extra Ecclesiam Nulla Salus," *Ex Auditu Verbi,* 1965, pp. 87ff.; and *The Church,* pp. 313ff.
62. Küng, *The Church,* p. 316.
63. Cf. the earlier accent: "outside which *no one at all (nullus omnino)* is saved" (Denz., 430; *TCT,* 151).
64. That is also the case, for instance, with K. Barth (*C.D.,* I/2, pp. 214f.). He adopts the words in the sense of "outside the circumference described by this meeting." Cf. p. 217: "by belonging to Christ we belong to all who belong to Him." These last words, particularly, contain a clear aspect of interpretation, since the starting point is no longer exclusively the institutional form of the *ecclesia*.
65. Westminster Confession, chapter 25, 2: *extra quam quidem ordinarie fieri nequit, ut quivis salutem consequatur.*

interpretation. The words were maintained in order to accentuate the significance of the Church along the way to salvation; therefore, one continued to speak of a certain "necessity" of joining oneself to the Church.[66] The dictum was placed in the context of the calling to follow and to serve Christ with the Church.[67] Evidently, a new formulation was not felt to be necessary, since it was clear from the whole life of the Church that one did not want to speak institutionally and exclusively. A short, traditional formulation is also, naturally, easier than a new one with many nuances. But, as a matter of fact, there is greater interest today in the problem of boundaries, and that interest concerns the others, the *many others*.

Extra ecclesiam does not in itself involve discrimination, since it corresponds to a free, negative choice with regard to the Church. Speaking about the boundaries of the Church can indicate a refusal to annex the others. It is necessary to analyze the resistance at the boundaries, without minimizing the depth of that resistance. The Church must understand the background and motives, whether conscious or unconscious, of that *extra*.[68] For we are speaking of people who live in the same life as Christians do. They participate in suffering and disappointment, in unsolved questions and mysteries, and also, sometimes, in problems of theodicy. Obviously, the Church, in proclaiming the gospel to all, must ask herself whether and to what extent she herself has been a hindrance for those who remained outside. Does standing outside always signify a stumbling over the

---

66. Cf. *Humani Generis* (Denz., 2319; *TCT*, 281) against those who reduce the necessity of membership in the Church to an empty formula *(vana formula)*. The Hungarian Confession (K. Müller, *Bekenntnisschriften*, p. 426) also says that the Church is necessary *(hanc Ecclesiam necesse est)*. See also the Belgic Confession, Article 28, in opposition to all isolation.

67. The emphasis in the Reformed confessions and in Rome on the significance of the Church *along with* maintenance of the *extra* is interesting for the problem of interpretation. Usage of traditional words, but with a shift in their signification, occurs also in the Reformation — also with regard to Christ's descent. Hence, one must be cautious about judging Roman Catholic "interpretations" too quickly as false reinterpretations.

68. Sometimes one cannot get any further than an impression of the reasons, since the deepest motives do not always come up for discussion. There are only a few witnesses like that of Bertrand Russell, *Why I am not a Christian*, 1967, who gives a wide-ranging list of reasons. The Church plays a role here (a brake on progress), as do the "good maxims" of Christ, which are not put into practice by Christians.

skandalon of the gospel? Or is it possible that the Church, as well as theology, is also responsible for the fact that other *skandala* have played a significant role?[69] For instance, the division of the Church can be influential, because this fellowship seems neither impressive nor new. So, at the boundaries, the first requirement of all is that the Church reflect on how she testifies to her faith and makes it concrete in her whole existence.

It is certainly not a symptom of false humility when one's eyes are opened more and more for this boundary problem, which is revealed already in the New Testament.[70] No one is capable of searching out the manifold reasons for which men "of like nature" (James 5:17) as all those in the Church stand outside. At the boundaries, too, only the spirit of a man which is in him knows a man's thoughts (I Cor. 2:11). Obstructions can arise in many different ways. The preaching of the gospel can be reduced to a general world-view or to an expression of what is already present in human life, so that it can scarcely give the impression of a saving, liberating message — the power of God for salvation (Rom. 1:16) any longer.[71] Moreover, a dubious complex of "notions" can arise that, through the modern communications media, penetrate to practically everyone as "representative" of the Christian faith. Aversion or opposition here cannot be directly identified with unbelief. Stumbling blocks can be strewn along the way, whereby interest is stifled before the actual questions — the actual question — come up for discussion. There are many examples of such notions and caricatures with respect to the Church's confession, for instance, in misunderstandings of election, original sin, the authority of the Church, and the relationship between present and future.[72] Such caricatures can become so imbedded that it is hardly possible any longer to see the need for removing shadows from the doctrines.

69. Cf. H.M. Kuitert, "Heilsboodschap, Skandalon en Geschiedenis," *Vox Theol.*, 1965, p. 41, on robbing the message of salvation of its character as a stumbling block.

70. Cf. G. Th. Rothuizen, *De Oude Man van Hoy*, 1969, p. 49, on caution with regard to opposition against the way that the doctrine of the trinity has been defended.

71. Cf. the warning against saltlessness in Matt. 5:13. Cf. also Col. 4:6.

72. Cf. the discussions in *Christendom en Marxisme*, 1966, and R. Garaudy, *From Anathema to Dialogue*. There is extensive literature on the question of whether the eschatological expectation does away with concern for the world.

Moreover, we become conscious of our limited ability to fathom the reasons for remaining outside the Church, so that, when various considerations replace simplistic ascertainment of those who are outside,[73] the desire is not to relativize the boundaries, but to do justice to the nature of those boundaries. Pope Pius IX's hesitation as he took this route places him with Bavinck, who admitted that he was not able to determine "the measure of grace with which man can still be bound to God among many errors and sins."[74] There is not only an unbreakable connection between preaching, hearing, and faith,[75] but the *mode* of preaching is also of the highest importance. On account of God's way towards men — through men — it is unjustified to eliminate one's own responsibility and to deliver a rash judgment. We cannot speak of a definitive decision, for because of the gospel itself various real and concrete "possibilities" arise at the boundaries of the Church. Only a "natural" pessimism can minimize these possibilities, but that is in direct conflict with the gospel, which speaks of the possibilities precisely where it seems that only impossibility can be spoken of (cf. Matt. 19:24ff.). Paul's reserve in I Cor. 5:12 is determined by his knowledge of these real possibilities at the sharply delimited boundaries. If anything seemed "definitive," then it was Paul's pattern of life (Acts 9; Phil. 3:6; I Tim. 1:15), but that was unexpectedly eliminated in a radical "correction" of his insight into the gospel.

Anonymous Christianity

We need not be surprised that, in times when believers stand less and less isolated in the world, interest in the others has strongly increased as many begin to realize the many influences that determine life. Gradually, one becomes more cautious in one's judgment, not in order to blur the actual difference between belief and unbelief, but to understand it in connection with decisions that are made in the depths of the heart. One begins to ask if there are not more perspectives in the lives of the others than are expressed in the words "unbelief" and "un-

73. Cf. Rothuizen, *op. cit.*, pp. 142ff., on hesitations in a concrete case.
74. Bavinck, *Geref. Dog.*, IV, 708. Cf. also his *Katholiciteit*, 1968, p. 26. See also *Gaudium et Spes* (*DV II*, p. 227): "But it is necessary to distinguish between error, which always merits repudiation, and the person in error."
75. Rom. 10:14. Cf. H.N. Ridderbos, *Aan de Romeinen*, p. 240, on not being able to believe.

believers." This puts us in the middle of some involved problems, presently being discussed, especially in Roman Catholic theology, as "anonymous" Christianity.[76] One recalls Kuyper's statement here that the Church does not go as well as expected, and the world goes better than expected. The problems are different, though, since Kuyper related the "better than expected" not to salvation, but to common grace.[77]

With the rise of discussions about anonymous Christianity, the question is asked whether justice is done to the deep resistances at the boundaries of the Church. The name itself raised questions, since we are accustomed to understanding "Christians" in connection with a conscious choice, the decision for Christ and His Name in the midst of the world. Is it possible here to distinguish between explicitly anonymous and implicitly anonymous? These questions arise because of the very positive pronouncements made about anonymous Christians, and because these pronouncements are made especially by the very same Church that had originally employed the statement *extra ecclesiam nulla salus* so rigorously in regard to Jews and Gentiles, schismatics and heretics! In the gospel we meet with a scribe who, because of his insight into the depth of the commandment, hears that he is not far from the Kingdom of God (Mark 12:34). Is there something similar in the view of anonymous Christianity, or is it an unfounded "optimism"? Or still another possibility: is all that is intended a *humanum,* which is interpreted as an "anonymous" form of faith?

The questions here are specifically concerned with the problem of what is implicit or unconscious in the relation with God.[78] It is a problem that the Church has often been concerned

---

76. Cf. already my *Nabetrachting op het Concilie,* 1968, pp. 18ff. Since then, the discussion has taken a remarkable turn, which we will go into further now. Incidentally, the problem is not being discussed only among Roman Catholics. Cf. the views of D. Sölle, *The Truth is Concrete,* 1969, pp. 101ff. (on the manifest and the hidden Church, and on the inside and outside in connection with doing the will of Christ). Cf. p. 106, on "the anonymous form of Christianity." The problem of anonymity is connected immediately here to that of love for God and for the neighbor, to the cup of cold water in Matt. 10:42, and to the parable of the two sons (Matt. 21:28ff.).

77. Cf. H.M. Kuitert, "De Wereld Valt Mee," *Kerk Buiten de Kerk,* 1969, pp. 55ff.; A. Kuyper, *Gemene Gratie,* I, 11ff.

78. H. Vorgrimler ("Theol. Bemerkungen zum Atheismus," *Mysterium Salutis,* III, 2, 1969, p. 600) prefers the expression "implicit" to "anonymous." On possible misunderstanding, cf. B.A. Willems, *op. cit.,* p. 111.

with, but current idiom includes a whole world of thought immediately related to reserve in our judgment of others. The intention is not to speak generally or definitively. With Rahner, at least, anonymous Christianity has an avowed background in God's general saving will, which puts all men's lives in a new light. Since Christ, the lives of men can no longer be thought of apart from that general saving will. The conclusion is not automatically drawn that there are no longer any boundaries and that everyone participates in salvation, but more "possibilities" are now reckoned with than was the case earlier. Moreover, Rahner emphatically says that he does not intend an annexation or triumphant imperialism that would remove the necessity even of "urging" them to enter. Nor does he intend to attach a Christian predicate rashly to others who do not value that predicate and whose real lives do not accord with it. Rather, the word "possibility" is used in a different outlook at the boundaries between Church and world. Participation in salvation is no longer dependent on conscious, explicit faith in the sense of a deed done by a person placed before a decision. The summons sounds for us to be measured in our "judgment" and not to lose sight of possibilities through Christ.

Rahner sharply opposed the rigorous interpretation of the *extra ecclesiam nulla salus,*[79] and has given the clearest form to the idea of anonymous Christianity. He rejects indignantly the reproach that this possibility abolishes the meaning of proclamation and mission, since it is neither an automatic conclusion nor a generalizing pronouncement. Whether there is real relatedness to God depends on what "basic decision" *(Grundentscheidung)* has occurred in man's heart. Although no general pronouncement can be made about everyone,[80] the Church

---

79. For Rahner ("Dogmatic Notes on Ecclesiological Piety," *Theological Investigations,* V, 353), the Church "naturally...is the Ark of salvation, the people of the redeemed." And it goes without saying that the *extra* continues to be valid, but the consciousness of faith has passed through an important development that now takes on existential significance.

80. With Röper *(The Anonymous Christian,* 1966), who agrees with Rahner, there is a clear problem here. She writes, "Every human being is a Christian, and he is one not always expressly but very often anonymously" (p. 126). Yet she also speaks of a general possibility of salvation that is given to every man, which "is, however, not a certainty of salvation." Whether anyone inside or outside public Christianity accepts the possibility of his salvation or not is unknown: "the answer to this question remains the secret of God's judgment" (p. 138). Cf. Rahner's *Grundentscheidung.*

can be seen more broadly, with respect both to other churches and to "unbelievers." Abstract possibilities are not meant when such "possibilities" are mentioned; the implication is that one expectantly meets the others on account of the universal significance of Christ for salvation. One cannot speak of hard exclusivity, but rather of hopeful inclusivity.[81] With Rahner, the motif of saving catholicity also plays a very strong role: in the history of humanity, the Church is the leaven "always and for each and every age, and especially also where the flour has not (yet) changed into the leavened dough in a way tangible to us."[82] For Rahner, that does not mean "in a modernistic sense — merely the conscious realization of natural religious need," but an outlook on the grace of God, which goes forth to all and can conquer where the Church does not conquer, even where she is rejected.[83] This view may sound presumptuous, since the non-Christian is seen as "a Christian who has not yet come to himself reflectively."[84] But the Christian can approach the others only in this way, because of the great possibility that accompanies their lives, the "possibility" of God's grace.

To clarify the discussions about anonymous Christianity, it is important to take cognizance of a conflict on this point between two theologians who have always stood close to each other in the whole framework of the new theology. We mean the sharp criticism of anonymous Christianity by Hans Urs von Balthasar, who attacks Rahner on this point.[85] Von Balthasar believes that this view detracts from the earnestness of

---

81. Cf. H. Ott, "Existentiale Interpretation und anonyme Christlichkeit," *Zeit und Geschichte*, 1964, p. 372: "But the boundaries of this true Church, which mediates salvation, are now [i.e., by Rahner] stretched out beyond the visibly, historically, and sociologically palpable Church in a way that almost causes dizziness." In addition to the concept "possibility," Rahner also uses "probability." On account of God's saving will, it is "absolutely possible and probable that man has already accepted this reality, without being conscious of that fact" (*Theological Investigations*, V, 361). Cf. also Rahner, "What Does Vatican II Teach About Atheism?", *Concilium*, 23, 1967, pp. 7ff.
82. Rahner, *Theological Investigations*, V, 361.
83. Rahner, "Christianity and the Non-Christian Religions," *Theological Investigations*, V, 134. Cf. God's "secret grace." So the rejection occurs "on the surface of existence."
84. *Ibid.*, p. 134.
85. H. Urs von Balthasar, *Cordula oder der Ernstfall*, 1967. The strange title comes from the legend of the 11,000 virgins, one of whom (Cordula) hid herself from the Huns at first because of fear, but then offered herself voluntarily and received the martyr's crown (p. 113).

decision for the Christian faith. This earnestness implies the
readiness to suffer martyrdom and is inseparable from Christian
faith.[86] According to von Balthasar, anonymous Christianity does
separate Christian faith from that readiness. On account of his
fierce attack, he has been reproached for sarcasm; he nevertheless refused to retreat because of this accusation, saying that both
the prophets and Paul have taught us "to employ this style" in
particular cases "as the correct manner of treatment."[87] Why
is von Balthasar so concerned? Why is he filled with the fear
that, for many, it is already too late, since they assume that a
concrete confession is not necessary for being a Christian, but
simply "openness"? He turns sharply against those confessions
that inscribe the word "implicit" on their banner and reduce
religion to ethics, the love of God to love for the neighbor.[88]
Von Balthasar's attack is concentrated in the charge that this
view separates itself from the catholic tradition and "contradicts the Church's whole canon of sainthood."[89] In his view,
the significance of the cross of Christ for salvation is minimized
here.[90]

    This conflict is so serious that one must ask whether von
Balthasar has correctly understood Rahner. Some of his questions must be taken seriously. They concern the way Rahner

---

86. *Ibid.*, p. 121: "Should martyrdom be brought forward as a proof for
the truth of the Christian faith?" See, moreover, Rahner himself on
martyrdom as belonging to the Church's essence, in *Zur Theol. des
Todes*, 1958, pp. 72ff., 91.

87. Von Balthasar, *op. cit.*, p. 125. There is indeed sarcasm in the conversation between the police inspector and the Christian. After a
caustic rejection of Christianity, the Christian says: "You are with *us!*
I know who you are. You mean it honestly; you are an anonymous
Christian" (p. 112).

88. *Ibid.*, pp. 84, 125. Cf. "Neo-Catholicism." In this connection he mentions Rahner, who wrote an article entitled "Reflections on the Unity
of the Love of Neighbour and the Love of God," *Theological Investigations*, VI, 231ff. Balthasar's conclusion definitely does not tally with
Rahner's analysis, since Rahner emphasizes that the love toward the
neighbor is not something "secondary" and *really* loves the neighbor
(Rahner, p. 247). Cf. von Balthasar's remark (*op. cit.*, p. 92): "Karl
Rahner was once a strong advocate of the veneration of the heart of
Jesus." Rahner apparently considers himself seriously misunderstood
by this criticism. Cf. his articles on the "Theology of Devotion to the
Sacred Heart," *Theological Investigations*, III, 1967, 321ff. and 331ff.

89. Von Balthasar, *op. cit.*, p. 125.

90. *Ibid.*, p. 91: "Clearly, a *theologia crucis* is lacking here, which Rahner
has owed us up till now." Cf. the "skipping over of the cross."

combines possibility and probability in a clear, concrete optimism about salvation.[91] Von Balthasar points especially to the meaning and significance of explicit faith and confession,[92] but this stress on the explicit contains many problems and questions in the light of a long Roman Catholic tradition — more problems and questions than Rahner brings up. He admits, although only in a footnote, that it is "self-evident" that implicit faith *(fides implicita)* and supernatural love "outside what is Christian" can exist.[93] Further, it cannot be denied that, apart from the name "anonymous," there are clear points of contact in the last 100 years of the Roman Catholic tradition for Rahner's views. There has been a long development, which goes back to the "desire for baptism" *(votum baptismi)* in Trent and became significant later especially through the "desire for the Church" *(votum ecclesiae)*.[94] The question is no longer the express desire for the Church, but the implicit desire. Moreover, positive things outside the Church are pointed to, particularly, living in harmony with one's conscience. These motifs have played an important role especially in the Second Vatican Council, where attention is called to the concrete deeds of "men of good will" and to the striving to live a "good life."[95] So it is

91. That optimism is expressed in the peculiar names *"anonymous* Christianity" and *"anonymous* Christians." According to E. Schillebeeckx, less has been written recently about anonymous Christianity, because Christian faith naturally is explicit (in *Ketters of Voortrekkers?*, 1970).

92. Von Balthasar's book frequently reminds one of the passionate reference to the earnestness of one's own decision of faith in K. Barth (*K.D.*, IV/4, 1967), in connection with his criticism of infant baptism in the national church, where this earnestness fades away (cf. Mark 16:16).

93. Von Balthasar, *op. cit.*, p. 95, with reference to the Canaanite woman (Matt. 15:21ff.). Cf. also with "theoretical atheists" (Rom. 2:14-16).

94. Denz., 796. Cf. W. Dietzfelbinger, *Die Grenzen der Kirche nach römkath. Lehre*, 1962, chapter 4.

95. *Lumen Gentium, DV II*, p. 35. The encyclical speaks of those who sincerely seek God and His will through the dictates of conscience, although they do not know the gospel of Christ or His Church. We mention further *Ad Gentes Divinitus (DV II*, pp. 595f.), on the truth and grace that "are to be found among the nations, as a sort of secret presence of God"; *Nostra Aetate (DV II*, p. 662), on respect for rules as "a ray of that Truth which enlightens all men"; and *Gaudium et Spes (DV II*, p. 221), on "all men of good will in whose hearts grace works in an unseen way." In all of this there are many points of contact with Kuyper's doctrine of common grace, although there is a difference, since Kuyper explains the "positivity" on the basis of the Holy Spirit without relating those outside to salvation. Cf. Kuitert on this in *Terzake. Kerk Buiten de Kerk*, 1969, pp. 63ff., especially on

understandable that Rahner appeals to this development as catholic tradition in view of all that is actually implied in it.[96] The connection that is made between the "good will" (bona voluntas) and the "good life" (recta vita) is striking, giving rise to the question of what conception of grace is involved here. For there is a correlation between morality and salvation here, even though morality is spoken of as under the influence of grace and even though humanism, because of the exclusive human initiative, is rejected. An ancient tradition is important here, namely, that of the facere quod in se est ("to do what one is capable of"), with all the problems that are connected with it.

This correlation problematic has remarkably not gone unnoticed in Roman Catholic circles either, as appears when Ratzinger holds the formulations of Lumen Gentium to be "quite questionable" and "easily bordering on Pelagianism." Man's seeking of and directedness to a recta vita are seen as "constituents of salvation."[97] This strong criticism touches the purity of the correlation between man and his salvation, and it is of far-reaching consequence when we think of a similar criticism of the facere quod in se est made by Luther.[98] It can also have important consequences for the view of implicit Christianity, which can no longer be founded on human, moral activity, but must be connected to grace. Thus, the whole problematic of the bona fides confronts us. And although the reference to John 16:2 does not say everything on the issue,[99] the correlation of bona fides, recta vita, and morality cannot lay the foundation for implicit Christian faith. For that matter, this does seem to be realized, since grace is constantly brought to the fore. Great emphasis is placed on God's love for mankind (philanthrōpía)

Kuyper's generous acknowledgment of the goodness of man and world — definitely a mystery, but not a mystery of salvation.

96. Both A. Röper and Rahner have used logical thinking without knowledge of logic as an illustration.

97. Cf. in H. Vorgrimler, "Theol. Bemerkungen zum Atheismus," Mysterium Salutis, III, 2, 1969, pp. 600f., with the addition: "with which an influence of grace only joins." Cf. also Vorgrimler's criticisms of "the well-meant but, with regard to content, empty notion of human good will."

98. Luther, too, in his Disputio contra Scholasticam theologiam, saw Pelagianism in this. See especially H.A. Oberman, "Facientibus quod in se est Deus non denegat gratiam," The Harvard Theol. Review, 1962, pp. 334ff.

99. Thinking that one is offering service to God by putting Christ's disciples out of the synagogue. Dietzfelbinger, op. cit., p. 105.

and on the salvation that has appeared for all men.[100] Human life is continuously accompanied by that salvation and cannot be separated from it.[101] Although it is not admissible to draw automatic conclusions from all of this,[102] catholicity can be more widely spread than was thinkable with the earlier boundaries, and the Church can see signs of God's grace and presence in this human life that is *extra ecclesiam*. Thus, Pius IX, whose decision about the boundaries of the Church had such profound influence, emphatically refers to the infinite mercy of God *(misericordia Dei)*, which makes it unlawful to draw boundaries on the basis of our human judgment.[103] We find this same warning over and over again in Rahner.

"Possibilities" for those outside

No one, not even critics of "anonymous" Christianity,[104] will claim that a simplistic answer to the question of the many others who are outside the Church is possible. For this problem

100. Titus 2:11. Rahner speaks of a Christian "existential" — thus not on the basis of a neutral analysis of man's being, but on the basis of God's saving action in Christ. For the new situation of salvation, see also L. Boros, *Mysterium Mortis. Der Mensch in der letzten Entscheidung*, 1964, pp. 116ff., in close connection with Rahner's *Grundentscheidung*. With Boros it is especially connected to dying, and he wants to avoid a *Deus ex machina* (p. 190).

101. This point of view does not come up in von Balthasar.

102. Hence Rahner combats the doctrine of *apokatastasis*, or universal restoration (e.g., "The Christian Among Unbelieving Relations," *Theological Investigations*, III, 371) and opposes the presumptuousness of optimism. Cf. "Dogmatic Notes on Ecclesiological Piety," *ibid.*, V, 364: for the child of God, optimism about others "will always find its limit and correction in this endured pessimism about himself." Moreover, psychology does play a role, for instance, in distinguishing between culpable and nonculpable atheism (*Concilium*, 1967, pp. 9ff.). See also the many other articles on atheism in this volume.

103. "Far be it from Us, Venerable Brethren, to dare set limits to the divine mercy, which is infinite. Far be it from Us to want to penetrate the secret plans and judgments of God, which are a great abyss (see Ps. 35:7), impenetrable to human thought" (Denz., 1646; *TCT*, 173).

104. For Rahner (*op. cit.*, V, 364), it becomes "less of a vexation that so few in the world belong to the number of the Christians of this church." Cf. *ibid.*, III, 355ff., on "the most obscure and difficult part" in these questions and "the Diaspora situation within the family," which already finds a prelude in I Cor. 7:12-16. It is also important here to recall what Rahner says about the fright that participation in salvation brings because "more is demanded of those to whom more is given." Rahner refers to Matt. 8:11f. (*ibid.*, V, 357) and to A. Dekker, *Homines Bonae Voluntatis*, 1969, pp. 134ff.

of the boundaries — and of judgment — is not only under discussion in Roman Catholic theology, but concerns the whole Church. There are striking attempts in our time to show that the Church does not pass hard sentences on the others and that, while the significance of the Church is not underestimated and the correlation between faith and salvation is not broken, diverse "possibilities" are considered. In reflection on what happens in and with those who are not liberated from the *massa damnata* or the *massa perditionis*,[105] we are struck by the attempt to maintain the correlation and the belief that Christ is the only way to the Father.[106]

Some suspect that there will be a "possibility" of repentance after death, especially for the many who have been deprived of the gospel.[107] This automatically leads to the question of whether, where there was no explicit faith, an implicit relation to God and His salvation could be deemed present. One is confronted with this question all the more when one realizes that the "necessity" of faith does not mean that faith constitutes salvation. Faith has a non-creative character: it is directed to salvation given by grace and is not an *opus meritorium* that takes the place of good works. Since the *misericordia Dei* is not "dependent" on human, explicit faith, one's attention is drawn to various possibilities. These questions have always played an important role in reflection on the salvation of children who die in infancy. Because of the correlation between faith and salvation, one may ask whether implicit faith did not have to be assumed for the administration of baptism to be meaningful. Or, if one is not ready to go that far, one asks if regeneration, at least, does not have to be assumed.[108] One must appreciate this interest in children and may not see these questions simply as theological speculation. But there are dangers here, and they can entangle us in even more complicated problems than those we already have.[109]

---

105. Cf. Augustine, *The Enchiridion on Faith, Hope and Love*, XXVII (Gateway Edition, p. 33). Cf. A. Adam, "Das Fortwirken des Manicheismus bei Augustin," *Sprache und Dogma*, 1969, pp. 156ff.
106. Cf. Zwingli's emphasis that "no one can come to the Father except through Christ *(nisi per Christum)*," in R. Pfister, *Die Seligkeit erwählter Heiden bei Zwingli*, 1952, pp. 66ff.
107. Cf. Bavinck, *Geref. Dog.*, IV, 706ff.
108. Cf. my *Karl Barth en de Kinderdoop*, 1947, p. 55 (on Luther) and 59ff. (on Calvin).
109. Nowhere is the problem of the boundaries "solved" in a stranger way than in the Roman Catholic idea of the *limbus parvulorum* for chil-

Within this complex of questions, there is often a conviction that the Church may not be guided by "narrow-mindedness."[110] In this respect, Bavinck even compares the different churches, concluding that Reformed theology "is in much better condition than any other with regard to these serious questions." He has the conviction in view that God is not bound to Word and sacraments and that one may not reflect on salvation without respecting the freedom of His grace. To come to a softer judgment, the Reformed view did not have to renege on a doctrine of the complete necessity of the means of salvation or to weaken the gravity of sin. Rather, the sovereignty of grace was confessed, and that was understood to mean that every calculation or fixing of the boundaries according to our insight had to be excluded.[111] This was not an escape to a *potestas absoluta* (absolute power) that disrupts and abolishes the *potestas ordinata* (ordained powers) of actual life, but cautious reflection and concern for the freedom of God's grace, which may not be approached from an antithesis between explicit and implicit. To set boundaries here can only be the result of a view that attaches a meritorious character to faith, making it the "con-

dren who have not been baptized and have not reached the age of decision because of premature death. The hypothesis of limbo designates an in-between situation where there is natural blessedness, but no *visio Dei*. Although this hypothesis is intended against "the zealots for damnation" (Boros, *op. cit.*, p. 122), it multiplies the boundary problem with new boundaries! Because that is unsatisfying, Boros was led to a "hypothesis of decision" that applies also to children: for them too everything is concentrated in one moment (*op. cit.*, p. 121). As is well known, no dogma of limbo has ever been pronounced, but the Jansenist reproach of Pelagianism was rejected (Denz., 1526). The idea of limbo is dying out in contemporary Roman Catholic theology and cannot get away from the eschatological reduction of tradition (von Balthasar, *Fragen der Theol. Heute*, p. 415).

110. According to Boros (*op. cit.*, p. 118), the intention of the idea of limbo was "preference for the more gentle solution."

111. Bavinck (*Geref. Dog.*, IV, 708f.) refers to Calvin, *Inst.*, IV, 16, 19, where Calvin speaks of faith through hearing in connection with children who are not yet capable of knowing God. For him that is not an unvarying rule *(perpetua regula)* "so that he may use no other way." Another way in calling many is the illumination of the Spirit — by inward means — "apart from the medium of preaching." For instance, children can receive "some part of grace" and, although they do not have the same faith and the same knowledge of faith, they pass over into eternal life when they die prematurely. Cf. also the Helvetic Confession, article 1; and the Westminster Confession, chapter 10, 3, with reference to salvation in spite of being incapable of outward calling by the ministry of the Word.

dition" for salvation. And so, when Bavinck speaks of the wide heart and the broad outlook, he is not assuming *apokatastasis*, but is locating "the deepest cause of salvation" in God's eternal pity and unsearchable mercy.[112] No correlation exists here between a supposed *bonas voluntas* and salvation; rather there is a reference to God's grace, which does not follow on the *bonas voluntas*, but is grace for sinners! Thus, Bavinck's conclusion need not surprise us: "With Scripture in hand, we can go no farther than that we abstain from a definite judgment either positively or negatively in regard both to the salvation of the heathen and to that of children who die in infancy."[113]

The impression of deep uncertainty that we receive here is caused because theoretical knowledge is denied us at the boundaries. The Church's charge is to proclaim God's salvation, so that the boundaries are broken through. Then the boundary problem opposes all self-assurance and pride. In this connection, Bavinck's recollection of Christ's answer to the question about the small number is meaningful: "Strive to enter!"[114] If one thing is clear here, it is that the Church may not function as a fearful border guard, but rather as one who brings good tidings (Rom. 10:15; Isa. 52:7). This is not only a result of her clear commission, but is also in harmony with her own life, which stands or falls with the perspective of changeable boundaries. For Christ died for us "while we were yet sinners, while we were enemies" (Rom. 5:8, 10). All hardness, imprudence, and rashness can only be signs that she has forgotten the gracious overstepping of the boundaries at her birth.

112. "The Reformed confession is wider of heart and broader of outlook than any other Christian confession" (*Geref. Dog.*, IV, 709). Bavinck appreciatively mentions the quotation of "invincible ignorance" (*Katholiciteit*, 1968, p. 19). His words about God's pity and mercy look almost like a summary of those of Pius IX (Denz., 1646-48).

113. Bavinck, *Geref. Dog.*, IV, 708.

114. *Ibid.* Luke 13:24. We find one of the most alarming consequences of theological conceptions in the analysis of whether the *numerus electorum*, the number of the elect, is "more" or "less." Cf. the statement of the cardinals of the Congregation of the Index in 1772 against Gravina, who considered it probable that "those who are saved are by far more numerous": "They are altogether condemned" (*omnino damnatur*). Cf. W. Schamoni, *Die Zahl der Auserwählten*, 1965, p. 33. That is a terrible "statistical" procedure that teaches us even more the danger that surrounds all reflection on the *cor ecclesiae*, the heart of the Church (i.e., the doctrine of election). Only a return to the gospel and to Paul allows us to breathe again!

The Church may not draw conclusions outside of the proclamation, but must testify to all nations of this salvation that oversteps all boundaries. On account of this gospel, the necessity of preaching is laid upon Paul (I Cor. 9:16), and the Lord Himself is subjected to a "necessity" with respect to the other sheep that are not of the fold (John 10:16). The dark enigma of unbelief in its many forms is neither denied nor minimized for the sake of a wider catholicity. Paul's passionate apostolate does not blur his sight with regard to the reality of many resistances, which he qualifies as enmity to the cross of Christ (Phil. 3:18). But it is precisely the seriousness of the resistance that stimulates the fervor of the proclamation. Also, within the Church, the gospel is constantly concerned with crossing boundaries, with the destruction of every proud obstacle. The goal is the Church's obedience (II Cor. 10:5f.). She is admonished against crossing the boundaries in the wrong direction,[115] and it is a profound misunderstanding for one to think that this admonition has lost its significance for the Church because of "the perseverance of the saints."[116]

The Church's function of proclaiming the gospel, which is inseparably connected to her own life, cannot be fulfilled in timidity, despair, and pessimism. Rather it must start from that "irresistibility" of "coming and seeing" that she herself has experenced. It is an irresistibility that seeks to break through misunderstanding, opposition, and every argument through a concrete reference to the reality of Christ (John 1:46). Whenever the Church seeks for wider catholicity in another way, she bypasses the mystery of true catholicity. The understanding of catholicity is diametrically opposed to all pride and discrimination. Therefore, there is no reason to "celebrate" catholicity,[117] but neither is there reason to turn away from it in bitterness because of the deep shadows that fall on it again and again.[118] Rather, the *credo ecclesiam catholicam* means that one must

---

115. Cf. Heb. 6:4ff.; 10:29ff.; II Pet. 2:20ff. We see this wrong direction also in Israel's longing to return to Egypt. Cf., among other places, Ex. 16:3 and the tremendous drama of Ps. 106.

116. Cf. my *Faith and Perseverance,* 1958.

117. *In Signo Sanctae Crucis,* 1964: "Here the Catholic *nota* of the Church is celebrated," because of her "unique ability" and her "marvelous power" to unite men with each other as brothers.

118. Cf. Bavinck, *Katholiciteit,* 1968, p. 31, on these undeniable shadows, which result in an extremely critical judgment "after a history of eighteen centuries."

exhort the Church to catholicity in urgent "trust." Then it will be possible not to celebrate catholicity, but to practice it in fear and trembling and in an ever new calling that is full of expectation.

CHAPTER SEVEN

THE CONTINUITY OF THE CHURCH

NO ONE WILL BE SURPRISED THAT, IN THE FRAME-work of the Church's catholicity, we also give attention to her continuity. If catholicity is more than a geographical, quantitative "universality," and if there is the added dimension of depth, then our thoughts must also encompass the temporal aspect: the Church of all ages, not limited by the horizon of a particular time or generation.[1] In view of this continuity, various epithets have been attached to the Church: unassailability and indestructibility in past, present, and future. Since the institutional forms of the Church, among other things, are being questioned today, we sometimes perceive fear for the Church of tomorrow. But the problem is wider than the horizon of our time. In earlier ages, too, the life and meaning of the Church was often questioned in times of crisis and danger. Usually, the notion of continuity continued to play a role in various crisis situations, even during serious persecutions.[2] Is there not a margin of reassurance about the whole history of the Church, since continuity is not based on indestructible qualities of the phenomenon "Church," but on an unshakable promise? Is not the Church the Church of Jesus Christ, Who is the same yesterday, today, and forever (Heb. 13:8)? The statement in Matt. 16 about laying the foundation and building the Church has played a great role in this "reassurance," since Christ will build His Church and the gates of hell will not prevail against her (vs. 18). This statement suggests imperishability and invincibility. Continuity no longer seems to be a "problem," for it is enclosed in the promise — not only because its founda-

---

1. Cf. W. Beinert, *Um das dritte Kirchenattribut*, II, 526, 531.
2. The saying that the blood of the martyrs is the seed of the Church also contains the element of the continuity of light vis-à-vis shadow.

tion has been laid in the past, but also because Christ's presence continues in all times: "I am with you always, to the close of the age" (28:20).

When one spoke of the continuity of the Church, no trivial concept of unchangeability was intended. Such a trivial concept is always a danger, but it is just as illegitimate as the appeal of the Jews to continuity with Abraham. John the Baptist emphatically denied it by referring to what God can do without demonstrable continuity: He can raise up children to Abraham from stones (Matt. 3:9; cf. John 8:33, 39). Whoever reflects on continuity in the light of Scripture quickly discovers that something other than rigid unchangeability is meant. One of Israel's greatest misunderstandings was in thinking that God, confronted by the changeability of her own life, would remain unchangeable. But in the dynamic history of God and His people, much can change. Suddenly, there can be words announcing rupture and discontinuity: "Thus says the Lord: behold, what I have built I am breaking down, and what I have planted I am plucking up" (Jer. 45:4; cf. 1:10). It is evident from Israel's history that the faithfulness of God does not make it possible to draw lines to the future. Israel could not conclude from the presence of the ark in the camp that they were unconquerable.[3] Israel's existence as a people — along the ways of God's faithfulness and promise — can be given over to need and threat, to fright and captivity. No simplistic statements can be made about this history, such that the present lies in the past and the future in the present.

What is striking in all the biblical statements about continuity is that there is no possibility of making a theoretical or practical claim out of it.[4] There is no basis for superficial, reassuring conclusions in the ark, in the temple, or in God's earlier deeds of salvation. And whenever, in the midst of sin and injustice, such conclusions are drawn, there is the threat of judgment; and the continuing value of city and temple is taken away. Radical discontinuity existed in spite of all the scorn by Israel's enemies (Ps. 89:41). The reflection of this need, which can develop into desperation (88:15), is visible again and again in the Psalms where complaints are made that God has

---

3. I Sam. 4:4ff. It is striking that the Philistines think fearfully of the gods who smote the Egyptians with plagues in the wilderness, but find a stimulus in that to battle to their utmost. They win and take away the glory from Israel (4:21f.).

4. A.D.R. Polman, *Onze Nederlandsche Geloofsbelijdenis*, III, 320ff., 376ff.

forgotten (42:9), cast off (88:14; 43:2; 89:38), hidden Himself from (88:14; 89:46), and forsaken (22:1) the writer.[5] True, we also discover perspectives in the Old Testament of a new beginning, of a re-establishment of the booth of David (Amos 9:11), and of a new "exodus." But such renewal assumes the serious reality of discontinuity[6] and may never be deduced from the past. It is not a self-evident conclusion from God's earlier presence and blessing; rather, it is a divine surprise, wonder, and gift, a hearing of prayer that again arises from the depths. Psalm 90 begins with great, positive trust: "Lord, thou hast been our dwelling place in all generations." But this trust does not exclude prayer for God's faithfulness and favor, for His glory on the coming generation (vss. 14-17).

Continuity in the Reformation

When the Church speaks of her continuity in various confessions, she does so in terms of a wide, catholic perspective embracing all ages. For example, the Belgic Confession states that the Church has been from the beginning of the world and will be to the end thereof (Art. 27). The seemingly placid perspective on the future here is not based on some analysis of history guaranteeing that perspective. The confession is immediately connected to Christ, since this continuing to the end is said to be evident because "Christ is an eternal King, which without subjects He cannot be." Thus, the confession does not go from history to the future, but from Christ to the continuity of the Church. One can also speak of divine preservation and support (Art. 27). Deeper dimensions than are present in the "what has been is what will be" of Eccl. 1:9 become visible here. The Confession does not speak of a continuity without tensions, but puts the outlook on the future in the framework of need and danger. The continuity seems to be severed when the Church occasionally appears very small and reduced to nothing (Art. 27). This description hardly suggests

5. Ps. 89 contains at the same time a strong emphasis on continuity (cf. vss. 29, 33, 36), with sun and moon as witnesses (vss. 36f.).
6. That is apparent from the judgment: Ephraim will return to Egypt (Hos. 9:3). Cf. Ezek. 15. Ezek. 20:32ff. speaks of the impression of having become like the nations, to which the reply is that there will be a new "exodus" from the peoples "with a mighty hand and an outstretched arm." See especially W. Zimmerli, "Der 'neue Exodus' in der Verkündigung der beiden grossen Exilspropheten," *Gottes Offenbarung*, 1963, pp. 192ff.

static unchangeability. As an illustration, the Confession recalls the perilous reign of Ahab, when even Elijah was so disheartened that he desired death (I Kings 19:4, 10, 14). But this reign is placed in the light of a "nevertheless": 7000 who had not bowed their knees to Baal (19:18). Remarkably, the Confession does not refer to a mysterious preservation, but sees that preservation become manifest in the reality of human faith and human decision — the 7000 believers. This preservation is not simply due to human perseverance, but to a divine act and initiative: "Yet I will leave 7000 in Israel" (19:18). These perspectives determined the statements in the Confession about continuity, and the words about Christ as eternal King are attached to the ancient confession of the Church that His Kingdom shall have no end.[7]

In the Reformation, the confession of this continuity in the midst of danger and threat had concrete, real significance. No thought was given to a national placidity that would assure one of continuance. The earnestness of the Belgic Confession can be understood only against the background of the tensions that are evident everywhere in the Confession.[8] Calvin recalled the 7000 when he confessed continuity: although the melancholy desolation, present on every side, cries out that no remnant of the Church is left, "let us know that Christ's death is fruitful, and that God miraculously keeps his Church as in hiding places."[9] Lutheran confessions, too, speak of the continuity of the Church. For example, the Augsburg Confession states that the one holy Church will remain forever.[10] Even though there are *multi hypocritae et mali admixti* in the Church in this life, the continuity of the *congregatio sanctorum et vere fidelium* is neither affected nor abolished. In the Lutheran churches, too, the reference to the 7000 plays an important role as a reference to the wonder of continuity, the "nevertheless" of divine preservation.[11]

---

7. The Nicene Creed in connection with Luke 1:33.
8. Cf. Art. 28 on edicts, and Art. 29 on persecution.
9. *Inst.*, IV, 1, 2. Cf. "it cannot be extinguished; nor can Christ's blood be made barren." Calvin also points to the oath to David and the promise "forever" in Ps. 89:35ff. *(Inst.*, II, 15, 3). Christ will live on with His members as "eternal King" in the "everlasting preservation of the church."
10. *Item docent, quod una sancta ecclesia perpetuo mansura sit* (Art. 7). Cf. the Schwabach Articles, 12.
11. Cf. W. Höhne, *Luthers Anschauung über die Kontinuität der Kirche*, 1963, pp. 17ff.; W. Maurer, *"Ecclesia Perpetuo Mansura"* im Verständnis

The unanimous affirmation given to this confession about the Church came at a time when the question of the Church's continuity was of first importance. It was constantly in dispute during the whole controversy between Rome and the Reformers. One need think only of the struggle between Sadolet and Calvin to see its importance. Calvin denies Sadolet's reproach that he did not honor the Mother Church and her continuity, replying that he cannot think of the Church apart from listening to the voice of the Church's Lord. Seen historically, however, to deny rupture and discontinuity was difficult, and the Reformers were very conscious of the seriousness of that rupture. With some justice, Luther's so-called "temptation of continuity" (*Kontinuitäts-Anfechtung*) has been noted because of the following accusation: "With your preaching of reformation, you put the entire, previous Church in the wrong and give the lie to God, Who has promised His Church eternal continuation."[12] The question of continuity had to arise, since the concern was neither a vague, romantic idea, nor an "invisible Church," but the historical reality of the Church. Luther found danger threatening the Church not only from without (the Turks),[13] but also and especially from within, from the Church's own life — specifically in the papacy, "in the temple of God."[14] In such a situation, was it still possible to speak of the continuity of the Church? Nevertheless, Luther came through doubt and temptation to a positive conviction, finding great significance especially in the declaration in Isaiah that the Word of God which goes forth from His mouth will not return empty, but shall accomplish that which He purposes and prosper in the thing for which He sends it (55:11). Luther's trust in this continuity had nothing to do with placid, unassailable constancy, and one misunderstands the promise by drawing rash conclusions from it. Perhaps we can summarize the whole problematic by saying that, in the view of continuity, the nature of the promise was in question. Was it a guarantee? Or is that already a misunderstanding of the promise?

Luthers," *Erneuerung der einen Kirche. Festschr. H. Bornkamm*, 1966, p. 35. Reformation considerations of the Church often remind us of the Old Testament perspectives of the remnant, not in the sense of an elite (the minority), but on the basis of divine grace. Cf. Mic. 4:7; 5:7.
12. Höhne, *op. cit.*, pp. 140ff.
13. Cf. my *The Return of Christ*, pp. 263f.
14. II Thess. 2:4. Calvin (*Commentaries on the Catholic Epistles*, p. 191) speaks of the greater danger from those who "went out from us" (I John 2:19) — greater "than when a thousand aliens conspire against us."

An objective guarantee?

The attention which has been given to the continuity of the Church is closely connected to the progression of time and generations: "A generation goes and a generation comes" (Eccl. 1:4). This temporal dynamic poses the question of constancy. If everything "here below" is liable to change, how is the constancy to be understood? In Scripture, our eyes are set on Him, with Whom there is no variation nor shadow due to change (James 1:17). But can one also use such words when reflecting on the history of the Church? When Moses reached the end of his life, he asked emphatically about continuity; he requested someone else "that the congregation of the Lord may not be as sheep which have no shepherd" (Num. 27:15ff.; cf. I Kings 22:17; Matt. 9:36ff.; Mark 6:34). The changing of the generations means that that problem is always relevant,[15] and in every phase of the Church, one has reflected on it. We are struck by the common usage of the same words, even in profound controversies. Continuity is always connected to Christ as the King of His Church. The *perpetuo mansura* in the Augsburg Confession is not especially Lutheran or Reformed at all, but stands at the fore of Roman Catholic ecclesiology. It is confessed precisely in opposition to the Reformed, and reference is made to the mystery of Christ's Church, to the singular, definitive laying of the foundation of that building of which Jesus Christ Himself is the cornerstone (Eph. 2:20; cf. I Pet. 2:6), and which is joined together as a dwelling place of God in the Spirit.[16] Nearly all of the conclusions of Roman Catholic ecclesiology are related to this outlook because of the conviction that Christ's Church has been removed once and for all from the situation of scattered sheep without a shepherd. Did this concrete, ecclesiastical continuity not disappear in the Reformation?

This question is so critical because we frequently meet statements and motifs in the New Testament that seem to border closely on the idea of an "objective" guarantee.[17] Are

---

15. In the New Testament, too, we discover the concern for continuity both when officers are appointed and when Heb. 13:7 says to remember the leaders who have brought the word of God.

16. Eph. 2:21f. *(sunarmológouménē).* The problem is illuminated by the rendering of Grosheide (*De Brief van Paulus aan de Efeziërs,* 1960, p. 48), who translates it as "sturdy," concluding that "no accidents can happen to it." See also Eph. 4:16.

17. Bavinck (*Geref. Dog.,* IV, 309) uses the word "guarantee" in connection with Jesus' promise.

some conclusions not possible because of Christ, and did the confessions not feel justified in drawing them? Does the form of the Good Shepherd not show continuity clearly? Does His goodness not come to expression in that He does not — as did the hireling — abandon the sheep, because He cares for them (John 10:11ff.)? Does the image of the shepherd not give great reassurance, putting the Church in the light of a blessed, "static" continuity?[18] Does it not make the image of the sheep without a shepherd an inner impossibility? Remarkably, however, this aspect of "caring for the sheep" is not pictured in a sphere of static continuity apart from tension and danger.[19] Christ's concern as Shepherd is that the sheep hear His voice, that they continue to listen to Him (10:16). The flock is tended and must continue to be tended in the light of the manifestation of the chief Shepherd.[20] All existence is related to Christ as the Shepherd along the way of care and the admonition to hear, to remain, and to follow. We are confronted with the same connections in the image of the vine (John 15:4-6). It encompasses peace ("I am the vine, you are the branches") and mentions a deep fellowship. But that does not eliminate the Lord's reference to a crossroads of remaining or not remaining in Him. Being branches of the vine includes rather than excludes the warning to "abide in me." And we hear an echo of that in a statement that has an especially correlative form: "If what you heard from the beginning abides in you, then you will abide in the Son and in the Father. And this is what he has promised us, eternal life" (I John 2:24f.).

Especially in our time, the question of continuity has come strongly to the center of attention again, with the attempt to focus in on the problem of the guarantee. Specifically, the Roman Catholics have given attention to what is radically new about the Church. In contrast to all that could "happen" to the people of God in the old covenant, reference is made to a totally new situation: the possibility of apostasy has been excluded. Rahner, especially, has laid great emphasis on the decisive significance of

18. Cf. Ps. 23 with the outlook on dwelling (23:6); Isa. 40:11; and Isa. 49:10 on springs of water and on not hungering or thirsting. Cf. Zimmerli, *op. cit.*, p. 199.
19. In addition to the care of the Good Shepherd, one can think of Paul's care for the Galatians. And it is care also in the sense that he is perplexed about them (Gal. 4:19f. — *aporoúmai en humín*).
20. I Pet. 5:2ff. Cf. John 21:15ff.; and J.B. Soucek, "The Family of God," *Ecumenical Review*, IX, 1956-57, pp. 145ff.

this newness. The situation of the Church is entirely different from that of the people of Israel, where there was rupture, discontinuity, and judgment. Particularly in the constitution of the Church, the possibility of discontinuity is graciously taken away. The starting point here is the contrast between synagogue and Church: the former could commit apostasy, but the latter cannot. As an effect of the divine deeds of salvation, a guarantee is given to the Church; therefore, she participates in indefectibility, which is closely connected to her infallibility: the Church is an eschatological reality that can no longer fall from the truth and thus stands in the light of a mysterious continuity.[21] Israel as the people of God is confronted with a serious crossroads-problematic, containing the possibility of discontinuity and change. But an emphatic change is announced: "Therefore, I tell you, the kingdom of God will be taken away from you and given to a nation producing the fruits of it."[22] Is this not a radical transition from old to new? Have not some "possibilities" in Israel been eliminated in the Church? For that matter, does not the Reformed view of the Church and her perpetuity encompass the same faith in gracious continuity?

Indeed, one continually meets this aspect of definitiveness in the Reformed view of the Church — i.e., a clear finality (*Endgültigkeit*) because Christ's work has been accomplished "once-for-all." This is brought to expression in many ways not only by the Roman Catholics, but also by the Reformers: "The faith of the Church is final and insurpassable in the sense that it is the connection to, and it proclaims, the grace of God in Christ, which saves for the Kingdom."[23] Considering this state of affairs, is controversy about continuity and indefectibility still possible? Bavinck refers to the same words of promise that dominate in Roman Catholic doctrine and names indefectibility as an attribute along with the four well-known attributes.[24] However,

---

21. See K. Rahner, *Über die Schriftinspiration*, 1958, p. 54, in connection here with the closing of the canon, which could not yet occur because the synagogue could still commit apostasy. Only with the Church could the canon take on definitive form. Cf. my *Holy Scripture*, pp. 70ff.
22. Matt. 21:43 *(arthḗsetai aph' humṓn)*. Cf. in the parable (21:33-41): the renting of the vineyard to other tenants *(állois geōrgoís)*. Cf. 21:18ff. on the cursing of the fig tree in connection with fruitlessness (cf. also 7:19).
23. W. Joest, "Die Kirche und die Parusie," *Gott in Welt*, I, 1964, p. 547.
24. Bavinck, *Geref. Dog.*, IV, 308f. Bavinck also mentions infallibility — recognized gladly by Protestants — with reference to Christ's care "that there will always be an assembly of believers on earth."

he rejects the conclusion that Rome draws from this. He does find a guarantee in the promise of the Lord, but finds that it may not be used rashly. He thinks of concrete churches ("a particular church in a particular land"), for which no guarantee has been given. Actually, Bavinck's criticism is aimed only at local or national aspects, for which the historical claim to the promise is impossible; but, at its deepest, this criticism seems similar to the question about whether the promise withdraws the Church from profound testing, criticism, and judgment. May one speak about "the Church" as possessing a guarantee based on the work of Him Whose word does not return empty (Isa. 55:11) and Who does not forsake the work of His hands (Ps. 138:8)? Or are testing and judgment of decisive significance for the discovery of the way of continuity?

Joest points out that the Church may not have a static consciousness of perfection on the basis of "finality," and he says that the Church must be ready "to purify herself and to let herself be trained."[25] This applies not only to individual believers but also to "the total life of the Church," which is not exempt from temptation and lives in expectation of the Judge. The "failure, lukewarmness, and error" of the office-bearers is also a warning against any self-assurance, since the proclamation of the parousia becomes an urgent admonition (*paráklēsis*) for the Church. In connection with this emphasis that the Church still remains subject to the critical testing of God's judgment, it is necessary to take account of the well-known statement of I Pet. 4:17, that judgment begins with the household of God.[26] This statement is provocative because it relates future judgment not only to individual believers, but also to something that belongs to God — viz., His household.[27] This qualification of the Church as God's possession has often led to totally unique praise for the Church. Far-reaching conclusions can be drawn from this statement: for instance, that the Church can never become the object of serious criticism. She

25. Joest, *op. cit.,* pp. 548ff.
26. Cf. my *Second Vatican Council and the New Catholicism,* p. 207.
27. This characterization does not only appear in I Peter. Cf. also I Tim. 3:15 (behavior in the household of God, which is the Church); 3:5 (managing one's own household and God's Church); I Pet. 2:5; Heb. 3:6 ("we are his house"). According to *TDNT,* V, 125, house (*oîkos*) is "an early Christian image for the community." Cf. what is said about the flock of God (*tò poímnion toû theoû*) in I Pet. 5:2 and Acts 20:28. There is mention of the "possession of God" (Minear, *Images of the Church in the New Testament,* 1961, p. 84).

is exempt from it. Likewise, on account of the salvation given to her, she is also exempt from every possibility of judgment![28] But Peter's statement puts us in an entirely different sphere. We certainly do not get the impression of exemption from all criticism, testing, and judgment; hence, one must reflect more closely on the nature of the "praise" for the Church as God's possession.[29] Her constitution obviously gives no reassurance in the sense that she no longer has to trouble herself about judgment. Rather, judgment *begins* in the Church; it then extends also to "the impious and sinners" (I Pet. 4:18).

This judgment of the Church first, rather than last, recalls the same motif in the Old Testament. Jer. 25:29 speaks of evil which Yahweh will bring "at the city which is called by my name."[30] This appears even more emphatically in the commission to judgment in Ezek. 9:6: "Begin at my sanctuary."[31] Naturally, the question about continuity also played a great role then, and the question arises in a cry, "Ah, Lord God! Wilt thou make a full end of the remnant of Israel?" (Ezek. 11:13). Since this same motif reappears in the New Testament, it is unjust to contrast the continuity of the Church with the discontinuity of Israel because of the difference beween old and new covenants. For that matter, this discontinuity did not have the last word even in the days of Ezekiel. His cry in the midst of judgment receives an answer that is full of the promise of gathering from scattering, one heart, and a new spirit: "They shall be my people, and I will be their God" (11:17ff.). That

---

28. We notice the elevation of the Church above criticism and judgment particularly in the Greek Catholic ecclesiology. Cf. N.A. Nissiotis, "Die qualitative Bedeutung der Katholizität," *Theol. Zeitschrift*, 1961, p. 259; and R. Slenczka, *Ostkirche und Ökumene*, 1962, pp. 157ff., on the essence of the Church for Bulgakov as divine *sophia*, or wisdom, in the world.

29. For this praise of W. Löhe, *Drei Bücher von der Kirche*, 1845: "a unique hymn of praise for the Church" (in G. Barczay, *Ecclesia Semper Reformanda Eine Untersuchung zum Kirchenbegriff des 19. Jahrh.*, 1961, p. 137).

30. Cf. G. Ch. Aalders, *Jeremia*, II. *Korte Verklaring*, p. 24: the people of His possession. Jerusalem and Judah are dealt with first, after which all the nations are judged (25:31ff.).

31. Cf. I Pet. 4:17: "For the time has come for judgment to begin with the household of God" *(ho kairos toú árxasthai)*. Ezek. 9:6 (LXX) reads: *kaì apò tôn hagíōn mou árxasthe*. Michel (*TDNT*, V, 127) points out rabbinic parallels concerning this beginning point. Cf. further Ezek. 11:10 on judgment "at the border of Israel': "and you shall know that I am the Lord."

new and surprising perspective, however, does not weaken the significance of judgment, since it becomes visible along the way of Yahweh's judging of, as well as gracious intercourse with, His people. Thus, the earnestness of judgment is understandably incorporated in the admonition that goes forth to the New Testament Church. Just as with Israel, the Church is taken more seriously because she is the chosen people of God.[32]

Any view of continuity that does not retain the possibility of calling the Church to order, because she is the "definitive" reality of salvation, is illegitimate. It may appear that we are putting old and new covenant, shadow and reality, on the same level. But that is only apparently so, because the structure of admonition in salvation does not change; it only becomes clearer in the new covenant, since the beginning "set in a new light by the Christ event."[33] That is not a denial of continuity, but the rejection of a perverted continuity. What happened in Israel can be used to admonish the Church, as we see pointedly in I Cor. 10:1ff. What happened to Israel is not an arbitrary example, which Paul accidentally notes, but a salvation-historical, typological connection. The drama and catastrophe of what occurred in Israel are warnings *(túpoi)* for us not to desire evil (10:6). And they were even written down for the sake of the Church, upon which the end of the ages has come (10:11). Paul is very conscious of the specific situation of the New Testament Church. But that insight into the end of the ages urges him to refer to Israel, to baptism into Moses, and to eating and drinking of supernatural food and supernatural drink, reminders of baptism and the Lord's Supper in the Church.[34] What happened in Israel must guard the Church from thinking she stands while not taking heed lest she fall (10:12). Such freedom from threat is in flagrant conflict with God's style of dealing with men or with His Church, and His style of being present in His "household" and tending His flock. There is no suggestion that the situation of the Church in the New Testament presents an entirely different structure of admonition. Rather, there

---

32. Cf. especially Amos 3:2: "You only have I known of all the families of the earth; *therefore* I will punish you for all your iniquities." Diametrically opposed to this is the desire for the day of the Lord (5:18ff.), which rests on one great, culpable misunderstanding. Cf. Jer. 7:4, 8, against deceptive words.

33. *TDNT*, V, 127.

34. Cf. H. Conzelmann, *Der erste Brief an die Korinther*, 1969, pp. 195ff.; H.N. Ridderbos, *Paul*, pp. 405, 419ff., on the description of the Old Testament gift in New Testament terminology.

is a striking continuity here in the call to faith and obedience.[35] Thus, the Church can be admonished by means of Israel's history,[36] and one cannot exalt oneself above this admonition, claiming that the admonition endangers the riches of the Church's constitution. Only in understanding and practicing this admonition does true continuity become evident.

Whenever there has been a tendency in the history of the Church to visibly and objectively fix the guarantee,[37] the offices of the Church have played an important role; their obvious, continuing presence is well-fitted for the task of verification. The simple rule, "wherever the Pope is, there is the Church" most eloquently exemplifies this.[38] One used to think that indefectibility could only be maintained in this way. Therefore, apostolic succession has played such a dominant role in Roman Catholic ecclesiology. The intention of this ascertainable continuity and legality was not to oppose the institution of charisma, or the Church's structure to fellowship with Christ, but rather to indicate the framework within which the Church's mystery

35. Cf. also Rom. 4:24 (written for our sake also); 15:4; Gal. 3:14, 16. Goppelt (*Typos. Die typologische Deutung des A.T. im Neuen*, 1939, p. 165) speaks of a "typological intensification." In Hebrews we see the wilderness generation as a "type": Heb. 3:7ff. quotes Ps. 95 with the conclusion, "Take care, brethren." Cf. Goppelt, p. 205: "God's rule over Israel as the admonishing and strengthening type for the Church." That does not imply that Old and New Testaments are put on the same level (cf. Heb. 3:1-6 — Moses and Christ), but it is directed to a "more" that stimulates to greater responsibility. See *TDNT*, V, 795 on the frequent admonition in the New Testament, specifically concerning its being qualified by "this reference back to the work of salvation."

36. Cf. R. Hummel, *Die Auseinandersetzung zwischen Kirche und Judentum im Matt. Evang.*, 1963, pp. 156ff.: "What elevates her (the Church) beyond Judaism, therefore, signifies just as much task as gift."

37. Erasmus pointed to this continuity in opposition to Luther when he asked, "Who could believe that this Spirit would have intentionally overlooked an error in His Church for so many centuries?" In essence, it is the same question that C.J. de Vogel later asked (*Eccl. Catholica*, 1946, pp. 74ff.). Luther went into Erasmus' question in *The Bondage of the Will* (trans., J.I. Packer and O.R. Johnston, 1957), pp. 119ff., denying that "God tolerated this error in His church." He refers further to Scriptural statements about continuity and then says, "what is hard and problematical is just this: ascertaining whether those whom you call the church were the church." And again reference is made to the seven thousand in Elijah's day: "But who saw them, or knew them to be the people of God?"

38. On Irenaeus' much more complex formulation of this dictum, see chapter 10 below. Cf. also my *Second Vatican Council and the New Catholicism*, p. 170; Bavinck, *Geref. Dog.*, IV, 266, 269.

THE CONTINUITY OF THE CHURCH

can endure unshaken and unthreatened. We do not yet want
to go into the problems connected with apostolic succession,[39]
but we do want to point out that the reference of the Reformers
to the "succession of the Word," while raising various new questions, did, in any case, try to give a deeper insight than the one
that resulted from ascertainable, continuous succession. One
could speak of a more dependent — and more critical — continuity, which cannot be "visible" apart from the life of the
Church in obedience. By using this verification principle — the
guarantee — there is a clear motif: guidance and protection
through the centuries. But one has to end up with the Church
functioning as a guarantee apart from any discussion or criticism, and acting as a pillar of cloud no matter what path is
taken.[40] Even though an unspiritual automatism was not intended, the nature of the guarantee made this danger inevitable.

To the degree that the spiritual character of the Church is
better understood, resistance to this form of verification gradually increases. Automatically, a view of apostolic succession
with more nuances also develops. To observe this shift is especially fascinating. One not only puts up resistance to petrified
fixations and automatism, but also examines the nature of continuity more closely. For instance, Küng points out that apostolicity may not be understood as a static attribute that lends
itself to demonstration.[41] A critical element also penetrates into
reflection on apostolic succession: reference is made to the
unique, foundational, and irrepeatable apostolic office, which
must be understood as normative for the Church of all ages.[42]
A critical dimension is therefore indicated in continuity, and
the reference to normativity is unmistakably similar to the
Reformed view of the *successio Verbi*. Since the whole structure
of continuity changes, traditional ecclesiology understandably
rejects this new structure as too dynamic, too actualistic, too
arbitrary, and especially too uncertain. The fear is that con-

39. Cf. below, chapter 10.
40. See especially the definitions of the First Vatican Council on the "pro-
    tection of the flock" and the "true doctrine concerning the establish-
    ment, the perpetuity, and the nature of the sacred apostolic primacy."
    It is affirmed that "in this primacy all the *efficacy* and all the *strength*
    of the Church are placed" (Denz., 1821; *TCT*, 201).
41. H. Küng, *The Church*, p. 358. See also his *Structures of the Church*,
    pp. 177ff.
42. Cf. G. Hasenhüttl, *Charisma. Ordnungsprinzip der Kirche*, 1969, pp.
    177ff., especially p. 182 on the "once-for-allness" as of decisive signifi-
    cance "for the whole structure of the Church."

tinuity will not be usable as directly and authoritatively as was the case earlier with office, hierarchy, and primacy. Yet this idea of guarantee can only give less and less resistance to the obviousness of the biblical witness that the Church stands under the authority of her Lord, Who rules her by Word and Spirit. The reality of the promise of His presence and blessing cannot be approached from a guarantee to the Church that is understood apart from her concrete life in faith and obedience.[43] Only in this way is the answer that was given in Isaiah's day to the messengers of the nation clearly seen: "The Lord has founded Zion, and in her the afflicted of His people find refuge" (Isa. 14:32).

A distinction between individuals and the Church?

Roman Catholic ecclesiology has increasingly seen the extreme difficulty of placing the actual situation of the Church on earth simply in the light of unthreatened unchangeability. Yet, often, one still admits the "possibility" of sin and apostasy only for individual believers, while denying it for the Church. In contrast to individual believers, "the Church" has an all-embracing guarantee against a lapse into apostasy.[44] "As a whole," she will not disappoint God; thus, she can no longer incur judgment. Although the Church's great light can be obscured, she can never become a "synagogue" again, and a "minimum" will always be preserved as a guarantee of indefectibility.[45]

In the Roman Catholic Church of the 16th century, one frequently called attention to that essential outlook on abiding and continuity, when the individual way of salvation was mentioned. One recalled the problematic of the crossroads, specifically in connection with preparation for grace, with the free will, and even with life after the reception of grace, since it could always be lost. Strikingly, though, Rome has always understood this individually and has considered it to be of no significance ecclesiologically. With respect to individual believers,

---

43. Cf. A.D.R. Polman, in *De Apostolische Kerk*, p. 186: "Whoever forges these strong promises for the Church into aprioristic safeguards changes the essential character of these firm pledges." Cf. in detail on apostolicity and continuity, O. Noordmans, *Gestalte en Geest*, 1955, pp. 335ff.
44. Cf. R. Schnackenburg, *The Church in the N.T.*, 1965, pp. 176ff.; *idem*, "Kirche und Parousie," *Gott in Welt*, I, 577. The aspect of judgment "opens the outlook primarily, though, on the unbelieving world."
45. Cf. my *Second Vatican Council and the New Catholicism*, p. 208.

there was no certainty of the perseverance of the saints,[46] but the situation was totally different with respect to the perseverance of the Church. In the individual sphere, one wanted to maintain human cooperation, while rejecting the reproach of synergism; but in the Church, there was an objective guarantee that put everything in the full light of unassailable continuity. It was an accomplished fact—both a fact and a mystery —manifest through the office of the shepherd as the vicar of Christ, caring for, tending, and protecting the sheep. In light of this view of the guarantee, one understandably could not see Luther other than as the rebel who attacked the continuity of the Church and thus dishonored Christ. Luther's conviction that what happened in the Reformation had not arisen from purely human initiative or arbitrariness, but "from divine counsel" (divino consilio),[47] was not adequate for making his stance believable in light of the Roman Catholic way of experiencing the Church.[48] Over and over again, there is surprise at this dynamic and alarm in the Reformation, which was open to the possibility of deterioration and disturbance with respect to the Church. Was it not unbelievable and inconceivable that the Holy Spirit would abandon the Church to error and deterioration for so long? We are confronted here with one of the deepest questions in connection with the continuity of the Church. The Reformers, too, knew all the texts to which Rome appealed, but nevertheless it seemed that Roman Catholic ecclesiology neglected essential aspects of the biblical approach to the Church.

The distinction between individual believers and the Church as a whole has never been made clear. How can the Church be isolated as a different reality from individual believers as the congregatio fidelium? The problem is expressed most strikingly in the formulation that the Church will never again disappoint God. We read of that disappointment in the Old Testament, where Israel causes Yahweh weariness (Isa. 43:24; Mal. 2:17) and disappointment at the well-tended vineyard from

---

46. Denz., 833.
47. Cf. H. von Campenhausen, "Reformat. Selbstbewusstsein und Geschichtsbewusstsein bei Luther," Tradition und Leben, 1960, p. 323.
48. The change in the later Roman Catholic view of Luther and the Reformation not only has to do with greater personal appreciation for Luther's religious motives, but is also related to hesitations about the evidentness of the antithesis that is postulated between rebellion and unassailable continuity.

which good fruit is expected.[49] When it does not result, the vineyard becomes a waste. But does a new and unprecedented stability in the Church make all of that only a past possibility?

In seeking to answer that question, we are struck that the way and the life of the Church in the New Testament is placed in the light of a very earnest and thoroughgoing admonition. One could even say that this admonition is not weakened, but strengthened! For, according to the Bible, the Church is subject even more strongly to testing because of the solution presented to her. To the degree that light has penetrated, responsibility grows (cf. Heb. 10:26ff.). And so, varied warnings are issued against wickedness, apostasy, and resistance, against grieving or extinguishing the Holy Spirit. And no distinction is made between believers (fideles) and the Church (congregatio fidelium). Moreover, shocking deformation is reported, for instance, in the letters to the churches of Asia Minor, where the central point is frequently in question: the abandonment of the first love (Rev. 2:4) and false tolerance of sin (2:20). Testing is related to what is most essential, since a church had the name of being alive, but was dead (3:1), or thought that she was rich, but in reality was poor and wretched (3:17f.). This church faces sharp testing and the threat of judgment, and the "possibility" exists that the lampstand will be removed (2:5). The testing is sharp because Christ, the faithful witness (1:5), is in the midst of the lampstands, i.e., in the midst of the seven churches (1:13, 20). This testing is done by Him Who searches mind and heart (2:23). The continuous reminders of such thoroughgoing testing automatically lead us to think of the Old Testament, where Yahweh punishes Israel, His people, for her iniquities (Amos 3:2), and He searches Jerusalem with lamps (Zeph. 1:12).

The question of what can happen in the Church is continually raised. What possibilities surround her? Nowhere do we meet any self-evidence or conclusions that are valid apart from the struggle of faith. Rather, we meet an urgent "if" in the New Testament, for instance, when Paul directs himself to the Gentile Christians and says that their continuity will be broken off if they do not continue in God's kindness (Rom. 11:21f.). Apparently we cannot speak about continuity as such. No matter how "synergistic" it may sound, an "if" resounds here with respect to true continuity. Frequently, one has shrunk

49. Isa. 5:1-7. This expectation is mentioned three times (vss. 2, 4, 7).

back from this "if," fearing that continuity would once again come to lie in our hands and that God's faithfulness would follow upon our faithfulness. Nevertheless, it is of the highest importance that we correctly understand the connections of continuity; otherwise, we may become caught in an objectivistic ecclesiology in which various conclusions are drawn that are not justified in the reality of the Church. These conclusions have often had a paralyzing function, for "the Church" was raised above her sin and faults. Those who hold such an objectivism lack appreciation for what Luther called the "most spiritual promise," which is understandable only by way of faith and obedience.[50]

The strong emphasis on the gratuity of grace clearly shows that the Reformers fully realize that the Lord rules His Church by Word and Spirit (cf. H.C., Q. 54). Hence, there has to be concern for Paul's "if."[51] For example, Calvin can write that it is not sufficient to accept God's grace once "except thou followest his call through the whole course of thy life."[52] And Calvin applies this not only to individuals, but also to the Church. According to him, this admonition is certainly not superfluous, since the danger of apostasy always threatens the Church: "Our course in the world is like a dangerous sailing between many rocks, and exposed to many storms and tempests; and thus no one arrives at the port except he who has escaped from thousand deaths. It is in the meantime certain that we are guided by God's hand, and that we are not in any danger of shipwreck, *as long as* we have him as our pilot."[53] This "as long as," which is parallel to Paul's "if," does not signify doubt about the foundations of the Church or her continuity. Rather, Calvin starts from the true nature of continuity, which does not lend itself in any respect to apologetic considerations;

50. Cf. Höhne, *op. cit.*, p. 141; K.E. Skydsgaard, "Vom Geheimnis der Kirche," *Kerugma und Dogma*, 1964, p. 150 (on dangers and temptations for the Church); and especially O. Weber, "Die Treue Gottes und die Kontinuität der menschlichen Existenz," *Gesammelte Aufsätze*, I, 1967, pp. 99ff.
51. Per Erik Persson, "Das Amt des Geistas. Eine kontrovers-theol. Skizze," *Kerugma und Dogma*, 1959, pp. 99ff., particularly on the Church and the Spirit, and the mode of the Spirit's working.
52. Calvin, *Commentaries on the Epistle of Paul to the Romans*, pp. 432f. There is no constancy "except thou humbly recognisest the mercy of God."
53. Calvin, *Commentaries on the Catholic Epistles*, p. 141 (*quamdiu illum habemus gubernatorem*).

rather, it can only be practiced in fear and trembling.[54] To isolate the Church from her members here or to see the Church's guarantee in her offices apart from critical testing[55] conflicts not only with the Church's reality, but also with the nature of continuity itself.

When Kuyper reflected on deformation, he thought not only of individual guilt, but of a guilt that "infects the whole of the body of Christ." Kuyper maintained that this guilt can go so far that ultimately the churches of the new covenant are told: "If you spread out your hands, I will hide my face; and if you multiply your prayers, I will not hear."[56] Kuyper speaks of a process of deformation that finally ends "because all life leaves the Church. Then there is nothing more about the Church that can be deformed, because all her life is lost."[57] Only a pseudo-church is left as "an absolutely deformed Church." Kuyper concludes this blunt picture with a prayer: "May God Almighty guard us, that our churches may not serve as instruments for Satan and in order that Satan may not animate our churches with his demonic influence."[58] Are such statements only emotional outbursts in a historically situated ecclesiastical struggle? Or do they express a realization of danger for the concrete Church, denying, as did the Reformers, all claims to unchangeable continuity on the basis of an office or on the basis of charisma? This latter is definitely the case, since the outlook on God's promise includes — not excludes — concern for various "possibilities" amid the reality of God's critical judgment. "He who has an ear, let him hear what the Spirit says to the churches" (Rev. 2:7, 11, 17, 29; 3:6, 13, 22).

Reformation and continuity

In times of crisis, conflict, and rupture, reflection on continuity always receives new impulses. Because of the historical development, we have grown accustomed to the concept "ref-

54. Cf. A.D.R. Polman's formulation (*op. cit.*, III, 162ff.). After the reference to continuity, there is a defense against all presumptuousness, since continuity is disclosed along the Church's way in confession of guilt and prayer.
55. The distinction between individual members and the Church had to lead to reflection on the safeguarding "objectivity" of the Church's offices.
56. A. Kuyper, *Traktaat van de Reformatie der Kerk*, p. 95.
57. *Ibid.*, p. 112.
58. *Ibid.*, p. 115.

ormation," but it is good to remember that "reformation" automatically leads to questions about the nature of the Church's perpetuity. That is especially the case when serious deformation, decay, and degeneration — the accusation made by the Reformers of the 16th century against the Roman Catholic Church — is under discussion. Deeper questions then come to the fore — i.e., deeper than what Pope Paul VI, following other popes, describes as the errors of members of the Church and deeper than what Rome understood already in the 16th century about the necessity of reformation. Yet it is also worthwhile to notice the general realization that permanent renovation and reformation are necessary. This realization found expression in the well-known words *ecclesia semper reformanda* ("The Church is always in need of being reformed").[59] Sometimes this has been amended to *ecclesia reformanda, quia reformata* ("Because the Church has been reformed, she is always in need of being reformed"). This statement was usually intended to indicate the Church's imperfection, parallel to the confession of believers about their imperfect lives. That realization has often been sharply outlined in individual life, for instance, when the Heidelberg Catechism speaks of a small beginning of obedience (Q. 114) or about the defilement of good works (Q. 62).

The critical question that must always be asked is this: is this indeed a confession of guilt, or only a general admission — without much existential earnestness — of a state of affairs? Naturally, this question is significant with respect to the *ecclesia semper reformanda*. The *quia reformata* intends to place the Church in the revealing light of the gospel, so that there is a permanent readiness to be corrected and called back from wrong paths. No matter how profound this *semper* may be, we are also confronted with the phenomenon of "reformation" that intervenes deeply in the whole life of the Church at particular dividing points in history. If one asks what the deepest intention of the 16th century Reformation was, one does not get very far with the word "reformation." The con-

---

59. On the origin of the words, cf. G. Barczay, *op. cit.*, p. 19. We find a Roman Catholic parallel in the Second Vatican Council (*Lumen Gentium, DV II,* p. 24): "at the same time holy and always in need of being purified *(semper purificanda),* and [she] incessantly pursues the path of penance and renewal." Cf. E. Schillebeeckx, "Ecclesia Semper Purificanda," *Ex Auditu Verbi,* 1965, pp. 216ff.; and my *Holy Scripture,* pp. 299ff.

cept can be filled with a greatly varied content,[60] and that may be the reason that Luther himself did not use the word frequently. In the concrete situation, however, the meaning became clear: there were accusations of abusing, neglecting, and obscuring the gospel of sovereign grace, while adding human traditions. The Reformers called the Church back to the gospel. There was no profound, theoretical analysis of "essence" and "form" in order to give the essence a good, restored form.[61] The Reformers were concerned with something more serious than the restoration of a "form," assuming thereby that the "essence" has remained pure. This comes clearly to light, for instance, in the struggle about indulgences, the mass, and papal authority. One could also speak meaningfully of "renewal," but here too different degrees are conceivable. Hence, renewal means something other than new creation. Yet it can hardly be denied that the Reformation intended something very radical; and therefore, the problem of the Church's continuity arises.

In concrete, reformation can mean criticism of a dangerous process of "deformation," as when Kuyper speaks of a process of deformation that ends with a pseudo-church.[62] How long can one speak of a continuity, renovation and reformation in such a process? The question is extremely important, for Luther and Calvin were strongly convinced that they did not want to establish a "new" Church. Rather, they believed that, in the strict sense of the word, the "innovators" were in the Roman Catholic Church. The Reformers were protesting precisely against this "newness."[63] In the struggles about whether the Reforma-

60. Cf., for instance, R. Radberg, "Reformatio Catholica. Die theol. Konzeption der Erasmischen Erneuerung," *Volk Gottes. Festgabe für J. Höfer,* 1967, pp. 237ff. C. Augustijn (proposition 1 of *Erasmus en de Reformatie,* 1962) does not call Erasmus a reformer or forerunner of the Reformation. In *Erasmus, Vernieuwer van Kerk en Theologie,* 1967, p. 35, however, Augustijn does say that *aggiornamento* is the question that ruled his life. Cf. p. 68: "the ideal of a reformation of the Church according to the standard of the early Christian Church is enticing." Cf. also Höhne, *op. cit.,* pp. 156ff.; P. Brunner, "Reform-Reformation. Einst-Heute," *Kerugma und Dogma,* 1967, p. 175.

61. For the words in connection with "form," we recall Paul's appeal to be transformed "by the *renewal* of your mind" (Rom. 12:2 — *metamorphoústhe tē̜ anakainṓsei;* Vulgate: *sed reformamini in novitate sensus vestri*). Preceding that is not being "conformed" to this world (*suschēmatízesthe;* Vulgate: *conformari*). Cf. *schêma* also in I Cor. 7:31 ("the form of this world").

62. A. Kuyper, *Traktaat van de Reformatie der Kerk,* p. 1.

63. See especially Luther in his *Wider Hans Worst,* 1541. Cf. E. Wolf, "Leviathan," *Peregrinatio,* I, 135ff.

tion had deviated from the original pattern of the historical Church, the Reformers often pointed to the strong relationship between themselves and the ancient Church.[64] Whether their Reformation could perhaps be described in the categories of nostalgia for the past, for the original model of the ancient Church, is a question that has been asked.[65] Was it in fact their view that the continuity had been broken since the ancient Church and that, at present, the broken line was once again extended? Was the Reformation the restoration of the ancient form of the Church after a phase of discontinuity? The answer to this question must be negative. It is true that the protest against the "innovators" had a defensive aspect, but the deepest impulse of the Reformation was not a radical theory of decay, as was the case with Joachim of Fiore (the Church of the Spirit in contrast to the historical Church), but a confession of continuity. The recollection of the 7000 in the Lutheran and Reformed confessions is a decisive indication of that. It was meant neither as a reassuring testimony that minimized the seriousness of the deformation, nor as a reference to some vague continuity, but as a recollection of God's testing judgment of the Church to the depths of her heart.

That the language about the Church used during the Reformation recalls the Old Testament idea of remnant has frequently been point out. Naturally, the important thing is how that "remnant" is understood. It could be interpreted in the sense of a small elite that survived and came to light again in the Reformation. Then the "small flock" can signify haughty self-complacency vis-à-vis the many who have committed apostasy. However, it is also possible for the idea of the remnant to function critically. It is not accidental that the Reformers saw the Church as continuing "from the beginning of the

64. Cf. R. Mooi, Het Kerk- en Dogmahistorisch Element in de Werken van Joh. Calvijn, 1965, pp. 355ff. on the historical argument beside the main argument. It would be interesting to compare Calvin's interest in the ancient Church and continuity with that of Newman, especially since Newman's conclusions led him to convert to the Roman Catholic Church.
65. See especially E. Wolf, "Erneuerung der Kirche im Licht der Reformation. Zum Problem von 'Alt' und 'Neu' in der Kirchengeschichte," Peregrinatio, II, 139ff., 149ff.; idem, "Leviathan," Peregrinatio, I, 135ff.; and, very enlightening, W. Maurer, "Die Geschichtliche Wurzel von Melanchtons Traditionsverständnis," Zur Auferbauung des Leibes Christi. Festg. P. Brunner, 1965, pp. 166ff.

world to the end thereof."[66] Thus, it acquired an outlook on the critical, promising aspect of the remnant. This possibility is indicated by the example of Paul at the historical dividing line between Israel and the Church (Rom. 11:2ff.), and it was also understood this way during the Reformation. One totally misunderstands the remnant if one connects it to praise and self-complacency. The recollection of the reality of the remnant does not give one a weapon to use against others, but refers to the critical testing of all, of the whole existence of the Church. Therefore, the Reformation was not nostalgia for the past, but a passionate, critical concern for the present and future of the Church. Höhne has pointed out that Luther contradicted his humanistic opponents, who longed for the past, with "nothing other than his view of continuity."[67]

In the midst of the history of the Church, continuity can be understood only from God's testing judgment. Therefore, there has always been a struggle about the true and false Church, about being in and of the Church, about dangers and temptations, so that the important thing was to listen to the Shepherd's voice. The idea that continuity revived after the Reformation is a contradiction in terms. But because of this, the Reformers' outlook on continuity takes on an extremely critical character, because the decisions — concerning whether the Church is truly the Church — now occur before God's eyes. The promise that God does not forsake the work of His hands does not remove all tension, calling, and responsibility from the Church's history.

66. B.C., Article 27. Cf. Y. Congar, "Ecclesia ab Abel," *Abh. über Theol. und Kirche, Festschrift für K. Adam*, 1952, pp. 79ff. This article has frequently played a role in later ecclesiological reflection in connection with the relation between the *ecclesia* and the (essential) hierarchy. Cf. pp. 95ff. on Bellarmine's definition.

67. There is a nostalgia in the longing for the past that can develop into pessimism, since it has lost the outlook on continuity. Moltmann (*Die Kategorie Novum in der Christl. Theol. Perspektiven der Theologie*, 1968, pp. 175ff.), especially, has criticized this romanticism, postulating in its stead the *novum* (something new, unheard-of) of renewal *(renovatio)*. When he says that the "re-" in reformation is directed more to the past than to the future, he is perhaps correct with respect to the Renaissance, but not with respect to the Reformation, which thought in the categories of both the *novum* and the present. When Höhne (*op. cit.*, p. 163) writes that the Reformation of the Church "was finally irreconcilable with his [Luther's] view of continuity," his judgment is, in my view, determined too much by a reaction, for the Reformation of the Church is identical with critical testing for the manifestation of true continuity.

Rather, the opposite is the case, for the promise of not forsaking the work of God's hands appears in the form of a fervent prayer (Ps. 138:8)! This framework of the promise of God's faithfulness, which is not nullified by human unfaithfulness (Rom. 3:3f.; II Tim. 2:13), was of decisive significance for Israel; but it is also of decisive significance for the Church. Continuity can never be founded on human conclusions or *a priori* propositions. The point of continuity is aimed at the present and, thus, also at the future. In that light, the *ecclesia semper reformanda* is not as innocent as it appears. For what is confessed in it — and it can only be understood as a confession of guilt — cannot be localized *a priori* in the Church's periphery. Above all, the consequences of the Church's guilt in individual and common life can never be ascertained and noted down; therefore, they are incalculable. The *semper reformanda* may never degenerate into a vague admission that is more like an excuse than a confession of guilt. And where the confession of guilt does become real, it is related to renewal and implies the radical calling to be truly the Church. Apart from this calling, the way of continuity cannot be walked.

From the nature of the case, this renewal cannot be separated from the renewal of individual believers. One cannot hypostatize the Church.[68] It is good to remember, though, that the Church does not stand or fall with the individual; there are wider and deeper horizons than those of our individual lives. The connection between the perseverance of the saints and the perseverance of the Church has been discussed in the past. Both have often been seen as deterministic interpretations of salvation, and one cannot say that there has never been reason for this misunderstanding. But the light of the gospel clearly shows that both are the opposites of self-evident unchangeability. With respect to the perseverance of the saints, the deterministic view clearly fails to give comfort and ultimate confidence in the pastorate. But the confession of the Church's perpetuity, too, is not exempt from the pastorate, especially in times when the future of the Church is in question.

We are reminded here of Luther's idea of the *ecclesia latens,* the "concealed Church." The expression is not without danger, and it can be seen as an escape into some vague continuity in an "invisible Church." However, there is another possibility

---

68. E. Schlink, "Christ and the Church," *The Coming of Christ and the Coming Church,* 1967, p. 96.

which was definitely present in Luther: the *ecclesia latens* can function as a critical concept,[69] recalling Him Who is "in the midst of the lampstands" (Rev. 1:13) and Who searches the heart (2:23). Every verification principle — no matter how subtly fixed it is — that casts shadows on this privilege does not appreciate that the mystery of the Spirit applies also to the Church: the Spirit is like the wind, which "blows where it wills, and you hear the sound of it, but you do not know whence it comes or whither it goes" (John 3:8). This statement has sometimes been used as the *locus classicus* of spiritualism, but continuity is not in the least threatened because of the Spirit's "arbitrariness."[70] But the statement is and remains a reminder along the Church's way. It does not make her a "hidden" reality that has no blessing for the world — thus not a city on a hill, not a light, and not the salt of the earth. Rather, it sets her life, her pilgrimage, and her blessing in the light of the Spirit, Who is the deep content of the promise. Along the ways of this promise, God does not forsake the works of His hands. With an eye on the long history of the Church, we can better understand that what Paul says about election shaming the wise and strong becomes visible in the true Church in order that no human being might boast in the presence of God (I Cor. 1:26-31).

Unchangeability

If we honestly take cognizance of the many changes in the life, thinking, and deeds of the Church throughout history, we may wonder if this continuity can be maintained.[71] Frequently, some have tried to distantiate themselves from this historical

69. See on the statement in Luther's *The Bondage of the Will* (p. 123), "The church is hidden away, the saints are out of sight" *(abscondita est ecclesia, latent sancti)*, E. Kinder, *Der evang. Glaube und die Kirche*, 1960, pp. 96ff.

70. Neither is that the case with the much discussed statement in the Augsburg Confession in connection with the office of preaching (Art. 5): *wo und wenn er will*. Cf. H. Diem, *Die Kirche und ihre Praxis*, 1963, pp. 167ff.; E. Wolf, *Peregrinatio*, II, 159.

71. The sense of this changeability has increased in our time more than ever before. Still, the experience of changes and new situations is not absolutely new. For example, Bavinck wrote in 1888 that, for the most part, "modern" culture has nothing to do with Christianity and the Church. "We are faced with a whole new state of affairs. Powers have arisen against which Christianity has never tested its strength; phenomena, which the Church has never taken into account" *(Katholiciteit,* 1968², p. 31).

problematic by pointing out that the Church's unchangeability belongs to her supratemporal structure, which never changes in character and always participates in the "once-for-allness" of salvation. This way of thinking about the Church suggests a different contrast between changeability and unchangeability, which the biblical witness lays on our hearts: "All flesh is like grass and all its glory like the flower of grass. The grass withers, and the flower falls, but the word of the Lord abides forever."[72] This contrast can also function in ecclesiology, because the word that abides turns out to be the Word that is "the good news which was preached to you" (I Pet. 1:25). Does this abiding, this unchangeability, not determine the Church? Does she not stand, therefore, as a rock in the breakers of time? In the same connection, one can think of the identity implied in Christ's being "the same yesterday and today and forever."[73] Although the Church cannot be identified with Christ, one has still often drawn various conclusions from the Church's participation in Him Who is always "the same"; for, directly after that statement, there is a warning against being led away by strange teachings (Heb. 13:9).

One cannot deny the suggestive element in this view of the Church and her unchangeability, and there is a direct point of contact for it in the New Testament admonition that warns sharply against introducing "change" into the proclaimed gospel. There is continuous resistance against any other name (Acts 4:12), another God (I Cor. 8:4), a different gospel (Gal. 1:6), another Jesus and another spirit (II Cor. 11:4), and another foundation (I Cor. 3:11). The warning is sounded against submitting to what is "other."[74] One could ask whether there is not an avowed "supratemporality" in all of this that remains unaffected by anything that occurs in history. For that matter, does not speech about the Church of all ages imply radical unchangeability? And is it not in opposition to the diverse attempts at accommodation, which have always changed the structure of the gospel and have removed the *skandalon*-character from it? Is it not that stability and unchangeability upon

---

72. I Pet. 1:24f. *(ménei eis tòn aiôna)*. Cf. Isa. 40:6-8.
73. Heb. 13:8. Cf. F.V. Filson, *Yesterday. A Study of Hebrews in the Light of Chapter 13*, p. 13, who indicates how far removed this "identity" is from all rigidity. Cf. Heb. 5:8f.; 2:9; and so forth.
74. Paul notes that the Corinthians "submit readily enough" (II Cor. 11:4 — *kalôs anéchesthe)*.

which one can depend[75] and in which one will not be ashamed? The background of all this is the apostolic mandate (Gal. 1:1) that is contrasted to what arises from one's own originality and authority — even Paul's own (1:8) — since the gospel is not man's gospel (1:11), but transcends all his thoughts and feelings. This dimension of unchangeability cannot be removed from the New Testament, and all forms of traditionalism have always lived from this dimension and have seen it as the end of all discussion.

Nevertheless, one has not yet finished when one has referred to the unchangeability of the Church's life and confession, for it is never possible to separate this unchangeability from what is transmitted through the ages.[76] Unchangeability cannot be compared to propositions or truths in science, which are discovered and proclaimed and then are carried along through the ages "unchanged." Such a petrified concept of unchangeability has often played an important role because of the fear that the Church would be dragged along by something that was alien to her essence, by a human, contemporary understanding of the world and one's own life. Then, in fear, the stable content of the Church's doctrine and teaching, which supposedly preserved her continuity, is pointed out. Particularly when the speech and testimony of the Church were connected to the leading of the Holy Spirit and dogma was given an infallible character, an attempt had to be made to show that the development of dogma, which was undeniable, was not a discontinuous, but a harmonious process. All the problems of more recent interpretation of dogma are connected very closely to this search for continuity.[77] Pope Paul VI's statement that "what was has remained" plays a role everywhere.[78] Obviously, though, it is

75. Cf. the image of the pillar in I Tim. 3:15 ("pillar and bulwark" — *stúlos*) and Gal. 2:9 (James, Cephas, and John, who "were reputed to be pillars" — *stúloi*). Is there "a slightly ironical note" (*TDNT*, VII, 735) in the Galatians passage, or is there a relationship with the *stúlos* of I Timothy?

76. Cf. on preservation my *Verontrusting en Verantwoordelijkheid*, 1969, pp. 64ff.

77. The many different interpretations of the development of dogma point out how complicated the problem is, since the intellectualistic approach to the development (from implicit to explicit), in any case, could not be maintained. Many factors turned out to have decided the development. Cf. my *Nabetrachting op het Concilie*, pp. 53ff. on "syllogistic logic" (*Syllogismuslogik*). For recent literature see H. Hammans, *Die neueren kath. Erklärungen der Dogma-entwicklung*, 1965; and *Mysterium Salutis*, I, 1965, pp. 727ff.

78. *Post Duos Menses* (1964).

one thing to pronounce these words and another to make them credible. If the development was observed without bias, was it indeed "homogeneous," or was it a "transformation"?[79] Many different answers have been given to this question, but it is realized more and more that one may not explain all the differences in the process of development as simply a different formulation of the same thing. Thus, the question of the nature of continuity had to be faced. The insistence that this problematic not be put under the table did not arise from an irrational opposition to all knowledge or to the concrete content of faith; it did not arise from allowing the *fides qua creditur,* the act of faith, to prevail over the *fides quae creditur,* the content of faith. Rather, it arose from the realization that the gospel is the power of God for salvation (Rom. 1:16); therefore, it can never be approached from a purely intellectual understanding of truth.

The big question that the Church must always deal with is this: in what way can she be of service to this power in her proclamation of this gospel? How can it be passed on faithfully, so that life comes under the power of a liberating message? The radical reversal (Acts 17:30; cf. 26:18) for which that message calls does not signify that the Church remains above the world like a drop of oil on top of water.[80] Rather, she stands in the midst of life, in countless encounters and confrontations. The fear of accommodation to changed times and to changing human insight has often led to petrification, and many attempts have been made to protect the unchangeable against the destruction of adaptation. But this "unchangeability" can hardly be distinguished from that of the talent hidden in the ground and eventually taken away from the slothful, wicked servant because it was unchanged and unfruitful. That the gift of the talent involved striving for a goal had not been understood by the servant (Matt. 25:25-30). There is a kind of unchangeability or continuity that lacks perspective — an archeological phenomenon that lacks fruitfulness and is powerless to be a blessing in new, changed times. The images of pillar and bulwark and even of the city on the hill and the light of the world can be isolated from the salt of the earth. Then they lose their dynamic significance. But the gospel has nothing to do with this unchanging petrification. There is an appeal to preserve the faith

79. The antithesis is mentioned by M. Marin Sola, *L'Evolution Homogène du Dogme Catholique,* 1924.
80. A well-known image from A. Kuyper.

that was once for all delivered to the saints, but that signifies contending for it (Jude 3) and living expectantly (21), so that one is preserved from falling (24). And continuity is disclosed in many ways by which one can keep oneself in the love of God (21) and can build oneself up on the most holy faith (20).

It was unavoidable that the gospel, which was preached everywhere and always, repeatedly confronted the Church with her calling and responsibility to interpret the good news purely for new worlds of thought, new historical experiences, and other languages. The gospel did not fall like rain in a barren wilderness, but entered into a rich, human life. The history of the Church bears undeniable marks that she has not been taken out of the world (John 17:15; cf. I Cor. 5:10), but rather has found a place in life. Her history shows the influence of particular times, historical situations, and contemporary experiences. Thus, the Church is forced to reflect on her own identity, on her ways in Christ (I Cor. 4:17), and on the central meaning and implications of the message of salvation. Naturally, it is always relevant to ask whether understanding is truly deepened, rather than blurred or obscured. One may never accept the declaration of continuity *a priori* and apart from closer examination.[81] The words "symbiosis," "contemporary," and "relevance," also do not in themselves guarantee that continuity has been preserved. Nevertheless, especially in times of shocking changes and in confrontation with new questions of Scriptural criticism and science, one has often discovered elements in tradition that had been carried along in the call to an unchangeable gospel, but do not really belong to the message of salvation. In such situations, it is always the task of the Church to listen to Paul's admonition, enclosed in a prayer for the Church, to "approve what is excellent."[82] The seriousness of that approval is clear,

---

81. Discussions understandably arose when A. Kuyper (*Principles of Sacred Theology*, p. 679) spoke of the calling "to raise the special form of its own confessional consciousness to the level of the consciousness-form of our age." For Kuyper, continuity was not broken by that, although he repeatedly felt the changes which, in his view, were necessary to be profound indeed. We think of his criticism of "a decided mistake" in earlier Reformed views of predestination. In this connection, cf. the neglect of common grace also in the Reformed confessions (*Gemene Gratie*, II, 95, 101ff.), along with which there is a very far-reaching remodeling that contains strong elements of discontinuity. Cf. p. 97 on inertness of the best Reformed theologians at this point for two centuries.

82. Phil. 1:9f. *(eis tò dokimázein humás tà diaphéronta).* Cf. the same formu-

since it cannot be a logical or theoretical procedure, but it is incorporated in fellowship with the Lord, in the abundance of love, in knowledge and all discernment (Phil. 1:9), and in the light of the day of Christ (1:10). Apart from this approval, it is impossible to bring the continuity of the Church into view. There is a double threat. On one hand, there is the danger of a plus: human additions to the unchangeability that place burdens too heavy to bear on new eras, thus throwing a stumbling block along the ways of the gospel.[83] On the other hand, there is the danger of a minus: a reduction that also destroys the unchangeable message of the gospel. In the midst of these dangers, the Church must constantly ask why and in what way she is a pillar and bulwark, a city on a hill, the light of the world, the salt of the earth, the household of God in the world, and a refuge in all needs. It will not suffice for her to refer to these as "qualities" that testify to her unchangeability. Rather, in every new situation,[84] the Church must seek her own "identity," so that by continuing from generation to generation and by going forth and producing fruit she will be clear and unambiguous.

Continuity and hope

We often see that anxiety for changeability leads one into a sterile, formal concept of unchangeability. But then the Church becomes powerless and without blessing; her bond with the past shows the signs of deep poverty.[85] However, if the Church's words can be taken seriously — truth, salvation, light, liberation, perspective — she cannot avoid the questions that she is asked about the continuity and reality of her message in new times. Shrinking back and being afraid here can only be the result of a deep uncertainty about one's own faith and about the continuing, true significance of the Church. Such uncer-

---

lation in an extremely critical context in Rom. 2:18-24 (dokimázeis tà diaphéronta).

83. One may think of the additions to the law mentioned in Matt. 23:4 ("heavy burdens") and Luke 11:46 ("burdens hard to bear"), in contrast to the light burden of Jesus (Matt. 11:30).

84. Cf. H.N. Ridderbos, Aan de Romeinen, p. 64, on approving "what is excellent in every situation."

85. We find the saddest side of the attachment to the past in Matt. 23:29ff. The scribes and Pharisees "build the tombs of the prophets and adorn the monuments of the righteous," while pridefully elevating themselves above that past.

tainty cannot simply be taken away by words, just as a child's anxiety does not disappear by acting "grown-up" in the dark. We do hear words that originate in deep certainty, such as the triumphant statements in the Old Testament about not fearing though the earth should change and the mountains shake in the heart of the sea (Ps. 46:2). They are words of continuity and unshakability, of continuing perspective on account of the city of God (46:5; cf. Isa. 26:1-4) and the refuge (46:7, 11). The outlook on the future rests on a profound foundation and thus goes beyond all experiential limits (46:5; Hab. 3:2, 16-19). In this outlook on the future, the Church becomes aware of her continuity; and, in that awareness, she is "present" in the world as the light and the city, testifying to the faithfulness of God's promise. Hence, this expectation cannot be kept hidden in one's heart, but must be public in the world. The New Testament says that a defense *(apología)* must be given to "anyone who calls you to account."[86] The apology here is concentrated in the hope "that is in you." It is not a scientific apologetic, but an apology for a way along which one will not be ashamed. This readiness to make a defense does not isolate hope from love and faith, but it does manifest the certainty of continuity; and, already in the New Testament, the controversy about faith and truth is often concentrated in hope (cf. Acts 17:31f.; 24:15, 21; 26:7; 28:20).

This hope is neither a vague, optimistic expectation for the future, nor an expectation projected on the basis of "openness" to the future. Rather, this hope manifests itself in threat and temptation,[87] and the continuity of the Church becomes visible in hope. This expectation is so closely connected to the whole life of the Church that she is summoned to hold fast the confession of hope without wavering.[88] This continuing hope is determined by its foundation[89] and also by that to which

---

86. I Pet. 3:15 *(pantì tõ̂ aitoúnti humás lógon)*. The "always" *(aeì)* signifies that "This possibility must be reckoned with perpetually" (R. Schnackenburg, *Die Petrusbriefe*, p. 100).

87. Cf. Rom. 4:18: "In hope he believed against hope" (in connection with becoming the father of many descendants and nations). Cf. the promise, 4:21 and Heb. 11:19.

88. Heb. 10:23 *(homología)*. The confession is flattened out seriously if its connection to hope is no longer fully understood and honored. Cf. also the firm trust in Heb. 3:6; 6:11, 18; 7:19; 11:1.

89. Cf. the foundation of hope in I Cor. 15:17. Apart from Christ's resurrection, there is continuity in sin: then "you are still in your sins." Cf. I Pet. 1:3, 8. In this connection we recall a point of discussion re-

it is directed.[90] Only in this way does it obtain its structure and unchangeability. It is directed to the God of hope (Rom. 15:13); and thus, the confession of hope becomes one of the most far-reaching points of confrontation in times of catastrophe and danger. That is especially the case because this abundance of hope (15:13) is also concerned with the world. Practically all the questions of eschatology can be concentrated in the question of the significance of this hope for this world and of godliness, which holds promise "for the present life and also for the life to come" (I Tim. 4:8). That is a sure and comforting word, which sets our eyes on the living God Who is the Savior of all men (4:10). The outlook on Him Who makes all things new (Rev. 21:5) does not mean that the continuity of the Church and hope have nothing to say for today and tomorrow and have no perspective or commission in the world. That was passionately denied not only by Kuyper,[91] but also by Bavinck, who saw the catholicity of the Church as a radical rejection of all defeatism with respect to responsibility for this world. He protested against a posture without hope and perspective, in which we, "with the pretense of Christianity, perhaps might reject the civilization of the century as demonic."[92] In contrast, he saw the gospel as filled with perspectives, a re-creating and renewing power. Only the one who understands this has an outlook on true catholicity,[93] an outlook on Him "Whose good pleasure it is to save man in his need."[94] According to Bavinck, the sense of life has gradually changed, with the result that life

garding Moltmann's *Theology of Hope*, 1967, p. 16. He was accused of a formalization in the directness toward the future in connection with the "primacy" of hope and of being too influenced by the universal, human "existential" of hope (E. Bloch), because of which the unique foundation of the Christian hope ends up in the shadows. Cf. G. Sauter, in *Diskussion über die Theologie der Hoffnung*, 1967, p. 117; cf. also H. Berkhof in the same work, pp. 176, 183. Moltmann's answer is connected to the *praesens*, the present (p. 207). Cf. p. 213 on the starting point in saving faith and on looking out from there toward the future.

90. Cf. John 5:45 on hoping on Moses. The connection between "hope" and "hope" structures the Christian expectation (K. Barth, *C.D.*, IV/3, 2, pp. 902ff.

91. Cf. H.M. Kuitert, *Sociale Ethiek en Geloof in Jezus Christus*, 1967, p. 20, on Kuyper's "not an inch" (with respect to how much of the inheritance of social and political life may be withdrawn from Christ's lordship).

92. H. Bavinck, *Katholiciteit*, p. 38.

93. *Ibid.*, p. 23. Cf. pp. 33ff. on pietism. Cf. also Bavinck's *De Algemene Genade*, 1894, pp. 29ff.

94. H.N. Ridderbos, *De Pastorale Brieven*, 1967, p. 119.

"on this side of the grave" has gained its own, independent value and is more than a preparation for heaven. And using an expression from Holtzmann, he refers to the Reformers as founders of a "worldly Christianity."[95]

These strong emphases do not mean that Bavinck has been captured in an unfruitful dilemma of horizontality and verticality; rather, they make room for a concern about life in this world. Bavinck was captivated by the aspect of catholicity, by the Church's continuing presence and continuing witness, her confession of hope; and he was convinced that he was not moving about outside, but inside Christ's universal domain. Naturally, one can make the error of haughty activism, which loses all connections of hope and overarches gnawing doubt about God's action now and in the future by means of human initiative and the work of our hands.[96] The circle of the history of eschatology in the last fifty years would then again be closed at the point where Barth fulminated against the "builders" of God's Kingdom, calling them back to the majesty and righteousness of His judgment and grace.[97] The danger will always exist that the connections between present and future will be violated. And no one has been given the definitive insight into the connections between human service to the Kingdom[98] and God's promise which fulfills everything. But this lack does not make the way impassable. If the Church is truly the Church, the problem of two kinds of ecclesiology, in which stress is laid either on the Church's being or on her functionality in the

---

95. Bavinck, *Katholiciteit*, p. 21.
96. Even the *pro Rege* ("for the King") cannot legitimize every language of expectation. We are thinking, among other things, of Kuyper's view that Calvinism "is such an all-embracing system of principles, as, rooted in the past, is able to strengthen us in the present and to fill us with confidence for the future" (*Calvinism*, 1898, p. 16).
97. K. Barth, *The Epistle to the Romans;* and "Die Gerechtigkeit Gottes," *Das Wort Gottes und die Theol.*, 1925, pp. 5ff.
98. Cf. human work as not useless, I Cor. 15. A. Kuyper, especially, was fascinated by these connections, specifically with regard to common grace, when he spoke of its fruit (abiding gain) for the Kingdom of glory (*Gemene Gratie*, I, 458ff., with reference to Rev. 21:26). Although there is no mention of a gradual transition, there is mention of "the hidden germ of life, the fundamental significance of things." K. Schilder (*Wat is de Hemel?*, pp. 234ff.) opposed Kuyper's appeal to Rev. 21. None of Kuyper's images offers much clarification. Cf. *Calvinism*, p. 72, on the all-embracing organism that will manifest itself as the center of the cosmos at the second advent. At present on earth, though, only its silhouette can be dimly perceived.

world, dissolves.[99] For the Church's being cannot be split up, since the Church *as the Church of Jesus Christ* is the light of the world and the salt of the earth. The confession of continuity is possible only from this inseparableness; otherwise, the perpetuity of the Church, her continuing presence in the world, becomes unfruitful. The Church's interest in the world becomes illegitimate only if it deteriorates into a prideful human "vicariate" that takes everything on itself because of God's "absence" and does not cherish any expectation for the glory of God's Kingdom. That kind of glory — the glory of righteousness (II Pet. 3:13) — is not in the hands of anyone and cannot be the crowning keystone in the vault of our actions! Here, if anywhere, it is clear that ecclesiology is inseparably related to the doctrine of justification, for justification forever determines the structure of the Church's continuity. If this connection is not violated, the embittered protest made against the many uncatholic failings of the Church, which abandons every expectation for the Church, can be resisted. The gospel rejects this way as too easy. Over and over again, it gives a new commission reminding us of the relationship between the Church's unity and catholicity.

It is not accidental that, already terminologically, catholicity and division are opposites of each other and mutually exclusive. Even those who see that the adage "in unity there is strength" is often used to describe the Church in a worldly sense may not ignore the fact that, because of division, catholicity cannot be seen as desirable in the world. Human calculations cannot answer the question about the future of the Church, but one cannot deny that the question is connected to the unity of the Church — her confession of the one hope (Eph. 4:4) — and, thus, also to the catholicity of the Church.[100] The calling to catholicity cannot be borne or practiced in the midst of fragmenta-

---

99. Cf. on this H. Berkhof, "Tweeërlei Ecclesiologie," *Kerk en Theologie*, 1962, pp. 145ff. Cf. p. 147 on the two accents (static and functional). The choice turns out not to be a choice in a dilemma, since "starting from Christ" does not cause the world to disappear from sight. Cf. p. 155 on being and function, and p. 158 on introvert and extrovert.

100. H.A.M. Fiolet's statement, "The relevant problem of the twentieth century is not the unity of the Church, but the question of whether there will still be a Church in the near future" (*De Tweede Reformatie*, 1969, p. 102), is often cited. In regard to the "one-sidedness" of this statement (isolated on the jacket of the book), one should consider that directly after this statement there is a reference to the "test case" of this future: the Church's unity.

tion. John writes revealingly that "whatever is born of God overcomes the world" (I John 5:4). And so, in all darkness and shadows that fall over the history of the Church, there remains a reason to recall the question "Do you not know?" in Paul's admonitions. For, in all the darkness, it speaks of the light and opens new ways along which the frustration of broken unity and violated catholicity can be withstood.

With respect to the one reality of the Church in all her facets — unity, catholicity, apostolicity, and holiness — there can be no excuse that her commission is too great. The excuse of powerlessness does play a great role when commissions are given, but the divine mandate overrides such sensible hesitations. It gives the commission anyway and creates the readiness to fulfill it.[101] Only in this connection can one correctly understand the abundance of words about the Church. They point us to a gift that does not allow pride, self-complacency, or boasting in the Church.[102] Rather, this gift belongs to the mysteries of the Kingdom: "Everyone to whom much is given, of him will much be required; and of him to whom men commit much they will demand the more" (Luke 12:48). Whoever sees this as a new law and a heavy burden has not understood what the gift signifies. For the depth of the gift gives a basis for the broad commandment. Only so is it meaningful to maintain the *credo ecclesiam* rather than to flee from it as from a commission that is too great. The Church must follow her way in humility, prudence, and resoluteness; she must be receptive to every criticism that reminds her of her "attributes," her reality; and she must be prepared to be recalled from division and narrowness to the clear ways of God — ways of unity and catholicity, of fruitfulness and perspective. Then she may also listen to the promise to the faithful servants who were faithful over "a little" and are placed over "much" (Matt. 25:21, 23). The eschatological perspective of joy — "enter into the joy of your master" (25:21, 23) — is exempt from every misunderstanding. One discovers it only in the context of the mystery of the seven stars and the seven lampstands (Rev. 1:20), and it manifests itself on earth in manifold repetition: "He who has an ear, let him hear what the Spirit says to the churches" (Rev. 2:7, 11, 17, 29; 3:6, 13, 22).

101. We recall Moses' "Who am I?" Cf. Ex. 4:1, 10-15; 5:22ff.; 6:29ff.; Isa. 6:5ff.; Jer. 1:6ff.
102. See especially I Cor. 4:7: having and having received. The conclusion is: "why do you boast as if it were not a gift *(hōs mē labόn)?*" In the exceptionality that comes with having received gifts, the question is applicable: "For who sees anything different in you?"

III. The Apostolicity
of the Church

CHAPTER EIGHT

THE MEANING OF APOSTOLICITY

A S WITH THE WORD "CATHOLICITY," THE WORD
"apostolicity" has become very familiar in the Church's
usage. This does not necessarily mean, however, that its essential significance is so clear that further reflection and analysis
are superfluous. Whoever asks what it means concretely to
say that the Church is "apostolic" faces a series of far-reaching
questions that are closely connected to the content of the concept "apostolicity." Just as was the case with catholicity, apostolicity is so closely connected to the history of the Church that
one can hardly reflect meaningfully on it if one does not consider those complications of history. Moreover, the designation
of the Church as apostolic contains an element that is not
present in the other "attributes" of the Church. What characterizes the Church in all eras — unity, catholicity, and holiness
— is not only confessed, but her particular relationship to the
past is also included. The designation "apostolic" emphatically
recalls that past, the apostolic past. A historical aspect becomes
visible. True, we also discover the perspective of wideness and
universality in catholicity, but apostolicity displays a unique,
peculiar aspect of the Church. Even though apostolicity does
not imply a minimal interest in the Church's present and even
though apostolicity is confessed in that present, neither detracts
from the fact that the relation to a unique past has been incorporated in the *credo* and is considered to be of great significance.

The human component

When we reflect on this relation, we are immediately struck
that a human aspect of the Church appears within our horizon
in a way different than in the other attributes of the Church.
Even if the gracious, divine origin of the Church of Christ is

201

confessed, interest nevertheless appears in the historical relatedness to men — apostles. They are seen not simply as a possible
historical aspect, but as something essential to the Church, something about which the Church herself feels she must speak
confessionally. She has always been conscious of herself as a
reality imbedded in human history. Even though the Nicene
Creed is the only creed of the ancient Church that mentions
apostolicity,[1] the Church has been aware from the earliest eras
of "the apostolic definiteness of the Church."[2] Strikingly, that
profession is made not only of the fundamental relation of
the Church to Christ and of her determination by His grace
and reconciliation, but also of a relation to human apostles.
And this relation is obviously understood as of decisive significance for the understanding of the Church. Hence, there
is every reason to give attention to it. This self-designation by
the Church is definitely not intended to let her dwell on an
illustrious past, as is the case with many historical recollections, when the glory of the present is derived from the origin.
But the Church, which lives in the present and is on the way
to the future — she has no lasting city (Heb. 13:14) — is reminded of a unique past, and the human aspect in it is pointed
to emphatically. This is not simply an interesting question
of "origins," scarcely of relevance to the Church's present, but
a "remembrance" that intervenes decisively in the present, placing the Church face to face with the deepest questions.[3] The
Church does not come into view here as a contingent phenomenon or as a transcendent "event" apart from any earthly
connections and components, but she is shown and confessed
in all her earthly, historical, and human connections in the
course of time.

This unmistakable aspect of the Church's human component has played a role in countless questions concerning the
Church, questions concerning her origin and continuity, questions about the nature of tradition and succession. As is evident
from the *credo*, one cannot think and speak meaningfully and
legitimately about the Church by thinking only of her divine
origin or by desiring to eliminate every human component on

---

1. Cf. J.N. Bakhuizen van den Brink, "Apostolische Traditie en Autoriteit in
   de Vroege Kerk," *Ecclesia*, II, 1966, pp. 120, 125; F. Kattenbusch, *Das
   apostolische Symbol*, I, 1894; II, 1900.
2. Cf. H.N. Ridderbos, in *De Apostolische Kerk*, 1954, p. 68.
3. Cf. H. Berkhof, "De Apostoliciteit der Kerk," *Nederlands Theologisch
   Tijdschrift*, 1947/48, pp. 146ff.

account of the danger of "competition." Undoubtedly, there has always been an awareness in the Church that no shadows may be thrown on Christ as Lord of the Church and on the divine origin of the Church. One can always recall various New Testament qualifications of the Church as Christ's "building" (*oikodomě* — cf. Matt. 16:18; Col. 2:7), as a dwelling place of God in the Spirit (Eph. 2:22), as the household of God (I Tim. 3:15; cf. Heb. 3:6), and as God's field and building (I Cor. 3:9; cf. II Tim. 2:19). One knows that the essence of the Church has not been rightly expressed when she is seen as "the legacy of the apostles" and not as "the legacy of Christ and the dwelling place of the Holy Spirit."[4] But the clarity of this decisive dimension does not make it right to oppose this relation. Whenever the Church of Christ becomes manifest in this world, our full attention is also called to an event in which men — with their dynamic activity — play a significant role.

It is undeniable that we meet continuously — without any notion of a dualistic origin[5] — with an emphatic apostolicity functionality, which makes it impossible ever to minimize the human aspect in the Church's reality. Because this human functionality is never made independent and is always related correlatively to Christ, it can be spoken of so frankly. For example, it can be said that the Church is built "upon the foundation of the apostles and prophets" (Eph. 2:20). Since this "building" in the proclamation of the gospel is understood so realistically, Paul can write that he has laid a foundation as "a skilled master builder."[6] Every misunderstanding is out of the question here, for the only foundation is Christ, and no one can lay another foundation (I Cor. 3:11). Within this horizon one can speak emphatically and without "competition." Paul can ask the Church of Corinth: "Are not you my workmanship in the Lord?" (9:1). The "in the Lord" does not abolish, but qualifies one's own work. Whenever one's own work is mentioned, we are continuously struck by a deep realization of smallness

4. A. Harnack, *History of Dogma*, III, 237. Cf. Bakhuizen van den Brink, *op. cit.*, p. 138.
5. Cf. H. Schlier, *Der Brief an die Epheser*, 1958[2], p. 142; Harnack, *op. cit.*, II, 76.
6. I Cor. 3:10 (*architéktōn*). Cf. F.W. Grosheide, *De Eerste Brief aan de Kerk te Korinthe*, 1957[2], p. 103: "To lay the foundation is to bring Christ, to preach Christ." Cf. II Cor. 4:5; 1:19 ("Jesus Christ, whom we preached among you").

and humility.[7] Radical, revealing formulations warn against misunderstanding. Paul recalls that neither he who plants nor he who waters is anything, because God alone gives the growth (3:7; cf. 3:5). By itself, the concept "fellow workers" (3:9) could conjure up all the dangers of competition. In this connection, however, it does not obscure the outlook on God's work. One could say, somewhat paradoxically, that the significance of apostolic activity is understandable only when one fully honors what Paul says about not being anything — the "incommensurableness" of God's work and human work,[8] which excludes all hubris and identification forever. The human work is totally directed, both dimensionally and correlatively, to God's work;[9] and in that way it receives its meaning and its real significance.[10]

When the Church confesses her apostolicity, while at the same time asking for attention to "how Christ and his Apostles had exercised their ministry,"[11] she expresses a deep realization of her continuing subjection to a norm. Precisely on account of this, the recollection of the past becomes relevant and concrete, and the reference to the attribute of apostolicity can no longer become a triumphant self-designation. In the history of the Church, whenever a struggle about true apostolicity broke out, it was always concentrated on the question of whether or not conformity to apostolic authority was present. Thus, apostolicity automatically became a critical fact.[12] The relation to apostolicity as the decisive, normative authority made it possible for one to avoid difficulty with the eschatological per-

7. Cf. the healing in Acts 3, which occurred not "by our power or piety" (vs. 12), but by the name of Christ (vs. 16). Cf. J.K.S. Reid, *The Biblical Doctrine of the Ministry*, 1955, pp. 43ff.
8. H. Conzelmann, *Der erste Brief an die Korinther*, 1969, p. 92.
9. Cf. especially Calvin, *Inst.*, IV, 3, 1, on God's kindness in using instruments in connection with the whole life of the Church and the office bearers. Here "a puny man risen from the dust speaks in God's name." The treasure is hidden in earthen vessels (IV, 1, 5), but the scantiness of men does not confound the authority of their teaching. Where the correlative directedness to God's work is obscured, though, this "mediation" is perverted.
10. That is apparent also from the wages that are promised (I Cor. 3:8).
11. Harnack, *op. cit.*, II, 76.
12. Bakhuizen van den Brink, *op. cit.*, pp. 127ff.: "The origin is decisive and the present Church must be judged by it." Cf. pp. 88, 127 on the citation from Tertullian (*De praescr. haer.*, 20, 7): "Every sort of thing must necessarily revert to its original for its classification." One must bear in mind, however, that the generalizing "every" runs the danger of blurring the uniqueness of apostolicity.

spective of Revelation. A wall becomes visible here with respect to the Church of Christ; it has twelve foundations, and "on them the twelve names of the twelve apostles of the Lamb" (21:14).

Throughout the whole history of the Church, there has been a great deal of interest in apostolicity. In the gospel, we are impressed by a human functionality that is of decisive significance for the whole life of the Church. Attention for what Christ is doing and will do does not make the Church into a kind of "mysterious" event through which she becomes the object only of "monergistic" divine action. Rather, from the beginning on, we see various perspectives of service, calling, commission, and mission. Great activity unfolds around Christ Himself when He begins to call the twelve (Matt. 10:1, 5). They are sent with the charge to go forth and to preach that the Kingdom of God is at hand (10:7). This human service and functionality is not minimized in any respect, although it is evidently surrounded by many dangers. That is the case not only in the later history of the Church but also already in the environs of the Lord Himself. Emphatic warnings are issued against the dangers of perversion, and reminders are given of the significance of being an instrument, being taken into service. There is no place here for any self-praise, since all that is said and done by those who have been called and sent is governed by the rule: "You received without pay, give without pay" (10:8; cf. I Cor. 9:18). Their works may never become a power that is at their disposal apart from the Lord. When the seventy return with joy on account of their power over the demons (Luke 10:17-20), the Lord reminds them of what lies behind this power as a gift from the Father. Only so can their power be purely understood. What is decisive is the perspective in this real power (10:18), this authority that has been given them (10:19). On account of this perspective, there is no place for a divine *Alleinwirksamkeit,* a divine sole activity, that sees all human activity as a threat to God's own glory. No reason is left for minimizing or relativizing this human activity, since its meaning and origin have been illumined once and for all.

Christ Himself gives human work such a place that, in the perspective of the harvest, He laments that there are few laborers. He does expect everything from God; but, in that expectation, He calls for prayer to the Lord of the harvest to send out laborers (*ergátēs*) into His harvest (Matt. 9:35-38; cf. Luke 10:2). This prayer stands in the context of the gospel of the Kingdom and of Christ's compassion for the sheep without a shepherd. This compassion is the origin that explains everything, the dominant factor in all the activity called for and blessed here, since He called and chose "those whom he desired" (Mark 3:13) to a service that is related wholly to Him and is fulfilled by Him: "to be with him, and to be sent out" (3:14). He chose the twelve after a night of prayer (Luke 6:12f.) and their empowerment is full of the mystery of the Kingdom. Human work is totally distinguished from all self-righteousness,[13] from human, independent achievements; for it is placed in the clear light of calling and election.[14] This light designates human work in the midst of many dangers — sheep among the wolves (Matt. 10:16) — as a testimony to the Kingdom (10:18). The Spirit of the Father will speak through them (10:20). What they hear whispered they must proclaim upon the housetops (10:27). A Kingdom is appointed to those who have continued with Him (Luke 22:28f.), and following Him qualifies their whole life (Mark 1:17; 2:14). The Lord's "nearness" is also of decisive significance after the resurrection when apostolic service is pictured in connection with that nearness: the apostles appear as eyewitnesses of what has happened, of the unique event of Christ's resurrection. When Judas fell out of the circle of apostles, another was chosen from among those who belonged to the circle during Jesus' earthly ministry, in order that "one of these men become with us a witness to his resurrection" (Acts 1:21ff.). As eyewitnesses, the testimony of the apostles is in contrast to all "cleverly devised myths" (II Pet. 1:16f.). It is described as a hearing and seeing, an observing and touching that is to lead to complete joy (I John 1:1-3). The unique mission is related to what has happened, to His manifestation "not to all the people but to us who were chosen by God as witnesses, who ate and drank with him after he rose from the dead" (Acts 10:41). The nearness here, the close relation to the living Lord, becomes a guarantee for an unprecedented certainty concerning the salvation that has been made manifest and now preached with full empowerment by men. In it all distances are bridged over: through the word of preaching, this salvation is no longer faraway, but near.[15]

13. Cf. *TDNT*, II, 648f. on the negative sense of human work (*érgon*) in Paul.
14. Cf. the warning against the misunderstanding in John 15:16 about going and bearing fruit.
15. Rom. 10:4ff.; Deut. 30:11, 14. The word that is near is "the word of

Representation

How must the empowerment for the apostolic proclamation be understood? Various studies appeared many years ago attempting to trace the contours of this empowerment. Attention centered especially on the connection with the messenger (*šāliaḥ*) in Israel, who is sent out with a definite commission. In fulfilling that commission, he represents the one who sent him. The New Testament concept of apostles was thought to attach itself to this and, at the same time, to imply a certain identification between the Sender and the one who is sent: the authority of the messenger is the authority of the Sender. Rengstorf, especially, attracted a large following with this hypothesis.[16] Gradually, though, objections arose because the *šāliaḥ* receives only a limited commission, while the apostolate does not have that limitation.[17] For that matter, even Rengstorf himself indicated that difference. The idea of representation, and the full empowerment implicit in it, undeniably belongs to the core of the apostolate. Clearly, one can acquire a right view of the apostolate only by analyzing its peculiar nature and structure. What is peculiar to the New Testament apostolate is determined by a unique empowerment "from above," which involves absolute normativity. In a world where there are so many "empowerments," many questions will self-evidently arise about the legitimacy of this empowerment, and we will see later how far-reaching these questions already are in the New Testament itself.[18]

However, in connection with the apostolic structure of the Church, it is the nature of the empowerment itself — in human hands — that calls for our attention. The New Testament empowerment contains a being sent, a going forth, and a bearing of fruit that rules the whole life of the Church — i.e., doing so on account of Him Who Himself is called the apostle of our confession (Heb. 3:1) and Who builds and leads His Church

faith which we preach" (Rom. 10:8). In the parable of the rich man and Lazarus (Luke 16:19ff.), the rich man judges the words of Moses and the prophets to be insufficient to convince men. Full power would be present only if someone were to rise from the dead (vss. 29-31).

16. *TDNT*, I, 414; K. Rengstorf, *Apostolate and Ministry*, 1969, pp. 21ff.; P.A. van Stempvoort, *Eenheid en Schisma in de Kerk van Korinthe;* R. Schippers, *Getuigen van Jezus Christus in het N.T.*, p. 132.

17. Cf., among others, W. Schmithals, *Das kirchl. Apostelambt*, 1961, pp. 87ff.

18. Heb. 3:2. Cf. B. Klappert, *Die Eschat. des Hebr. Briefes*, 1969, pp. 53ff.

in and through that empowerment. Thus, it is important to ask this question: in what way are we to think of the relation beween Christ's empowerment and the empowerment of those whom He has called? A certain identification has frequently been mentioned here, because we are told that to hear or to reject the disciples is to hear or to reject Christ Himself. This is an indication of a deep, direct connection in the empowerment.[19] On the basis of this identification, a substitution, an expression surrounded by many dangers, has also been frequently mentioned. "Substitution" seems to suggest that someone *takes the place of another* who can no longer fulfill this commission or, in any case, does not fulfill it.[20] In the history of the Church, this problematic of substitution comes up especially in the so-called vicariate of the pope as the deputy of Christ on earth between the ascension and the second coming.[21] Even though the intention is not to declare Christ's own rule to be insufficient or to eliminate it, such a thought can easily play a role nevertheless. So, understandably, when the word "substitution" is used to characterize the salvation-historical transition,[22] there is a warning especially against interpreting it in its usual sense for normal life.[23] Christ's empowerment in no sense disappears from the Church's sight, because it manifests itself precisely in the human empowerment.[24]

19. Luke 10:16. Cf. Matt. 10:40 ("He who receives you receives me"); John 13:20 ("he who receives any one whom I send receives me"); I Pet. 4:11. Luke 10:16 is cited by Pius XII in *Humani Generis* (1950) to describe the authority of encyclicals. On Luther's emphatic language about the identity, cf. K.G. Steck, *Lehre und Kirche bei Luther*, 1963, pp. 52ff. Barth, in *C.D.*, I/2, pp. 746f., takes back his earlier criticism of Luther's emphatic identification (*Prolegomena*, 1927, pp. 415ff.).
20. For instance, cf. the substitution of Judas by Matthias in Acts 1:25: "to take the place in this ministry and apostleship." Cf. Acts 1:20 in connection with Ps. 109:8.
21. Cf. A. Harnack, "Christus Praesens-Vicarius," *Sitz. Berichte der preuss. Akad. der Wiss.*, 1927, pp. 415ff.
22. One may also think of the *other* Counselor Who is to come (John 14:16).
23. Calvin (*Inst.*, IV, 3, 1) speaks of a sort of delegated work (*quasi vicariam operam*), since "he does not dwell among us in visible presence ... to declare openly his will to us by mouth."
24. Cf. K. Barth, *C.D.*, I/1, pp. 106ff.: *vicarius Christi*, but apart from Christ's "yielding His right and His honor to man." Cf. also *TDNT*, VI, 682f. in connection with II Cor. 5:20; and Rengstorf, *Apostolate*, p. 59. A. Kuyper dealt with the same questions in connection with the rule of Christ and God in contrast to the idea of abdication. See my *The Providence of God*, 1952, p. 109.

To escape from the many dangers of misunderstanding,[25] one usually does not speak of identification and substitution, but of representation. Representation indicates that there is no suggestion of independence or isolation,[26] and it brings to expression the relation to the empowerment of the Lord Himself.[27] The word "representation" allows the intention of the word "identification" to emerge clearly: in human, empowered speaking, the full seriousness and reality of Christ's speaking is present. A warning is given against the misunderstanding that it is only a human voice. The depth of human, empowered speaking is indicated in a sharp contrast: "Therefore whoever disregards this, disregards not man but God, who gives his Holy Spirit to you" (I Thess. 4:8). The empowerment is real and is not relativized by its human character.[28] So there is also mention of a stewardship of the mysteries of God entrusted to man.[29] That this "stewardship" is given from above does not make it unreal and without authority, but founds it. The apostles are ambassadors for Christ (II Cor. 5:20), and when Paul writes "as though God were making his appeal through us," he does not intend the "as though" as a fiction. Rather, it indicates a deep relation of representation, since the *vox Dei* sounds in the *vox humana*.[30] Therefore, Paul can relate the word of reconciliation

25. There are many illustrations of these dangers in the history of the Church with regard to the designation of the pope as *vicarius Christi*. One example is the gradual concentration of the "vicariate," which at first was understood more broadly, in the pope. Cf. H. Küng, *The Church*, p. 468.

26. Cf. Calvin, *Inst.*, II, 12, 6, in connection with the creation of angels and men: "he willed that his glory be represented both in angels and in men" *(representari suam gloriam voluit);* and especially IV, 1, 6, on being a co-worker of God, which does not mean that Paul intends "to credit to himself even a particle apart from God," since that would be a sacrilege. Cf. in detail, M. de Kroon, *De Eer van God en het Heil van de Mens*, 1968, pp. 160ff.

27. Cf. O. Weber, *Grundlagen der Dogmatik*, II, 630.

28. On the word of preaching, cf. I Thess. 2:13. There is a parallel in I Sam. 8:7: "they have not rejected you, but they have rejected me." Cf. also Gal. 4:14: at first the Galatians received Paul, in spite of all his weakness, as an angel of God, as Christ Himself. Later that insight was lost to their detriment because of "bewitchment" (3:1).

29. I Cor. 4:1 *(oikonomia).* Cf. 9:17; Tit. 1:7; I Pet. 4:10; Col. 1:25. Cf. also J. Roloff, *Apostolat-Verkündigung-Kirche*, 1965, pp. 112ff.

30. *Hōs* (KJV: "as though"; RSV: omitted; Vulgate: *tamquam Deo exhortante per nos).* Cf. *TDNT*, VI, 283: "in the word of the ambassador Christ Himself speaks." Cf. the reference to Luke 10:16 in the Apology to the Augsburg Confession (J.T. Müller, *Die symb. Bücher der ev.*

to God's deed and can fully honor its power. Paul can write that the Corinthians came to belief through servants (I Cor. 3:5) and that he himself "became your father in Christ Jesus through the gospel."[31] One may not derogate in any respect from the power and significance of human functionality because of a fear of identification and substitution; for this human "meditation," this being taken into service, is expressed very clearly in the New Testament. It does not limit, but indicates the full empowerment of Christ.

Spiritualistic objections to this real functionality only seem to further God's honor, since they do not appreciate true human empowerment. By transcendentalizing the empowerment, they obscure the outlook on the ways of God, as the empowerment does not truly enter into human life. Spiritualism is understandable, and its great influence can be explained by its intention to see salvation fully in the hands of God and to withhold it from all human usurpation.[32] Undeniably, where salvation comes into view in the New Testament, men also come into view; and they have an exceptional functionality in speaking authoritatively of this salvation. We confront a forceful expression of that when we hear that the keys of the Kingdom of heaven are given into human hands (Matt. 16:19), accompanied by the pronouncement that what the apostles bind or loose on earth will be (éstai) bound or loosed in heaven. The parallel here is striking. Bounds are trespassed that on account of the divine, sovereign privilege do not seem to us to be trespassable. There have always been people who had more appreciation for a different statement about the keys, one which is full of exclusivity with respect to the exalted Lord: "I have the keys of Death and Hades" (Rev. 1:18). He has the key of

luth. Kirche, 1928, p. 158) in connection with "Christi vice et loco": id docet nos illa vox Christi, ne indignitate ministrorum offendamur.

31. I Cor. 4:15 (egénnēsa). Cf. Gal. 4:19 on "my little children" and Paul's travail "until Christ be formed in you!" On this passage Calvin (Commentaries on the Epistles of Paul to the Galatians and Ephesians, p. 132) writes: "this is a remarkable passage for illustrating the efficacy of the Christian ministry." Beside this "motherly" aspect, there is a fatherly aspect too. Cf. II Cor. 6:13; Philem. 10.

32. Cf. W. van 't Spijker, De Ambten bij Martin Bucer, 1970, pp. 350f., on the reasoning behind human mediation, which was not clear to Bucer. Cf. in this connection Calvin (Inst., IV, 1, 5) on the human medium — its familiarity — vis-à-vis the unbearable direct speaking that would overwhelm us. Therefore, it is ungratefulness to drag down the authority of the Word on account of the baseness of men.

David, "who opens and no one shall shut, who shuts and no one opens" (3:7). Is there not something strange in those keys in human hands? However, resistance to various popular notions of Peter as the "keeper of the keys" of heaven may not blind us to a unique stewardship, a far-reaching human empowerment in which there is no fear at all of obscuring the divine privilege. The parallel between earth and heaven in Matthew is related not only to Peter but to all the apostles (18:18). Naturally, it can be misunderstood and misused — such is the case with every empowerment — by being made into one's own "possession." Then it can take on horrible forms.[33] But one may not undermine or minimize the mystery and the reality of this empowerment because of that; rather, one must take full account of it.[34]

This equal "validity" both on earth and in heaven is more striking when the empowerment is related to the forgiveness of sins. The Scriptures speak of the forgiveness of sin as a human deed: "If you forgive the sins of any, they are forgiven; if you retain the sins of any, they are retained" (John 20:23). Kümmel considers it "hardly thinkable that Jesus would have granted such full empowerment, binding God, to a man," and he refers to the protest against the oath that "seeks to bind God."[35] Such a view does point out that the reality of the human empowerment automatically brings up many questions. The view is related to what von Campenhausen calls "the complete identity of the ecclesiastical and the divine judgment," which "is brought to expression with unsurpassable vigor."[36]

33. One may think of the lawyers who hindered those who were entering (Luke 11:52). Cf. Christ's reproach in Matt. 23:13: "you shut the kingdom of heaven against men." Cf. above, chapter 6, in connection with setting human boundaries that are not God's boundaries.

34. There has been much discussion whether the power of binding and loosing is related to the rabbinic usage of the power of the keys. In spite of varying interpretations of the object of binding and loosing, however, there is clearly a far-reaching parallel; and it is decisive for the human functionality. Cf. K. Adam, "Zum ausserkanonischen und kanonischen Sprachgebrauch von Binden und Lösen," *Gesam. Aufs.*, 1936, pp. 17ff.; *TDNT*, II, s.v. *déō (lúō)*, pp. 60f.

35. In connection with Matt. 5:33ff. W.G. Kümmel, *Kirchenbegriff und Geschichtsbewusstsein in der Urgemeinde und bei Jesus*, 1943, p. 40.

36. H. von Campenhausen, *Ecclesiastical Authority and Spiritual Power in the Church of the First Three Centuries*, 1969, p. 126. Von Campenhausen speaks of "ratification," since there is not first of all a divine judgment, in accordance with which the Church must give her judgment, but the starting point is the human, empowered judgment. Cf. *TDNT*, III, s.v. *kleís*.

Retreat from the seriousness of human empowerment   out of
fear that divine forgiveness would be made into a human thing
is frequent. It sometimes occurred in reaction to the Roman
Catholic institution of penance, for which Trent appealed to
John 20.[37] In the New Testament itself, we encounter a shrinking away from too close a connection between the divine and
human judgment. Then forgiveness is designated as exclusively
a divine privilege. In opposition to the reality of Christ's forgiveness of sins, the accusation is made: "It is blasphemy! Who
can forgive sins but God alone?"[38] Is forgiveness not a "transcendent" event, an exclusive divine privilege apart from any
human cooperation? Is not any "immanent" aspect to the power
of forgiveness in flagrant conflict with true, comforting forgiveness? However, this seeming obviousness is broken through
by Christ. Perceiving their questionings (dialogismoi), He asks
why they question these things in their heart (Luke 5:22). And
when forgiveness comes to pass through the man Jesus Christ,
the crowds are afraid and glorify God "who had given such
authority (exousía) to men" (Matt. 9:8). One should not build
a theology of human empowerment on this striking reaction,
but it is good to remember that the transcendentalizing of the
empowerment is eliminated by the emphatic way in which the
New Testament entrusts true empowerment to men in God's
order of salvation. The words "I absolve you from your sins"
(ego te absolvo a peccatis suis) are not necessarily an expression
of pride or a magical misuse of one's office. Moreover, because
the New Testament is so emphatic, the words cannot be minimized. One can ask whether the meaning of this empowerment
is purely interpreted when it is said that the God-man Christ
"wanted to share this power with the priests."[39] But it is irrefutable from the New Testament that an apostolic empowerment has been given and that statements sound forth, reaching
even to heaven, to the ears of God. There is no suggestion in
this that Christ's place is taken, but only that what happens
"on behalf of Christ" (II Cor. 5:20; cf. Acts 3:6) is the mode of

---

37. Denz., 894.
38. Mark 2:7 (ei mè heis ho theós). Cf. Luke 5:21; Matt. 9:3. Grosheide (Het
    Heilig Evangelie volgens Johannes, II, 1950, p. 538) speaks of forgiveness
    as "the work of God, which He does not let out of His hands." Cf.
    Luke 7:49: "Who is this, who even (hòs kaì) forgives sins?"
39. Thus the encyclical Ad Catholici Sacerdotii, 1935, with the addition:
    "one does not behold so much the hand of a man, but rather the
    hand of God, Who brings about a great wonder."

His empowerment in earthly, human reality. Pius XI speaks in this connection of a dreadful power[40] that belongs to God and now is given to men who themselves must also listen to this word of empowerment. Although history proves that one can land in strange, impassable ways because of this empowerment, there is a real, valid divine consolation that becomes manifest in the human form of the empowerment. And all the real dangers of misusing it and of making it independent cannot throw any shadows on its reality.[41]

Mutual subjection?

If the apostolicity of the Church is connected to the real functional character of the apostles — and thus also, to the salvation that has appeared in Christ, to His appearance "once for all at the end of the age" (Heb. 9:26), to the revelation of the mystery that was kept secret for ages and is now disclosed to all nations according to God's command (Rom. 16:26) — speaking about the apostolic structure of the Church is clearly more than a historical consideration related to her origin or beginning. Rather, in her *credo,* the Church wanted to give an outlook on the uniqueness of the *vox humana* which bore testimony to this reality in the last days, and wanted to test the conformity of that testimony with these human voices that God made to sound forth over the whole world. What holds good with respect to all the attributes of the Church holds good to a special extent with respect to apostolicity. It is removed from all self-evidence and must be understood apart from every false lyric that is indistinguishable from ecclesiastical self-complacency. That is possible only in the outlook on the nature of apostolicity as the "concrete spiritual criterion" that points to normativity and subjection.[42] This aspect of the *credo* proposes the question whether the Church truly lives under the

40. *Reformidanda potestas, Ad Catholici Sacerdotii.*
41. Calvin (*Inst.,* III, 4, 14) warns against dreaming up some power that is separate from the preaching of the gospel. One may think here of Trent's declaration, which implies a view of the Reformation, that absolution "is not merely a simple *(nudum)* ministry that consists in announcing the gospel or of declaring that the sins are remitted; but it is like a judicial act *(actus judicialis)* whereby the sentence is pronounced by the priest as a judge" (Denz., 902, 919; *TCT,* 795, 808).
42. K. Barth, *C.D.,* IV/1, p. 712. Naturally, such an aspect of testing is also present in the other attributes of the Church (cf. above, chapter 1), but it is present concretely in apostolicity.

empowerment of the apostolic testimony, and that question is so urgent that it is impossible to pronounce this *credo* other than in fear and trembling: " 'Apostolic' means in the discipleship, in the school, under the normative authority, instruction and direction of the apostles, in agreement with them, because listening to them and accepting their message."[43] This testing does not imply a rupture between the apostles and the Church on her way through the centuries, but does postulate a very special relation, because the Church knows that she is confronted here with concrete, human voices that have empowerment and authority.[44]

It is good and necessary to give full attention to the significance of this *vox humana*. In what way is it essential for the Church, since the starting point of all reflection on the Church is her relatedness and subjection to the Lord of the Church? Does this structure leave room for a special, human, and mediating empowerment by which a relation of subjection and obedience arises between men and other men? The New Testament is full of the subjection of all to Christ and warns against everything that threatens this structure. The "lordship" of one over another is such a threat, because the total, single subjection to the Lord can be overshadowed. For instance, Christ pointed out that various facts from the lives of men in the world could not simply be transformed "by analogy" to the life of the Church.[45] We are thinking of the distinction between the rulers and great men of the people, who have power and lordship over their subjects, and the disciples of Jesus, whose existence in the world is characterized in this way: "But it shall not be so among you" (Mark 10:43; cf. Matt. 20:28f.; Luke 22:24-27). Here everything is totally different, since whoever wants to be great must be the servant and slave of all. Therein lies the decisive order that characterizes the Church.

Subjection to Christ does leave room for a general subjection of the many members of the one body to one another:

43. *Ibid.*, p. 714. The sense of being tested is the defense against all self-glorification; as such, it has penetrated more and more into the Roman Catholic notion of the Church. Cf. H.U. von Balthasar, "Kirchenerfahrung dieser Zeit," *Sentire Ecclesiam*, p. 753, on the Church as the "handmaid of the Lord," not called to "weave earthly crowns" for herself.
44. This relation is obscured when the spectacle of the Church is spoken of as Paul VI does as the apostolic army, gathered from the whole world (*Salvete*, 1963).
45. Cf. O. Weber, *Grundlagen der Dogmatik,* II, 625ff., on the order in the Church: "not a mere application of general principles of order."

we must be subject to one another out of reverence to Christ
(Eph. 5:21). The decisive order of the Church stands in the
light of service directed to one another. Instead of selfishness
and conceit (Phil. 2:3), there is to be mutual affection, love,
and a show of honor (Rom. 12:10) toward one another for the
upbuilding of the one body. This mutual aspect also functions
in admonition (Col. 3:16; cf. I Thess. 5:11), and it contains
no one-sidedness. The background and foundation is the humiliation, the emptying, and the service of Jesus Christ, which
embraces an appeal to live in that same like-mindedness (Phil.
2:5; cf. Matt. 11:29) for the revelation of the participation in
the Spirit (Phil. 2:1). In that light we must ask the question:
within this circle of fellowship, can there be anything other
than this mutual subjection? Does a localization of empowerment and authority, along with the subjection and obedience
that are correlates of it, seem to abolish this mutuality? Our
interest becomes even more intense since the New Testament
carries on such sharp opposition against the self-exaltation of
some above others. We perceive that, for instance, with the Pharisees and scribes, who sit on Moses' seat (Matt. 23:2) above the
crowd and who, in their places of honor, take up the best
seats in the synagogue (23:6). Christ opposes all such pretensions
and the self-evidence of such "priority." One may not be called
rabbi (23:8), because One is the teacher of all; and one may
not be called father or master, because One is the father and
master (23:9f.), and they are all brethren (23:8). All of this
comes to a climax for Matthew in a warning against self-
exaltation (23:12).

All these forms of defense and criticism have reference to
the decisive structure of the Church. So, it would certainly be
unjust to interpret contemporary interest in this radicalness too
quickly as "modern" democratization, as an attack on all authority in the Church, or as a rebellion by the laity against
the officebearers. Rather, it is necessary to devote full attention to this structure. It is inseparably connected to the perspective of fulfillment in the coming of the new covenant. That
new covenant is characterized in such a way that God's law
is put upon the heart, and it is said of the people of God: "And
no longer shall each man teach his neighbor and each his
brother, saying, 'Know the Lord,' for they shall all know me,
from the least of them to the greatest" (Jer. 31:34; Heb. 8:11).
Are we not faced here by a structure in which each is "independent" of the other, not in the sense of isolation, but due

to the reality of a spiritual fellowship and to the gifts of the Spirit[46] in a beneficial "pneumatocracy"?[47] The charisma seems to eliminate all "localization" and every fixation or channeling of authority and office that would apply only to individuals.

In addition to Paul, attention is given in this connection especially to the Johannine letters, where there are references to an anointing of all: "you have no need *(ou chreian échete)* that any one should teach you" because the anointing "teaches you about everything" (I John 2:27). Likewise, being "taught by God" is also mentioned.[48] It is not a protest against authority and submission, but a recognition of the filling by the Holy Spirit and the authority contained therein.[49] An emphatic warning is issued against the desire for superiority as it becomes visible in the horrible form of Diotrephes, whose pretended empowerment — to the point of excommunication — appears in wanting to be first.[50] In the Gospel of John, the riches of the Church are pictured as the continuance of *all* in the vine; that is the decisive structure of the Church (15:1-8). Our attention does not seem to be called to auxiliary structures that are also necessary within this fundamental structure. It will always be necessary to acknowledge fully this striking dimension in John, the central relatedness of all to the same reality of salvation, in which all individualism is out of the question because of the pneumatic power of fellowship.

Charisma and office

All of this is so clear and radical that one can ask how there can be any dependence with respect to human empowerment. This question concerns not only all forms of office in the Church, but also the *credo*, which speaks of the apostolic structure of the Church. Is not every human *Gegenüber* a per-

---

46. Joel 2:28; cf. Acts 2:17. Cf. J. Ratzinger, "Bemerkungen zur Frage der Charismen in der alten Kirche," *Die Zeit Jesu. Festschr. H. Schlier*, 1970, pp. 257ff.; *idem, Das Volk Gottes. Entwürfe zur Ekklesiologie*, 1970, pp. 116ff.
47. The expression comes from R. Sohm, *Wesen und Ursprung des Katholizismus*, 1912², p. viii, to indicate the rule of the whole people by the Spirit. "Therefore, no Christian is subject spiritually to another."
48. John 6:45, referring to Isa. 54:13 ("all your sons"). Cf. I Thess. 4:9 ("you yourselves have been taught by God to love one another"); I Cor. 2:13 ("not taught by human wisdom but taught by the Spirit").
49. R. Schnackenburg, *Die Joh. Briefe*, 1953, p. 24. Cf. John 14:26.
50. III John 9. Cf. E. Käsemann, "Ketzer und Zeuge," *Exeg. Vers. und Besinn.*, I, 170ff.

version of this new fellowship and of the Johannine outlook on the Church?[51] Frequently, tension, or even an antithesis, is noticed between the charismatic depth of the Church and her structure in office and institution. Supposedly, the Church was originally charismatic by nature (spiritual, mutual subjection in the one body), but diverse circumstances and factors landed the Church in a wholly different climate of life and thought — namely, that of institutionalization and of official structures of authority. The explanation for this is sought in fear of arbitrariness, chaos, and disorder: consistent, unhampered individualism could lead to a spiritual anarchy where there would no longer be any checks and the appeal to the Spirit could not be refuted or contradicted by anyone. Gradually, therefore, the *charismata* were restricted, if not replaced, by official structures which channeled the workings of the Spirit.

In this line, Käsemann points especially to Paul, the great charismatic, who saw the Church as the domain of the Spirit. No other "order" may rule there than the order of grace, which links everyone.[52] Naturally, Paul was not sanctioning individualism or disorder. He knows that God is not a God of confusion (I Cor. 14:33 — *akatastasía*) and that all things must be done decently and in good order (14:40 — *euschēmónōs kaì katà táxin*). But that in no sense signifies the restraint provided by "official" structures, because the opposite of confusion is peace as the manifestation of grace and as harmony with the living Lord. Order is not a necessary "antipole" of the Spirit, but the peace of directedness to one another, which bans all individualism.[53]

51. G. Hasenhüttl (*Charisma. Ordnungsprinzip der Kirche,* 1969, pp. 263ff.) speaks with regard to John of "the eschatological reduction" and of the immediate connection with Christ — with the continuity that it implies. Further, see W.G. Kümmel, *The Theology of the N.T.,* 1973, pp. 261ff.; and E. Schweizer, "Der Kirchenbegriff im Evangelium und in der Briefe von Johannes," *Neotestamentica,* 1963, pp. 259ff., on the radical newness of the Church, which appears in simply abiding in Jesus. This does not indicate in the least a lack of interest in the *ecclesia* (cf. I John 2:19), although the word appears only in III John 6 and 9; but the Johannine ecclesiological dimension is definitely unique.

52. E. Käsemann, "Amt und Gemeinde im N.T.," *Exeg. Versuche und Besinn.,* I, 1960, pp. 109ff., with reference, among other things, to the manifestation of the Spirit (*"phanérōsis toú pneúmatos"*) that is given to each for the common good (I Cor. 12:7).

53. Cf. on peace versus disorder also H. von Campenhausen, "Recht und Gehorsam in der alten Kirche," *Aus der Frühzeit des Christentums;* and E. Käsemann, "Sätze heiligen Rechtes im N.T.," *Exeg. Versuche und Besinn.,* II, 1964, pp. 81ff.: "not order as such and in the formal sense."

According to Käsemann, there is no longer a place for a holy
sphere with a cultic nature or for a specific privilege for some,
because the pneumatic charisma structures the whole Church.[54]
And it is this fundamental structure that, according to Käsemann,
was not preserved. It was replaced by other structures in a shift
from charisma to office. Käsemann shows a large measure of
understanding for this shift[55] and also speaks of "a historical
necessity" vis-à-vis "the enthusiasm fermenting in the churches."
But the shift is striking and has had far-reaching consequences.[56]
Even though one can speak of a legitimate aspect to this development,[57] the Church was from then on caught in the grasp
of necessary "regulations and structures." We touch here upon
the much discussed problem of "early catholicism." Early catholicism means that what later became the official structure of
the Church in the Roman Catholic Church already had a clear
place in the New Testament: official regulation in opposition
to the dangers of spiritual anarchy.[58] The Pauline and Johannine
aspects of the Church, Spirit, and charisma faded away. True,
the intention was not to oppose office and structure to the
Spirit, but rather to preserve His work from confusion and to
escape spiritualistic intangibility.[59] A principle of order was
introduced to structure the Church. First of all, it was beside,
and later in place of, the charismatic structure. Just as everything
in God's world-order has a firm place, a position, a particular
order, so it also is in the Church: charismatic life — life deriving
from the Spirit — must be inserted into this order.[60]

54. Käsemann, *op. cit.*, I, 121.
55. *Ibid.*, II, 82, on "ecclesiastical law" and the ensuing casuistry.
56. According to Käsemann, it was "a revolutionary change that occurred
    within a half century after Paul."
57. Käsemann, "Paulus und der Früh-katholizismus," *op. cit.*, II, 249. It
    is legitimate because the Spirit stimulates the search for new ways in
    the need and timidity of men." Cf. also p. 250 on "the struggle against
    enthusiasm."
58. For this early catholicism, see also W. Marxsen, *Der Früh-katholizismus
    im N.T.*, 1958, p. 8, in connection with, among other things, II Pet.
    1:19-21 on the interpretation of prophecy, which is no longer a "pri-
    vate matter," but becomes a "matter for the teaching office." Cf. my
    Holy Scripture, pp. 115ff.; and K. Beyschlag, *Clemens Romanus und
    der Früh-katholizismus*, 1966.
59. Käsemann, *op. cit.*, II, 250ff.
60. In spite of the recognition of a certain legitimacy, Käsemann sees the
    shift as a transition to "the religious metaphysics of the heavenly-
    earthly orders." One considers this element to be present especially in
    Clement of Rome. Cf. Beyschlag, *op. cit.*, pp. 276ff.; A.F.J. Klijn, *Apos-
    tolische Vaders*, II, 1967, p. 18; Hasenhüttl, *op. cit.*, pp. 288ff.

It is clear that the background of these considerations is a contrast between charisma and office as two completely different experiences of the Church. Offices arise when one can no longer breathe on the mountainous heights of charismatic life. So one ties down the life of the Spirit. That the Spirit blows where He will (John 3:8) becomes a past tense, and the Spirit has entered into the firm structures of the Church. We touch here upon a captivating aspect of the entire history of the Church. We see tensions arise over and over again between charisma and office. Even where the official structures of the Church do not deny the charisma,[61] the fear frequently arises that the charisma will stifle the offices, blurring the significance of the Church's institutional life.[62] The solution is then sought in the idea that the *charismata* belong to what is extraordinary, or exceptional, in the Church. No matter how much recognition they are given as spiritual gifts, they may never detract from the "common" life of the Church, which cannot exist apart from official structures.[63] Because of that, the *charismata* became less and less significant in reflection on the structures of the Church, at the most continuing to be respected as luxuries "that can be lacking without any harm at all."[64] But the problematic of office and the charisma, charisma and office, continued to exist and could always give occasion to new reflection. Calling attention to the significance of the charismatic life of the Church continued to be legitimate, for it had to be given its due on account of the double structure of the Church — viz., the charismatic and official structure. Charisma and office could not be placed in opposition to each other, but both had to be honored in harmony with each other.[65]

---

61. The encyclical *Mystici Corporis Christi* of 1943 denies that "this ordered or 'organic' structure of the body of the Church contains only hierarchical elements and with them is complete" (Denz.-Schönm., 3801; *TCT*, 241). There is great interest in life in the world as an honorable and humble place in the Christian fellowship. Cf. H. Kraemer, *Het Vergeten Ambt*, 1962.

62. Cf. Paul VI's fear (*Ecclesiam Suam*, para. 47) of the desire "of renewing the structure of the Church through the charismatic way."

63. Cf. Hasenhüttl, *op. cit.*, pp. 321ff. on resistance to the American reform Catholicism, which wanted to stimulate the laity to active cooperation in the Church (Hecker).

64. *Ibid.*, p. 322.

65. Cf., among others, K. Rahner (*Das Dynamische in der Kirche*, 1958, pp. 61ff.), who speaks of "a divinely willed dualism between charisma and office" and of "antagonism." But he does not have any disharmony in view here.

This interest in the charisma, which breaks out over and over again, recalls the spiritual character of the Church. In the New Testament, the *charismata* are concentrated in Christ's one gift of salvation.[66] They can take on particular form in a great variety of ways without breaking up into a disparate multiplicity: in gifts, service, and working, which all find their connection in the one Spirit (I Cor. 12:4). He manifests Himself in the gift (12:7), and He gives, apportions, and inspires it (12:8, 11) as "grace which was given you" (1:4 — *cháris dotheísa*). Because of the fundamental relation to the Spirit,[67] it is impossible for the gift of salvation to be transferred to the command of men in such a way that the prayer *Veni Creator Spiritus!* would be superfluous because the Holy Spirit had come. No matter how many ways are cleared by the power of the Spirit, it is not possible to tie down and channel His work. That is the background of the various protests in the history of the Church against the dangers of institutionalization. The recollection of the charisma of the Spirit certainly did not always intend to call attention to spectacular phenomena in the Church, but to the boundaries of the Church's official structure. Over and over again, threats to the Church because of institutionalization were apparent in the history of the Church. When her life was caught in the grasp of fixed structures, it became possible to determine where the Church was present — namely, in the firm framework of fixed offices.[68] In spite of the good intentions of the official structure, the danger of automatization

66. Rom. 5:15ff.; 6:23. Cf. O. Perels, "Charisma im N.T.," *Fuldaer Hefte,* 1964, pp. 39ff.; J. Ratzinger, "Bemerkungen zur Frage der Charismen in der Kirche," *Die Zeit Jesu. Festschr. H. Schlier,* 1970, pp. 257ff.; *idem, Das neue Volk Gottes. Entwürfe zur Ekklesiologie,* 1970², pp. 116ff.

67. Paul speaks also of "spiritual gifts" (I Cor. 12:1; 14:1 — *pneumatiká*). The context in which the spiritual gifts are mentioned makes it impossible to see the spectacular charisma as what is proper to the Spirit and His working. For what is proper always lies in the charisma as the central saving gift of grace, to which all the gifts are related. Cf. Ratzinger, *Die Zeit Jesu. Festschr. H. Schlier,* p. 262. See also his comments on glossolalia and on the "eruptions of *agápē*" as "the actual Christian wonder."

68. Cf. K. Rahner, "Do Not Stifle the Spirit!," *Theological Investigations,* VII, 72ff., especially on our time as "hostile to all that is charismatic," because "the only effective and valid factors are those which are the outcome of plan and design" (p. 76). Cf. the dangers of centralism, which can forget that the activity of the Spirit "can never find adequate expression simply in the forms of what we call the Church's official life, her principles, sacramental system and teaching" (p. 75).

and channeling appeared over and over again. The Spirit as the "soul of the Church" could be found and acknowledged only within a fixed framework, and thus the deep earnestness of the admonition not to quench the Spirit was no longer understood and honored fully.[69] Protests against quenching the Spirit can develop into passionate opposition to all offices and institutional forms. Then the voices sound nostalgically for the Spirit whom one misses more and more in the institution. This was the case in the Middle Ages with Joachim of Fiore, who looked forward to a new era of the Spirit when the "priestly" Church would come to an end.[70] However, the protest does not always have to appear in these revolutionary forms; it can also arise from nostalgia for a new understanding of the offices, for a religious catharsis of the concept, so that the offices no longer stand in the way of the Spirit's power, but are totally serviceable to it. Clearly, this motif strongly dominates in contemporary Roman Catholic ecclesiology; and, naturally, it can adopt extremely critical forms. But it is different from Joachim of Fiore, because the critical motif is taken up in expectation for the Church. There is no longer a dilemma or antithesis between charisma and office, since they are related to each other in a meaningful and fruitful connection. The offices no longer have to be seen as a threat

69. I Thess. 5:19. Cf. *TDNT*, VII, 168 ("to suppress," "to restrain"); and Calvin, *Commentaries on the Epistles of Paul to the Philippians, Colossians, and Thessalonians*, p. 298, on "an exceedingly useful admonition." Calvin speaks of a "dreadful blindness," opposing those who are of the opinion that it is "in man's option" to quench the light of the Spirit; for "God works efficaciously in his elect," although they are still threatened by slothfulness. Especially Rahner (*op. cit.*, p. 73) has accentuated the seriousness of quenching the Spirit with regard to "the burning fire of God." It is a "terrible danger" that the Spirit has been given "into our power, made subject to the inertia of our spirit, brought under the control of our cowardice, placed at the disposal of our empty, earthly, loveless hearts." The Spirit *can* be stifled "not indeed throughout the entire Church, but still over so wide an area, and to such a terrible extent that we have to fear that judgment which begins with the house of God" (p. 80). The citation here from I Pet. 4:17 was not incorporated in the Constitution on the Church, even though it was dealt with in many commission discussions.

70. Cf. K. Löwith, *Weltgeschichte und Heilsgeschichte*, 1953², pp. 136ff.; E. Benz, *Ecclesia Spiritualis. Kirchenidee und Geschichtstheologie der Franzisk. Reformation*, 1964, especially pp. 32ff., 256ff.; H. Grundmann, *Studien über Joachim von Fiore*, 1966, pp. 106ff. Joachim did not want a "translation," but a "severing" in an "abruptly operative, spiritual existence (*Dasein*)."

to the Spirit, but rather are directed to His work and power. Criticism of the institutional degeneration of the office asks for concern for the truthfulness and purity of the human empowerment according to its apostolic structure. Such concern is due not to an anti-institutional inclination, but to a recollection of the body of Christ and the power of the Spirit. In crisis situations concerning the authority of the Church, there can be a certain uneasiness[71] that the new interpretation of office — and specifically of the hierarchy — will lead eventually to a minimizing of the Church's firm structures.[72] At the same time, though, we confront this new view of offices and institution that intends to recall the apostolic structure of the Church. In that structure, the *vox humana* does not frustrate the blowing of the Spirit, but is subject and serviceable to Him, and "authority" does not abolish, but serves and affirms the communion. The *Gegenüber* of authority remains subject to the Lord Himself.

Only in this connection is it possible to answer someone who raises the question: "Who made you a prince and a judge over us?" (Ex. 2:14). It is apparent in the New Testament that this irritated question is totally illegitimate vis-à-vis true empowerment. For that matter, the *Gegenüber* is separated distinctly from any usurpation. The latter is constantly warned against and, therefore, is qualified religiously. In this sphere, the exercise of empowerment itself stands under the test of submission (cf. Matt. 7:1ff.; Rom. 14:4). Where obedience to authority is called for, there appears to be no thought of rigid, blind obedience: esteem and love for the bearers of the empowerment are required because of their work (I Thess. 5:12f.; I Cor. 16:11, 18), and they must be received with joy (Phil.

---

71. Cf. Paul VI in opposition to charismatic attempts at renewal, in *Ecclesiam Suam*, para. 47. In this context he refers to "the Church's original structure" (*"germana Ecclesiae conformatio"*).

72. G. Hasenhüttl's study (*op. cit.*, pp. 334ff.) ends with a discussion of the *hierarchy*. He does not contest the hierarchical structure of the Church, but founds it in the charismatic structure (thus, not a dualism of structures, namely, the hierarchical and the charismatic). Hence, the Church is not absorbed structurally in the hierarchy, but the hierarchy comes into view in the relatedness to the Church as the body of Christ and as communion: "where the charismatic fellowship is, there is the Church of Christ" (p. 338). In the original form of Vatican II's Constitution on the Church, the hierarchy preceded the people of God. Later, the order was reversed, and Hasenhüttl sees that as a new aspect that is full of promise for reflection on the structure of the Church.

2:29; cf. Heb. 13:7, 17). That the empowerment comes "from above" cannot in any sense be compared to an "authoritarian" order. Certainly, there is mention of real authority — with subjection and obedience as the subjective correlate — but the question of decisive significance is: within what contours does the authority manifest itself? In the New Testament, it possesses a totally unique structure. There is no hint of a formal, empty, or aprioristic relation of authority that demands submission as such.

Service

In our time, the emphasis has fallen more and more on the mode of empowerment and authority. In order to separate the empowerment from all perversions, one has emphasized especially that service characterizes office and authority. One wants to avoid an interpretation of office and authority based on a general *Vorverständnis* of "lordship," by which the outlook on the blessing and liberating power of the empowerment would be obscured.[73] In discussions on the usage of the concept "service," the danger has been pointed out that the sovereign *Gegenüber* can be blurred by a general work of ministry, or service, so that its being "on behalf of God" is scarcely seen any longer. For instance, van Ruler speaks of "violent systematizing" when one speaks not of offices, but of services, because then "important elements of the New Testament kerygma concerning God's action" fall away.[74] Naturally, such a replacement could conceivably arise, but it would be unjust to explain the replacement as such on the basis of that meager view, since the New Testament concept of "service" *(diakonia)* is often used in an attempt to contrast the office to all authoritarianism and hypostatization. Thus, there is no antithesis between office and authority,[75] and the "on behalf of God" is not in the least ex-

---

73. See in detail H. Dembowski, *Grundfragen der Christologie. Erörtert am Problem der Herrschaft Jesu Christi,* 1969, pp. 323ff., and pp. 37ff., 55ff. (in opposition to all "ecclesiocracy"). Further, cf. R.J. Bunnik, *Dienaren van het Aggiornamento,* 1967; H. Bouchette, *Leek en Ambt,* 1963; and H. Küng, *The Church,* pp. 388ff.
74. A.A. van Ruler, *Bijzonder en Algemeen Ambt,* 1952, pp. 11f.
75. Van Ruler (*op. cit.,* p. 22), for that matter, also speaks of the serviceability of the Church in her apostolic position and function — namely, "serviceable to this affair between God and His world. That is the origin of the Christian concept of service." Cf. p. 75 in connection with Jesus' serving and ruling. Van Ruler intends to warn against

cluded, since this service is founded precisely in it. So, the word
can also illuminate purely the meaning of offices.[76] It can recall
Christ, Who characterized His coming into the world as "service"
(Mark 10:45), and it can recall the authoritative service of the
apostles. Their service is compared to the servant who is not
above his master and to the messenger who is not above the
one who sends him (John 13:16). In all empowerment, service
to the Lord is essential; and thus, it is directed to men. Therefore, this service can never take on the form of an office that
is concerned basically with itself, thus becoming an abstract
empowerment above the Church.

It is very remarkable that it is in the Pastoral letters,
which have been discussed a great deal because of their institutional aspect, that the living, practical context of empowerment comes to light so clearly. The bearers of empowerment
are called to reflect the service of the Lord in their personal
lives. For instance, the bishop must satisfy certain "conditions"
(I Tim. 3:2; 4:14; 6:11). There may not be any "stumbling
blocks" in his life that would hinder the power of his empowerment and service.[77] The office is not thereby personalized, but
it is denied any "supra-personal," authoritarian form. Only in
these connections[78] can the outlook on the power of the empowerment be preserved and can authority manifest itself in
the speaking of the Word of God (I Pet. 4:11), while at the
same time requiring imitation of the faith of those who have
received the commission (Heb. 13:7). Submission is the subjective correlate not of an empowerment in itself, but of an

"the one-sided and passionate predilection for the word service" (p. 76).
Cf. O. Weber, Grundlagen der Dogmatik, II, 628, on the emotional
misunderstanding of the word service.

76. Cf. Lumen Gentium, DV II, pp. 46f., on the duty committed to the
shepherds as "true service." M. Löhrer ("Die Hierarchie in Dienst van het
Christenvolk," in Barauna, De Kerk van Vaticanum II, II, 13) sees this
emphasis as the fruit of present-day exegesis and of ecumenical dialogue.
He correctly points to the two-fold aspect of this servitium, since it is
on behalf of Christ and, thus, is service to the Church. Cf. for the
former, I Cor. 4:1: servants (hupērétas) for someone, who "willingly
learns his task and goal from another who is over him in organic order"
(TDNT, VIII, 533). That is in opposition to all arbitrariness (p. 542);
and so it is akin to being an apostle. Cf. K. Barth, C.D., IV/2, pp. 676-726.
77. Cf. H.N. Ridderbos, "Kerkelijke Orde en Kerkelijk Recht," Ex Auditu
Verbi, 1965, pp. 194ff.; idem, De Pastorale Brieven, pp. 90ff.; H. Machlum,
Die Vollmacht des Timotheus nach den Pastoralbriefen, 1969, pp. 59ff.
78. Cf. the connection between managing one's own household and caring
for the Church (I Tim. 3:5).

authority that is full of blessing and salvation. It can be designated as keeping watch over souls (13:17). The empowerment
separates itself from any hubris on the part of the bearers, who,
for that matter, themselves are in a relation of submission:
they too must give account (13:17). Paul pointedly indicated
the nature of empowerment in the Church when he characterized it as follows: "Not that we lord it over your faith; we
work with you for your joy."[79] In the context of communion,
there can be distinctions so that "some" come to the fore: the
70, the 12, or the many. The empowerment is then concentrated in their service.[80] This empowerment does not attack
the communion, but is a sign of a beneficial *Gegenüber*. It
becomes audible in the concrete *vox humana*, which itself is
tested as to whether it truly serves and consolidates the communion.

The normative past

If confessing the apostolicity of the Church means continuing subjection to the apostolic witness, then it definitely does
not signify an inert clinging to a faraway past that has scarcely
any significance in the present.[81] Rather, the New Testament is
full of the opposite; for, starting precisely from this normative
beginning, the Church is set in motion, and only in this way
can it be recognized as a truly apostolic Church.[82] Apostolicity
incontestably reaches back to this beginning, the beginning of

---

79. II Cor. 1:24. Cf. I Pet. 5:2f. on tending the flock vis-à-vis domineering
    over it *(katakurieúō)*. Cf. this same word also in Mark 10:42. Cf.
    further I Thess. 2:5ff.: without flattery, greed, or seeking glory from
    men, but with gentleness, "like a nurse taking care of her children."
    O. Weber *(op. cit.,* p. 627) speaks about offices as a "benefit." One may
    also think of the antithesis with making men slaves, parallel to preying
    on someone and taking advantage of him (II Cor. 11:20). G. van
    Leeuwen ("Bijbels-theol. notities bij het Gezagsprobleem," *Rondom
    het Woord,* 1968, p. 62) speaks of the *kābôd,* the glory in authority,
    but "this line of the *kābôd* is not drawn uncritically."
80. Cf. Luke 10:1. The distinction is expressed explicitly in Acts 10:41f.:
    "not to all the people but to us who were chosen by God as witnesses."
    Cf. R.P. Meye, *Jesus and the Twelve. Discipleship and Revelation in
    Mark's Gospel,* 1968, pp. 118ff.; O. Noordmans, *Gestalte en Geest,* 1955,
    pp. 105f., on "the crowd": "The form that the gospel adopts with respect
    to the crowd is the apostolate."
81. Cf. O. Noordmans, *op. cit.,* pp. 335ff., on antiquarian and mystical
    apostolicity. Cf. below, chapter 10, on the movement in the history of
    the Church.
82. Cf. K. Barth, *C.D.,* IV/1, pp. 712ff.

the gospel of Jesus Christ (Mark 1:1). It is the gospel that was proclaimed and delivered once for all and for which one must contend (Jude 3). This aspect of apostolicity as the outlook on the living Lord of the Church along the way to the future manifests itself from the start in a passionate defense against heresy, since it obscures the continuing outlook on salvation.[83] Over and over again, normativity comes to the fore in direct connection to the present and the past. This temporal aspect is not to be understood in the sense of a formal category that postulates the value of what is old as such, but as a concrete boundary along a way that must be walked. Hence, a warning is given not to go "beyond" Scripture[84] and not to "go ahead" in a wrong direction (II John 9). The Church hears many apparently "conservative" admonitions, just as in the Old Testament where the people are admonished to ask for the ancient paths, while they do not want to give heed to or to walk along the good way (Jer. 6:16). Progress can only occur in holding true to what has been attained (Phil. 3:16), in abiding in the doctrine (didachê) of Christ (II John 9), and in not abandoning what was received. All of this is in a recollection of the "beginning" that governs the structure of what comes later.[85] There is no hint here of a formal, inert conservatism, since the temporal dimension is filled with the outlook on Him Who was from the beginning (I John 1:1). It is the category of a very specific origin, which must continue to determine the Church's life. That salutary beginning involves the disclosure precisely of what is radically new (I John 2:8); therefore, it must continue in concrete remembrance if the Church is to remain truly the Church. Conzelmann sees all of this as ecclesiastical traditionalism.[86] In itself, though, this characterization says little,

---

83. On heresy cf. chapter 5, pp. 115ff. above.
84. I Cor. 4:6 (Dutch; RSV: "live according to Scripture"). On this phrase see O. Linton, Theol. Stud. u. Krit., 1930; M.D. Hooker, "Beyond the Things Which are Written. An examination of I Cor. IV, 6," New Testament Studies, 10, 1963/64, pp. 127ff. H. von Campenhausen (The Formation of the Christian Bible, 1972) speaks of an "enigmatic passage."
85. II John 5; I John 2:7, 24. Cf. H. Conzelmann, "Was vom Anfang war," N.T. Studien für R. Bultmann, 1954, pp. 194ff. See I John 1:1 as the content of the abiding kerygma; 2:7 (the commandment from the beginning); 2:24; II John 5f.
86. Conzelmann, op. cit., pp. 197, 199. J. Brosch (Das Wesen der Häresie, 1936, p. 93) speaks incorrectly of a Roman Catholic "principle of tradition" here.

since what is new summons up this continuing interest. The necessity of continuance is filled with the fervor of the great mystery, and its background is a different "earlier," when the mystery was still kept secret, while it is *now* (in the beginning!) disclosed (Rom. 16:25f.). On account of this "now," the Church must remain in what she has heard and understood (Col. 1:6; Phil. 4:9) and in what was delivered to her (I Cor. 11:2, 23; 15:1ff.; I Thess. 4:1).

That definite forms can play a role in the historical progress of the Church (cf. Rom. 6:17; II Thess. 2:15) in no way derogates from the fact that this "tradition" structurally differs from every idealization or romanticization of the past.[87] A critical light often falls on human traditions, so that tradition and preservation as such are certainly not placed beyond all suspicion.[88] The decisive questions are: which "doctrine" is in question? What way must one continue walking? In "abiding," one's sight is directed to understanding the grace of God in truth (Col. 1:6) as the decisive turn from falsification and darkness. The unique tie to "the beginning" is directed to the hope of the gospel which has been heard[89] and to life in the world. It can even be said that the teaching and tradition that must be preserved is sound doctrine (Titus 1:9), not as a middle-class phenomenon, a rigid and immovable possession, but as the revelation of the liberating and healing power of salvation.[90]

---

87. Cf. *TDNT*, I, 482 on the danger of the "romantic aura." The significance of Tertullian's statement (see above, chapter 8, p. 204, n. 12) is also connected with this. In the reference to the *omne genus,* the question of the uniqueness of the origin does not in the least come into view. In this connection see P. Stockmeier, *Handbuch der Dogmengeschichte,* I, fasc. 1a, 1971, p. 55, which parallels Tertullian's thought on tradition with that of Cicero (the holy prehistoric era, to which one must return). See also H. von Campenhausen (*Tradition and Life in the Church,* 1968, pp. 7ff.), who stresses that "the inner meaning of the Christian idea of tradition can be understood only in its demarcation from Judaism" (p. 10).

88. Cf. Paul's blameless "traditional" life in the light of the new life (Phil. 3:6); and the contrast between the tradition of the elders and the attitude of the disciples, who do not follow this tradition (Matt. 15:2ff.). The traditions of men can make the commandment of God inoperative (15:6). Cf. also the empty deceit "according to human tradition" (Col. 2:8); the teaching of the Pharisees (Matt. 16:12), of Balaam (Rev. 2:14), and of Jezebel (2:24); and strange teachings (Heb. 13:9).

89. Col. 1:23. Cf. I Tim. 6:20 on guarding what has been entrusted *(parathēkē)* in connection with the future (6:19). II Tim. 1:12 speaks of the divine guarding of the *parathēkē.* Cf. *TDNT,* VIII, 163f.

90. Cf. the sound words of Jesus Christ (I Tim. 6:3; cf. 2:8).

This sound doctrine is opposed to the violation of life that can occur in all sorts of forms (I Tim. 1:10; cf. II Tim. 4:3; 1:13). Whoever formalizes tradition can never get a correct view of true apostolicity. He lacks appreciation for the virtuality and dynamic of tradition that is separated from faith, hope, and love. Where apostolicity is isolated and the power of the apostolic testimony is not understood, the *credo* loses its luster; it is without responsibility, subjection, and obedience.[91]

The question is asked whether such usage of the criterion of the beginning, the "apostolic" witness, is really possible. Earlier, because of the general acceptance of a normative canon, this recognition did not seem to be very complicated: this limitation had been given to the Church along her way through the centuries.[92] Also, the limitation of the number of gospels to the well-known four was closely connected to this aspect of testing.[93] Particularly in the Reformation, this distinguishing and sifting function of the canon acquired great significance in the face of the overgrowth of human traditions and was decisive in the outlook on the apostolic structure of the Church and her doctrine.[94] One began simply from the unity and harmony that was thought to be present in the canon and that offered, therefore, a criterion for the rejection of all heresy.[95] Reflection on the rule of faith *(regula fidei)* reached its height here in firm trust in a clear criterion for the Church on the way to the future.[96] In later times, a far-reaching change occurred here because of historical-critical research, which concerned itself

---

91. That A. Seeberg's *Der Katechismus der Urchristenheit*, 1903, was reissued in 1966 can serve as a warning against every simplistic identification of definite fixations and this loss of luster.

92. The aspect of limitation and testing on the basis of the original gospel comes to expression already in the fixing of the canon. Cf. H. von Campenhausen, *The Formation of the Christian Bible*, 1972, pp. 147ff., particularly on the second century. Further, cf. H.N. Ridderbos, *Heilsgeschiedenis en Heilige Schrift*, 1955.

93. Von Campenhausen, *op. cit.*, pp. 210ff., particularly on the "expansion" of the gospels. Cf. Tj. Baarda, *Vier = Eén. Enkele Bladzijden uit de Geschiedenis van de Harmonistiek der Evangeliën*, 1969, pp. 12ff.

94. Cullmann (*Die Tradition*, 1954, pp. 45ff.) has pointed out that there was no place left in the process that resulted in the fixing of the canon for tradition as something independent, since it had to prove itself according to a concrete norm. Cf. my *Second Vatican Council and the New Catholicism*, pp. 106f.

95. Cf. S.L. Greenslade, "Der Begriff der Häresie in der alten Kirche," in Skydsgaard-Vischer, *Schrift und Tradition*, 1963, pp. 32ff.

96. Cf. P. Stockmeier, *op. cit.*, pp. 45ff., 55.

with the origin of the canon and, further, with the whole content of the Holy Scriptures. One concluded that it was impossible to maintain the unity and coherence of the Scriptures and, thus, to start from one concretely usable criterion in order to guarantee the Church against all erroneous ways.[97] One found great differentiation especially within the books of the New Testament. One discovered that it was not possible to put all the books of the New Testament simplistically under the one denominator of an original "apostolic" witness, because they contain different approaches (now usually designated as "different theologies," for instance, those of Paul, John, and Luke). For many people, the clarity of that "from the beginning" began to become indistinct. Thus, it lost its abiding normativity. The distinction between earlier, original purity and later deviation seemed to become more and more dubious, requiring an untenable harmonization to maintain it.[98] The temporal characterizations, "unbelief, right belief, wrong belief"[99] became less and less usable. Heresy could no longer be seen as a clear disruption of original purity, as was first thought when heresy was seen as the bad seed thrown by the devil into the originally good field. Unbiased historical criticism made it impossible to speak of the "priority of true faith."[100] One pointed to motifs — for instance, in Paul — "which appeared to the later Church as condemnable heresy." That raised the question of the criterion, since unity began to fade and became increasingly diffi-

---

97. On the canon cf., among others, G. Hornig, *Die Anfänge der hist.-krit. Theol. Joh. Sal. Semlers Schriftverständnis und seine Stellung zu Luther*, 1961. On historical criticism cf. further G. Ebeling, "The Significance of the Critical Historical Method for Church and Theology in Protestantism," *Word and Faith*, 1960, pp. 17ff.; K. Scholder, *Ursprünge und Problemen der Bibelkritik im 17. Jahrhundert. Ein Beitrag zur Entstehung der hist.-krit. Theol.*, 1966; W. Pannenberg, *Basic Questions in Theology*, 1971.

98. E. Käsemann, "Begründet der N.T. Kanon die Einheit der Kirche?" *Exeg. Vers. und Besinn.*, II, 214ff.

99. Cf. W. Bauer, *Orthodoxy and Heresy in Earliest Christianity*, 1971, p. xxiii. G. Strecker has added a section to this edition on "the reception of the book," on, among other things, the sharp rejection of Bauer's influential book by Roman Catholic and Anglican writers.

100. H. Koester, "Häretiker im Unchristentum als theologisches Problem," *Zeit und Geschichte*, 1964, pp. 61ff.; *idem, Religion in Geschichte und Gegenwart*, III[2], 17-21; *idem, "GĒŌMAI DIAPHOROI,"* The Harvard Theol. Review, 1965, pp. 279ff. Cf. also E.L. Allen, "Controversy in the N.T.," *N.T. Studies*, 1955, pp. 143ff.; Chr. Dietzfelbinger, *Was ist Irrlehre?*, 1967.

cult to indicate clearly and concretely.[101] Nevertheless, in the midst of that awareness of greater complications, we also meet with an awareness of a central relatedness and normativity that has been given by the "origin." And there is a search for the recognition of "the essential characteristics of that which is distinctively Christian."[102] This recognition cannot be brought about simplistically and harmonistically, but only by listening patiently to all the different aspects of the message.

These problems now give definition to both Roman Catholic and Protestant exegesis in interpreting the one gospel.[103] It goes without saying that this is of decisive significance for the apostolicity of the Church. We often hear the complaint today that the life of the Church seems to be determined more by an uncertain "seeking" than by a "having found." One can have different opinions about this analysis, but it is certain that the intention of the *credo* is to start from great positivity in the readiness to subject itself to the authority of the gospel. This clearly does not eliminate the continuing seeking, which, for that matter, is not without promise (Matt. 7:7); but there is also an unmistakable realization in the *credo* of "knowing" and "having found." Therefore, one must say that the repetition of these words will always test the Church with respect to her seeking and her finding. Even if one does not use the apostolicity of the Church in an irritating self-complacency[104] and knows that the Church must not be haughty, but must associate with the lowly (Rom. 12:16), one still may not deny that there is a certain fascination in the *credo* of apostolicity. This fascination has often caused one to speak lyrically about the Church.[105] Such language does have direct points of contact with the New Testament witness. But the legitimacy of all lyricism is dependent on the understanding directed both to the

---

101. Koester, *Zeit und Geschichte,* p. 61. According to Koester, Christianity was originally syncretistic because there was no one uniform language. Language cannot be separated from content.

102. Koester, *The Harvard Theol. Review,* 1965, p. 282.

103. Cf. H. von Campenhausen (*Tradition and Life in the Church,* 1968, p. 15) on the complications in the "purely factual elucidation of Christian origins for us today" as "tremendously difficult" (in connection with the layers of the gospels).

104. Cf. on this H.U. von Balthasar, "Kirchenerfahrung dieser Zeit," *Sentire Ecclesiam,* 1961, pp. 746ff. Cf. p. 753 on earthly-integralistic self-glorification.

105. See further on this in chapter 12, in connection with the Church's holiness.

promise and to the admonition present in the *credo* of apostolicity. In times when the question is asked about truth and truthfulness with respect to every statement about the Church, and when the Church herself gives everyone the criterion — her *credo* — to judge her life, there is no more urgent question than that of the truth of that *credo*. And that is especially the case when it is concentrated in the Church's life, which wants to be bound to the living Lord via the apostolate.

CHAPTER NINE

APOSTOLICITY AND TRUTH

THE QUESTION OF TRUTH HAS ALWAYS PLAYED A
determinant role in the history of the Church. It was not a
purely theoretical or intellectual concept of truth, but truth
in its blessing and liberating character (John 8:32). This truth,
which is truth in Christ and is identical with Him (14:6; cf.
1:14; 15:26; I John 5:7), was the stimulating power of the apostolic witness: "we cannot do anything against *(katà)* the truth
but only for *(hupèr)* the truth" (II Cor. 13:8). This is not a
disinterested ascertainment of the harmony of thought and
being, but a fullness of riches and life, a being of the truth
(John 18:37; I John 2:8; I John 3:19), and a walking in the
truth (II John 4, III John 3f.; cf. II Tim. 2:18; John 3:21). It
involves imitation of Him Who was born and came into the
world in order to bear witness to the truth.[1] It goes without
saying that one cannot speak meaningfully about the *credo* of
apostolicity apart from thinking about these perspectives, and
the Church that confesses herself to be apostolic can be nothing
else than a center of truth, an alluring house of light and blessing. Involuntarily, one thinks of the fire that Christ came to
cast on the earth (Luke 12:49), a fire that spreads and reflects
itself in the unmistakable fervor of the apostolic proclamation
and dynamic. In the *credo,* the Church puts her whole life in
word and deed at the disposal of this power of the truth and
offers everyone a measuring rod that can judge her life. This
is the great risk of the Church, when, in the midst of much
resistance and criticism, she persists in her confession: *credo
apostolicam ecclesiam.* From the beginning, one knew that this
truth would not be accepted directly or as a matter of course

1. John 18:37. On the concept of truth in Scripture, cf. H.J. Vrielink, *Het
   Waarheidsbegrip,* 1965; A. Szekeres, *Kernwoorden van het Christelijk
   Geloof,* 1970, pp. 61ff.

by everyone. It was the truth of a new message that was not "according to man" (Gal. 1:11) and was often spoken against (Luke 2:34). In the apostolic proclamation, therefore, we often come across a struggle between lies and truth. However, there is never any irrational reference to an esoteric, inaccessible mystery, but only a clear apology, a defense (cf. I Pet. 3:15). It is directed against attack and criticism and against the reproach of impossibility, irrationality, and foolishness (cf. I Cor. 1:23; Acts 17:22ff.; 28:17ff.). From the beginning, we see the apology connected to many problems, specifically with respect to the question whether it is possible to demonstrate the rationality of faith.[2] The temptation to think only about one's own, internal truth was thwarted by inescapable contacts that automatically made defense necessary.[3] The background of the varied apologies in the history of the Church is the dynamic apostolic testimony, which does not withdraw into an anxious defense, but is bent on refutation and persuasion. Apology started from the conviction of an unshakable authority, but it did not stop simply with postulating that authority; rather, it went into all contradictions. This apology was by nature deeply religious. It touched the whole life in the readiness to make a defense for the hope to everyone who might call it to account (I Pet. 3:15). Every apology contains an urgent appeal to give up prejudices. Faced with the criticism that the gospel message is "madness," Paul testified to the "sober truth" (Acts 26:25f.). All refutation and defense contain the facet of creating room for new interest, in order thereby to penetrate to the heart.[4] Paul considered himself fortunate to be able to make his defense before Agrippa (Acts 26:2 — makários), and all apology is filled with great boldness (26:26; 28:31).

   It is self-evident that true apology is possible only on the basis of such a strong conviction. In times of hesitation, un-

2. Cf. A. Adam, *Lehrbuch der Dogmengeschichte*, I, 137ff., on the Apologists in the ancient Church and their defense of the faith in "attestation of the Christian truth on the field of reason."
3. Cf. J. Gauss, "Anselm von Canterbury und die Islamfrage," *Theol. Zeitung*, 1963, pp. 250ff., with the hypothesis: " '*Cur Deus Homo*' was a doctrinal and polemic writing against the Mohammedans." Cf. also *idem*, "Glaubensdiskussionen zwischen Ostkirche und Islam im 8-11 Jahrh.," *Theol. Zeitung*, 1963, p. 142.
4. Cf. Christ's apology in Mark 3:23 against the interpretation of the Pharisees concerning the casting out of demons. Their interpretation is both an inner impossibility and senseless. Cf. Peter's sober answer in Acts 2:15 (the third hour!).

certainty, scepticism, and crisis, the power of apology automatically diminishes. One should not think here exclusively of
the shifts in apologetics that we perceive in the history of theology. The question whether a reasoning, demonstrative defense
of the Christian faith is possible has often been discussed. Aversion to rational apologetics need not signify a crisis in Christian
apology. But there can also be a feeling of uncertainty that
undermines the élan of apology, since much of what was earlier
defended with conviction has come to be encircled by many
question marks. As a result, various earlier "bulwarks" have
been abandoned.[5] For example, in the time of the Enlightenment and in the historical criticism of the 18th and 19th centuries, questions arose that began to throw shadows along the
whole line of defense. Refutation no longer seemed so problem-
less, but became an acute problem. Was there still really a link
present in the Church to the fervent, convincing, and bold proclamation and apology that we find continuously in the apostolic
witness? We recall that Paul was not ashamed of the gospel
(Rom. 1:16) and that the gospel warns against such shame (Mark
8:38; Luke 9:26; II Tim. 1:8), which is an indication of alienation, uncertainty, hesitation, or anxiety, because of which "pub-
licity" is shunned.[6] In such shame, what is whispered is no
longer proclaimed on the housetops (Matt. 10:27). We perceive
nothing of this shame in the apostolic proclamation. Knowing
that the gospel is not according to man does not pave the way to
timid silence, but rather to a penetrating proclamation characterized by a positivity that continually amazes us. This positivity, on account of the *credo,* places the Church before the
question of whether she still knows and understands this fervor
of conviction, this dynamic of proclamation. Does she still know
in all the difference with the apostles that the Church of the
living God is called "the pillar and bulwark of the truth"?[7]

5. Cf. V. Hepp, *Geref. Apologetiek,* 1922.
6. See in contrast not being put to shame before kings (Ps. 119:46), before
councils, governors, and kings (Matt. 10:18; Mark 13:9); and speaking
before the nations in a manner that cannot be withstood or contradicted
(Luke 21:15).
7. I Tim. 3:15. W. Pannenberg (*Basic Questions in Theology,* 1971) sees
the crisis that has arisen — concerning that positivity — in connection with
the traditional Protestant principle of Scripture, specifically, its "supra-
natural" starting point, which makes one defenseless against exact analysis and criticism. For Pannenberg, this means a way to a different, new
apology, as that comes to expression in his view of "reason." Cf. the
articles "What is Truth?" and "Faith and Reason" in the same volume.

Verification

Whoever reflects on the positivity and certainty evident in the apostolic proclamation is faced with a complex of questions that is present everywhere today as the problem of verification. Naturally, this word is not intended as the substantiation of something that is in itself uncertain, but as a refutation of the criticism that the truth of the gospel is pretense and lies. The Church has dealt with this problematic in many situations. True, we often see a certain mistrust of the idea of verification, because of the fear that it is an attempt to transfer the truth of God to the domain of purely human thinking and reasoning, which then has the last word. It has been pointed out that the decision for or against the truth reaches deeper than human thought. However, it would be incorrect to look at the questions about verification exclusively from this angle. There is a kind of apology that is aware of the problematic of the heart and is nevertheless connected to a penetrating persuasion.[8]

There have been times when one was convinced of a common basis for contact and communication — and thus for meaningful apology — in human thought, specifically with respect to the existence of God. Verification of Christian belief in God hardly seemed to be a problem because of numerous "proofs" for His existence. General human verification seemed possible for the convinced apostolic proclamation of "one God," from Whom all things are, in contrast to all the so-called gods in heaven or on earth (I Cor. 8:4ff.; cf. Gal. 4:8). A certain obstinacy and positivity is contained in these proofs concerning the conviction that ground and motives removing this belief in God from all irrationality can be pointed out. One was not content with the statement that the fool says in his heart "there is no God" (Ps. 14:1; 53:1), but pointed to general human insight, which showed that belief in God was different from a leap into an irrational, defenseless belief. Kant's criticism of the proofs for God has never been able to detract from this interest entirely. After a crisis in traditional apologetics, which was never completely satisfied with the unfruitfulness of conclusions "from the things that are created,"[9] interest in these

8. When the Canons of Dort (III-IV, 12) say that regeneration is not effected "merely by the external preaching of the gospel, by moral suasion . . . ," they are rejecting trust in reason to the exclusion of the work of the Spirit.
9. Denz., 1785.

proofs has again returned.[10] One searches continually, not necessarily for strict proofs, but at least for arguments, indications,
and pointers[11] which have force, if not with respect to the full
content of the Christian confession, then nevertheless with respect to the belief in God that is essential in the Church's confession. That confession never meant an isolation of belief in
God — His existence — any more than that was the case in Israel,
where the question about God never concerned His "existence,"
but only adopted the form of where God was and why He
hid Himself.[12] In all her reflection on belief in God, the Church
always found herself faced with the calling of indicating that
Christian faith in God is something totally different from what
is discussed in natural theology and the proofs for God as
"prime cause," "prime mover," or "absolute being." Confrontation with atheism could not only involve the question of believing or not believing in "God." Rather, as Israel confessed
the irrefutable incomparability of Yahweh in a question: "Who
is a God like thee, pardoning iniquity?" (Mic. 7:18), the question "Who is God?" also had to be discussed. Theology dealt
in many ways with the concrete content of belief in God;[13] but,
at the same time, one began to reflect on possible "experiences"
of the reality of God that could function to a certain extent as
points of contact for the Christian message. By placing those
experiences in the context of Christ, one wanted to create some
room again in modern life for verification instead of a defenseless, vulnerable reference to irrational faith in God containing
no possibility of discussion or apology.[14] This did not signify
a simple return to the old natural theology with its proofs, but
opposition to the criticism of all natural theology by Ritschl,
Hermann, and especially Barth, whereby they withdrew to
revelation in Christ.[15]

10. Cf. R. Slenczka, "Gottesbeweise," *Kerugma und Dogma*, 1968, pp. 83ff.;
    O. Huonder, *Die Gottesbeweise. Geschichte und Schicksal*, 1968; W.
    Pannenberg, "Types of Atheism and Their Theological Significance,"
    Basic Questions, pp. 184ff.
11. H. Bavinck, *Geref. Dog.*, II, 62ff., on arguments in distinction from
    proofs and on testimonies that make an impression. The testimonies
    that proceed from God are "summarized in the so-called proofs."
12. Cf. H.J. Kraus, "Der lebendige Gott," *Evang. Theol.*, 1967.
13. Cf. H.G. Geyer, "Gottes Sein als Thema der Theologie," *Verkündigung
    und Forschung*, 1966.
14. In connection with the non-Christian religions, see Pannenberg, "Toward
    a Theology of the History of Religions," *Basic Questions*, pp. 65ff.
15. Cf. E. Kinder, "Das vernachlässigte Problem der 'natürlichen' Gottes-
    erfahrung," *Kerugma und Dogma*, 1965, pp. 316ff.; C. Gestrich, "Die

Nevertheless, one cannot say that the problem of verification simply began to play a new role in reflection on God's existence. Rather, attention was directed to the total "claim to truth" (*Wahrheitsanspruch*) of the Christian witness,[16] and one can ascertain a growing inclination to a rational apology. For instance, Pannenberg warns against "ghetto theology," which shuts itself up in a defenseless and contextless belief as an unapproachable, unverifiable house,[17] making all apology superfluous and impossible and excluding all possibilities of contact between belief and disbelief.[18] Hardly any other single subject receives such intense reflection in our day as the relation between faith and reason,[19] and the theses of the "God is dead" theology have greatly increased interest in the problematic of apology and verification. Naturally, it is of great interest to know in what way the question of verification is answered,[20] because the apostolic witness, to which the Church is subject, was faced with this question from the beginning and has given an answer to it.

In the gospel, there is tension connected to Christ's empower-

unbewältigte natürliche Theologie," *Z.Th.K.*, 1971, pp. 82ff.; G.C. van Niftrik, *Het Bestaan van God in de Kentering van deze Tijd*, 1971.
16. Cf. P. Brunner, "Der Wahrheitsanspruch des apostolischen Evangeliums," *Kerugma und Dogma*, 1968, pp. 71ff.
17. Cf. W. Pannenberg, "Insight and Faith," *Basic Questions*, pp. 28ff.
18. Cf. also J. Moltmann, "Theologie in der Welt der mod. Wissenschaften," *Perspektiven der Theol.*, 1968, pp. 269ff. See also the application to the relation of theology and the natural sciences in Pannenberg, "Kontingenz und Naturgesetz," *Erwägungen zu einer Theologie der Natur*, 1970, pp. 34ff., particularly on the "cleft that often seems unbridgeable today." His conclusion is that modern knowledge of nature and faith in God are not incompatible (p. 72). Cf. Pannenberg, *Basic Questions*, against the idea of double truth. The breaking of all contact has the result, via the blurring of the "meaningfulness" of faith, that the Christian message cannot regain "its missionary character" (pp. 51ff.).
19. See, among others, G. Otto, *Vernunft. Aspekte zeitgemässen Glaubens*, 1970; J.A.B. Jongeneel, *Het Redelijk Geloof in Jezus Christus*, 1971.
20. Moltmann ("Offenbarung und Gottesfrage," *Parrhesia*, 1966, pp. 150ff.) designates three schemes of verification that attempt to demonstrate that belief is "meaningful and necessary," namely, the "cosmological-world historical" (from reality), the anthropological (God as the answer to the questionableness of man), and the onto-theological (following Anselm and Barth, the *Deus dixit*, in which Revelation proves itself). Cf. also *The Theology of Hope*, 1967, pp. 37ff. In contrast, Moltmann points to the eschatological character of revelation, in which verification and fulfillment are related and verification is not possible "through illumination of a reality that is under discussion and is already incipient" (*Parrhesia*, p. 172). In the contemporary discussion, however, the concern is precisely apology and verification in the present.

ment when He appeared in the midst of His people. The statement of John that He came "to his own home" (1:11) definitely did not have such evidence for Israel that all verification was made superfluous. He was questioned continuously about His empowerment, His legitimacy and authorization, about the foundation for His statements "but I say to you."[21] What competency is behind His words and deeds? From whom has He received that competency (Matt. 21:23ff.; Mark 11:28ff.)? One wants to have this question answered *before* believing, and this "before" plays a role in the *passio magna:* "Let him come down now from the cross, and we will believe in him" (Matt. 27:42). This request for verification can arise from a desire to test Him (16:1; cf. John 2:18; 4:48; 6:30); in that case it is the request of an evil and adulterous generation (Matt. 16:4; 12:39) and is rejected[22] because one never comes to true faith in that way.

By requiring an incontestable sign apart from genuine expectation that it will come, the intention is wholly different from that described in the Old Testament when, in need and threat, a sign of God's favor is requested for comfort and encouragement.[23] The rejection of verification as a demand is closely connected to this. It does not arise from weakness, but from knowledge of the only way that the empowerment can be truly understood.[24] It is noteworthy that verification is not always rejected, but the mode of verification is wholly unique

---

21. Matt. 5:20-32. Cf. E. Lohse, "Ich Aber Sage Euch," *Der Ruf Jesu und die Antwort der Gemeinde. Festschr. J. Jeremias,* 1971, pp. 189ff.

22. Cf. Matt. 21:24 (the baptism of John); 12:39 (no sign except that of Jonah); Mark 8:12 (no sign). Cf. *TDNT,* VII, 235: "The point of the demand is that Jesus should undertake to show thereby that God, in whose name He works, has unequivocally authorized him," because the sign "will prove that any doubt concerning His divine authority is wrong."

23. Cf. Ps. 86:17. The temptation can also be seen in John the Baptist's question in Matt. 11:3: "Are you he who is to come, or shall we look for another?" Christ's answer discloses the specific nature of true verification, since it does not transcend what John already knew, but calls attention to it anew (11:2-6). The possibility of the *skandalon,* of offense, is not excluded, but included (11:6).

24. How little power the sign has on the basis of the preceding demand comes to expression in a revealing way in John 9:17ff. After the healing of the one born blind — the sign! — the question of verification is again asked in great confusion, specifically in not knowing "where he comes from" (9:29). Cf. 9:39 on seeing and not seeing. Cf. also the "if" of verification in the demonic question in Matt. 4:3, 6.

and, over and over again, is totally different from what was asked for or intended. In terms of Pilate's question about Christ's kingship, the Lord's answer is incommensurable. It places everything in the light of verification, but in a wholly unique way: "Every one who is of the truth hears my voice."[25] The surprising light of the unique empowerment, of truth that manifests itself, falls continuously on both verification and the manner in which it is recognized and accepted. A way is indicated along which the meaning of verification is not denied, but disclosed.

A criterion for testing?

But does not all of this mean that it is impossible to reflect further on empowerment and verification, since the empowerment can be accepted only in faith? Is the acceptance only a seeing of what others do not see, a conviction so obvious and free of doubt that there is no need for proof and verification? It would be wrong to end reflection on verification like that, because we live in a world where there are many pretensions to empowerments and to seats of honor (cf. Matt. 23:6). Hence, the problem of recognition and testing arises automatically. Since a pretension can be connected to mistake or imagination,[26] it is necessary to have one's eyes and ears open wide in critical testing. For instance, the Church is not left to the pretensions of the "spirits" and is not allowed to trust every "spirit"; rather, the spirits must be tested (I John 4:1; cf. II John 7; Matt. 24:11, 24; Mark 13:22). The question of verification is outlined clearly for us here. Israel already faced this confrontation in the conflict between true and false prophecy. A simple distinction was not always possible, for the false prophets also put their proclamation under the shield of divine empowerment: "Thus says the Lord."[27] The pretension to empowerment always seems to

---

25. John 18:37. On Pilate's question, see K. Barth, *C.D.*, IV/3, 1, pp. 78ff., specifically on the "special confirmations" and the "crystal clear" *thema probandum* (p. 80). Cf. also John 7:16ff.: doing the will of God and knowing where Christ's teaching comes from. We point out in passing that the problem of verification also has a directly personal aspect, as appears from "knowing that one is of the truth" (I John 3:18ff.) in direct connection with what is usually called the *syllogismus practicus* (cf. I John 3:14; and my *Divine Election*, 1958, chapter 9).

26. Gal. 6:3: "If anyone thinks he is something, when he is nothing" *(einai ti mēdèn ön)*.

27. In Matt. 7:15-23, the possibility of verification lies in knowing the *fruits* of the false prophets. Cf. Jer. 28.

bring a certain defenselessness with it.[28] The prophets themselves show a deep conviction of their calling. Faced with a denial of their empowerment, they can do nothing other than what Amos did when he asserted that his call came not from his own initiative, but "from above."[29] The phenomenon of prophecy does not bear transparent signs of legitimacy that eliminate all doubt for everyone.[30] Thus, struggle and discussions are possible about the empowerment that comes in the form of the *vox humana!*[31]

We also touch upon this problematization of the empowerment in the conflict that Paul points to between apostles and pseudo-apostles. There were those who disguised themselves as apostles, testing and tempting the Church.[32] As a result, the question arises as to what the criterion is for distinguishing between pretense and reality, between usurpation and empowerment (cf. Rev. 2:2). How is the deceitful work (II Cor. 11:13) to be discerned? The question is urgent on account of the conscious intention to mislead by pretending to be apostles of Christ and servants of righteousness — messengers of light just like Satan, who disguises himself as an angel of light (11:14). In the "phenomenal" world of pretension and empowerment,

28. One may also think of the problem of recognition in Deut. 18:21f.: whether or not the prophetic word is fulfilled. The conclusion is not to be afraid of the false prophet, whose word is not fulfilled. Cf. A.S. van der Woude, "Waarheid als Leugen," *Vox Theol.*, 1970, p. 65; C.L. Labuschagne, *Schriftprofetie en Volksideologie*, 1968; *idem*, "De Valse Profetie in Israël," *Rondom het Woord*, 11, 1969, pp. 142ff.; *TDNT*, VI, 807f.

29. Amos 7:15. Cf. C. van Gelderen, *Amos*, p. 217, on "something violent in Amos' call." Cf. 3:8: "The Lord God has spoken; who can but prophesy?" Cf. also H.W. Wolff, *Die Stunde des Amos. Prophetie und Protest*, 1969, pp. 15ff.

30. Cf. Jeremiah, who goes his way after Hananiah's renewed prophesying (Jer. 28:11). See also Jer. 23:16, 26, and the radical disqualification in 23:32 ("I did not send them"). Cf. Wolff, *op. cit.*, pp. 14ff., on the possible misunderstandings about the prophet, the *seer*, as Amaziah calls Amos (Amos 7:12).

31. Cf. Paul's constant thanksgiving that the Thessalonians received the word of God "as what it really *(alēthōs)* is, the word of God" (I Thess. 2:13). Interest in the humanity of the Scriptures has often led historically to a lack of appreciation for their *theopneustos* and full authority. But one cannot offer resistance to that by relativizing the humanity, since the full authority reaches us through the *vox humana*. Cf. my *Holy Scripture*, chapter 12.

32. II Cor. 11:12 *(metaschēmatizómenoi)*: in a different *schēma* — form, shape, mask (cf. *TDNT*, VII, 957f.).

recognition and distinguishing are necessary. Obviously, too, they are possible, as in the Church at Ephesus, which tested the false prophets and found them to be false (Rev. 2:2). In this activity of testing, the question of the criterion looms automatically.

Paul, the apostle, did not encounter the questions of verification, authorization, and legitimacy only in connection with the threat to the Church in general, but especially in connection with his own apostleship. His apostolic empowerment was denied over and over again. He himself was convinced that he had been called (Rom. 1:1; I Cor. 1:1; Gal. 1:1), that he had been set apart by grace according to the will of God (Rom. 1:1; Gal. 1:15), and that he had received the gospel through a revelation of Jesus Christ (Gal. 1:12). In his defense he laid strong emphasis on the directness and immediacy of his calling, which was independent of men. After his calling, he did not confer with flesh and blood (1:16) and he did not go to Jerusalem, but went to Arabia.[33] His apostolate is "independent" (Gal. 1:1) and is not explainable from a human chain of tradition or human instruction.[34] Understandably, this express accentuation that Paul's apostolate came "from above" seemed to render him defenseless. Was he not an easy object for suspicion and criticism, since every simple "criterion" was absent? He could not point to any "authority," and he could not prove that he had not himself imagined his apostolic dignity.[35]

Is any other verification possible than that via tradition and

---

33. Gal. 1:17. On Rom. 15:20 (Paul's ambition), cf. K. Barth, *The Epistle to the Romans*, p. 533; O. Michel, *Römerbrief*, p. 330 (not "personal ambition"); H.N. Ridderbos, *Aan de Romeinen*, p. 333; G. Klein, "Gal. 2, 6-9 und die Geschichte der Jerus. Urgemeinde," *Rekonstruktion und Interpretation*, 1969, pp. 110ff.

34. What Paul says about his independence is not directed against other relationships in the Church — other apostles, for instance. Cf. Paul's later visit with Cephas and James in Jerusalem (Gal. 1:18f.), although the same accent continues here too ("none of the other apostles except"; what is stated "before God"). In I Cor. 11:23, the directness of his call evidently does not exclude the *parádosis* (tradition). "From the Lord" does not signify a breaking of all the chains of tradition in his teaching, but a reference to the deepest origin (see on this Grosheide, *De Eerste Brief aan de Kerk te Korinthe*, 1957², p. 307). Cf. also I Cor. 15:3: "what I also received." Cf. H. Conzelmann, *Der erste Brief an die Korinther*, 1969, p. 231, in opposition to Lietzmann, who derives the content entirely from Paul's experience at Damascus.

35. Cf. the high priest who does not take the honor *(timé)* on himself, but is called, as Aaron was (Heb. 5:4f.; Ex. 28:1; Num. 3:10).

succession? Paul knows that he does not belong to the row of "the 12" and has no connection with those who were "originally" sent out by the Lord. He admits that *expressis verbis* in his self-characterization as "one untimely born," to whom Christ appeared last of all (I Cor. 15:8 — *ektrŏma*). Is that not a beautiful starting point for all of Paul's critics, who make his life and pretensions suspect as irregular? And if they are irregular, are they not also illegitimate? Paul knows about this irregularity.[36] He recognizes it and describes it in the context of deep humility (cf. I Cor. 15:9; I Tim. 1:13-16) on account of his appointment by grace to the row of witnesses. In contrast to all arrogance, Paul realizes also that his apostolate is totally underivable from his own disposition or capability. The relation to the Lord due to mercy rules all of this thinking about being appointed as a servant (I Tim. 1:12). It is the exclusive foundation of all his sufficiency (II Cor. 3:5; cf. 2:16). Nevertheless, there is no trace of hesitation or doubt in this, but rather of being driven, of having necessity laid upon him (I Cor. 9:16; cf. Acts 4:20): his life in weakness (II Cor. 10:1, 10; 11:21), suffering, and abnormality. But precisely this drivenness "from above" seems to raise the question of verification in order that it be distinguished from arbitrariness and presumption. The appeal to an inescapable "necessity"[37] does not contain a rational proof for Paul's apostolate, but a reference to an inscrutable superior power such as we meet with in Amos and Jeremiah.[38] Paul knows that there is testing, but it is a *divine* testing: it is not the man who commends himself, but the man whom the Lord commends who is accepted (II Cor. 10:18, 12; 12:11). But, at

36. That Paul, in using *ektrŏma*, adopts a "term of abuse" from his opponents was suspected already by Harnack and later accepted by many others. See *TDNT*, II, 466; E. Güttgemans, *Der leidende Apostel und sein Herr. Studiën zur paulin. Christologie*, 1966, p. 87; and also H.J. Schoeps, *Paul*, 1961, p. 77, on "this abusive phrase" as the key word in the polemic of the Judaizers.

37. I Cor. 9:16 *(anánkē)*: "For necessity is laid upon me," and "Woe to me if I do not preach the gospel!" Cf. E. Käsemann, "Eine paulinische Variation des 'amor fati,'" *Exeg. Vers. und Besinn.*, II, 1964, pp. 223ff., on this "astonishing" expression *(anánkē)*. His opposition to what he calls "the edifying understanding" ("a holy must," inner pressure) is not convincing, since Käsemann himself interprets: "the power of the will of God, which demands utterly, succeeds in relation to man with its demand, and makes its servant its instrument" (p. 234). Cf. "inexorable and inescapable."

38. Cf. Amos 3:8; Jer. 1:6ff.; 20:9 as meaningful parallels (otherwise Käsemann).

the same time, it is clear to him that this "necessity" makes him unassailable. He is not "subject to human categories of judgment."[39] In this connection, one has spoken of Paul's self-consciousness, a term that can be interpreted in many ways.[40] It may be used only if it is borne in mind that this "self-consciousness" is *sui generis*. Only in the context of a very humble apostolate can it be understood. There is a definite implication here vis-à-vis every request for verification. That explains why Paul did not appeal to mystical or ecstatic experiences in order to legitimize his "abnormal" apostolate by reference to something exceptional.[41] Paul knows the question about authorization and is faced with it also in the Church: "you desire proof *(dokimĕn zēteite)* that Christ is speaking in me" (II Cor. 13:3). To this question he can only answer that "Christ is powerful in you." Neither in visions and revelations (II Cor. 12:1) nor in the way of appearance and preaching (cf. I Cor. 2:1) is there a proof that is sufficient for every critical or uncritical observer. But that does not mean defenselessness, since Paul knows of the empowerment and the power of Christ that works in and through him (Rom. 15:18). Thus, one can say that he does not reject verification, but recognizes it, not in an *a priori*, but in an *a posteriori* context: the Church is the seal of his apostleship (I Cor. 9:2; cf. Phil. 4:1) as the demonstration of the Spirit and power (I Cor. 2:4). The Church is his letter, knowable and readable by all men, and she shows that she is a letter from Christ "delivered by us."[42] The legitimacy and verification are not placed outside the proclamation and its power but are real only in and through the proclamation. This is not a neutral problematic of criticism using an *a priori*, independent cri-

---

39. *TDNT*, II, 258, and III, 651.
40. *TDNT*, VII, 898, and III, 650 ("Apostolic Self-Boasting"). Further, see G. Bornkamm, *Paul*, 1971, pp. 157ff.; H. von Campenhausen, *Tradition und Leben*, 1960, pp. 318ff., with reminders of "Paulinische Wendungen" (p. 332).
41. Cf. K.H. Rengstorf, *Apostolate and Ministry*, 1969, pp. 87f.; and *idem*, *TDNT*, I, 439f. Rengstorf, speaks of a "renunciation of any ecstatic basis for the apostolate" with reference to II Cor. 12:1ff. (boasting from which nothing is to be gained). Paul's "experience" is not "organically linked with his apostolate." Cf. J.P. Versteeg, *Christus en de Geest*, 1971, pp. 225ff.; G. Bornkamm, *Paul*, pp. 88ff.
42. II Cor. 3:1-3 *(phaneroúmenoi)*. The "readableness" does not imply a self-evident ascertainment. Cf. E. Käsemann, "Die Legitimität des Apostels," *Z.N.T.W.*, 1942, pp. 59ff.

terion.[43] The legitimacy is discovered only in the Church, since she is not blinded to it by all the contradictory cases of shadows, weakness, and suffering;[44] instead, she bows before this empowerment and finds joy in it.[45] One can say, then, that the lack of spectacular, directly convincing glory is incorporated in a unique, rather than self-evident verification.[46] It has a "paradoxical" appearance but points essentially towards the true empowerment.[47] What is unique about the empowerment manifests itself in the effective power that is given with it, and Paul is not "defenseless" in the face of the so-called "superlative" apostles, who pretend to have a special "uniqueness" but have only seemingly solved the problem of verification.[48]

The content of the gospel

Paul's empowerment can never be spoken of apart from the content of the proclamation.[49] This decisive dimension in no

43. The appearance of absolute independence in I Cor. 2:15 (the spiritual man is "to be judged by no one") is taken away by the relatedness to Christ (2:16) and by the limitation that Paul is subject to: "we will not boast beyond limit, but will keep to the limits God has apportioned us" (II Cor. 10:13 — *katà tò métron* versus *tà ámetra*). Cf. Käsemann, *op. cit.*, pp. 57ff., in connection with the formal analogy between Paul and the pneumatics, who also do not want to be judged by anyone. God's limits are "at the same time the foundation of his freedom and the barrier to his arbitrariness."

44. See especially Gal. 4:14 on the trial (*peirasmós*) that Paul's weakness (ailment) caused and on the reaction of the Galatians (earlier, at least), who did not scorn him, but received him "as an angel of God, as Christ Jesus."

45. See Gal. 4:15 (Paul's readiness to do anything); John 3:33 (the sealing that lies in the reception of the testimony). Cf. R. Bultmann, *Glauben und Verstehen*, III, 19.

46. Cf. II Cor. 4:7 on the treasure in earthen vessels "to show that the transcendent power belongs to God and not to us."

47. Cf. II Cor. 6:4-10. On the paradox cf. *TDNT*, III, 651. Cf. Güttgemans, *op. cit.*, pp. 170ff., on the changed attitude of the Galatians (Gal. 4:14) as the loss of the sense of the "*theologia crucis*" (in connection with Paul's ailment).

48. Cf. II Cor. 12:12: Paul's irony in connection with his not being inferior in signs, wonders, and mighty works. Cf. 11:5: superlative (*huperlían*) apostles. Cf. E. Käsemann, *op. cit.*, pp. 41ff.; G. Bornkamm, *Paul*, p. 180.

49. Cf. H.N. Ridderbos, *Paul*, p. 241: "Paul does not first ask obedient recognition of his authorization and thereafter of the content of his message: his commission and authorization consist in the proclamation of the revelation of the mystery, and the nature of his apostolic authority is to be inferred from that." A different verification is impossible for Paul on account of all the connections of sealing in the fulfillment of the promises, which find their Yes in Christ: "That is why we utter

sense implies a denial that the apostolic empowerment is *a priori*.[50] The opposite appears from the way in which the radicality of the proclamation comes to light in the functioning of the empowerment. It occurs in the full earnestness of the apriority, but this earnestness can never be isolated from the proclamation itself. Nowhere is this radical seriousness more visible than in Paul's letter to the Galatians, especially in opposition to all who preach a different gospel "contrary to that which we preached to you" (1:8-9; cf. II Cor. 11:4). There is an antithesis between Paul's gospel and every other "gospel" (Gal. 1:6). The formulation does not signify that there are two "gospels," because Paul adds that there is no other gospel.[51] For him, the one gospel is the "measure and point of orientation for all proclamation."[52] It is directed against an inconceivable, quick alienation from the riches of the crucified Christ, which amazes Paul (3:1f.). It is a deviation not from "Paul," but from his gospel,[53] whose content is the antithesis between the way of works and the preaching of faith (3:5, 11; 5:5). The apostolic empowerment is never discussed "in itself," as if subjection to this empowerment were asked for first — in order to appeal thereafter, by way of conclusion, for obedience to the message. In order to protect empowerment one has often thought in these categories, but they result from what Paul would see as an unreal abstraction. Paul's empowerment is always concrete and filled with content; his goal is to win men for his Lord by making the significance of the gospel transparent, the objective evidence of the gospel.[54] Exactly in this way, Paul can speak so radically

the Amen through him, to the glory of God" (II Cor. 1:20-22; cf. Rev. 3:14). Cf. also *idem*, "Gezag en Ambt," *Rondom het Woord*, 1969, pp. 168ff., against formalizing the offices and against maintaining the authority of offices on the basis of "a formidable, formal structure of authority." In addition, see W. Schmithals, *Das kirchl. Apostelambt*, 1961, p. 202.

50. Cf. S. Kierkegaard, "Of the Difference Between a Genius and an Apostle," in *The Present Age*, 1962, pp. 89ff.: for apostleship "divine authority is, qualitatively, the decisive factor" (p. 93); authority comes "from elsewhere" (p. 96). Cf. on this K. Barth, *C.D.*, I/1, pp. 125f.

51. Gal. 1:7 (*hó ouk éstin állo*). Cf. the different Jesus, a different spirit, and a different gospel in II Cor. 11:4. Cf. D.W. Oostendorp, *Another Jesus*, 1967.

52. E. Grässer, "Das eine Evangelium. Hermeneutische Beträchtungen zu Gal. 1, 6-10," *Z.Th.K.*, 1969, p. 313.

53. Paul speaks of "my" (Rom. 2:16) or "our" (I Thess. 1:5; II Cor. 4:3) gospel.

54. Grässer, *op. cit.*, p. 320.

with apostolic authority — even to the extent of an "anathema" — about the impossibility of an alternative.[55] Naturally, this is not a matter of "opinions" — not even of Paul's (Gal. 1:18) — but of a decision that touches everything, for "only the destruction of the truth produces the anathema."[56] Neither a man — the gospel is not according to man (Gal. 1:11) — nor an angel can place himself in opposition to the gracious, authorized content of this concrete gospel, which designates every attempt to achieve one's own righteousness as a way that leads to a dead end. Whoever wants to speak here of circular reasoning, and wants to separate empowerment from the message, does not understand that this "circular reasoning is required for the sake of the matter itself."[57]

In the light of what has been said above, one can say that, although there need not be a contrast between person and thing, there is never any possibility of anchoring the empowerment in particular persons and, on account of their qualities, fastening it in human structures. We often see such a process begin in the Church when various traditions and achievements lead to fixations that seem so self-evident that they are withdrawn from all testing. The track of apostolicity is abandoned then, and the validity of true normativity begins to fade. Then the structures themselves as the framework of the Church's life become the guarantee of empowerment, while the critical question of conformity with the gospel no longer functions constantly. In this connection, Paul's attitude to various states of affairs in the Church, which became concrete in particular persons, is mentioned frequently. We are thinking especially of Paul's statement about James, Cephas, and John, "who were reputed to be pillars" (Gal. 2:9 — hoi dokoúntes stúloi einai), and about those who were "reputed to be something" (2:6 — apò dè tôn dokoúntōn einai ti). One has concluded from this that Paul was never impressed with any positions of prominence in the Church and, in such words, "may have implied, at least hinted some doubt, about the 'repute' of those, who were styled pillars," knowing that "reputations may be false."[58]

Paul is certainly not thinking of men who have raised them-

---

55. *Ibid.*, p. 341.
56. *Ibid.*, p. 343.
57. *Ibid.*
58. C.K. Barrett, "Paul and the Pillar-apostles," *Studia Paulina*, 1953, p. 3. Barrett points out that *dokein* appears in Paul 14 times apart from Galatians, implying a certain doubt 8 or 9 times.

selves to a function as pillars, because he values their recognition that the gospel to the Gentiles had been entrusted to Paul and added nothing to him; thus, we cannot speak of a conflict here. Yet the formulation is remarkable; and although it is better that one not speak of mockery here,[59] a reference is nevertheless made to the necessity of continuous testing on the basis of the gospel, lest the empowerment of the gospel be endangered.[60] Certainly, this is never clearer than in the conflict between Paul and Peter in Antioch. The problem was not solved via a formally understood authority (Peter as pillar or Paul as apostle), but only via the decisive criterion of the gospel of God's grace.[61]

When the Church qualifies her own reality as apostolic, by subjecting herself to the apostolic witness, she cannot see her office and empowerment in isolation. There can be no a priori, unfilled, prefatory verification, which in itself would be unassailable as "an authoritative structure."[62] The functioning of the Church's authority implies directedness to the saving message of the gospel. When one reflects on the truth and power of this authority, one inescapably avails oneself of the word "evidentness" with respect to verification.[63] Although this word certainly does not answer all questions — those about seeing and discovering — it does express that God's truth takes on form in and through the vox humana. Along that way it intends to lead to the discovery and the perception of the shining light that forces all presuppositions, prejudices, and arguments to yield to it, a light "brighter than the sun" (Acts 26:13). The evidentness of the gospel as a convincing power is the unique

59. K. Barth, The Epistle to the Romans, 1933, p. 533, writes that "he is strangely suspicious, even sarcastic, with reference to already existing pillars."
60. Cf. what Paul writes about those who were reputed to be something: "what they were makes no difference to me; God shows no partiality" (Gal. 2:6).
61. On this conflict see further in chapter 10 below.
62. H.N. Ridderbos, "Gezag en Ambt," Rondom het Woord, 1969, p. 171. That Ridderbos' rejection of formalizing does not exclude apriority is completely clear from various of his publications.
63. Cf. ibid., "We may conclude, therefore, that the offices must derive their credibility from the evidentness of the gospel." Cf. the confrontation of the offices in the Church "with the evidentness of their calling, which is also to say, with the evidentness of the gospel." In connection with the evidentness, one may also recall the remarkable statement in III John 11f. about the good testimony to Demetrius from every one "and from the truth itself.'

focus where the lines of apriority and faith come together. That the truth of God is not delivered into the grasp of human, testing rationality is beyond all doubt in light of the apostolic witness. Discovery and growing insight are not in conflict with the testimony that what God has prepared is beyond the reach of eye, ear, and heart (I Cor. 2:9; cf. Isa. 64:4); and in this connection, the revelation through the Spirit is recalled (2:10). But the light shines in the darkness and is experienced there as light — in all its newness and surprise, in its radiating riches and liberation. The prejudice yields in a new judgment, a new and disclosing insight, which is experienced not as an "anthropological" verification, but as a wonder and a gift (cf. Isa. 64:1ff.). Philip answers Nathanael's prejudice about Nazareth not with an *a priori* request for subjection, but with an appeal: "Come and see!" Then the prejudice is conquered in an actual encounter.[64] The directedness to this discovery, this seeing, is not in the least concerned with a subjectivizing of the relation of faith or with a testing of authoritative revelation by human experience.[65] But one definitely must consider that the gospel does not penetrate into life apart from touching the heart through the truth of the gospel itself,[66] and it is quite impossible to picture a way from *a priori* authority to an acceptance that would be characterized as the way of blind obedience.[67]

64. John 1:46f. Cf. the belief of the Samaritans after they had believed because of the Samaritan believers' words (4:42). Jesus had stayed with them for two days (4:40). One should not read this as implying the insufficiency of human words, but should definitely do full justice to this dimension of discovery. Cf. F.W. Grosheide, *Het Heilig Evangelie volgens Johannes*, I, 319ff.; H. Strathmann, *Das Evang. nach Johannes*, 1968, p. 89.
65. Cf. H.M. Kuitert, *The Reality of Faith*, 1968, pp. 108ff.
66. Cf. Bavinck's interesting discussion of the experiential theology of Frank, who "tried to give an account of why the Christian accepts everything as truth that his faith contains" (*Geref. Dog.*, I, 493ff.). Although Bavinck has criticism, he guards Frank against misunderstandings, calling his question "of the greatest importance" (p. 494). It is the question of the way to certainty, and Bavinck speaks of "an important truth" here (p. 495).
67. In the vicinity of the heavenly vision, to which Paul was not disobedient (Acts 26:19), there is mention of blindness, but in that blindness light begins to shine and the way becomes free for joyful proclamation of the gospel. Cf. in connection with the "enlightenment," K. Barth, *C.D.*, IV/3, 1, p. 202. In what happens to Paul (Acts 22:6), he comes to sight and knowledge, thus becoming a witness against all the blinding caused by the god of this world (II Cor. 4:4).

Radical obedience to authority?

Frequently, one has passed off this way to faith and certainty too easily and shoved all the problems of coming or not coming to faith aside by a reference to "believing on authority." Everything depends here on the way this belief is understood. It must be understood that this authority truly penetrates life as a light and as a liberating authority.[68] In connection with the relation between authority and belief, one has often referred to faith as an unmediated, wondrous gift of God, thereby putting aside every element of verification. This belief, which could be described as assent, acceptance, or obedience, seemed to resolve all problems and to offer a direct link to the normativity of the apostolic witness. One did not trouble oneself with Bavinck's interest in "the way along which" or with the nature of the "experience" (*Widerfahrnis*) by which the evidentness of the gospel summoned up discovery. However, one must say that what becomes visible in the apostolic activity has direct significance for the right understanding of the Church's *credo*[69] if her authority is to be truly the expression, or form, of her apostolicity. The mode of all ecclesiastical authority belongs essentially to the normativity of the apostolic witness. The contrast appears via the pointed distinction between the obedience of faith and all slavish obedience, where the concrete content of God's revelation does not have significance from the beginning on. Then the obedience becomes a heavy burden that must be accepted in subjection. Rather, the New Testament speaks of an easy yoke and a light burden of Christ (Matt. 11:30) and of commandments that are not burdensome (I John 5:3) in distinction from the burdens of the lawyers that are hard to bear (Luke 11:46; Matt. 23:4). This does not minimize either authority or obedience (cf. B.C., Art. 28), but both become visible in the context of a new discovery. It is the impressiveness of the message itself that repeatedly

---

68. O. Noordmans' plea for "belief on authority" (*Serie Practisch Christendom*, 1921) is not a plea for blind obedience, but for the necessary "tempering of knowing-everything-oneself" (p. 5). Cf. his citation from Harnack (*History of Dogma*, V, 82) on faith that always appeals to "an external authority" and not only to "its own inner impulses." Noordmans' "belief on authority" has nothing to do with blind obedience. Cf. K. Schilder, *Heidelbergsche Catechismus*, II, 563; my "*Sacrificium Intellectus?*," *Gereformeerd Theologisch Tijdschrift*, 1968, pp. 189ff.
69. Cf. K. Schilder, *loc. cit.*, on faith as assent "to what is said about God and has been understood, considered, and known by us."

comes to expression in the apostolic testimony[70] and that causes Paul's astonishment when the picture of the Christ portrayed before the eyes of the Galatians begins to fade (Gal. 3:1ff.). One cannot escape the conclusion that the apostolic empowerment, to which the Church subjects herself in her credo, implies that the Church knows and makes known that her authority is radically different from every isolated pretension to authority, which would obscure the concrete outlook on the Lord of the gospel Himself.

To accentuate the sovereignty and apriority of revelation, obedience is often pictured as an act of radical subjection. One thought that everything could be made clear by referring to the motivation for this subjection: because of the authority of God.[71] One supported this aspect of radical subjection with the clear emphasis in the New Testament on the abandonment of one's autonomy, on capitulation and captivity.[72] Paul can even use the picture of "slavery" to describe this obedience without misgivings. He is obviously fascinated by the unheard-of bond of being in the "possession" of Another. This bond of being obedient slaves (Rom. 6:16) — correlated to the "from the heart" (6:17) — is directed to righteousness and sanctification (6:18f.). The scope of the slavery does not need to be balanced with freedom;[73] it is filled with the perspective of eternal life (6:22), and it points to the obedience to Christ (II Cor. 10:5), the obedience to the truth (I Pet. 1:22), the obedience of faith (Rom. 1:5), and the obedience of childhood (I Pet. 1:14). All of this brings the nature of obedience to light.[74] It is far removed from the frustrating associations of being a "slave" in Paul's time.

---

70. One may recall in this connection the discovery and astonishment in Matt. 7:28f.: Christ's teaching "as one who had authority, and not as their scribes." Cf. Mark 1:22.

71. *Propter auctoritatem Dei,* Denz., 1789. This authority is set in opposition to seeing with natural reason: "not because its intrinsic truth is seen with the natural light of reason *(naturali rationis lumine),* but because of the authority of God who reveals it, of God who can neither deceive nor be deceived" (*TCT,* 63). Cf. also Denz., 1811. One must bear in mind the background of this *propter,* though, which is the defense against rationalism. Cf. U. Gerber, *Kath. Glaubensbegriff,* 1966, pp. 73ff.

72. Cf. the radicality in Paul's description in II Cor. 10:5f.

73. The new Dutch translation (1969) renders the "slavery" *(doúloi* and *edoulóthēte)* with respect to sin and righteousness in Rom. 6:18 as "slaves of sin" and "taken into the service of righteousness." The New English Bible and the RSV, on the other hand, read in both cases "slaves."

74. Cf. John 15:15 on no longer being servants *(doúloi),* but friends.

There is no hint of joyless, powerless, and unwilling subjection to a decreeing power. In the apostolic gospel many radical words can be used, because this radicality is withdrawn from all the darkness of a demonic, authoritarian force that is powerless to win hearts. This gospel does not ask for blind obedience, nor for a *sacrificium intellectus*. It is a serious misconception to believe that the value of faith and obedience increases to the degree that the object of faith becomes more inconceivable and more enigmatic. The not seeing and nevertheless believing to which Jesus refers when speaking to Thomas (John 20:29) has nothing to do with this irrational subjection.[75] Whoever sees faith as blind obedience must eventually see it as a meritorious work, an achievement of subjection as "formal renunciation."[76] Then it is often viewed as the deepest core of belief and as the proof of esteem for the sovereignty and authority of God's truth.[77] In this way, not only the apostolate but also the apostolic structure of the Church becomes a superior power that bounds authority off first of all from human reason. Appreciation is lacking for the fact that, although believing does imply that one no longer belongs to oneself (I Cor. 6:17; Rom. 14:7), it does not mean the closing of ears and eyes. Rather, what is important is precisely the opened ears and eyes.[78] The recognition

---

75. Cf. Pannenberg, *Basic Questions*, pp. 49ff., on Luther in connection with Heb. 11:1. That the submission does not eliminate the believing witnesses, but includes them in a dynamic way, is as clear as day in the entire New Testament witness, which cannot be conceived of apart from the understanding and interpretation after the appearance of salvation in Christ (letters and gospels).

76. Cf. R. Bultmann, *Theol. of the N.T.*, p. 315. Faith is an abandonment of oneself, but not an achievement or merit. Cf. the context of the work of faith in I Thess. 3 and Philem. 6. Cf. further *TDNT*, VI, 219f.; and my *Faith and Justification*, chapter 4.

77. We encounter a striking example of this in the encyclical *Mysterium Fidei* (1965), where Pope Paul VI cites Bonaventure in connection with the acceptance of transubstantiation. Bonaventure points out the very great difficulty in accepting the true presence of Christ in the sacrament and then adds: "And so believing this is especially meritorious" (*"maxime meritorium"* — para. 20). This obedience is termed *humble* (*"humili obsequio"*), since it arises on the strength of the revelation of God. Cf. also the reference to John 6:60 (the reaction of the Jews to Jesus' saying as *hard*).

78. Cf. K. Rahner, "The Concept of Mystery in Catholic Theology," *Theological Investigations*, IV, pp. 36ff., especially on the negative approach of the theology of the schools, which resulted in a plurality of mysteries (pp. 46ff.). Cf. his "Intellectual Honesty and Christian Faith," *ibid.*, VII, 47ff., in opposition to irrationalism.

of the apostolic gospel is allied to insight and to trust with the
whole heart.[79] All legalizing of faith — subjection to a new law
— is out of the question. True, the mystery that has been revealed "according to the command of the eternal God" is made
known to bring about the obedience of faith (Rom. 16:26), and
all of the dynamic of the apostolate is connected to that. But
in this way, hearts are won for the mystery in obedience, love,
and trust. It is the way of authoritative persuasion, of penetrating conviction, along the way to salvation. That faith is
the gift of God is in no sense denied here, but room is made
for the functional nature of the proclamation of the gospel
and for the discovery of its significance, both alarming and
blessing, both accusing and liberating.

Spirit and word

Via the reference to faith and enlightenment as the gift
of God, the work of the Spirit is often isolated as a "miraculous"
event.[80] Then faith is spoken of only in the words of the one
born blind: "One thing I know, that though I was blind, now
I see" (John 9:25). This made all verification and all apology
superfluous. To go this way is to go the way of spiritualism,[81]
which does not give the proclamation of the gospel any essential,
decisive place, devaluing it more and more as only the "external"
word.[82] The revelation of God and the preaching about it could
function at most as an occasion for the actual mystery of enlightenment, and hence it became only a silent mystery that

79. Cf. *TDNT*, VI, 220.
80. In the Heidelberg Catechism (Q. 65), this isolation in the reference to
the dimension of the Spirit is clearly rejected (preaching and sacraments).
81. With the motif of "the perception of this innate Word of God," whereby Scripture is only the "testimony of faith" rather than "the power
that produces it." Cf. K. Holl, *Luther und die Schwärmer. Aufs. zur
K.G.*, I, 431ff. Cf. p. 448 on Luther's reaction.
82. Pannenberg, especially (*Basic Questions*, pp. 40ff.), has warned against
evading the question of truth by the appeal to the Spirit. Cf. p. 43
("no 'haven of ignorance' for pious experience") and p. 41 (on truth
"which is realized by means of conviction"). The problematic in Pannenberg's accents lies in the "unbiased" perception of God's truth (p.
42). Not seeing — as blindness — is not denied (cf. "a banal fact," p.
40). It can be taken away only by "enlightenment" (p. 42). His protest
against the "attendant" enlightenment that is supposedly necessary
because revelation is unintelligible in itself contains worthwhile motifs,
but leaves the nature of the "unbiasedness" too much in the dark.
Further reflection on I Cor. 2:10-16, especially, is important here.

left no room to speak of responsibility. This train of thought draws on the biblical preaching about the Spirit of God as the Spirit Who convinces men of the truth, but it does not honor the ways of the Spirit, along which the Word of truth is proclaimed and seeks to penetrate into hearts. Only in this way is subjection stripped of all frustrations to true humanity. Then Paul's crass images — even those of capitulation and captivity — can be of service, since they are related to the proclamation of the gospel, which illuminates this obedience as an obedience of faith and trust.

Thus, the wonder of the Spirit does not blur attention for the Word, for the proclamation. Rather, the significance of the mode of proclamation becomes more important. Paul lays such strong emphasis on the proclamation, pointing out that faith comes "from what is heard, and what is heard comes by the preaching of Christ" (Rom. 10:17, cf. 10-14), that the danger of spiritualism was repeatedly detected. Faith is never a "mysterious" given that provides an irrational link to the truth of the gospel and thereby renders the content of the revelation and of the proclamation unimportant. Rather, the full functionality of the proclamation itself is acknowledged. Only when the Church understands the power of this functionality and practices it in the proclamation will she be truly able to confess her apostolicity. When hermeneutical questions concern theology more than ever before, there is a danger that one, out of fear for the "hermeneutization" of theology, will not acknowledge fully the significance of the understanding of the proclamation. One is then captive to the fear that the understanding becomes the deepest criterion for the truth of revelation and that the latter will be limited on the basis of our horizon of understanding. Undeniably, this is always a danger. A verification problematic can arise, which one could call an "anthropological" verification, in so far as revelation is measured by anthropological suppositions. It is a correlation that constitutes the finding from the seeking and the answer from the question! Revelation must then verify itself to man as a confirmation of what is, or is supposed to be, present in man himself. On the basis of this correlation, revelation is limited in a far-reaching way.[83] For Paul, understanding itself clearly could never

83. H. Thielicke (*The Evangelical Faith*, I, 1974, pp. 84ff.) has criticized this form of theology in detail as consciousness theology. It has been filled on the basis of the correlation and reduces theology to anthropology (p. 81), although this danger may not take away interest in

become the criterion of truth. Paul knows that "not all" have heeded the gospel (10:16), and the question of whether they have not heard is answered with the conviction, "indeed they have," because the Word went out to them (10:18). However, that understanding as a human approach is not in itself capable of resolving the problem of verification in no sense relativizes the significance of this understanding.[84] The New Testament apostolate — specifically Paul's — is full of penetrating power. It is directed to understanding and conviction[85] on the basis of the empowerment of the gospel, as a joyous message, and in expectation of the Spirit.

Understandably, then, one repeatedly recalls Paul's statement that seems to indicate, as it were, a certain "method" in his preaching. In order to win as many as possible, he became "to the Jews as a Jew, and to those outside the law as one outside the law."[86] Yet this is not a dominating "technique," but a genuine approach, the goal of which is to penetrate to the one who is confronted with the gospel. This forceful penetration is described in the context of the necessity of preaching the gospel (I Cor. 9:16). The gospel is not transformed; rather, the intention is to let it be experienced as genuine, living truth.[87]

the addressee in the gospel (p. 23). The normative meaning of the "anthropological analysis of existence" must be opposed (p. 47). We meet with a similar criticism in Moltmann, "Anfrage und Kritik zu G. Ebelings 'Theol. u. Verkündigung,'" *Evang. Theol.*, 1964, pp. 25ff. In connection with the correlation between human need and the kerygma, Moltmann accuses Ebeling of seeing revelation in Christ verified anthropologically. Cf. also H. Schmidt, "Das Verhältnis von neuzeitl. Wirklichkeitsverständnis und Chr. Glaube in der Theol. G. Ebelings," *Kerugma und Dogma*, 1963, pp. 71ff.

84. In spite of the "endless circles" in which one can become trapped hermeneutically, van Ruler ("Schriftgezag en Kerk," *Rondom het Woord*, 1968, p. 361) says that one must reflect on the hermeneutical question "a great deal and for a long time, and also deeply."

85. Paul's conviction is spoken of in II Cor. 5:14 ("we are convinced that" — *krínantas toúto*). The love of Christ enables him to discover coherence (that one has died for all). Cf. I John 5:20: understanding *(dianoia)* to know Him Who is true.

86. I Cor. 9:20f. Cf. W.C. van Unnik, "De Grieken een Griek," *Vox Theol.*, 1969, pp. 7ff. Cf. Calvin, *Commentaries on the Epistles of Paul to the Corinthians*, I, 305: "To *become all things* is to assume all appearances, as the case may require." Calvin also uses the word accommodation here.

87. Cf. F.W. Grosheide, *De Eerste Brief aan de Kerk te Korinthe*, p. 251, on "coming close to those who are under the law" in order to win them. Cf. van Unnik *(loc. cit.)* on making oneself understandable, also in reaction to questions and objections by the environment, with new forms of expression in order to express what is special about the message.

Conzelmann calls Paul's statement "surprising," since, in view of his letter to the Galatians, he cannot enter into any compromise with respect to being "under the law."[88] Paul certainly does not have a compromise in view,[89] but he knows that the word of the gospel does not come into a vacuum but into a life that is totally full. There it is to sound forth as a knocking on the door. Therefore, the Church's apostolicity is effected in the way of the urgent, understandable word, which does not penetrate as a totally alien "power,"[90] but wins men for God's salvation. Whoever does not acknowledge this penetration of the apostolic proclamation because of fear for accommodation and does not understand the sense of breaking through all misunderstanding violates true apostolicity. The tragic result is petrification, no matter how much one seeks to preserve the unassailable apostolic truth.

The *credo* of apostolicity does not give the Church a reason for self-complacency; rather, it sets her face to face with the most critical question of her existence: the question of the power, the clarity, and the boldness of her proclamation.[91] Apart from all of this, tradition degenerates to a *corpus alienum* in the modern world. The results for the Church's authority are catastrophic, because no theory or ecclesiology can hide the lack of boldness and apostolicity forever. Thus, not surprisingly, the Church, in reflecting on her *credo,* always comes more deeply and widely into contact with the question of the content, the essence, the "substance" of the gospel. The lack of boldness is certainly due not only to hesitations concerning the nature and technique of carrying the message to others. The significance of these questions — to be all things to all men for the sake of the gospel (9:22f.) — may not blind our eyes to the danger of a deeper hesitation, the danger that we do not know, at least not as positively as the Church's *credo* does. The last book of the Bible warns against addition (adding to) and re-

88. H. Conzelmann, *Der erste Brief an die Korinther,* 1969, p. 189. Cf. Gal. 2:4f.: not yielding submission even for a moment to those who spied out his freedom in Christ.

89. Cf. I Cor. 9:23 (for the sake of the gospel)!

90. "Alien" can be used only in the vicinity of the Reformation's *aliena justitia,* or alien righteousness, and of the "alien acquittal" (the title of a book by K.H. Miskotte — *De Vreemde Vrijspraak).*

91. The high degree to which the word is related to what is put into words is clear from the rejection of lofty words (I Cor. 2:1) and plausible words (2:4, as the caricature of persuasion). Cf. 4:20 (power vis-à-vis talk) and Lam. 2:14 (oracles false and misleading).

duction (taking away) with an eschatological earnestness that corresponds to a divine addition and reduction (Rev. 22:18f.). The mystery of truth can obviously be violated in two directions. The *credo* of apostolicity will be able to preserve its meaning and truth only if it does not lose its apostolic luster, if the Church remembers how concretely this *credo* has intended that subjection, and, finally, if the outlook is preserved on that gospel toward which all apostolicity is directed and with which it must remain filled to the end.

CHAPTER TEN

APOSTOLIC SUCCESSION

IF THE CONFESSION OF THE CHURCH'S APOSTOLIC-
ity recalls us to her normative origin and foundation, that
means she is continuously related to this past. The continuity
of the Church has already drawn our attention in connection
with catholicity, and we tried to trace the meaning of the
Church's confession concerning her continuity through the ages.
We pointed especially to the danger of misunderstanding this
continuity as an automatic, self-evident guarantee.[1] To indicate
the line of continuity is obviously not so simple, and one can
easily go astray with the claim of continuity. That not only
applies to the Jews, who refer to the continuity with Abraham
as their father,[2] but also has significance in the whole life of the
Church; for warnings also sound there against misunderstanding
the continuity.[3] Against this background, the question of how
this continuity could be thought of concretely continually arose.
If one does not want to lapse into a vague concept of continuity,
must it not be fixed visibly and historically? We have already
pointed out that this question received a clear answer in the
well-known Roman Catholic doctrine of apostolic succession. In
contrast to every ecclesiological docetism, one wants to take the
promise of Christ for His Church completely seriously by
drawing inevitable conclusions about the Church's concrete
historical life from it.[4]

---

1. Cf. chapter 7 above.
2. Matt. 3:9; John 8:33. Cf. Isa. 41:8: Israel as "the offspring of Abraham,
   my friend." Christ relativizes the Jews' claim and points to a different
   father (John 8:39, 44). Cf. the discontinuity: the other tenants in Matt.
   21:41 and Mark 12:9.
3. Cf. above, pp. 179ff.
4. Cf. above, pp. 176f.

Infallibility

At the background of apostolic succession, there lies the conviction that a guarantee given and preserved by God is necessary.
Understandably, all the problems concerning this guarantee are
always brought up in connection with the infallible guide that
has supposedly been granted to the Church. The problem has
not only played a role with Rome but also evidently kept Reformed ecclesiology busy as self-evident reflection on the *ecclesia
perpetuo mansura*.[5] That explains why the word "infallibility"
is employed here too and why Bavinck has no objections to
speaking of the infallibility of the Church. He even says that it
is recognized gladly by Protestants.[6] In his view, it is immediately connected to *indefectibilitas* and has its foundation in
Christ's promise in Matthew 16. Bavinck does raise objections
to the Roman Catholic view of infallibility, which relates it to
the "papal" church and finds the guarantee of continuity in the
pope as the vicar of Christ. But Bavinck does not hesitate to
use the word "guarantee." Van Ruler, too, speaks emphatically
of the Church's infallibility.[7] This "verbal" agreement is quite
striking. With a closer observation, however, the disagreement
is obviously still present. To the Roman Catholics, obvious
protestations like those of Bavinck and van Ruler are too vague
and not concrete enough — one could also say too docetic — to
truly be able to guarantee the Church's infallible guide. For instance, Bavinck sees the Church's infallibility as implying "that
there will always be a gathering of believers on earth,"[8] and
van Ruler distinguishes between christological and pneumatic
infallibility. The latter — not on the basis of the *anhypostasis*
(impersonal human nature) but on the basis of "inhabitation" —
adopts the form of mutuality: the Spirit includes man, so that
"the fallibility of man has not been excluded, but included in
the infallibility of the Spirit."[9] Such statements clearly cannot
satisfy traditional ecclesiology, because infallibility is not understood demonstrably, visibly, and concretely in history. There-

5. Augsburg Confession, Article 7. For other confessions, see above, pp. 167f.
6. H. Bavinck, *Geref. Dog.*, IV, 309.
7. A.A. van Ruler, *Reformatorische Opmerkingen in de Ontmoeting met
   Rome*, 1965, pp. 107ff.
8. Bavinck, *Geref. Dog.*, IV, 309.
9. Van Ruler, *op. cit.*, p. 108. One may compare H. Küng's view *(Infallible?,*
   1972, p. 158) that the Church "will persist in the truth *in spite of*
   all ever possible errors!" Cf. p. 163 on the "fundamental remaining of
   the Church in truth, which is not annulled by individual errors."

fore, it does not give sufficient outlook and certainty for the actual visible Church. For Rome, the infallible leading is demonstrable in the Church's whole history. For her safety, one cannot allow less.

The intention here is not to glorify specific persons, but rather to guarantee continuity through a charisma, a privilege, that can be described as "divine assistance." It is not an inherent attribute[10] and does not rest on revelation or inspiration,[11] but is assistance in order to protect apostolicity and to give an effective guarantee and sanction to the Church's historical life. One can think of various aspects of the Paraclete where the idea of the helper also plays a role.[12] The divine assistance designates the Church as needing help and as receiving help.

That the scope of infallibility is continuity is clear from the First Vatican Council, where the *custodia* (safe-guarding) comes to the fore as the central theme.[13] At the deepest, it is the *custodia* of Christ Himself with its blessing and preserving effect. It is the foundation for definitive reassurance with respect to the Church's life through the ages. One can think here of the story of Moses' prayer that Yahweh go with them along the dangerous way (Ex. 33:16). For him, Yahweh's going along is a *conditio sine qua non* (33:15), and the divine answer says that God will give Israel rest along her way (33:14). So, according to Rome, the *custodia* is the "first condition of salvation"[14] of the Church, because it is possible through that *custodia* for her to

10. Cf. *Lumen Gentium (DV II,* p. 48) on the endowment "in defining a doctrine." Cf. G. Thils, "La Locutio ex cathedra et l'Esprit Saint," *Ecclesia a Spiritu Sancto Edocta; Mélanges Theol. Hommage à Mgr. G. Philips,* 1970, pp. 122ff.
11. Cf. Denz., 1638. Much attention is devoted in theology to the defense against misunderstandings. Cf. J. Mulders, "De Term Onfeilbaarheid," *Onfeilbaarheid. Annalen van het Thijmgenootschap,* 1968, p. 5; K. Rahner, "Zum Begriff der Unfehlbarkeit in der Kath. Theol.," *Stimmen der Zeit,* 186 Bd., 1970, pp. 18ff.
12. Cf. G. Bornkamm, "Die Zeit des Geistes," *Gesch. und Glaube,* I, 1968, pp. 90ff.; *idem, Der Paraklet im Joh. Evang.,* pp. 68ff.; E. Käsemann, *The Testament of Jesus,* 1968, pp. 11ff.
13. Cf. Denz., 1793 *(TCT,* 67): on perseverance and the Church as "guardian and teacher" *(custos et magistra);* 1798 *(TCT,* 78): the Church "received the office of safe-guarding the deposit of faith" *(fidei depositum custodiendi);* and 1821 *(TCT,* 201): protection, perpetuity, and strength *(custodia, perpetuitas, soliditas).* Cf. further Denz., 1827, 1836, and 1839.
14. *Prima salus,* Denz., I, 1833 (cf. Denz., 171).

"cling without fail to the faith."[15] Therefore, the charisma can be compared to the pillar of cloud by day and the pillar of fire by night that safeguarded Israel's journey through the wilderness and that continued to live on in Israel's recollection as a wonderful mystery: "By a pillar of cloud thou didst lead them in the day, and by a pillar of fire in the night to light for them the way in which they should go" (Neh. 9:12).

This hymn of praise to preservation and safeguarding is in the context of the comforting promises in Israel's history that God had fulfilled (9:8), of signs and wonders by God's name against Israel's enemies (9:9ff.). They were promises of continuity, also in the face of guilt, since Israel was not abandoned in the wilderness and the pillar of cloud did not depart (9:19), because the good Spirit led them (9:20; cf. Ex. 13:21f.; 14:19; 33:10; Ps. 99:7). This salvation-historical recollection sought to remove the static aspect from the *custodia*.[16] It is a custody that is full of content along a way where life is safeguarded, as the cherubim on the ark overshadow the mercy seat with their wings (Ex. 25:20; 37:9), bringing to light the mystery of grace at the place where God meets with His people and speaks with them (25:22). This continuing *custodia* gives unassailable constancy to the Church. The promise has eliminated error and the dark threat of alienation. The consequence is that, on account of this definitiveness, there can never be any actual "reformation," at least not in the radical sense.[17] The First Vatican Council postulates that the "irreformability" of the pope's infallible pronouncements is in harmony with the decisive gifts of the Holy Spirit.[18] The *custodia* implies this "irreformability," since

15. *Indefectibiliter adhaeret, Lumen Gentium (DV II*, pp. 29f.), in connection with the sense of faith *(sensus fidei)* that is aroused and sustained by the Spirit.

16. The *custodia*, as far as its intention is concerned, can be compared with the watchmen in Ezek. 33:1-20 and with the "watchmen" who have been set by God on Zion's walls and shall not be silent all the day and all the night (Isa. 62:6).

17. The necessity of "renovation" can be spoken of in many ways, but it is kept within clear boundaries. Cf. Y. Congar, "Comment l'Eglise Sainte Doit se Renouveler sans Cesse?", *Sainte Eglise. Etudes et Approaches ecclésiologiques*, 1963, pp. 131ff.; idem, *Vraie et fausse Réforme*, 1950. We will return to this renovation later in connection with the Church's holiness and sin (chapter 13 below). See already pp. 182ff. above.

18. Denz., 1839 (*TCT*, 219) says of infallible pronouncements: "irreformable *because of their nature (ex sese)*, but not because of the agreement of the Church." There has been much discussion of the last phrase here;

the whole Church continues to walk along the *good* way because of the special "watchful care" *(vigilantia)* of the Spirit.[19] In that light, Rome, understandably, will always continue to deny that there is an "automatic" guarantee, since the promise of the Spirit as the *anima ecclesiae* condemns and eliminates all audacious trust.[20]

Nevertheless, this view of the Church implies that the *custodia* and *vigilantia* must also be demonstrable in the Church's history.[21] They are not related to an imperceptible "invisible Church," but affect the Church's concrete life in such a way that they lead to fixation and perceptibility, with all the possibilities of verification and legitimacy. The apostolic tradition goes with the Church; it is the *plenitudo veritatis*, which is preserved "by a continuous succession."[22] The Church "in her teaching, life, and worship, perpetuates and hands on to all generations all that she herself is, all that she believes."[23] The word "help" *(assistentia)* reappears here too with a reference to the Church's actual history.[24] There can be no tension between that history and the promise of *assistentia* and *custodia!*[25] Since

sometimes it is interpreted as a rejection of approval and ratification afterwards, and sometimes as a concentration of the infallible authority in the papal charisma. Cf. J. Mulders, *op. cit.*, p. 16; H. Küng, *Structures of the Church*, pp. 368ff. The words were added at the last moment in opposition to Gallicanism, and the discussion centers on the question of whether it is clear that the actual consensus with the Church as the people of God, in any case, may not be lacking. In this context, one may also recall the "Prefatory Note of Explanation" added to *Lumen Gentium*, where there is sharp emphasis on the *ex sese (DV II,* pp. 98ff.).

19. Cf. *Dei Verbum (DV II*, p. 126). Cf. also J.G. Geenen, "Ecclesia a Spiritu Sancto edocta," *Mélanges Théologiques*, 1970, pp. 169ff.
20. Cf. G. Philips, *Leergezag en Onfeilbaarheid*, 1934, p. 35.
21. "This See of St. Peter always remains untainted *by any error"* (Denz., 1836, *TCT*, 216).
22. *Continua successione, Dei Verbum (DV II*, p. 115). "Divine Providence" can also be spoken of *(Lumen Gentium, DV II*, p. 46). Cf. O. Rousseau, "Divina autem Providentia. Histoire d'une Phrase de Vatican II," *Mélanges Théol.*, pp. 281ff.
23. *Dei Verbum (DV II*, p. 116).
24. *Ibid.*
25. Understandably, therefore, the First Vatican Council had to deal with a few facets of the Church's history that were difficult to harmonize with the *custodia*. One may recall the well-known question of Pope Honorius, whose statement about monotheletism in the 7th century was later condemned by other popes. Cf. W. Plannett, *Die Honoriusfrage auf dem Vatik.-Konzil*, 1912; Granderath, *Geschiedenis des Vatik. Konzil*, III, 173ff.; *Theologisch Woordenboek*, II, 2269 (not a formal

the harmony was designated as unbroken guidance, inductive facts from Church history could only affirm the charisma of truth. In this light, naturally, every appeal is out of the question, since an appeal assumes the possibility of error. This unassailability as a guarantee in the head of the Church[26] comes to expression clearly in the well-known formula: "The most distinguished See is judged by no one."[27] Such a "judgment" would endanger the whole way of the Church, causing a crisis of the pastorate of the Lord Himself.

Peter and his successors

This pneumatic view of continuity in the Church leads automatically to concretization in apostolic succession, which manifests the work of the Spirit in a way that has had great consequences for the Church's whole history. The promise given to Peter in Matt. 16 is at the center of these considerations. The promise of invincibility in connection with him implies an outlook on the empowerment of his successors. In 1870, one appealed for this idea to the earlier decisions of the Church where succession already had an important place.[28] The statement "you are Peter" *(tu es Petrus)*, engraved in large letters in the Church of Peter at Rome, recalls this comprehensive prom-

heresy). Others have said that it was not a statement *ex cathedra*. The case of Honorius is often viewed as a confirmation of Manning's saying: "Dogma must vanquish history" (Plannett, p. 90). See in more detail my *Het Probleem der Schriftkritiek*, 1938, pp. 220ff.

26. *Lumen Gentium (DV II*, p. 49): not as a "private person." The conclusion is: "Therefore they need no approval of others, nor do they allow an appeal to any other judgment." Neither can the assent of the Church, therefore, ever be lacking *(numquam deesse potest)*.

27. *Prima sedes a nemine judicatur, Codex Iuris Canonici*, canon 1556. Cf. also canon 1558 on the "absolute incompetence" of all other authorities. On *a nemine*, see also Denz., 1830 *(TCT*, 210): "the judgment ... is not subject to review by anyone" *(judicium a nemine fore retractandum)*, with reference to a letter of Nicholas I (858-867) where these words appear (Denz., 330ff.). The *a nemine judicatur* appears in I Cor. 2:15 (Vulgate; Greek: *hup' oudenòs anakrinetai)*. The English reads: "is to be judged by no one." According to *Unam Sanctam* in 1302, this text is applicable to the pope and his successors (Denz., 469). Cf. H. Küng, *Structures of the Church*, p. 250; and *idem, Infallible?*, 1972.

28. Denz., 1824 *(TCT*, 204), where Ephesus (431) is cited: Peter "lives even to this time and forever in his successors." Cf. Denz., 466 *(TCT*, 152) on Peter as the Prince of the Apostles "whose successor is the Roman Pontiff." Cf. S.E. Hof, *Populus Christianus. Kerkstrukturen volgens Leo de Grote*, 1970, pp. 156ff. See p. 181 on the *per Petrum* and the *in Petro*.

ise to Peter as the "Prince of all the apostles" and as the "visible head of the whole Church militant."[29] That promise cannot be isolated on account of the continuance of the Church to the end of the ages. The Reformed tradition has repeatedly viewed the rock on which the Church would be built not so much as the person of Peter, but as his confession.[30] But one saw this as an escape from the evidence of the story, which places Peter fully in the light. Cullmann points out that the exegesis has usually been greatly determined by the controversy; one has gradually come to see that there is no antithesis between the relatedness to Peter and to his confession.[31] In his view, there must be full room for recognition of Peter's first place and, from the Reformed standpoint, it is not in the least necessary to minimize its significance.[32]

But this interest in the person of Peter must not lead us to neglect the context of the promise to Peter, especially when we consider that we confront a moving problematic about continuity in the gospels precisely in Peter's life. After Peter's confession we read about the announcement of Christ's suffering. Peter's reaction to that is to designate a different way than the way of suffering: "God forbid, Lord *(hileōs soi kúrie)!* This shall never happen to you" (16:22). Under God's mercy *(éleos)*, Christ's way will not be that of such a great passion. Peter has apparently not in any sense been withdrawn from all dangers and threats after the confession. Rather, such dark shadows

29. Denz., 1823 *(TCT,* 203). Cf. Denz., 1824 *(TCT,* 204): "most Blessed Peter, Prince and head of the Apostles, the pillar of faith, and the foundation of the Catholic Church."
30. Cf. Calvin, *Inst.,* IV, 6, 6; and Cullmann, *Peter,* 1962, p. 168. Calvin believed that dispute about "the meaning of the words" is impossible: "nothing clearer or more certain can be said." He refers to I Cor. 3:11 (Christ as the foundation). According to F. Kattenbusch, *Der Quellort der Kirchenidee. Harnack-Festschrift,* 1921, p. 165, it is not possible, "it seems to me, to reach one's goal purely exegetically."
31. In addition to Cullmann's book on Peter, see the (Roman Catholic) work by F. Obrist, *Echtheitsfragen und Deutung der Primatstelle Mt. 16, 18ff. in der deutschen protestant. Theol. der letzten dreissig Jahre,* 1960; J. Ringger, "Das Felsenwort. Zur Sinndeutung von Mt. 16, 18 vor allem im Lichte der Symbolgesch.," in M. Roesle-O. Cullmann, *Begegnung der Christen,* 1959, pp. 271ff. Bavinck also rejects this dilemma, because the words cannot refer to anything but the person of Peter *(Geref. Dog.,* IV, 320). Cf. also Barth, *C.D.,* II/2, p. 441, on "the words of Mt. 16:18 are spoken."
32. Cf. *prōtos* in Matt. 10:2: "first, Simon." Cf. Cullmann, *Peter,* on the New Testament data on Peter. Bavinck *(Geref. Dog.,* IV, 321) calls Peter *"primus inter pares."*

occur that he comes under Christ's judgment that he is not on the side of God but of men and, therefore, is acting like Satan and like a stumbling block for Christ (16:23). This event had to become an occasion for new reflection on the question of the relatedness of the Church to the person of Peter. Apparently, one must be cautious with various ideas about the rock and with conclusions that are drawn from Christ's word of promise. After Peter's confession, even though it was not given by flesh and blood, the things of God were not in good hands with Peter. They were anything but safe. He does set himself up here — just as later in Gethsemane (26:51ff.) — as "a guardian," but this *custodia* is not legitimized. Rather, it is disqualified and rejected along the *via dolorosa*. In the form of a rebuke *(epitimán) of* Christ (16:22), this *custodia* is the object only of a rebuke *(epetímēsen) by* Christ Himself (Mark 8:33)! That implies an urgent warning against every rash conclusion.

No matter how different Peter is from Judas, whose place is taken by another after his betrayal,[33] and although Peter again receives a place in the Church, Peter's life is nevertheless not under the sign of an unbroken guarantee and continuity. Naturally, this has not been asserted by Roman Catholic exegetes, but it has practically never shocked them into the new reflection on the rock, Peter, and his significance for the Church. When the First Vatican Council founded the primacy, these shadows scarcely played any role. In connection with Matt. 16, the primacy is designated with reference to the later commission to tend the sheep.[34] Neither the darkness after the confession in Caesarea Philippi, the total misunderstanding of the *theologia crucis,* nor the later denial is mentioned. And Christ's intercession that Peter's faith not fail (Luke 22:32) is mentioned as an aside. The recollection of this prayer has a clear scope: the designation of the continuity in Peter's life.[35] But it is clear that we do not escape by using the word "continuity"; for the intercession is pictured against the background of such a dangerous situation that there is a new commission through a new

---

33. Christ's statement to Peter ("Satan") does, however, remind us of His statement about Judas in John 6:70. Cf. Barth, *C.D.,* IV/2, p. 431.

34. Denz., 1822. Cf. John 21:15ff.; and *Lumen Gentium (DV II,* p. 43).

35. Denz., 1836 *(TCT,* 216): the See of St. Peter remains free of any error "according to the divine promise of our Lord and Savior made to the prince of his disciples, 'I have prayed for thee, that thy faith may not fail; and do thou, when once thou hast turned again, strengthen thy brethren' (Luke 22:32)."

event: "and when you have turned again, strengthen your brethren" (22:32). There is no hint that Christ's intercession takes anything at all away from Peter's way in darkness and denial. The satanic temptation plays a decisive role in both Matt. 16 and in Christ's intercession. All four of the gospels picture the denial of Peter for us and show how deeply the "discontinuity" penetrated into his life, where it climaxed in a curse[36] as Peter separated himself from the Lord, denying His name "before men" (Matt. 10:33; cf. II Tim. 2:13). The tension in the satanic temptation — sifting like wheat — is unprecedented.

One can say, though, that in this darkness a new perspective becomes visible of a fellowship that will not always be broken: "that your faith may not fail" (Luke 22:32 — *hina mè eklipę pistis sou*). On account of this statement, the question whether Peter was only partially lost from fellowship with the Lord has been raised. Did he not continue to believe? What is the nature of the new perspective on Peter's life? Can the continuity be pictured — as has often happened — as "enduring"? And does that not imply the correctness of the Vatican paraphrase?[37] Whoever wants to continue to speak of "continuity" here is confronted in any case with a wholly unique structure to continuity. It cannot be clarified from the general category of continuity — continuance, constancy, and unbrokenness. The gospel story points us to a deep discontinuity, which may not be transformed into continuity, as though the pattern of Peter's life could be described as a "continuance" of what was present, like

36. "But he began to invoke a curse on himself and to swear, 'I do not know this man of whom you speak'" (Mark 14:71 — *anathematizein*). G. Bornkamm ("Das Wort Jesu vom Bekennen," *Gesch. und Glaube*, I, 1966, p. 34) sees *anathematizein* as "a formula of excommunication on Jesus," thus not a curse on himself. That there is a "toning down" *(Milderung)* of the situation in Luke 22:60 ("I do not know what you are saying") is difficult to prove.

37. Bavinck (*Geref. Dog.*, IV, 320) has a remarkable view. He writes that Peter proved he was a rock in his confession, and the allusion to Christ's naming him (John 1:43) is related to "his loyal character that, despite his sanguine, emotional nature, was proper to him and came out most clearly at Caesarea Philippi." That is a characterological analysis that is difficult to reconcile with the New Testament picture of Peter. Along such paths one can also judge differently: Peter as without "the inflexible will power of a Paul" in connection with Peter's "unstable" character (J. Schmid, "Petrus der Fels," in Roesle-Cullmann, *op. cit.*, p. 252).

the firmness of a rock.[38] If continuity is mentioned in this story, then it is in the form of Peter's own announced continuity when he asserts his readiness to go to prison and to death (Luke 22:33) in contrast to the possible discontinuity in the case of the other disciples (Matt. 26:33). The rupture that is conceivable for them is, according to Peter's own words, out of the question for him: "I will never *(oudépote)* fall away," and "I will not *(ou mḗ)* deny you" (26:34f.; cf. Mark 14:29). Two sorts of continuity face each other: that of Peter in the normal contours of unbrokenness, and that of Christ's intercession, which, in the rupture and discontinuity, is directed to restoration and renewal. The rupture is pictured in this way: the shepherd is struck and the sheep are scattered (Mark 14:27). Peter's way is not in the least the right way, but a dark way, on which the light of God breaks through unexpectedly and incalculably, graciously and surprisingly.[39] Peter remembers Christ's word, turns, and receives a new commission.[40]

So, what happens in Vatican I is not permissible: passing by the deep shadows quickly for the sake of a reference to continuity and the uninterrupted primacy, and then concluding to the charisma of truth for Peter and his successors. In Vatican I, the drama of Peter's life in confrontation with the *passio magna* is scarcely considered worth mentioning. It is hidden behind the reference to the continuity that had to be indicated with respect to this empowerment in the hands of men.[41] But true continuity

38. That is also in conflict with the disclosure of discontinuity in Christ's glance, resulting in Peter's weeping bitterly (Mark 14:72). Various constructions about whether Peter's denial was historical or unhistorical do not tally, in my view, with this experience of guilt in the discontinuity.

39. We find a deep realization of this outlook in the Canons of Dort (V, 4f.), where Peter's fall is described as "deadly guilt," with the perspective of the shining of the light of God's fatherly countenance on those who have fallen when they change their course by serious repentance. David, too, is recalled here. The continuity was broken in his life, and he was the man after God's own heart along the way of shocking prophetic admonition (II Sam. 12), perhaps reflected in David's prayer that the joy of salvation be restored to him (Ps. 51).

40. One may recall the "solemn triple repetition" in John 21:15ff. as "a reference to the triple denial," which was held by "almost all scholars" in the ancient Church (J. Ringger, *op. cit.*, p. 341). Cf. the use of the name Simon and the call to follow Christ. Cf. K.H. Miskotte, *Geloof bij de Gratie Gods*, p. 48, on Christ's knowledge of Peter in contrast to Peter's lack of knowledge of Christ.

41. *Lumen Gentium*, too, simply refers back to Vatican I. Christ's intercession can be omitted here also.

can only be experienced as a wonder of preservation. It never lends itself to *a priori*, linear conclusions.[42] The contours of Peter's life look different than a simplistic demonstration of the continuity,[43] since in his life the *custodia* is perverted because of blindness for the things of God. The promise of Christ cannot be summarized in the single word "guarantee" as though everything did not depend on Christ's real prayer in the dark hour of the *passio magna*. It breaks through the sphere of factuality and self-evidence and precludes forever speaking simplistically of the efficacy of the apostolic office.[44]

One cannot save the "common" concept of continuity by finding the problematic before, but not after, Christ's resurrection. Also after the resurrection, we meet with a problematic that is extremely instructive for true continuity in the Church. The Reformers were understandably interested in the far-reaching conflict in Antioch, where Paul openly opposed Peter because he was wrong (Gal. 2:12ff.). Reformed interest in this did not arise from an anti-papal feeling, but from the realization of the central role that testing plays here. Since Peter pleads for unchanged continuity with tradition, it is obvious here, if anywhere, that the problem of good guidance, of true *custodia,* remains of the greatest significance along all the Church's ways.[45] The decision is made not on the basis of a simplistically ascertainable and formally understood authority (Peter or Paul?), but on the basis of the content of the gospel. And the conflict is so arresting that the many attempts to invalidate the Reformed appeal to Galatians 2 have not made a credible impression.[46] The attempt, specifically, to place the critical testing

42. That the powers of death will not prevail (Matt. 16:18) does not lie in Peter's power or in that of the other apostles. Rather, their lack of power is pictured all the way through Gethsemane. The *custodia* fails precisely in Gethsemane!
43. Cf. on numerous problems, E. Dinkler, "Petrusbekenntnis und Satanswerk," *Zeit und Geschichte*, 1964, pp. 132ff.; G. Klein, "Die Verleugnung des Petrus," *Rekonstruktion und Interpretation*, 1969, pp. 62ff.; E. Linnemann, "Die Verleugnung des Petrus," *Z.Th.K.*, 1966, pp. 1ff.
44. *"Efficacia apostolici muneris,"* Denz., 1888.
45. Cf. the influence of Peter's action on the rest of the Jews and Barnabas in Gal. 2:13.
46. Cf. F. Overbeck, "Über die Auffassung des Streites des Paulus und Petrus in Antiochiën (Gal. 2, 11ff.) bei den Kirchenvätern," *Sonderausgabe*, 1968; K. Holl, "Der Streit zwischen Petrus und Paulus zu Antiochië in seiner Bedeutung für Luthers innere Entwicklung," *Ges. Aufs. z. K.G.*, III, 134ff.; O. Cullmann, *Peter*, pp. 42ff.; G.H.M. Posthumus Meyer, *De Controvers tussen Petrus en Paulus*, 1967.

that takes place in the light of a distinction between orthodoxy and orthopraxy has not been satisfactory.[47] Undoubtedly, Peter's attitude is under discussion, but it is related to the truth of the gospel. And precisely because of that, the outlook was preserved on the meaning and mystery of the *custodia*.[48]

The nature of succession

It goes without saying that the discussion about continuity has not simply been closely connected to the texts about Peter, but has been concentrated in the question of the nature of succession.[49] The *a priori* view of succession does admit errors and lacks in the Church, but the continuity rests in a "nevertheless" of fulfillment, which can be concretely grasped in history.[50] This apriority determines the *successio* decisively, making its specific mode into an inescapable postulate that takes the tension out of the normativity of the apostolic gospel to which the Church subjects herself.[51] That history — the progression of gen-

47. Cf. H. Schlier, *Der Galaterbrief*, p. 50: practical in contrast to theoretical.
48. Overbeck *(loc. cit.)* points out that Luther "shuns completely the quicksand of the question of what Peter answered." In his view, this question was not relevant; he was concerned only with the question of testing. Cf. M. Luther, *Komm. zur Gal. brief (Calwer Ausg.)*, 1968, p. 81. For Calvin, see especially W. Nijenhuis, "Paulus en Calvijn," *Rondom het Woord*, 1971, pp. 82ff. (on Calvin's Bible discussions of Gal. 2 in 1562).
49. At the Second Vatican Council, one did not feel the need to reconsider the manifold exegetical problems concerning the twelve, the apostles, and the remaining "offices" and "services," because the fundamental idea of succession was elevated above all doubt. Cf. H. Küng, *Infallible?*, 1972.
50. This motif clearly comes to expression not only in the Roman Catholic, but also in the Greek Catholic Church. K. Bonis, for example, points to the ecumenical councils and the "spiritual director" of the decisions that were made there ("Zur Frage der Tradition und der Traditionem," in Skydsgaard-Vischer, *Schrift und Tradition*, 1963, p. 65). The act of handing down, the *actus tradendi*, is not "abandoned to what is human — all too human." There are real shadows, for instance, at the Robbers' Synod of 449; but Chalcedon followed in 451, bringing the truth to light again.
51. Cf. Cullmann, *Peter*; K. Barth, *C.D.*, II/2, pp. 440f.; E. Schlink, "Die apost. Sukzession," *Kerugma und Dogma*, 1961, pp. 79ff. The postulate appears in Rahner in the statement that the apostolic succession, as "the criterion of the true Church," cannot be given up, "because otherwise the Church is changed from a historical, tangible reality into an abstract idea" (Rahner-Vorgrimler, *Kleines Theologisches Wörterbuch*, 1963, p. 345). Cf. *idem, s.v. Papst*.

erations — comes into view in the New Testament as well as in the Old Testament (cf. Ps. 22:30f.; 78:3-5) is undeniable. But precisely in that progression of ages, the Lord prays for those who will believe in Him through the word of His disciples. Therefore, the outlook is preserved fully on the words about continuity and perspective to which one has always appealed for apostolic succession. They are the words about the faithfulness of God (Rom. 3:2f.), Who does not forsake the work of His hands (Ps. 138:8; Phil. 1:6; cf. Heb. 6:16-19), and about the new age of the Spirit of truth, Who will guide into all the truth (John 16:12f.; cf. 14:16f.), thus continuously connecting the Church to Christ.[52] Confronted with the Roman Catholic idea of succession, the Reformers had to deal with this clear testimony of Scripture. They did not deny the significance of all such words; but, obviously, they understood them differently. Perhaps one can best characterize the controversy by saying that the Reformers consistently refused to turn this promise into a starting point for a series of conclusions that would make the guarantee an "objective" factuality. Nowhere in the whole of the New Testament does the promise lend itself to such a series of conclusions. Rather, the promise comes into sight in the context of admonition, and it excludes every a priori identification of the Spirit with the Church.

The confession that we often meet with in the ancient Church that the Spirit is the anima Ecclesiae[53] can refer to the Church's life along the way of expectation — Veni, Creator Spiritus. But it can never involve any claim or pretension that has validity "in itself," as though the Church's being is present in the world unthreatened and as a matter of course.[54] In the Reformation this different pneumatic view gave reflection on the Church a different hue. The Reformers did not oppose contingency and arbitrariness to continuity and firmness, and they were even prepared to speak in a certain way of a guarantee and a safe guide.[55] But all these words were related to the Church under the lordship of the Lord of the Church. With

52. John 14:26. Cf. H. Schlier, "The World and Man According to St. John's Gospel," The Revelance of the N.T., pp. 156ff.
53. Cf. J.N. Bakhuizen van den Brink, Ecclesia, II, 30.
54 Cf. the important article by Per Erik Persson, "Das Amt des Geistes. Eine kontrov. theol. Skizze," Kerugma und Dogma, 1959, pp. 99ff., especially on the Spirit as "the inner, constant principle of life" of the Church in traditional Roman Catholic dogmatics and on petrification. Cf. Bakhuizen van den Brink, op. cit., 31.
55. Bavinck, Geref. Dog., IV, 309.

that, one did not place continuity in human hands, but one did designate the only way along which the promise could be understood and preserved.[56] As a result, the Church's history was no longer seen as sanctioned in its whole, actual course, but as full of tension: it was not legitimized *a priori* because of the *assistentia divina*. Even the appeal to the Spirit — in the actuality of Church history — was placed emphatically under the test of faith and obedience in order to draw attention to the constancy of the Church. The conflict between Calvin and Sadolet was concerned not with the contrast between acknowledging or not acknowledging the promise of the Spirit, but with a different insight into the work and way of the Spirit. When Calvin confronts the assertion that the Church cannot err, he discusses the promise of John 14 and 16 in the context of the Church's relationship to the Word and to Christ Himself. Boasting in the Holy Spirit is not lacking, but attention is called to the mode of this boasting. Calvin is very critical here in comparison to his opponents, who have uncritically misunderstood this boasting *(Inst.,* IV, 8, 13f.). That appears most sharply when Calvin speaks about councils. He points out that they have not been legitimized *a priori*, but are tested according to the rule that Christ is "in our midst" when we are gathered in His Name *(Inst.,* IV, 9, 2). Apart from this dimension, the promise degenerates into an "objective" prediction. Not in antithesis to the promise of the Spirit, but in conformity with that promise, Calvin discovers a balance on which to judge men and angels *(Inst.,* IV, 9, 9) that can test the Church in all ages. And therein, "the whole empowerment of the apostolate is implied."[57]

Therefore, the *a nemine judicatur* is unacceptable to Calvin, no matter what ecclesiastical authority it is postulated of, because the leading of the Spirit is experienced only in "voluntary captivity."[58] The unprecedented testing that is implied in this is evident from the way Calvin describes his insight into the testing. It is — for the sake of the dangerous situation — almost in a provocative way. For example, he speaks of the "council" (the 400 prophets) convened by Ahab (I Kings 22:6, 22), which flattered a godless king and, through a lying spirit, condemned Micaiah as a heretic *(Inst.,* IV, 9, 6). Calvin also speaks of the

---

56. Cf. H. Küng's statements *(Infallible?,* p. 163) when he considers the nature of the promise and cannot escape — any more than can Calvin — the "so far as" in opposition to every static ecclesiology.
57. Cf. Calvin, "Reply to Sadolet," *Library of Christian Classics,* XXII, 242ff.
58. Calvin, *Commentaries on the Epistles of Paul to the Corinthians,* II, 324.

"council" that convened against Christ (John 11:47). We also hear this extremely fierce criticism in the reference to the warnings against the shepherds and watchmen in Israel, who sometimes became *blind* watchmen (Isa. 56:10; cf. Jer. 6:13; 14:14), while there was "hatred in the house of God" (Hos. 9:8; cf. *Inst.*, IV, 9, 3). Then Calvin also answers the objection that this was possible in Israel but is no longer conceivable in the Church. He points to the necessity of continuous testing because of false teachers and to the dangers that can threaten the Church from the side of the pastors *(Inst.,* IV, 9, 4). As Calvin explains emphatically, he in no sense wants to undermine the authority of the pastors *(Inst.,* IV, 9, 5), but discrimination and testing are necessary to guard against all arbitrariness. Calvin is not concerned with an anti-conciliar and anti-papal disposition. He even appears willing to go very far, because he exclaims: "Let the Pope be the successor of Peter, if only he also performs the service of an apostle."[59] This statement connects directly to present-day ecclesiological thought about the service of Peter. In that light, Calvin can understandably speak in a provocative way and at the same time can mention the "majesty" of a council as long as Scripture "stands out in the higher place" *(Inst.,* IV, 9, 8).

The Reformers, with their different understanding of the promise of the Spirit, had a wholly different view of the primacy and of the idea of succession. Although the place of Peter in the founding of the Church was not neglected, much wider interest in the whole life of the Church arose in connection with the commission and empowerment conferred on men. That the promise is given not only to Peter, but also to the other apostles played a role here too. Matthew mentions binding and loosing with regard to *all* (18:18). And in John, *all* receive the Spirit in connection with forgiving and retaining guilt (20:23). From the nature of the case, the Roman Catholic doctrine of the Church has also dealt with this, as is obvious from many far-reaching discussions about the relation between primacy and episcopacy. The tendency to give a place within the hierarchy to the episcopacy led to its being recognized (just as in 1870), but it receives the function of strengthening the primacy — especially via the

59. Calvin, *Om de Eenheid en Vrede der Kerk*, trans. D.J. de Groot, 1953, p. 56. Cf. Calvin, "Reply to Sadolet," *L.C.C.*, XXII, 243, on the boasting in the succession of Peter by "your pontiff." Obedience is due to him "so long as he himself maintains his fidelity to Christ and does not deviate from the purity of the gospel." Cf. Nijenhuis, *op. cit.*, pp. 232ff.

"Prefatory Note of Explanation" to *Lumen Gentium*.[60] This specific and primary "petrine" accent is connected to the clear perceptibility of the empowerment and the custody. It signifies much more than a sign of unity,[61] because, in the primacy, the wide arch of tranquillity and guarantee spans the whole history of the Church. Understandably, then, the many questions in our time about the specific petrine form of the Church cause a certain suspicion, for the Church's being is thought to be inseparably connected to what for centuries has been seen as the point of concentration of office, empowerment, authority, and safety.[62]

The new reflection on the petrine character of the Church should not be seen as a replacement of the petrine character by the Pauline. Rather, the new reflection is much more synthetic by nature because of a re-evaluation of the office of Peter. Motives of a very differing nature play a role here. First of all, there is greater impartiality with respect to the real history of the Church. In the First Vatican Council, the *custodia* was concretized especially in the infallible guide, but the realization has grown more and more that the *custodia* must also be seen in connection with a doctrinal authority that is not infallible. Precisely in that custody, far-reaching questions are repeatedly brought up for discussion and, therein, guidance is given to the way one must walk in the Church. Not simply "cathedral" orthodoxy, but also guidance in the practical lives of priests and laity[63] was discussed. Here the question about the true *custodia* came to the fore, and the conclusion was drawn that

60. Cf. my *Nabetrachting op het Concilie*, 1968, chapter 5.
61. Calvin (*Inst.*, IV, 6, 4) spoke of the promise directed especially to Peter as intended to commend unity to the Church (appealing to Augustine and Cyprian).
62. The petrine character of the Catholic Church was much discussed at the time of Jansenism, when the relation between Peter and Paul was at the center of interest, especially with Arnauld. Cf. J.N. Bakhuizen van den Brink, "Paulus bij Jansenius en Pascal," *Rondom het Woord*, 1971, p. 110. A "tremendous commotion" ensued, resulting in a decree by the Holy Office in 1647, which judged as heretical an equality between Peter and Paul "without subordinating and subjecting St. Paul to St. Peter in the supreme power and government of the universal Church" (Denz., 1091; *TCT*, 170).
63. One may think of the guidance with respect to celibacy and birth control. The latter, in the encyclical *Humanae Vitae*, was the reason for Küng's publication on infallibility.

the Church had failed in important points. Hence, the concept of *custodia* was gradually illuminated critically.[64]

In addition to this, a second motive can be distinguished. It is emphasized that this office would not summon up so much opposition in other believers if it displayed the serviceableness intended by Christ. Therefore, it is of the greatest importance for the Church that this form again become visible in the ministerial primacy.[65] Thereby, "Peter" — the pope — comes much closer to all the other bearers of office, since the point of concentration for all is in this service. Then the office cannot be juridicized, leading to all the aspects of power that have appeared in history.[66] And so, the office of Peter would not need to disappear, but it would lose its offensive aspects, since the care and guidance of the Church receives a different, salutary structure.

Finally, we meet with the most important motive. It concerns succession itself, because the unique significance of the apostolate (testimony to the life and work of Jesus Christ) is accentuated and designated as unrepeatable.[67] The essential relation between "the original phase" and "the following period" could not be recorded in the mere sense of "succession," since all that followed is founded on the testimony concerning the unique past. Thus, it is not that there is a simple continuation of the original line, but rather a normative attachment of the whole "following period."[68] With that, succession was used less and less as a formal, empty category. Attention was still directed to history, but this return and relatedness to the once-for-allness of the time of salvation was sharply separated from all "antiquarian" interest.[69] This viewpoint, which always dominated in the

64. The broadening of the *custodia* is due also to the great significance that is frequently attributed to non-infallible pronouncements. That is very clear, for instance, in the encyclical on celibacy, *Sacerdotalis Coelibatus*, where the papal duty and mission are illuminated with the light that radiates from Christ. Cf. my *Nabetrachting op het Concilie*, pp. 166ff.

65. H. Küng, *The Church*, p. 462.

66. *Ibid.*, p. 465. Cf. on John XXIII, who, according to Küng, took the primacy of service totally seriously, pp. 471f.

67. Cf. H. Küng, "What Is the Essence of Apostolic Succession?", *Concilium*, 34, 1968, pp. 28ff.

68. See also *TDNT*, VI, *s.v. Petros*, on "what continues in what is once-for-all." Cf. G. Hasenhüttl, *Charisma. Ordnungsprinzip der Kirche*, 1969, pp. 181ff.

69. Cf. O. Noordmans, *Gestalte en Geest*, 1955, pp. 326ff., on historical interest, which in itself is legitimate, but can reach too high a degree,

Reformed view too,[70] made it impossible to see succession as a self-evident, historical "succession" that followed from the promise of the Spirit and was, as it were, recordable.[71] Thus, one was not entitled to make historical decisions on the basis of formal succession.[72] All attention was directed to tradition as content, the act of transmission of this tradition, which is one-for-all. Thus, the life of the Church could no longer be withdrawn in any respect from testing and norming. Whenever "succession" is approached in this way — either by the Roman Catholics or by the Reformation — the approach to the New Testament data also changes in character. The urge to systematize the various different services and offices decreases. Then, too, more account is taken of situational determinedness, which need not be a continuing "model" for the Church in all ages but, nevertheless, offers a continuing outlook on the nature of the normativity that must rule the structure of the Church in all her forms.[73]

so that one thinks one has the leading and the truth through the Spirit in one's grasp. Cf. the remarkable views of Noordmans on the possibility of a discontinuity in the papacy that does not exclude an evolution "in the near future" (pp. 339ff.). That Noordmans sees an anomaly in the succession of Peter by the pope is understandable (*Het Koninkrijk der Hemelen,* 1944, p. 197).

70. Cf. L. Goppelt, "Tradition nach Paulus," *Kerugma und Dogma,* 1958, pp. 213ff.; E. Schlink, "Die apostl. Sukzession," *Kerugma und Dogma,* 1961, pp. 80ff.; K. Boon, *Apostolisch Ambt en Reformatie,* 1965, p. 68; J.N. Bakhuizen van den Brink, "Tradition im Theol. Sinn," *Ecclesia,* II, 60ff.

71. H. Küng, *The Church,* pp. 463ff., on what is decisive in the succession, namely, the Spirit, in the petrine mission and task, witness and ministry. Cf. pp. 355ff.: "As direct witnesses and messengers of the risen Lord, the apostles can have no successors.... What remains is a task and a commission," obedience to the normative apostolic witness.

72. Cf., among others, the standpoint of Leo XIII on Anglican ordinations (*Apostolicae Curae,* 1896). They are declared to be invalid because of the insufficient form of the priestly ordination.

73. One may recall the discussion of the New Testament data in all their variations of service, leading, care, and empowerment with relation to the question of whether there is a model here that is to be imitated by the later Church. Cf. H.N. Ridderbos, *Paul,* p. 475: no clearly worked out doctrine of offices. Naturally, the situational variation does not justify arbitrariness, since the point of concentration in all the variation is obviously defined by the outlook on the government of the Church through the Word and the Spirit. Cf. further G. Sevenster, "Het Kerkelijk Ambt in het Licht van het N.T.," in Kuitert-Fiolet, *Uit Tweeën Eén,* 1966; *idem,* "Problemen betreffende het Ambt in het N.T.," *Nederlands Theologisch Tijdschrift,* 1963.

The successio Verbi

This is especially the background of concern for the *successio Verbi* or *doctrinae*. It was not intended to depersonalize the office and empowerment. Nor was it meant as a docetic, contingent ecclesiology that opposes the *successio doctrinae* to the *successio personarum*. But it did contain a reference to subjection to the apostolic gospel, which makes it impossible to approach the legitimacy from a normal, self-evident succession. The Reformation did not separate the *successio doctrinae* from the *successio personae*, since the former is determined precisely by permanent responsibility from generation to generation. The normativity functions in the progression. Thus, Calvin can speak without bias about that progression and succession, saying that a "holy, inviolable, and perpetual law" is imposed "upon those who took the place of the apostles" *(Inst.,* IV, 3, 6 — *succedunt).* There is no hint that the bearers of the *successio Verbi* disappear from view, as though they are of no significance because of the supra-personal power of the Word of God and as though, starting from an isolated concept of purity, no schism can be criticized legitimately. Rather, one will have to say that, since the progression of the gospel has been so normatively qualified, the Church's responsibility not to place "purity" above legitimacy in arbitrariness or an unfounded schism becomes even greater. From the Reformed point of view, such a two-fold normativity is unacceptable, for apostolicity is that of the one Church. Whoever makes a separation between purity and legitimacy here must end in ecclesiasticism or in a sphere of formal legitimacy that endangers apostolicity and catholicity.[74]

These dangers are avoidable without neglecting the aspect of progression and preservation. The New Testament sharpens our attention for this perspective, which is related to a *cura* (care) and *custodia* that preserves apostolicity. It is in that connection that the laying on of hands, which we meet in the New Testament in concrete, historical connections, comes up for discussion. Here the "succession" displays its personal, human, and communal character. A technical, automatic, or magical "transfer" is evidently not intended, since attention is constantly called to the dimension of depth in the laying on of hands. And it is

74. Cf. D. Nauta, "Calvijns Afkeer van een Schisma," *Ex Auditu Verbi,* 1965, pp. 131ff.

related to prayer;[75] hence, it shows the "transfer" to be a meaningful sign of commission, blessing, and responsibility.[76] Human connections become visible, but they must be protected against dangers.[77] The human functionality (cf. II Tim. 1:6) cannot be understood as a causal, realistic event that one has at his disposal (cf. Acts 8:18ff.) and that guarantees continuity. True, in the New Testament there is a clear connection between the laying on of hands and the gift of the Spirit (cf. 8:17; 19:6), but it is encircled by the living and praying Church and is thereby directed to the progress of the gospel. In all of this, the Church is continuously warned against a lifeless mechanization, whereby the outlook on salvation is lost and the river of the Church has no living water (cf. Ps. 65:9). Then, clearly, various dilemmas — such as symbolic or realistic, for instance — do not help to illuminate the meaning of the laying on of hands.[78] Only in the context of the living Church does it acquire its concrete meaning and significance.[79]

Finally, we want to look at the much-discussed saying of Irenaeus where "demonstrability" seems to play a great role: "Wherever the Church is, there is the Spirit of God; and wherever the Spirit of God is, there is the Church; and there is every grace."[80] We are not concerned here with a discussion of Irenaeus' ecclesiology,[81] but with his striking formulation. At first sight it gives the impression of a simple ascertainment and indicator with respect to the relation of the Church and the

---

75. Acts 6:6 and the fasting and praying in Acts 13:3. Cf. 1:24 (Judas-Matthias); Num. 27:18; Deut. 34:9 (Moses-Joshua). See H. Küng, *The Church*, p. 426; A.D.R. Polman, *De Apostolische Kerk*, pp. 190ff.

76. See Hasenhüttl, *op. cit.*, pp. 250ff., against mechanical sacramentalism and automatism.

77. Cf. the warning to Timothy not to neglect the gift that was given to him via the laying on of hands (I Tim. 4:14 — *mè amélei*) and the calling to "rekindle the gift" (II Tim. 1:6).

78. H.N. Ridderbos (*De Pastorale Brieven*, 1967, pp. 123, 125) writes correctly: "not simply symbolic," although the words "but represents in a solemn and visible way" do not make everything clear either. Cf. p. 125: "not simply symbolic, but as an individualizing allotment of the gift of Christ." See further P.A. Elderenbosch, *De Oplegging der Handen*, 1953, pp. 70ff.; J. Behm, *Die Handauflegung im Ur-christentum nach Verwendung, Herkunft, und Bedeutung*, 1911, pp. 188ff.

79. Cf. Calvin, *Inst.*, IV, 3, 16, with a continuous "provided." It can be called a sacrament, although not one of the ordinary ones (*Inst.*, IV, 14, 20).

80. Irenaeus, *Adversus Haereses*, III, 24, 1. Cf. IV, 26, 2; III, 38, 1. See also Polman, *De Apostolische Kerk*, p. 212.

81. Cf. Polman, *op. cit.*, pp. 202ff.

Spirit. This reminds us of Saint Peter's in Rome, where these words appear in a different form: "Wherever Peter is, there is the Church."[82] In this fixation, the twofold direction of Irenaeus' saying is missing: the Church to the Spirit and the Spirit to the Church. That two-fold direction means that the saying cannot become a "spatial" ascertainment that no longer stands under the testing of the phrase, "where the *Spirit of God* is."[83] Naturally, the saying in the cathedral is not intended "unpneumatically," but it is illustrative of a view of succession where one has lost interest in the pneumatic aspect of testing. Therefore, one can transmit Irenaeus' saying in such a short version. However, only in the correlative two-foldness of the *"ubi–ibi"* will it be possible "to live with the apostles"[84] along the Church's way through the ages. Then the outlook on the apostolic definiteness of the Church's *custodia* can be preserved in fear and trembling under the promise of the living Lord.[85]

82. *"Ubi Petrus, ibi ecclesia."* Cf. P. Th. Camelot, *Die Lehre von der Kirche. Handbuch der Dogmengeschichte*, III, Fasc. 3b, 1970, p. 56; my *Second Vatican Council* and *the New Catholicism*, p. 170; *Nabetrachting op het Concilie*, pp. 98ff.
83. Although one can say that the breakup of the apostolic office and tradition was "an inconceivable thought" for Irenaeus (E. Flesseman-van Leer, "Tradition, H. Schrift und Kirche bei Irenäus," Skydsgaard-Vischer, *op. cit.*, 1963, p. 52), the two-foldness is striking and has profound meaning. Cf. J.N. Bakhuizen van den Brink, *Ecclesia*, II, 90ff., on M. Werner's interpretation.
84. K. Barth, *C.D.*, II/2, pp. 430f.
85. H.N. Ridderbos, *De Apostolische Kerk*, p. 68.

CHAPTER ELEVEN

APOSTOLIC CONFESSION

WHEN WE REFLECT ON APOSTOLIC CONFESSION, we do not have the Apostles' Creed especially in view, but the Church's confession in various times and in variation. This confession is intended to be related "apostolically" to the apostolic testimony via continuing directedness to the normative gospel. But do the Church's "confessions," which have grown up historically, truly display this directedness? And is there continuity in the apostolic confession? These questions are urgent since so much in the Church has changed and is still changing. Frequently, the impression is given that she believes and confesses differently than in earlier days. Must it not be said in all honesty that the Church has been seized by a far-reaching process of reduction, whereby much from the past has been abandoned? In itself, the word "reduction" need not frighten us. Faced by many human additions to the gospel, the Reformers also wanted to lead the Church back ("reduce") to the original, apostolic gospel. It was a clear limitation on the earlier "abundance" of many truths, and Rome saw it as an arbitrary attack on what belonged to the essence of the gospel and the Church. Was this a gradual process of destruction or a reduction to the apostolic gospel? This question is especially acute today, because there is much unrest and uncertainty about the earlier confession of the universal, Christian, and undoubted faith.

Before dealing with the question of reduction, further interpretation, and new understanding, we must account for the fact that the Church, in her confession, has wanted to reach back to what is said in the New Testament about the confession of the Name of the Lord. It is a very existential and far-reaching confession, and its seriousness becomes clear from the contrast between confession and denial: "Everyone who acknowledges me before men, I also will acknowledge before my Father who is in heaven; but whoever denies me before men, I also will deny before my Father who is in heaven" (Matt. 10:32f.; cf. Luke 12:8). The parallel between what men (can) do and what Christ will do, indicates the deep aspect of confession in contrast to "being ashamed" (Mark 8:38; Luke 9:26; John 12:42f.). The whole of life is determined directly by it. Not only is this earnestness of decision mentioned in the situation of the first witnesses,[1] but the contrast is general: confession rather than denial in the midst of all testing (Rev. 2:10), and struggle even to the point of martyrdom (2:10; cf. 2:13).

In confession, the deepest decisions are made and the widest perspectives are implied,[2] since the believer's faith is no longer hidden and internal, but fully public and explicit.[3] The "confession" (homologia) is not a "truth" in itself, but is directed truth. It spreads out as a testimony, as speaking because of faith (II Cor. 4:13), as a good confession (I Tim. 6:12), that is connected to believing in the heart (Rom. 10:9). That the confession is before men does not mean that it has no significance for the believer himself. It is called a confession with the lips for salvation (10:10) and stands vis-à-vis the dark reality of denial in word and deed (cf. Acts 3:13; I John 2:22; II Pet. 2:1f.), of the unfaithfulness that concerns the whole man in his deepest decision.[4] There is great seriousness here as well as great concentration on what is confessed and on Him about Whom this decision is made. There is no place for "indifferent things"[5] in this confession, because it is made in statu confessionis ("in a state of confession") in the context of not fearing (Matt. 10:19, 26) and of the promise of the Holy Spirit (10:20). The Name of Christ is in the center — i.e., saying that Jesus is Lord (I Cor. 12:3). All of this occurs in continuous confrontation with "men," a confrontation in which the disciples of the Lord will receive "a mouth and wisdom" (Luke 21:15).

In light of this central significance of confession, there is every reason to ask whether the way we have become accustomed to speak about confession and the confessions actually lies on

---

1. Cf. G. Bornkamm, "Das Wort Jesu vom Bekennen," Gesch. und Glaube, I, 30ff.
2. Cf. Matt. 16:17; Rev. 2:10 (the crown of life); 2:17 (the hidden manna, the white stone with a new name). Cf. H. Diem, "Das Bekenntnis in der Kirche des N.T.," Evang. Theol., 1934/35, p. 420.
3. F. Haarsma, "Het Actuele Belijden der Kerk in Theol. Perspectief," Vox Theol., 1966, p. 284.
4. Cf. TDNT, I, 470.
5. Bornkamm, op. cit., p. 32.

the same level as this New Testament confession. Now and then we hear radical words of confrontation in the confessions, specifically in sharp pronouncements such as "the rejection of errors," "we condemn" *(damnamus)*, or even "anathema." But, at the same time, a more "morphological" understanding of confession has understandably been mentioned in later times; the many "differences" are not experienced as a radical rupture,[6] as an antithesis between for and against, between confession and denial.[7] Frequently, one speaks with a certain ease about different confessions as a manifestation of the Church's "pluriformity." But is this not a devaluation of the confession of the New Testament? Are the confessions of the Church still truly concerned with confessing the Name "before men"? Or has the Church not been able to endure this high tension of an inescapable *status confessionis* in the power of the Spirit? Has she thus passed over to a less radical, less existential, and less pneumatic understanding of confession?[8] Interest in these questions is due not to a relativizing of the confession, but to the striking fact of an unmistakable change that one must, in any case, place in the sharp light of the radical scope of New Testament confession.[9]

Centrality and concentration

Sometimes this radicality emerges all at once in reflection on an ecclesiastical confession, particularly when the religious commitment involved in a confession is accentuated. Kuyper expressed the wish that a confession would pronounce only "what was settled and sealed with the blood of martyrs,"[10] in order

6. Cf. H. Gollwitzer, "Die Bedeutung des Bekenntnisses für die Kirchen," *Festschr. für E. Wolf*, 1962, p. 153.
7. Whoever recalls the *anáthema* of Paul in Gal. 1:8 and sees how the anathema is used later — often with the addition that the intention is only to reject the error — feels the difference in seriousness and radicality.
8. Cf. K. Barth, *C.D.*, I/2, p. 630 on not being "ripe for confession" if one is afraid to pronounce the *damnamus*.
9. On the confession, beyond "all the non-obligatoriness of mere opinion," cf. *TDNT*, V, 212. One may recall the later problematic about the possibility of examination and revision of the confession. Cf. Bavinck, *Geref. Dog.*, IV, 401; I, 6, 63. In my *Verontrusting en Verantwoordelijkheid*, 1969, p. 143, I pointed out that our almost self-evident usage of the possibility of revision and gravamen with regard to the New Testament confession is conceivable only in the form of apostasy, a clear indication of the problem.
10. A. Kuyper, *Voorrede van de Verklaring van de N.B.G. van Ds. A. Rotterdam*, I, 1890, p. xiv.

that it be a watchword in life and death,[11] under the animation of the Holy Spirit.[12] Such statements are connected consciously to the decision-character of Christian confession and of the confession of Christ, which leaves no room for what is secondary next to what is primary.[13] One could speak of a tendency to simplicity, to concentration on what is most "essential." This limitation — not in order to minimize but in order to maximize — summons up the question of the nature of the Church's confession in later centuries, especially when it is apparent that not all "confessional" differences are of equal importance.[14] Thus, the question of the relation between that centrality and the total extent of what was expressed in the confessions had to arise. Did not a relatedness of faith still exist in the midst of what were sometimes radical differences? The realization grew that not all of what was pronounced could be unhesitatingly spoken of as being *in statu confessionis*.[15] Because of that, one was forced to give account of the centrality of the Church's confession, which then summoned up recollections of the full earnestness of New Testament confession.[16]

When "concentration" is used to indicate the unity in the many words of the Church's confession, discussion about the further definition of that "center" can immediately begin. No one will want to deny the gravity of this problematic of center

11. A. Kuyper, *Encyclopaedie der Heilige Godgeleerdheid*, III, 371.
12. A. Kuyper, *Calvinisme en Revisie*, p. 25. Cf. also on the confession as "a cry of distress of the soul and a cry of delight at the greatness of God's mercy" and as an affliction of the soul (*Revisie der Revisielegende*, 1879, p. 80). It can contain nothing "but that of which one can testify before God that it is conclusive for salvation" (*Confidentie*, 1873, p. 97). Cf. also A.A. van Ruler, *Hoe Functioneert de Belijdenis?*, 1954, on the confession as the breath of the body of Christ; and Gunning (in W.F. Dankbaar, "Nieuwe Belijdenissen in Oude Kerken," *Vox Theol.*, 1966, p. 258) on the confession as the "birth cry" of the Church.
13. Cf. J. Koopmans, *Het Oudkerkelijk Dogma in de Reformatie, Bepaaldelijk bij Calvijn*, 1938; Th.L. Haitjema, *Gebondenheid en Vrijheid in een Belijdende Kerk*, 1929, pp. 45ff.
14. Cf. H. Diem, *Theologie als kirchliche Wissenschaft*, 1951, p. 133.
15. Cf. K. Barth, *C.D.*, I/2, pp. 831f. on *theologoumena* that do not necessitate separation and on the *Aufhebung der Gegensätze*, with reference to Calvin and the Consensus Tigurinus of 1549. Cf. H. Gollwitzer, *op. cit.*, p. 183; W. Nijenhuis, "Paulus en Calvijn," *Rondom het Woord*, 1971, pp. 82ff.
16. Cf. K. Barth, *C.D.*, I/2, p. 624: "We can confess only if we must confess."

and periphery.[17] Nevertheless, almost no one, at least not in practice, has been able to avoid this tendency to concentration. That comes to expression in the attempt to designate what is unabandonable as the central content of the gospel.[18] No one has yet found a word that can clarify this legitimacy apart from all dangers. No matter what words were used — essence, core, center, fundamental — questions always arose about such words. But in spite of these questions, the importance and urgency of the topic remained in opposition to all atomizing of the truth.[19]

"Concentration" did not first arise in the time of ecumenical dialogue between churches. It emerged aiready during the Reformation in the well-known distinction between fundamental and non-fundamental articles of faith. There has been much concern with this distinction because of the connection of non-fundamental with articles of faith,[20] especially with respect to the criterion of distinction and the arbiter.[21] One can summarize all the objections in this question: via such an "arbitrary" distinction, does not the fundamental end up in the sphere of the peripheral and the secondary? Does that not herald the decline of Protestantism?[22] One cannot deny the critical significance of

17. Van Ruler (*op. cit.*, p. 20) calls the question of "what is fundamental in the confession and what is peripheral" a meaningless question; however, that does not mean that his entire work is not directed explicitly and implicitly to what is "fundamental."
18. Cf. Dankbaar, *op. cit.*, p. 253.
19. One may also think of the relation between the ten commandments and the "sum of the law," which does not relativize the commandments, but explicates their meaning through their relatedness to the center. Cf. Rom. 13:8f. (the fulfillment of the law by love, with the remarkable addition of a number of commandments: "and any other commandment"). Cf. H.N. Ridderbos, *Aan de Romeinen,* p. 297: put under one common denominator; reduce to the main point.
20. Cf. my *Holy Scripture,* chapter 6.
21. Calvin (*Inst.,* IV, 2, 1) spoke already of errors that ought to be pardoned — namely, those "which do not harm the chief doctrine of religion." The Church's death occurs only when falsehood breaks into the citadel of religion. The word "fundamental" alternates with "necessary" (cf. IV, 1, 12). Not all articles of doctrine have the same character and break unity. In the 19th century, too, the distinction of fundamental and necessary played a large role. See for the frequent usage, G. Groen van Prinsterer, *Het Regt der Hervormde Gezindheid,* 1848, pp. 58ff.; *idem, Confessioneel of Reglementair?,* 1864; and many other examples in D. Nauta, *De Verbindende Kracht van de Belijdenisschriften,* 1969.
22. Thus K. Barth, *C.D.,* I/2, pp. 654f., on the danger of one's own choice as the principle of distinction, so that one rules over the truth and ends up with an "essence" of faith "in the thin formulae." It is re-

this question. Questions of criteria always have something alarming about them; they urge us to watchfulness, continuous reflection, and caution.[23] The distinction is concerned with difficult questions, and use of it has sometimes involved obvious arbitrariness. The problems become visible whenever one tries to fix what is fundamental in a definite enumeration. The well-known proverb: "Unity in the essentials, freedom in the non-essentials, love in both" seemed to spread a clear light in the midst of all ecclesiastical division but, over and over again, it met with great difficulties whenever it was concretely applied.[24]

Bavinck, especially, connected reflection on the center and periphery directly to the nature of faith and thus also to the central understanding of the articles of faith in connection with the person of Christ. That constituted a clear point of contact with the New Testament confession, which is confession of Christ as the truth. Belief cannot be described as the intellectual acceptance of a series of individual truths; rather, it is related to "an especial central object, the grace of God in Christ."[25] If faith is not "a sum of articles, the knowledge and acceptance of which is necessary for salvation,"[26] then a wholly different view becomes visible from that of the Roman Catholics, where the question had to arise about which truths at the least had to be accepted and believed for salvation. Bavinck is not concerned with a more or less obvious and successful enumeration. According to him, the Reformation was not concerned with a meager

markable that Barth wants to speak, nevertheless, of "a certain distinction in dogmatics . . . between the essential and the non-essential, the central and the peripheral." Thus, Barth sees the decline in the actual mode of usage in Protestantism. See in detail on the distinction, O. Ritschl, *Dogmengeschichte des Protestantismus*, IV, 306ff.

23. Cf. H.G. Hubbeling, *Criterium als Kenmerk en Norm*, 1968.

24. Cf. A. Eekhof on this proverb: "*In necessariis unitas, in non-necessariis libertas, in utrisque caritas,*" *Oorsprong, Betekenis en Verbreiding*, 1931. The motto was still employed by Pope John XXIII (*Ad Petri Cathedram*, 1959) in this form: "There must be unity in the essentials, freedom in the doubtful, love in everything." There have been profound differences, though, about what is "necessary." Calvin (*Inst.*, IV, 1, 2) sums up the problem with his addition "and the like" (*et similia*). Cf. what Bavinck (*Geref. Dog.*, I, 581) writes about orthodoxy's not wanting to limit the fundamental articles of faith to a small number.

25. In spite of all his objections, Bavinck considered the distinction between fundamental and non-fundamental to be "very important" (*Katholiciteit*, p. 26). Cf. his *Geref. Dog.*, I, 583ff.

26. Bavinck, *Geref. Dog.*, I, 183. Cf. also Calvin, *Inst.*, III, 2, 2-6.

"minimum,"[27] but with the decisive directedness in faith and confession to the message of salvation. He felt that he clearly perceived this centrality in the Holy Scriptures.[28] Apart from that outlook, all fellowship in the Church could be impossible and sectarianism would be fostered in the most frightening way.[29] The point at issue in concentration is believing trust in Christ and relatedness to Him.

That it is impossible to escape reflection on centrality and concentration is clearly evident from the attention given by the Second Vatican Council to a certain relief in the "truths" of faith when it spoke of a "hierarchy of truths" and of a certain "order." Earlier, scarcely any distinction was tolerated among the catholic truths,[30] but now it is postulated that not all the truths of the catholic faith are connected in the same way to the foundation of the Christian faith.[31] Strikingly, no distinction is made between fundamental and non-fundamental. Rather, in close connection with the ecumenical dialogue,[32] an order is spoken of that does not disturb the relation to the foundation, but confirms it. We need not be surprised that, just as in the case of the Protestant distinction, discussions quickly arose about the criteria for this "hierarchy."[33] In spite of the relatedness to the foundation, there can be a relativizing of the importance of particular truths. Nevertheless, one clearly does not want to go

---

27. According to Bavinck (Geref. Dog., I, 581), the distinction made during the Reformation took the place of the Roman Catholic doctrine of fides implicita, implicit faith.

28. Ibid., 582. Among other places, in I Cor. 2:2; Gal. 6:14; I Pet. 2:6.

29. Bavinck, Katholiciteit, p. 26.

30. Cf. especially the encyclical Mortalium Animos (1928), directed against the ecumenical movement, which was seen as a destruction against which the Roman Catholic Church had to be protected.

31. Decree on Ecumenism (DV II, p. 354). Cf. U. Valeske, Hierarchia Veritatum, 1968; my Nabetrachting op het Concilie, pp. 103ff.

32. It was the background of Pangrazio's proposal. In his view, the order gave an outlook on "all Christians as a family, already united in the primary truths of the Christian religion." Cf. his speech in Congar-Küng, Konzilsreden, 1964. Interestingly, Occam (not discussed in Valeske, loc. cit.) already wanted to order the different truths of faith "hierarchically."

33. That can occur especially if the mariological and ecclesiological dogmas are said to be peripheral dogmas, distinguishable from the salvation concentrated in Christ (P. Schoonenberg, "Historiciteit en Interpretatie van het Dogma," Tijdschrift voor Theologie, 1968, pp. 293ff.). Pangrazio himself (Konzilsreden, p. 64) distinguished from the trinitarian and christological dogmas those which are related to the means of salvation (seven sacraments, the hierarchy of the Church, apostolic succession).

the way of a quantitative reduction. In the relief, attention is called not to a "reminder-faith," but to a "core-faith."[34] In the turn from the quantitative to the qualitative, from the atomistic to the "organic," we recall how emphatically the one thing that is needful and the one thing that is essential are indicated in the New Testament. Paul, for example, effected a striking concentration by writing: "For I decided to know nothing among you but Jesus Christ and him crucified" (I Cor. 2:2). Does the conscious choice, the decision,[35] that we encounter here perhaps imply — expressed somewhat anachronistically — a canon within the canon, preference, selection, and reduction? In any case, Paul saw that this emphasis was necessary here and did not need to be complemented by other "emphases." The striking thing is that Paul spoke in detail about the resurrection of Christ in this same letter, pointing to its decisive significance (15:14-17). Cross and resurrection are not "truths" next to each other, but are related in a unique way. Nevertheless, exactly because of that, I Corinthians 2 is of great value for all reflection on the center, the "middle," of the gospel as the radiating light contrasted to the dispersion of the unrelated multiplicity of individual truths. For Paul, the cross cannot be isolated; it is not one proposition among others in his preaching in such a way that the others have to be added to it.[36]

The reference to the decisive relief has always warned the Church against atomizing her doctrine and preaching. In many variants and emphases, Paul could speak about the one mystery of reconciliation, the reconciliation of the world (II Cor. 5:19), and the forgiveness of guilt in prevenient grace, whereby all is lost if justification by works is again set up vis-à-vis justification

34. F. Haarsma, *De Leer van de Kerk en het Geloof van Haar Leden*, 1968, p. 19. See on the hierarchy of truths further, W. Dietzfelbinger, "Die Hierarchie der Wahrheiten," in J.C. Hampe, *Die Autorität der Freiheit*, II, 619ff.; H. Müller, "Die Lehre des Vatik. II über die 'hierarchia veritatum' und ihre Bedeutung für den ökumenischen Dialog," *Theol. und Glaube*, 56 (1966), pp. 303ff.

35. *Ékrina* (I Cor. 2:2). Cf. Grosheide, *De Eerste Brief aan de Kerk te Korinthe*, p. 72; Conzelmann, *Der erste Brief an die Korinther*, p. 69.

36. Cf. Paul's not glorying except in the cross of Christ (Gal. 6:14). Cf. P.A. van Stempvoort, *De Brief van Paulus aan de Galaten*, p. 189, on "one of his most pointed confessions"; Bavinck, *Geref. Dog.*, I, 583, on faith that has laid aside all "addition"; and Barth, *C.D.*, IV/1, p. 557, on the *theologia crucis* and *theologia gloriae* in alliance against an abstract *theologia crucis*. See also the vehement discussion of E. Käsemann with Künneth on the "theology of the resurrection" (*Perspectives on Paul*, 1971, pp. 32ff.).

by faith (Gal. 2:21). This message is so "central" that it forces the Church to remove every suggestion that there are "many" things that must be believed. From the multiplicity of the possible words, the message tends toward a clear concentration in which decisions are made. This way was apparently not so difficult for the apostles as it has been in later reflection on the "core" of the message. Such a decision can be made in a few words, as in the statement "Jesus is Lord" versus "Jesus be cursed" (I Cor. 12:3), where there is a direct outlook on the Holy Spirit in this "speaking." Following the line of this apostolic concentration, the Church has always attempted "summaries" in order to clarify the situation that arises because of the gospel. It is attention for the one thing that is needful in contrast to a multiplicity that could entangle one.[37]

Whenever this concentration comes up for discussion, the deepest questions of the Church always come to the fore. That was the case in a striking way when, specifically in the Lutheran Reformation, justification by faith was indicated as "the article upon which the Church stands and falls" (*articulus stantis et cadentis ecclesiae*). This phrase is in complete harmony with what Luther wrote: "Nothing in this article can be given up or compromised, even if heaven and earth and things temporal should be destroyed. On this article rests all that we teach and practice against the pope, the devil, and the world."[38] This locus of justification is the foundation of the Church, and "without this article the Church does not stand." The intention is clearly not a quantitative reduction, but a concentration. Although it does arise in a polemical situation, it calls attention to the substance of God's salvation, which comes to stand in the center in a definite way as the unabandonable mystery of divine grace.[39] Attention for this substance always implies also the conviction of the continuing relevance of this doctrine. In later times,

---

37. Cf. Luke 10:42: "one thing is needful" (*henòs dé estin chreía*). One may think of the loss of relief in the Pharisees' view of the law: the neglect of "the weightier matters" of the law (Matt. 23:23 — *tà barútera*).

38. *Smalcald Articles*, II, 1. For many citations from Luther, cf. F. Loofs, "Der articulus stantis et cadentis ecclesiae," *Th. Stud. und Krit.*, 1917, pp. 323ff. One may not entertain any doubts about this "principal article": "Otherwise all is lost, and the pope, the devil, and all our adversaries will gain the victory" (*Smal. Art.*).

39. Cf. E. Wolf, "Die Rechtfertigungslehre als Mitte und Grenze reformatorischer Theologie," *Peregrinatio*, II, 11ff. On the concept "center," cf. F. Mussner, "'Evangelium' und 'Mitte des Evangeliums,'" *Gott in Welt*, I, 492ff.

struggle about that relevance can arise and the concentration comes to be at issue. That is also the case today with respect to Luther's "standing and falling." The question is whether "justification" as the center of salvation is relevant in the full sense of the word. This problem usually comes up for discussion in connection with Luther's question about the gracious God. We find in Barth a prelude to this discussion already in 1938. He calls attention to the shift that appears in the proposition that "the Reformation confession was right," but we are concerned with different questions.[40] Barth fears that the relativizing of the Lutheran "standing and falling" could be "the wings behind which the old enemy, against whom the Reformation drew up its confession, will make a triumphant return into the Church in a new form." Criticism of Luther's "concentration" clearly involves more than a protest against salvation-egoism and salvation-individualism. At issue is not only the narrowing in the *pro me*, but also the question of salvation in that concentrated form in which we meet it in the Reformation and in which one misses attention for and directedness to the world around us, in threatenedness, need, and terror. D. Ritschl saw this concentration as an inheritance from Augustine, who has fatally determined the thinking and believing of many Christians by a typically Western concentration on confession and belief.[41] It cannot boast of continuing relevance, but must give way to a different concentration of attention, by which the earlier concern with one's own life and one's own salvation recedes into the background.[42] We see here how suddenly the

40. K. Barth, *C.D.*, I/2, p. 655. In this connection Barth names the questions, which many consider to be more important, of social and political life. Cf. on the interest in the question not of the gracious God, but of the gracious neighbor and in the question "whether there is a God at all." Cf. E. Leppin, "Luthers Frage nach dem gnädigen Gott heute," *Z.Th.K.*, 1964, pp. 93ff.; and my *Holy Scripture*, pp. 339f.
41. D. Ritschl, "Die Last des Augustinischen Erbes," *Parrhesia*, 1966, pp. 470ff.
42. Cf. K. Stendahl's criticism of the interpretation of Paul that made justification central on the basis of the "introspective conscience" ("The Apostle Paul and the Introspective Conscience of the West," *Harvard Theol. Review*, 1963, pp. 199ff.). He refers to the radical difference between Paul and Luther (in connection with the exegesis of Rom. 7). Paul opposed Judaism, and this opposition does not lend itself to lasting centralization. See E. Käsemann's pointed criticism ("Rechtfertigung und Heilsgeschichte," *Perspectives on Paul*, 1971, p. 139). He sees this as a break with the Reformation. Judaism gave rise to something lasting, so that Luther's question "retains its enduring justice" (p. 138).

question of concentration can become a very profound affair. Various reactions can easily begin to play a role as the concentration comes into the discussion as directedness of attention. In such discussions the Church is always urged not to lose herself in new reactions,[43] but to designate the meaning of true concentration in a conscious recognition of the center in opposition to all onesidedness.

Moreover, all of this is concerned not simply with questions about the Church internally, but also externally — with the right confession of the Church before men, with her accountability in the face of explicit and implicit questions that touch her faith (I Pet. 3:15 — apología). This "accountability" has led to reflection on the aspect of concentration also starting from that "externally." In this connection, we are thinking of many considerations on the so-called "short formula" (Kurzformel). Such a Kurzformel is requested neither because one cannot say much about faith and the gospel (cf. Acts 20:9, 11), nor in order to reduce the gospel to a number of propositions, but for the sake of the clarity of the message. According to Rahner, the important thing is "to express what is essential in brief to today's highly preoccupied men"[44] in an atheistic world. In this confrontation one cannot consider his responsibility discharged by pointing to the Church's confession as the answer to the request for an account. What is at issue is not simply a particular content of knowledge, but a testimony, a message, to which the witness, the confessor, is related with his own life in the defense concerning his hope (I Pet. 3:15). In her confession, the Church is directed to the realization of her hope (Heb. 6:11). This hope is not simply of significance "futuristically," but marks her life in the world through expectation (6:18; cf. 10:23; Col. 1:5; Rom. 15:13; II Cor. 1:7, 10).

The confession of this hope cannot be isolated, but forms the canvas for the confession. Apart from this canvas, confession becomes a knowledge in competition with other knowledge. It is praised in the market of life but has no significance for life

43. Cf. K. Barth, C.D., IV/2, pp. 798f., especially on Mary's deeds of love (Luke 7; Mark 14; John 12) and the annoyance at this "luxury" toward the Lord in the light of the saleability of the ointment.
44. K. Rahner, "The Need for a 'Short Formula' of Christian Faith," Theological Investigations, IX, 1972, 117; and "Reflections on the Problems Involved in Devising a Short Formula of the Faith," Theological Investigations, XI, 1974, 230ff. Rahner himself gives different Kurzformeln (pp. 238ff.).

itself. If the confessing Church cannot come to an understandable account concerning life in this expectation, she is doomed to powerlessness. Speaking about and discussing one's own confession within the bounds of the Church is simpler than truly giving an account confessionally. Faced by the many questions about the content of faith and its relevance, which moves the Church to be concerned with the world,[45] only an answer with the clear relief of concentration is meaningful and fruitful. No matter how paradoxical it may sound, the concern in the brevity is precisely to say "everything" in its qualitative richness. Here there is no hint of propositions thrown abruptly into the world, but of that unity that wants to manifest itself also in long conversations. The tendency to point to the voluminous "quantitative" can be an escape from one's own responsibility toward those who are "outside." The directedness of the many words to the one word does not degrade the tradition and the confession, but forms the touchstone for true confession. It gives an outlook on the fullness of salvation, just as limitation in the Gospel of John does not signify impoverishment, but points the way to life (20:30f.; 21:25; cf. Heb. 11:32).

Further interpretation

But can there be a real connection between present-day confession and the fixed confessions of earlier centuries? The question is meaningful, since one can indicate a clear historical coloration of polemic and defense in the confessions. Moreover, do all the forms of theological reflection in the confessions have direct, clear significance for the Church? Can they ever have a truly binding character for her?[46] Yet one cannot say that this automatically makes a connection impossible, since the defense is not concerned first of all with the antithesis, but with the thesis. Theological reflection is also concerned with calling attention to that thesis, even though, for many people, much in the

45. Cf. Rahner, *ibid.*, IX, 236, on what "is of fundamental importance, and on the basis of which the totality of the faith can in principle and in itself be attained."
46. Cf. the report of A.D.R. Polman, *Acta Gener. Syn. 1969-70*, p. 227, on Article 19 of the Belgic Confession and Question 48 of the Heidelberg Catechism with regard to the relation of dogmatics and catechism. Cf. also M.P. van Dijk, *Nieuw Credo*, 1970, p. 6; D. Schellong, *Theol. im Widerspruch von Vernunft und Unvernunft*, 1971, p. 68. Schellong writes that a "refinement of doctrine" and a "complication of false doctrine" often go together.

polemic will remain latent in spite of intense catechism.[47] The big question with respect to contemporary confession, however, remains that of whether there is not a far-reaching problem in the fact that the confessions were drawn up in a totally different time than ours. Is the connection to contemporary belief and confession not made difficult because of these fixations? All reflection on the possibility of a new confession has this question at the background. The desire for a new confession is not meant as a break with the past, but as an attempt to speak and to testify in such a way that the confession is understood in a new time. One usually expresses the continuity in this way: it is the core of the earlier confession, and its relevant significance must come out.[48]

Even if one does not see much perspective in a new confession, and even if such a new confession is threatened by the danger of very time-bound ideas about what cannot be lacking here and now, the question about the connection between past and present remains relevant. The impulse for a new confession has its background in the realization that the old confessions are imbedded in the life and thought of their time. One began to reflect more and more on that time-boundness and on the framework of fixation as the horizon of knowledge and understanding of the confession in earlier centuries, which was also determinative for the formulation of the confession. Along with that came the question of whether or not a particular philosophical way of thinking had not placed its stamp on particular points. What was often said during the Reformation with respect to Roman Catholic dogmas — namely, that they exhibited philosophical presuppositions — now also received a place in reflection on the Reformed confessions.[49] But the possibility especially came to the fore that changes had appeared in the under-

---

47. One may recall difficult passages, such as B.C., Art. 35 (on the Lord's Supper); Art. 15 (baptism and original sin); and H.C., Q. 48 (the so-called *extra Calvinisticum*). Cf. G. Groen van Prinsterer, *Het Regt der Herv. Gezindheid*, 1848, p. 59, on the Canons of Dort: in themselves an irrefutable refutation, but — as a "theological treatise" — for most people "without harm and even to their advantage a closed book."

48. Cf. D. Nauta, *De Verbindende Kracht*, p. 38, on the desire for a new confession already with Da Costa: "a new confession on the old foundations" as a prime, also ecclesiastical, need. Cf. p. 53: a confession for our time, if need be against our time, but in any case *of* our time.

49. For example, the Aristotelian philosophy (double predestination and the divine exclusive causality) was brought up for discussion in a report to the Synod of the Gereformeerde Kerken on the Canons of Dort (*Bijlagen Acta Gen. Syn. 1969-70*, 75a, p. 463).

standing of the Holy Scriptures. Was it not plausible that the changing understanding of the Holy Scriptures entailed consequences also for the understanding and interpretation of dogma?[50]

Not only the progress in understanding the Scripture, but also the unmistakable fact of the limitedness and inadequacy of all human formulations, with which one tries to interpret the truth, plays a role here. In the Reformation, one did not have difficulty with that. One always held open the possibility of deeper and more meaningful expression — and even of the correction of what was no longer serviceable to pure interpretation. But also in Roman Catholic theology in our time, the realization of this inadequacy has broken through more and more powerfully in new reflection on "infallible" dogma.[51] The unmistakable "historicity," the time-boundness, came clearly to the fore, not only on account of the avowedly polemical directedness of the confessions, which wanted to accentuate one central aspect of the truth,[52] but also on account of the discovery that different statements were understood in a different way in the course of time due to the material employed in earlier times for thought and conception. It was perceived that the language and era of dogma could not be approached as "supratemporal," even apart from the fact that human formulations can never grasp and exhaust the truth of God. In other words, the realization grew more than ever before of the "relativity" of dogma; as a treasure in earthen vessels, it had to be taken account of in new times and implied further nuancing of infallibility. In that situation, many feared that this approach would eventually endanger the certainty of the Roman Catholic Church and her dogma, her preservation of the goods of salvation.[53] But the

---

50. One may think of the way the Canons of Dort employ definite texts, especially Matt. 11:25f. (C.D., I, para. 8) and Matt. 20:15 (C.D., I, 18). Cf. my "Het Schriftbewijs in de Canones," *Gereformeerd Weekblad*, April 11, 1969; *Acta Gener. Syn.*, 1969-70.

51. That is what Rahner means when he says that "Every formula transcends itself" ("Current Problems in Christology," *Theological Investigations*, I, 1961, 149), not because it is false, but because it is true and is directed to "a statement right into mystery" (*Myst. Salutis*, I, 696). Cf. B.C., Art. 9, on surpassing "all human understanding"; and, further, Bavinck, *Geref. Dog.*, II, 74ff., on inadequate knowledge with reference to seeing in a mirror and walking by faith, not by sight.

52. Cf. H. Küng, *Structures of the Church*, 1964; and *idem, Infallible?*, 1972.

53. Although K. Rahner had already indicated very emphatically the inadequacy of all, including ecclesiastical, formulations, he criticized H. Küng's book for, in his view, going too far. See the discussion between

problematic was so obvious that it began to arrest the attention of practically all churches. In all of this, one has tended more and more to admit honestly and frankly many shifts with respect to the earlier confession. But, at the same time, one has denied that a rupture has occurred in the Church's consciousness of faith.

In this combination of motives — changeability and continuity — we encounter a phenomenon that has called up much discussion — namely, that of further interpretation. It is one of the most far-reaching aspects of the Church's confession in our time because apostolicity and the truth of that confession come especially into the center. That further interpretation of dogma is not intended as a rupture, but as relatedness is evident already from the word "interpretation." The intention is to interpret the previous confession. It is to build bridges between earlier times and the present.[54] Heated discussion has arisen about this further interpretation. Is it really still interpretation of the ancient confessions? Or is it a radical, destructive transformation, since ancient words are filled with such a new, modern content that hardly any harmony between earlier and now can be perceived? Sometimes strong words such as "dishonesty" and "duplicity" are used in the discussion, and it is pointed out that it would be more honest to acknowledge the rupture than to go the way of further interpretation, suggesting that, essentially, little has changed.

One will not be able to pass by the seriousness of these questions because they bring us into contact with an important question, which touches on the legitimacy or illegitimacy of a "hermeneutics" of doctrinal pronouncements.[55] To speak rashly here of dishonesty and deception would be unjust, for there will

Rahner and Küng in *Stimmen der Zeit*, 1970, pp. 361ff.; and 1971, pp. 43ff., 105ff., 145ff. For the conflict see my articles, "Het Conflict Küng-Rahner," *Geref. Weekblad*, Mar. 19, 1971 and following; E. Jüngel, "Irren ist Menschlich," *Evang. Kommentare*, 1971, pp. 51ff.; L. Bruce van Voorst, "Küng and Rahner. Duelling over Infallibility," *The Christian Century*, May 19, 1971, pp. 617ff.

54. Cf. P. Schoonenberg, "Historiciteit en Interpretatie van het Dogma," *Tijdschrift voor Theologia*, 1968, p. 281.

55. Cf. M. Löhrer, "Zur Interpretation lehramtlicher Aussagen als Frage des ökumenischen Gesprächs," *Gott in Welt*, II, 502ff. As an example one may think of the interpretation of the descent into hell and the Heidelberg Catechism. See G.P. Hartvelt, *Patronen van Interpretatie*, 1966; idem, "De Nederdaling ter Helle," *Rondom het Woord*, 1970, pp. 237ff.; D.A. du Toit, *Neergedaal ter Helle. Uit de Geschiedenis van 'n Interpretasie-probleem*, 1971, pp. 30ff., 181ff.

possibly be a certain distantiation in later times in the historical interpretation of the confession. That distantiation is connected to the relation between past and present, to nuancing in understanding, and to one's own directedness to what must now be confessed. The history of the fixation of the symbols, which frequently is very complicated, raises many questions that can contain interpretative difficulties for the Church.[56] Then there is always concern for what the Church intended and the way it was brought to expression. It is the problem of the matter and the formulation, a distinction that no one who wants to do justice to the facts can escape totally. We see clearly that continuing interpretation plays an important role in the process of understanding. In Scripture itself, for that matter, one sees various interpretative aspects. They are not aimed at destruction and transformation, but precisely at the disclosure of the deep meaning of Christ's work of salvation.[57] Even he who does not identify further interpretation of dogma with this interpretation nevertheless discovers elements in it that are connected to the way of expressing things in human language at a particular time and that make it necessary to interpret the same mystery continuously, thus confessing it in living faith. Naturally, one can stumble on these ways, even to the extent of total transformation and destruction; but that does not take away the meaning of this interpretative understanding. Change *in* the unchangeability is not a paradox or a contradiction, but a meaningful thing that has always been understood and accepted in the Church in principle — even if it was often only intuitively[58] — although one can say that reflection on the problem came clearly to light first of all in the 19th century.[59]

56. One can perceive this clearly in the discussions later about the *extra ecclesiam nulla salus* in B.C., Art. 28. See above, chapter 6, pp. 148ff.
57. One may think of the Gospel of John (cf. F.W. Grosheide, *Het Heilige Evangelie volgens Johannes*, II, 226) and the element of interpretation with regard to the Old Testament by New Testament writers (the proof from Scripture).
58. Cf. K. Rahner-K. Lehmann on "Geschichtlichkeit der Vermittlung," *Mysterium Salutis*, I, 731.
59. Further interpretation is decidedly not a modern or modish phenomenon. One may recall the continuous further interpretation of the christological dogma. One sought, usually polemically, in ever new formulations to express what is peculiar to Christ's person and work, especially when, starting from the *unio personalis*, one attempted to clarify the problem of union in the post-Chalcedonian development (among other things, the *anhupostatos*). Cf. W.C.H. Driessen, "Dogmainterpretatie in de Vroege Kerk," *Tijdschrift voor Theologie*, 1968, pp.

In considering that problem, we must begin by admitting that there can be no simplistic technique here that operates with the concepts of matter and formulation, content and form. For, undeniably, there is no clear "distinction" between form (formulation) and content in the older formulations, and, in any case, the "scope" of a confession — in connection with continuity — cannot be found outside that which was formulated.[60] Is the distinction, the dissociation,[61] between the formulation and the essential content of the confession not a discovery of later times due to gradually sharpened insight into the differences between then and now? May one force these later distinctions on the earlier confessions in order to be able to indicate continuity?[62] This question arises from the possibility that further interpretation may do violence to the text or may be constructive, with the result that the continuity becomes unbelievable.

In answer to this and similar questions, one points to the inevitability of further interpretation and, at the same time, postulates that it is not based on arbitrariness. The text that is interpreted is not without a context and background; rather, at issue is a confession of the Church, which, in various different forms, wanted to confess Christ. Therein lies the justice of further interpretation, which seeks to hear and interpret this voice. If the word "intention" is sometimes used here, it is not meant to designate a psychological problem, as though one's concern were not actually with the text but with the intention of its framers. Rather, one's concern is with an intentionality in the confessions themselves, which often comes clearly to light. But this directedness is concretized in a definite time, which is connected to the understanding of Scripture then. Often, too,

---

243ff. One may also think of the *filioque* added to the Nicene Creed, intended not as something new, but as further interpretation.

60. Cf. G.P. Hartvelt, "Sacra Scriptura sui ipsius interpres," *Gereformeerd Theologisch Tijdschrift*, 1964; H.J.H.M. Fortmann, "Onrust rondom het Dogma," *Vriendengave B.J. Alfrink*, p. 52 (on the lack of a distinction between the content that is absolutely valid and the relative, time-bound formulation).

61. The term has been used especially by Schoonenberg.

62. Cf. E. Schillebeeckx, "De Eucharistische Wijze van Christus' Werkelijke Tegenwoordigheid," *Tijdschrift voor Theol.*, 1965, 1966, in my view, on the further interpretation of transubstantiation. Cf. especially 1965, p. 141, on the distinction between what is actually affirmed and the aspect of clothing with regard to what earlier was a "question of life and death." Cf. also *idem*, "Naar een Katholiek Gebruik van de Hermeneutiek," *Geloof bij Kenterend Getij*, pp. 78ff.

it is connected to limited ideas and thoughts, which were characteristic of that time but can now be reflected on critically — unless one believes that all formulation of dogma has taken place under the special, providential leading and sanction of the Holy Spirit.[63] The limitedness of human formulations can be indicated already in the ancient Church, when she wrestled with language in the Greek and then in the Latin world in order to confess salvation in Christ in an understandable way.[64] When we look back at that confession in later times and trace its intentionality, tensions can arise concerning continuity. However, they cannot be abolished by starting from an abstract idea of "unchangeability" and minimizing the differences, but only by acknowledging the differences and seeking the confessional continuity in those differences.

We find a clear example of such tension and of the Church's concrete action in the Reformed Churches in Holland (Gereformeerde Kerken) with respect to a gravamen submitted against a few statements of the Canons of Dort. Naturally, the central point was the correct view of the election of God, but the problem of confession —and subscription to the confession — also came clearly to the fore. The Synod concluded that reprobation from eternity "is not based on clear Scriptural data and that, thus, one has the right to have objections to the said passages and to express them." Obviously, the background of this decision lies in a dissociation carried out within the text of the Canons. The decision is made with reference to the clear scope of the Canons, namely, the sovereignty of God's grace for men. According to the judgment of the Synod, that scope comes to light clearly in the Canons themselves, even if it is within a definite framework that is unacceptable.[65] This is an important example of a combination of criticism and interpretation in connection with the scope and historical background of confession.[66] Considerations with regard to the core, scope, and intention of confession are connected to the recognition of the centrality of the truth in the midst of the limitedness and in-

---

63. We can trace this tendency clearly in the encyclical *Humani Generis,* 1950, by Pius XII, and in *Mysterium Fidei* by Paul VI.
64. Cf. W.C.H. Driessen, *op. cit.,* pp. 243ff.
65. Cf. *Acta Gen. Syn. 1969-70,* art. 376, p. 324, on the philosophical-theological background. Cf. the report of the commission on "not speaking rightly about the Lord God" (p. 467).
66. Cf. A.D.R. Polman, "De Leer der Verwerping van Eeuwigheid op de Haagse Conferentie van 1611," *Ex Auditu Verbi,* 1965, pp. 176ff.

adequacy of the earlier confessions, which speak of the great
mystery but certainly do not describe it exhaustively.[67] Undoubtedly, we are always required to make necessary distinction
with respect to what comes to us in human language, just as
Paul summons the Church to "approve what is excellent" (Phil.
1:10 — tà diaphéronta). According to Paul, discernment must be
present in this centralizing approval. The summons does not
point to a technical procedure, but is connected to the abundance of love and opens perspectives for the day of Christ.[68]
All further interpretation of the Church's confession is connected very closely to this approval or distinguishing. That in
no sense denies the legitimacy and the meaning of the historical
interpretation of the confessions; but, in this interpretation, the
Church is not in a detached situation, for it remains the
Church's confession founded in understanding of the gospel.
Thus, tension is always present, at least according to the Reformed confession, when dealing with the old confessions, since
the Church knows that her subjection to the apostolic witness
is decisive for her whole life. Along this way she will have to be
conscious of all the dangers of transformation and destruction,
as well as of the difficult commission of distinguishing, in order
that, in the midst of many voices, she continue to hear the voice
of the gospel. The difficulty is increased even more by the historical development of confessions: the multiplicity that confronts us later in the Church displays much variation in the
formulation of the central content of the confession,[69] and we

67. Rahner ("The Prospects for Dogmatic Theology," Theological Investi-
    gations, I, 5) calls the idea that "theology has pretty well exhausted
    divine revelation and translated it all into theological intelligibility"
    blasphemous.
68. Cf. H.M. Matter, De Brief aan de Philippenzen, 1965, p. 22, who points
    out the contrast with the approval in Rom. 2:18, which is concerned
    with a minimizing (via casuistry) rather than with the maximum of
    obedience that Paul requires. Cf. the Pharisaic neglect of the weightier
    matters of the law, that with which the law is concerned (Matt. 23:23).
69. We see the variation in the many formulations of Groen van Prinsterer
    (op. cit., pp. 58f.) when he speaks of "the main point and essence of
    the formulas" as, for example, "unconditional sovereignty and the free
    grace of God" (for the Reformed Church). For the Church as the
    Protestant Church, it is subjection to the Scriptures; and for the
    Church as the Christian Church, it is human corruption, adoration of
    God, Christ's sacrifice, etc. Cf. Confessioneel of Reglementair?, p. 3,
    for concrete application with regard to a preacher who "proclaims the
    Christ of Renan, the doctrine of transubstantiation, or the system of
    Proudhon concerning property as theft and thereby ceases de facto
    to be a teacher in the Reformed Church."

are also faced with many new questions that were outside the
Church's horizon at the time of the confessions, so that one
cannot expect answers to them from those confessions.[70] Thus,
we see various shifts that induced new reflection on whether the
Scriptures were correctly understood in earlier times.

As one of the most striking examples of all of this, one can
point to the discussions about the doctrine of original sin. The
situation here has been especially complicated because there
have always been questions as to whether it can be brought into
harmony with man's own responsibility and guilt.[71] In addition
to that, other complications arose later in connection with the
exegesis of Genesis 1-3, leading to further interpretation, as in
countless Roman Catholic publications of our time. The concern here is not simply with scientific questions of evolution,
monogenism, and polygenism, but also with new reflection on
the nature of sin, its universality, its character as power and as
guilt.[72] The questions of further interpretation increased interest
in what — both in the Roman Catholic and Protestant churches,
and especially in their preaching — was scarcely mentioned in
detail anymore. It seemingly became a latent dogma that was
assumed as a confessional given more than justified and confessed "before men." Other questions took the place of the
explanation of the human situation in sinfulness as "heredity."
They dealt especially with the power and superiority of sin in
persons and contexts, thus clearing the way for the outlook on
the liberating salvation, on the light that has appeared in this
darkness. To speak here of fashionable actualizing is nothing
else than to lack appreciation for what was described religiously
and dogmatically as guilt before God. It became less and less
possible to reject out of hand various new reflections on the
basis of "the doctrine of original sin," since it is evident on

70. This motif plays an important role especially in Schoonenberg.
71. Cf. my Sin, 1971, chapter 12.
72. It is striking that Roman Catholic publications, especially, have appeared in this area. The most recent is that of Urs Baumann, Erbsünde?
Ihr traditionnelles Verständnis in der Krise heutiger Theologie, 1970.
If one asks the reason for this special Roman Catholic interest, we can
point out that Humani Generis (1950) made a choice amid modern
questions with its reference to the doctrine of original sin "as this
is guaranteed to us by Scripture and tradition, and proposed to us
by the Church." The sin committed by one man named Adam has
been handed down by descent (generatione) to all (Denz., 2328; TCT,
366). The stream of publications began after that. From the side of
Protestantism, see E. Kinder, Die Erbsünde, 1959; my Sin, 1971.

closer inspection that the meaning and biblical foundation of this doctrine is definitely not elevated above all unclarity.[73] In further interpretation, one was aware of diverse motifs in the church's confession, connected especially to power and superiority, the significance of which had to be recognized. The analysis and further interpretation of the doctrine of original sin were no longer primarily directed to the explanation of the present situation, but to what was esteemed to be fundamental also in our time, for us personally, and for all life. Here the superiority, the inescapability of sin for us, came strongly to the foreground and thus was connected to the confession of the Church.[74]

In this situation of criticism and interpretation, there can be groping progress for a long time in order to do justice to all aspects. Because there is much less positivity than seemed to be present in earlier ages, a certain nostalgia can arise for that earlier time, and one can begin to speak of decline and disobedience with regard to the clear language of Scripture. However, one then forgets that the earlier positivity did not always go with equally great clarity. All confession — but certainly also the confession of guilt — must undeniably be concerned with that clarity! Therefore, one can only greet the many new ques-

---

73. Hence, one may not overestimate the significance of the earlier positivity, in view of the perplexities in the centuries-long discussion of inherited guilt, hereditary corruption, inheritance, imputation (cf. my *Sin*, especially chapters 13 and 14), and, in Roman Catholic circles, the character of original sin as actual guilt. We are thinking also of the fluctuating differences in the exegesis of Rom. 5:12 (in Calvin, Greijdanus, and H.N. Ridderbos, for instance), especially on whether "all" is to be understood as "personal or corporative sin." Ridderbos points out that the context of Rom. 5:12 deals "not with original sin as moral corruption, but with the inclusion in Adam's sin and in Adam's death" (*Aan de Romeinen*, p. 117; cf. *Paul*, p. 99). Clearly, the idea of the "corporate personality" is also an entirely different level than that of "inheritance" — which is hard to connect with it and was expressed in H.C., Q. 7 (the depravity of "our nature" in Paradise), as an explanation for our depravity. On the questions surrounding the corporate personality and inheritance see especially Urs Baumann, *op. cit.*, pp. 214ff. The perplexing character of all the differences is highlighted by Freundörfer's comment that Rom. 5 is "the single document for the existence of a biblical dogma of original sin" (*Erbsünde und Erbtod beim Apostel Paulus*, 1927, p. 105).

74. Cf. Ridderbos, *Paul*, with strong accents on the power of sin. Cf. Schoonenberg, "De Macht der Zonde," *Het Geloof van ons Doopsel*, IV, 1962; *idem, Mysterium Salutis*, II, 845ff.; J.T. Bakker, "Zonde en Schuld," *Kernwoorden van het Chr. Geloof*, 1970, pp. 27f.; E. Kinder, *op. cit.*, pp. 46ff.

tions about "original sin" and its interpretation thankfully, since they erect a dam against the danger that we might come gradually to a latent dogma. What always seemed to many people to be a strange, inhuman doctrine — the height of unacceptability — would then become a *corpus alienum* for the Church herself, in direct contradiction to that same Romans 5, where the light and grace of Christ have this darkness as a background. We may not deny the significance of reflecting anew on the various questions about original sin in connection with the Church's confession, her "knowledge" of guilt and of her forgiveness.

In statu confessionis

From these examples in the Church's concrete life, it is evident that, over and over again, one seeks for that continuity in the Church's confession which gives it relevance also in one's own time. All protests against actualizing — sometimes justly and sometimes unfairly — cannot undo the fact that the confession itself encompasses this actuality before men. Apart from it, the confession is relativized to a *gnosis*. We touch here on a problem that has repeatedly come up for discussion, namely, that of the so-called *status confessionis*. Although, on the basis of the New Testament, one can speak of a continuing *status confessionis* (gospel and Acts!), one has always had an eye also for specific situations when the Church was summoned *ad hoc* to make necessary decisions in order to elucidate a confused and dangerous time, full of concrete temptation at one definite point. The Church was then of the opinion that she could not stop with a recollection of her confession and its implications, but felt herself forced to a confessional answer for this time, in new temptation. There are times when there seems to be no such acute tension, at least not in a direct, spectacular sense. Unexpectedly, though, the course of events can disturb this "rest," and the Church can be faced with a *status confessionis*.[75] The declaration of Barmen in 1934 is often recalled as an exam-

---

75. Although there was certainly not rest everywhere in the ancient Church, the persecutions that came upon her did place her in new situations that had to be coped with. D. Schellong's distinction (*op. cit.*, pp. 58ff.). between a "confessional stand" (*Bekenntnisstand*) and the *status confessionis* does contain an element of truth historically, but it is not a change into a different genus (p. 61), since the Church is tested in the *status confessionis* on what she had confessed in times of more rest.

ple of this.[76] The Church became conscious of an acute threat and thus gave a warning confession in opposition to the "false doctrine" of the "German Christians." This occurred in the realization that everything was suddenly at stake, since other powers, events, and truths demanded a place as "revelation" next to the revelation in Jesus Christ (II, 1), other "lords" and other "leaders" (II, 2, 4) than the one Lord of the Church. Later one asked whether Barmen was not concerned simply with an "ephemeral heresy" and whether it had not lost all significance for us.[77] However, this question has little meaning on account both of the unpredictability of history, where an error can repeat itself again in another form, and of the clarity that can come to light for a long time in a *status confessionis*, whereby it maintains continuing and direction-giving actuality.[78] In a *status confessionis*, a confession can sometimes bear a startling character with a clear *damnamus*. That is not always because the words are completely new. The confession of Barmen can scarcely be called a new confession. It consists of a number of well-known texts from Scripture, which one wanted to let re-sound anew in that situation as a reminder that decisions are necessary and that they affect whether the Church is "to be or not to be."

Clearly, the Church's speaking here may not be related *a priori* to the official-institutional aspect of the Church. Frequently, there is charismatic and intuitive insight into the dangers of a special situation, which then can acquire significance in the whole Church.[79] Naturally, the analysis of the situation —

76. See E. Wolf, *Barmen. Kirche zwischen Versuchung und Gnade*, 1957; K. Barth, "Barmen," *Bekennende Kirche*, 1935; and in detail *idem, C.D.,* II/1, pp. 172-178.

77. On this question see K. Scholder, "Die Bedeutung des Barmer Bekenntnisses für die evang. Theol. und Kirche," *Evang. Theol.*, 1969, pp. 435ff. Cf. also D. Schellong, "Barmen II und die Grundlegung der Ethik," *Parrhesia*, 1964, pp. 491ff.

78. Cf. A. Szekeres, "Barmer Thesen in 1968," *Kerk en Theol.*, 1968, pp. 269ff., with application to the situation of the Church in Hungary (the political directives of the State as a second source of revelation). For the rest, the question of actuality is influenced also by the judgment of Barmen, particularly if one is of the opinion, as Szekeres is, that Barmen "has shut the world out of the Church" due to the Christological concentration (Barth). What Szekeres contrasts to that (in virtue of the concentration on Christ) is not in the least in conflict with Barmen.

79. One may recall the Dutch publication "What We Do and What We Do Not Believe" in 1941, a clear parallel to Barmen, but with the

either individually or as a community — plays a decisive role. Precisely because the Word of God is recognized not as a general category, but as related to actual life — where it is to be a light and a lamp, an answer to all implicit and explicit questions[80] — analysis is indispensable. Therefore, it is not meaningful to approach the Church's speaking from the distinction between the Church as institution and as organism.[81] This aspect played a great role in earlier times via the distinction between office and laity. It was thought that the "office" had its own "sources" at its disposal, so that serious analysis was scarcely necessary and the Church's whole life could be led with authority. Since then it has become more and more clear that actually giving direction is possible neither "in general" nor in the abstract. At the Second Vatican Council, there was strong opposition by conservative theologians to a conciliar analysis of our time, because of fear that the Church's authority would be subject to such an analysis and thus would lose influence.[82]

When one's own sources become more and more dubious in the course of history, in that one cannot draw all solutions from revelation, and when reflection on the ways that could and had to be walked occurred more and more often apart from the "official" Church, a new problem loomed up — namely, that of competence. That problem of the relatedness of the Church's speaking to the concrete situation does not lose anything of its seriousness and its complications if it, on account of the questions of competence, is referred from one authority to another, for instance from the institution to the organism, from the office to the laity. For no matter where the relatedness comes

addition of a rejection of anti-Semitism and the ideology of race. An interesting example of a "personal" confession from an earlier time, which later became significant for the Church, is the Second Helvetic Confession by Bullinger, which was written as a testament "in anticipation of death." See H. Ott, *Glaube und Bekennen*, 1963, pp. 54ff.

80. Fear for the problematic of question and answer on account of the danger that the answer will be washed away by the questions or by the situation is superfluous for anyone who acknowledges without bias that the Word of God unfolds its power precisely here. Cf. the defense to anyone who calls to account (I Pet. 3:15 — *pantì tõ̧ aitoúnti humâs lógon*); knowing how to answer everyone (Col. 4:6); and Paul's answer on the Areopagus (Acts 17:22ff.).

81. Cf. H.M. Kuitert, "Het Spreken der Kerk," *Anders Gezegd*, 1970, pp. 179ff.

82. Cf. K. Rahner, "Over de Theol. Problematiek van een 'Pastorale Constitutie,'" *De Kerk en de Wereld van deze Tijd*, 1967, pp. 327ff.; my *Nabetrachting op het Concilie*, pp. 182ff.; and Kuitert, *op. cit.*, p. 175.

into view, reflection on the Word of God is always necessary, that Word of God proclaimed by the Church. This explains why the Church was never satisfied with a "general" preaching, but sought to place life in the world in the light of the gospel in order that her preaching not deteriorate into a meager preaching.[83] Conscious of many complicated situations and entanglements, she nevertheless did not hesitate to enter upon the way of reflection.[84] Along that way it was evident again and again that the situation — and the powers and motives that came to light in it — were not so inextricable as was frequently suggested with reference to the Church's incompetence. True, every pronouncement by the Church apart from analysis and information is meaningless and unbelievable, but this condition may not barricade the way to disclosing, witnessing, and warning, signifying not a fashionable "actualizing," but relating to actual life and, therein, wanting to point out the good way.[85]

Even the tensions of the modern world can force the Church into a *status confessionis*.[86] Does she still understand what Luther wrote: "If he have faith, the believer cannot be restrained. He breaks out. He confesses and teaches this gospel to the people at the risk of life itself."[87] A confession must not only be correct;

83. Cf. Kuitert, *loc. cit.*
84. One should think of the presupposition of all ecclesiastical reflection on the question of war and the problem of race. It is the meaning of, the competence for, and the right to such reflection.
85. For many years J. Verkuyl has stood tirelessly in the breach for this kind of speaking. Cf. his *The Message of Liberation in Our Age*, 1970; and J.T. Bakker, "Onderweg naar Eén Wereldsamenleving," *Gereformeerd Weekblad*, August 20, 1971 (on the impossibility of isolating salvation within Church walls and inner rooms). When J. van Genderen (*De Reform. Belijdenis in Discussie*, 1971, p. 51) writes that a confession in answer to questions of present interest about the consequences of faith in Jesus Christ in today's world is a way "along which one is busy estranging oneself from the Holy Scriptures," he may want to indicate a danger of secularization ("less about God and more about the consequences of faith and the present," p. 52), but he does not offer much clarity; for he himself does not want to say that the Church "can be silent about the consequences of faith" (p. 53). To that he adds, "but the confession is concerned primarily with faith itself" — as if the concern in the consequences of faith were not faith itself!
86. Van Genderen (*op. cit.*, p. 54), too, speaks of situations "in which a powerful witness must be heard." It is quite apparent, therefore, that the nature and the content of this witness are in question, but not the calling itself.
87. *Martin Luther: Selections From His Writings*, J. Dillenberger, ed., 1961, p. 18.

it must also be important: definitive for the Church's whole life, for her walking in the truth, her "being" as the light of the world, a city on a hill, the salt of the earth. Whoever restricts the Church's confession to an esoteric mystery has robbed it of its power, paving the way toward the saltlessness that no longer serves anything (Mark 9:50). That impoverishes not only her confession externally (cf. Col. 4:6), but also her own life internally (from preaching to liturgy). Confession can retain its significance only if it continues to be "proclaimed by a herald."[88] Where the confession gets a place in the Church's doctrine and teaching, it will always be directed to the completeness of the man of God, equipped for every good work (II Tim. 3:17). This speaking must be confessional and instructive, explanatory, often polemical, and, if need be, challenging. The relationship of this confession to life does not make the gospel "dependent," but rather fruitful. Otherwise, the Church's life is cut off from her root, from love and from the command, from the presence of the Lord, which is decisive for every confession, both old and new.[89] Apart from this outlook, the confession may perhaps remain for a long time as a traditional inheritance, but, in the long run, its lack of a connection with "men" causes a rupture in the Church's apostolicity, since it is not related to true discipleship.

Confession and instruction

In this connection, it is good to recall the earlier discussions about the difference between a confessional Church and a confessing Church. That there need be no dilemma here is definitely correct. But the rejection of this dilemma implies also that confession is possible and meaningful only in the light of living confessing.[90] We touch here on the danger that Bavinck described as the replacement of the confession of faith by faith

88. K. Barth, *C.D.*, I/2, p. 641.
89. With regard to a new confession, there is always a danger that it will be determined by a theological situation (what must and what must not be in it?). But that does not condemn interest in a new *credo*. One can say that this endeavor is meaningful on the condition of the normative structure of true confession. The Church is urged to give an account of that confession which is still experienced as relevant. Cf. M.P. van Dijk, *Nieuw Credo*, 1970.
90. On the varied mode of confession and unity, cf. H.G. Jung, "Bekenntnis und Konfession," *Evang. Kommentare*, 1971, pp. 159ff., on the "Church's critical task of accountability."

in the confession.[91] That is a warning against petrification, since confession "is from the very beginning an act."[92] That is not an emotional protest against the formation of confessions, but rather a touchstone for its significance. That the confessions have come to be connected to intensive "instruction" need not conflict with that confessing, if the "instruction" does not threaten true confessing. In the history of the Church, we discover a complicated process in the growth of confessions. In that process, a connection comes about between confession and instruction. The Nicene Creed reads "we believe,"[93] and the Chalcedonian Decree reads, "we confess and teach."[94] This way to instruction, which one walks in association with Scripture, definitely need not be a deflection from the just way of the Church; but there is a danger that, in the historical development, the doxological element, and the confession founded in it, will end up in the background, if doctrine — relevant in Acts in the midst of a *status confessionis* (cf. 2:42) — begins to give the impression of a law that isolates the confession from the Church's proclamation. Every facet of confession loses its significance if it becomes a terminal point in place of a stimulus in the continuous listening to the gospel.[95] In confession, the Church is referred to a multitude of words by which she must seek to understand the one voice and to make it understood.

The dangers that threaten here in connection with a fixed confession have often come up for discussion in connection with the so-called Athanasian Creed, which gives an answer to "Whoever wishes to be saved" *(Quicumque vult salvus esse)*. The Creed points to the universal belief in the triune God. To this a detailed trinitarian and christological exposition is attached with respect to the faith that must be preserved "whole and entire," since without this faith salvation is impossible (Athan. 1, 2, 44). We get the impression that very much is "necessary," very much explicit belief. After the formulation of the trini-

---

91. Cf. also C. Veenhof, *Prediking en Uitverkiezing*, 1959, p. 193 (on Kuyper).
92. O. Weber, *Grundlagen der Dogmatik*, I, 39.
93. *Credimus*, Denz., 86.
94. *Confiteri ... docemus*, Denz., 148. Cf. E. Schlink, "The Structure of Dogmatic Statements as an Ecumenical Problem," *The Coming Christ and the Coming Church*, 1967, pp. 28f.
95. One may think of the formulations at Chalcedon. They lose all value if they begin to function apart from the proclamation concerning Jesus Christ; then they can do nothing but give a meager impression of a "two-natures doctrine." Cf. my *Het Laatste Woord? Opstellen Aangeboden aan Dr. D. Nauta*, 1968, pp. 134ff., 146ff.

tarian confession, we hear that it is also necessary to believe steadfastly in the Incarnation of our Lord Jesus Christ (29), which includes the "true God and true man," His eternal generation, His birth from Mary, His suffering, descent, resurrection, ascension, sitting at the right hand of God, and second coming (30-44). Because of this, the Athanasian Creed has been involved in many discussions, especially in connection with the necessity of belief for eternal salvation. Is this a "doctrine of law" imposed on one? Is it intellectual assent and knowledge *(assensus* and *notitia)?* Harnack speaks of the "obscure history of the origin and reception" of this symbol, which was adopted by the Church along with the Apostles' Creed."[96] According to him, no symbol has gone so far in the "necessity of belief" as this one did[97] along the way to an ecclesiastical legal statute upon which salvation depends, as consent to transmitted formulations that are protected warningly.[98] The impression can arise here that the object of belief is not a unity, but a multiplicity. Crystallized in these formulations, it becomes a *sine qua non* and is related to a dogmatic elaboration that, in the time after Augustine and with the help of his doctrine of the trinity, is incorporated in the correlation of salvation.[99]

This correlation has to leave a different impression behind — and does — than that other call to belief in Mark 16:16, where the outlook on the gospel remained fully preserved and was related to the promise of salvation.[100] The Reformed affiliation in its confessions to the ecumenical symbols points to relatedness with the trinitarian and christological confessions, but not to their acceptance as a law whereby faith stands or falls with

96. Harnack, *History of Dogma,* IV, 135f.
97. In spite of the designation "psalm of Athanasius" (Bakhuizen van den Brink, *Kerkgeschiedenis,* I, 271).
98. A. Adam, *Lehrbuch der Dogmengeschichte,* I, 339, on the symbol as a "formula of guarantee," since the ancient tradition could be saved only "through the armor of the letter." The later attempt to weaken the introductory words does not recognize the solemnity of these words. Cf. J.N.D. Kelly, *The Athanasian Creed,* 1964, p. 71.
99. See, among other places, Athan. 36. Cf. the elucidation of the unity of Christ's person with the analogy of the union between man's reasonable soul and flesh into one man (37), an analogy of the analogy-less mystery of the incarnated Word!
100. Compare the Athanasian Creed to H.C., Q. 2 ("How many things are necessary for you to know?"), where "three things" constitute a single answer which is directed to comfort in life and death.

these formulations.[101] More important than the question of how the Athanasian Creed intended these elaborate formulations concretely[102] is the discovery that belief cannot be an *assensus* in the sense of an ecclesiastical law separated from the depth and riches of the gospel. Apart from the gospel, the confession is always quantitatively "too much" and can become a stumbling block along the Church's way.[103] The way of confession is a different way, because the multiplicity can be mentioned here only as the radiation of the one great light. Whenever the Church speaks of that mystery, she will have to be conscious of this nature of confession. Otherwise, the multiplicity will be in conflict with the one confession of the disciples of the one Lord and will be lacking in power.[104] Naturally, conformity with the content does play a decisive role in the confession, and the *homo-logia* is undoubtedly and essentially *assensus,* or affirmation. But whenever even the impression is awakened that the *assensus* alone, on account of its "usableness," can define and protect the ways of the Church, we face a dangerous process of impoverishment and minimizing. The aspect of being or not being in agreement with the confession is then abstracted from its deep context and can be interpreted as *notitia* and *assensus* on the analogy of other forms of belief and acceptance.[105]

With that, one was far removed from biblical belief and confession as the answer to the proclamation of salvation. That does not mean knowledge has no place in belief and confession. But everything depends on how it is understood. The important thing in every concept is the content given it and its context. Even the word "knowledge" *(cognitio)* can point to the divine

---

101. See B.C., Art. 9; Formula of Concord, Part I, no. 2. Calvin's refusal of Caroli's demand that he subscribe to the Athanasian Creed was directed against the compulsion of such a law of faith as the criterion of orthodoxy. Cf. J. Koopmans, *op. cit.,* p. 37; W. Nijenhuis, *op. cit.,* pp. 98ff.; D. Nauta, "Een Geloofsbelijdenis van Calvijn," *Schrift en Uitleg,* 1970, pp. 141ff.

102. Cf. the report to the Synod in *Acta Gener. Syn. 1969-70,* p. 226, on the Athanasian Creed as a "one-sided Western speculation." Further, cf. A.A. van Ruler, *Hoe Functioneert een Belijdenis?,* p. 14, against the absolutizing of formulations.

103. "Rock of offense," in contrast to others who saw a sort of world catechism in the Athanasian Creed, comparable to the "Marseillaise" — a very strange comparison (Kelly, *op. cit.,* p. 124). Cf. O. Weber, *op. cit.,* II, 300.

104. H.M. Kuitert, *The Reality of Faith,* pp. 120ff.

105. Bavinck, especially, warned continuously against this misconception.

benevolence,[106] where others used two words: "not only a sure knowledge, but also a firm confidence" (H.C., Q. 21). This knowledge, this trust, does not believe "in what is uncertain."[107] Rather, it is a knowledge that is itself life (John 17:3) and can be described by the Belgic Confession as "embracing Christ" (Art. 22). This belief with the heart can be mentioned in one breath with confession with the mouth (Rom. 10:10). The life of the Church must avoid every appearance that conformity in content with the apostolic witness already guarantees the Church's apostolicity. Orthodoxy has not always been conscious of that danger. One did theoretically take account that a break is possible between verbal confession and the heart, but one referred then to the hiddenness of the heart that lay outside the Church's judgment. In practice, the result was that conformity was the exclusive criterion, in flagrant conflict with the gospel, which allows conclusions to be drawn from the connection between the tree and its fruit: "Thus you will know them by their fruits" (Matt. 7:20; cf. James 3:11f.). That is why all confession by the Church is so vulnerable, for it is the object of unprecedented testing. The Church is reminded that clear "acceptance" of truths can be connected to dead faith apart from fruit (James 2:19). There can be no separation between orthodoxy and orthopraxy.[108] Therefore, isolated attention for knowledge and assent does great damage to the Church's life and testimony in the world; it deforms what comes into view in the New Testament as believing confession.

If belief and confession cannot be examined from the isolated relation of the subject who knows and the object that is known, and if Paul's radicality signifies a break with an earlier abundant knowledge and zeal for the traditions of the fathers

---

106. Calvin, *Inst.*, III, 2, 12: "faith is a knowledge of the divine benevolence to us and a sure persuasion of its truth." Cf. III, 2, 2: "Faith rests not on ignorance, but on knowledge"; I, 10, 2: the description of Jehovah's powers in Ex. 34 shows us Him "not as he is in himself, but as he is toward us." See also John 17:3 and Phil. 3:10.

107. Weber, *op. cit.*, II, 312. Cf. p. 293; Bavinck, *Geref. Dog.*, I, 591.

108. Cf. the contrast between saying "Lord, Lord," and doing the will of the Father (Matt. 7:21); professing to know God, but denying Him by deeds (Tit. 1:16 — *homologoúsin* and *arnoúntai*); and holding the form of religion but denying its power (II Tim. 3:5). In opposition to this separation is the harmony of obedient acknowledgment of the gospel of Christ by a deed of the Church (II Cor. 9:13). On the indissoluble connection, cf. E. Schillebeeckx, "Het 'Rechte Geloof,' zijn Onzekerheden en zijn Criteria," *Tijdschrift voor Theologie*, 1969, pp. 140ff.

(Gal. 1:14 — *perissotéros zēlōtḕs*), then a dimension is indicated that is of decisive significance for believing confession. All formal analogies of knowledge and assent are thwarted by a deep-going, total change, which structures all believing confession and from which what is abiding is tested. One has always noticed how remarkably Paul places knowledge in a revealing light: "now that you have come to know God, or rather to be known by God" (4:9). This "rather" does not rob human knowledge of its significance. Nevertheless, Weber is not wrong in speaking of "the mystical sound of such declarations,"[109] since a dimension is designated here that is of decisive significance for the understanding òf belief and confession. True knowledge in the light of this "rather" eliminates all isolated attention for verbal conformity; and this dimension of knowledge qualifies the only, true orthodoxy,[110] in which the Church herself is tested in all knowledge and confession with respect to her living belief. This is not a minimizing, but a maximizing of knowledge, belief, and confession, since true belief and confession are possible only in and from this dimension. Confession is torn loose from its root if this confession gives way to a secularization that robs the "confessing" Church of her power, in spite of the fact that she is perhaps confessing "the truth." In all the Church's confession, her own whole life before God and before men is at stake. Here, in the midst of the appearance of unassailable truth, she is more vulnerable than anywhere else. Here she is tested not only by "men," who judge the Church's life according to her words, her confession, but also by Him Who summons the Church to confession before men and then proves and tries her (cf. Ps. 26:2;

109. O. Weber, *op. cit.,* I, 216. Cf. K. Barth, *C.D.,* IV/3, 1, p. 185 on "the bold expression of Paul" ("in which the object becomes the subject"). Cf. knowing and being known in I Cor. 13:12. Further, see John 10:14; I Cor. 8:2f.: "If any one imagines that he knows something, he does not yet know as he ought to know. But if one loves God, one is known by him." On Gal. 4:9, van Stempvoort (*De Brief van Paulus aan de Galaten*, 1961², p. 112) speaks of the Johannine ring in Paul's voice.

110. H. Schlier (*Der Brief an die Galater*, p. 143) speaks of an "intensifying correction of what has been said" with respect to the "or rather" in Gal. 4:9. It does not seem to me that there is any suggestion of a correction here — it would sooner be present in I Cor. 8:1f. (in connection with the knowledge that puffs up). Luther (*Commentary on St. Paul's Epistle to the Galatians*, 1930, p. 361), in his consideration of Gal. 4:9, writes that "our knowledge is rather passive." He writes this in contrast to the belief that all thinking starts from our righteousness.

Jer. 11:20; 17:10; 20:12; Rev. 2:23) in that confession with a
measuring rod that discloses everything, placing it in the light
of the Name that is confessed in the Church and before men.
The testing of that confession corresponds to another confession
— that of Christ before the face of the Father and before the
angels of God (Matt. 10:32; Luke 12:8).

IV. The Holiness
of the Church

CHAPTER TWELVE

THE MEANING OF HOLINESS

WHEN THE CHURCH CONFESSES HER OWN HOLI-
ness in the *credo* (*credo sanctam ecclesiam*), there is
every reason to reflect seriously on this "attribute," especially
when we think of what is commonly understood by "holy"
and "holiness." Words like "catholicity" and "apostolicity"
are not immediately understood by everyone from a certain
Vorverständis. They do not need, as it were, immediate elucidation, as is especially the case with the word "catholic." But
holiness immediately conjures up all sorts of associations for
practically everyone. It is usually connected to other qualifications, such as spotlessness and perfection, to exemption from
the sphere of evil and contamination, which in so many respects
rules the lives of men in the world. The *credo* of the Church
resounds in this world with this *Vorverständnis,* asserting that
she too is a fellowship of saints. But can this unmistakable claim
be proved? Is it not flagrantly contradicted by countless facts?
What does it signify concretely that the Church has given everyone who will listen not only the criteria for judgment of unity,
catholicity, and apostolicity, but also that of holiness? After the
credo of unity, the credo of holiness, especially, seems to be
exceedingly vulnerable. With respect to unity, one can still
point, in the midst of all division, to a unity in Christ and can
call attention to ecumenism in and in spite of the disunity of
the churches. But holiness does not seem to lend itself at all to
"further interpretation."

How is it possible that the Church characterizes her life, her
"being" in the world, so positively and so emphatically, apparently without hesitation and audible for all men, as the holy
Church and the fellowship of the saints? Was the *credo* really
intended as seriously as it sounds? Or does the Church perhaps
mean something entirely different with "holy" than what one

313

commonly understands by holiness? But it is not true that what the Church intends by holiness has nothing at all to do with that general *Vorverständnis* that is found in the world. Holiness is usually thought of as perfection and cleanness, the radiation of a deep, striking purity; and the Church has always spoken about holiness in such a way that it, in any case, has something to do with that. Theology may sometimes have spoken of a *hidden* holiness of the Church, as Luther did, but that does not mean that there is a total misunderstanding of what the Church means by holiness here, since, precisely with respect to holiness, many can understand that "hiddenness" only with difficulty.[1] It is not unjust that holiness is always connected to what becomes visible in the world in one way or another and can be perceived by human eyes as a light that shines in the darkness. Generally, the Church too has realized that not everything is said with that "hiddenness." Nor is everything said with the conclusion from an analysis of the *credo* that "one could even say that the holiness that is confessed here is the forgiveness of sins."[2] It may be correct that the *credo* of holiness cannot be separated from faith in the Holy Spirit and from the forgiveness of sins, but that does not mean that the general understanding of holiness and holy lies on a totally different level than the understanding contained in the *credo*.

This impression was strengthened for many by the way in which the Roman Catholic Church spoke about the saints and their veneration: the radiation of holiness, perfection, and exceptionality in the concrete life of those saints gave occasion to the veneration. The martyrs, especially, with their radically devoted lives have played an important role here as the "primary" saints of the Church.[3] The presence of miracles was superfluous for their canonization, because their death counted as the sufficient, spectacular sign, as the testimony of God Himself.[4] "Saints" formed a separate, very specific group in the Church. They obtained veneration through special merits during their lives on earth. Nevertheless, the *sancta ecclesia* is not at all a special Roman Catholic concept. When the Reformers rejected the veneration of saints, they in no sense intended to

---

1. Cf. V. Vajta, "Die verborgene Heiligheid der Kirche," *Gedenkschrift für W. Elert*, 1955, pp. 296ff.
2. *Ibid.*, p. 296.
3. Cf. H. von Campenhausen, *Die Idee des Martyriums in der alten Kirche*, 1964[2], pp. 95ff.
4. K. Rahner, *Zur Theol. des Todes*, 1958, p. 104.

deny the holiness of believers and of the Church. Rather, one can say that the Reformers spoke in a still wider sense of believers as saints by not connecting holiness to a specific, separate group. Holiness was confessed in the midst of life, as Luther, according to the statement of Karl Holl, "brought the saints from heaven down to earth."[5] By so doing, they come to stand much closer to us in the form of all believers. Instead of being removed from earth or being a faraway future, holiness became a nearby reality. And to the degree that it came closer, the question of the meaning of the *credo* became more urgent.

The connection of the concept of holiness with perfection and completion seems to make it almost inevitable that the *credo* be seen as a form of self-praise and self-complacency: it automatically seems to be paired with discrimination against others outside the Church, who lack this holiness. Does this perhaps recall the Pharisees, who trusted in themselves that they were righteous and despised others (Luke 18:9)? Even if one accepts that such a sense of self and such discrimination are not the intent of the *credo,* since the *credo* also recognizes the forgiveness of sins, it is still meaningful to ask how the *credo* can be distinguished from this self-praise. Must one not think directly of a halo of holiness that encircles the Church? That is a question for which one has become especially sensitive in our time due to a growing aversion to all ecclesiastical narcissism,[6] whereby the Church loses herself in her own life and then speaks about her whole existence with such "grand" words.

An external, "objective" holiness?

In reflecting on the *credo,* one must first recognize that the Church meant to remain in the clear track of the New Testament, where the holiness of the Church is mentioned continuously. Believers are called saints (II Cor. 1:1; Eph. 1:1; Col. 1:2), sanctified in Christ Jesus (I Cor. 1:2; Phil. 1:1), called to be saints (Rom. 1:7); and they find themselves in the midst of earthly, everyday reality in Corinth, Rome, or Colossae. They are continually reminded of this special qualification, and the whole Church is addressed as God's own people and as a holy nation, called out of darkness into His marvelous light (I Pet.

5. K. Holl, in P. Althaus, *Communio Sanctorum,* I, 27. Cf. K. Holl, "Die Entstehung von Luthers Kirchenbegriff," *Ges. Aufs.,* I, 322. Cf. Luther on Rom. 12:13 (*Lectures on Romans,* ed. W. Pauck, 1961, p. 351).
6. J.B. Metz, *Theology of the World,* 1969, p. 81.

2:9). Even though there is clearly no suggestion here of one's own achievement and quality — holiness is in the context of election, calling, and mercy (2:10) — nevertheless, the Church becomes visible in her holiness. Because this holiness is spoken of so emphatically, the charge has often been made that the Church did not take her own *credo* with full seriousness any longer and had ended up in a compromise of unholiness and toleration of evil. In the light of the New Testament, she was reproached for tolerating sinners in her midst when they had fallen into sin again after baptism or had not remained firm in persecutions. We are thinking specifically of the Novatians, who wanted to maintain the purity of the Church "at any cost,"[7] as well as of the Donatists, who, in connection with the administration of the sacraments by the "traitors" *(traditores)* — "Who will distribute what he himself does not possess?" — saw the dawning of the end of this Church and then wanted to realize the ideal of a holy Church themselves.[8] The Church did not have an easy time with this criticism from the New Testament. She was constrained to give account of the meaning of her *credo*. In the New Testament, for that matter, holiness is not in the least a faraway, abstract thing, but a reality that is inseparably connected to what has happened in a radical transition from the former manner of life to a new life (Eph. 4:22), in being set free from the law of sin and death (Rom. 8:2), and even in passing from death to life (I John 3:14). The Church is called holy in these radical connections, in this rupture that arose through the call out of darkness into marvelous light (I Pet. 2:9).

This rupture and transition contains the outlook on the holy Church, distantiated from all vanity and pollution, darkening and uncleanness, and described in comparison with the heathen: "You did not so learn Christ!" (Eph. 4:20). Here there is mention of the new man, created after the likeness of God "in true righteousness and holiness" (4:24 — *hosiótēs*), and of a new creation in Christ: the old has passed away and "behold, the new has come" (II Cor. 5:17; Gal. 6:17). If one considers all this, one will have to be cautious and may not speak too quickly

---

7. Novatian recalled the New Testament characterizations of the Church (bride, temple, holy, and blameless). Cf. H.J. Vogt, *Coetus Sanctorum. Der Kirchenbegriff des Novatianus und die Geschichte seiner Sonderkirche*, 1968, pp. 94ff., 133ff.

8. E. Altendorf, *Einheit und Heiligkeit der Kirche*, 1932, pp. 117ff.; H.B. Weyland, *Augustinus en de Kerkelijke Tucht*, 1965, pp. 26ff., 33 (on the *corpus permixtum* in Augustine).

of "endeavors for holiness" in *malam partem* or of old streams in the Church as "rigoristic" heresy.[9] Rather, there is every reason to reflect on the *credo* in the light of the New Testament, especially because we meet with many interpretations that can be called nothing other than relativizations. One of the most striking interpretations is the understanding of the holiness of the Church as a so-called "objective" holiness which has been given to the Church "in Christ." Then a certain parallel is made with forensic justification, which points to *favor Dei,* supposedly denoting a changed, new relation. In this objective holiness, then, the solution was sought for the tension that becomes visible again and again between the Church's confessed holiness and her empirical "appearance." A deep-going problem was brought to discussion here, because it was thought that the objectivizing could answer all questions. But objections always arose against this "solution." Did the glorious aspect of holiness signify a reference to holiness in Christ — outside us *(extra nos)* — without the Church's concrete existence reflecting this holiness as a shining light in the world? It is clear that the distinction between objective and subjective holiness can never disclose the meaning of the *credo,* at least not if one still wants to admit some connection between the *credo* and the message of the New Testament about the Church's holiness.

The question whether the *credo* did not have everything to do with the Church's concrete life on earth had to repeatedly arise. The background for this is the clear way in which the New Testament speaks about holiness in the sense of a light radiating in the world, where believers are called to extreme concentration and activity.[10] That attention was nevertheless directed again and again to "objective" holiness is closely connected to the seemingly clear point of contact with the way Holy Scripture often speaks about holiness. "Holy" and "holiness" point frequently to separate, to a setting apart for a particular purpose or for a particular service. Holiness is spoken

9. Cf. K. Rahner-H. Vorgrimler, *Kleines Theol. Wörterbuch,* p. 264 (on Novatianism).
10. When J. Ratzinger *(Introduction to Christianity,* 1969, pp. 261f.) writes that the Church is called holy not because her members were all without exception holy, sinless men, but because sanctification is the power that God exercises in her in spite of human sinfulness, he deals implicitly with the question of the reality of this exercise of power, so that the dilemma of objective or subjective is abolished. Cf. on the dream of all the ages, which will not become a reality until the new earth.

of not only in a "personal" context. Diverse things and affairs are designated in their separateness as holy: for example, holy ground,[11] a holy city (Isa. 48:2; Matt. 4:5; Rev. 21:2, 10), a holy mountain (Isa. 11:9), a holy temple (Isa. 64:11), or holy offerings and things (I Sam. 21:4; Neh. 10:33). Also when holy persons are spoken of, the aspect of separation dominates — the directedness to a particular goal.[12] Not wrongly, holiness has often been spoken of as a relational concept. In contrast to a moral or ethical interpretation, an objective, relational holiness was spoken of on the grounds of the Old Testament data, and opposition was offered against the moralistic endeavor for holiness. No matter how correct this defense against moralism may be, one may clearly not conclude from the relational aspect of separation to an isolated "objective" holiness as a relation separated from God's intention in the setting apart. The relation that becomes manifest in the setting apart is full of a holy, unique dynamic; it takes on concrete form in the service of the Lord. It may not be understood from a dilemma between external and internal. This "relation" has nothing to do with emptiness and formality, which belong to many human relations, but it is creative and re-creative, dynamic-relational. That appears clearly when warnings are often sounded against isolation of the "external," as if the relation in that sense has religious significance. This warning has been especially directed against deterioration to the "external" cult.

Bavinck points out that many in his time began to conceive of sanctification in an external, cultic sense. In contrast, he points to its "ethical" meaning on the basis of the indwelling of the Spirit.[13] Thereby, a direction was pointed out beyond many dilemmas (external-internal; cultic-ethical), and the New Testament gives clear confirmation of it in many ways. No escape is possible here anymore into an external objectivity, which could be placed in opposition to the personal sanctification of life. But the New Testament definitely does not stand in contrast to the Old Testament on this point. When Israel is

11. Ex. 3:5; Josh. 5:15; Matt. 24:15; Acts 6:13; 21:28. Cf. *TDNT*, I, 90f.; Bavinck, *Geref. Dog.*, II, 185; IV, 236ff.
12. Cf. Num. 16:7: "the man whom the Lord chooses shall be the holy one." Cf. F. Kattenbusch, *Das Apostolische Symbol*, II, 684ff.
13. H. Bavinck, *Geref. Dog.*, IV, 237. Cf. on what the relation brings with it and on conformity and glorification. Sanctification consists fully in being conformed to the image of the Son. Cf. further R. Schippers, "Cultus en Ethos in het N.T.," *Arcana Revelata*, 1951, pp. 105ff., 117; H.K. La Rondelle, *Perfection and Perfectionism*, 1971, pp. 120ff.

set apart, we perceive nothing of an externality that characterizes this relation. Rather, this relation is inseparably connected to Israel's concrete life on earth. And because it is so much the opposite of all abstractness and emptiness, it can be said: "The Lord will establish you as a people *holy to himself*, as he has sworn to you, *if* you keep the commandments of the Lord your God, and walk in his ways" (Deut. 28:9; cf. Lev. 20:7f.). The unique relation of being "God's own people" is focused directly on Israel's conduct. We find this same directedness in the whole of the New Testament, where we meet with the call to sanctification and perfection as a summons to intense activity in the midst of life as the holy people of God.[14] The command "You shall be holy, for I am holy" appears in the New Testament as a citation from the Old Testament (I Pet. 1:16; Lev. 11:44; 19:2; 20:7), where it already stands vis-à-vis uncleanness (Lev. 11:44) in reference to concrete life in all human relationships (19:34). In the New Testament, the will of God for sanctification is contrasted emphatically to all life in darkness and sin (I Thess. 4:3f.). The way to sanctification is designated in the "conduct" of the saints in harmony with their "being set apart," which must take form in countless ways (cf. Rom. 16:2). Therein lies the unprecedented urgency of all New Testament admonition, which is directed to sanctification of the whole life as the clear purpose of calling and election (cf. John 15:16). Likewise, election in Christ is directed to holiness and blamelessness before God (Eph. 1:4). And the believers as saints and loved ones will put on inner mercy, goodness, lowliness, meekness, and patience (4:2, 24). There can be no doubt about the profound origin of this concrete sanctification in the New Testament, since the new man is described as created in righteousness and holiness (4:24). There is no dilemma anywhere, because precisely this origin, which is full of depth and grace, calls life out of darkness.

14. E. Fuchs ("Die volkommene Gewissheit," *N.T. Studien für R. Bultmann*, 1954, pp. 130ff.) opposes Matt. 5:48 ("You must be perfect") to the "ethical" interpretation and points to the rich young ruler (Matt. 19:16, 20: "What must I do?" and "What do I still lack?"). That Matt. 5:48 refers to the relation to God excludes isolated "human self-development," but not sanctification of life in and on the basis of this new relation. On this passage see further La Rondelle, *op. cit.*, pp. 159ff.; P.J. du Plessis, *Teleios. The Idea of Perfection in the N.T.*, 1959.

The concreteness of holiness

Frequently, in reaction against moralism and legalism, sanctification has been made secondary, as an "application" of forensic justification, whereby one really thought of a duality more than of a unity. Then, in exegesis of many biblical texts, the intention, it is said, was not so much moral or ethical as "religious." There is a motif in this that must be recognized in contrast to a new works-righteousness, but the concreteness of sanctification, so clear in the New Testament, unintentionally fades here. And the unbreakable unity that is evident from the image of the good tree with good fruit is broken. It is fruit that befits the great repentance *(metánoia* — Matt. 3:8; cf. 7:19) — in contrast to the fig tree that is without fruit (Matt. 21:19, 43). The relation between the radically new relationship to Christ and the fruit is so close that the tree can be known by its fruits (7:20; Col. 1:10; Titus 3:14; II Pet. 1:8). They are fruits through fellowship with Christ (John 15:4) and by the power of the Spirit (Gal. 5:22). The creative relation is never neglected and the disciples are called clean "by the word which I have spoken to you" (John 15:3). But precisely at this point, abiding in the vine becomes visible in the critical, warning analysis of the vine and branches (15:2). In the New Testament, life is important in the eyes of God. Discipline on that life is related ultimately to sharing in God's holiness,[15] as in the exceptional statement in II Peter, where partaking in the divine nature is related to sanctification, which takes on visible form in the midst of life.[16] Due to numerous factors and feelings, we may find it strange that the summons resounds in the New Testament to sanctify oneself.[17] But this lack of worry is possible because of

15. Heb. 12:10: "that we may share his holiness." The phrase reminds us also of becoming partakers of the Holy Spirit already in this life (Heb. 6:4 — *métochoi*). R. Asting *(Die Heiligkeit im Urchristentum,* 1930, p. 255) speaks of a "mystical-ethical quality' in connection with the promise of seeing the Lord (Heb. 12:14). In II Cor. 1:12, Paul speaks about behaving in the world "with holiness and godly sincerity . . . by the grace of God." The union of holiness and godly sincerity *(eilikrineia)* pointedly designates the concreteness of sanctification. Heb. 12:10 accentuates this concreteness — in the usefulness of discipline — in a special way.

16. II Pet. 1:4 *(theias koinōnoì phúseōs).* Even when one does not see this in the least as a "deification," one cannot minimize the significance of this outlook. Cf. the contrast with the blindness in II Pet. 1:9.

17. I John 3:3 *(hagnízei heautòn).* Cf. K. Barth, *C.D.,* IV/1, p. 101, against the "self-sanctifying as the filling out of the justification which comes to man by God."

deep connections — namely, those of hoping in Him. Interest in concrete conduct is not in the least an emptying of the concept of holiness,[18] but an understanding of the meaning of being set apart, which seizes life and sets it in motion, admonishing it to strive for that holiness without which no one will see the Lord.[19] And that striving is contrasted to failing to obtain grace (Heb. 12:15)!

In the reality of this power of grace, of being led along under Christ's liberating lordship,[20] everything depends on whether or not this liberation is understood along the way that is clearly marked. It is the way of an innocent and blameless life in the world, without grumbling or questioning, and without blemish (Phil. 2:14f.) — "in all your conduct" in contrast to earlier conduct (I Pet. 1:15, 18). In spite of all the dangers of "moralism," the separation is without doubt directed to another, different life,[21] as light versus darkness: "once you were darkness, but now you are light in the Lord" (Eph. 5:8), sons of light and of the day (I Thess. 5:5), in wakefulness and soberness, and thus belonging to the day that is coming (5:8 — *hēmeis dè hēméras óntes*). Clearly, every escape into an "objective" or "cultic" framework is out of the question. It is an externalization that overlooks life, because the relation becomes a contentless affair.[22] Every externalization or ritualization neglects the warning of the Old and New Testaments against the misunderstanding that cleanness is separate from life. Conduct is mentioned con-

18. Cf. O. Michel, *Der Brief an die Hebräer*, p. 301.
19. Heb. 12:14 (*diōkō*). Cf. I Thess. 5:15 (seeking to do good). Cf. also my *Faith and Sanctification*, 1952, pp. 101ff.; *TDNT*, II, 230, on "the striving of Christians." That this language "is a feature shared with OT and Rabbinic piety and Hellenistic moralism" and is carried out further in "greater intensity and depth" does not offer any clarification of this striving.
20. Cf. P. Stuhlmacher, *Gottes Gerechtigkeit bei Paulus*, 1965, with important points of view with regard to the nature of God's liberating justice and with regard to "synergism" in distinction from the activity that is called up in this justice — although, in my view, Stuhlmacher sees too many symptoms of a falling back into synergism, for instance, in James (pp. 191ff.) and in Luke (pp. 194ff.).
21. When Barth, with others, sees the difference as "not something positive," but as the "with fear and trembling" (Phil. 2:12), it is difficult to see this as a dilemma (the conduct), although what Barth means is clear: "in the renunciation in principle of wishing to surmount other persons" (*Erklärung des Philipperbriefes*, p. 71). Cf. his exegesis of Rom. 12 in his *The Epistle to the Romans*.
22. Cf. the sharp polemic in the New Testament against externalization (Matt. 23:25ff.; Luke 11:41). Cf. *TDNT*, III, s.v. *katharós*.

tinuously "in newness of life" (Rom. 6:4; cf. I Kings 8:58; Ezek. 33, 34), in restoration of life "full and unreserved self-offering to God"[23] in the midst of all the relations of earthly life. How much God's call is directed to that life is evident from the negative boundary: "God has not called us for uncleanness, but in holiness" (I Thess. 4:7). This concreteness of the new life,[24] which is called on the basis of the promise to make holiness perfect in opposition to all pollution (II Cor. 7:1), perhaps comes to the fore most pointedly in the reference to the possibility of a striking holiness that can be seen in concrete deeds. Via that seeing, concrete life is related to a specific goal: glorifying God, since light shines in the darkness and is recognized as the light of God.[25] There is something undeniably impressive in the new life of sanctification, something radiating that automatically draws attention to itself (cf. Acts 5:13f.; I Pet. 3:2).

One has frequently asked how this seeing and perceiving, this recognition of the origin, is possible. How are ways opened here to the glory of God? But the scope of sanctification is designated in a very clear way;[26] and, as preaching, it precedes all reflection when the new life is designated as the place of far-reaching decisions.[27] However, this is not simply a seeing of light as contemplation of a remarkable phenomenon of light, but this light is also experienced in human relationships. That

23. *TDNT*, III, 425.
24. Cf. James 1:27; Eph. 5:26. Concrete life in contrast to "merely relational" life has always played an important role in discussions about justification. Cf. my *Faith and Sanctification*, 1952, pp. 90f., on the change due to grace. The "relation" also played a large role in Rome's earlier polemic against the Reformation. The Reformation supposedly did not know any "inherent righteousness" (*justitia inhaerens*), but only a relation that remained external (the cloak of righteousness on an unchanged life). Cf. below, chapter 13, on the *simul justus et peccator*.
25. Matt. 5:16. Cf. my "Heiliging en Dienst," *Kernwoorden in het Christelijk Geloof*, 1970, pp. 55ff.
26. That seeing does not automatically lead to recognition is evident from the interpretation of what is seen when, for instance, Christ casts out demons (Mark 3:22). But Christ exposes this interpretation as senseless and contradictory (3:23ff.). In Church history seeing came up for discussion in connection with the heretical martyrs besides those from the Church (von Campenhausen, *op. cit.*, pp. 164ff.). Cf. Rahner (*op. cit.*, pp. 76ff.), who speaks of "an inner uncertainty and embarrassment"; and W. Bartz, "Heroische Heiligkeit und Martyrium aüsserhalb der Kirche," Ratzinger-Fries, *Einsicht und Glaube*, 1962, pp. 321ff.
27. Cf. H.M. Matter, *De Brief aan de Philippenzen*, 1965, pp. 63ff., on the shining light and the missionary motif it contains.

happens when, against all the expectations of the persecutor, he is blessed (Rom. 12:14), evil is not repaid with evil (12:17), and the enemy is fed and given drink (12:20). This is not a Pharisaic desire to be seen (Matt. 6:1; 23:5), but a dynamic of sanctification in deeds of mercy and love, truth and peace, which must go out to all men (Rom. 12:17), since evil is overcome with good (12:21), falsehood with truth, and hate with love. What happens here has nothing to do with a striving for a heroic, spectacular holiness, but has to do with the Church's readiness for that sanctification by which life is blessed.[28] When we consider all of this — i.e., the clarity of sanctification in its radical, all-embracing character,[29] whereby the utmost is required because the utmost was given[30] — the question arises as to how the Church has dared to speak so positively and emphatically in her credo. If every escape into a sterile objectivity was out of the question for the Church on account of the evidentness of the New Testament, and if it was also unthinkable in the context of faith in the Holy Spirit and the forgiveness of sins, then the confession of holiness and the communio sanctorum must be taken seriously. We pointed out earlier that there are different interpretations of the article about the communio sanctorum — namely, whether the intention is a fellowship of saints (sancti) or a fellowship of holy things (sancta), particularly the Lord's Supper. Even when the possibility of the sacramental aspect of communion is not excluded, an interpretation is not thereby legitimized that would put the statement of the credo in an "objective" or "institutional" framework. One may assume — also on account of the concern

28. We are in a different sphere here than in the subtle distinction of common or mediocre holiness (Balduinus, De Heiligheid der Kerk, pp. 34ff.). Cf. on heroic, charismatic, and higher holiness "in some souls" as the highest triumph of Christ in the "heroes of virtue," to which only a few belong.

29. See especially H.N. Ridderbos, Paul, pp. 265ff., on the totalitarian point of view vis-à-vis sin as a totalitarian regime, on the posse non peccare (p. 272), perfection (p. 271), and not being tempted beyond one's strength (p. 269; I Cor. 10:13). Further, see idem, "De Heiligheid der Gemeente Volgens het N.T.," Vox Theol., 1948, pp. 187ff. See below, chapter 13.

30. One clearly derogates from this if one, in the discussions on sanctification and justification, warns against accentuating sanctification too strongly. In the light of the New Testament, it is not a question of accents — the totalitarian New Testament — but sanctification can be spoken of wrongly. Indicative and imperative are not mutually limiting aspects of the salvation in Christ.

for the concrete form of holiness in the Church — that the *credo* has not ended up in an external escapism, neglecting all personal aspects of sanctification. Thus, reflection on the emphatic *credo*, without further interpretation, retains its urgency. That is even more the case since we meet such further interpretation in practically all instances where the *credo* is mentioned. For instance, it can be pointed out that the Church is rightly called holy, but that it is nevertheless not a "perfect" holiness![31] One can even speak of a universal admission which expresses itself in the striking phenomenon that one hastens to remove every misunderstanding that can arise about the seemingly simple and univocal "holy Church."

We sometimes get the impression that what has been given with one hand is taken away with the other. For instance, van Ruler speaks about the Church as the cathedral of love[32] and the reality of love in the world, filled as she is with an immeasurable light, the embodiment of joy.[33] But he adds that the Church is the place where Christ desires to dwell with sinners, and "therefore, one must not expect too much from the Church and Christians."[34] That is a remarkable conclusion for those who, from these characterizations of the Church and from the *credo*, do expect much from the Church! Again and again, we perceive something of a certain lyric in language about the Church, but this lyric obviously does not exclude something more, something that seems to be in tension with that lyric, from being said. Just as Bavinck calls catholicity "of arresting beauty" and then, nevertheless, complains about what has come of it "after a history of 18 centuries,"[35] it seems to be the same also with respect to the Church's holiness. We hear continuously of tension, and the distinction between an ideal Church and the empirical Church describes what the Church ought to have been and what she is in reality.[36] We get the

---

31. Cf. the "Catechism of the Church of Geneva," *Library of Christian Classics*, XXII, 103: "But is this holiness which you attribute to the Church now perfect? Not yet: that is, so long as it battles in this world." Cf. H.C., Q. 114, on the "holiest men" and the small beginning of obedience.
32. A.A. van Ruler, *Ik Geloof*, 1968, p. 132.
33. Van Ruler, "De Pretentie van der Kerk," *Wending*, 1958.
34. Van Ruler, *Ik Geloof*, p. 132. Cf. the warning not to speak about the Church too romantically and too idealistically.
35. H. Bavinck, *Katholiciteit*, 1968², pp. 10, 31.
36. Cf. H. Küng, *The Church*, pp. 3ff., without thereby intending two Churches, because the essence of the Church can be seen only in the historical form (p. 5).

impression everywhere that the *credo* of holiness is surrounded
by question marks and the "lyric" is disturbed by dissonance.
Apparently, the *credo* cannot be understood apart from further
elucidation.[37] What does this frequently "dialectical" speech
about the Church signify? For, apparently, the *credo ecclesiam* involves much concern and shame and "it can and necessarily will
be a very critical *credo*."[38] Is the *credo* perhaps more an expression of hope, nostalgia for the ideal Church, the recognition of a normative standard, than it is a description of a real
Church? The nostalgia and shame can be clearly perceived in
nearly all ecclesiological considerations and, precisely because
of that, the simple word "holy" attracts our attention again
and again. That the Church has confessed holiness in spite of
all the shadows is undoubtedly connected to the New Testament
picture, where the Church is also spoken of lyrically as the holy
people, the temple of the Spirit, the bride, the body of Christ.

Fascination and newness

If the Church formulated her *credo* in this light, referring
to that unique dimension of the Church, and if she knew of
the forgiveness of sin and of the Holy Spirit, then this credo
will only have meaning and significance if the Church, in spite
of all the question marks, exhibits something of that reality in
Christ which gave occasion to the aspect of fascination in New
Testament speech about the Church. In connection with the
forms of appearance of "the holy" in the world, Rudolf Otto
has spoken on one hand of the tremendous, the numinous, and
the awe-awakening, and on the other hand of the fascinating.
He considered both of these elements *(tremendum* and *fascinans)*
to be united in a "harmony of contrasts."[39] Without going into
Otto's view of the holy and the Holy, one can ask, in light of
the New Testament, whether there is not reason to bring the

37. Cf. K.H. Miskotte's splendid "lyric" on the Church, betrayed by all
human powers and, nevertheless, the ark "in which men from all nations embark for God and His Kingdom" (*Om de Waarheid te Zeggen*,
1971, p. 57). Thus we can return consoled "to our place and our work
in the Church." Cf. Huub Oosterhuis, "Hymne aan de Kerk," *Wending*,
1958, pp. 516ff., on the Church as our daily bread, table and cup,
silver-fleet and property, the perfect house, the pillar of fire in the
night of time, and God's new beginning. The descriptions end in a
prayer for forgiveness on account of blindness and error.
38. H. Küng, *The Church*, p. 36.
39. R. Otto, *The Idea of the Holy*, pp. 31ff.

holiness of the Church into connection with the *fascinans*.[40] In our time the question seems to be strange indeed, for the attitude of the world to the Church is more one of rejection and criticism than fascination. The connection with the *fascinans* seems even less possible, since the Church has learned more and more that opposition to and displeasure with her cannot be explained *a priori* from the relationship to Christ and from an appeal to His word, "If the world hates you, know that it has hated me before it hated you" (John 15:18f.). Indeed, there is a parallel here between Him and His disciples, since there is a stumbling block in His revelation that can affect His disciples too. But that does not give the Church a key to explain all opposition against her and her suffering in the world.[41] What Christ says of Himself cannot be said *a priori* of the Church: "They hated me without a cause" (John 15:25; cf. 8:46; II Cor. 5:21). Whoever draws rash conclusions here must lapse into self-praise and self-complacency in the Church, understanding the *credo* from an ecclesiological apologetic that simply points to the Church in her glorious aspects, in her unquestionable holiness as a sign of truth and credibility.[42]

Nevertheless, even he who sees the gigantic dangers surrounding the "holy Church" will have to give account of the aspect of fascination of holiness about which Otto, not unjustly, has spoken and which confronts us so clearly in the New Testament. We are thinking of the relatedness indicated in the *credo* by Kattenbusch "with heaven, with the Spirit, with God Himself" and with mystery.[43] Whoever considers that mystery with its aspects of fascination must ask the question of whether the Church's *credo* does not also compel us to think in this direction, no matter how strange it may seem. In the face of the dangers

---

40. Otto *(ibid.)* describes the *fascinans* also with the words "as something uniquely attractive" or "a potent charm."

41. Cf. the distinction between suffering reproach "for the name of Christ" and suffering differently because of one's own guilt (I Pet. 4:14f.). In the first case, the suffering is connected with glory: "the spirit of glory and of God rests upon you."

42. In my view, this danger was real when Vatican I spoke of the Church and what is present in her "to make the credibility of the Christian faith evident," namely, her "marvelous propagation," her "exalted sanctity," and her "inexhaustible fruitfulness" — all of which are an "irrefutable proof" (Denz., 1794; *TCT*, 68).

43. F. Kattenbusch, *Das Apost. Symbol*, I, 683: "When the Church is termed *hágia*, it means that she is of a station that has something mysterious to it — even displays in some way something wondrous; where a *hágion* is, there is at the same time a *mustérion*."

of self-praise and self-complacency, a tendency can be traced in the Church to speak about the Church only in whispers, due to a realization of the contrast between the Church and the *fascinans*. Perhaps one can still be impressed by the eschatological aspect of holiness and glory that we see in a remarkable statement in the New Testament: at the second coming, Christ will be marveled at in all who have believed and so will be glorified in His saints (II Thess. 1:10 — *thaumasthénai*). But this direct relatedness of the "saints" to Christ and His glory[44] seems to be faraway, strange, and scarcely capable of being brought into connection with the Church in the present. Whenever we reflect on the *fascinans*, we are inclined to think not of the Church, but of the appearance of Christ with all those facets that show us, in the midst of much opposition and aversion, that there are reactions of astonishment correlate to the *fascinans* that has gone out from Him. Not only is He recognized as the Holy One of God (Mark 1:24; Acts 3:14; Rev. 3:7), but also — not in radiating glory, but in His humility — He evokes amazement, as with the disciples, who followed Him along the way of suffering with amazement (Mark 10:32). Likewise, we read that the multitude marveled at the revelation of His power and glory (5:20; 7:37; Luke 11:14). This "motif of astonishment"[45] becomes visible in confrontation with surprising, impressive, extraordinary things (Luke 5:26 — *parádoxa*), but also in reactions of deep humility in the light of Christ's revealing presence (5:8). It is the *fascinans* that lights up also in reactions of exuberance about and delight in the salvation that has appeared in Him. The result is countless superlatives, which are signs of the *fascinans* of salvation.[46]

With respect to this *fascinans*, there is no mention of a critical *credo* but only of a *credo* that leads to glorifying God (Luke 5:26). But when we reflect on the Church, the connection with the *fascinans* seems to become much more difficult, if not impossible. Nevertheless, with respect to the *credo* in the light

44. Cf. Calvin, *Commentaries on the Epistles of Paul to the Philippians, Colossians, and Thessalonians*, p. 318: Christ will come to be glorified in the saints, "that is, that he may irradiate them with his glory." Cf. H.M. Bolkestein, *De Brieven aan de Thessal.*, 1970, p. 183, on the glory of Christ "not outside of the Church, but precisely in the Church."
45. *TDNT*, III, 37.
46. This is so especially in the Pauline letters, where salvation becomes visible in its unutterable, incomparable, and overwhelming aspects, for instance, in Eph. 1:19; 2:7; 3:18ff.; Phil. 3:8; I Cor. 2:9; II Cor. 7:4; 9:14. Cf. I Pet. 1:8, 12.

of the New Testament, one must reflect on this *fascinans*. Whoever shrinks back here implicitly submits a gravamen against the *credo*, thus withdrawing the Church from the marvelous light to which she has been called out of darkness, full of calling and responsibility. Naturally, it is possible to transpose Christ's statement and promise, "You are the light of the world" (Matt. 5:14), into a pretentious declaration: "*We are* the light of the world." As the history of the Church proves, anything can happen here, and all is lost in a Church that glorifies herself, thereby turning the *fascinans* into the opposite. But there is a different *fascinans*, which rests in the acceptance of the gift, the nearness of the Lord,[47] in humility, in nostalgia, and in striving for the sanctification that is seen and experienced by others. One must not think here of the formal category of the "extraordinary," although that can be an inducement to astonishment in the New Testament. There can only be a *fascinans* that makes the Church transparent in the outlook on what her reality in this world in Christ signifies. Then the stumbling block can be conquered. Then it is also clear that this *fascinans* can only be a reality in all the connections in which it appears in the New Testament. They are the connections of deep humility, of an understanding of indicative and imperative, of the confession of guilt and nostalgia, and of the blessing on concrete, everyday life by the power of the Spirit. In the New Testament, the life of sanctification is brought into connection not only with eschatological salvation — the vision of God *(visio Dei)*[48] — but also with the light that radiates in this world and causes the darkness to pass away.

In analyzing what is actually fascinating, one has pointed out that the *fascinans* has usually been connected to what is new, to something surprising that was outside our horizon of expectation, and, especially, to "what had never before been."[49]

---

47. In John 17:22, after all that has been said about the glory of Christ (17:1, 5, 10), Christ speaks of the glory that has been given to Him as given to His disciples, namely, "to do things that could not happen by the power of men, a power which he who exercises it causes to operate for the glorification of God" (H. Kittel, *Die Herrlichkeit Gottes,* 1934, pp. 258ff.). Cf. the opposite in falling short of the glory of God (Rom. 3:23).

48. Heb. 12:14; Matt. 5:8; Rev. 22:4. Cf. my *The Return of Christ,* chapter 12.

49. Cf. H. Mühlen, *Entsakralisierung. Ein epochales Schlagwort in seiner Bedeutung für die Zukunft der Chr. Religion,* 1971, pp. 20ff. (with reference to technology and space travel).

If that new and surprising element undeniably belongs to the *fascinans*,[50] then one can ask whether the Church should be brought into connection with it, since she seems to be so closely connected to the past as the guardian of tradition. Undeniably, the Church has often had difficulty in interpreting the "old" and the "new," particularly when the impression was aroused that she could not cope with other times, becoming confused by them rather than making clear that the newness in Christ contains a promise "for the present life and also for the life to come" (I Tim. 4:8) and that, therefore, the Church had the calling to distinguish herself radically — the setting apart — from the glorifying of "the old" and "the past." No matter how difficult the Church's way frequently seems to be in analyzing the visible and invisible motives of history — the spirit of the times — her unique setting apart forces her to a continuous defense of the power and splendor of newness, which, in Christ, characterize life and make her capable of breaking through all the caricatures of a false conservatism.

In every historical development, we encounter a process of old and new, tradition and transformation. Tradition always plays a role, as does the way in which the past is thought to have significance for present and future.[51] With respect to the Church, which does not stand apart from the historical process, one can see clearly that a dangerous dilemma often arose between emphases on the old or on the new. That dilemma has always led to strong polarizations in the history of the Church. One could shrink from the dimensions of a new time, withdrawing within the boundaries of what was old and trusted; or one could be captivated by the fascinating aspect of a new time,[52] then forgetting that the words "old" and "new" are restamped by the gospel and thus refer to a clarity that elimi-

50. Cf. the new things that Yahweh will do (a way in the wilderness and rivers in the desert; cf. Isa. 42:9), leading here already to a new song (42:10; 48:6-8), and requiring that one's glance be turned away from former things (43:18ff.).

51. Cf. G.W. Locher, *Transformatie en Traditie*, 1971; J. Verkuyl, H.G. Schulte-Nordholt, *Responsible Revolution*, 1974 (the subtitle includes the word "transforming").

52. One can perceive that clearly in Kuyper, who was captivated by the "consciousness-form of our age" — to which he wanted to raise one's own confessional consciousness (*Principles of Sacred Theology*, p. 679). He had an open eye for the power of what is new versus blindness for new commissions (*Conservatisme en Orthodoxie*, 1871, pp. 7ff.).

nates every polarization.[53] Only if newness is rightly understood can the suggestion be resisted that the Church is related exclusively to the past. This resistance finds its foundation in the fact that, in the New Testament, salvation is connected with unmistakable clarity to radical newness. That newness may be a decisive aspect in the eschatological perspective — the *new* Jerusalem (Rev. 3:12), the *new* earth (II Pet. 3:13), *new* wine (Mark 14:25), and the *new* name (Rev. 2:17). But that does not mean that this fascinating newness of "the glorious end of the revelation of God's salvation"[54] is of no significance for the Church, which is on her way to this disclosure when God will make all things new (Rev. 21:5). This connection has come to expression in many ways, as a "shining" of that glory of newness into this life.[55] but no one has expressed it in a more radical and more fascinating way than Paul did when he beckoned to behold: "the old has passed away, behold, the new has come" (II Cor. 5:17).

In light of this Pauline "lyric" about new life (Eph. 4:24), the new creation (II Cor. 5:17; Gal. 6:15), and the new man (Col. 3:10; Eph. 2:15), one can say that, although "the past" and "tradition" are not lost in oblivion for Paul, whatever is "venerable"[56] still has to legitimize itself for this new time. Only so can it be incorporated in the continuity of life in Christ on the way to the future. For this life is no longer characterized by what is "old" and "antiquated," but by a radical newness. Paul connects it to the freedom received in Christ (Gal. 5:1), another aspect of those wonderful qualifications of the time of salvation that has dawned. They take away the impression that the Church is concerned with the old in a way that would limit

---

53. Various polarizations can be related to characterological and personal components, both in the direction of the old (preference for every status quo because of the stubborn virulence of what is well known and habitual; cf. J. Moltmann, "Die Kategorie Novum in der Chr. Theol.," *Perspektiven der Theol.*, 1968, p. 175) and in that of the new. Cf. the interest of the Athenians for Paul's new teaching and the strange things that he brought to their ears, because of their continual desire to hear or tell something new (Acts 17:19ff.). They end up mocking the one thing that is new: the resurrection of the dead (17:32).

54. *TDNT*, III, 449.

55. *Ibid.*, on *kainós* as "a slogan of the reality of salvation which we know already in Christ." Cf. Ridderbos, *Paul*, pp. 52ff., 223ff.; P. Stuhlmacher, "Gegenwart und Zukunft in der paulin. Eschatologie," *Z.Th.K.*, 1967, pp. 423ff.

56. *TDNT*, I, 486f., *s.v. archaios.*

joy about what has come.[57] Evidently, holiness — the setting apart of the Church *in* Christ and *for* newness of life — has been radically misunderstood if the impression is given that the Church hangs inertly on to the past as such, taking it along the way without true perspective and without the powers of the coming age.[58] The calling to take away this misunderstanding in the world can be fulfilled only in the midst of life under the warning that a "tear" *(schisma)* occurs when a piece of unshrunk cloth is sewed on an old garment or new wine is put into old wineskins, by which the wine is lost (Mark 2:21f.). When we think of "schism," we usually think of the division of the Church, but there is also another schism — although it can be closely connected to schism in the Church! — that is connected to old and new and to the way newness is understood as the mystery of the Church's life. Here, if anywhere, a gravamen against the *credo* has obviously been denied us, since the Church in the *credo* stands under the depth of the indicative. Whenever that is forgotten, the outlook is also lost on the commandment that is not burdensome (I John 5:3). Then it is experienced as a yoke and burden, and that same impression is awakened in all who are outside.

Just as Israel could "forget" the exodus (its meaning and liberation) and could desire to return to the land of Egypt, preferring to die there (Ex. 16:3; Num. 14:2), or could ask in the present: "Where is the Lord who brought us up from the land of Egypt?" (Jer. 2:6), so too, the splendor of the new can fade in the Church. This "falling back" is portrayed by the Word of God as dangerous to life, because there is a fundamental misunderstanding of the gospel, which places the Church in the great transition: "The darkness is passing away and the true light is already shining."[59] This newness of light and of the commandment (I John 2:8) puts the Church under the high pressure of a new responsibility. It is this responsibility that she accepts in the *credo* of holiness and must learn over and over again. Apart from this newness, the Church walks along

---

57. Therefore, there is no antithesis in the relation of old and new in the Old and New Testaments. Cf. Lam. 3:22f. (God's mercies are new every morning). This text reminds one involuntarily of Kierkegaard's views on the meaning and joy of "repetition."

58. Heb. 6:5. The apostasy is designated here in the warning about not being able to be restored again *(pálin anakainízein)*.

59. I John 2:8. Cf. G. Klein, "Das wahre Licht scheint schon. Beobachtungen zur Zeit- und Geschichtserfahrung einer urchristlichen Schule," *Z.Th.K.*, 1971, pp. 216ff.

ways of tradition without light, of words without power, of customs without surprising, liberating deeds. The "humble" gravamen against the credo is an escape from this "being" of the Church, from this commission and this nostalgia, from the recollection of the Church's origin. It makes room for a return of darkness (cf. Luke 11:24-26), which expresses itself in life in hate of brothers and in not knowing where one is going (I John 2:10f.). In contrast to this darkness stands the light of the setting apart, of sanctification as the light of the Church, full of remembrance of the house founded by God for an unlimited escape, in which the afflicted of His people can hide (Isa. 14:32). At the same time, it is the perspective of the salutary presence of God,[60] the outlook on the remarkable event that is pointed to by Zechariah in the midst of the transition from the old to the new temple: ten men from the nations of every tongue will take hold of the robe of a Jew, saying, "Let us go with you, for we have heard that God is with you" (8:23). This perspective is not that of an "objective" setting apart, for it becomes visible against the background of life: truth versus lies, salvation versus evil, judgments that make for peace in the gates, veracity and the love of truth and peace (8:16-17, 19). Here is a promised and awaited *fascinans* as the prelude along the ways of the Church, which lead not to her own glory, but to the glorifying of God (Matt. 5:16).

The caricatures of the *fascinans* are countless; they are correlates of false boasting. In watchfulness against these dangers, the *fascinans* will not become a pretentious, worldly attitude, whereby one's own claim takes away more and more attention from the claims placed on the Church.[61] But, for the sake of the Church's whole life, one will also have to preserve, pronounce, and clarify the *credo*, precisely in the midst of many disappointments and many "experiences of the Church."[62] In

---

60. This presence of the holiness of God signifies the radical "no" against all darkness and fruitlessness. This holiness is not to be understood as sinister *tremendum*, but as directed salutarily. Cf. K. Barth, *C.D.*, II/1, pp. 363ff.

61. O. Weber, *op. cit.*, II, 619.

62. Cf. H. Urs von Balthasar, "Kirchen-erfahrung dieser Zeit," in Daniélou-Vorgrimler, *Sentire Ecclesiam*, 1961, pp. 743ff., in a in many respects disconcerting honesty and in a protest against all self-glory, without abandoning the *fascinans*: "where the darkest tragedy of universal history splits open, the deepest fountain of love must also bubble up" (p. 767). See also K. Rahner, "Dogmat. Randbemerkungen zur 'Kirchenfrömmigkeit,'" *Sentire Ecclesiam*, pp. 769ff.

that way, one will love the Church, placed under the discipline of that *fascinans* that is no longer a hindrance to the true shining of the light, but coincides with that light. After all that has been considered with respect to the meaning of holiness, one can ask whether all of this nevertheless does not fall under the judgment of romanticism and idealism. Can it be viewed as anything other than unreal? Must we not reflect deeper and longer about this "holy"? Is it not intriguing that this word — especially next to the word "unity"! — has always needed further interpretation? From the *credo,* one cannot suffice with a recollection of a certain self-evidence of sin and the lack of sanctification; one cannot reassure oneself by ascertaining a riddle of sin *(mysterium iniquitatis)* that has remained and will remain in this dispensation. Rather, one must reflect seriously on questions that constantly come up for discussion in the Church and that are related to what presents itself to us as the strange complex of holiness and sin.

CHAPTER THIRTEEN

HOLINESS AND SIN

IF IT IS APPARENT FROM THE CHURCH'S LIFE IT-self, especially from her speaking about her holiness, that she constantly thinks it necessary to interpret the *credo* further, then there is every reason to reflect on this remarkable fact. Even if this further elucidation is obviously connected to the reproach of self-complacency and self-overestimation, the actual problematic is not yet explained fully. Precisely if the Church is not prepared to abandon the *credo* at this point (and thinks she can produce good reasons for not doing so), one can still not deny that there is something strange and unexpected in the admitted connection of holiness and sin and in the characterization of holiness as "imperfect holiness." One can recall here what Kuyper once wrote. He said that the world goes better than expected, and the Church goes worse than expected.[1] He speaks of a conflict between our notion and reality. That applies with respect to the world, where we meet many good, beautiful things. They waken jealousy and force the question on us of how they can be harmonized with the confession of the radical, total character of the corruption of sin. In explaining this state of affairs, the starting point of Kuyper's doctrine of common grace, Kuyper deals also with the notion of the Church and her reality. From the suppositions of what the Church is, according to the Church's confession, one could expect that the Church, in contrast to the world, would be determined "by an ideal, holy life of love."[2] But, understandably, the opinion that the Church was worse "than one from the side of Christianity wanted to have believed in theory" became established. Kuyper speaks here not only of a conflict but also of a "mystery," lying

1. A. Kuyper, *De Gemene Gratie*, II, 9; cf. I, 11.
2. *Ibid.*, II, 9.

in the fact "that the Church remains so much below her esti-
mated value."[3] We get the impression "of a saving, divine grace,
but in such a way that its fruit and effect *disappoint* us."[4] Thus,
Kuyper is captivated not only by a world that goes better than
expected, but also by a Church that is disappointing.[5] On
account of that, Kuyper considers it necessary to reflect more
deeply on the confession, for faith as a world-conquering power
does not seem to tally with the conclusions that can be drawn
from this "power."[6] There is "an unknown power in play"; it
is a mystery "to whose disclosure you continue to be called."

In the history of the Church, we do encounter interest in
the world's "going better than expected." Nevertheless, the
Church was faced first of all by her own problematic — sin and
imperfection in the light of her positive *credo*. Sometimes we
even get the impression that there is a certain self-evidence
here. We are thinking of many witnesses who are somewhat
amazed that the feeling exists that there is a possibility of total
perfection during earthly life. Even if one does not use the word
self-evidence, one is still inclined to speak of the "inevitability"
of sin, the "remaining" sin in the individual believer and in
the Church. Not unjustly, the remark has been made that the
Church has still not reflected enough on sin in the Church and
that we face a far-reaching problem here that could be of great
significance "existentially-religiously."[7] In any case, one does not
get any further by referring to "the mystery," the *mysterium
iniquitatis*.[8] And Kuyper wants to "unveil" the mystery, obviously intending to indicate connections that will make the facts,
at least to some degree, clearer. Naturally, that applies not
simply to the imperfection of individuals but also to that of the
Church with her "attribute" of holiness. Due to undeniable
criticism from outside and from internal experience, the Church
has to give account of the penetrating, alarming power of sin.
What did it mean that her whole existence had been characterized as in radical contrast to "earlier" and as a transition
from death to life (I John 3:14; John 5:24)? How are we to
understand the shadows that are so clearly indicated also in the

3. *Ibid.*, II, 5.
4. *Ibid.*, II, 10 (italics from Kuyper).
5. Cf. H.M. Kuitert, "De Wereld Valt Mee," *Terzake. Kerk Buiten de Kerk,*
   4, 1969, pp. 63ff.
6. Kuyper, *op. cit.*, II, 5.
7. K. Rahner, "De Zonde in de Kerk," in Barauna, *De Kerk van Vaticanum
   II*, II, 434ff .
8. Cf. my *Sin*, chapter 5.

New Testament with respect to the churches in Corinth, Galatia, and Asia Minor, which fell under penetrating admonition and sharp criticism? It is admonition against the dangers of sin or pollution (Eph. 4:21ff.) and against grieving or quenching the Holy Spirit (Eph. 4:30; I Thess. 5:19). Where does this vulnerability to unholiness and impurity come from?

In this connection, one often recalls James's statement that "we all make many mistakes,"[9] as well as John's statement that it is self-deception to say that we have no sin.[10] For many people, this expressed an almost inevitable "structure" of the life of the "saints," an undeniable "not yet" in all Christian life, which could be denied only because of self-overestimation. So, opposition was mounted continuously against those who did not want to recognize this inevitability or necessity[11] or were convinced that sanctification was "realizable," that the completely devoted answer to the totalitarian admonition of the New Testament was possible.[12] One rejected this expectation as a form of untenable optimism, referring to the frequent "not yet" in the New Testament[13] and to the prayer for forgiveness in the Lord's Prayer.[14] True, one also recalled the radical words of I John, which connect being born of God with not sinning and not being able to sin,[15] but such texts were usually not understood "absolutely." Hence, in many confessions we read of something other than this "not being able to sin." Even though the intention was not to postulate the invincibility of the power of sin when speaking of the "remnants of sin" (reliquiae peccati), they were real and were not to be underestimated as belonging to the life of the Church on earth.

This recognition sometimes gets strong formulation: for instance, when it is said that even the holiest men in this life

9. James 3:2. Cf. Dr. Theotimus, *In Multis Offendimus Omnes. Werkg. Kath. Theol. in Nederl.*, 1956, pp. 111ff. The text is cited, among other places, in Carthage (Denz., 107). Cf. further, Trent (Denz., 805, 833). James also warns against superficial isolation of a particular sin (2:10f.; cf. Gal. 5:3).
10. I John 1:8. Cf. Denz., 106.
11. Theotimus (*op. cit.*, p. 111) describes the doctrine of the Church in contrast to the Catharite error in this way: "being liable to daily sin with a certain *necessity.*"
12. See chapter 12 above.
13. Cf. H. Bavinck, *Geref. Dog.*, IV, 248.
14. Thus Augustine (in Theotimus, *op. cit.*, p. 19).
15. I John 3:9 (Vulgate: *peccatum non facit* and *non potest peccare*). Cf. I John 4:20. On the discussions, cf. H.K. La Rondelle, *Perfection and Perfectionism*, 1971, pp. 227ff.

have only a small beginning of obedience (H.C., Q. 114; cf. B.C., Art. 24) and that God has the law preached so strictly for the deeper knowledge of sin — our sinful nature[16] — and for diligence and prayer toward the goal of perfection after this life (H.C., Q. 115). Both the calling to perfection and the totalitarian character of the commandment are recognized in general (Q. 113), but that is not thought to imply realizability, either for individual believers or for the Church as a whole. One cannot say that this further interpretation — the problematic of holiness and sin — has evoked much reflection. The shadows are pointed out and constantly assumed in confession and liturgy. They seemed to correspond to daily experience and to the confession of guilt of believers,[17] as well as to correlate with the Church's humility. That holiness and sin go together was seen as an undeniable fact. Although one warned against tolerating the *reliquiae peccati*, Isaiah's saying was constantly recalled: "all our righteous deeds are like a polluted garment" (64:6). This saying is related to Israel, which has been abandoned by the wrath of the Lord into the hand of her iniquities (64:7).

The way sin is spoken about makes it extremely difficult to distinguish between actuality, inevitability, and necessity. When Kuyper speaks of the "deep, sinful error" of the doctrine of perfectibility, he sees it as arising from superficiality. He points to a psychology of conversion in contrast to it and then points to God's omnipotence, which "has sovereignly fixed a boundary for itself in the limited nature of the creature."[18] Perfectionism is overturned by "a good knowledge of souls" and Romans 7. On account of the "still unfinished, spiritual creature," the believer needs Christ's substitutionary righteousness as a supplement "for what is lacking."[19] In these considerations, we find a certain explanation of the inevitability of the *reliquiae*, by which it becomes, at least to some degree, understandable. We could not expect anything else, because a certain connection

---

16. H.C., Q. 115: *Unser sündliche Art.* The Latin reads: *quanta sit naturae nostrae ad peccandum propensio* ("how great our natural propensity to sin is"). This formulation already raises questions terminologically in connection with what Q. 8 says about regeneration, which breaks through the inclination to evil.

17. Cf. the Augsburg Confession, Art. 12; the Formula of Concord, Part 2, VI, 7.

18. A. Kuyper, "Volmaakbaarheid," *Uit het Woord*, III, II, 1878, pp. 9, 48.

19. *Ibid.*, p. 49. Kuyper also argues that the admonition does not imply realizability, giving a number of everyday examples that bear little resemblance to the indicative and imperative in the New Testament.

with the will and action of God is accepted,[20] for example, when the general viewpoint is introduced that one does not find the full working of the Spirit in anyone: the power of grace has been retarded, delayed, reduced in speed, restrained.[21] But even where there is no attempt at an explanation and where there is no reflection on the why of remaining sin, warnings are nevertheless issued constantly against perfectibility. One considers the believer, the saint, also in the light of the shadows, although, of course, there can be much difference as to the depth of those shadows.[22] Naturally, many questions can arise here in connection with particular statements in the New Testament, where the Church is dealt with as "in splendor, without spot or wrinkle or any such thing" (Eph. 5:27). In exegesis, the solution is often to understand such statements "eschatologically" — or better, futuristically. They are related to the later reality of the Church in spotless holiness, which is not yet present or attainable in this life.[23] But now and then, one perceives some hesitation in referring to the Church's future,[24] for the New Testament speaks

20. Cf. Kuyper, *ibid.*, p. 52, in this connection on "what is decreed according to God's adorable order." One may also recall the remarkable formulation in the Canons of Dort (V, 1): God does regenerate by the Spirit and delivers from the dominion and slavery of sin, but "in this life He does not deliver them altogether from the body of sin and from the infirmities of the flesh." Cf. V, 2: "Hence spring forth the daily sins of infirmity."

21. K. Schilder, *Heidelb. Cat.*, IV, 103. Cf. "retardation of the power of sanctification."

22. *Reliquiae* does not usually point to a minimizing, since it implies a comparison with the previous domination of sin. Cf. for instance C.D., V, 3. We find strong accents in Kuyper, *Nabij God te Zijn*, II, 91ff., on the pure in heart. With reference to Ps. 51, he speaks of pollution, of the "painful wrestling" through all ages, a hopeless wrestling with the impurity of one's own heart.

23. Especially Augustine in his defense against the Donatists and Pelagians (with an appeal to I John 1:8). Cf. H. Riedlinger, *Die Makellosigkeit der Kirche in den lateinischen Hoheliedkommentare des Mittelalters*, 1958, pp. 59ff. The polemic against Pelagius played a role, since he, via Ambrose's commentary on Luke, pointed to Zechariah's and Elizabeth's being righteous *(díkaios)* and blameless *(ámemptos)*, walking in all the commandments of the Lord (Luke 1:6). Cf. R.F. Evans, *Pelagius. Inquiries and Reappraisals*, 1958, pp. 25, 95ff.

24. Calvin (*Commentaries on the Epistles of Paul to the Galatians and Ephesians*, p. 321) calls Augustine's defense against the Pelagians, using Eph. 5:27, a successful answer, since "Paul does not state what has been done, but for what purpose Christ has cleansed his church." Nevertheless, Calvin speaks of cleansing (in connection with baptism) here too, "that we may retain through our life the purity which we have once received."

in many ways about cleanness, spotlessness, and blamelessness in direct connection with earthly life. In any case, therefore, there is no hint of a futuristic mystery that has nothing to do with this life.[25]

A distinction between the Church and her members?

In the history of the Church, we meet with various attempts to speak in such a way about imperfection and unholiness in the Church that the *credo* does not become meaningless and illusory. One knew that the Church was summoned to perfection (Matt. 5:48), to an undivided heart (cf. Gen. 6:9; 17:1), to action in which nothing is lacking, to steadfastness that has full effect (James 1:4), and to perfect love (I John 4:18). How is this light — present now in contrast to the darkness that once was present (Eph. 5:8) — not taking part any longer in the unfruitful works of darkness (5:11), being awakened from sleep (5:14), belonging to the day (I Thess. 5:4f.), to be understood in the midst of the Church's shadows? What does it mean to say that the renovation of the world has been decreed irrevocably and that the Church has already been marked "with a genuine though imperfect holiness," but yet, as the "pilgrim Church" (*ecclesia peregrinans*), dwells among creatures who groan and travail in pain?[26] What does this "imperfect sanctification" signify?[27] In reflection on these questions, we meet continuously with attempts "to exhibit an aspect untouched by sin" in the Church.[28] One of the most well-known and influential ways of interpretation is to deem

25. Cf. Eph. 5:25ff.; 1:4 (holy and blameless). Cf. on letting steadfastness have its full effect (*érgon téleion*), "that you may be perfect and complete, lacking in nothing" (James 1:4; cf. I Pet. 1:15; 2:15). Cf. M. Dibelius, *Jakobus*, 1958[8], p. 73. H. Schlier (*Der Brief an die Epheser*, 1958, p. 258) sees *paristêsai* ("to present," Eph. 5:27; cf. II Cor. 11:2) as a continuing event and considers the question "present or future?" as basically useless. The Church in herself is already "spotless," but only eschatologically will she be spotless "in full beauty."

26. *Lumen Gentium, DV II*, pp. 78ff.

27. In *Lumen Gentium (DV II*, p. 93), we read that the Church has already reached perfection in Mary, "whereby she exists without spot or wrinkle" — which implies the imperfection of the others. Although the Church is the "spotless spouse" (*sponsa immaculata*, p. 19), she, in her sacraments and institutions, takes on the appearance of this passing world (p. 79).

28. H. Riedlinger, *op. cit.*, p. 461. Cf. Harnack, *History of Dogma*, V, 41f., on the attempt "to regard the Church primarily as an *institution* whose holiness and truth were inalienable, however melancholy the state of its members."

the Church in the full sense of the word "holy" and then to relate sin to the individual members of the Church. This distinction plays an important role even in our day in traditional Roman Catholic ecclesiology.[29] One saw the "holy Church" as bringing the essence of the Church to expression. It had been exempted from all sin as God's work, His temple, the body of Christ, and God's house. Christ was present by His Spirit in this Church, and there could be no mention of imperfection in her. Nor could there be mention of deformation which would make reformation necessary. The holy Church no longer stood under judgment because of Christ's will in constituting the Church as an irrevocable given of salvation, and she would not be confronted in the future by judgment either. This definitive constitution has always played an important role in the view of the Church, since the Church has no longer "been accepted conditionally, as was ancient Israel, but absolutely: her acceptance and non-rejection no longer stands on the conditionality of human morality which is always fluctuating."[30] Therefore, with respect to sin, one must speak differently about the Church than about the Church's members. Only for them is there reason to continue to pray with David: "Lord, enter not into judgment with thy servant; for no man living is righteous before thee" (Ps. 143:2). This prayer may not be transposed to the Church "as a whole," to the "essence" of the Church, which possesses her unassailable holiness in Christ.

This distinction between the Church and her members has a long tradition of usage. It seemingly provided a solution to the problematic of the confession, *credo sanctam ecclesiam*. It could be pointed out that the Church was and would remain a *corpus permixtum*, because chaff would always be found among the wheat and the Church would always comprise both the righteous and sinners. But one distinction was made especially to show that the Church is not simply the sum of individual believers, a conception that is rejected as "nominalistic." She

29. Cf. especially the intriguing book by M. Schwintek, *Die Kirche der Sünder. Eine kontroverstheol. Untersuchung zum Verhältnis von Kirche und Sünde*, 1969. Cf. also my *Nabetrachting op het Concilie*, pp. 257ff.; R. Schnackenburg, *The Church in the N.T.*, 1965, p. 176; and M. Labourdette, *Heiligheid Roeping van alle Leden der Kerk*, Barauna, *op. cit.*, II, 371, with the remarkable formulation that the *Church* feels sorrow for the sins of her *members*.

30. J. Ratzinger, *Das neue Volk Gottes. Entwürfe zur Ekklesiologie*, 1970, p. 254. Old Testament prophetic criticism "is no longer possible in this final radicality," since the conditionality no longer exists!

is "an organic reality," and it can be said of her: "There is
no more sin in the Church than in Christ, of Whom she is
the body; and she is His mystical personality."[31] The problem
clearly is not solved by the defense against nominalism, for
the question is whether that which is more than this "sum,"
the Church, has been exempted from all sins. Yet the distinction
seemed to give light, and it returns in various formulations.
In our time, Paul VI has reaffirmed this tradition. He speaks
of the renewal of the Church as necessary, but then interprets
this "need" further: "correcting the defects of its own members."[32] At the same time, he pronounced: "This reform cannot
concern either the essential conception of the Church or its
basic structure."[33] And when the Council itself dealt with the
sin to which the people of God on their pilgrimage are still
liable, a papal intervention added "in its members."[34] It is
recognized that the visage of the Church, although it displays
purely the features delineated by the Spirit, is "never as perfect,
as lovely, as holy or as brilliant as that formative Divine Idea
would wish it to be."[35] But, at the same time, we perceive the
anxiety that criticism of the Church will go too far, relativizing
her mystery.[36] Especially when the analogy between Christ in
His incarnation and the Church plays a role, the emphasis on
this "essence" of the Church becomes stronger, since one can
more easily declare this "mystery" to be inaccessible for sin
and pollution. When the "essence" of the Church — frequently
seen as the prolongation of the incarnation — comes into view,
there is actually no mention of sin any longer. Nor is there
any real possibility of criticism, since the Church is the apple
of God's eye (Deut. 32:10; Zech. 2:8), His people and possession.
In this light, the Church is holy, spotless, pure, and perfect. She
can be compared to the bride in the Song of Solomon: the only

31. Y. Congar, "Comment l'Eglise doit se renouveler," *Sainte Eglise*, 1963,
pp. 144ff. Cf. "a juxtaposition of individuals." Congar agrees with Ch.
Journet's statement that "the Church is not without sinners, but she
herself is without sin."
32. *Ecclesiam Suam*, para. 11.
33. *Ibid.*, para. 46.
34. Cf. *Decree on Ecumenism, DV II*, p. 346.
35. *Ecclesiam Suam*, para. 10.
36. Cf. *Lumen Gentium, DV II*, p. 93 (the Church is perfect in Mary, but
"followers of Christ" must still conquer sin). Cf. Rahner, in Barauna,
op. cit., I, 442: "The editors were evidently suspicious here of saying
that *the Church* still had to conquer sin in herself and, thus, increase
in holiness."

one, the perfect one, the flawless one (6:9), as fair as the moon and bright as the sun.[37] In all sorts of ways, the consequences of the identity of Christ and His Church are further unfolded, and it is denied that there is any pride or self-complacency here.[38] The impression can grow that, with respect to the Church, there is a certain perfectionism, a spotless holiness and perfection. Therefore, the *credo sanctam ecclesiam* is a veritable, legitimate confession.[39]

But in our time, this view of the Church is rejected from various sides as a romanticization and idealization. It is replaced by a different view of the Church which contains many more possibilities for necessary and legitimate criticism of the Church.[40] These possibilities are connected to the experience that it is difficult to speak of the Church's blamelessness, of her being totally exempt from reproof and reproach. When Scripture speaks of the blamelessness of believers, it speaks of what is valid before the eyes of God (cf. I Thess. 3:13), but this also seems to imply invulnerability before the eyes of men. Can such a blamelessness truly be spoken of with respect to the Church?[41] If not, is criticism of the Church not only legitimate, but also necessary? And is that criticism not stimulated by the Church's

37. Song of Sol. 6:10. For the reference to the Song of Solomon, see especially the revealing book by Riedlinger. Origen already, in connection with Eph. 5:27, distinguished the ideal form of the Church from the mass of simple believers (Riedlinger, *op. cit.*, pp. 29ff.). No other text is cited so frequently in these commentaries on the Song of Solomon as Eph. 5:27 (p. 36), especially in reference to Song of Sol. 4:7 ("there is no flaw in you"). According to M.A. van Oudenrijn (*Het Hooglied,* 1962, p. 27), Paul may have had this text in mind when he described the Church in Eph. 5 as without spot or wrinkle.

38. Cf. *Ecclesiam Suam*, para. 46: "Oh, it is neither pride nor presumption nor obstinacy nor folly but luminous certitude...."

39. Cf. F. Malmberg, "Enige Aspecten van de Zonde als Christologisch Probleem," *Jaarb. Kath. Theol.*, p. 16: just like Mary, the Church is "indefectibly holy." Cf. *Mystici Corporis Christi:* one cannot fault the Church "if some of her members are weak or sick."

40. Cf. B. Schneider, "Bemerkungen zur Kritik an der Kirche," *Gott in Welt*, II, 246ff.; L. Baas, "Über das Ärgernis," *idem*, 267ff. We recall that Calvin (*Inst.*, IV, 8, 12) already knew and rejected the distinction between the Church and her members: "But to consider the church already completely and in every respect holy and spotless when all its members are spotted and somewhat impure — how absurd and foolish this is!"

41. Blamelessness can also be taken in the sense of "legalistic" blamelessness. Cf. Phil. 3:6 as an expression of Pharisaic self-assurance (*TDNT*, IV, 573).

professed holiness, which offers a measuring rod to judge the Church? It has been pointed out that the background of this criticism was not inner alienation or prideful distantiation from the Church,[42] but opposition to the idea that, where the Church (her essence) is concerned, only individual believers can be spoken of with respect to sin and guilt.

Clearly, we meet here with a far-reaching problem. True, criticism may not consist of generalizations without any notion of variation. But that is not to say that "individualizing" sin implies that the Church as fellowship stands above and beyond sin. One need think only of the critical letters to the Church in Asia Minor. Here, too, there are moments of individualizing: "some" (Rev. 2:14ff.) and "a few" (3:4). But there are also more general reproaches against the Church herself, which has the name of being alive but is dead (3:1). This realization is growing in our time because the concrete Church comes into view as fellowship. Hence, we also encounter criticism of a too simplistic interpretation of the Song of Solomon. The Church comes into view much more clearly with her sin and lacks, her visage, her comings and goings, and her speaking and being silent. All of this stands under the responsibility of the Church's whole life in the light of her calling which can be understood only along the way of promise and admonition. Through the growing realization of the significance of these connections, the recognition of sin in the Church takes on a much less innocent character.[43] The traditional distinction between the Church and her members as a solution to the problem of holiness and unholiness is even opposed explicitly. In connection with various sins in the New Testament communal life, it is said that these are not simply "single transgressions of individuals, which thus do not actually affect the Church as such."[44] Not only is the impossibility of attaching meaning to this distinction recognized

---

42. K. Barth (*C.D.*, IV/1, p. 691) speaks of criticism of the Church as "always a responsible and dangerous matter." The starting point must be: "I myself am in the *ecclesia semper reformanda*, and responsible for it" (p. 692). The result is "a final brotherly mildness," reserve, and respect. In Barth's view, much criticism of the Church has "failed simply" due to lack of solidarity. Cf. p. 693 on Luther.

43. E. Schillebeeckx (*Ex Auditu Verbi*, 1965, p. 226) sees difficult and delicate problems in "the synchronous affirmation" of the *ecclesia indefectibilis* and the *ecclesia semper purificanda*.

44. B. Schneider, *op. cit.*, p. 249. Cf. H. Küng, *The Church*, pp. 322ff., on the evasion in this distinction.

since it bears an abstract character,[45] but it is also seen to be untenable on account of the shocking experience that the Church herself is burdened by sin. The sin of its members "sullies the body of Christ itself, shakes the spiritual building itself."[46] One begins to see the distinction as a "hypostatization" of the Church — the "essence" of the Church, the Church "in herself" — whereby holiness is guaranteed. The result is that there can be no participation in guilt on the part of the Church.[47] The problem of sin was no longer experienced as relevant for the Church, and it was no longer understood that the sin of the individual "has an importance for the Church and affects her being." So, in practice, one proceeded on the assumption that "in the case of the Church everything is always all right, because she is without any doubt 'holy' and no shadow of the short-comings of her members can ever fall upon her."[48]

This new reflection on the holiness of the earthly Church had to raise various questions about the offices, the structure of the Church. Specifically, could this office be placed outside the effect, the pollution, of the power of sin?[49] Sin in the Church: there is every reason to experience this "theme" as "one of the most agonizing questions of ecclesiology which persistently recurs throughout the history of dogma." The question thus became inescapable "where this Church is to be found which so confidently declares itself to be a holy Church, therefore the Church illuminated by the light of God's own holiness."[50]

45. M. Schmaus, *Die Lehre von der Kirche*, pp. 636ff.: "It is difficult to link a feasible meaning to this thesis." Cf. Küng, *The Church*, p. 322: an "unreal distinction."

46. Küng, *op. cit.*, p. 323. Cf. K. Rahner, "The Sinful Church in the Decrees of Vatican II," *Theological Investigations*, VI, 270ff.

47. Cf. M. Schmaus, *loc. cit.*, on "a substance with a personal stamp"; and K. Rahner, *op. cit.*, p. 277: "almost like an independently existent 'entity,'" with reference to *Mystici Corporis Christi*.

48. Rahner, *op. cit.*, p. 278. According to Rahner, therefore, the Protestant question about the Church as an objective institution and the "Luciferian *theologia gloriae*" — in place of an *ecclesia crucis* — must be taken seriously.

49. Cf. H. Urs von Balthasar, *Herrlichkeit*, I, 544ff., among other things, on the errors of the institutional Church, with all their consequences, in the direction of secularization and misuse of power. Cf. *idem, A Theology of Anthropology*, 1967, pp. 75ff.

50. K. Rahner, "The Church of Sinners," *Theological Investigations*, VI, 253. It is striking that this emphasis on the impossibility of disposing easily of sin in the Church appears in the same theologians who give very strong emphasis to the absolute impossibility that the constitution of the Church should ever become antiquated. Besides Rahner, see

Earlier, there was scarcely mention of a question or problem here. The Church's holiness often fulfilled an important function in apologetics, as in the First Vatican Council.[51] In our time, we do not often hear that the Church and her holiness is spoken of in this way, since attention is directed to sin in the Church as something real, "a blot and a blemish on the holy mystical Body of Christ itself."[52] Sin cannot be minimized by localization, and it is evident that the official representatives are sinners "in a very noticeable way." According to Rahner, there is no dogma of the Church that holds that the influence of sin extends only to their personal lives and not to what is called "the activity of the Church."[53] Whoever isolates and localizes here operates with an abstract "essence" of the Church, neglecting the influence of sin in the Church. Sin in the Church is not separate from individual members; but precisely because of that, it can become a power in the Church, leading her along unimaginable ways in the midst of real, unperceived dangers. During the Reformation, this problematic was perceived sharply, even in the highest regions of the Church. The criticism of the Reformers was indebted not to an anti-papal disposition, but to this insight, which placed the whole Church under the permanent testing of the gospel. In Roman Catholic circles recently, much greater interest in this insight has arisen due to much greater impartiality with respect to the Church in history, her dangers and threats, her real life in the light of her *credo*.

Simul justus et peccator

In this connection, it is perfectly understandable that there is much more appreciation by Roman Catholics now for the formulation *simul justus et peccator* ("at the same time righteous and sinner"). This formulation was concerned especially with justification; the aspect of the individual believer came especially to the fore, while the Church was not directly visible within the horizon. However, the *simul* clearly has a great deal to do

also J. Ratzinger, *op. cit.*, p. 255, on the Church as "the authentic site of the divine acts of salvation" — although the Church is not yet "final" and must still pray for forgiveness (Augustine).

51. Denz., 1794.
52. K. Rahner, *op. cit.*, p. 260.
53. *Ibid.*, pp. 260f. Cf. p. 277: one must view the so-called institutional holiness in doctrine, sacrament, and law not "in abstraction but in their historical reality and in their actual realization by human beings in the Church."

with the questions that now concern us, for it is directly connected to the relation between being righteous and being sinful in believers: holy and sinner.[54] The earlier Roman Catholic criticism of the *simul* started from the notion that justification was viewed by the Reformers as a purely external, declaratory judgment, a "forensic" deed of God that did not involve any actual change in man, since only the relation to the *favor Dei* was in question. Others saw the *simul* as, at the most, a construction that balanced off the "righteous" and the "sinner" against each other in an unsettled battle, a sort of indecisive tie without the superiority of grace.[55] We see this interpretation still at work in Karl Rahner when he first speaks of a catholic "no" to the *simul* formulation, because, according to him, there can be no thought of a "suspended dialectic between sinfulness and holiness," and because grace dominates and triumphs in the life of believers.[56]

From a voluminous series of studies, it has become clear that the *simul* in the Reformation — especially in Luther — had nothing to do with such a state of equilibrium, and there has been renewed interest in his religious motives, also in this formulation.[57] There is such obviousness here that the sad connection of the *favor Dei* to "the external" and to "only" — only faith rather than being — became less and less credible. The result is that, after Grosche's plea in 1935 for a catholic interpretation of the *simul*, others such as Küng and Pesch now also freely push aside all sorts of caricatures and call attention to an extremely important and shocking problematic: holiness and sin.[58]

54. Cf. E. Schott, "'Zugleich.' Mensch und Zeit in Luthers Rechtfertigungslehre," *Vierhunderdfünfzig Jahre Luther-Reformation. Festschr. F. Lau,* 1967, p. 324.
55. Cf. my "Simul Peccator et Justus," *Gereformeerd Theologisch Tijdschrift,* 1947, pp. 174ff.; and "De Critische Functie van het Sola Fide," *idem,* 1957, pp. 137ff.
56. K. Rahner, "Justified and Sinner at the Same Time," *Theological Investigations,* VI, 223.
57. From Protestant theology we mention W. Joest, "Paulus und das Luthersche simul justus et peccator," *Kerugma und Dogma,* 1955, pp. 269ff.; *idem, Ontologie der Person bei Luther,* 1967, pp. 265ff.; J.T. Bakker, *Coram Deo,* 1956, p. 219; H.J. Kouwenhoven, *Simul Justus et Peccator in de nieuwe R.-K. Theol.,* 1969, pp. 67ff.
58. R. Grosche, "Simul Peccator et Justus. Bemerkungen zu einer theol. Formel," *Catholica,* 1935, pp. 132ff.; H. Küng, *Justification,* 1964, p. 239 (who sees the *simul* as defined already at Carthage); O.H. Pesch, *Theol. der Rechtfertigung bei Martin Luther und Thomas von Aquin,* 1970, pp. 170ff. Cf. Pesch, p. 114: "The *simul* is not an actuality, but

The insight has grown that Luther did not see sin as an "undisputed reality governing the field," but as "sin that is assaulted and fought against."[59] The *simul* is not an equilibrium, an inevitable "existential" of the Christian; rather, it is a "formula of battle"[60] along a way, in movement: a transition in which the glance is directed in humility to Christ and His saving, superior grace. This insight automatically gives a connection with Roman Catholic authors who began to understand the problems of the *simul* — not only individually, but also with respect to the Church — in a new way. Also with Rahner, after his misunderstanding of the Reformation's *simul*, there is once again room for a Catholic "yes." Properly understood, the Reformation formula has "a perfectly positive meaning for Christian existence."[61] Via this "yes," the interpretation of the *simul* is clearly concerned not simply with a theoretical problem, but with the highest actuality. It is concerned with the actual Church, with her light and her shadow, for the "communion of sinners" has not been excluded by the "communion of saints."[62]

Thus, we see that there is intense concern everywhere again for the *simul*. On one hand, one does not want to derogate from the power of the Spirit and the newness of life in Christ; on the other hand, one refers to sin and continuing imperfection. In the Reformation, the traditional exegesis of Romans 7 played a large role in the emphasis on being a *peccator*, a sinner. One supposed that one saw clearly a tension within the Christian life. This is reflected in various confessional statements which lay strong emphasis on abiding sin and the struggle connected with it.[63] In our time, many have given a different exegesis of

a constant event that takes place in a venture"; and p. 115: "Sin and righteousness do not exist with equal right." For H. Urs von Balthasar, see Kouwenhoven, *op. cit.,* p. 67.

59. Pesch, *op. cit.,* pp. 114ff.
60. Thus Joest as well as Pesch.
61. Rahner, *op. cit.,* p. 229.
62. That the *simul* totally wipes out the disagreement is an incorrect conclusion. Cf. the discussion between H.A. Oberman ("De Rechtvaardigingsleer bij Thomas en Luther," *Kerk en Theol.,* 1969, pp. 186ff.) and Pesch ("Nogmaals de Rechtvaardigingsleer bij Thomas en Luther," *idem,* 1969, pp. 389ff.). This discussion is concentrated on the interpretation of the *simul,* but it also discloses the new affinity that is of far-reaching significance for the view of the Church.
63. Cf. H.C., Q. 127 (Rom. 7:23); Q. 126 (the transgressions and the evil that always cleaves to us, miserable sinners); B.C., Art. 15 (the sense of corruption that often makes believers sigh); Art. 24 (the punishableness of all our works); C.D., V, 2 (the blemishes on the best works of

Romans 7 than that which we meet in Augustine, Luther, Calvin, Kohlbrugge, Noordmans, and Barth. Romans 7 is no longer seen as a description of tension within the Christian life. Naturally, we cannot go further into this divergence here, but it is of importance to note that this new exegesis implies a different insight into the *simul*. The *simul* does still play a role in this new exegesis, however. In the first place, it comes to the fore as a critical question with respect to the comparison between Romans 7 and 8. Is it really possible to reconcile the Christian life as it is described in Romans 8, as being set free from the law of sin and death (8:2), with the picture that, according to the old exegesis, was drawn of believers in Romans 7? There believers are described as sold under sin (7:14), as wretched men (7:24) in whom nothing good dwells (7:18). We meet with this problematic of the *simul* when Ridderbos writes that Romans 7:14-25 and Romans 8 "are at the deepest not coexistent."[64] One may not illuminate the present-day discussion about the exegesis of Romans 7 directly by means of Luther's sharp criticism against the conception that Romans 7 speaks about the "fleshly" man. Luther calls that conception "foolish": "a false, dangerous view." But he is carrying on a polemic against the idea that people after baptism "are at once without any sin," which he sees as "a most harmful deception"[65] in which there can be no mention of the tension and discord in Romans 7. However, this point of view is lacking in the new exegesis. It does not consider any *simul* to be possible with respect to what Romans 7 says about being lost and sold under sin.[66] However,

the saints); V, 11 (doubts and grievous temptations). Cf. the detailed citation of Rom. 7 in the Formula of Concord, Part 2, VI, 7.

64. H.N. Ridderbos, *Aan de Romeinen*, p. 154. Cf. p. 164 ("in inescapable conflict" with what Paul says in Rom. 6 and 8 about the new life) and p. 140, on Rom. 6:18 (the Christian has already escaped the slavery of sin *in principle*). Cf. *idem, Paul*, pp. 151f., 124ff., 144ff. On the question of coexistence, one should consult, in the Lutheran opposition to the new exegesis, the considerations of A. Nygren, *Commentary on Romans*, 1949; Joest, *loc. cit.*; and E. Ellwein, "Das Rätsel von Römer VII," *Kerugma und Dogma*, 1955, pp. 247ff.

65. Luther, *Lectures on Romans*, ed. W. Pauck, p. 212.

66. Ellwein's answer (*op. cit.*, p. 255) to the question "Is Rom. 7:14ff., therefore, characteristic for his Christian present?" is in the negative, naturally (especially with regard to what is characteristic). For Ridderbos (*Aan de Romeinen*, p. 167), this is the principal argument. Cf. p. 163: in Rom. 7 "not one word is spoken about the Spirit." Cf. W.K. Groussouw, "De Verscheurde Mens van Romeinen 7," *Vriendengave voor Kard. B.J. Alfrink*, p. 73, with reference to Calvin's exegesis. Rom. 7 is concerned with more than "remnants" of the flesh.

this is not seen as implying sinlessness apart from struggle and tension. Compared to earlier exegesis, the picture of the believer does change, since Paul's decisive view about "the power of the Spirit that conquers all sins" implies that "the idea that believers must always remain broken down in a small beginning is certainly not harmonizable with his indicative and imperative pronouncement about perfection."[67]

One may not postulate an antithesis between pessimism (the traditional exegesis) and optimism (the newer exegesis). One cannot speak of pessimism in the traditional exegesis, since it is explicitly rejected, especially with reference to Romans 7:25.[68] And the newer exegesis cannot simply be characterized as optimism, because everything is related emphatically to the power and grace of the Spirit as constitutive for the nature of life in Christ. Unmistakably, there is a moderation of the tension and discord, but discord has remained! For example, we hear that "the temptation of sin has not lost its relevance for believers."[69] And again, the conflict has not "been ended all at once," on account of the struggle of the flesh against the Spirit, even though the believer is "no longer powerless like the man under the law of Romans 7."[70] He, too, who takes Romans 8 — liberation — completely seriously must thus be on his guard against a lack of appreciation for the dangers. It is apparent that, also in the newer exegesis, the struggle still remains. What Paul says in Romans 8:9 about being not in the flesh but in the Spirit is not nullified by — and thus, can be "coexistent" with — the desire of the flesh against the Spirit in Galatians 5:17. Being "in the Spirit" does not mean "that the Spirit takes hold of the human ego to such an extent that it is no longer exposed to the power of the flesh."[71] That means we are dealing here not with a "remnant" which can be neglected, but with a relevant

---

67. Ridderbos, *Paul*, p. 272. Cf. H.C., Q. 114; Q. 126; C.D., V, 2. Ridderbos agrees that there is no *non peccare* or *non posse peccare* in Paul, but there is a *posse non peccare*.

68. Cf. Luther, *op. cit.*, p. 207, on the "fighter who stands in between two opposite laws, but not as a defeated one." Cf. R. Hermann, *Luthers These 'Gerecht und Sünder zugleich,'* 1960, p. 11; A.F.N. Lekkerkerker, *De Brief van Paulus aan de Romeinen*, I, 1962, p. 322, on the "*de profundis.*"

69. Ridderbos, *Aan de Romeinen*, p. 165.

70. *Ibid.*, pp. 179f. Cf. also Ridderbos, *Paul*, p. 130, with reference to Gal. 5:17.

71. Ridderbos, *Paul*, p. 269. Cf. his *Aan de Romeinen*, p. 36 ("the abiding gateway of invasion") and p. 137 (struggle as "the distinguishing mark of the present situation of believers").

reality. Hence, Ridderbos can write that "the forbidding and pitiable picture" set by Paul before the eyes of his readers with respect to "the moving seriousness and the lack of prospects of the I wrestling in its own power" is still necessary for believing readers.[72]

The reality that comes into view here, in the Christian life, always calls up recollections of Psalm 51 and other psalms. In both exegeses, the believer is characterized in such a way that he does not have justification behind him: it is not a station that has been passed forever, which he can forget along his continuing way, and to which he no longer needs to return. The possibility remains that he "can be brought back so violently to this situation from which he starts."[73] That is what comes repeatedly to expression in the humble statements of the confessions because of the imperative, which remains necessary as well: "Let not sin reign" (Rom. 6:12). We will have to remain conscious that Luther's distinction between the *peccatum regnans* ("sin which rules") and the *peccatum regnatum* ("sin which is ruled")[74] — actually, it also plays a role in Ridderbos — does not provide final clarity, since letting sin reign is warned against. The problem of what can be coexistent is certainly not simple, and from Ridderbos's exegesis it is apparent that, in one way or another, the *simul* remains. If it is not related to Romans 7, then it is nevertheless included within the reality of Romans 8. The Christian life is characterized as a "polarity full of tension" of the "already" and the "not yet" and as a continuing struggle between flesh and spirit.[75] That is what — even apart from the exegetical decision concerning Romans 7, therefore — is intriguing about the problematic of the *simul* or of what can be "coexistent."

There can be no disregard for "indwelling sin" or for the "remnants of the flesh," although this latter phrase could give

---

72. Ridderbos, *Aan de Romeinen*, p. 154.
73. K. Barth, *C.D.*, IV/1, pp. 581ff. Groussouw (*op. cit.*, p. 80), in spite of a sharp rejection of the traditional exegesis, writes: "Only faith in the Lord saves him and *continues* to save him from the abyss."
74. Cf. R. Hermann, *op. cit.*, pp. 60ff., 65.
75. Ridderbos, *Aan de Romeinen*, p. 277. According to Groussouw (*op. cit.*, p. 80), Gal. 5:16ff. does not prove, in spite of the striking similarity with the terminology of Rom. 7, that Rom. 7 speaks about the Christian. However, there is, in his view, an element of truth in the traditional exegesis in connection with "a possibility that is still real and can pervert his Christian existence." The thankfulness that the Rom. 7 stage is past does not mean that the past has been completely liquidated.

rise to that.[76] Precisely when we are speaking about confessed sin, such a "quantitative" minimizing in the experience of guilt is evidently not possible on account of the nature of sin before God.[77] Thus, the *simul* is understandably spoken of with such deep seriousness. It is connected to accusation, confession, and prayer; and its meaning is preserved only as long as it does not become a self-evident, generalizing "formula of being"[78] or an ascertainment of facts. Only then is quantification of the experience of guilt *coram Deo* out of the question, as is the case also in the Church's confessions. Remarkably, in the *credo* of the "perseverance of the saints" in the Canons of Dort the way of humility and of the confession of guilt is designated with a recollection of David and Peter. There is still a possibility of enormous sin, called deadly guilt in spite of all criticism of the distinction between venial and mortal sin, and of grieving the Holy Spirit. But reference is also made to that way along which the light of God's Fatherly countenance again shines (V, 5). Naturally, the *simul* can be perverted into a complaining, joyless Christianity. The result can easily be antinomianism, a simplistic generalization without seriousness and consequences,[79] or, finally, an excuse on account of the "necessity" of "remaining" sin. But these caricatures may not divert our attention from what can be called not the meaning, but the seriousness of the *simul*.

76. *Reliquiae carnis*. When Calvin speaks about *reliquiae carnis*, he does not aim at a minimizing. Whoever bears them in himself feels the "strife" of Rom. 7 (*Inst.*, II, 2, 27). Therefore, Augustine was right, according to Calvin, in abandoning his earlier view of Rom. 7. It is clear that this does not decide the question of the exegesis of Rom. 7. Cf. P. Althaus, *Paulus und Luther über den Menschen*, 1951.

77. One may recall Luther's "allegorization" of the entry into Canaan: the conquest as well as the "remaining" Jebusites, Canaanites, and others (Judg. 1:21, 28, 30ff.). Nevertheless, Luther polemicizes against minimizing and criticizes "all attenuating expressions" (cf. Hermann, *op. cit.*, pp. 13, 56).

78. Cf. Joest, *op. cit.*, pp. 269ff.

79. Cf. H. Scholz, "Zur Lehre vom 'armen Sünder,'" *Z.Th.K.*, 1896, pp. 463ff., with valuable thoughts on the context in which "miserable sinners" are spoken of and the spirituality of it. Cf. the expression in H.C., Q. 126 (in prayer). See also K. Barth, *C.D.*, IV/2, p. 577, on the danger of the false tax collector who has become a Pharisee and on vivification as the meaning and intention of mortification. These questions have always played a role with regard to Kohlbrugge's exegesis of Rom. 7, especially verse 14. Cf. G.W. Locher, "Paulus en Kohlbrugge op de Komma," *De Dertiende Apostel en het Elfde Gebod*, 1971, pp. 153ff.

The simul and the Church

In the new concern for the *simul* in Roman Catholic theology, the significance not simply for the individual believer but especially for the Church plays a decisive role, even into all the levels of her existence. Paired with that is the protest against triumphalism, which can play a role in individual life,[80] but now comes into view especially as ecclesiological triumphalism. It does not rest in personal pride, but in an ecclesiastical self-esteem that is difficult to put one's finger on.[81] The rejection of the "hypostatizing" of the Church gives rise to a very profound problem. For that matter, it functioned already in the Reformation in reflection on the Church, her dangers and threats.[82] The statement that the well-known distinction has no real, historical meaning[83] is not simply a theoretical, innocent theme. As an illustration of the far-reaching change, we point out that the Song of Solomon can again come up for discussion, but now it has a different scope than in the Middle Ages when it was the spotlessness of the bride. Its new scope can be seen in reference to a different statement by the bride: "I am very dark, but comely" (1:5). For that matter, Tyconius already referred to this statement for the two sides of the Church. This dual aspect of the Church, which must be taken seriously, is beginning at present to influence the interpretation of the glory of the Church. Reference is made not only to the power of God, but also to the power that becomes visible in human weakness, for instance in Peter as rock *and* as Satan. Further, attention is called to a striking paradox in the Church's whole life which belongs to the fundamental tensions of faith.[84] Then tension of the *simul* is accentuated so strongly that the impression of an inevitability on the part of the sins of the Church arises. For

80. Cf. R. Budiman, *De Realisering van de Verzoening in het Menselijk Bestaan,* 1971, p. 178.
81. One may think of Greek Catholic ecclesiology in connection with the "divine-human" character of the Church, encompassed in the praise of God as the manifestation of divine wisdom. Cf. R. Slenczka, *Ostkirche und Ökumene,* 1962, p. 91, on the members of the Church as the human side vis-à-vis "the real Church."
82. Especially in Luther and Calvin in their concern with the Church and the threat of the Antichrist in the temple of God. Cf. my *The Return of Christ,* pp. 262ff.
83. J. Ratzinger, *op. cit.,* p. 259.
84. *Ibid.* Cf. with regard to Luther, who "recognized (the shadows) overwhelmingly clearly" as the tension of the *simul justus et peccator.* Ratzinger recalls Gal. 2:11ff. here too: "Peter still a rock and stumbling block in one."

instance, sin finds a certain explanation on account of the Church's taking part in the divine self-emptying as a mystery.[85]

It is reasonable to ask whether too much honor is not given here to the "mystery of sin" in the "mystery of the Church," and whether the Reformation's *simul* will not always have to protest against it. According to Joest, there is no mention in Paul of reflection on this "inevitability" nor on "the why of the continuation of sin."[86] Joest believes that this reflection is present at the periphery in Luther, so that the *simul* is no longer only a "battle formula," but threatens to become an explanation. The result is that others conclude to the powerlessness of the Christian life in the Reformation's view; the *simul* is "an unavoidable existential of the earthly state of the Christian."[87] However, what Luther was concerned with, according to Joest, was not this "necessity," but the struggle in the transition to full salvation. All of this is a warning for all reflection on the *simul*. But, at the same time, it is a reference to a problematic for the whole Church. Every excuse and every explanation that would in one way or another incorporate sin in the Church's mystery is out of the question. The power of the apostolic surprise on the basis of the depth of indicative and imperative[88] confronts this again and again whenever the Church enters upon ways that, in contrast to salvation, can only be characterized as not understandable, senseless bewitchment (Gal. 3:1). It is the struggle that is pictured in the New Testament over and over again in the midst of the dangers of the *simul*. Therein lies the impossibility of a *simul* as "a state of rest or equipoise as between two coordinated factors."[89] That would be to stimulate inertness and to incorporate the *simul* in the Christian life without struggle and directedness to liberating grace, which is the touchstone of all recognition of the "not yet." Whoever elevates the "not yet" to a structure apart from the context of struggle and prayer[90] has not understood the power of the indicative and the imperative.

85. Cf. H. Urs von Balthasar, *Herrlichkeit*, I, 544ff.
86. W. Joest, "Paulus und das Luthersche simul justus et peccator," *Kerugma und Dogma*, 1955, p. 320.
87. Joest, *Ontologie*, pp. 309ff. Cf. pp. 315ff. on the permission of God with humility as the goal. Cf. Luther, *op. cit.*, p. 212: "Sin is left in the spiritual man for the exercise of grace, for the humiliation of pride, and for the restraint of presumptuousness."
88. Cf. Rom. 6:2 ("By no means!") and I Cor. 6 ("Do you not know...?"). Cf. my *Sin*, chapter 5.
89. K. Barth, *C.D.*, IV/2, p. 649.
90. Cf. R. Hermann, *op. cit.*, chapter 3.

When Kuyper writes that perfectionism is contradicted by a cloud of witnesses,[91] it is good to recall that in Heb. 12 the cloud of witnesses observes the believers in their struggle. Thus, it becomes a motive for laying aside every weight and sin which clings so closely (12:1). And here, with respect to the race set before us, the admonition sounds to look to Christ in all the dangers of weariness and faintheartedness (12:3). We hear also of a "not yet." However, it is not contrasted to "already," but is connected to *not yet* resisting sin to the point of shedding blood (12:4), and it ends finally in the reference, via discipline, to sharing in God's holiness (12:10). Whoever does not understand the warning against this "not yet" cannot conceal himself behind the "not yet" in distinction from the "already" in the eschatological perspective. There can be no mention of an ascertainment of an inevitable *simul* full of resignation,[92] but only of a protest against all that would divert one's gaze from Him Who is the pioneer and perfector of faith (12:2). No appeal to discord as an inevitable given, no reference to anthropological structures — as if Romans 8 did not have everything to do with them! — and also no escape into the eschaton can legitimize the *simul*. Apart from the race and apart from the "awakening to conversion,"[93] the Church loses all credibility in her reference to the *simul*. Her credo becomes meaningless, pretentious, and contestable on all sides. That applies to everyone who wants to be and to remain forever a living member of the Church (H.C., Q. 54), but also to the Church in all her aspects of dispersion and solidarity, of her responsibility, of the seriousness and effects of her failings, of her speaking where she ought to be silent, and of her silence when she ought to proclaim from the housetops (Matt. 10:27).

In the history of the Church, those figures always attract attention who have given account of the seriousness of the *simul* and have not related it only to the individual members of the Church to the exclusion of the threat to the Church and her offices. In our time, the Dutch pope, Adrian VI (1522-1523), is recalled again and again. He spoke about the disaster of the schism that had come over the Church, stating that God had

91. A. Kuyper, "Volmaakbaarheid," *Uit het Woord*, III, II, 1878, p. 9.
92. Heb. 12:2. It is the tension of the race that the *simul* implies, and, apart from that context, it always becomes a dangerous *theologoumenon*. This race stands in the light of Christ's way through the cross and shame (12:2).
93. Barth, *C.D.*, IV/2, p. 577.

caused that disaster on account of the sins of the Church and, especially, on account of the sins of the spiritual and ecclesiastical authorities. He mentioned frightful things, misuses of religious authority, that had occurred. This led to complete pollution, which passed from the head to the members, from the popes to the lower bearers of authority.[94] Here the sin of the Church and its consequences are spoken of in honest self-criticism and in plain terms. This is an exception in language about the Church,[95] but interest in such statements is coming to the fore more strongly at present. That is due to a deepened realization of solidarity in opposition to all "individual" localization, which does not affect the Church. Meanwhile, we also see the Church spoken of in analogy to the confession of guilt of individual believers. How could it be otherwise in the *congregatio fidelium?* Wherever the guilt is suppressed, no matter for what reasons, life wastes away (Ps. 32:3). No self-evident, humble *simul* will be able to offer defense against that. This is not a danger with which one church can reproach another. The relationship of guilt to the Church may have been a problem in the Roman Catholic Church until the Second Vatican Council,[96] but the danger threatens everywhere that the Church has been called in word and deed to the light of the day, to concern for the gospel, to love and to service — in one word, to that sanctification that the Church sings about nostalgically in a way that should exclude all misunderstanding: "Make your Church a pillar of your truth, a refuge in the wilderness, a house where your peace is."[97]

That the *simul,* the complexity of holiness and unholiness, may never be understood as an inevitable, necessary "structure" of the Church in this life and that it is never possible to attribute meaning to sin in the Church appears most clearly from the way in which the Church is placed under the calling to walk in the truth. Apostolicity and holiness concern each other di-

---

94. Cf. C. Mirbt, *Quellen zur Geschichte des Papstthums und des röm. Katholizismus,* 1934.

95. Cf. also Pope Paul IV on the miracle that the Church, in view of the corruption of the Holy See by his predecessors, has maintained herself (Schneider, *op. cit.,* p. 256).

96. Cf. the hesitation, in spite of the *ecclesia semper purificanda (Lumen Gentium),* to relate sin also to the Church. Cf. K. Rahner, *Theological Investigations,* VI, 284ff., on the reserve with regard to the Church as "subject of guilt."

97. Hymn 54, verse 4, *Honderdnegentien Gezangen* (The Gereformeerde Kerken in the Netherlands).

rectly in this admonition, and they cannot be isolated from
each other. Orthodoxy and orthopraxy are inseparably connected. That walking in the truth is connected to the radiating
light of holiness appears not simply from James' warning
against the faith that, although it is correct "in itself," nevertheless lacks everything and can be compared to the belief of
the demons (James 2:19). Rather, it appears also from the testimony that proceeds from following the truth (III John 3-4), and
which John speaks of as his greatest joy (III John 4; II John 4),
because service is rendered loyally "especially to strangers" (III
John 5). The break between orthodoxy and orthopraxy as a
danger is not a theme of moralism, but rather opens one's eyes
for the attack on the testimony of the truth, for the threat not
only to the holiness, but also to the apostolicity of the Church.
The new concentration on the concrete *simul* brought the aspect
of the Church's credibility more and more to the fore, and the
credo of holiness became an urgent appeal. Precisely because
the gospel is not man's gospel (Gal. 1:11), it is of decisive significance that its own unclouded meaning come to light. This
meaning is threatened by every discrepancy that accompanies
the testimony to the truth.

Paul brought the dangers of this discrepancy to light in a
revealing way. He did not objectify the prohibition against
stealing "in itself" and apart from the preacher, but indicated
the threat of uncredibility: "While you preach against stealing,
do you steal? You who say that one must not commit adultery,
do you commit adultery? You who abhor idols, do you rob
temples? You who boast in the law, do you dishonor God by
breaking the law?" (Rom. 2:21-23). Undoubtedly, there is an
inner disunity in the discrepancy between preaching and teaching (Rom. 2:21 — *kērússein* and *didáskein*) and deeds, but Paul's
concern is directed first of all to something else. He points out
that, through these contours of preaching, the Name of God is
blasphemed among the Gentiles "because of you, as it is written" (Rom. 2:24; cf. Isa. 52:5; Ezek. 36:20-23). The Jewish
testimony was directed to being a light for those in darkness, a
corrector of the foolish, and a teacher of children (Rom. 2:19f.).
The power of this testimony in warning and admonition gives
way when there is an obvious break in the Church's own life,
thus giving an occasion for blasphemy.[98] On the basis of an

98. Cf. the prayer in H.C., Q. 122 ("on our account"). Calvin (*Commentaries on the Epistle of Paul to the Romans*, pp. 104ff.) points to the
warning power of Paul's words to the Jews *also for us*. The opposite

isolated concept of truth — agreement with a particular state of affairs and correctness in citing the Decalogue — the truth cannot conceivably become a lie. But one must have an eye for the warning that "what is true — also God's truth — can, at particular moments, become a lie in the mouths of men."[99] The unbreakable connection between the different aspects of the one *credo* is apparent here, if anywhere, and one thinks involuntarily of what James says about the consequences and implications of failing in one point (2:10). The *credo* involves such profound responsibility that the Church must always understand it anew. Therefore, the *credo* is possible only in the context of struggle, prayer, and nostalgia. Outside this context, the Church's speaking becomes meaningless and unfruitful, and her existence gives no light to the world. But within this context, the *credo*, in fear and trembling, keeps its meaning. That is not on account of self-evident tolerance with regard to the *simul*, but on account of visible intolerance with regard to it. Only in this progress, this visible transition, can the Church be preserved from the suspicion that she is not in the least a house of peace. The enticing light of this house, of this refuge, can become visible only in vivification, in surprise at the *simul* within the Church herself, and in ever-new acceptance of the commission which that surprise entails.

is the putting to shame of those who revile (I Pet. 3:16). Cf. also 2:12: the Gentiles' seeing good works, which leads to glorifying God. Cf. above, chapter 4, pp. 101f.
99. Cf. A.S. van der Woude, "Waarheid als Leugen," *Vox Theol.*, 1970, p. 69.

CHAPTER FOURTEEN

HOLINESS AND DISCIPLINE

WHOEVER HAS REFLECTED ON THE HOLINESS OF the Church in the *credo* is faced automatically with the question of what attitude the Church should adopt toward sin in her midst. If there is no suggestion in the *justus et peccator* of patient recognition of or acquiescence to an inevitable state of affairs, but rather of an expression filled with the summons to struggle and opposition, then the Church cannot withdraw from continuing reflection on the illegitimacy that comes into the open here. Frequently, one has distinguished between sin and the sinner; but because sin is hardly an abstract thing, this distinction, which in itself is meaningful, does not provide a solution. The living, concrete man always confronts us in sin, and thus the problem of what the Church's attitude must be arises. Clearly, there can be no recognition of sin — nor any excuse for it. Such recognition always involves a lack of appreciation for the destructive power of evil, which will always raise questions about the *credo* of the Church, which is confessed so emphatically. Moreover, sin clearly does not bear a less serious character because it is found in the Church. Rather, according to the biblical witness, the opposite is the case.

In light of divine electing grace, the prophets point to the specific responsibility of the people of God (Amos 3:1f.; Zeph. 1:12). That is the foundation of all reflection on the holiness of the Church and her discontinuity. There can be no indulgent tolerance of sin in her midst, as if a meaningful place could be conferred on such sin. With respect to the darkness at the sanctuary of Shiloh, Eli is reproached through Samuel for not restraining his sons (I Sam. 3:13). And Paul, in a concrete case, reproaches a church for a tolerance that endangers the existence of the whole Church. He speaks of arrogance where there should be mourning, and it should have led to a deed (I Cor. 5:2).

358

Likewise, he himself mourns "over many of those who sinned before and have not repented" (II Cor. 12:21). Because of a relativizing and minimizing of the destructive evil, there can be tolerance whereby it is not taken seriously. But also, even when one did not want to underestimate sin, one has often recalled Him Who is the only Knower of hearts as well as the admonition not to participate in any chain reaction of evil — not to avenge ourselves, but to leave it to the wrath of God (Rom. 12:19), His unique and holy privilege, which we may not arrogate to ourselves.[1]

In various discussions about discipline, a role was often played by the idea that evil did have to be undermined and withstood, but that this was possible only by good, as could come to light concretely in the attitude to one's enemy (12:20f.). In reflection on sin and in the defense against it,[2] we meet with the expression "passed over sin" with respect to God Himself. We read in Rom. 3:25 that God "in his divine forbearance had passed over former sins." In this new translation, we meet with terminology that recalls various forms of toleration. Earlier, one translated the text to say that these sins had been "forgiven"; but the Greek word that is used here — *páresis* — justifies the new translation, since it contains an element of not punishing, of permission and tolerance, of "passing over."[3] What is remarkable is that this terminology does not in the least imply toleration or indulgence of sin. The text points to the demonstration of God's righteousness in Christ (3:25f.), Whose life and death make manifest how seriously God takes sin. Paul says that God, by sending His Son, has condemned sin in the flesh (8:3) and that, by the crucifixion of the old self with Christ, the sinful body is destroyed (6:6). There appears to be no hint of pretending not to see or overlooking sin as a factor in life that can be neglected.[4] The motive of this "passing over" and

1. H.N. Ridderbos, *Aan de Romeinen*, p. 285. The degree to which the "chain reaction" falls under judgment is evident from the call to imitate Christ, Who, when He was reviled, did not reply with reviling and threats (I Pet. 2:23).
2. Overcoming evil with good assumes hatred of what is evil (Rom. 12:9) in connection with genuine love. Cf. in detail K. Barth, *The Epistle to the Romans*, on Rom. 12:9-21. Cf. also Ridderbos, *op. cit.*, p. 287, on the double victory of evil and the propagation of sin.
3. Cf. Ridderbos, *op. cit.*, p. 85: "let it go." The earlier translation was: "for the remission of sins" (KJV).
4. The New English Bible translates Rom. 3:25 as follows: "because in his forbearance he had *overlooked* the sins of the past." "Overlooked," just

God's forbearance is different from many human motives of "letting it go"; it is a different one than that of Eli in his powerlessness. The divine restraint has nothing to do with not being able to react to sin, and it definitely does not indicate sin as something tolerable. So, everything depends on the nature of the forbearance.

In many ways, the Church has been confronted with all these problems of "tolerance." She was forced to reflect on sin in the Church, not because of a natural indignation at evil in itself, but because of the knowledge of mercy and forgiveness, of the justification of the ungodly (4:5), and of God's not counting sin (II Cor. 5:19). Because of this biblical proclamation, she had to reflect on her own attitude to sin. She became conscious that her attitude was different and had to be different from that of a moral aversion and condemnation due to a legalistic view of evil. Otherwise, not only would her own existence be endangered — the origin of the Church — but also, she would reflect on sin apart from considering mercy and divine forgiveness as the great light in deep darkness. From the beginning on, the Church's attitude has been more complicated than one would expect in general considerations of "evil." Here and there in the New Testament, we meet a view of sin that is uncomplicated, when the Pharisees condemn Jesus on account of His attitude to sinners. They saw His association, His eating and drinking with sinners, as a tolerance that contradicted the essence of the holy Torah, as a relativization of the seriousness and dangers of sin: "This man receives sinners and eats with them" (Luke 15:2). The only possibility here is distance, and the only excuse that Simon the Pharisee can think of for Jesus' relation to "sinners" is that Jesus does not know "who and what sort of woman this is" (7:39). Here mercy and forgiveness are understood as tolerance of evil, a view that is in direct conflict with the whole New Testament, where not only Jesus but also the apostles bring to light the degree to which forgiveness is connected to condemnation of and liberation from sin (cf. Rom. 6; John 8:11). There is no way from this mercy and forgiveness to a tolerance that does not take sin seriously. No matter how great the danger may be of throwing stones without oneself being free of blame (cf. John 8:7), the "not counting of

like "passed over," requires elucidation from the context. Cf. "to demonstrate his justice now in the present" (NEB). In contrast to indulgence, cf. the *kratein* ("retain") in John 20:23 in distinction from *áphesis* ("forgiveness").

sin" in II Cor. 5:19 has led the Church to deny any legitimacy to sin. And she herself, according to the testimony of the whole New Testament, is not free from her own, human responsibility in that denial, nor from the struggle and defense involved in it.

The letter to the Hebrews

The Church has been confronted with this problematic of forbearance, toleration, forgiveness, and condemnation of sin in many ways, and particularly when she had to reflect on sin breaking out in the Church herself. For the background of belonging to the Church was a radical transition from darkness to light and from death to life. Liberation in Christ was pictured as dying to sin, as being crucified and raised with Christ. Could a renewed manifestation of sin be anything other than a radical form of apostasy? We meet with this problematic in Heb. 6:4ff. with respect to those who have once been enlightened, have tasted the heavenly gift, have become partakers of the Holy Spirit, have tasted the goodness of the Word of God and the powers of the age to come, and afterwards have committed apostasy. We are told that it is impossible to restore them again to repentance, "since they crucify the Son of God on their own account and hold him up to contempt" (6:6).

These statements, which have such a radical tone, as well as other statements about apostasy after enlightenment,[5] later occasioned many discussions. With respect to the perseverance of the saints, for instance, was such an apostasy of saints possible? But in the ancient church, one was concerned especially with that word "impossible," which seemed to exclude a repetition of conversions: every vice versa of conversion-apostasy-conversion. . . .[6] Such statements guarded the Church against thinking in the framework of self-evidency, since, if not renewal after apostasy, then at least that apostasy itself came into sight within the Church's horizon. One had to reflect on the dangers here, which appeared in the context of an urgent warning. In this reflection we see a tendency, on one hand, to recognize something of the radicality of Heb. 6 — against the multitude of possible conver-

5. Cf. II Pet. 2:20 (having escaped the defilements of the world through the knowledge of the Lord and Savior and once again becoming entangled in and overpowered by them — the last state worse than the first); Luke 11:23-26; Heb. 10:26 (deliberately sinning after the knowledge of the truth). Cf. my *Faith and Perseverance*, 1958, pp. 116ff.
6. Cf. K. Barth, *C.D.*, I/2, pp. 399f.

sions — yet, on the other hand, to hold open at least one possibility of a new conversion. For instance, that is the case with the pastor of Hermas. After apostasy there is only one more repentance *(mía metánoia)* possible.[7] And he makes no distinction between great and small sins. Therein lies the problem of the nature of the realization of salvation, which is not bound to the first radical transition from death to life. Understandably, others also continued to reflect on this new conversion. For instance, Tertullian reaches back to that radicality when he, in his montanistic period, sees all doors closed to apostates after illumination. He sees the pastor of Hermas as lacking in earnestness, since he is also favorably inclined to an adulterer.[8] Tertullian wants to listen to a different "shepherd" and to John the Baptist, who asks for fruits of repentance.

The Church did not follow Tertullian in this, but spoke of a continuing perspective of God's mercy even after sin and apostasy. Because there were several possibilities, the way became less clear and more complicated. It may be correct to say that one may not introduce the later struggle about penance into the ancient Church,[9] but the problem of sin in the Church came up for discussion already in the ancient Church. Did not the acceptance of new possibilities imply that sin was taken less seriously? Moreover, in reflecting on sin in the Church, one could not deal only with individuals or with abstract possibilities, but one had to reflect on the admonition that was addressed to the whole Church. The letter to the Hebrews, which speaks so radically about enlightenment and the powers of the coming age, indicates an urgent danger zone when it admonishes against failing to obtain grace (12:15), against lacking sufficient resistance (12:4), against growing weary or fainthearted (12:3), and against weak knees and drooping hands (12:12). The pastoral character of the admonition is striking; it has nothing to do with rigorous legalism. Rather, hearts are comforted in the

7. Cf. B. Poschmann, *Handbuch der Dogmengeschichte*, IV, Fasc. 3, 1951, p. 16; H.F. von Campenhausen, *Ecclesiastical Authority and Spiritual Power*, 1969, pp. 222ff.
8. *De Pudicitia*, 20.
9. Cf. von Campenhausen, *loc. cit.*, who says that if one does do this, one has to understand Heb. 6 rigoristically and that "all efforts to soften [the passages] down" are impossible. In his view, the impossibility in Heb. 6 does not signify a prohibition against readmission, but that new repentance and renewal are not reckoned with when one has become apostate and turned one's back on the Church. Thus, the radical words of Heb. 6 are to be understood primarily parenetically.

struggle through the outlook on the great high priest who can
"sympathize" with our weaknesses, since He has been tempted
in every respect as we are.[10]
Therefore, one may, in the midst of danger, draw near with
confidence to the throne of grace (Heb. 4:16). But the context
of all of this is not inactive ascertainment, but urgent admonition to a way, the way of the Church. In the reference to weakness *(asthéneia)*, a different picture confronts us than that of
radical apostasy and schism, when boundaries are transgressed
consciously (Heb. 10:26; cf. Num. 15:22ff.). The Church is pictured in the aspects of weakness, ignorance, and waywardness,
and we are reminded that she is not, on account of that, re-
pudiated by Christ. Remarkably, we even hear — even if the
weakness and vulnerability are not minimized[11] — of the Old
Testament high priest who "can deal gently" *(metriopathéō)*
with the ignorant and wayward, "since he himself is beset
with weakness" (Heb. 5:2). Even though the Old Testament
priest is also "weak," there is still a reference to Christ: He is
"moderate,"[12] taking underlying motives and gradations into
consideration.[13] The Church has also been frequently concerned
with this when she has reflected on the total process of the life
of believers. In that reflection she did not start from a black-
white schema, but from the complexity in the life of the believer,
which was later described as *simul justus et peccator*.

Under the influence of the Church's history, the word "discipline" in the phrase "ecclesiastical discipline" is often associated
with punishment — sometimes even to the extent of excommunication. However, to take this negative aspect as one's starting
point would be incorrect, since discipline must be seen first of
all in the framework of deep concern for the Church, for preserving her along the way of life. That does not eliminate the
aspect of punishment, but it does illumine its significance. This
comes to light especially clearly in Hebrews, which speaks of
the discipline of the Lord. The element of punishment and

10. Heb. 4:14ff. Cf. O. Michel, *Der Brief an die Hebräer*, on this text.
   Cf. the Spirit's help in weakness in Rom. 8:26. In Rom. 5:6 *asthéneia*
   is spoken of in a different context — with regard to Christ's dying while
   we were yet helpless, parallel to the "while we were yet sinners" (5:8)
   and to ungodliness (5:6).
11. Without lacking appreciation for the "seriousness of the situation"
   (TDNT, V, 936).
12. *TDNT, V, 938*.
13. Cf. H. van Oyen *(Christus de Hogepriester, 1939, p. 85)* speaks of the
   "golden mean," the fair judgment. Cf. O. Michel, *op. cit.*, p. 131.

chastisement (12:5f.) plays an important role here, but it stands
in a very clear framework. The Church may not regard discipline lightly, since, as punishment and chastisement, it strikes
those who are God's sons and whom God loves (12:6f.). Being
left without this discipline (chōris ... paideías) is an indication of
being outside the sonship (12:8), parallel to the Old Testament
saying that he who spares the rod hates his son, while love takes
hold of discipline (Prov. 13:24; cf. 3:12). Discipline drives folly
from his heart (22:15) and saves his life from Sheol (23:14). No
matter how great the danger is that the connection between
discipline and love become an easy, a priori justification of every
disciplinary action, it is, nevertheless, an essential connection;
and the directedness of discipline belongs to its essential structure: "that we may share his holiness."[14] Apparently, pain is
connected to discipline, but later it produces the fruit of righteousness (Heb. 12:11).

Already in Israel, this beneficial teleology of discipline plays
a role as a disciplining action of Yahweh: He humbles Israel by
hunger, directing the people to the good land and acting as a
man who disciplines his son.[15] Obviously, the discipline because
of God's mercy has a limit, since its goal is not ruin, but life in
His fellowship (cf. Ps. 118:18). Therefore, it is also connected
to the admonition to follow straight paths in order that there
be healing (Heb. 12:13). Grace is the origin of discipline; thus,
it fills it with the perspective of salvation.[16] Even when there
is mention of very serious and far-reaching sin in the Church,
the directedness to a goal comes clearly to light. When Paul
warns the church of Corinth on account of her tolerance and
then himself "excommunicates" the sinner, he indicates the
perspective: the deliverance of the sinner to Satan happens "for
the destruction of the flesh, that his spirit may be saved in the

14. Heb. 12:10. The directedness of discipline to a goal also plays a role
    in Elihu's address (Job 36:9ff.). To what degree it is an "orthodox"
    framework or a deep mystery of discipline because of the love of God
    in the totality of God's revelation depends on the judgment especially
    of Elihu's train of thought (cf. N.H. Snaith, The Book of Job. Its
    Origin and Purpose, 1968, pp. 86ff.).
15. Deut. 8:3-7. Cf. also 11:2. The thought also appears in the speech of
    Eliphaz as a blessing: "happy is the man" (Job 5:17f. LXX — makários
    dè ánthrōpos).
16. "His chastisement arises from His grace" (O. Michel, op. cit., p. 297).
    Cf. Rev. 3:19 ("Those whom I love, I reprove and chasten"— elénchō
    kaì paideúō); and II Sam. 7:14f. (the father-son relationship in con-
    nection with chastening as well as with steadfast love). Cf. K. Barth,
    C.D., IV/1, p. 537.

day of the Lord Jesus."[17] It may be unclear to us precisely what Paul meant by this extremely positive deliverance to Satan, but there can be no misunderstanding about the teleology. No self-exultation is contained here either, but only a reflection of what God Himself intended with discipline. The Church must be guarded and protected against dangers, since she is so weak and vulnerable; and discipline is directed to repentance. This directedness to a goal is the decisive starting point for all reflection on discipline, and it constitutes a pointed protest against allowing discipline to deteriorate. A moralistic discipline may not be allowed to darken the splendor of grace and mercy; otherwise, the meaning of empowerment is lost due to a lack of appreciation for the teleology of discipline.[18]

The dangers in discipline

In the New Testament, this discipline is related to human empowerment, and the words of admonition and forgiveness are heard through the *vox humana*. We touch here particularly on the power of the keys, which are called by the Smalcald Articles "an office and a power of the Church given by Christ to bind and to loose sin."[19] Already with respect to empowerment to forgiveness, questions can arise about the certainty of the *vox humana*,[20] but at least we are dealing with a joyful message that comes via human mediation (Rom. 10:15). However, when admonition, warning, and discipline come into view, we seem to have landed in an all-too-human sphere. Has there not been reason for the tidal wave of irritation at this kind of empowerment?

In 1937, von Campenhausen wrote that the doctrine of the power of the keys "has played no role any longer in the general,

17. I Cor. 5:5. Cf. the cleansing out of the old leaven (5:7) in the Church, not the judging of those who are outside (5:12f.). For the "so that" of discipline, cf. finally I Cor. 11:32: chastening by the judgment of the Lord "so that we may not be condemned along with the world." Cf. *TDNT*, V, 624f. The purpose is designated also in I Tim. 1:20 (learning not to blaspheme). Cf. Matt. 18:15ff., with listening as the purpose and expectation.
18. Cf. II Tim. 2:25 (gentleness in correction); I Cor. 14:25 (the disclosure of the secrets of the heart in worship and confession).
19. J. Müller, *Bekenntn.schr.*, 1930, p. 321.
20. We are thinking of the longing to hear it "from His mouth" itself (cf. the old Dutch rhymed version, Ps. 56:5) and the unprecedented certainty that rests on it in this Psalm.

theological movement of the last 150 years."[21] That may be connected to a greater sensitivity to the danger of human judgment above others. The realization of the unsearchableness of human life, especially, has played a role here — the lack of knowledge of what is in a man in distinction from the man's own spirit (cf. I Cor. 2:11). That has also determined reflection on the *extra ecclesiam nulla salus*,[22] and it has given new impulse to the earlier *de intimis non judicat ecclesia* ("the Church does not judge what is innermost"). Not judging lest we be judged seemed to lead more and more to the Church's shrinking back from a definitive "judgment." In addition, the empowerment to discipline in the Church's history was frequently misused and perverted into an exercise of might that had no interest in what stands in the foreground of the New Testament as the grace of God.[23] Because of a sense of "power," doors can be closed that are not closed on God's authority, for instance, when the disciples hindered children from approaching the Lord (Matt. 19:14; Mark 10:14; Luke 18:16) or wanted to bring down fire from heaven on the Samaritans.[24] Those who wield the authority of the keys must also undergo the judgment of God. They, too, stand under the absolute test of divine purity. To recognize the dangers of the power of the keys has nothing to do with relativizing the earnestness of sin or with tolerance.

On account of all the possible dangers, discipline has often been seen as basically impossible for the Church. Again and again, one shrank back from this judgment of men, which could end fatally with the loss of the realization of what had originally determined the Church herself — namely, forgiveness.[25] In this connection, one has recalled the parable of the weeds. They were sown in the field next to the good seed, and the servants were not permitted to gather them on account of the danger that the wheat might also be rooted up (Matt. 13:28ff.; cf. 13:47). The admonition to let both grow together until the harvest was

---

21. H.F. von Campenhausen, "Die Schlüsselgewalt der Kirche," *Evang. Theol.*, 1937, p. 143; cf. A. Kuyper, *E Voto*, III, 264ff.
22. Cf. above, chapter 6, pp. 139ff., and, as an example, the nuances in the word "extra" in Pope Pius IX in the 19th century, especially in the distinction between *ignorantia* (ignorance) and *pertinacia* (obstinacy).
23. Cf. K. Barth, *C.D.*, III/4, pp. 282f.
24. Luke 9:51-56. Cf. also Acts 10:14; Mark 9:38-41; Luke 9:49f.
25. Cf. Paul on the punishment that may not be continued, but must be replaced by forgiveness, comfort, and love — all of which is in radical defense against Satan's designs (II Cor. 2:5-11).

seen as an indication of the problematic element in all human discipline. It always runs the danger of being corrupted by the kind of human pride that Calvin writes about in connection with Romans 12:19: "innate pride, which makes us very indulgent to our own faults and inexorable to those of others."[26] Others, though, recalled correctly that the parables are concerned with the Kingdom of God. According to Christ's interpretation, the field is the world.[27]

Although it is correct that we cannot resolve the problem of discipline in the Church by an appeal to this text, we must consider the reference to God's final judgment as a serious matter. The parable of the weeds in the field is probably aimed at those who wanted to "separate" the holy remnant of the messianic Church in purity and holiness, grasping in advance at God's judgment.[28] That, however, is impossible, since this eschatological judgment, which bears a definitive character, is not given to men. Hence, what is forbidden in the parable cannot determine the character of discipline, since discipline cannot be concerned with a final, definitive separation. That does not remove the serious character of discipline, but it can never be a closed judgment, because what is characteristic of all human exercise of discipline is precisely that it is not definitive. If it is closed, it loses its meaning entirely and is separated from its root, its relatedness to God's grace and mercy. Where discipline adopts this form, we can speak only of "errors of judgment" and a "premature separation."[29] Lacking patience, one usurps God's pure judgment, with the result that all the perspectives of restoration and repentance are excluded. Paul warns urgently against such a final "eschatological" judgment by men; they are reminded that they are *in time,* that time in which the history of God with man occurs. And no judgment may be pronounced before the time that the Lord comes, when the purposes of the heart will be disclosed (I Cor. 4:5). Discipline has its place, meaning, and significance along this way through time in the midst of all the complications of situations and motivations, of stumbling and standing up, of alienation, apostasy, and return. According to its deepest intention, it is related to this time, to the time that has been filled with God's patience and mercy. While men like Jonah no longer have any perspective and want

26. Calvin, *Commentaries on the Epistle of Paul to the Romans,* p. 473.
27. Matt. 13:38. Cf. R. Schippers, *Gelijkenissen des Heren,* 1962, p. 65.
28. Cf. J. Jeremias, *The Parables of Jesus,* p. 157.
29. *Ibid.*

to pronounce a definitive, irrevocable judgment,[30] God's mercy intends to fill all deeds, even those of admonition and discipline, with deep expectation.

The Church has always wanted to do justice to all of this by giving attention to the character of discipline as a process. We see that process with its many possibilities and perspectives in Matt. 18:15-17, where different phases are mentioned in punishment: first in the personal sphere, then in the presence of witnesses, and finally in the Church. These phases can end in the dark phenomenon of not listening. Process and restraint is reflected also in Tit. 3:10, where we read of an admonishment "once or twice." Such discipline in human actions and considerations can be nothing else than a reflection of God's forbearance, "not wishing that any should perish, but that all should reach repentance" (II Pet. 3:9). Thereby, all the Church's activity and care is given its essential scope. When this context is respected in a living Church, there is extreme patience in all her discipline. Apart from intense expectation, the process is inconceivable. It becomes a regulated, lifeless technique, taking on a business-like character as the application of a number of legal rules. Then, too, the purpose of all admonition is forgotten: love which issues from a pure heart (I Tim. 1:5). However, when discipline is understood, it can receive a serious character in alarm at concrete disturbances by men who do not want to know of this discipline (Titus 1:10, 16) because of alienation from the grace of God. And within this discipline, sharp rebuke can have a place, since its aim is salvation and soundness in the faith (1:13). But as a flower that is pulled from the stem withers, so discipline that is not understood will always disclose its deadly character and wake irritation. For it gives the impression of human meddling and human discrimination!

A judicial act?

There has been much concern with the nature of ecclesiastical empowerment and discipline. Does discipline bear a judicial character, or is it absorbed in the proclamation of the gospel? On the basis of John 20:22f., Trent spoke of "the power (*potestas*) of forgiving and retaining sins," calling it a distortion

---

30. Jonah 4. Cf. the magnificent section on "Mission without a Missionary" in K.H. Miskotte, *Als de Goden Zwijgen*, 1956, pp. 352ff., on the perspectives in connection with the Gentiles who suddenly no longer believe in "the immutability of God."

of this power to apply the words to the authority of preaching the gospel.[31] It is clear from this how Trent pictured the Reformed view of the power of the keys.[32] In contrast to the power of the keys as only a declarative act, the judicial deed was highlighted: the priest makes a pronouncement as a "judge." The contrast suggests that the declarative proclamation of the Word can only be a "verbal" affair. It does not actually affect man in his sinfulness, as is apparent from the dilemma: *only* proclamation or actual empowerment.[33] The Reformers indeed reacted sharply against separating the power of the keys from the proclamation of the Word, as we see clearly in Calvin.[34] He is not concerned to deny the right that Christ has granted His Church, but he wants to point out that "any right of binding or loosing which Christ conferred upon his church is bound to the Word" (*Inst.*, III, 4, 14; cf. IV, 2, 10). The whole power of the ministry of the keys lies in the grace of the gospel, which is sealed in the hearts of believers. That can happen "only through preaching." However, preaching is not a "bare ministry," but the empowered authority of the proclamation as the actual power of the keys. Here the dilemma is broken through.

The word "judicial" is obviously not decisive. Calvin, too, can use this word and other words to refer to the reality of the power of the keys. He can speak unbiasedly, for instance, about the "jurisdiction of the Church" ("and its abuse") and about

31. Denz., 913: *detorserit autem ... ad auctoritatem praedicandi Evangelium.*
32. See especially the remarkable context of the polemic against the Reformation. Not only is it postulated that absolution is "not merely a simple ministry (*nudum ministerium*)" but a "judicial act" (Denz., 902; *TCT*, 794), but also the characterizations are employed of absolving "in jest and without a serious intention" and not requiring "the confession of the penitent" (Denz., 919; *TCT*, 808). On this remarkable polemic, see K.J. Becker, *Der Priesterliche Dienst, II, Wesen und Vollmachten des Priestertums nach dem Lehramt*, 1970, pp. 77ff. On the *actus judicalis*, cf. further K. Lehmann, "Das dogmatische Problem des theol. Ansatzes des Amtspriestertums," *Existenzprobleme des Priesters*, 1969, pp. 135ff.; L. Olt, "Das Weihesakrament," *Handbuch der Dogmengeschichte*, IV, Fasc. 5, pp. 119ff.
33. History plays a role in this, specifically, the polemic with Abelard, who laid strong emphasis on the subjective disposition of contrition and on intercession for the forgiveness of sins and denied the power of the keys as an *actus judicalis* — an influential view "for more than a century" (B. Poschmann, *Handbuch der Dogmengeschichte*, IV, Fasc. 3, 1951, p. 85). Abelard's view was rejected at the synod of Sens in 1141.
34. Cf. Calvin, *Inst.*, III, 4, 14: "But when it is a question of the keys, we must always beware lest we dream up some power separate from the preaching of the gospel."

"ecclesiastical power" *(Inst.,* IV, 11, 1). When such words are viewed in themselves, one could think of various Roman Catholic characterizations of the power of the Church as "a perfect society,"[35] but, with Calvin, this "power" stands in a framework that is directed to the spiritual rule of the Church by the gospel. The terminology intends to give an outlook on the reality of the power of the keys, which stands in the framework of an absolute, saving relatedness to the Lord. In that way — and only in that way — can there be empowerment. Then Calvin can point out that no one may despise the judgment of the Church or consider the vote of believers unimportant, because God testifies "that such judgment by believers *is nothing but* the proclamation of his own sentence" and that "whatever they have done on earth is ratified in heaven" *(Inst.,* IV, 11, 2). We meet with this breakthrough of the dilemma also in the Heidelberg Catechism. The preaching of the gospel is not spoken of here as an external, verbal event, but as a witness to the forgiveness of sins along the way of faith and repentance in the conviction that God will judge according to this gospel (Q. 84). Moreover, it is said that the Kingdom of heaven is opened and shut by the power of the keys (Q. 85).

Frequently, one has let everything depend on the use of the word "judicial" as it appears in Trent. For example, Bohren grants that the Reformers were wrong to deny this "judicial" aspect, and he even joins Trent in speaking of an action of the Church that "is more than the mere proclamation of the Word."[36] Thus, the impression is given that everything becomes clear with the words "judicial act" and that the reality of empowerment is maintained only by it. However, analysis of the word "judicial" is of greatest importance. One must constantly ask oneself in what framework this word functions. Bavinck believes that the empowerment to open and close the Kingdom of heaven is made by Rome "totally unjustly" into a judicial power, particularly in the sacrament of penance.[37] In his opinion, the true power of the keys has been concentrated in the competency to proclaim the gospel, which opens and closes. There is no power that transcends it, earning as such the name

35. *Mystici Corporis Christi, TCT,* 262.
36. R. Bohren, *Das Problem der Kirchenzucht im N.T.,* 1952, p. 58.
37. Bavinck, *Geref. Dog.,* IV, 152. Cf. also *idem, Magnalia Dei,* 1931, pp. 539ff., on the robbing of the power of the keys of its spiritual character, namely, "in a worldly administration of justice." Cf. H. Bouwman, *De Kerkelijke Tucht,* 1912, pp. 12ff.

"judicial act." That is a usurpation, since bishops and priests become judges in an institutional understanding of power that is characteristic for Catholicism. Such a "juridical" power is inconceivable, because a limited, fallible man cannot judge "the deepest motives of the heart of his brother." No one can place his trust about eternity in "such a superficial judgment," and God alone is the Knower of hearts. According to Bavinck, empowerment is disclosed in the proclamation, which points a way of faith and conversion. Along that way, there is an outlook on the reality of salvation; and naturally, the opening and closing can never bear a definitive character.[38]

The temporal aspect of the power of the keys is not an inner inconsistency, but belongs to its essential meaning and directedness. It is the reflection of God's mercy in time, where the appeal to conversion rules everywhere. And so, it can be said that empowerment is not a purely human judgment, but a witness that corresponds to God's judgment — His wrath and condemnation *"so long as* they are not converted"* (H.C., Q. 84). When Thurneysen criticizes the Catechism on this point because the power of the keys is not seen only as proclamation of the gospel but is also connected to excommunication, the underlying idea is that the Catechism has two independent keys in mind.[39] He points out that the element of "denial of forgiveness" is then incorporated in the power of the keys, and he sees a contradiction between questions 84 and 85. He does recognize that repentance and renewed reception as members of the Church and of Christ also have a place in question 85, but he concludes that there was only a "seeming exclusion" which cannot have been meant seriously. In my view, this criticism lacks appreciation for the active aspect of the power of the keys. There can be no mention of a "relapse into the Catholic practice of penance," since the power of the keys remains inseparably connected to the proclamation. Thus, it cannot become a closed, ecclesiastical judgment. The connection of the power of the keys to the proclamation is not a "bare ministry," but an empowered ministry that is always directed to new ways and to opened doors. Thus, it manifests its conformity to God's judgment. Thereby,

---

38. Bavinck cannot be combatted by what M.J. Arntzen (*Biecht en Vergeving der Zonden,* 1961, p. 54) writes in defense of a juridical power that transcends "a defining of the relation of someone to the Kingdom of God." For Bavinck (and Calvin), the proclamation is much more than such a "defining."

39. E. Thurneysen, *A Theol. of Pastoral Care,* 1962, pp. 32ff.

the power of the keys is differentiated from all usurpation and pride, since it is inconceivable apart from the correlation with the Word of the gospel, which points out and opens ways.

Frequently, in sharp opposition to Sohm, a plea has been made for the juridical aspect of the power of the keys in order to accentuate the reality of the power of the keys. Then this power automatically got the character of a juridical plus, of an addition to the proclamation, with the result that the proclamation was externalized and minimized. The understanding of power was no longer founded totally on the correlation between penitence and forgiveness. In the Roman Catholic Church, this power was always mentioned as not autonomous, but as granted by God, which led to feelings of emotion and humility in connection with one's own priestly unworthiness.[40] But that does not detract from the fact that the empowerment begins to rule the Church's life as a juridical structure. In discussions of Church and law in connection with Rudolf Sohm, concern is always with that juridical structure. We already saw earlier that no one wants to deny that disorder must be excluded from the Church, because it endangers peace (cf. I Cor. 14:33, 40; I Thess. 5:13). But that is totally different from a "system of Church government that operates judicially" as a "purely formal, completely neutral scheme of order."[41] Everything is determined by the "matter of the church," the gospel, which is the ruling authority in all things.[42]

Although Sohm's fierce polemic is not a plea for the abstract equality of all and although he recognizes a "superiority and subordination willed by God,"[43] it is apparent that he postulates the contrast between Church and law on the basis of a specific conception of law that he calls attention to in the Roman Catholic understanding of power. He discovered an attack in it on all freedom[44] and on the Church "in the religious sense."[45] We are

---

40. Cf. the encyclical *Ad Catholici Sacerdotii*, 1935: *commotus vehementer.*
41. E. Kinder, *Der evang. Glaube und die Kirche*, 1960, pp. 165ff. Cf. D. Nauta, *Verklaring*, pp. 10ff. (on peace and concord); Calvin, *Commentaries on the Epistle of Paul to the Corinthians*, I (on I Cor. 14:40).
42. Cf. R. Sohm, *Kirchenrecht, I, Die geschichtl. Grundlagen*, 1892, p. 3.
43. *Ibid.*, p. 26.
44. *Ibid.*, p. 27. Cf. p. 28: "duty of love" versus "duty of law." Cf. Sohm's *Wesen und Ursprung des Katholizismus*, 1922, p. 18, on the Church as a "body of law" and as a "perfect society" and on the jurisdiction as "judicial coercive authority" and "hierarchical coercive authority" in the name of God.
45. Sohm, *Kirchenrecht*, I, 24.

not concerned here with an analysis of the motives of Sohm's ecclesiology, but the law that Sohm usually has in view clearly is not in harmony with what God intended for the Church and her empowerment. It is in conflict with what Paul says vis-à-vis caricatures — viz., that empowerment and authority are not out to lord it over the Church's faith, but rather to work together for her joy (II Cor. 1:24). So, real caricatures induced Sohm, and especially Brunner,[46] to fierce defense, but they did not rise above the caricatures to reflect without reaction on that reality of empowerment that, on the basis of the relation to the gospel and to the Lord Himself, places the Church's life under empowerment and testing according to God's judgment. For then it is no longer necessary to oppose every connection of Church and law, since the empowerment is directed and serviceable precisely to the upbuilding of the Church.

If the gospel remains the focus of all empowerment, the power can never be independent as if it were inherently at the disposal of the Church, for that would obscure the outlook on the empowerment of the Lord Himself. Understandably, warnings were issued at the Second Vatican Council not only against triumphalism, but also against all juridicalism. Both are closely connected and can appear in an "ecclesiology of glory."[47] Then the realization of the total dependence of the Church's whole life on the Spirit, Who "withdraws Himself from all rational legal thinking," disappears.[48] To recognize this is in no sense to escape into an irrational ecclesiology, but to recall the dependence of the Church on the Holy Spirit. The power of the keys is never excluded from testing. No matter how greatly — in fear and trembling — the "applicability" of human judgment before God is emphasized, as in both Calvin and the Heidelberg Catechism, it must be recognized that there can be no a priori automatic identification, inherently present in the Church apart from all testing. Even if one brings the power of the keys into direct connection with "divine law," meaning by that the commission in human functionality in the midst of the Church's threatened life and holiness, this divine law can never legitimize a kind of thinking about power that does not acknowledge per-

46. E. Brunner, The Misunderstanding of the Church, 1952; and Dogmatik, III.
47. Cf. the speech by Stephen Laszlo at the Council (Konzilsreden, 1964, pp. 36ff.).
48. J.N. Bakhuizen van den Brink, Jus Ecclesiasticum. Historische Beschouwingen over Kerk en Recht, 1968, p. 39. Cf. p. 35.

manently and fully the outlook on the Lord Himself and on His empowerment and living presence.[49] It is understandable and legitimate that Rome, faced with various spiritualistic conceptions of the Church as "a Church of love" — in opposition to institutionalization, authority, and empowerment — rejected "mystical" ecclesiology as not in harmony with Christ's intentions.[50] The Church is truly more human than came to light in this ecclesiology, and there can be no dilemma in the communion of the Church between love and empowerment, love and order, love and institution. But the outlook on the nature of empowerment, authority, and institution is obscured if they become usable givens. For the empowerment does not have legitimacy simply because of its factuality, and it may not be separated from the proclamation of the gospel.

Discipline and one's own life

Since the Church herself has not been elevated above all sin, the question can arise whether there can ever be justification for discipline in the Church. One is reminded unintentionally here of Jesus' words to the Pharisees who accuse and condemn the woman caught in adultery. He calls them to order with the pointed statement, "Let him who is without sin among you be the first to throw a stone at her." Apparently impressed by that statement, they go away one by one (John 8:7, 9). In view of the confession of guilt, is it possible to speak with empowerment about sin and to know that what is said has validity before God's face? Bohren understood the pericope in such a way that there is a clear indication for discipline. Jesus demands "that discipline be executed by the sinless."[51] In I Corinthians, like-

---

49. Cf. K. Rahner, "Reflections on the Concept of 'Jus Divinum' in Catholic Thought," *Theological Investigations*, VI, 219ff. Cf. the critical remark by Calvin *(Inst.,* IV, 2, 10), who does not doubt the "divine law" *(jus divinum)* of the power of the keys: "For if they are churches *(nam si Ecclesiae sunt),* the power of the keys is in their hands; but the keys have an indissoluble bond with the Word" — a critical pericope against every independent, inherent power.

50. Cf. *Mystici Corporis Christi, TCT,* 264.

51. On John 8:7, Calvin *(Commentaries on the Gospel according to John,* I, 320f.) points to Deut. 17:7 (the hand of the witnesses shall be first against him) with the conclusion: "here Christ demands from the witnesses perfect innocence, so that no man ought to accuse another of crime, unless he be pure, and free from every fault." Calvin does not deduce a veto on discipline of sinners from this, but he sees it as a criticism of hypocrisy.

wise, the sinner must be removed from the Church, in order that they be a "new lump" and the paschal festival be celebrated "not with the old leaven, the leaven of malice and evil, but with the unleavened bread of sincerity and truth."[52] Even though one does not derive the total impossibility of discipline from these examples, it remains striking that Jesus does not "apply" the law to which the Pharisees appealed in a simple casuistry,[53] but refers to their own lives, which, according to their own "objective" procedure of discipline, were not under discussion! Jesus does not break through the one law or the other, nor the stoning as such, but uproots the whole technique in an unprecedented way in order to save the adulterous woman from imminent judgment.

It is good to take serious account of this correlation and to observe the problem here in order not to lapse into a superficial technique of discipline.[54] The background of the penal laws in Lev. 20 is that the people of God have been set apart. When concrete sins come into view, which defile the sanctuary and profane God's holy Name (20:1-7), the admonition follows: "Consecrate yourselves therefore, and be holy; for I am the Lord your God" (20:7). And that implies keeping God's statutes (20:8ff., 22ff.). In the New Testament, too, discipline is most closely connected to the Church's holiness. It is not simply that a number of individuals confer together on the exercise of the empowerment to discipline, but Paul speaks in a concrete case of a gathering "of you and my spirit with the power of our Lord Jesus" (I Cor. 5:4). The danger is not imaginary that one may forget this connection between the Church's holiness and discipline, thus devaluing discipline to a rule of order that does not take one's own life in concrete holiness into consideration. Then discipline is objectivized and can scarcely be distinguished from pride, self-overestimation, and discrimination. In the form for excommunication in the Reformed Church (Gereformeerde Kerken), attention is called emphatically to this correlation. Not

52. I Cor. 5:6-8. Cf. Bohren, *op. cit.*, p. 62: "The summons to ecclesiastical discipline is founded on the sinlessness of the Church."
53. Grosheide, *Het Heilig Evangelie volgens Johannes*, II, 3.
54. That the condemnation of sin is not relativized here is clear. Christ's not condemning (John 8:11) not only implies a new way (not sinning anymore), but is also a disclosure of the grace of Him Who is "without sin" and does not take up a stone. Cf. Calvin on this passage and K. Barth, *C.D.*, III/4, pp. 234f. The departure of the Pharisees (the only "likable" feature of the Pharisees in the whole gospel!) withdraws them from the sudden appearance here of the luminous circle of grace.

only is the Church admonished not to hold the one who has been disciplined as an enemy but as the object of admonition "as you would a brother," but the Church is also summoned to recall Paul's admonition: "let any one who thinks that he stands take heed lest he fall" (I Cor. 10:12). Moreover, in the prayer that follows, the confession of one's own guilt and the recognition of deserving excommunication also sound forth.

This remarkable concentration on one's own life and one's own guilt may not be interpreted as "pious" hypocrisy. Naturally, though, one must always ask whether the Church is truly acting in this disposition and in this prayer. Only if this correlation in word and deed — in the whole life of the Church — is present will it be possible to take away the stumbling blocks of human pride and discrimination from discipline. One cannot withdraw from the seriousness of this connection by pointing out that discipline is concerned only with public, grievous sins. Whoever does that in order to arrive at an "objective" discipline, thus seeing it as a self-evident right for the protection of the Church's "holiness," lapses irrevocably into the Pharisaic attitude, which classifies sinners in hard-hearted discrimination on the basis of the "moral" Torah. This attitude is exposed by Jesus through reference to what, although not always spectacular, can arise out of the heart (Matt. 15:19). Discipline is always threatened by the danger of pride and discrimination. It can appear that everything is going "legally" while there is total confusion in one's own life. In the gospel we read of an "excommunication" where one born blind is cast out of the synagogue (John 9:22, 34). The disciples, too, face the same threat (12:42; 16:2). Here the relation between the holiness and discipline of the people of God has been severed. The application of the Old Testament *ḥerem* ("devotion to destruction") can become a sinister affair that goes against the whole work of the Messiah and ends in His own excommunication outside the camp (Heb. 13:11f.). The "religious" foundation — thinking that one is offering service to God (John 16:2) — does not make this discipline any less serious, but increases the guilt; and Christ connects this exclusion directly to a blessing in order to take away every misunderstanding about what happens here through men (Luke 6:22; cf. John 12:42). Yet, when faced with the admonitions and warnings of the Church, one will have to think twice before one too hastily justifies oneself on the basis of this "blessing"!

The irremovable correlation between holiness and discipline

is disclosed in the contrast with all pseudo-empowerment and pseudo-discipline, for discipline is not only directed to holiness, but also presupposes it. Here there is testing not only of the lives of others, but also of one's own life.[55] Only in this way is it understandable that discipline has everything to do with the visibility of the Church, which is the light of the world, the sign of God's mercy in the world, and the witness of the restoration of grace. Exercising discipline here without also truly standing under this mercy — also in the saying, "Go and do not sin again" (John 8:11) — is nothing but an inner contradiction. Then the Church employs her empowerment in appearance only, without blessing and without admonition not to fail to obtain the grace of God, Who loves the world (3:16) and justifies the ungodly (Rom. 4:5).

Heresy

In the history of the Church, the potential necessity for the Church to intervene when she saw the proclamation of the gospel threatened by heresy always came up for discussion in connection with discipline too. One need not be surprised that this action of the Church, usually designated as doctrinal discipline, was often the occasion of moving, passionate discussions. For living men are always involved, men who are dealing with the gospel and the proclamation in their way and who are related very existentially to possible discipline. We are not thinking here of the problem of latent heresy, which can be unarticulated and hidden in the Church. It is a certain feeling about life that gradually becomes alienated from concrete points of the Church's confession. This heresy — usually more suspected than established, because it is connected more with what is suppressed or gets less stress than with what is discussed — is difficult to demonstrate as a concrete, threatening danger for the Church.[56] However, doctrinal discipline is concerned with what comes up for discussion explicitly. Heresy, no matter how time-bound it is,[57] is always after a different interpretation of

---

55. D. Nauta, *Verklaring van de Kerkorde van de Geref. Kerken in Nederland,* 1971, p. 359, on "continuous self-discipline."
56. Cf. K. Rahner, "What Is Heresy?" *Theological Investigations,* VI, 468ff.
57. Various transformations of heresy do not exclude continuity in heresy, naturally. A. Kuyper (*Het Modernisme een Fata Morgana op Christelijk Gebied,* 1871) believed that there was a close affinity between the modernism of the 19th century and Arius.

the gospel. It can adopt such forms that the Church must ask
whether the gospel is not robbed of its meaning. In the ancient
Church, when heresy did not adopt an antithetical position to
the witness of the Holy Scriptures, but rather intended nothing
else than to interpret this witness and constantly appealed to
it,[58] the Church was faced with the question of whether or not
various interpretations of the gospel were tolerable. The complicated problem of recognizing heresy was of decisive significance then, especially because heresy claimed that the Church
could understand and proclaim the gospel truly only in this
way.[59] There were countless complications in ideas about the
mystery and in the terminology that was used to express this
mystery. It is apparent from the long struggle about christological and trinitarian dogma that recognition of heresy was
anything but a simple affair.[60]

Sometimes in the course of history we get the impression
that that recognition is not so difficult after all. We meet with
a positive "rejection," a *damnamus,* or an *anathema sit.* But, at
closer inspection, it is apparent that one has not come to such
judgment except after an attempt at analysis. Such analysis is
a *sine qua non* for every judgment by the Church, and it is of
decisive significance for all concrete reflection on doctrinal discipline.[61] Naturally, in later times, deeper historical research
can lead to the question of whether the analysis was correct and
did justice to the adversaries.[62] But that does not take away the

58. With regard, specifically, to the mystery of Christ's person — *vere Deus,
    vere homo.* Cf. my *The Person of Christ,* 1954, pp. 59ff., 155ff. See pp.
    60f. on Arius' appeal to Scripture, among other places, to Deut. 6:4 and
    Prov. 8:22.
59. Cf. A.A. van Ruler, "Uitzichten in het Vraagstuk van de Leertucht,"
    Kerk en Theol., 1959, p. 11, on the attempt of heresy "to penetrate
    more deeply into the mystery and to express it better than the Church
    has so far been able to."
60. Bavinck (*Geref. Dog.,* III, 265) writes that the faith with which the
    Church made her appearance in the world knows "that in Christ God
    Himself had come to her and had incorporated her in His fellowship."
    The problem is that this conviction was basic for practically all who
    were involved in the christological struggle and who were convinced
    of the evidentness of their own view.
61. That has been understood by the Church, as appears from many de-
    fenses that are based on an analysis of the "deviating" opinion, for
    instance, at Trent, where many opinions were reproduced and then
    were answered with the *anathema sit.* Cf. also the detailed reproduction
    of the doctrine of the Remonstrants in the Canons of Dort.
62. The Roman Catholic Church pronounced that the condemnation of
    a particular opinion implies that the analysis of the heretics was cor-

urgency of analysis, especially when the dispute is not simply a theological discussion but a struggle about the proclamation of the gospel, with the result that the decisions that are made have great bearing on those who until now have had a place in that proclamation as servants of the Church. That gives a personal focus to the recognition of heresy, especially because the Church's defense was always also intended as an appeal to a return to purity in the confession. Naturally, such an appeal was out of the question if there was an incorrect analysis, a caricature. The realization of the necessity of correct analysis was often connected in later times to the question of whether the Church was really authorized to declare a radical *damnamus* or *anathema sit* against heresy. Was her insight not limited and her knowledge imperfect (cf. I Cor. 13:9f.)? Here and there, one asked whether doctrinal discipline was not possible only in a Church which had an infallible agency to pass the definitive judgment. Such considerations could lead to hesitation in the exercise of doctrinal discipline, and this hesitation was strengthened further by the recollection of the Church's history, since whatever diverged at first sight from tradition was often rejected as an alien innovation.[63] In that way, the confession and discipline could be formalized into something that had little or nothing to do with the original intention of discipline — the pure proclamation of the gospel. It could become an uncomplicated, intellectual procedure leading to discrimination and rash intolerance. For this to happen, it is not necessary that discipline adopt the form of power and force, as was often the case earlier with heretics, who were coerced with the dilemma: conversion or annihilation.[64] Even apart from coercion and force, it is possible for the Church as the Church, as the house

rect. The problem became acute in connection with the condemnation of Jansenism. Cf. my *The Second Vatican Council and the New Catholicism*, p. 50, on the so-called "dogmatic facts." In our day this analysis is seen with much less bias, for instance, with regard to the condemnation of Luther in the decree on justification at Trent. Cf. H. Küng, *Justification*, pp. 217f.: did Luther mean it in that way?

63. Concerning the *anathema* in the Roman Catholic Church, profound changes have arisen not only in a certain reserve (for instance, John XXIII: mercy rather than condemnation), but also due to the many complications in recognizing heresy within a new horizon of the Church. Cf. M.M. Bourke, "Should the Church Impose Sanctions for Errors of Faith?", *Concilium*, 51, 1970, pp. 21ff.

64. Cf. K. Aland, "Toleranz und Glaubensfreiheit im 16. Jahrh.," *Reformation und Humanismus. R. Stupperich zum 65. Geburtstag*, 1969, p. 77.

of God, as the temple, as the bride of the Lord, as the body of Christ, as light in the world, and as the sign of God's mercy, to become unrecognizable because of the absence of the spiritual character of discipline.

We touch here on the far-reaching problematic of tolerance and intolerance. In the course of the centuries, both words have acquired a certain emotional value and their precise significance cannot be simply described. It is possible, via an appeal to tolerance, for one to end up in an indifference that no longer takes the obscuring of the gospel seriously.[65] But it is also possible, via an appeal to the necessity of intolerance for the sake of the truth,[66] for one to become far removed from what God intended with the Church as "the pillar and bulwark of the truth" and as the light of the world. Therefore, everything depends on the concrete content that the concepts tolerance and intolerance are given. Many hesitations about doctrinal discipline are connected to the fact that it, at least at first sight, has the appearance of far-reaching intolerance, haughtiness, and narrowness. This appearance is strengthened further if a certain arbitrariness penetrates into discipline with respect to the preaching of the gospel, arousing doubt about whether the Church is truly concerned in her discipline with the gospel. Remarkably, doctrinal discipline has often been concentrated on the ascertainment and contradiction of explicit deviations in the Church's doctrine and confession, while there was no discussion of such discipline where the confession was not openly assailed, even though the preaching of the gospel as a *joyful* message was obscured. Then the impression had to arise that verbal conformity with doctrine alone was at issue. Moreover, concern with this verbal conformity can slacken concern for forms of heresy that penetrate under the seeming protection of orthodoxy: the life and thought of the Church can capitulate

---

65. Cf. E. Wolf, "Toleranz nach evang. Verständnis," *Peregrinatio*, II, 284ff. Gunning valued Trent's anathema on heretics higher morally than those who "esteem" all convictions as legitimate (cf. Noordmans, *Geestelijke Perspectiven*, 1930, p. 119).

66. This appeal to the "intolerant" truth played a large role in Rome's (earlier) view of religious freedom, particularly, of whether someone had the right to teach an error. The shift from the 19th to the 20th century on this question is striking (cf. the declaration of the Second Vatican Council on religious freedom, *Dignitatis Humanae*). See my *Nabetrachting op het Concilie*, pp. 35ff.; W.F. Golterman, "De Libertate Religiosa," *Nederlands Theologisch Tijdschrift*, XXIII, 438ff.

to particular ideologies, frequently even with an appeal to the gospel.[67]

We touch here on the danger of an inner inconsistency that is connected to the misunderstanding of doctrine, or teaching (didachē). There is interest in what Noordmans called the empirical heretic — in clearly demonstrable deviation from the confession — but there is little concern for other threats that, in spite of verbal conformity with the Church's confession, can stand in the way of the proclamation of the gospel.[68] When Noordmans points also to the ethical heretic,[69] he does not mean discipline of life in the traditional sense (the "morality" of the preacher), but that form of heresy "which hinders the Church in her revelation." Naturally, this can also be the case with respect to the empirical heretic, as a threat to the Church by a "higher" and "deeper" interpretation of the gospel, but the horizon of heresy is broader. It is as broad as life itself and it can also become visible with respect to the serviceability "to keep the gospel to its course."[70] Only on the basis of this broad horizon is it possible to take heresy in full seriousness, since the significance and consequences of the proclamation of the gospel come into view here.[71] Naturally, there can be much difference in insight about those consequences, but it is impossible to isolate doctrinal discipline, suggesting that "orthodoxy" in christology or in the confession of providence already guarantees the safety of the Church (Barmen). Where these connections are neglected and various forms of heresy remain "latent,"[72] or at least unnoticed as heresy, the full outlook on the appearance of the grace of God for the salvation of all men (Titus 2:11)

67. One may recall the conflict about the Barmen Declaration, which opposed false doctrine, and the profession of the Reich Bishop Ludwig Müller about his orthodoxy. Cf. K. Strijd, "Dimensies der Leertucht," Nederlands Theol. Tijdsch., 1961, pp. 447ff.

68. Van Ruler, especially, has warned against an intellectual formalization of discipline (in a plea for doctrinal discipline) when he protested against "the madness of the mutual charges of heresy" within the Reformed religion, for which there are not enough tears to lament them (Hoe Functioneert de Belijdenis?, 1954, p. 33).

69. O. Noordmans, Beginselen van Kerkorde, 1932, p. 11.

70. Ibid. Cf. F. Haarsma, Geest en Kerk, 1967, pp. 237ff.

71. One may recall the extinguishing of the light (the removal of the lampstand) in connection with the abandonment of the love that was held at first (Rev. 2:4f.).

72. Cf. K. Rahner (Theological Investigations, VI, 470ff.) on the danger of heresy for salvation and on the relation between heresy and apostasy (481ff.).

eventually disappears. Only in the relatedness of doctrinal discipline to this gospel can the relation between holiness and discipline be legitimate. Only here can it be evident that discipline has nothing to do with discrimination or self-exaltation, narrow-mindedness or contempt for others. In this framework there can be no doubt that the calling of the Church is to act in such a way that the light of divine grace and mercy is not obscured. It is the light to which she herself was called out of darkness, the light that she wants to make shine for all. Here, the posture of the Church can and must also have the form of discipline and defense.

Clearly, the Church is called to the greatest caution in this defense. The reason is not indifference to truth,[73] but the realization that too much is at stake for one to proceed carelessly here. One of the most moving facets of the Church's life is her defense in speech and action that she must later take back. There is always something irreparable about that, and it is among the darkest shadows in the Church's life.[74] Particularly in times of transition and change, the Church is cautioned even more against premature and incorrect judgments about doctrine. At present, ecclesiastical life is determined much more strongly than earlier by hesitation and restraint in making definitive judgments. Not only is one aware that in the past doctrinal discipline was often paired with further disunity, but also the idea plays a role that there can be defense and contradiction only on the basis of the unity and fellowship of the Church, which is Christ's body — on the basis of the one Church that confesses her holiness and therein opposes all darkness.[75]

73. Cf. in contrast Luther's plea for "assertions" in light of the statement: "The Holy Spirit is no Sceptic" (*Spiritus Sanctus non est Scepticus*). See my *Holy Scripture*, pp. 43f.
74. In the history of the Roman Catholic Church, the process against Galileo lived on up till the Second Vatican Council as a ghost; the decision was actually taken back, but it was usually in the form of "tacit revision." Cf. O. Loretz, *Galilei und der Irrtum der Inquisition*, 1966, pp. 143ff.
75. Cf. A.A. van Ruler, *op. cit.*, pp. 8ff., on the possibility of doctrinal discipline, resting on the restoration of the Church's unity and on the ecumenical question as an urgent matter precisely because of discipline! Cf. also his "Het Einde van een Huishoudelijke Twist," *Kerk en Theologie*, 1970, p. 13. The problem of doctrinal discipline in a particular church becomes especially visible when a conversion to another church (and her offices) takes place. Even though one can assume that doctrinal discipline is related to what is explicitly proclaimed and does not imply an "eschatological" judgment, this "prob-

The significance of this aspect of the Church and her discipline is even more pressing, since questions are being asked about the seriousness, the right, and the sense of the Church's division. Earlier, the *damnamus* and the *anathema sit*[76] seemed to answer all questions, but that answer became less clear and less serious in later times because of many shifts in the churches.[77] The analysis of actual heresy as a threat has become more complicated in a groping search for the continuity confessed by the Church and for the Church's unity under the promise of the Holy Spirit. In that situation, the fear can arise that all of this must lead eventually to indifference and boundless tolerance, resulting in a much greater "elasticity" that has no affinity to the clear defense of the New Testament. The word "elasticity" always has the sound of a far-reaching relativizing. Remarkably, though, Bavinck did not shrink back from this word when he came to the conclusion that "some elasticity in the purity of the administration of the Word must be accepted from a Protestant point of view, as otherwise nearly all life in fellowship would become impossible and sectarianism would be fostered in the most terrible way."[78] In this connection, he points out that heresy can only be related to obstinate error about what belongs to the foundation of the Church; and when he adds that heresy thus becomes "a fluctuating concept," all these words seem to be extremely vulnerable. However, Bavinck obviously does not intend to relativize the truth and the Church's confession, but to appeal to the true — and not always simple — recognition of heresy. He adds a warning against all lack of caution in judging others.[79] Naturally, in reaction to

lem of offices" nevertheless remains an indication of an unsolvable problem in the divided Church.

76. Apart from that, one should consider the riskiness of the *anathema sit* in light of the *anáthema* in the New Testament (Gal. 1:8; cf. I Cor. 16:22) with its radical aspects. Cf. the *anáthema* in the LXX as the translation for the Old Testament *ḥerem*. Cf. M.M. Bourke, *op. cit.*, pp. 19ff.

77. One of the many symptoms is Lord's Day 30 of the Heidelberg Catechism concerning the mass as "accursed idolatry." There are many other questions, too, in connection with the relation between Rome and the Reformation. They were discussed at the General Synod of the Gereformeerde Kerken. Cf. *Acta Gen. Syn. 1969-70*, pp. 271ff.; and the report on subscription to the confession (on H.C., Q. 80 and B.C., Art. 29).

78. H. Bavinck, *Katholiciteit*, 1968², p. 26.

79. "As long as others who differ from us attach value to the Christian name, there is no reason to dispute it with them and to drive them

"fanaticism for truth,"[80] this appeal to caution can be misused by indifferentism, but Bavinck's concern is just the opposite; attention is called to the substance of the truth, which must always determine the boundaries. Precisely because the Church is not a school of philosophy but a proclaimer of good news, a witness of God's salvation for the world, it is out of the question to think that one might have the right "to stick the dagger of intellectuality in this heart of the matter."[81] All simplistic usage of particular patterns is in conflict with the earnestness of the controversy about doctrinal discipline.

Particularly in times when new perspectives loom up in the understanding of the Scriptures, recognition of heresy also becomes more complicated. It is possible only against the background of the recognition of the truth. What was said in chapter eleven about concentration on the central apostolic witness returns of itself in considerations about the Church's defense. All that presents itself to the Church as new insight — sometimes in sharp reaction to earlier onesidedness — confronts the Church with the question of her own faith and her own interpretation of the gospel in our time. There is certainly no reason to complain about this new commission, since the Church is tested by it as to whether her own faith truly overcomes the world (I John 5:4). In this confrontation she may not capitulate uncritically to all that is new. In the midst of all the uproar of theology, the warning not to believe every "spirit," but to test all spirits to see whether they are of God (4:1), is valid. This commission applies both to oneself and to others, and all "personalism" that anchors truth in "angels or men" must remain out of the question (Gal. 1:8f.). This calling is endangered whenever the Church allows herself to be closed to the Scripture because of fear of new ways and because of a process of polarization that attempts to overcome various onesidednesses by other ones — a phenomenon that has always been a breeding ground for new heresy.

The struggle about the eschatological expectation is perhaps one of the most striking aspects of the discussion of the recogni-

---

forward along the path of negation with the whip of consistency. Rather, it is befitting, then, to hold them to the Christian name and to lead them back to the fullness of truth and life which is contained in the name" (*Verzam. Opstellen*, 1921, p. 29).

80. Cf. H. Küng, *Truthfulness: the Future of the Church*, 1968, pp. 51ff.
81. A.A. van Ruler, *op. cit.*, p. 13. It is clear that he is not in the least making a plea for irrationality here.

tion of truth and heresy. In opposition to all eschatological and individualistic salvation, which was already criticized sharply by Kuyper,[82] new reflection on the expectation has begun. It is stirring up nearly all aspects of theology and the Church by calling urgently for concern with this world. Earlier, too, the attempt was made to understand that the eschatological expectation is something totally different from a futurism that abandons the present. However, at present this conviction is coming to the fore in a new way in various questions about the Kingdom of God and this world. It would be a catastrophe for the Church if she were to be confronted unintentionally with a choice between salvation-egoism and attention for the world. Such a dilemma leaves no room any longer for a "collective finding of truth"[83] which goes back to the knowing *with all the saints* that Paul speaks of (Eph. 3:17f.). Rather there can only be reaction and separated ways. Nevertheless, the concern cannot be to find a "happy medium" or to harmonize "accents," but to maintain the one expectation of its foundation, structure, and calling. Faced with the threat of heresy in both directions, the Church has been called to test all spirits and to show that the meaning of the expectation, of the resurrection of the flesh and life eternal, does not frustrate, but stimulates interest in the present and in the world. If the Church does not break through the dilemma of accents, the only possibilities that remain are a dismal egoism, which has no interest in responsibility in this world, or a human vicariate, which sees itself as the instrument of divine concern with the world but ends in moralism, cultural optimism, and human hubris.

At present in "eschatology," the anthropological questions no longer appear in the foreground, as was the case earlier in connection with dichotomy, the *anima separata* ("the separate soul"), and the *status intermedius* ("intermediate state").[84] Rather, the discussion focuses on the relation between present and future, the nature of transcendence, and especially the functionality of human striving in relation to the coming King-

82. A. Kuyper, *E Voto*, II, 201: "most Christians by far," in connection with spiritual selfishness and egoism.

83. Cf. K. Rahner, "A Small Fragment 'On the Collective Finding of Truth,'" *Theological Investigations*, VI, 82ff.

84. From the nature of the case, such questions do continue to play a role, but it is always in a definite context that is most closely connected to the central concern. Cf. E. Schillebeeckx, "Leven Ondanks de Dood in Heden en Toekomst," *Tijdschrift voor Theol.*, 1970, pp. 418ff.

dom of God.[85] The Church is prompted in this process to confess her faith and to search for the background and motives that influence present-day eschatological thinking. The Church must understand her calling not to enter into the confusion of reaction, onesidedness and accents, but to make clear in word and deed that her eschatological expectation does not make her blind, but rather seeing — through the disclosure of the meaning of this life in the hands of God.

The doctrine of God

We need not be surprised that the questions about the recognition of heresy are always concentrated in the struggle that was carried on already in the ancient Church. That appears clearly from the extremely complicated struggle about the confession of Christ, about the depth of reconciliation, about His work of salvation in the world and His presence in our midst as the living God. This confession is under discussion not only implicitly in countless New Testament exegetical problems, but also in reflection on the Church's tradition, her christological decisions. Those are questions which often emphatically recognize the "true God and true man" of Chalcedon, but which at the same time legitimately call attention to the danger of a confession of Christ that involves a certain problematic of the personal union, the *unio personalis* — its possibility and conceivability — thereby running the risk of weakening interest in the reality of "God in Christ." Naturally, the far-reaching discussion about Chalcedon can call up new questions, even if there is complete appreciation for the defensive position of this council, which compelled it to go into the problematic of union. But all of this can also stimulate the Church anew to be open to the fullness and varied witness of the New Testament,[86] which no single formulation can replace. The Church should understand that many problems which, in a particular climate, perforce had to concern the Church — how the union was possible — end up in the background in the discovery which the preaching of the gospel seeks to evoke: "It is the Lord!"[87]

85. Cf. K. Rahner, "Marxist Utopia and the Christian Future of Man," *Theological Investigations*, VI, 59ff.
86. Cf. W. Pannenberg, *Jesus — God and Man*, 1964, pp. 287ff.
87. John 21:7. One may recall the affirmation of two wills in Christ (in opposition to the monothelites) and the unity of the New Testament's picture of Christ.

In our time many of the questions of recognition — truth and heresy — in connection with the confession of Christ are concentrated in the question about the living God. There are questions about His revelation in this world and its knowability, about His presence or His "absence"! Clearly, these questions also do not leave the congregation untouched; after a period of relative self-evidence, they are confronting her anew with great problems. This new interest has not been called up only by the so-called "God is dead" theology, but also by living questions in the congregation about the providence of God and prayer because of the existential power and seriousness of experience.[88] Rather suddenly, there is new interest in dogmatics for the confession of the trinity. For a long time it had been more supposed than discussed. Questions arose in dogmatics about whether it was possible to deal separately with the doctrine of God and that of the trinity — one after the other. This was more than a purely "methodological" problem.[89] Concern with these questions is in itself not a sign of threatening heresy, but is legitimate because of what Bavinck calls "the core of Christian faith, the root of all dogmas, the substance of the new covenant." It is not "a metaphysical dogma or a philosophical speculation," but "the heart and the essence of the Christian religion itself."[90] We are dealing here not with an attempt to fathom the living God so that He is made into "the crowning keystone in the vault of our thinking,"[91] but with an interpretation of the sense of our speech about and confession of the triune God. Unexpectedly, we are reminded here of the Belgic Confession, which speaks about the knowledge of the triune God not only from the testimonies of Holy Writ, but also "from their operations, and chiefly by those we feel in ourselves" (Art. 9). Although no two-source theory is intended,[92] the reality of experience clearly appears here in connection with God's revelation. This implies

---

88. Cf. P. Baelz, *Prayer and Providence*, 1968.
89. Cf. H. Bavinck, *Geref. Dog.*, II, 119: first on "the divine nature" and "*shortly*" in the locus of the trinity." Cf. K. Rahner, "Remarks on the Dogmatic Treatise 'De Trinitate,'" *Theological Investigations*, IV, 77ff., on the distinction, which is felt to be self-evident, between the treatises *De Deo uno* and *De Deo trio* and on the "splendid isolation" of the latter (p. 84).
90. Bavinck, *Geref. Dog.*, II, 300ff.
91. A phrase by Karl Barth to characterize the grasp of human thinking.
92. Thus A. Kuyper, correctly, in *E Voto*, I, 165. A.D.R. Polman (*Onze Ned. Geloofsbelijdenis*, I, 308ff.) is correct in seeing a contrast here with all speculations and with an abstract dogma.

that God comes to us in His revelation as the true God and that the aspects of "in Himself" and "for us" can no longer become a meaningful problem, any more than it is meaningful to interpret the Johannine outlook on the *visio Dei* (the vision of God) "as He is" further as "as He is in Himself."[93] Anxiety about an interdependence between God and man and about an attack on what one intended earlier with the aseity of God is ungrounded if one esteems God's revelation as trustworthy and, therefore, can have full interest in the reality of His trinitarian revelation.[94]

We are no longer in the habit of seeing the problems of heresy in connection with the doctrine of God, since they are usually concentrated in the area of christology, where they have played such a clear role. However, the Church in this time, in and because of the confession of Christ, is clearly and immediately confronted by the question of God. We saw earlier that this was the case with the confession of election, but along the whole line of thought and belief in this age, the Church is faced with the calling to responsible discourse about God. She must testify to the truth and reality of God, and therein she has the commission to "test the spirits" in a positive directedness to the message of the living God for the world.

In recognition of truth, and thus also of heresy, the Church is tested on her faith, her confession. All heresy contains not only a threat, but also a challenge, since it always wants to understand the truth of God more highly and deeply. Along these ways of distinction and recognition, it is possible for the Church to understand anew her calling to speak out where the gospel of the grace and love of God threatens to perish because of an old or new problematic that has no place any longer for the radical, disclosing *pro nobis*, the *sola fide*, and *sola gratia*. To pronounce the *damnamus* here in fear and trembling requires the most serious and far-reaching self-discipline from the Church. She will be able to defend against heresy meaningfully only if she actively undermines it. Therein, she does the greatest

---

93. *Ut in se est.* Cf. I John 3:2. Cf. my *The Return of Christ*, chapter 12.
94. For all the questions that have arisen here (ontological trinity and revelational trinity, "in itself" and "for us," salvation history, etc.), see the studies by E. Jüngel, *Gottes Sein ist im Werden*, 1965; and C.H. Ratschow, *Gott existiert*, 1966, both in connection with H. Gollwitzer, *The Existence of God as Confessed by Faith*, 1965. In all of this, as in every domain of the confession, there is the danger of recognizing heresy either too hastily or too late.

service possible to heresy. The Church, with respect to the problem of doctrinal discipline, has understandably never been able to escape into a "tolerance" without nuance. When van Ruler calls the "spirituality" of discipline a decisive condition for all discipline and calls discipline "an affair of the Spirit,"[95] he has touched on the deepest problem also of all doctrinal discipline. For it is not in the least an application of a number of rules via an objective technique, but an antithetical speaking that is founded in a thesis. Whoever keeps that in mind will be able to separate all defense from triumphalism and juridicism.[96] Only if the Church understands the gospel — to be interpreted again and again as joyful news — and throws open all the gates in the proclamation, may she (even militant terminology is acceptable here) stand in the breech as the witness to threatened salvation. And only where this salvation is obscured or limited may she be "intolerant," not in the sad sense of prideful discrimination, but as a reference to the "forbearance" of God, which radiates in the gospel to the whole creation (Mark 16:15).

And so, one may also speak without bias of concern for the purity of the proclamation. On the basis of ecclesiastical experiences in the divided Church, one has heard a connotation of introverted churchliness in this word — i.e., a boast of one's own "purity" without concern about its implications for the Church's life. Rediscovering its profound meaning is possible only if the Church's concern is with the sole "intolerance" that is thinkable in the Church — defense against threats to the gospel of grace. Naturally, one can ask whether discipline is safe "in human hands." Does it not inevitably degenerate into something all too human? Does not all of this perhaps explain why a "complete solution" to the problem of doctrinal discipline is not possible?[97]

In her holiness, the Church is tested on her thesis and her antithesis, which is directed to the thesis and which places her under the test of the pure proclamation of that marvelous light, the light of mercy (I Pet. 2:9f.). Thereby, all misunderstandings

95. Van Ruler, *op. cit.*, p. 16.
96. In all the nuances and distinctions within doctrinal discipline, such as juridical or medical, it must be borne in mind that the decision is made already in the fact of the defense itself, no matter in what form it occurs. On account of the seriousness and the responsibility in this positive defense — in the form of action and in that of the judgment — the gospel is always in question.
97. Van Ruler, *Hoe Functioneert de Belijdenis?*, p. 31.

can be taken away already in the earthly *visio Dei*. And all of this comes into effect along the way of election, which removes all false pretensions from the Church and assigns a place for her in the world via the decisive, constant reminder that "you did not choose me, but I chose you and appointed you that you should go and bear fruit" (John 15:16).

CHAPTER FIFTEEN

HOLINESS AND MISSION

WHOEVER REFLECTS ON MISSION IN CONNECTION with the holiness of the Church finds himself on well-known terrain. Although there has often been little interest in the Church's commission in the world, the New Testament is too clear about it for it to remain in the shadows forever. And it has increasingly been seen that the essence of the Church cannot be thought of apart from that peculiar movement towards the outside, the world. The distinction between the Church and the world can never signify that there is a separation such that, fundamentally, the Church and the world have nothing to do with each other. Rather, there is a centrifugal motive in the Church's existence. It is not something secondary; the Church's mission cannot be added to the reality of the Church as if it belonged to the "well-being" of the Church. Especially on the basis of the root idea of the Church's holiness — separation — it is necessary to reflect again and again on this striking outward movement of the Church. One could misunderstand this holiness, that "holy" people, to mean that the Church has already attained her ultimate destination, with no essential additions required. Then we find ourselves in the sphere of an introverted churchliness which finds its most actual and deepest life in meditation upon the Church as the mystery of Christ on earth. With respect to the Church as the holy nation of God, one would then see everything as summarized in the thankfulness of Ps. 147:20: "He has not dealt thus with any other nation; they do not know his ordinances. Praise the Lord!" Clearly, this view of the Church is diametrically opposed not only to various explicit statements about the Church's witness in the world, but also to the deepest intention of the Church's separation, or holiness. Apart from this separation, her meaning and directedness — her "being" — is inconceivable. Where this separation becomes reality because of God's electing action, a movement arises simultaneously that is crystallized in a commission to "go forth" as a witness to the end of the earth (cf. Acts 1:8). What is the reason for this movement, this never ceasing activity of witnessing? And how does the way lead from separation to mission?

In the Church's history, many problems have always been connected with these questions. The meaning of separation was repeatedly misunderstood, and one, whether expressly or not, had no eye for the essential missionary dimension of the Church. In general, one can say that the Church, at least theoretically, has always known that her separation does not signify a stand-still, but a movement. One could not ignore the well-known statement of Jesus before His ascension when He emphatically charged the disciples to "go forth" with the close of the age as the limit: "Go therefore and make disciples of all nations, bap-tizing them in the name of the Father and of the Son and of the Holy Spirit, teaching them to observe all that I have com-manded you; and lo, I am with you always, to the close of the age" (Matt. 28:19f.). Even though some have denied that this text applies to the Church of all ages,[1] one has generally felt that a connection to this universal, total commission, which embraces the whole world.[2] The so-called "great commission" was seen in connection with other statements about being wit-nesses "in Jerusalem and in all Judea and Samaria and to the end of the earth," a witness to which the coming Spirit would empower them (Acts 1:8; cf. Luke 24:48). The calling, with this wideness of perspectives, has a special urgency (cf. Mark 13:10; Matt. 24:14). It is in no sense accidental or secondary. Since the resurrection of the Lord and the "power" that has been given to Him, Jerusalem is not a stopping place for God's action, but the point of departure for a movement that embraces the whole creation.

In times when this movement seemed to have come to a standstill, such universal statements always caused a bad con-science. Urgent voices of protest sounded again, recalling that the Church cannot be truly the Church without this movement

---

1. Cf. in J. van den Berg, *Waarom Zending?*, 1969, p. 10 (on Beza).
2. Cf. K. Barth, *Auslegung von Matth. 28, 16-20*, 1954, pp. 13ff. One may think of the multiple characterization of *all*: all authority, all nations, all that has been commanded, and always. Cf. G. Bornkamm, "Der Auferstandene und der Irdische (Mt. 28, 16-20)," *Zeit und Geschichte*, 1964, pp. 173ff.

and perspective and that this dynamic belongs to her essential structure in the last days; thus, it is directly connected to the end, which supposes this universal preaching.[3] Karl Barth brought all of this to expression pointedly when he said that the actual Church becomes evident in that she fulfills this commission as a mark of the Church, an "external sign by which the true community of Jesus Christ may be infallibly known." If that is not present, it is an alarming sign that something is decisively wrong in the inward relation of the community to its own basis of existence and that under the cover of sacred zeal there is a process of defection from its Lord."[4]

No antithesis is possible between liturgy, doxology, experience, prayer, love of God, and rest in God's house on the one hand, and the outgoing movement to the world in the Church's witness on the other. It is not possible to view the Church's life "in itself" apart from all the dynamic connections that she has been placed in as the Church. That is connected to the fact that there can be no doubt about the being of the Church, since her commissions arise from what she is — the light of the world, a city set on a hill, and the salt of the earth (Matt. 5:13f.). She gets a summons to be what she truly is and must be more and more. Therefore, apart from this movement, the Church is not to be thought of as the Church of Jesus Christ.[5] The great commission of Matt. 28, too, is not to be understood as an accidental commission, a command that could not be expected from the reality of the Church.

According to Harry Boer, the stimulus for mission was not so much the great commission, as the reality of the outpouring of the Holy Spirit. An emphatic command, as if it were some-

---

3. Cf. Matt. 24:14: "and then the end will come." Cf. O. Cullmann, "Le Charactère Eschatologique du Devoir Missionaire et de la Conscience Apostolique de Saint Paul. Etude sur le *katéchon* de 2 Thess. 2:6-7," *Rev. d'Histoire et de Philos. Relig.*, 1936, pp. 210ff.; my *The Return of Christ*, pp. 126ff., on the "eternal" gospel (to every nation and tongue and people, Rev. 14:6f.); Bornkamm, *op. cit.*, p. 177; F. Hahn, *Mission in the N.T.*, 1965, pp. 47ff.

4. K. Barth, *C.D.*, IV/3, pp. 772f.

5. According to Barth (*ibid.*, pp. 764ff.), there is a "gap" in the doctrine of the Church — also the Reformation and post-Reformation doctrine — due to the isolation of the idea (in itself correct) of the *coetus* or *congregatio fidelium*. The error lies not in what is said, but in what is not said, with all the dangers of the Church as an "institution of salvation." The Protestant Church in the 16th and 17th centuries, according to Barth, had a "pronounced lack of joy in mission." See, however, J. van den Berg, *op. cit.*

thing new, was actually not necessary![6] The Church does not simply receive a commission or command from without, but is also moved by the Spirit from within.[7] However, the truth of this may not make us overlook the fact that one is not finished simply with a reference to the self-evidence of this movement. Much inertia and misunderstanding about her being are possible in the Church, and these show us that an admonition such as the *usus elenchticus,* the convicting function of the law, continues to be necessary here, just as the indicative never makes the imperative superfluous.[8] That we are not dealing with something "secondary" here is accentuated by the admonition. One may never withdraw via an untenable dilemma into the "primary," "inner" riches of the Church. Such an approach of primary and secondary, centripetal and centrifugal, always makes the missionary form of the Church something "secondary." The danger exists that the riches of the Church are no longer understood correctly. Then they become a horrid self-sufficiency as riches that do not need anything. But they are neither cold nor hot and therefore need refining by fire (Rev. 3:17f.). The riches of the Church cannot be understood unless the Church is in motion in the "going forth"[9] that Jesus commanded as "the most profoundly necessary step."[10] Therein it is clear that God loved the world (John 3:16), that He was in Christ reconciling the world to Himself (II Cor. 5:19), and that

6. H.R. Boer, *Pentecost and the Missionary Witness of the Church,* 1955, pp. 32ff. Cf. Proposition I: "The N.T. gives no reason to believe that the immediate post-Pentecostal Church was moved to the great missionary witness by conscious obedience to the Great Commission." The commission "derives its meaning and power wholly and exclusively from the Pentecost event" (p. 40). Cf. also the conclusion of H. Diem ("Der Ort der Mission in der system. Theol.," *Theol. Lit. Zeitung,* 1966, p. 163) that "it would not at all have needed that missionary command by the Risen One."

7. Discussion of the authenticity of Matt. 28:19f. has been carried on especially in connection with the trinitarian aspect of the commission to baptize. Cf. my *The Sacraments,* 1969, p. 102; K. Barth, *C.D.,* IV/4; Th. Ohm, *Machet zu Jüngern alle Völker,* 1962, pp. 428ff.; O. Michel, "Der Abschluss des Matth. Evang.," *Evangelische Theol.,* 1950/51; H. Luck, "Herrenwort und Geschichte nach Matth. 28," *Evang. Theol.,* 1967; and various articles by M. Kähler in *Schriften zur Christologie und Mission,* 1971, pp. 34ff.

8. Cf. K. Barth, *C.D.,* IV/3, p. 763, on "a powerful element of exhortation."

9. Matt. 28:19 *(poreuthéntes).* It is always a going forth under a *promise* on the strength of a *command* that is full of perspective. Cf. Jesus' statement to the paralyzed man (Luke 5:24) and Luke 7:50 (go in peace).

10. K. Barth, *C.D.,* IV/3, p. 874.

Christ is the Savior of the world (John 4:42). That is a continuing reminder of the *missio Dei,* the "mission of God," which radically excludes every religious or cultural absolutizing of work.[11] The origin and goal of holiness can never be neglected on account of its directedness to what is indicated clearly in universal perspectives.[12] Apart from those perspectives, the Church of Jesus Christ cannot be understood.[13]

Being meddlesome or compassionate?

To get a correct view of the Church's directedness to the world, it is important to pay attention to these undeniable perspectives. They touch immediately on the phenomenon of the congregation, which has not been taken out of the world but, *in* the world, must be kept from the evil one (John 17:15). The Church is placed in the world not as a passive observer of God's action in and with the world; rather, she is called to "involvement," or engagement, with the world — with the whole

11. This aspect is illuminated pointedly in the emphasis on the *missio Dei.* Although one cannot speak of a new motif in the history of missions, the broad interest in this characterization does point to an experience that can be threatened (the absolutizing of the "calling" church). See the book *The Mission of God* by G. Vicedom (1965) and *Missio Dei. Term en Functie in de Zendingstheol. Discussie* (Interuniv. Instituut voor Missiologie en Studie, ed. H.H. Rosin, G. van Winsum). There is something striking, in my view, about the large amount of agreement with this characterization, which, traditionally, has something self-evident about it. This is probably connected to the trinitarian aspects of the *missio Dei* that are indicated by, among others, Vicedom, and that direct attention to history in its concrete relatedness to mission, although the characterization "from rigorous Christo-centricity to thoroughgoing trinitarianism" as "the direction of missionary theology" is meaningful only starting from a wrongly understood Christocentrism (*Rapport Missio Dei,* p. 11). Cf. A.G. Honig, *De Kosmische Betekenis van Christus,* 1968, pp. 21ff.

12. The universal aspect appears also at the end of the Gospel of Mark. Cf. the differences between Matthew and Mark: "Go into all the world" (Mark); *kērúxate* (Mark); *mathēteúsate* (Matt.); *pánta tà éthnē* (Matt.); *páse̜ tȩ̄ ktísei* (Mark). Cf. also Matt. 28 and Mark 16:16 on baptism. On the (possible or probable) connection on the basis of Mark's priority, see E. Linnemann, "Der (wiedergefundene) Markusschluss," *Z.Th.K.,* 1969, pp. 270ff.

13. In the new Roman Catholic ecclesiological literature, much is said about the Church as "*sacramentum mundi*," the sacrament of the world. The term is not exclusively related to missions, but is especially directed against the isolation of the Church. Cf. Thomas O'Dea, "The Church As Sacramentum Mundi," *Concilium,* 58, 1970.

of human life in all its dimensions. In this aspect of the Church's life, we are faced with profound and far-reaching questions, all of which are connected with the nature of this "involvement." One can ask whether such "engagement" with the world will ever be understood differently than as "meddlesomeness," as the revelation of a sense of superiority that implies the world's inferiority.[14] We are thinking especially of the fact that the world does not present itself to the Church as a religionless world, full of anxiety and uncertainty, abandoned to the powers of death and destruction, but as a full — and in many senses "religious" — world of faith and reflection on the relation between God and man and between men and the world, reflection on the world's origin, present, and future. The question arose again and again here of what right the Church has to witness to the filled world. How can she make it clear that her call is meaningful, the call which reminds us of the radical calling that went forth to Abraham: "Go from your country and your kindred and your father's house to the land that I will show you" (Gen. 12:1)? Is there any expectation that such an appeal will be understood as anything else than superior "meddlesomeness"?

Frequently in the history of missions, Paul's nocturnal vision in Troas has been recalled. A Macedonian man besought him to "Come over to Macedonia and help us" (Acts 16:9 — *boêthēson hēmin*). It has been pointed out that it was evident later how much distress there was in Philippi in the phenomena of love of money, soothsaying, and suicide (16:16-19, 27). May this vision be seen as a justification of the Church's involvement and helpful going forth? And does it contain, explicitly or implicitly, a real request to be helped by the gospel? In the Old Testament we read of a parallel. The nations will take refuge in the God of Israel in the day of trouble because of deep disappointments about their own achievements: "Our fathers have inherited nought but lies, worthless things in which there is no profit. Can man make for himself gods? Such are no gods!" Then Yahweh is invoked as strength and refuge (Jer. 16:19f.). There is every reason to be realistic about the actual world; one must not look around too quickly for such a recognized need for help and then designate the Church's involvement as meaningful and acceptable to the world. Rather, we find, whether in the day of trouble or not, that few traces of this explicit call for help are

---

14. Cf. H. Kraemer, *Waarom Zending Juist Nù*, 1936, pp. 48ff., on the spiritual obtrusiveness that wakes — rightly — annoyance.

discoverable, and certainly not for the help of the Church! Rather, some religions have their own "sense of mission." That indicates clearly the problem of the Church's involvement in the world.

In Roman Catholic theology, the so-called *votum ecclesiae,* the "desire for the Church," has long played an important role in ecclesiology, along with the further distinction between an explicit and an implicit desire.[15] One could attach the proclamation of the gospel to this desire. So, the impression could arise that the world's doors were open for the Church's proclamation and that the heralds of the Kingdom could enter in to pluck the fruits of what could perhaps be interpreted as "preparation for the gospel."[16] Because of this, the "going forth" of the Church in her mission was filled with expectation.[17] Recently, there has been more silence about the *votum ecclesiae* on account of the danger of annexation. It can easily penetrate into the doctrine of anonymous Christianity[18] or into that of the *votum ecclesiae,* which could suggest the call of the Macedonian man or the prophecy of the servant of the Lord, for whose law the coastlands wait (Isa. 42:4). In the modern world situation, one was also forced to reflect on closed doors, so that the Church was confronted with many questions that had long been concentrated in the "absoluteness" of Christianity. These urgent questions came increasingly to the fore in immediate connection with the right and the meaning of the stepping over of boundaries that is implied in all the activity of mission.

In the New Testament there is no hesitation about the meaning and right of mission. Although the great commission of Matt. 28 was pronounced in a circle where "some doubted"

15. Cf. in *Mystici Corporis Christi* (Denz.-Schönm., 3871; *TCT*, 278): "unsuspectingly belong to the mystical body of the Redeemer by some kind of *desire* or *longing" (inscio quodam desiderio ac voto).* Cf. also Denz.-Schönm., 3870 (*TCT*, 275) on the *votum,* which does not have to be definitely explicit. See further on the *votum ecclesiae* my *The Second Vatican Council and the New Theology,* pp. 193ff.; W. Dietzfelbinger, *Die Grenzen der Kirche nach röm.-kath. Lehre,* 1962, pp. 74ff.
16. Cf. in this connection on the question of the meaning of mission, my *Nabetrachting op het Concilie,* pp. 24ff. (specifically Rahner's defense against doubt on this point).
17. Cf. J.C. Groot, "Theol. Bezinning op Motief on Doel van de Missie," *Tijdschrift voor Theologie,* 1965, pp. 49ff., on mission as "the bringing of what is already present, not yet in sacramental visibility and, to that degree, in a certain hiddenness or anonymity, to explication and fullness."
18. Cf. my *Nabetrachting op het Concilie,* pp. 18ff.; and above, chapter 6.

(28:17), there is no doubt or uncertainty about mission. At the same time, however, there is clearly no human hubris here. When the apostles "go forth," not shrinking back from any barrier, and even discovering material in various setbacks for the further working and the great power of the gospel (cf. Phil. 1:12ff.), there is no hint of a world-conquering heroism. Rather, all activity is performed in deep humility and in an uninterrupted realization of dependence. It is not that doors simply stand open, but that doors are opened. Paul speaks of a wide door for effective work that has been opened to him in connection with the proclamation of the gospel (I Cor. 16:8f.; II Cor. 2:12). He admonishes the Church to pray that God may open a door "to declare the mystery of Christ."[19] The fulfillment of the world-wide commission takes place through the midst of various resistance (cf. I Thess. 2:16, 18) and stands ultimately under the decisive rule of the Spirit (cf. Acts 16:7), Who here, too, leads the Church according to Christ's promise. The reason for all of this — humility as well as the courage, the dynamic, and the prayer — is faith in the uniqueness of this testimony, which qualifies absolutely the nature of the involvement that appears here geographically. It is concern with all nations and proclamation "everywhere" (Acts 17:30). The going forth is unbiased and confident. It claims validity in spite of the "fullness" of life, which does not drive back the proclamation but rather stimulates it (cf. 17:15-34). This involvement cannot be understood on the basis of formal, general categories of influence and propaganda for mediocre things and ideas, but only on the basis of the gospel "in all its radical novelty," without which it is "valueless and futile."[20] It is not a plea for a particular culture, ideology, or religious ideal, which is always accompanied by a sense of superiority.

But it has not always been clear that the Church is concerned with nothing else than this new message. One of the most serious dangers to all mission is that a different involvement can come to the fore — for example, one's own self-interest or imperialist, colonialist motives.[21] Then the meaning of mission is entirely obscured and made unrecognizable for the world.

19. Col. 4:3. For the prayers of the Church, cf. also II Thess. 3:1; I Thess. 5:25; II Cor. 1:11; Eph. 6:19.
20. K. Barth, *C.D.*, IV/3, p. 875.
21. Cf. J. van den Berg, "Een open Pad voor Handel en Christendom," *Christusprediking in de Wereld*, 1965, pp. 63ff., in connection with Livingstone.

Even if it is only that there is a combination of motives, the message becomes a different gospel (Gal. 1:6f.), propaganda for one's own affair and one's own interests. And whenever, in the historical course of things, all domination comes to an end, there is no danger to the power and working of mission. Rather, there is a possibility for a new calling and a new understanding.[22] Then there can again be an outlook on the nature of the gospel, which is designated centrally and clearly by Paul when he recalled Isaiah's joyful words: "How beautiful are the feet of those who preach good news!" (Rom. 10:15; Isa. 52:7). This is not a heavy yoke or heavy burden, nor a new law, morality, or new religion, but only "good news" *(eu-angélion)* that is preached to the poor (Matt. 11:5) and brings peace and liberty (Acts 10:36) in the forgiveness of sins. It is the message of God's mercy, authentically interpreted by angels; it is the gospel of Him Who is not the final point of human seeking, but Who is found by those who did not seek Him (Rom. 10:20; Isa. 65:1) and Who justifies the ungodly (Rom. 4:5). The gospel summons to a new day, to an arising from sleep (Eph. 5:14) in a new time (Luke 4:18, 43), the time of the testimony to grace (Acts 20:24).

If this gospel is protected against all misunderstanding (cf. II Cor. 4:5), an appeal can understandably be made here to repentance and conversion (Mark 1:4; Acts 17:30). These words have constantly evoked many reactions, because one sensed a feeling of superiority in them. It was not clear that the Church's only goal was conversion to joy[23] and that she knew that her own origin lay in that divine movement of mission, a visitation of and involvement with all who sat in darkness (Luke 1:79). But if that is forgotten, mission becomes only a ridiculous affair without the continuing sense of a transition from "not having received mercy" to "having received mercy" (I Pet. 2:10). Mission is the place where darkness yields. On account of this mystery, Mary is called blessed by all generations (Luke 1:48), for "Immanuel" brings salvation in the presence of all peoples,

---

22. Cf. H.W. Gensichen, "Die deutsche Mission und der Kolonialismus," *Kerugma und Dogma,* 1962, pp. 176ff.; H. Kraemer, "De Zending in de Wisseling der Tijden," *Uit de Nalatenschap van Dr. H. Kraemer,* 1970, pp. 77ff.; I.J. Hesselink, "The Christian World Mission Today," *The Reformed Journal,* 1971, pp. 19ff.

23. See especially J. Schniewind, *Das biblische Wort von der Bekehrung,* 1948, p. 3: "conversion to God is joy." The nature of "penitence," as in the Old Testament, is the turning away from all foreign gods. Conversion can be understood only in connection with Him to Whom one turns. Cf. Isa. 45:21ff.; 1:18ff.

a light for revelation to the Gentiles and for glory to Israel (Luke 2:31f.). The proclamation summons a conversion to this gospel. At this proclamation the whole country of Judea and all the people of Jerusalem go out to John the Baptist to be baptized, confessing their sins (Mark 1:5). Here is a deep mystery, that of the tender mercy of God (Luke 1:78). It can be understood only as emotion, as a wonderful movement of love and compassion. There are no presuppositions in man, no motives on the basis of religion or morality for it. God has compassion as the father in the parable of the prodigal son (15:20 — *esplanchnisthē*). Compassion is awakened in the heart of Israel's God: "My heart recoils within me, my compassion grows warm and tender."[24]

This inner compassion forms the core of the gospel. Everything is disclosed by the compassion of Christ as it is described for us in the gospel when He has compassion on the sheep without a shepherd.[25] It is not clear why this inner emotion is distinguished as a "Messianic characterization of Jesus" from "the mere depiction of an emotion,"[26] as if there could be an antithesis in the man Jesus between the two and as if the reference to this "messianic characteristic" would not involve all the waves of concrete, shocked emotion. Here we are in the midst of the gospel that must be preached to the whole world, and in this emotion the disciples go out to win disciples for this Lord. In contrast with the lack of interest of men for sinners, the light of the concentrated interest of the Lord for the blind, miserable, poor, lonely, and lost (Luke 19:10) shines forth. Such compassion has often been limited due to fear that doors would be opened too widely, since one shuddered at the idea of "cheap grace."[27] And via a horrible misunderstanding, the abundance and depth of this divine compassion was often placed in the constricted lines of a wrong view of election, which obscured the outlook on the mystery of divine love. A tension, a "dialectic"

---

24. Hos. 11:8. It clearly does not suffice to say that this is "simply anthropomorphic," since what follows here is: "for I am God and not man, the Holy One in your midst" (11:9).

25. Mark 6:34 *(esplanchnisthē)*. Cf. Mark 8:2; 1:41; Luke 7:13; Matt. 9:36; 20:34.

26. *TDNT*, VII, 554.

27. There is much misunderstanding about these words. They can be used critically against all rashness; but, at the deepest, this rashness can be opposed only by the mystery of the "as a gift" (Rom. 3:24; KJV: "freely") and of buying "without money and without price" (Isa. 55:1) that makes all rashness ridiculous.

between election and proclamation arose, and it often detracted from the power and expectation in proclamation,[28] even though one tried to hold both in "balance." Then it became extremely difficult to see that divine compassion is not a pseudo-emotion, but an inner, impenetrable mystery that led the throng to glorify God.[29] It is the mystery of all the universal perspectives of the Old and the New Testaments,[30] of the revelation of the form of the Shepherd, Who gathers the shepherdless sheep and brings them back into the fold. Only in these surroundings is it possible to reflect on the movement of the Church, on her "witness" in the world. That witness is real, trustworthy, and credible only in the imitation of God and in the imitation of Christ.

The connection between following the Lord and the movement towards the world is clearly expressed in the Gospel of Mark. The commission goes forth to the disciples to follow Him and He will make them fishers of men (1:17; cf. Matt. 4:19; Luke 5:10). This decisive viewpoint stamps all their work and tests all their activity, which must now be connected to the goal set by Christ. Along this way the remarkable promise sounds that they need not fear (Luke 5:10) because of the light and presence of the Lord (cf. 5:8). Henceforth (5:10), this way must be walked in faith and expectation under the positive promise. Everything is founded in the imitation of Christ. Being with Him and following Him is where the movement of the disciples that results in their world-wide commission begins. This being sent, then, belongs essentially to the structure of imitation, since the disciples are stimulated to tumultuous activity. Men are caught, and won, for this Lord.[31] The one who is lost is sought and found in "Jesus' movement of collection."[32]

28. Cf. C. Veenhof, *Prediking en Uitverkiezing,* 1959; my *Divine Election,* chapter 7; O. Noordmans, "Praedestinatie," *Geestelijke Perspectieven,* 1930, pp. 1ff.
29. Matt. 15:31. Cf. B. Citron, "The Multitude in the Synoptic Gospels," *Scottish Journal of Theol.,* 1954, pp. 408ff. All tension between the individual and the multitude is gone, as is the rupture between spiritual and physical need. Cf. Matt. 15:32 on the hungering multitude; and O. Noordmans, *Gestalte en Geest,* pp. 105ff.
30. Cf. H.N. Ridderbos, *De Pastorale Brieven,* p. 73, on "the desire for universal salvation," which must determine the prayer of the Church.
31. Mark 1:20. Cf. R. Pesch, "Berufung und Sendung, Nachfolge und Mission," *Zeitschrift für kath. Theol.,* 91 (1969), 15ff.; L. Grollenberg, "Mensen Vangen (Luke 5, 10) Hen Redden van de Dood," *Tijdschrift voor Theol.,* 1965, pp. 330ff.
32. Pesch, *op. cit.,* p. 22. Cf. for the image Jer. 16:16.

The depth and background of being sent is also illuminated
pointedly by the way mission is related to Christ's own sending:
"As thou didst send me into the world, so I have sent them into
the world" (John 17:18; cf. 20:21). This "as" is more than an
accidental analogy; it is an essential connection on the basis of
the same directedness of the same goal. The disciples' being sent
has its origin in His being sent. Thus, there is a necessity in
mission. It is not due to coercion, but to what is implicit in
Christ and qualifies His disciples. In this light, the sense of
"necessity" in the apostles is understandable: "We cannot but
speak of what we have seen and heard" (Acts 4:20). Paul knows
that he is under obligation to both Greeks and barbarians
(Rom. 1:14) and that necessity is laid upon him to preach the
gospel (I Cor. 9:16).

This proclamation, which rests in the wideness of God's
action towards the world, is in no sense comparable to exalting
oneself above others. The blame for resistance to this gospel
must not be on the stumbling blocks of pride and "meddlesomeness," since resistance is an offense to this proclaimed gospel
itself. It is the gospel that scatters the proud; certainly, therefore, the proclaimers of this gospel must keep themselves far
from this pride. That is possible only if the Church herself has
truly been grasped by God's mercy and has been taken along
on the way to the world, to all nations, and to the ends of the
earth. In her mission the Church must be the opposite of the
prophet Jonah, who is angry at God's mercy. He continues to
suspect mercy behind his sending, fearing that God does not
mean His threat and judgment completely seriously. He is prepared to do without mercy, something that Yahweh cannot do
without on account of His involvement with the great city
Nineveh (Jonah 4:10f.). Here, in contrast to the darkness of
Jonah's wrath, the light shines of that God Who sends not to
ruin but to save. He has a "different view of that city, that
Goyim complex,"[33] different from Jonah's "seeing" full of horror, different from the later Pharisees, and different from the
disciples, who want to call down fire on the Samaritans (Luke
9:51-56) and do not see as God sees and as Jesus sees the tax
collectors and the crowds. Only from this mystery of seeing is
it understandable that the disciples of the Lord, in all their
"going forth," are restrained from quick, natural deeds in re-

33. K.H. Miskotte, "Missie ondanks de Missionaris," *Als de Goden Zwijgen*,
1956, pp. 353ff.

action, restrained already in the presence of Jesus from grasping
the sword (John 18:11; Matt. 26:52), a misunderstanding of His
way through the world. Mission can be understood only when
the eyes are opened to this new seeing and when the movement
bears the stamp of the divine Sender, Who sends not to condemn the world, but to save it (John 3:17), and Who does not
have pleasure in the death of the wicked, but desires rather that
he turn from his way and live.[34] Being sent is the deed of Him
Who is the Father of mercies (II Cor. 1:3; cf. Rom. 12:1 —
oiktirmós), the God of all comfort (II Cor. 1:3). They who are
sent — i.e., the whole Church — must reflect (cf. Luke 6:36) that
mercy in inner compassion, precisely as holy and beloved ones
(Col. 3:12). In no respect may they be a hindrance to the outlook
on the eternal source of compassion.

Israel's place in mission

When we reflect on the meaning and background of the
Church's "going forth," we are confronted with various facets
of God's action in and with Israel. An avowed aspect of limitation and separation comes to the fore here, since Israel alone
is elected "from all the families of the earth" (Amos 3:2; cf. Ps.
147:19f.; Num. 23:9). This unmerited election excludes from
the beginning all self-complacency and every claim derived from
it.[35] Although God's attention is concentrated on Israel alone
(Ps. 147:20), it is also directed to the world from the beginning
on. The wide, universal perspective of the nations, the blessing
of this nation for all generations of the earth, is implied already
in Israel's origin as a nation.[36] In Israel's further history, too,
the perspective of a widening horizon is present. There is a
vision of the procession of the nations to Jerusalem, all the
nations and the many peoples.[37] One day, the covering that is
spread over all peoples (Isa. 25:6-9) will be taken away, while
the house of God will be a house of prayer for all peoples
(56:7; cf. Mark 11:17). Israel is given as a light to the nations

34. Ezek. 18:23, 32; 33:11. H.N. Ridderbos *(loc. cit.)* refers to this saying in
his exegesis of I Tim. 2:4.
35. Cf. Mic. 3:11: while giving judgment for a bribe, "they lean upon
the Lord and say, 'Is not the Lord in the midst of us? No evil shall
come upon us.'" Cf. also Jer. 8:4; Amos 9:7f. In place of this claim,
there is greater responsibility (Amos 3:1; Zeph. 1:12). Cf. my *Divine
Election*, chapter 10, on "The Great Misunderstanding."
36. Gen. 12:2f.; 18:18; 22:18; 26:4; 28:14.
37. Isa. 2:2-4. Cf. Mic. 4:1-4; Jer. 3:17; 4:2; 16:19.

that salvation may reach to the end of the earth (Isa. 49:6; 60:3). Again and again, the limitation is broken through by mysterious perspectives of an altar to the Lord in the midst of the land of Egypt as a sign to Him (19:19f.). Yahweh will make Himself known to the Egyptians, and Egypt will know Him (19:21f.). The ends of the earth are called by Yahweh, because He is God and there is no other (Isa. 45:22; cf. 65:1; Ps. 87).

All of this does not mean that Israel "goes forth," is sent into the world, as is the case later with the Church.[38] But there is a clear relationship, since Israel's existence has been given as a sign that must lead the nations to turn to Israel's God. The mystery of Israel's existence on the basis of God's love implies the perspective for the world.[39] It is the canvas for the later Messianic time of fulfillment, when all boundaries are crossed over. This widening of the horizon is one of the deepest aspects of the New Testament. It is the insight that this wide horizon was implied in God's intention when He took out a people from the Gentiles (Acts 15:14). But this new horizon certainly does not become visible above time and above history. It is not a logical conclusion from the Old Testament perspectives. Nor is it a placid progression from the implicit to the explicit. Rather, the wide horizon of the nations and the world comes into view in inseparable connection with the relation between Israel and the Messiah. That comes to light clearly when, in the synoptic gospels, the concentration of the Messiah and His disciples on Israel becomes very strongly visible. It is usually designated as an avowed particularistic emphasis: limitation to Israel alone. Not only are the disciples commanded to go

38. Cf. D. Bosch, *Die Heidenmission in der Zukunftsschau Jesu*, 1959, p. 19 (not an "explicit notion of mission"); F. Hahn, *Mission in the N.T.*, 1965, pp. 18ff.: "But there is an absence of any idea of going out to the nations." Israel is Yahweh's witness "solely by reason of its existence and of God's salvation which is given to it." See further J. Blauw, *Gottes Werk in dieser Welt*, 1961: not Israel's going forth, but the coming of the nations, is illuminated in the perspectives. "Israel itself is not a missionary, but its election, no doubt, does have a missionary sense" (Hahn, p. 20).

39. According to F. Wagner (*Über die Legitimität der Mission*, 1968, p. 14), the Old Testament has no significance "for the founding of mission," and the distinction between centripetal and centrifugal has little meaning. That everything depends on the meaning given to the words "particularism" and "universalism" is evident from many views of the Old Testament in the 19th century. Cf. R. Smend, "Universalismus und Partikularismus in der A.T. Theol. des 19. Jahrh.," *Evang. Theol.*, 1962, pp. 169ff.

nowhere among the Gentiles and not to enter a town of the Samaritans (Matt. 10:5f.; cf. 10:23), but also the Lord Himself knows that He has been sent only to the lost sheep of the house of Israel (15:24 — *ei mè*) This "only" does not imply that salvation is limited to Israel and that there are no perspectives outside Israel's boundaries. Whenever Israel sees her separation and election as self-evident on the basis of God's covenant, the horizon widens and a critical light falls on Israel.[40] We hear not only that God can raise up children for Abraham from stones (3:9), but also that Israel is distinguished from others, who will come from east and west to sit at the table with Abraham, Isaac, and Jacob in the Kingdom of heaven (8:11f.). Lights shine outside Israel that seem to be extinguished in Israel, lights of great faith vis-à-vis Israel's lack of faith.[41]

The specific limitation to Israel belongs in this critical framework of the first and the last, and the wider perspective can be alarming. The doors are obviously not closed, since Jesus sees the coming of the Greeks as a sign of the decisive hour, when the grain of wheat will die and bear fruit (John 12:20ff., 32). There is a historical tension in the Gospels that ends in a new state of affairs. All doors are opened by a transition that is directly connected in the whole New Testament to the rejection of the Messiah. Frequently, the changing situation is characterized as a transition from centripetal to centrifugal directedness. With respect to the change in the perspectives, opinions differ about the relation of Jesus to the mission among the Gentiles. With respect to Jesus, the centrifugal aspect was denied; only "later" could it have significance.[42] The tension becomes visible

40. Cf. already in the Old Testament against all claim and pretension, Jer. 7:7ff. and Mic. 3:11. Zion is plowed as a field and Jerusalem becomes a heap of ruins (3:12).

41. Matt. 8:10 (not even in Israel such faith). Cf. Luke 4:27 (the cleansing of Naaman the Syrian) and 17:18 (the thankful Samaritan as the only one who returned). For the critical light on misunderstood limitation, the idea of the holy remnant is of great importance already in the Old Testament. It is not a glorification of the small number, but a critical, wider outlook, as it becomes visible around Jesus for tax collectors and sinners. Cf. J. Jeremias, "Der Gedanke des Heiligen Restes im Spätjudentum und in der Verkündigung Jesu," *Abba*, 1966, pp. 129ff.

42. See especially the article by B. Sundkler, "Jésus et les Païens," *Rev. d'Histoire et de Philos. Relig.*, 1936, pp. 463ff., on particularism as "an insufficient alternative" (pp. 470, 481), with the solution that "Jesus was a particularist." That does not eliminate mission (p. 498), but Israel and Jerusalem are the starting point for mission. Sundkler denies,

in the New Testament in what "first" stands at the center versus the "later" centrifugal widening of the Messianic salvation for the world.[43] We perceive the perspective of the other sheep (John 10:16), of the Spirit Who will convince the world of sin, righteousness, and judgment (16:8ff.), and of the world's belief through the manifestation of the Church's unity (John 17:21). The transition becomes especially visible in the conflict in the parable, related by all the synoptic gospels, of the unrighteous tenants. It ends with the vineyard being given to others.[44] At the same time Christ is proclaimed as Savior of the world, a rupture becomes visible in a shocking progression from first to later. There is a change of direction,[45] and Isaiah is then cited in connection with it: "I have set you to be a light for the Gentiles that you may bring salvation to the uttermost parts of the earth."[46]

What happens here cannot be brought into a logical synthesis, such that one thing could be deduced from another. What Stauffer calls "the law of deflection"[47] with respect to God's providence dramatically comes to light here. Every deterministic view, which sees Israel's guilt simplistically as a necessary link on the way from the implicit to the explicit, or from first to later, lacks appreciation for the depth of God's ways toward the world.[48] It makes the deeds of God and those

therefore, the "universalistic" aspects of the New Testament gospels and gives much attention to Jerusalem as the center of the earth (p. 499). Cf. Ezek. 38:12; J. Jeremias, *Jesu Verheissung für die Völker,* 1956, pp. 9ff., 47ff.

43. Cf. Matt. 15:26 ("It is not fair to take the children's bread and throw it to the dogs") and Mark 7:27 ("Let the children first be fed"). Cf. Jeremias, *op. cit.,* p. 25: in Mark "a temporal, circumscribed, passing privilege" is made "from Israel's exclusive right (Matt. 24)." In his view, that is a "moderation."

44. Matt. 21:33-46; Mark 12:1-12; Luke 20:9-19. Cf. the opposition to this "giving it to others" in Luke 20:16: "God forbid!"

45. Cf. Acts 13:46: after the repudiation of the Word, Paul says, "behold, we turn to the Gentiles" (*idoù strephómetha eis tà éthnē*). Cf. also 18:6.

46. Acts 13:47; Isa. 49:6. Cf. Rom. 1:16 ("to the Jew first and also to the Greek" as a universal aspect: "to every one who has faith"); 10:12 (no distinction between Jew and Greek in connection with all who call upon Him); 3:29 ("Or is God the God of Jews only? Is he not the God of Gentiles also? Yes, of Gentiles also"). The purpose of the apostleship is to bring about the obedience of faith "among all the nations" (1:5).

47. *"Das Gesetz der Umlenkung."* E. Stauffer, *N.T. Theol.,* 1955, pp. 205f. Cf. my *The Providence of God,* 1952, pp. 90ff.

48. Cf. the rejected stone that has become the head of the corner (Luke

of Israel into a chain of necessities, so that Israel's fall also becomes "meaningful."[49] But in this context, the words "causal"
and "must" do not get us any further, at least if we do not
want to fall into the dark abyss of God's causing sin *(Deus
causa peccati)!* The subtle distinction in connection with guilt
"against, but not outside, the will of God" *(contra, sed non
praeter voluntatem Dei)* may point to a teleological illumination
of historical events, but the progress is never explicated on the
basis of the "necessity" of guilt. Rather, Scripture points to the
mystery of God's action directed universally to the world. His
action is disclosed right through the drama of history. Along
this "detour" the Gentiles come into view. They are no longer
far away, excluded from God's involvement, but are related to
full salvation as fellow heirs, members of the same body, and
partakers of the promise in Christ Jesus. It is not another "religion" than theirs, but the unsearchable riches of Christ (Eph.
3:6, 8) and the "plan of the mystery."[50] Along this way, it is re-
emphasized that their calling may not lead to haughtiness (cf.
Rom. 11:20ff.) or to a new feeling of superiority in the opposite
direction from that of the Pharisees (cf. Acts 11:17). Nor can
there be any thought that the boundaries are now indefinitely
closed to Israel.[51] Such a feeling would again threaten everything, since it would be a new misunderstanding of gracious
election, of which mission — from now on directed to all — is
the manifestation.

The motive of mission

Against this background one can ask what the concrete

20:17). Cf. Ps. 118:22 and Matt. 21:43 (to a nation producing the fruits
of it). The parable was understood by the Pharisees and chief priests:
"they perceived that he was speaking about them."

49. In Rom. 11:11, this problem of determinism is not in the foreground
when the question is asked whether Israel has stumbled in such a way
that she *had* to fall (New Dutch Translation, 1969; RSV: "so as to
fall"; Greek: *hina pésōsin*). But, in the teleology (via the jealousy), it
does become clear how far removed we are here from all fatalism. Only
in this climate can it be understood that "through" Israel's trespass
salvation has come to the Gentiles.

50. Eph. 3:8f. Cf. H. Schlier, "Die Kirche als das Geheimnis Christi nach
dem Epheserbrief" and "Die Entscheidung für die Heidenmission in
der Urchristenheit," in *Die Zeit der Kirche,* 1955, pp. 229ff., 90ff.; W.
Bieder, *Das Mysterium Christi und die Mission,* 1964, pp. 44ff.

51. Cf. Acts 9:15 (Paul as an instrument to carry God's Name before
Gentiles and kings and the sons of Israel); Luke 2:32 (Gentiles and
Thy people Israel); Rom. 11:1ff. (Paul on Israel's not being rejected).

motive of the activity of mission is. One can think of a variety of "motives"; however, these motives can never be separated from the directedness, the scope, and the goal of mission. There is an inner motivation of obedience and love,[52] but both are always in wide contours and are connected to God's intentions in the world-wide proclamation. A legalistic interpretation of obedience will never lead to true missionary power. Love, too, is meaningful only on the basis of the goal. The motives have content only when they are connected to, and directed to, the actual goal. That directedness is spoken of in the great commission when it refers to "making disciples" (Matt. 28:19 — *mathēteúsate*). All reflection on the goal of mission must also be concerned with that. Closely connected to this is the question of whether mission must first of all be directed "individually" — i.e., in the summons to personal conversion, a "personal revolution." In a time when attention is called especially to the community, to nations and continents, a danger exists that one will lose interest in the individual out of reaction to various forms of salvation-individualism. Little more is discernible here either of the pastorate of the good Shepherd, Who also calls the individual and brings him to conversion,[53] or of the apostolic zeal, which does not in the least neglect the individual because of its concern for the wide world.

Naturally, there can be a one-sided interest in individuals who are pulled away from the world, which is "in the power of the evil one" (I John 5:19) and is considered to be outside the horizon of mission. But this narrowing of the perspectives may never lead in reaction to a "collectivism" that considers concern for the concrete needs of individuals to be unimportant. According to the unbiased language of the New Testament, it is men who must be "caught" (Mark 1:16-20) and "won."[54] We can disregard the question of whether the frequent rejection of the so-called "pietistic" motive of mission does justice to pietism,

---

52. Cf. J. van den Berg, *Waarom Zending?*, 1959; E. Jansen Schoonhoven, "Critische Bespreking van enige Zendingsmotieven," *Nederlands Theol. Tijdschrift*, V (1950/51), 219ff.

53. Cf. J.H. Bavinck, *Mensen Rondom Jezus*, 1960⁵, a book by a man of missions who is obviously not caught in a dilemma here.

54. In all his interest in "the boundlessness of the addresseeship" (G. Eichholz, *Tradition und Interpretation*, 1965, p. 80) and in his thinking on "nations," Paul is not blind to the individual need that is close at hand. Cf. on winning: I Cor. 9:19ff.; Acts 26:29 (Agrippa). Cf. also on anyone who is brought back from the error of his way (James 5:19f. and Matt. 18:15).

but the reaction itself is undeniably not evangelical. The wideness of the perspective — also geographical (Macedonia, Spain, and Rome) — does not obscure the individual, for there is no suggestion of any individualism here. Rather, individuals are drawn into the way and work of the Lord in the new discipleship, which then is itself incorporated anew in the wide horizon. There has often been discussion also of the question whether there may be an ecclesiastical motive in mission, usually described as the "*plantatio ecclesiae*," the planting of the Church.[55] This motive has often been opposed because it was seen as lacking appreciation for the expectation of the Kingdom and as too strongly concentrated on the institution of the Church, so that mission found its terminal point in the Church. However, this criticism is based on the supposition that the ecclesiastical motive must of itself lead to this limitation of perspectives because of an introverted churchliness. But everything depends on whether the starting point for understanding the Church is the calling, discipleship, and imitation of Christ. If it is, mission will not founder on churchliness,[56] because this *plantatio* itself has been included from the beginning in the Church's movement — her "going forth." Then there can be no ecclesiastical-worldly striving to widen and consolidate ecclesiastical power.[57] There is every reason to assume that the "young churches," specifically, have not in the least neglected their call due to an ecclesiastical rest, exchanging their outlook on the coming Kingdom for the *plantatio ecclesiae*.

In connection with the motives and directedness of mission, the question has come to the fore today whether the Church is not being viewed in a very limited perspective. Does one not have salvation-history more than world-history in view? For example, Linz has said that Cullmann has a too one-sided interest in salvation-history and not in an "actual inclusion of the world and of history in salvation-history."[58] According to Linz, Cullmann sees the present as nothing else than "a salvation-historical

---

55. Cf. on this motif in Voetius, H.A. van Andel, *De Zendingsleer van Gisbertus Voetius*, 1912, pp. 148ff.

56. Cf. G.F. Vicedom, *op. cit.*, pp. 91ff.

57. When H.J. Margull (*Theol. der missionarische Verkündigung*, 1959, pp. 71ff.) opposes the *plantatio ecclesiae* as a goal, it is evident that this criticism is directed against a conception of goal (identical with end, stopping place) that is indeed untenable. That is apparent when Margull himself speaks of the *plantatio ecclesiae* as "the essential work of missiological proclamation" (p. 72).

58. M. Linz, *Anwalt der Welt. Zur Theol. der Mission*, 1964, pp. 158ff.

interim" in a world that is passing away. The dominant thing in this view is then the apocalyptic outlook, which expects an abrupt end to the world; it is a dualistic pessimism that no longer cherishes any expectation for the world and everything that belongs to it.[59] Obviously, Linz sees this view as entailing an empty history, a reduction of the biblical perspectives, according to which the Lordship of Christ has begun decisively with the resurrection of the Lord, His "enthronement."[60] Faced with this empty history,[61] we must recall the dethronement of the powers by the triumphant Lord. The power of liberation is to be made manifest not only in souls snatched away from the perishing world, but also in all the connections of life, in harmony with the signs of that power that will follow believers in their proclamation. It is power in opposition to all the powers of destruction and the demonic.[62]

Presence and proclamation

The intention of all of this[63] is not to establish a new cultural optimism,[64] but to refer to salvation in Christ, which becomes public in signs. The signs are not to be understood only "symbolically," but also as answers to real, concrete needs, thus leading men to glorify God. In times of deep need, this aspect of Christ's coming into the world can automatically attract greater attention to itself. It can make one seek ways

59. The new time that has dawned, between the resurrection and the parousia, then becomes "the time of the Church," with the result that mission receives a "meaning that is alienated from history"; for the horizon of the Church defines everything (ibid., pp. 155, 160ff.).
60. Ibid., p. 63.
61. Ibid., p. 158, against the "basileia that is to come and is already present only in the Church." Linz is prepared to speak with Dodd of "realised eschatology" and of "proleptic parusia" (p. 55).
62. Mark 16:17f. D. Bosch ("Heilsgeschichte und Mission," Oekonomia. Heilsgeschichte als Thema der Theologie, 1966, pp. 389ff.) argues that Linz has misunderstood Cullmann (salvation-history separate from world-history), because Cullmann, too, speaks of an event that changes the world.
63. Cf. also J. Moltmann, Theology of Hope, 1967, pp. 265ff., on what is promised and hoped with regard to "the new situation of the promised future." Cf. also H. Berkhof, Christ: The Meaning of History, 1962, chapter 7.
64. As is clearly apparent in Berkhof, also in his questions to Moltmann (Diskussion über die Theol. der Hoffnung, 1967, pp. 181ff.) about whether his dynamic directedness to the future does full justice to "fulfilled" time. Cf. also Vicedom, op. cit., p. 89.

along which the healing and helping powers of Christ's Kingdom become disclosed on account of the promise for life in the present and in the future (I Tim. 4:8). The many discussions about the possibility and credibility of Christian politics have often been concentrated in justice, not as an abstract concept, but on the basis of the gospel, which is directed to all need and to the way of Christ. This gospel is not exchanged for the kind of "social gospel" that makes the personal question of salvation irrelevant on account of the Church's world-wide concerns.

Through the attention for various clear aspects of the New Testament — no personalism nor individualism[65] — the question whether the Church's first and more important calling is still to proclaim the gospel explicitly can arise. Or is her actual presence in the world of the most significance now? Various considerations of that presence sometimes remind us of the position of Israel, which we dealt with earlier. She did not "go forth" into the world of nations as a missionary; nevertheless, there was a missionary dimension as the sign of God's power and presence as a magnet for the nations, who are immensely captivated by this presence (Zech. 8:23). This question seemed to be even more urgent because many people understood all explicit missionary proclamation as a sign of a feeling of superiority and because the Church's words were repeatedly interpreted as words without deeds. Was not a different way to be recommended — that of the deeds and service of the Church in solidarity with the manifold needs of men, summed up in the familiar phrase, the Church's "world diaconate"? This was not meant as a new, autonomous human achievement, but as the reflection of the one deed of true service of Christ, through which this concrete deed of "involvement" can be recognized and understood.[66] The presence of the Church in the world is then understood "from the knowl-

---

65. Cf. H.N. Ridderbos, "Het Koninkrijk Gods en ons Leven in de Wereld," *Het Woord, het Rijk, en onze Verlegenheid*, 1968, pp. 153ff., on sanctification with regard to life in its "larger connections" (p. 161) on account of the "leaven that permeates everything." All of this is in the "tremendous context" of the field: "not just the soul and not just the Church, but the field in the world" (p. 163). Cf. *idem, De Pastorale Brieven*, pp. 117ff. (I Tim. 4:8), on the (long) life in the present "in all of his existence as a man" as not in tension with, but in virtue of, godliness.

66. Parallel to the knowledge by what becomes manifest among the disciples (John 13:35).

edge about the preceding presence of Christ Himself."[67] The intention is not some new, worldly "strategy of mission," but the elimination of every illegitimate *skandalon* that can be connected to the Church's proclamation. That applies also to the *skandalon* in the suggestion that Christ and the Church are concerned only with the conversion of souls and have no actual interest in real need, except as a means to the "actual" goal of mission. This *skandalon* is in direct conflict with the Lord Himself, Who was full of compassion for men in need, in all their blindness and deafness, sickness and hunger, threat and death in the midst of all the powers (Heb. 2:14). Because of that compassion, Christ dethrones the powers and takes away all their rights.[68]

It is striking to note how many attempts are made to escape the danger of polarization in the discussion of proclamation and presence.[69] It would be a sad matter if one were to oppose all the aspects of the Church's presence in the world, which are getting such strong emphasis at present. And it would be just as sad if one were to flee from the proclamation to presence. There is a deep biblical truth in the interest in the presence of deeds, the service of the Church; and, understandably, one has spoken here, too, of the "language of the gospel," for the deeds say something and imply a "testimony." Earlier, we saw that the seeing of works in the New Testament can be serviceable and can be directed to giving glory to God (Matt. 5:16). The concentrated concern for the proclamation as the disclosure of the great mystery at God's command (Rom. 16:26) may not close our eyes to this. The New Testament speaks of the testifying power of that presence in a concrete case: wives may win husbands who are disobedient to the Word by their behavior "without a word."[70] Obviously, a light still shines that draws attention and breaks through dark resistance. But that hardly means one may flee from the proclamation to anonymity and silence. That would be in conflict with the whole New Testament. Winning itself — also in I Pet. 3:1ff. — cannot be understood apart from

---

67. W. Krusche, "Missio-Präsenz oder Bekehrung," *Kerugma und Dogma,* 1968, pp. 119ff.; and P. Beyerhaus, "Präesenz, Solidarität und Zeugnis im miss. Dienst," *Z.Th.K.,* 1968, p. 371.
68. Col. 2:15. Cf. H.N. Ridderbos, *Aan de Kolossenzen,* 1960, p. 188; J. Verkuyl, *The Message of Liberation in Our Age,* 1970, chapters 4 and 5.
69. See especially the many valuable characterizations in Krusche, *loc. cit.*
70. I Pet. 3:1ff. On the behavior of wives, cf. R. Schnackenburg, *Die Petrusbriefe,* 1961, p. 88: "the reality of the gospel, which presents itself in the behavior of the wife" *(epopteúsantes).*

the knowledge of that for which one is won. It is precisely the testimony that comes to expression in the presence that must disclose the meaning of this presence. Therein lies the responsibility of all presence. It cannot be of significance as a desire for solidarity, since this solidarity must not be "played at but aimed at."[71] Only so can it be truly serviceable. At a particular time, hesitation about the meaning of the explicit proclamation can arise due to the realization that words — including those of preaching — can be devalued and become unintelligible. Moreover, the idea can take hold that, on account of the Church's division and the distance that can exist between her words and deeds, the Church's words can scarcely have power any more. Then there can be an inclination to silence, which can be authentic and meaningful if it is embodied in the active presence of the Church. Then we are dealing with a certain reservation about words. In that context one has often recalled warnings against absolutizing human words: "the kingdom of God does not consist in talk but in power" (I Cor. 4:20), or in "righteousness and peace and joy in the Holy Spirit" (Rom. 14:17). Moreover, it is important to bear in mind that seeing can play an important role in testimony for the Lord, as in the emphatic charge to let good works be seen (Matt. 5:16 — *lampsátō tò phôs humôn*).

The problem of presence and testimony was dealt with especially by Bonhoeffer in his well-known reflections on the so-called "secret discipline" (*Arkandisziplin*). In the ancient Church that referred to the silence of the baptized about the mysteries of the Christian faith. With Bonhoeffer this secret discipline is in the context of modern life. It is connected to the high degree of unintelligibility, according to him, of many central ideas and words in the Christian faith, such as atonement and redemption, regeneration and the Holy Spirit, cross, resurrection, and imitation of Christ. Of these he writes: "All of these things have become so problematic and so remote that we hardly dare any more to speak of them."[72] The Church is guilty for this, since she lost her chance "to speak a word of reconciliation to mankind and the world at large." He points to meaningful Christian existence in our time as "praying for and doing right by our fellow men." Bonhoeffer does not see that as a continuing replacement of proclamation by presence, but a temporary "reserve," and he hopes — "the day will come" — that it will be

71. Beyerhaus, *op. cit.*, p. 375.
72. Bonhoeffer, *Letters and Papers from Prison*, p. 160.

possible to speak once again in "a new language" which is liberating and redeeming.[73] One could think of what was described already in 1938 as "the apologetic of deeds": the clarity of the deed and the influence that it can bear are "an unambiguous means of expression" and a "testimony to genuine being and living faith."[74]

There is probably no one who does not have at least some sympathy for this problematic, especially when it is not connected with anxiety and shame for witness through the word, but rather with an analysis of modern man and the Church, and when an emergency situation is spoken of that will sometime pass away. In any case, one will have to take into account that the intention of the idea of an authentic silence is to bring the connection between the Church's speaking and her whole life up for discussion. It is only her life that can make it clear that her words are not the same as the "windy," although in many respects "true," words of Job's friends (16:2f.; 42:7f.). In this connection, present-day language about the gospel has often dealt with Israel, after the horrors for the Jews and the tidal wave of anti-Semitism that also did not pass by the Church. The Church's speech is in this context of darkness; hence, it is more difficult and complicated than when Paul, in bringing the gospel to the Jews, speaks of the wish to be *accursed and cut off* from Christ for the sake of his brothers (Rom. 9:3 — *anáthema*) and of his great sorrow and unceasing anguish (9:2 — *lúpē megálē kaì adiáleiptos odúnē*). And whenever one seeks to go on to the explicit word of proclamation, the dangers that threaten are not only those of misunderstanding.[75] There are dangers, too, because things must not only be said but also lived out in deeds, so that one does not fall under the judgment of worthlessness and fruitlessness.[76]

---

73. Cf. G. Ebeling ("The 'Non-religious Interpretation of Biblical Concepts,'" *Word and Faith*, 1960, pp. 98ff.), who points out that, at the deepest, the contrast in Bonhoeffer is not "the carrying out of existence" versus "word," since everything that is said about the "arcane discipleship" "pushes towards the question of the proclamation, the coming to expression of the Word of God."

74. E. Koehler, "Apologetik der Tat. Zur weltanschaulichen Bewegung der Gegenwart," *Evang. Theol.*, 1938, p. 41.

75. Cf. the striking misunderstanding at the healing in Lystra (Acts 14: 8-18): "The gods have come down to us in the likeness of men!" The apostles reply not only by tearing their garments, but also by a new proclamation, which is intended to eliminate all misunderstanding.

76. Cf. Koehler, *op. cit.*, p. 41. Cf. perhaps — the text is difficult — James 2:18.

Dialogue

In this connection it is important to point out also that, if words may not be replaced by silence, the nature of this speech automatically acquired great importance. We are thinking of various discussions about the question of whether the proclamation must not first of all adopt the form of dialogue, conversation with others, in solidarity with all and in community with respect to the great questions of life. We find an ancillary dilemma to that of "proclamation or presence" here, namely, "proclamation or dialogue"! Due to various factors, interest in dialogue has increased greatly in our time, especially in opposition to all "superiority" in contacts with others. Many see this interest as a fashion arising because of the weakening of the Church's certainty of faith. However, one clearly makes it too easy for oneself by approaching all of this suspiciously because of the fear of syncretism and relativization. For there can be no doubt about the fact that, when the gospel first "went forth," the Church spoke not only *to*, but also *with* others. There was no "monological" proclamation, to which only "listening" corresponds, but a deeply penetrating way of approach. It deals with living men in diverse connections and seeks the Word that can be understood and heard in that variation. For Paul, the proclamation does not approach "man" apart from any context and, thus, apart from variation and specific application. Paul knows that he is entering upon ground where, already before his appearance, God has not left Himself without witness and has given food and gladness (Acts 14:17). It is the God Who is present with those who are determined by a "that": that they might feel after Him and find Him, although "He is not far from each one of us" (17:27). The one who is sent encounters this reality and this world. How could he not feel for their feeling and seek to understand it, then speaking of the new message of the God Who is at hand? How could he not listen here, as Paul does in the city full of idols, then disputing not only in the synagogue (17:17 — *dielégeto;* cf. 28:23f., 30f.), but also with Epicurean and Stoic philosophers (17:18 — *sunéballon autǫ̃*)?

None of this occurs if one starts from the idea that "the proclamation" alone is important, rather than conversation, dialogue, true human contact, and the way to persuasion. The concrete man is taken seriously in all his questions and disputes, in his opposition and "closedness." Thus, there is also "deliberation" in all proclamation, in contrast to monologue, which sees only "man in general."[77] If proclamation truly wants to reach the real man, it is impossible to avoid dialogue. That leads to the deepest problem in the relation of proclamation and dialogue, especially when dialogue is recommended as a "missionary method." Does it not become clear that such a method is not truly concerned with genuine dialogue, but only with an appearance of dialogue in the form of the agonal motif, the motif of struggle?[78] Is dialogue not simply a means to a goal? Does the danger not always threaten that dialogue, on closer inspection, will be nothing other than "the postulated and anticipated victory of one's own principle"? Is it not simply a "demonstration of superiority" by those who possess beatitude (beati possidentes) without any true interest in listening to a beating heart?

Nevertheless, one may never capitulate to the dilemma, proclamation or dialogue. Rather, one must reflect on that human contact that is incorporated in the proclamation of the gospel, because of which it can be nothing else than true human contact. Whoever understands that will automatically begin to reflect on the mode, meaning, and significance of dialogue, and that person will never be able to escape into an unreal, monological proclamation, which would appeal to shaking the dust off one's feet if the Word is not received and listened to (cf. Matt. 10:14; Mark 6:11; Luke 9:5; Acts 13:51). The connection of dialogue and proclamation seems to involve an impossible, paradoxical situation, and one cannot say that we have a simple solution at our disposal. The realization that the human solidarity present here cannot be a "purposeless" solidarity[79] does not free us for a moment from the seriousness of conversation. We sense that seriousness in the countless encounters of Jesus with His contemporaries, which begin with Jesus and discharge themselves in a history of emotions (cf. John 3; 7:45-52; 19:39). They are encounters in which neither proclamation nor dialogue excludes the other. What is decisive here is true directedness to

---

77. Cf. G. Eichholz, "Der missionarische Kanon des Paulus (I Kor. 9, 19-23)," *Tradition und Interpretation*, 1965, pp. 114ff.
78. Cf. K. Goldammer, "Zur Idee des Dialogs und des dialogischen Denkens," *Erneuerung der Kirche. Festschrift G. Bornkamm*, 1966, p. 317. In the papal encyclical *Ecclesiam Suam*, dialogue plays a large role, namely, in all human relations, the Jewish people, the monotheistic religions, and the separated brothers. Cf. my *Nabetrachting op het Concilie*, 1968, p. 12; see also *Gaudium et Spes*, DV II, p. 306.
79. Cf. Beyerhaus, *op. cit.*, p. 383, also on "the insufficiency of the purely dialogical method." Cf. also W. Holsten, "Verkündigung und Gespräch," *Evang. Theol.*, 1958, pp. 76ff.; A.G. Honig, *op. cit.*, p. 20.

the other. Lacking any appearance of an "exhibition," it receives a place in the proclamation, in which the nonparadoxality of witness and dialogue are understood and practiced.

In her going forth and speaking and in her apology and refutation, the Church must be aware that every dialogue which misrepresents the feeling and seeking of the other will be unfruitful. Much is at stake here because, in the widening horizon of mankind,[80] the explicit connections and contacts grow steadily, urging the Church to unprecedented conscientiousness. The Church herself has become the Church as the object of proclamation. In all her feelings and seeking, she has been understood and, thus, found — not as a "miracle" of surprise, but "persuaded" as Jeremiah was.[81] She herself knows how great the resistance against the gospel is in her own midst. She knows her own guilt, her own history, her own division, and her lack of attentive listening, which has so often made her proclamation assailable and uncredible. She must know that she can speak only in the deepest humility, for she has nothing that she has not received (I Cor. 4:7). She must know that she herself sees in a mirror dimly (13:12). Certainly she does not have the answer to all the questions of men and the world. One could speak here of shyness,[82] particularly in times when the Church is confronted with difficult questions and realizes that she can find and show the good way — the way of life — only with difficulty.

In times when many turn away from the Church in disappointment and when she seeks restlessly for the causes and for new "forms" through which the gospel can again be a new, surprising light, the Church will have to be ready for true dialogue. And in that dialogue, she will have to concern herself with the positivity of the message that has been entrusted to her from above, and she must constantly subject herself to it anew. The dialogical motive will always embrace the agonal motif, but the Church will have to remember that only when the weapons that are used here are not used to carry on a "worldly war" can they have divine power (II Cor. 10:3ff. — *sarkikà* versus *dunatà*). In all the army of Christ, both inside and outside, there can be no doubt about the nature of these

80. Cf. O. Köhler, "Missionsbefehl und Missionsgeschichte," *Gott in Welt*, II, 346ff.
81. Jer. 20:7 (New Dutch Translation, 1969). Both the RSV and the KJV read "deceive": "O Lord, thou hast deceived me, and I was deceived."
82. Cf. G.Th. Rothuizen, *Schema 13*, p. 27, on the shyness about which the Church knows more than does the world.

"weapons." The militant aspect in all the images that are employed includes the equipment of the gospel of peace (Eph. 6:15) and the sword of the Holy Spirit (6:17). In this *militia* "praying with all prayer" is not a pious pretense, but is itself the structure of the *militia* (6:18). The Church is tested in her dialogue not only as to the purity and understandableness of her proclamation, but also as to her faith and love, her confession of the Name, and her whole life in that imitation to which she summons others. Therefore, the Church's "going forth" can never be isolated from her own responsibility — also in all the institutional aspects of her existence.

The expectation for the Church — for her "institution," her inwardness, her concern for herself and her "ecclesiology" — can be obscured by a fierce, emotional reaction to all introverted churchliness. Then there can be an inclination to declare an exodus; the Church's true being is experienced elsewhere as a new reality.[83] And no longer is the "Church" postulated as the starting point and goal of mission. From numerous of Hoekendijk's ideas, it is evident that he opposes especially all introverted churchliness, the identification of the Church with the Kingdom of God, which results in loss of sight with respect to the world and the Kingdom of God. Thus, he appeals to the exodus, which is hazardous but full of promise. It is not first of all an exodus from social structures, but from a churchliness that has withdrawn into herself;[84] and its goal is to be the mes-

---

83. Cf. J.C. Hoekendijk, *Kerk en Volk in de Duitse Zendingswetenschap*, 1948, pp. 223ff., in connection with the Church as a function of the apostolate. Cf. *idem, The Church Inside Out*, 1966, pp. 47ff. On Hoekendijk, cf. H.D. van Loor, *Hoekendijk en Verder*, 1966; G. Brillenburg Wurth, *De Apost. Kerk*, 1954, pp. 98ff.; K.H. Kandler, "Kirche und Exodusgemeinde," *Kerugma und Dogma*, 1971, pp. 244ff. Kandler sees Brunner as "informant and teacher" (p. 252). It does not seem to me to be correct to place Hoekendijk and Brunner so close to each other, although there is a point of contact with regard to "the misunderstanding of the Church."

84. That is not in the least to deny the point of contact between the exodus in Hoekendijk and the exodus in Moltmann, as is apparent from the eschatological perspectives as well as from the *shalom* and justice in the world. Here, too, it is evident that Brunner is not the "teacher," and not only not of Moltmann (cf. *The Theology of Hope*, pp. 321ff.). For various dilemmas, see Chr. Hinz, "Feuer und Wolken im Exodus," *Diskussion über die Theol. der Hoffnung*, 1967, pp. 125ff. Moltmann's answer is: smashing down "open doors" (p. 210). Through these "open doors," however, all the questions return. They are questions also about the Church in the present, her institution and proclamation, which goes toward the future on the basis of the "once-for-all." The same is true

sianic nation and the salt of the earth. This "ecclesiology" — in the striking characterization, "the Church inside out" — is certainly due partially to disappointments about the Church, which has postulated her institutions and offices not only as the stable point of departure, but also as the goal of mission, stressing her isolated piety and liturgy, her inner riches, instead of wanting only to be the sign of the coming Kingdom. In contrast to this exodus-motif, others have emphasized the testing of the Church within her life as it has grown historically.[85] That does not have to be rigid conservatism; rather, the critical attitude is directed to the renewal of the Church and to looking for Church forms that can be made serviceable to the proclamation of the gospel in a changed world-context. Until now there were far-reaching differences of opinion about the various approaches. These were determined partially by the analysis of the Church's place in the midst of the world and of the negative posture of many towards her.[86] But the outlook on the return to in place of exodus from the Church is a sign of an expectation, not as triumphant optimism, but as an expectation that is filled with new responsibility. It is responsibility in answer to the question of whether the Church, in all her actions, has truly understood her calling.

That this proclamation cannot contain any element of "compelling them to enter" hardly needs reminder here. We have known for a long time already not only that nothing can be compelled here, but also that the gospel has nothing to do with such coercion.[87] Thus, more and more attention has been given to countless problems of reflection on world religions, points of contact and accommodation, intelligibility, proclama-

with respect to Hoekendijk, who, for that matter, often speaks not simply antithetically, but also correlatively.

85. Cf. H.D. van Loor, op. cit., pp. 103ff.

86. Cf. G. Dekker, Wat is er met de Kerk aan de Hand?, 1971, p. 72 (perspective!), on the ways of the institution. Reflection on the forms of the Church in connection with sociology in no sense implies the "holy sociology" against which Barth (C.D., IV/3, pp. 740f.) polemicizes, warning against structures that are defined by parallels from aristocracy, monarchy, or democracy.

87. Augustine considered the appeal to Luke 14:23 ("compel them to come in" — anánkason eiselthein) to be justified by the direction of the constraint, namely, toward the good. Cf. H.B. Weyland, Augustinus en de Kerkelijke Tucht, 1965, pp. 203ff. Cf. Bavinck, Katholiciteit, p. 20, on the fatal fruits "against his intention and against his interpretation." Cf. Calvin, Commentary on a Harmony of the Evangelists, p. 173: "I do not disapprove of the use which Augustine frequently made of this passage against the Donatists."

tion, and dialogue. Clearly, though, all of the Church's work becomes senseless and unbelievable apart from her own life of imitation, because then there is no connection between what is proclaimed from the housetops and what the Church has heard whispered (Matt. 10:27). Then there is a blurring of expectation, an abandonment of one's own surroundings and the world due to lack of hope, an overestimation of the powers (as if nothing had happened to them!), and a creeping sense of a Manichaean "antipole" to divine love and mercy. Nothing is more dangerous for the Church than that her expectation collapse in defeatism about herself and about the world. Then John Mott's expectant phrase sounds strange and overstrained to us, directed in 1900 to evangelizing "the world in this generation."[88] Mott did not want to romanticize, but was filled like Paul with an ardent zeal. He deserves more than to be labeled an unrealistic idealist who obviously did not know the world and its resistances.[89] He did not in the least start from some ecclesiastical triumphalism, and he connected his expectations to "the awakening of the sleeping Church."[90] To rediscover this expectation, this nostalgia, is never a psychological technique by which the Church attempts to raise herself above all the cares and worries about the Church and about her Lord. Her only foundation is the relatedness of the commission to the gracious declaration of His presence (Matt. 28:20). This declaration is full of admonition, calling her to see with open eyes — "and behold, I am with you always" — during the "interim," which is not a "lordless time,"[91] not a time of despondency and sarcasm about the Church of others and about crumbling discipleship. Rather, it is the time when the shock of recognition, as so many times previously, again indicates the way in order that the Church go in it. To go this way is the way of discipleship, which — one and catholic, apostolic and holy — knows of the experience of the great, universal mystery, of the unique account about the many things and signs which inspired the enraptured, unexaggerated statement: "were every one of them to be written, I suppose that the world itself could not contain the books that would be written" (John 21:25; cf. 20:30f.).

88. John R. Mott, *The Evangelisation of the World in this Generation*, 1900.
89. On Mott, see W.A. Visser 't Hooft, *Heel de Kerk voor Heel de Wereld*, 1968, pp. 20ff.
90. J. Mott, *op. cit.*, p. 210.
91. K. Barth, *Auslegung von Matth. 28, 16-20*, 1945, p. 22.

INDEX OF PRINCIPAL SUBJECTS

421

INDEX OF PERSONS

Aalders, G. C. 174
Aalders, W. J. 22
Abelard 144, 146, 369
Adam, A. 123, 143, 160, 233, 305
Adam, K. 211
Adrian VI 47, 354
Aland, K. 379
Allen, E. L. 229
Altendorf, E. 316
Althaus, H. L. 31
Althaus, P. 92, 315, 351
Ambrose 338
Anselm 237
Aquinas, T. 144
Arius 377, 378
Arnauld 272
Arntzen, M. J. 371
Asendorff, U. 22
Asting, R. 320
Athanasius 305
Augustijn, C. 184
Augustine 110, 133, 142, 146, 160, 272, 287, 305, 316, 336, 338, 345, 348, 351, 419

Baarda, Tj. 228
Baas, L. 342
Bacht, H. 38
Baelz, P. 387
Bakhuizen van den Brink, J. N. 106, 142, 143, 202, 203, 204, 269, 272, 274, 277, 305, 373
Bakker, J. T. 298, 302, 346
Balduinus 323
Barauna, G. 148, 224, 335, 340, 341
Barczay, G. 174, 183
Barrett, C. K. 246
Barth, K. 23, 30, 31, 34, 40, 43, 46, 47, 61, 89, 90, 91, 100, 111, 128, 149, 157, 195, 196, 208, 213, 224, 225, 236, 237, 239, 241, 245, 247, 248, 263, 264, 268, 277, 280, 281, 282, 283, 285,

287, 288, 300, 303, 308, 320, 332, 343, 348, 350, 351, 353, 354, 359, 361, 364, 366, 375, 387, 392, 393, 394, 398, 419, 420
Bartmann, B. 13
Bartz, W. 322
Bauer, W. 229
Baum, G. 42, 70
Baumann, U. 297, 298
Bavinck, H. 9, 13, 15, 16, 17, 18, 24, 31, 37, 43, 44, 46, 47, 54, 55, 61, 62, 85, 87, 89, 106, 110, 111, 115, 119, 120, 133, 134, 143, 145, 146, 152, 160, 161, 162, 163, 170, 172, 173, 176, 188, 195, 196, 236, 248, 249, 258, 263, 265, 269, 280, 283, 284, 285, 291, 303, 306, 307, 318, 324, 336, 370, 371, 378, 383, 384, 387, 419
Bavinck, J. H. 408
Becker, K. J. 369
Beckmann, K. M. 31, 83
Behm, J. 276
Beinert, W. 106, 110, 165
Bellarmine 17, 37, 38, 186
Bensdorp, Th. 60
Benz, E. 123, 221
Berkhof, H. 30, 80, 82, 90, 108, 110, 111, 113, 114, 115, 195, 197, 202, 410
Berkouwer, G. C. 16, 32, 33, 50, 85, 91, 92, 100, 119, 122, 135, 141, 144, 147, 153, 160, 163, 169, 172, 173, 176, 178, 183, 190, 208, 218, 228, 239, 240, 249, 251, 262, 272, 273, 277, 280, 282, 284, 287, 291, 292, 297, 298, 301, 304, 321, 322, 328, 335, 340, 346, 352,

353, 361, 378, 379, 380, 382, 388, 393, 394, 397, 401, 403, 406, 416
Bernard of Clairvaux 66
Beyerhaus, P. 412, 413, 416
Beyschlag, K. 218
Bieder, W. 127, 128, 407
Blauw, J. 404
Blei, K. 115
Bloch, E. 195
Boer, H. P. 393, 394
Bohren, R. 370, 374, 375
Bolkestein, H. M. 327
Bonaventure 251
Bonhoeffer, D. 83, 92, 94, 413, 414
Bonis, K. 268
Boon, K. 274
Bormann, P. 18
Bornkamm, G. 243, 244, 259, 265, 279, 392, 393
Boros, L. 159, 161
Bosch, D. 404, 410
Bouchette, H. 223
Bouma, C. 44
Bourke, M. M. 379, 383
Bouwman, H. 370
Brandenburg, A. 18
Brosch, J. 33, 117, 226
Brunner, E. 115, 373
Brunner, P. 184, 237
Bucer 210
Büchsel 138
Budiman, R. 352
Buizer, C. M. 149
Bullinger 301
Bultmann, R. 44, 48, 244, 251
Bunnik, R. J. 223

Calixtus 126
Calovius 126
Calvin, J. 10, 15, 33, 41, 64, 65, 66, 67, 68, 83, 85, 87, 102, 118, 122, 143, 160, 161, 168, 169, 181, 184, 185, 204,

SCRIPTURE INDEX